W9-BAA-649

Maryland

Maryland

Leonard M. Adkins
with photographs by the author

FOURTH EDITION

The Countryman Press ✳ Woodstock, Vermont

For Ann and Denny Messick. Thank you for your friendship—and for Laurie.
—L. M. A.

Interior photographs by the author unless otherwise specified
Maps by Erin Greb Cartography, © The Countryman Press
Text and cover design by Bodenweber Design
Composition by PerfecType, Nashville, TN

Explorer's Guide Maryland
978-1-58157-175-2

Published by The Countryman Press, P.O. Box 748, Woodstock, VT 05091

Distributed by W. W. Norton & Company, Inc., 500 Fifth Avenue, New York, NY 10110

Printed in the United States of America

No entries in this book have been solicited or paid for.

10 9 8 7 6 5 4 3 2 1

Also by Leonard M. Adkins

50 Hikes in Maryland: Walks, Hikes, and Backpacks from the Allegheny Plateau to the Atlantic Ocean

West Virginia: An Explorer's Guide

50 Hikes in West Virginia: From the Allegheny Mountains to the Ohio River

Wildflowers of the Blue Ridge and Great Smoky Mountains

50 Hikes in Northern Virginia: Walks, Hikes, and Backpacks from the Allegheny Mountains to the Chesapeake Bay

50 Hikes in Southern Virginia: From the Cumberland Gap to the Atlantic Ocean

Hiking and Traveling the Blue Ridge Parkway: The Only Guide You Need with GPS, Maps, and More

The Appalachian Trail: A Visitor's Companion

Wildflowers of the Appalachian Trail

Best of the Appalachian Trail: Day Hikes

Best of the Appalachian Trail: Overnight Hikes

Images of America: Along the Appalachian Trail: Georgia, North Carolina, and Tennessee

Images of America: Along Virginia's Appalachian Trail

Postcards of America: Along Virginia's Appalachian Trail

Adventure Guide to Virginia

The Caribbean: A Walking and Hiking Guide

Seashore State Park: A Walking Guide

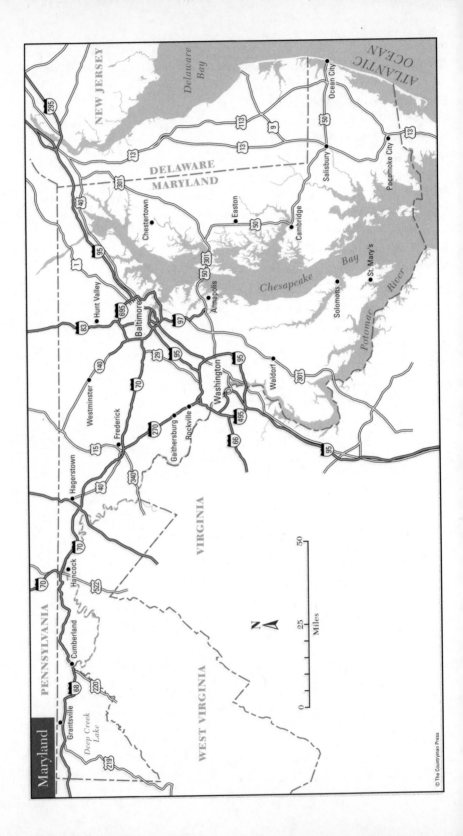

EXPLORE WITH US!

Welcome to the fourth edition of *Explorer's Guide Maryland,* the state's most comprehensive travel companion. All attractions, inns, and restaurants are chosen on the basis of merit, not paid advertising. The organization of the book is simple, but the following points will help to get you started on your way.

WHAT'S WHERE

In the beginning of the book is an alphabetical listing with thumbnail sketches of special highlights, important information, and advice on everything from where to obtain the best homemade ice cream to what to do if you get stung by a jellyfish.

LODGING

Lodging establishments mentioned in this book are selected on the basis of merit; no innkeeper or business owner was charged for inclusion. When making reservations, which almost all B&Bs require, ask about the policy on children, pets, smoking, and acceptance of credit cards. Many B&Bs do not accept children under 12, and some places have a minimum-stay policy, especially on weekends, holidays, and during special events.

Rates: The rates are for two people to stay in one room for one night and are weekend rates during what the establishment considers its high season. Weekday and off-season rates may be lower. However, please do not hold me or the respective innkeepers responsible for the rates listed as this book went to press. Changes are inevitable. State, local, and room taxes (which, when added together, can be well above 10 percent) have not been included.

RESTAURANTS

Please note the distinction between *Dining Out* and *Eating Out.* By their nature, restaurants in the *Eating Out* section are less expensive and more casual. Many restaurants change their menus often; the specific dishes mentioned in this book may not be available when you dine. They are cited to give you a general idea of the cuisine offered. Like the lodging rates quoted in this book, menu prices were current when it went to press. However, as we all know, prices never go down; be prepared for them to have risen somewhat.

KEY TO SYMBOLS

☺ **Special value.** The special-value symbol appears next to lodgings and restaurants that offer a quality not often found at the price charged.

🐾 **Pets.** The pet symbol appears next to places, activities, and lodgings that accept pets. Almost all lodging accommodations require that you inform them of a pet when you make a reservation and often request an additional fee.

✎ **Child-friendly.** The crayon symbol appears next to places or activities that accept and/or appeal to young children, or have a children's menu.

♿ **Handicapped access.** The wheelchair symbol appears next to lodgings, restaurants, and attractions that are partially or completely handicapped accessible.

☂ **Rainy-day activity.** The rainy-day symbol appears next to places of interest and things to do that are appropriate for inclement-weather days.

💍 **Weddings.** The wedding-ring symbol appears next to establishments that specialize in weddings.

🍸 **Bars.** The martini-glass symbol appears next to establishments that have choice selections of beers, wines, and other alcoholic beverages.

We welcome any comments or corrections on this guide. Please address correspondence to Explorer Guide Editor, The Countryman Press, P.O. Box 748, Woodstock, VT 05091, or email countrymanpress@wwnorton.com.

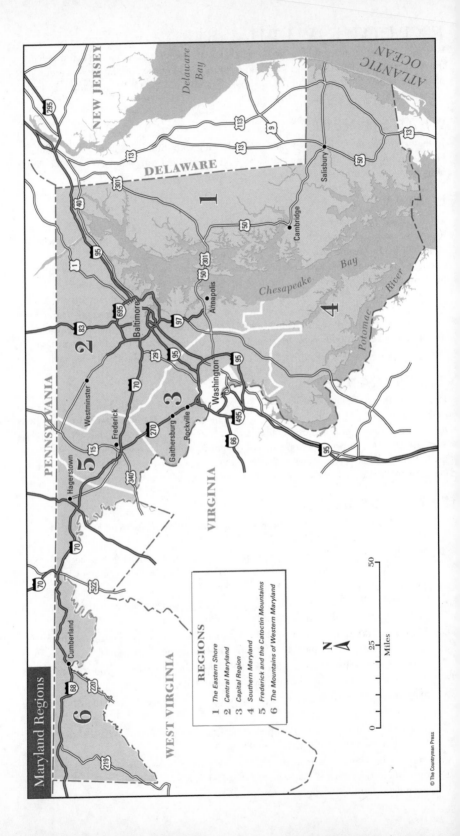

Maryland Regions

REGIONS

1 The Eastern Shore
2 Central Maryland
3 Capital Region
4 Southern Maryland
5 Frederick and the Catoctin Mountains
6 The Mountains of Western Maryland

N

0   25   50
Miles

© The Countryman Press

CONTENTS

ACKNOWLEDGMENTS

I relied upon hundreds of people to help me along the way, to make arrangements, point me in the right direction, and introduce me to other people, places, and activities I would have overlooked. Without your unselfish aid, this book would never have been completed. May it reflect the confidence you had in me:

Barbara J. Beverungen, JoAnna Crone, and Heather Johnson, Carroll County Office of Tourism; Kathy Mackel and Christina Lipponcott, Caroline County Office of Tourism; Deb Clatterbuck and Sarah Duck, Garrett County Chamber of Commerce; Lisa Challenger and Debbie Keitt, Worcester County Tourism; Martha Clements, Town of Ocean City Department of Tourism; Mary G. Galloway, Amanda Fenstermaker, and Jill Jasuta, Dorchester County Department of Tourism; Sheila Crites, Allegany County Convention and Visitors Bureau; Norma Dobrowolski, Donna Abbott, Debbie Travers, and staff, Ocean City Convention and Visitors Bureau; Debbi Dodson, Barbara A. Reisert, and Gayle V. Keen, Talbot County Office of Tourism; Beverly Brown, Dianne Gleissner, Rebecca Lira, and Carolyn Laray, St. Mary's County Department of Economic and Community Development/Division of Tourism; Bethany Mattocks and Kelly Groff, Conference and Visitors Bureau of Montgomery County; Julie Widowson, Beth Somers, Wendy Robertson, and staff, Somerset County Tourism; Deborah Ing, W. Edward Lilley, Lori Paddy, and Rachelina Bonacci, Howard County Tourism Council; Sandy Maruchi-Turner and Bob White, Cecil County Tourism; Diane Molner, Winifred Roche, Kathleen Whitehead, and Susan Hanna, Discover Harford County Tourism Council; Larry Noto, Monee Cottman, and Kristin Symes, Baltimore Area Convention and Visitors Bureau; Terry B. Nyquist, Steven Miller, Kristen Conn, Michelle Wainwright, and Sandy Fulton, Wicomico County Convention and Visitors Bureau; Craig Peddicord and Marge Saunders, Baltimore County Conference and Visitors Bureau; Beth Finneyfrock Rhoades, Michelle Kershner, and Tiffany Wilms, Tourism Council of Frederick County; Catherine Carroll, Donna Dudley, and Joanne Roland, Charles County Tourism Office; Herman E. Schieke Jr., Joyce A. Baki, and Erica Stone, Calvert County Department of Economic Development; Kim Shirer, Allegany County Department of Tourism; Barbara Siegert, Heather Taylor, Debbie Birch, and Terry M. Miles, Queen Anne's County Office of Tourism; Ngina Jackson and Carl Smith Jr., Prince Georges County, Maryland, Conference and Visitors Bureau; Bernadette Van Pelt and Jen Davis, Kent County Office of Tourism; Anedra T. Wiseman, Susan Steckman, Sarah Todd-Evans, Tina Judd, and Clare Vanderbeek, Annapolis and Anne Arundel County Conference and Visitors Bureau; and Gigi Yelton, Betsy DeVore, Clarissa Stanton, and Thomas Riford, Hagerstown/Washington County Convention and Visitors Bureau. Every entry in this book represents hours that someone was willing to take out of a busy schedule to assist me. To those many hundreds more who can't be named here, thank you.

Connie Yingling, Maryland Office of Tourism Development—was I ever lucky that you stepped in to help. Dr. Stephen Lewis, Caroline Charonko, Terry Gumming, and Susie Surfas—life goes on, thanks to you. Nancy Adkins, Kathleen, John, Tim, and Jay Yelenic—thank you for understanding why my visits became so infrequent. Laurie—thank you for sharing Maryland with me, and me with Maryland. Life with you is all it should be.

ACKNOWLEDGMENTS

INTRODUCTION

Istarted the introduction to my book *50 Hikes in Maryland* with the tourism-bureau-inspired slogan, "So many things to do. So close together." I stand by that phrase to introduce you to this fourth edition of *Maryland: An Explorer's Guide*. From the waves of the Atlantic Ocean rolling onto the sands of the Eastern Shore to the heights of the Allegheny Plateau shadowed by a setting sun in western Maryland, all areas of the state are within a few hours' drive of one another.

As you head to the beach in Ocean City, you could stop to take a fishing trip on the Chesapeake Bay, visit a maritime museum (or two, or three, or more) to learn how people make a living from those waters, watch migrating waterfowl fly overhead by the thousands, kayak a tidal stream, and still have time for an evening ride on a 1902 carousel and a fresh seafood dinner.

In Baltimore, you can take in the exhibits at the city's world-renowned art museums, watch dolphins at play in the aquarium, stand upon the parapets that gave birth to America's national anthem, dine on Spanish food in a jacket and tie, and finish the day munching a freshly made cannoli as you stroll the alleyways of Little Italy.

Within a 30-minute drive of this cosmopolitan atmosphere, you could be bicycling a 20-mile rail trail through rural countryside, swimming in the Chesapeake Bay, or betting on a horse at Pimlico, home of the Triple Crown's Preakness Stake.

Half a day's drive to western Maryland can introduce you to the 184.5-mile C&O Canal, Civil War battlefields at Monocacy and Antietam, one of the state's finest fine-arts museums, and the opportunity to go underground. You could learn of the upheaval of the land when Africa collided with North America ages ago, enjoy a historic steam-train ride through the forested mountains, go downhill skiing, and exhilarate in white-water rafting.

To facilitate your explorations, this guide, the most comprehensive of its kind, has been divided into broad geographic regions. Individual chapters then cover areas that can easily be explored from their listed overnight accommodations.

Each chapter begins with an overview of the area, taking in its geographic features, historic aspects, and attraction highlights. There are listings on how to obtain further information, how to get to the area and get around once there, and places to obtain emergency help should the need arise.

Following those are the *To See* and *To Do* sections, which provide you with enough information to decide if a particular museum, historic home or site, family attraction, guided tour, golf course, hiking trail, lake, or other place or activity should fit into your travel plans.

I then give descriptions of places to stay, including B&Bs, inns, resorts, cottages, vacation rentals, and a few motels and hotels. Having stayed in them, or at least visited, I have based my descriptions on firsthand experiences and a propensity to snoop into hidden areas and out-of-the-way places. I try to be as honest as possible in my appraisals. What I saw and experienced is what I wrote about.

The same is true for the dining options provided. I gained quite a few pounds sampling the fare of the upscale restaurants (*Dining Out*) and that of the everyday places (*Eating Out*), in addition to bakeries, candy shops, ice cream parlors, and coffeehouses.

Listings of entertainment venues, outstanding businesses worthy of some of your shopping time, and special events that take place annually round out each chapter.

Within all of these hundreds of listings and descriptions you will find very few negative remarks (and those are usually small comments about something trifling). The reason is that I visited and dined in a few places that I simply did not include in the guide. If I was uncomfortable in a place or found it lacking in cleanliness, I felt that other lone travelers, couples, or families would, too. If a meal was not worth the calories consumed, or the atmosphere made for an unpleasant dining experience, the restaurant was not included. This does not mean that an inn had to be palatial or a restaurant serve five-star cuisine. It just means that you should get a good and fair experience for the time and/or money you spend.

I became acquainted with Maryland on an intimate basis when I first hiked the Appalachian Trail as I followed the state's 40 miles of the pathway along the crest of South Mountain. I came to appreciate more of what the state has to offer after I married Laurie, who was born and raised in Annapolis. Journeys to visit her relatives introduced me to the places important to her childhood, while further explorations enabled both of us to discover boundless hiking, biking, canoeing, and other outdoor adventures.

History permeates the air over this land. The first settlement in the New World dedicated to true religious tolerance was established here in 1634. George Washington and many other movers and shakers of the American Revolution traveled throughout, fighting and preaching for the cause. Four of the state's citizens signed the Declaration of Independence, and when the new country needed a place for its capital, Maryland graciously donated the land on which Washington, DC, is built.

As a border state, Maryland was the site of some of the most bitter fighting during the Civil War. The Battle of Antietam was the single bloodiest day in American war history, while the fight along the Monocacy River is credited with having saved Washington, DC, from Confederate invasion.

I had fun doing the field research for this book. I had already experienced many wonderful adventures in Maryland, but the need for current, firsthand knowledge of the state set me off on new explorations. From fly-fishing in a western Maryland creek to touring the hallowed halls of the capitol building in Annapolis, I had the perfect excuse to go to new places and engage in activities I had always wanted to explore but had lacked the time. A walk along the C&O Canal, an afternoon nap upon the Ocean City beach, and a visit to the Calvert Marine Museum in Solomons returned me to places I had long yearned to see again. In addition, since the human body demands fuel and rest, I became privileged to sample the sumptuous offerings of some of the world's most innovative chefs and engage in friendly and intriguing conversations with the guests and hosts of the state's excessively relaxing and historically rich B&Bs.

George Washington traveled often throughout Maryland and really did sleep here—in many places, in fact. You should, too. Happy exploring.

WHAT'S WHERE IN MARYLAND

AREA CODES More than five areas codes exist in Maryland, with new ones to be added in the future. You must dial the area code on all phone calls, including those made locally. This means that every call is at least a 10-digit proposition.

ADMISSION FEES Admission fees of less than $10 per person are simply listed as "small admission fee." The actual cost is provided if higher. Please keep in mind that, as this book went to press, the rates quoted were accurate but are always subject to change.

AIR SERVICE The state is serviced primarily by three airports clustered around the Baltimore–Washington, DC area. **Baltimore/Washington International Thurgood Marshall Airport** (1-800-I-FLY-BWI; www.bwiairport.com) is located between Baltimore and Annapolis. **Ronald Reagan Washington National Airport** (703-417-8000; www.metwashairports.com /reagan/reagan.htm) is in Virginia across the Potomac River from the District of Columbia. **Washington Dulles International Airport** (703-572-2700; www.metwash airports.com/dulles/dulles.htm), in northern Virginia, may be a bit farther away but often has lower airfares. All three have airline companies with connections around the world.

Philadelphia International Airport (215-937-6937; www.phl.org) may be a good choice for those traveling to central Maryland or the northern part of the Eastern Shore, while **Pittsburgh International Airport** (412-472-3525; www.fly pittsburgh.com) may be best for those wanting to explore western Maryland.

Smaller, regional airports have commuter connections and are noted in their respective chapters.

AFRICAN AMERICAN HERITAGE Maryland has been the site of key events in the history of the country's African Americans. The first blacks forcibly brought to the British colonies were indentured servants, while the first slaves arrived in Maryland in 1640, with the largest percentage of them subsequently made to work on the state's tobacco farms. When Maryland's farmers changed from tobacco crops to grain production, the need for a large workforce diminished, and many owners began selling their slaves to plantations in the deep South, breaking apart families.

With the outbreak of the Civil War, and Pennsylvania and Delaware representing freedom to a slave who could make it across the states' borders, Maryland was used by many a slave as an escape route. Since the Underground Railroad was operated in secrecy, it is hard to know exactly how many sites there were in the state. However, one documented place is the **Baltimore Harbor,** where a freedom seeker could possibly acquire false documents showing he or she was a freed slave, or obtain secret passage on a ship bound for Northern states. **Harriet Tubman** escaped from her slave owner on the Eastern Shore and, in an amazing display of courage, fortitude, and selflessness, returned to Maryland so many times that she was able to guide at least 70 more people to freedom along the Underground Railroad. The **Harriet Tubman Museum** in Cambridge tells her story and conducts guided tours of sites important in her life.

Frederick Douglass managed to escape by dressing in a sailor's uniform. This famous orator became such a driving force in America that a number of places in Maryland commemorate his life. The **Frederick Douglass Museum and Cultural Center** in Highland Beach is located in his modest summer home, and exhibits provide insight into the man, the experiences of other African Americans, and a bit of history on the local community. The **Frederick Douglass–Isaac Myers Maritime Park Museum** in Baltimore's Fell's Point district focuses on two of the neighborhood's most noted residents. There are items from the lives of Douglass, an orator, and Myers, who established the country's first black owned and operated shipyard.

In Baltimore's Inner Harbor, the impressive **Reginald F. Lewis Museum of Maryland African American History & Culture** celebrates how skills brought from Africa shaped the lives of those kidnapped to America, along with examinations of African American families and their creative spirits. Also in Baltimore, the **National Great Blacks in Wax Museum** is the country's first and only wax museum of African American history. The **Eubie Blake Jazz Institute and Cultural Center** honors the life and music of this Baltimore native.

Although small, the **African American Heritage Society of Charles County** in La Plata does a nice job of paying homage to a number of notable local African Americans, including Matthew Henson, the first person to reach the North Pole, arriving there almost an hour before Robert Peary. Located in Fulton, the **African Art Museum of Maryland** and the **Howard County Center for African American Culture** in Columbia focus on artistic

achievements, both on the African continent and in America.

A brochure available from the **Maryland Office of Tourism Development** (see *Information*) directs you to scores of additional sites throughout the state. The local tourism offices can supply even more detailed information pertinent to their areas.

AMTRAK Despite its many troubles through the years, AMTRAK (1-800-USA-RAIL; www.amtrak.com) service for Maryland is quite extensive. It can get you close to the northern part of the Eastern Shore by dropping you off in Aberdeen or take you deep into western Maryland at Cumberland. There is, of course, service to Baltimore; Washington, DC; and several towns close to the two big cities.

ANTIQUES New Market has close to two dozen antiques shops, while other areas with heavy concentrations of dealers include Havre de Grace; Kensington; Historic Savage Mill in Savage; and Fell's Point, Federal Hill, and Antique Row in Baltimore. Head to the Eastern Shore to find shops filled with nautical items of yesteryear.

The **Antiques Dealers Association of Maryland** (www.antiquesinmd.com), P.O. Box 303, Olney, 20832, publishes a pamphlet describing more than 50 of its members. A calendar of shows is included.

APPALACHIAN TRAIL The Appalachian Trail follows the crest of the Appalachian Mountains for more than 2,000 miles from Georgia to Maine. Forty miles of the pathway are in Maryland, entering at the C&O Canal across the Potomac River from Harpers Ferry, West Virginia. After following the canal eastward for a few miles, it climbs Weverton Cliffs for a spectacular view of the confluence of the Shenandoah and Potomac Rivers. Staying along the crest of South Mountain, the trail passes by several places of historical interest and one viewpoint after another. It leaves the state at the Mason-Dixon Line near Pen-Mar.

The Appalachian Trail Conservancy (304-535-6331; www.appalachiantrail.org), P.O. Box 807, Harpers Ferry, WV 25425, is the source for the *Appalachian Trail Guide to Maryland and Northern Virginia; The Appalachian Trail: A Visitor's Companion; Wildflowers of the Appalachian Trail;* and other publications and information.

AQUARIUMS You could spend hours, even days, experiencing everything the multilevel, multibuilding **National Aquarium** in Baltimore has to offer. Smaller, but still engaging, are the aquariums in the **Ocean City Life Saving Museum** and at the **Calvert Marine Museum** in Solomons.

ART GALLERIES Baltimore is the state's epicenter of art with the world-class **Baltimore Museum of Art** and **Walters Art Museum.** The eccentric exhibits in the **American Visionary Art Museum** enhance the reputation. The **Annapolis Marine Art Gallery** displays only works of living artists who portray life in and around the water. The architecture of the **Washington County Museum of Fine Arts** in Hagerstown is almost as impressive as its extensive collection of old masters and American works.

Smaller in size, but still impressive, are **Strathmore Hall** in North Bethesda, **Gudelsky Gallery** in Silver Spring, and **African Art Museum of Maryland** in Fulton. **Mattawoman Creek Art Center** near Marbury is in one of the most peaceful settings you will find, while the presentation of artwork in the commercial **Ocean**

Gallery World Center in Ocean City fits in with the chaos and activity of its boardwalk location.

Many artist-owned galleries have become destinations unto themselves. Places such as **Troika Gallery** in Easton contain the works of some of the state's best creators. Most colleges and universities also have a gallery or two, and do not overlook the *Crafts* section in each chapter.

The Web site www.delmarweb.com /maryland/artgallery.html has an extensive list (but no descriptions) of galleries throughout the state.

ARTS COUNCILS Every county has an arts council that is funded, at least in part, by the **Maryland State Arts Council** (www.msac.org). As individual organizations, they vary greatly in how large they are and what they do. Most do sponsor classes in various media, theatrical and musical productions, and festivals. All of them have a gallery where the works of their members are displayed in changing exhibits. Several of the largest and most active are: **Academy Art Museum,** Easton; **Carroll County Arts Council Gallery,** inside a refurbished 1928 art deco movie house in Westminster; and **Washington County Arts Council,** Hagerstown.

The **Elkton Arts Center** in Elkton is a real standout. The **Garrett County Arts Council** has the only fine-arts gallery in its region.

BALLOONING Hot-air balloon rides are available from **Friendship Hot Air Balloon Company** (410-442-5566; www .ballooningusa.com) in West Friendship.

BEACHES **Ocean City** is, of course, the beach that comes to mind when you think of Maryland. And well it should. With its thousands of motel rooms, attractions by the score, and 10 miles of sand, it is the quintessential East Coast resort town. Just south of it is **Assateague Island** and 30 miles of beach with far fewer people (and amenities). If you are looking for even fewer people, know that hardly anyone ever takes advantage of the small public beach in **Public Landing.**

The beach on **Janes Island** in the Chesapeake Bay offers great seclusion, as it can only be reached by boat. Other beaches along the bay are easier to get to. **Betterton Beach** is the only one that has been completely free of sea nettles (jellyfish) for decades. **Sandy Point** near Annapolis is considered by many to be one of the bay's finest. **Chesapeake Beach** and neighboring **North Beach** were resort destinations in the early 1900s and are still nice, but now quieter, places. You have to take a hike to reach their beaches, but you can search for fossils once you are upon the sands of **Calvert Cliffs State Park** and **Flag Ponds Nature Park** near Lusby, and **Purse State Park** close to Marbury.

Many state parks have beaches along their lakes, and other small public beaches are mentioned throughout this book.

BED & BREAKFASTS I don't list every one that is in operation, but I have stayed in more than 100 B&Bs in Maryland and visited and inspected scores more. My selection ranges from modest homes to palatial mansions and includes working farms, waterfront cottages, historic town houses in busy downtown areas, rustic lodges in isolated woodlands, and more.

Each B&B is different, and it is this diversity that makes each place a new experience. As opposed to staying in a hotel or motel, a visit at a B&B is a much more personal way to get to know the locals and the area in which they live. Although you can make reservations by other means, I like making mine over the phone, as it gives me a chance to chat with the host and establish a relationship before I arrive.

Rates were current when this book went to press, but as in all things monetary, they will probably be a bit higher by the time you visit. Be aware that a number of B&Bs do not accept credit cards or children.

BICYCLING The relatively flat terrain of the eastern portion of Maryland has always made it popular with bicyclists, and the activity's growth in recent years has made the state even more biker-friendly. The *Maryland Bicycle Map* provides information on more than 50 places to road and/or mountain bike, describing several major long-distance trails and even bike-friendly ferry and transportation systems. The pamphlet *Bicycling in Maryland* contains additional biking and contact information. Both are available from the **Department of Transportation** (1-800-252-8776; www .mdot.maryland.gov). Local tourism offices usually have detailed information about their respective areas, such as the **Great Delmarva Bicycling Trail,** a 2,500-mile route that takes riders past the farmlands, swamps, marshes, creeks, and small towns of the three states located on the peninsula.

The 184.5-mile **C&O Canal** is probably the most popular biking route, but do not overlook the **Northern Central Railroad Trail, Baltimore and Annapolis Trail, Capital Crescent Trail, Rock Creek Trail, Western Maryland Rail Trail, Great Allegheny Passage,** and **ViewTrail 100 Bike Trail.** Also, many of Maryland's Scenic Byways (see *Scenic Drives*) are great road-riding journeys.

Adrenaline High (410-749-2886; www.adrenalinehigh.com) puts together customized bicycle tours in and around Somerset County on the Eastern Shore. **Mountainside Bike Tours** (301-722-4887; www.mountainsidebiketours.net) provides tours and a variety of services on the C&O

Canal, Great Allegheny Passage, and other places in Maryland and Pennsylvania.

BIRDING **Waterfowl** migrating through Maryland during spring and fall may be observed by the hundreds of thousands on the Eastern Shore in places such as **Blackwater National Wildlife Refuge, Eastern Neck National Wildlife Refuge,** and **Deal Island Wildlife Management Area.** *Birdwatcher's Guide to Delmarva* provides details on these and other Eastern Shore sites. **Sandy Point State Park** and **Point Lookout State Park** are a couple of hot spots on the Chesapeake Bay's western shore.

In addition to waterfowl, wide varieties of birds are often seen in **Merkle Wildlife Sanctuary, Greenwell State Park,** and **Patuxent Research Refuge. Clyburn Arboretum** is a favored Baltimore-area birding site, while a number of state-rare breeding species have been observed in **Finzel Swamp** and **Cranesville Swamp** in western Maryland. Rock outcrops along the route of the **Appalachian Trail** on South Mountain are the places to be for the **fall hawk migration.**

The Audubon Society leads bird walks at **Pickering Creek** and **Woodend.** The Wildfowl Trust of North America sponsors a number of walks each year in the **Chesapeake Bay Environmental Center.** Held annually, usually in late April, the **Delmarva Birding Weekend** (1-800-521-989) is a celebration with dozens of events throughout the three states. Activities include canoe and kayak trips, boat excursions, day and night hikes, and rallies where birders mingle on an informal basis. This is one of the country's premier birding events, attracting thousands of ornithological enthusiasts.

As stands to reason, the Baltimore oriole is the state bird.

BOATING AND SAILING EXCURSIONS To explore Maryland without taking a boating excursion of some kind or another is to miss an essential element of the state. Many of the outings are narrated (and are the ones I think you gain the most

from), and you can go onto the water in everything from sailboats to working fishing boats to boats built solely to thrill with speed. The Eastern Shore towns of Ocean City, Cambridge, Hurlock, St. Michaels, Stevensville, Grasonville, Chester, Rock Hall, North East, Solomons, Chesapeake City, and Tilghman Island all offer excursions. Two boats I especially enjoyed were the *Nathan of Dorchester* in Dorchester and the *Lady Patty* in Tilghman Island. Look to the harbors of Havre de Grace, Baltimore, Chesapeake Beach, and Annapolis for trips originating on the Chesapeake Bay's western shore.

A boating excursion of a different kind is the one-hour round-trip ride on a mule-powered boat on the C&O Canal at Great Falls.

BOAT RAMPS, PUBLIC The map *A Fisherman's Guide to Maryland Piers and Ramps* is available from the **Fisheries Service** (1-800-688-FINS; www.dnr.state.md.us) and highlights more than 240 public water-access areas throughout the state. *The Chesapeake Bay, Susquehanna River*

and Tidal Tributaries Public Access Guide provides even greater detail to those particular areas and can be obtained from the **Chesapeake Bay Program** (1-800-YOUR-BAY; www.chesapeakebay.net).

BOOKS It is always a good idea to read a few books to help you gain a greater awareness, enjoyment, and understanding of your surroundings. *Maryland: A Middle Temperament, 1634–1980*, by Brugger, Requardt, and Cottom, is an in-depth survey of the state's history. *Maryland: A New Guide to the Old Line State*, by Brugger and Papenfuse, covers the state's history by leading you on different driving tours; it would make a good companion to this book. It can be a little heavy on the technical aspects, but Edwin Danson's *Drawing the Line: How Mason and Dixon Surveyed the Most Famous Border in America* chronicles the task of delineating Maryland from Pennsylvania. *Maryland in the Civil War: A House Divided*, by Robert I. Cottom Jr. and Mary Ellen Haward, may be the best way to learn about the state's role during the war without having to read multiple volumes. *Home on the Canal*, by Elizabeth Kytle, is interesting for its historical information, but even more so when it provides firsthand accounts of those who lived and worked on the C&O Canal.

James Michener wrote what may be the best-selling Maryland novel of all time, *Chesapeake*, which describes life around the bay through the eyes of the early settlers and on up to those inhabiting the land in later years. William Martin's novel of intrigue and romance, *Annapolis*, uses the city as a background.

Tom Horton lived and worked among the local people so that he could write his intimate portrait, *An Island Out of Time: A Memoir of Smith Island in the Chesapeake*. *Chesapeake Almanac: Following the Bay Through the Seasons* is a collection of newspaper columns by John Page William Jr. that takes you through a year's worth of natural world events around the bay. *Chesapeake Bay: Nature of an Estuary*, by Christopher P. White, is another good book about the environment of the bay.

Baseball fans will enjoy Lois P. Nicholson's *From Maryland to Cooperstown: Seven Maryland Natives in Baseball's Hall of Fame.*

Maryland author Nora Roberts has sold more than 280 million copies of women's novels, a number of them set in Maryland, while mystery writer Martha Grimes turns out one book after another, some of which also feature locations in the state. The comments of the great Baltimore newspaper writer H. L. Mencken have been gathered into several volumes and should be looked over for their caustic wit and ironic observations.

If planning outdoor activities, I recommend you consult my guidebook *50 Hikes in Maryland* (Countryman Press Guides), as well as *Hikes in Western Maryland* by the Potomac Appalachian Trail Club; *Birdwatcher's Guide to Delmarva;* and *Finding Wildflowers in the Washington, DC/Baltimore Area. Hiking, Biking, and Canoeing in Maryland*, by Bryan MacKay, focuses on outings appropriate for families with children.

BUS SERVICE Greyhound (1-800-231-2222; www.greyhound.com) services the Eastern Shore towns of Ocean City, Princess Anne, Easton, and Salisbury. Greyhound also serves Baltimore, Annapolis, Frederick, Hagerstown, New Carrollton, and Silver Spring.

CAMPING Reservations for campsites and cabins in state parks can be made by calling 1-888-432-CAMP or online at http://reservations.dnr.state.md.us. A few are open year-round, but most of the parks' campgrounds are open from early spring to late fall. Backcountry camping is permitted in many state forests, but information (and payment of a fee) must be obtained from each state forest office.

More than 30 campsites, with chemical toilets and drinking water (in-season), are strung along the **C&O Canal National Historical Park** (301-739-4200; www .nps.gov/choh). Only two, Antietam Creek and Fifteen Mile Creek, charge a fee; all others are free, and all are operated on a first-come, first-served basis. Reservations can be made for camping in **Assateague Island National Seashore** and **Greenbelt Park** by calling 1-877-444-6777 or logging onto www.recreation.gov. Call 301-663-9388 for camping reservations in **Catoctin Mountain Park.**

The largest percentage of commercial campgrounds listed in this book have hookups and other facilities for those traveling and camping with trailers or RVs.

CHESAPEAKE BAY If there is any one thing that defines Maryland, especially its eastern portion, it is water—and the Chesapeake Bay is the state's most immense body of water. As America's largest bay, it is the catch basin for a far-reaching drainage system that covers 64,000 square miles. Snowmelt that begins its downstream journey near Cooperstown, New York, meets and mingles in the bay with rainwater that fell on the higher elevations of the Allegheny Mountains on the western Maryland–West Virginia border. The bay is considered an estuary—a body of water in which tidal movements bring salt water upstream, where it comes in contact with the fresh water being carried toward the ocean by river currents.

There are many other estuaries throughout the world, such as Puget Sound in Washington, Cook Inlet in Alaska, and the fjords of Norway, but none of them is nearly as productive as the Chesapeake Bay. Millions of pounds of seafood are harvested

from the bay most years, including a large percentage of America's supply of **blue crabs** and **oysters.** A number of conditions combine to make the bay this productive. Probably the two most important factors are the large amounts of fresh water coming into the bay and the vast acreages of marshlands surrounding it, which produce an abundance of detritus and other nutrients. These wetlands are home to numerous shorebirds and are also major resting areas on the **Great Atlantic Flyway** for migratory waterfowl.

The **Chesapeake Bay Gateways Network** (1-866-229-9297; www.baygateways.net) is a system of parks, refuges, historic towns, and museums (most of which are described in this book), each of which tells a part of the bay's natural history and impact on Maryland's way of life. The brochure is available from the **Maryland Office of Tourism Development** (see *Information*).

CHESAPEAKE & OHIO (C&O) CANAL The 184.5-mile C&O Canal, running from Georgetown to Cumberland, has excellent opportunities for hiking, biking, canoeing, camping, horseback riding, insights into history, and more for the entire family. I have included information on these activities in the appropriate chapters. Please consult the **C&O Canal National Historical Park** sidebar on page 309 to learn more about the colorful history of this national treasure and how you can best explore it.

CHILDREN, ESPECIALLY FOR The crayon symbol ✐ identifies activities and places of special interest to children and families.

CIVIL WAR As a border state, Maryland was a hotbed of activity during the Civil War. **Antietam National Battlefield** at Sharpsburg and **Monocacy National Battlefield** near Frederick preserve the sites of two of the war's most important battles. In Cambridge, **REI Heritage Tours** (410-820-8350; www.the-rock-newsmagazine.com/harriet.tubman.tours.html) sponsors

guided tours that reveal the story of Ms. Tubman, who led scores of slaves to freedom along the Underground Railroad.

Baltimore Civil War Museum tells of the city's part during the war and in the Underground Railroad. The **National Museum of Civil War Medicine** in Frederick vividly portrays medicine's role. Other sites, battles, and museums of Civil War significance are detailed in their respective sections of each chapter.

A brochure detailing a statewide **Civil War Driving Trail** and another about individual **Civil War trails,** plus other information concerning Maryland's role in the conflict, can be obtained from the **Maryland Office of Tourism Development** (see *Information*). The local tourism offices can provide Civil War information and trail brochures pertinent to their own areas, such as the *1862 Antietam Campaign* in Frederick and Washington Counties and *John Wilkes Booth: Escape of an Assassin* in southern Maryland.

COVERED BRIDGES Spanning a waterway within the Fair Hill Natural Resources Management Area is the **Big Elk Creek Covered Bridge.** About 3 miles north of North East on MD 272 is the **Gilpin Falls Covered Bridge,** the longest covered bridge still standing in the state. The circa-1865 **Jericho Covered Bridge** is near Kingsville. **Utica Covered Bridge, Loy's Station Covered Bridge,**

and **Roddy Road Covered Bridge** are all north of Frederick.

CRABS **Blue crabs** can be found from North America's Cape Cod to South America's Uruguay, and even in Egypt's Nile River. It is in the Chesapeake Bay, however, that they had historically reached their greatest numbers, and Maryland crabs have the reputation of being the finest. The harvest fluctuates from year to year—and has been on a downward trend for a while—yet thousands of pounds are still caught and eaten each year. Crab houses serve up bushels of heavily spiced steamed crabs, and soft-shell crabs are considered a real delicacy, while the state's succulent **crabcakes** are known far and wide. I find it amusing that, as you travel around the state, you will find almost every restaurant that serves seafood has "the region's best crabcakes," "the Eastern Shore's best crabcakes," "the best crabcakes in Maryland," or even "the world's best crabcakes."

One of the most fun activities a visitor to the Chesapeake Bay can do is to go **crabbing** by becoming what the local folks call a "chicken necker." This is done by attaching a chicken neck (or any other bony piece of meat) to a string and casting it a few feet out into the water. Gradually pull the string in when you feel a tug on it. With luck, a crab will be hanging tenaciously on to the bait, and you can slip a net under it before you lift it out of the water. Be careful of the claws when you turn the net over to gently shake the crab out! No license is required for recreational crabbing (if you take less than two dozen hard-shell crabs), but I suggest you follow what is the law for commercial crabbing and not keep a crab that is less than 5 inches from shell point to shell point.

The interesting lives of blue crabs are described in superbly entertaining and nontechnical detail in William Warner's Pulitzer Prize–winning *Beautiful Swimmers: Watermen, Crabs, and the Chesapeake Bay.* "Beautiful swimmers" is the English translation of the blue crab's genus/species name, *Callinectes sapidus.*

tinctive event or celebration takes place almost every day of the year. Leading annual events are noted in the *Special Events* section at the end of each chapter. A brochure published each year by the **Maryland Office of Tourism Development** (see *Information*) describes hundreds of events that will take place within the calendar year; a number of them are one-time occurrences.

FACTORY OUTLETS There are a number of modern, mall-type outlets, and they are noted in their respective chapters under *Selective Shopping*.

FARMER'S MARKETS Farmer's markets can be found in every region of the state and are listed in the *Selective Shopping* section of each chapter. I love going to them, but be aware that the locations and operating days and times of farmer's markets have been known to change frequently.

FERRIES Relics of the past, only a few ferries remain in Maryland. Their historic aspect and the scenic beauty of the waterways they cross make using one as much of a fun excursion as a utilitarian necessity. The **Whitehaven Ferry** is connected to a fixed line and crosses the Wicomico River about 18 miles west of Salisbury. The **Upper Ferry** crosses the Wicomico River less than 10 miles west of Salisbury. The **Oxford–Bellevue Ferry** enables a circular driving tour of Easton, Oxford, and St.

DECOY CARVING AND WILDLIFE ART **Steve and Lem Ward** are generally acknowledged as being the ones who elevated decoy carving into an art form. Their workshop in Crisfield has been preserved, while the **Ward Museum of Wildlife Art** in Salisbury exhibits their work and chronicles the history of decoy carving. Other significant decoy displays are in the **Upper Bay Museum** in North East and the **Havre de Grace Decoy Museum.** The **Ward World Championship Wildfowl Carving Competition,** held each spring in Ocean City, is the world's largest carving competition.

DELMARVA The word *Delmarva* refers to the entire Eastern Shore peninsula, which is composed of portions of Delaware, Maryland, and Virginia.

EMERGENCIES Hospitals with emergency rooms are noted near the beginning of each chapter. A few urgent-care facilities that can handle minor emergencies are also listed. Dialing **911** anywhere in the state will connect you to an emergency service. For highway accidents or assistance, the **state police** can be reached at 410-653-4200, on **CB Channel 9,** or **Cellular #77.**

EVENTS County fairs, arts and crafts demonstrations, fishing tournaments, skill competitions, historic reenactments, music concerts, crab festivals: Some kind of dis-

Michaels by making a crossing on the Tred Avon River. **White's Ferry,** the only remaining ferry across the Potomac River, permits you to come into Maryland near Poolesville from US 15 just north of Leesburg, Virginia.

Much larger, the **Cape May, New Jersey–Lewes, Delaware, Ferry** (1-800-643-3779; www.cmlf.com) can save you hours and many miles of driving if you are arriving on the Eastern Shore from New Jersey.

FISHING The **Department of Natural Resources/Fisheries Service** (1-800-688-FINS; www.dnr.state.md.us) can supply the information you need about regulations and licenses, and has free publications geared toward tidal, freshwater, trout, fly-, and other types of fishing.

Within the *Fishing* section of the chapters are places to fish on your own, or companies and individuals who provide guided trips. The Web site for the **Maryland Charter Boat Association** (www .marylandcharterboats.com) contains the largest list of charter-boat captains on the Chesapeake Bay, while local tourism offices (see *Guidance* in each chapter) maintain lists of reliable captains and fishing guides.

GOLF The courses listed under the *To Do* section in each chapter are public courses that do not require payment of a membership fee. The *Maryland Golf Guide,* available from the **Maryland Office of Tourism Development** (see *Information*), outlines public, semiprivate, and private courses.

HANDICAPPED ACCESS
The wheelchair symbol ᕕ appears next to lodgings, restaurants, and attractions that are partially or completely handicapped accessible.

HIGHWAY TRAVEL The speed limit on interstates is 65 miles per hour unless otherwise noted. Driver and passengers are required to wear safety belts, and children under the age of four or those weighing less than 40 pounds must be in approved child-

safety seats. Driving lights must be on whenever you are using windshield wipers. You may make a right turn at a red signal light after coming to a complete stop unless posted signs prohibit doing so.

Call the **State Highway Administration's Construction Hotline** (410-545-0300; 1-800-323-6742; http://sha.md.gov) Mon.–Fri. 8–4:30 to obtain the latest information on construction projects that may impact your travel plans. The commission's Web site provides up-to-date road conditions during inclement weather and a wealth of road-travel information.

The official state highway map can be obtained from the **Maryland Office of Tourism Development** (see *Information*). Available at bookshops and many convenience stores, the *Maryland and Delaware Atlas and Gazetteer* (published by DeLorme) is an invaluable navigation tool.

HIKING I have included the state's best hiking excursions under the *Hiking* section of each chapter; look at the *Bicycling, Birding, Parks, Gardens,* and *Nature Preserves* sections for additional opportunities to walk outdoors.

Recommended resources include *Weekend Walks on the Delmarva Peninsula,* by Jay Abercrombie; *Country Walks Near Washington,* by Alan Fisher; and *Country Walks Near Baltimore,* by Alan Hall Fisher. One of my own books, *50 Hikes in Maryland* (Countryman Press), covers the entire

There is often a line waiting to get into Havre de Grace's **Bomboy's Homemade Ice Cream.** **Hoffman's** in Westminster has been using the same recipes since it opened in 1947. **Mother's Federal Hill Grille** and **Maggie Moo's** are located in Baltimore. **Baugher's** in Westminster and **Queen City Creamery and Deli** in Cumberland serve their ice creams within a restaurant setting, while the peach ice cream at **Kent Fort Farm** in Stevensville is available only during the August Peach Festival. **Scottish Highlands Ice Cream** in Oxford should not be missed.

The crème de la crème is **Lakeside Creamery** at Deep Creek Lake. The owner is such a master at his craft that people travel from foreign lands just to take his classes on producing homemade ice cream.

INFORMATION Regional information sources are described under the Guidance section near the beginning of each chapter. The **Maryland Office of Tourism Development** (410-767-3400; 1-866-639-2536; www.visitmaryland.org), 217 E. Redwood St., Baltimore, 21202, publishes *Destination Maryland,* an annual guide to many attractions, outdoor opportunities, and lodging facilities throughout the state. The office can also be the source for numerous brochures on specialized topics such as golfing, biking, antiques, canoeing, fishing, and more.

Please Note: As this book went to press, the state of Maryland had closed most of its **Welcome Centers** due to budgetary reasons. That information has been left in this book in the hope that the centers will reopen when the fiscal situation improves. It is also to let you know that the restrooms at most of the sites have remained open.

state with outings ranging from easy, one-hour jaunts to multiday backpacking treks.

HORSEBACK RIDING Places to ride your own horse and businesses offering guided rides are listed under the *To Do* section of a chapter; additional places to ride can often be found by looking in the *Bicycling, Hiking,* and *Parks* sections of a chapter. **The Equiery** (1-800-244-9580; www.equiery.com) publishes a directory to rental stables and guided trail rides in the state.

HUNTING A comprehensive booklet, *Hunting and Trapping in Maryland,* can be obtained from the **Department of Natural Resources** (410-260-8540; www.dnr.state.md.us).

If you like the outdoors but are not a hunter, be aware that hunting is permitted in wildlife management areas, state forests, and some state parks. Although the law is under pressure to change, Sunday hunting was still prohibited in most places as this book went to press; be sure to check local regulations.

ICE CREAM, HOMEMADE When I started adding them up, I was amazed at just how many places produce homemade ice cream; no wonder I put on a few pounds researching this book. **Dumser's Drive-In** at Ocean City serves it within a few hours of making it. **Canal Creamery** is on the waterfront in Chesapeake City.

INSECTS Warm weather brings no-see-ums, gnats, fleas, sand fleas, deerflies, mosquitoes, ticks, and more. Although the mountains have their fair share, the lowlands, marshes, and beaches of the eastern part of the state, especially southern Maryland and the Eastern Shore, can be nearly swarming with them at times. Bring lots of repellent on any outing from late spring through midfall. (And remember that one of the pleasures of travel during the colder months of the year is the absence of insects.)

KAYAKING AND CANOEING
The kayaking and canoeing are soft and easy along the streams and creeks of the Eastern Shore and southern Maryland, while winds across the Chesapeake Bay can test the mettle of an experienced kayaker. The rushing waters of western Maryland can require such technical skill that they have been used for national and international competitions and by athletes training for the Olympics.

Included in the *Kayaking and Canoeing* section of the various chapters are guided trips by outfitters as well as places to paddle on your own. Also consult the *Boat Rentals* and *Parks* sections.

Administered by the National Park Service, the **Captain John Smith Chesapeake National Historic Trail** commemorates the captain's early 1600s explorations of the Chesapeake Bay and its many tributaries. Like Smith, you could easily spend years on these explorations. This is America's first national water trail, and much of it is still in the planning stage, so consult www.nps.gov/cajo for the most up-to-date information.

LIGHTHOUSES
Lighthouses have helped provide safe passage for commercial and recreational boats navigating the Chesapeake Bay and other state waters for well over 100 years. Of the 44 once in Maryland, only about 25 remain, and most are no longer in service. **Hooper Straight Lighthouse** in St. Michaels and **Drum Point** in Solomons have been moved to museums and are two of the most visited. **Cove Point,** the oldest continuously used lighthouse in the state, is at the mouth of the Patuxent River north of Solomons.

Concord Point is along a waterside walkway in Havre de Grace, while **Turkey Point** is reached by a 1-mile hike in Elk Neck State Park. **Sevenfoot Knoll,** now in Baltimore's Inner Harbor, was moved from its original location at nearby Pier 5. **Piney**

Point has an adjacent museum, while **Point Lookout** is open to the public only on special occasions; both are at the tip of southern Maryland where the Potomac River meets the bay.

MARITIME MUSEUMS
The **Chesapeake Bay Maritime Museum** in St. Michaels is the state's largest and one of the finest on the East Coast. The **Calvert Marine Museum** in Solomons is another standout. At the head of the bay is the **Havre de Grace Maritime Museum,** while Cambridge on the Eastern Shore has the **Richardson Maritime Museum. Baltimore Maritime Museum** has no real walls, as it consists of three ships docked about a block from one another.

MOTELS AND HOTELS
For the most part, chain motels and hotels have not been listed because information about them is easily obtained from many sources and because their architecture and amenities tend to have a cookie-cutter sameness. Those that are included are in areas where lodging options are few, are in a desirable location, or are outstanding places to stay.

THE NATIONAL ROAD
In 1775, British forces under Gen. Edward Braddock, accompanied by a young George Washington, widened a Native American trail through Turners Gap to facilitate their march westward, where they were

ambushed (and Braddock killed) by French and Indian troops in Pennsylvania. With funds provided by the state in 1806, the route was improved, extended from Baltimore to Cumberland, and named the **National Pike.** At the same time, the U.S. Congress also authorized federal funds for another road, this one to begin in Cumberland and head westward. Eventually the two roads came to be known as the National Road. As one of the major thoroughfares of the day, it was traveled by such luminaries as Abraham Lincoln, Daniel Webster, Henry Clay, and Presidents Jackson, William Henry Harrison, Polk, Taylor, and Van Buren.

US 40 in Maryland follows the route of what was once the National Road and was named an **All American Road** in 2002. As you explore Maryland, take a break from the interstate to travel the roadway and discover historic sites you would otherwise pass by. A map guide that provides more details about the route may be obtained from local tourism offices or the **Maryland Office of Tourism Development** (see *Information*).

NATURE TOURISM The **Department of Natural Resources** has embarked upon what I think is one of the most exciting and farsighted ventures to come along in years. By using state employees, contracts with private outfitters, and some volunteers, the Nature Tourism program offers recreational and educational

opportunities for adults and children of all skill and fitness levels to experience the outdoors. Hiking, biking, rock climbing, caving, horseback riding, kayaking, canoeing, rafting, fishing, bird-watching, camping, and day camps are just a few of the many organized and guided activities the program has offered—usually at a fairly low cost. New ones are being added all the time. Call 1-800-830-3974 or log onto www.dnr.state.md.us/outdooradventures for detailed information.

OLD LINE STATE One of Maryland's nicknames is the Old Line State. It does not refer to the Mason-Dixon Line as many people believe but goes back to the Revolutionary War. Maryland's Governor Smallwood had led a group of state volunteers to help George Washington in New York. The Marylanders held their line of defense against the British long enough to permit Washington's troops to escape and regroup to fight another day. He was so impressed that Washington ever after referred to Maryland as the "Old Line State."

PARKS, NATIONAL Assateague **Island National Seashore** shares the barrier island with Maryland's **Assateague State Park** and Virginia's **Chincoteague National Wildlife Refuge.** Undeveloped, except for a couple of campgrounds and a few visitors centers, the island offers close to 30 miles of unbroken sandy beaches on which to beachcomb, swim, sunbathe, surf, or fish. A hike of 25 miles can be accomplished by making use of designated campsites (and carrying plenty of water!). **Greenbelt Park,** close to Washington, DC, has a campground and a trail system within a forest bordered by four-lane highways. **Catoctin Mountain Park,** north of Frederick, is home to the U.S. presidential retreat, **Camp David,** and miles of pathways leading to spectacular viewpoints.

Among other components of the U.S. National Park Service are **Antietam National Battlefield, C&O Canal National Historical Park, Fort Washington, Glen Echo Park, Oxon Hill Farm, Piscataway Park,** and a number of historic

buildings and structures, such as the **Thomas Stone National Historic Site** near Port Tobacco.

PARKS AND FORESTS, STATE

With more than 280,000 acres of land, there is a state park or forest within a 40-minute drive of any location in Maryland. Admission to the state forests and some of the state parks is free, but some have a nominal entrance or parking fee, usually around $5. Many of the state parks have campgrounds and cabins for rent, and back-country camping is permitted in some of the state forests (see *Camping*, above). Consult the *Bicycling, Hiking, Kayaking and Canoeing*, and *Parks* sections in each chapter to find what is available in each region. The **Department of Natural Resources–State Forest and Park Service** (410-974-3771; 1-800-830-3974; www.dnr.state.md.us) can send you a packet brimming with all kinds of information.

PETS The dog-paw symbol 🐾 appears next to places, activities, and lodgings that accept pets. Always inform a hotel, motel, B&B, or other lodging that you will be trav-

eling with your pet; expect to pay an additional fee.

PICK-YOUR-OWN PRODUCE

There's just something about a strawberry, tomato, or peach picked ripe off the plant that grocery-store produce can't match. Farms and orchards that invite the public into their fields and orchards are listed in each chapter. Unless you don't mind just taking a drive in the country, it is a wise idea to call ahead to confirm what is ripe and at what time and day you may come out to pick.

POPULATION The state's population was 5,773,552 according to the 2010 federal census.

RAILROAD RIDES AND MUSEUMS

Rail fans, and children, enjoy the excursions offered by the **Walkersville Southern Railroad** near Frederick and **Western Maryland Scenic Railroad** in Cumberland and Frostburg.

Baltimore's **B&O Railroad Museum** has 40 acres of locomotives, cars, and artifacts. Built around 1830, the **Ellicott City B&O Railroad Station Museum** is the oldest railroad terminal in America. **Brunswick Railroad Museum** features a model layout of the B&O line from Washington, DC, to Brunswick. Hagerstown's **Roundhouse Museum** is from the days when five different lines converged on the city.

SAILING LESSONS **Annapolis Sailing School** is one of the world's most well-respected institutions of sailing knowledge. Also in Annapolis, **Womanship, Inc.,** has sailing instruction taught by and for women.

Rock Hall has the **Maryland School of Sailing and Seamanship.** North of Baltimore in Havre de Grace is **BaySail.** In western Maryland, you can learn to hoist a sail on a lake at the **Deep Creek Sailing School.**

SCENIC BYWAYS I had originally intended to point out quite a number of

Maryland's scenic drives (and I do include a few), but when I discovered the excellent *Maryland Byways* book and accompanying *Scenic Byways Map*, it seemed that the effort would be superfluous.

First of all, the nearly 200-page book is free and can be obtained from most local tourism offices, state welcome centers, the **Maryland Office of Tourism Development** (see *Information*), or the **Maryland Scenic Byways, Office of Environmental Design** (1-877-MDBYWAY; http://roads .maryland.gov).

Second, the book gives directions for more than a dozen drives throughout the state, with detailed background information on the human and natural history of the area driven through, sites along the route, recreational opportunities, and even side trips worth taking. The shortest byway is 7 miles in Baltimore; several are about 200 miles each, with a couple stretching from western Maryland to Baltimore and Washington, DC. The longest, more than 400 miles, is a thorough exploration of the Eastern Shore.

This is a great explorer's resource—and remember, it is available free for the asking.

SEA NETTLES A jellyfish with long tentacles, known as a sea nettle, increases in number as the temperatures of summer warm the Chesapeake Bay, its tributaries, and the Atlantic Ocean. Its sting can be a source of irritation for many hours. Alcohol, vinegar, baking soda, or meat tenderizer may help relieve the pain, but some people

have severe allergic reactions that require them to be hospitalized.

SKIING, CROSS-COUNTRY New Germany and **Herrington Manor state parks** have trails groomed and tracked just for cross-country skiing. The parks also provide ski rentals and warming huts. Information on the many miles of ungroomed trails around the **Deep Creek Lake** area can be obtained from the **Garrett County Chamber of Commerce** (301-387-4386; www .garrettchamber.com).

Piney Run Park near Sykesville, the **Catoctin Mountain Park, C&O Canal,** and **Appalachian Trail** all make for good cross-country ski outings when enough snow falls to cover the roots and rocks.

SKIING, DOWNHILL Wisp Resort, at Deep Creek Lake, is the state's only downhill skiing spot. It has what is considered to be one of the best snowmaking systems in the world, so all that is really needed is cold weather for the trails to be open. Snowboarding, cross-country skiing, tubing, night skiing, and children's programs are also available.

SNOWMOBILING The Deep Creek Lake area welcomes snowmobilers. **Deep Creek Lake, Garrett State Forest, Potomac State Forest,** and **Savage River State Forest** have a combined total of 75 miles of marked trails open for backcountry travel. The **Garrett County Chamber of Commerce** (301-387-4386; www .garrettchamber.com) can supply detailed information.

STAR-SPANGLED BANNER TRAIL A 100-mile scenic and historic driving tour that follows the route taken by the British when they invaded the Chesapeake Bay area in the 1814, the trail takes in numerous sites that highlight the events leading up to the Battle of Baltimore, which inspired Francis Scott Key to write the words that became America's national anthem. Some sites are identified by little more than a marker, others include extensive museums, while still others take in entire towns and cities, such as St. Michaels and Annapolis. A detailed, full-color brochure can be obtained from most state visitors centers or from the **Maryland Office of Tourism Development** (see *Information*).

TAXES The state sales tax is 6 percent; lodging, meals, and amusement taxes can be well in excess of 10 percent.

WATERFALLS Swallow Falls State Park near Oakland has a 1.5-mile circuit hike that will lead you to four different waterfalls. **Muddy Creek Falls** is considered the highest in the state, **Lower Falls** and **Swallow Falls** are on the Youghiogheny River, and there is a sandy beach at **Toliver Falls.**

The round-trip journey to **Cunningham Falls** near Thurmont is an easy 1-mile hike. **Falling Branch,** in Rocks State Park near Jarrettsville, and **Great Falls,** in the Potomac River, are on the fall line where the piedmont meets the Coastal Plain.

Incidentally, despite the name, there are no waterfalls in Gunpowder Falls State Park. *Falls* was a colonial term for "river."

WEATHER Maryland can have a wide range of temperatures and conditions. Winters can be unpredictably cold or relatively mild, while summers can become hot and humid or may be rather temperate. Spring and autumn can be the most pleasant times of the year, as days warm up to a comfortable degree, nights cool down for easy sleeping, and crowds are fewer.

Snow is common in the mountains, moderate in the Capital and Central

regions, and quite infrequent in southern Maryland and the Eastern Shore. When heat and humidity have taken the joy and fun out of the eastern portion of the state, the mountains will beckon with temperatures that can be 10 or more degrees lower. Exploring Maryland can be a year-round activity.

WHITE-WATER RAFTING **Precision Rafting** in Friendsville is the premier Maryland company that runs the Upper Youghiogheny River as it passes through a narrow, 5-mile gorge with nearly continuous Class IV and V rapids. **River and Trail Outfitters** in Knoxville and **Outdoor Excursions** in Boonsboro have runs along the (usually) calmer Potomac River. **Adventure Sports Center International** near Deep Creek Lake can change the difficulty of its mountaintop-constructed course with the push of a button.

The Eastern Shore

1

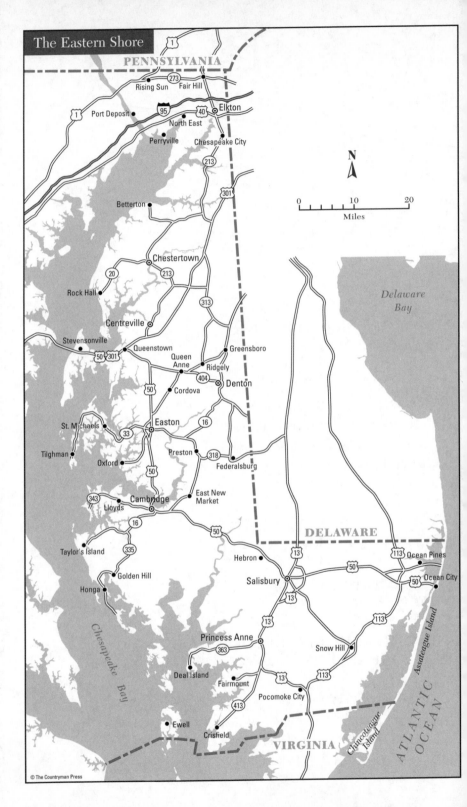

The Eastern Shore

© The Countryman Press

THE EASTERN SHORE

Maryland's Eastern Shore is a land where time has stood still—or at least slowed down considerably.

In search of flounder, crabs, clams, oysters, and other delicacies of the deep, watermen still rise before dawn to venture onto the Chesapeake Bay or the Atlantic Ocean. Moving about in small craft often with a crew of just one or two people, they use many of the same techniques that their fathers and grandfathers used decades ago.

The area is unmarred by huge malls and strips of fast-food restaurants; the only industry in many of the unpretentious fishing villages are small seafood-processing plants at water's edge. Thriving downtown districts still exist in a number of small towns. Blessed with a long growing season and fertile soil, the flat fields surrounding the towns produce a rich harvest of corn, beans, tomatoes, peppers, and other vegetables.

The completion of the Bay Bridge in 1952 opened the Eastern Shore to a rush of travelers and new residents. Although rising amounts of traffic and tourism have resulted in subtle changes in Eastern Shore lifestyles, outside influences have also helped bring about an increased awareness of the need to preserve the natural world.

Migrating shorebirds, waterfowl, raptors, and songbirds—including sandpipers, plovers, dowitchers, knots, whimbrels, ducks, geese, herons, egrets, swans, pelicans, falcons, and ospreys—make use of the islands, marshlands, and fields as major resting areas. Thousands of waterfowl, such as snow geese, black ducks, mallards, and pintails, winter here.

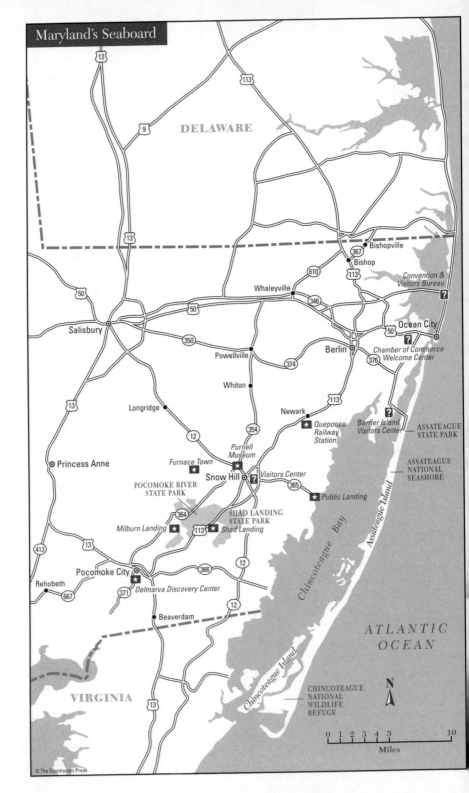

Maryland's Seaboard

MARYLAND'S SEABOARD

OCEAN CITY, ASSATEAGUE ISLAND, AND BERLIN

When Marylanders, especially those from the Baltimore–Annapolis area, say they are "goin' down'e ocean," they mean they will be spending time on the beach at Ocean City. My wife is a native Annapolitan, and her earliest vacation memories are of packing up the beach blankets and sand buckets and spending a few hours in the car anticipating the first whiff of salty air. It is such an entrenched tradition that generation after generation return here, going so far as to spend their vacation time in the exact same motel or B&B room as their parents or grandparents did.

The area began developing as a resort destination in 1869 when Isaac C. Coffin built the Rhode Island Inn. Within a few years, a group of developers received a land grant, and the Atlantic Hotel—still in operation—was opened in 1875.

The construction of a railroad bridge across the Sinepuxent Bay in 1880 connected the mainland to the resort, which was soon host to more than 5,000 visitors a year. Although Ocean City continued to grow in popularity, the city and surrounding area were struck by a major storm in 1933 that destroyed almost the entire infrastructure and nearly every building and road. The storm cut an inlet into the bay, separating the city from what is now called Assateague Island and creating ideal conditions for commercial and sportfishing. Boats could dock in the quiet waters of the bay but have quick access to the ocean for deep-sea fishing.

A four-lane bridge across the bay was constructed in 1941, and Ocean City has continued to grow in popularity since.

With its 10-mile-long beach, the city has many of the aspects of beach towns farther north, such as a 3-mile boardwalk, amusement parks and arcades next to and close to the beach, and an abundance of saltwater taffy and other goodies stores. Yet its waters are warmer and gentler, like those of the ocean resorts found in South Carolina and Georgia.

The southern end of the boardwalk, with arcades, amusement parks, many fast-food spots, and the widest part of the beach, attracts the most people, while the central portion of the boardwalk has the largest number of high-rise condos and hotels. Those looking for a quieter family atmosphere on the sand often book motels north of the boardwalk.

Almost everyone who visits Ocean City makes the short drive to Assateague Island to catch a glimpse of the wild ponies made famous by Marguerite Henry's popular series of children's books, beginning with *Misty of Chincoteague* in 1947.

A barrier island, Assateague is the farthest east you can go to take a hike or camp in Maryland. Formed by sand that constant waves have raised from the gently sloping ocean floor, a string of such islands extends along the East Coast from Plum Island, Massachusetts,

WILD PONIES GRAZE ON ASSATEAGUE ISLAND.

to Padre Island, Texas. Being prime beachfront property, many have been heavily developed and turned into typical high-rise resort areas.

The same thing almost happened to Assateague Island. Having purchased the largest majority of it in Maryland, the Ocean Beach Corporation began subdividing the island into small plots in the 1950s. Within a few years, there was a paved road running down the interior of the island, electric lines had been installed, close to 6,000 plots had been sold, and a number of houses already built.

Then a northeaster that struck in March 1962 drove the ocean completely across the island in several places. Almost every house was demolished, the power lines were downed and severed, and the road destroyed, with most of its pavement washed away. Realizing the enormous costs of trying to maintain a modern way of life on the island, private investors began to shy away, and the federal government was able to establish Assateague Island National Seashore in 1965.

Today the entire island is public land and administered as the national seashore by the U.S. National Park Service, Assateague State Park under the jurisdiction of the Maryland Department of Natural Resources, and, on the Virginia side of the island, Chincoteague National Wildlife Refuge within the auspices of the U.S. Fish and Wildlife Service. What this means to you is that the island's 37-mile beach has been left gloriously undeveloped, with just a few minor amenities, such as couple of campgrounds, visitors centers, and a few nature trails concentrated in two small areas.

COMMUNITIES **Berlin** has retained so much of its small-town look and atmosphere that Hollywood has chosen it as the setting for several movies. Two of the most recent are the Julia Roberts and Richard Gere film *Runaway Bride* and Disney's 2002 release of *Tuck Everlasting*.

The town dates from a 1677, 300-acre land grant establishing the Burley Plantation. It was not named in honor of the German city; most historians believe the name was derived from a local habit of quickly saying and slurring the name of one of the town's inns, the Burleigh Inn. Its fortunes were in many ways tied to those of Ocean City, as it slowly prospered by becoming a stopping-over point or an alternate destination for travelers headed to the beach.

Today the Atlantic Hotel, built in the late 1800s, sits in the center of the town's well-preserved historic district. Visitors now come to walk the tree-lined streets, stopping to

The town of **Snow Hill** was chartered in 1686, and only eight years later it was named a
Royal Port, reflecting its advantageous location. The Chincoteague Bay and access to the
Atlantic Ocean were only 7 miles to the east, while the Chesapeake Bay at Pocomoke Sound
was less than 30 miles down the river. Snow Hill retained its prominence long into the 19th
century, as the railroad came through the center of town. The town is the seat of government
for Worcester County, and many of its old homes and other historic structures remain along
its tree-shaded streets. The small business district is still located where it always was, close to
the river—now a playground for recreational boaters.

Pocomoke City, also located along the Pocomoke River, shares much of the same history as
Snow Hill. With deeper water, though, it was able to service much larger ships, which it still
does today. The Victorian Costen House helps preserve the town's history, while the board-
walked trail in Cypress Park is a great place to enjoy the area's natural habitats.

GUIDANCE The **Ocean City Convention and Visitors Bureau** (410-289-2800; 1-800-
OC-OCEAN; www.ococean.com) operates a large information center attached to the convention center at 4001 Coastal Hwy., Ocean City.

The **Ocean City Chamber of Commerce** (1-888-OCMD-FUN; www.oceancity.org) has a
welcome center just a few miles west of the beach on US 50 in West Ocean City.

The **Ocean City Downtown Association** (410-289-1413; www.downtownassociation.net)
has a small information center in its office at 605 Baltimore Ave.

Exhibits, an aquarium, and brochures about Assateague Island are available at the National
Park Service's **Barrier Island Visitors Center** (410-641-1441; 410-641-3030; www.nps.gov
/asis), 7206 National Seashore Lane, Berlin.

The **Worcester County Tourism Office** (410-632-3110; 1-800-852-0335; www.visit
worcester.org) is located at 104 W. Market St. in Snow Hill.

GETTING THERE *By air:* The **Ocean City Airport** (410-213-2471; www.oceancity
airport.com) is available to private planes, while the **Salisbury/Ocean City Airport** (410-
548-4827; www.flysbyairport.com), which is located about 30 minutes west of the ocean,
receives regularly scheduled flights.

By car: **US 50** is the route that will bring you into the city from points to the north, west,
and south. If possible, plan your arrival for times other than Friday afternoon or evening and
Saturday morning, and your departure other than Sunday. Doing so will permit you to avoid
miles of bumper-to-bumper cars moving at
a snail's pace. **US 113** and **US 13** are the
main arteries through Worcester County
and provide access to major side routes. US
13 also offers a shorter, less congested
travel alternative between Wilmington,
Delaware, and Norfolk, Virginia.

By ferry: If coming from New Jersey and
other places to the northeast, you can save
yourself a number of hours and many miles
by taking the **Cape May, New Jersey–
Lewes, Delaware, Ferry** (1-800-64-
FERRY; www.cmlf.com; for schedule and
reservations) and driving through Rehoboth
Beach to Ocean City.

ADDITIONAL SOURCES OF INFORMATION

A number of publications, such as *Sunny Day
Guide to Ocean City, Ocean City Visitors
Guide,* and *Ocean City: Sea for Yourself,* are
available free from the convention and visitor
bureaus, the welcome center, merchants, and
vending boxes on the streets. Not only do they
provide up-to-date information on stores,
restaurants, events, and points of interest, but
some also contain a plethora of coupons that
could end up saving you quite a few dollars.

PONY PENNING

One of the most exciting events of the year in this area takes place on the last continuous Wednesday and Thursday of July when Virginia's famous herd of ponies swims across the channel from Assateague Island to Memorial Park on Chincoteague Island in Virginia (call 757-336-6161 for more information). Actually owned by the Chincoteague Volunteer Fire Department, some of the foals are sold at auction, with proceeds aiding firefighting efforts. Legend has long held that the ponies are descendants of mustangs that swam ashore after a Spanish ship wrecked off the coast in the 16th century. More likely, their ancestors were placed on the island by mainland owners wanting to avoid taxation and the expense of fencing.

By bus: **Greyhound** (1-800-231-2222; www.greyhound.com) has a station at 12848 Ocean Gateway (the Park and Ride off US 50) in West Ocean City.

GETTING AROUND *By car:* Driving (and then parking) at any time during the summer season can be a real aggravation. To save driving into the resort area, you can park your car for free at the **Park and Ride** off US 50 in West Ocean City and take the shuttle bus to the South Division Street Transit Center in Ocean City for only $1 per boarding or $3 for a ride-all-day pass.

If you do drive into the resort area and happen to find a parking space, but don't want to drive anymore, you can ride a bus all the way from the Inlet to the Delaware state line for only $2, all day, 24 hours a day. During the summer, **buses** run about every 10 minutes during the day, about every 30 minutes at night; every 30 minutes at other times of the year. Routes include all of the major streets and roadways. Exact change required. Call 410-723-1606 for more information.

By train: The **Boardwalk Train** (410-723-1606; www.oceancitymd.gov), with open-air cars, runs the full length of the 2.9-mile boardwalk throughout the heaviest tourist months. $3, one way. Inquire about the multiride pass to save a few dollars.

By taxi: It is against the law to hail a taxi in Ocean City; you must call ahead for them to pick you up. **Abouttown Taxi** (410-208-9909); **Ace Taxi** (1-866-641-4280); **City Cab** (410-723-4222); **Dave's Taxi** (410-250-2400).

By bus: The local bus service, **Shore Transit** (443-260-2300; www.shoretransit.org), has a route that enables you to ride a loop from West Ocean City to Berlin. It is also possible to ride between the three lower shore counties.

PARKING Paid parking in all municipal lots in Ocean City is in effect 24 hours a day during the main tourist season; those on the street have varying times. No-parking zones are enforced, and businesses can be aggressive in their towing policies.

The Inlet parking lot has a gated time system. You get a ticket when you enter and pay when you leave; no need to worry about feeding the meter. It often fills to capacity early in the day, especially on weekends during the summer.

PUBLIC RESTROOMS In Ocean City, at the boardwalk at Worcester St.; boardwalk at Caroline St.; Third St. and St. Louis Ave. at the Skate Park; boardwalk at Ninth St.; boardwalk at 27th St.; and the South Division Street Transit Center.

MEDICAL EMERGENCY *Ocean City:* **Atlantic Immedicare on 10th Street** (410-289-0065; www.atlanticimmedicare.com); **75th Street Medical Center** (410-524-0075; www.75thstmedical.com); **126th Street Medical Center** (410-250-8000; www.75thst

medical.com). *Berlin:* **Atlantic General Hospital** (410-641-1100; www.atlanticgeneral.org), located at the intersection of US 50 and US 113; available for 24-hour emergency services.

✳ To See

MUSEUMS

Newark

Queponco Railway Station (410-632-0950), 8378 Patey Wood Rd. Donations accepted. Open first and third Sat. 1–4, May–Oct. A local group rescued this abandoned passenger station in 1991 and is gradually restoring and outfitting it to look as it did from 1910 to the 1960s.

Ocean City

⚓ **Ocean City Life Saving Museum** (410-289-4991; www.ocmuseum.org), boardwalk at the Inlet. Open seven days a week June–Sept.; Sat. and Sun. in May and Oct. Very small fee. Once a lifesaving station, this museum chronicles the exploits of brave members of the U.S. Life Saving Service and Coast Guard who have saved more than 7,000 lives off the Maryland coast. In addition, there are items from Ocean City history, a whimsical look at bathing-suit styles through the years, several small aquariums, shipwreck items, and, what I found very interesting, over 200 samples of beach sand from around the world. Free family programs on the boardwalk during summer.

Pocomoke City

Delmarva Discovery Center (410-957-9933; www.delmarvadiscoverycenter.org), 6 Market St. Open daily 10–4 Memorial Day–Labor Day; see Web site for other times. Small admission fee. In the last edition of this book I said that things were still in the construction phase when I last visited, but that the Delmarva Discovery Center looked like it was going to be a quality museum. I was right. The timeline in the lobby does an excellent job of blending world and natural history with the regional history to help you put things in perspective. Dioramas portray what the environment and life along the Pocomoke River used to be like, what it is now, and what the future may hold. A small aquarium has local aquatic creatures, a real beaver lodge has been reconstructed as a display, and your chance to use oyster tongs will provide a vivid experience of what hard work this occupation can be. I strongly suggest you stop by; it will be worth your time. It's an experience where you will be immersed in sight and sound, and the kids will enjoy it as much, if not more, than you do.

THE QUEPONCO RAILWAY STATION

Sturgis One Room School Museum (410-957-1913), 209 Willow St. Small admission charge. Open Tues.–Sat. 1–4, May–Oct. The Sturgis one-room school served Worcester County's African American community 1900–1937. Moved from its original site in the late 1990s, it continues to undergo restoration and outfitting.

Snow Hill

Julia A. Purnell Museum (410-632-0515; www.purnellmuseum.com), 201 W. Market St. Small admission charge. Tues.–Sat. 10–4, Sun. 1–4, Apr.–Oct. Ms. Purnell created more than 1,000 needlework pictures during the last 15 years of her 100-year life. The works, most of them depicting the historic homes and buildings of Snow Hill, brought her such worldwide acclaim that she was inducted into the National Hobby Hall of Fame. Since its establishment in 1957, the museum has become a repository not only of her accomplishments but also of many items important to the history of the area. Exhibits include a general store, a tribute to local firefighters, and a display of Native American artifacts. The local museum of my childhood had a pair of dressed fleas that attracted many people from the surrounding area, and I was happy to see that the Purnell Museum also contains a pair, one of them carrying a parasol! Docents tell me this is the museum's most popular display.

Mt. Zion One Room School Museum (410-632-1265), Ironshire and Church Sts. Small admission charge. Tues.–Sat. 1–4, mid-June–first week Sept. Now moved from its original location, the Mt. Zion school served students from the northern part of the county 1869–1931. Many of the original coat hooks and shelves remain, as well as some of the students' metal lunch pails. Docents provide a short guided tour.

HISTORIC HOMES

Berlin

Calvin B. Taylor House (410-641-1019; www.taylorhousemuseum.org), N. Main and Baker Sts. Donations accepted. Mon., Wed., Fri., and Sat. 1–4, Memorial Day weekend–October. Like so many historic buildings in America, the Taylor House, built around 1832, was slated to be torn down to make way for a parking lot. Rescued from destruction by the Berlin Heritage Foundation, it opened to the public as a museum in 1983. Guided tours take visitors throughout the period-decorated house and focus on its two most prominent occupants. The Harrison family operated the country's largest mail-order nursery business, shipping seedlings from their fruit trees to destinations the world over. In 1890, Calvin B. Taylor established the bank bearing his name, which is still in business. His bank desk and chair are on display along with other items from the town's history. Most impressive are the original flooring and 1830s quilts in the upstairs bedroom, and the portico's butterfly modillions atop the fluted columns.

Pocomoke City

Costen House (410-957-3110), 206 Market St. Small admission charge. Wed. and Sat. 1–4, May–Oct. Dr. Costen was known throughout the Eastern Shore for his courageous works and travels to treat victims of typhoid fever. Built around 1870, his home now helps present the life of a small town and of the doctor and his family. The Hall-Walton Garden on the property re-creates a landscape similar to that of the doctor's days.

FURNACE TOWN

HISTORIC SITES Furnace Town (410-632-2032; www.furnacetown.com), Furnace Town Rd., Snow Hill. Small admission fee. Open seven days a week 11–5, Apr. 1–Oct. 31. Off-season the grounds and trails are open for walking during daylight hours. The smelting of iron during the 1800s was a labor-intensive process that required an entire village to support just one furnace. Through living-history demonstrations and reconstructed buildings, those days are brought back. Visit the old furnace, observe the blacksmith at work, or stand on

1872 RULES FOR TEACHERS

- Each teacher will bring a bucket of water and a scuttle of coal for the day's session.
- Men teachers may take one evening each week for courting purposes, or two evenings a week if they go to church regularly.
- Women teachers who marry or engage in unseemly conduct will be dismissed.
- Any teacher who smokes, uses liquor in any form, frequents pool or public halls, or gets shaved in a barber shop will give good reason to suspect his worth, intention, integrity, and honesty.
- The teacher who performs his labor faithfully and without fault for five years will be given an increase of 25 cents per week in his pay, providing the Board of Education approves.

—from the Worcester County one-room schoolhouses

the pulpit of the church and preach a sermon. The broom maker explained to me what a niddy-noddy is; be sure to find out for yourself. The easy, 1-mile Paul Leiffer Nature Trail wanders through the Nassawango Cypress Swamp.

HISTORIC CHURCHES The **Gothic Revival Makemie United Presbyterian Church** (410-632-1698), Market and Washington Sts., Snow Hill) was built in 1890 and serves a congregation that can trace its origin to the end of the 1600s.

There are both Gothic and Victorian aspects to the **All Hallows Church** (410-632-2327; www.allhallowssnowhill.org), Market and Church Sts., Snow Hill), built around 1750. The purple and yellow panes in the roundheaded windows were added near the turn of the 20th century. Take a step inside to see the 1701 Bible printed in London and given to the congregation by Queen Anne.

✷ To Do

AIR RIDES ♂ **O.C. Parasail** (410-723-1464; 410-289-BEST; www.ocparasailing.com), 54th St. or Talbot St. Pier, Ocean City. Certainly not cheap, but a thrill nonetheless, O.C. Parasail has single and tandem flights for kids and adults. It is Ocean City's oldest parasail company and has completed over 150,000 flights with a perfect safety record while providing a different perspective on the ocean and the beach.

♂ **Bay Sports Unlimited** (410-289-2144), 22nd St. and the bay, Ocean City. Bay Sports offers single, tandem, and triple parasail rides. Waverunners are also rented.

Cloud Dancer (410-641-2484; www.clouddancersightseeingtours.com), Ocean City Airport. Two-passenger open-cockpit flights over the area in a vintage biplane.

Ocean City Sky Tours (410-289-TOUR; www.oceancityskytours.com), Ocean City Airport. Day, sunset, and night flights.

ARCADES, AMUSEMENT AND WATER PARKS, GO-CARTS ♂ **Baja** (410-213-2252; www.bajaoc.com) **& Grand Prix** (410-213-1278; www.grandprixoc.com) **Amusements,** both on US 50, 1.5 miles west or less of Ocean City. If your children can't wait just another five minutes before starting their fun in Ocean City, pull into one of these two parks for a plethora of go-cart tracks (many different styles of tracks and cars), water rides, miniature golf, and arcade games. Mom and dad will get into racing just as much as the kids.

♂ **Jolly Roger Amusement Park** (410-289-3477; www.jollyrogerpark.com), 30th St. and Coastal Hwy. and at the Pier on the Boardwalk, Ocean City. One admission price gets you into both locations of the city's largest amusement park with the Sky Coaster, Giant Ferris Wheel, and Titanic Slide.

♂ **Ripley's Believe It or Not Odditorium** (410-289-5600; www.ripleysoceancity.com), on the boardwalk at 401 S. Atlantic Ave., Ocean City. Adults $12.99; seniors $10.99; children 6–12 years of age $7.99. If the items that Robert Ripley had collected throughout his lifetime of travels around the world were presented in a less sensationalist way, this could almost be a museum. Expect to spend an hour gazing at more than 500 exhibits, including a shrunken head, a commercially produced vampire-killing kit that travelers in the 1800s purchased by the thousands, a human-bone flute, masks and other artifacts from native tribesmen on various continents, and a disturbing array of torture items employed by those in power throughout the centuries (think twice about bringing small children). Additional attractions (with additional admission fees) are the Laser Race and Mirror Maze.

♂ **Splash Mountain** (410-289-3477), 30th St. and Coastal Hwy., Ocean City. Ten water slides, a lazy river, and a sea-creature walk. Adjacent to Jolly Roger (see above).

♂ **Speed World** (410-289-4902; www.jollyrogerpark.com), 30th St. and Coastal Hwy., Ocean City. Go-carts of every imaginable shape, such as Indy racers, LeMans, midget racers, family tracks, and even a speedboat course. Adjacent to Jolly Roger (see above).

♂ & **Trimper's Rides** (410-289-8617; www.trimpersrides.com), between S. Division and S. First Sts., on the boardwalk, Ocean City. Fans of old carousels will love this amusement park with its 1902 Herschel-Spellman carousel. In continuous operation since its 1912 installation, its hand-carved horses, camels, roosters, tigers, zebras, and more have been maintained in excellent condition. Trimper's is the center of activity on the southern end of the boardwalk in the evening.

BICYCLING Bicycle riding is permitted on Ocean City's **boardwalk,** but hours vary greatly according to the season, so check the posted signs.

♂ & **Jo's Bikes** (410-289-5298), Second St. and the boardwalk, Ocean City. Rents wheelchairs and strollers in addition to bicycles.

Bill's Bikes (410-289-2155), N. Division and Baltimore Ave., Ocean City. Open all year for bike rentals, sales, and service.

Dandy Don's Olde Towne Bike Rentals (410-289-2289), 12th St. and the boardwalk, Ocean City. Regular bike (and some other interesting pedal vehicles) rentals.

THE 1902 HERSCHEL-SPELLMAN CAROUSEL AT TRIMPER'S RIDES

HAND-NET DIPPING FOR CRABS AND CLAMS OFF ASSATEAGUE ISLAND

The **ViewTrail 100 Bike Trail** follows a circular path along country roads, through farms, woodlands, cypress swamps, and small towns for more than 100 miles in Worcester County. Numerous restaurants, historic sites, and accommodations along the way. See *Guidance* for places to obtain the trail brochure.

BOAT EXCURSIONS **OC Rocket** (410-289-9125; www.talbotstreetpier.com), Talbot St. Pier, Ocean City. A ride, at times up to 40 miles an hour, on this boat should be able to satisfy anyone's need for speed in the ocean. The 50-minute trip passes through the Inlet and goes along the beach almost to the Delaware state line. Hold on to your seat when you bounce across the waves! *Yee hah!* Be sure to ask for the discounted price.

✯ Located at the same pier as the *OC Rocket* and owned by the same company, the **Assateague Adventure** is an easy pontoon-boat ride/nature tour. The boat glides into the Ocean City Fishing Center and along Sinepuxent Bay, and lands on Assateague Island. In addition to possibly seeing the wild ponies and hand-net dipping for crabs and clams, you'll hear naturalists narrate tidbits about island migration, saltwater marshes, sea lettuce, and more. Adults may wish for more depth of information, but it's a good introduction to the local environment.

Sea Rocket (410-289-3499; www.searocket.com), 700 S. Phiadelphia St., bayside, Ocean City. Claiming to be the world's largest speedboat, the *Sea Rocket* competes with the *OC Rocket* for customers. It is the one with the large rooster-tail wake.

Pocomoke City

Bay Queen River Cruises (443-437-7235; 410-632-1415; www.thebayqueen.com), 2 Market St., Pocomoke City. A daily cruise during the heaviest tourist months takes passengers on a sight-seeing excursion of the Pocomoke River environs.

BOAT RENTALS **Bahia Marina** (410-289-7438; www.bahiamarina.com), between 21st and 22nd Sts. and the bay, Ocean City. Pontoon and skiff rentals.

Bayside Boat Rentals (410-524-1948; www.baysideboatrentals.com), 54th St. and the bay, Ocean City. Pontoon boats.

FAMILY ACTIVITIES *✯* **Pirate Adventures** (302-539-5155; www.pirateadventures oceancity.com), at Harpoon Hanna's, US 54 and the Bay, just across the Delaware line, Fenwick Island, DE. $20 a person. Reservations required. Young kids really enjoy this cruise on a pirate ship in search of sunken treasure. The crew is in costume, the kids get their faces painted, cannons are fired, the boat is attacked, and everyone gets to take home a share of the loot.

*⚓ **Duckaneer Pirate Ship** (410-289-3500; www.talbotstreetpier.com), 311 Talbot St. and the bay, Ocean City. If Pirate Adventures is full, you could always take the kids on the *Duckaneer.* $19–20 a person.

*⚓ ♿ **Frontier Town Western Theme Park** (410-641-0057; www.frontiertown.com), 3.5 miles south of US 50 on MD 611, Ocean City. Open 10–6 daily mid-June through Labor Day; gate closes at 4:30. Adults $14; children 4–10 $12. When my wife told me how much fun she had as a child coming here in the 1960s, my thought was that the children of today would look upon the theme park as a hokey bore. How wrong I was. Kids up to 12 years old were cheering on the good guy in the Gunfight at the OK Corral, joining in the (authentic) Native American dances, and hooting and hollering at the villain in the Trial of Lopez. The constructed frontier town houses gift shops, a western saloon complete with a cancan show, and stagecoach, steam-train, and pony rides. Separate additional fees (adults $14; children $12) provide access to the Frontier Town Water Park. Campers at Frontier Town Campground (see *Camping*) have free access to the water park.

FISHING

Ocean City

Headboats (first-come, first-served) and charter boats (reserved ahead of time) leave almost daily from nearly every marina in the Ocean City area. Most provide or rent the necessary equipment.

Ocean City Fishing Center (410-213-1121; www.ocfishing.com), West Ocean City. Just off US 50 on the mainland, the center claims to have the largest charter fleet in Ocean City.

Judith M (410-289-7438; www.judithmfishing.com), Bahia Marina between 21st and 22nd Sts. Possibly the most recognized headboat around Ocean City, the *Judith M* goes on deep-sea fishing trips twice a day during summer. In the evening she provides narrated 90-minute oceanfront cruises.

Bay Bee (410-213-1121; 1-800-322-3065; www.ocfishing.com), US 50 and Shantytown Rd., West Ocean City. In search of sea bass, flounder, trout, snapper, blues, and croaker, the *Bay Bee* runs half-day trips.

Snow Hill

Captain Bruce Wootten (410-251-9677; www.captbrucewootten.com), 6661 Snow Hill Rd. Captain Bruce, a licensed guide, specializes in bass fishing on the Pocomoke, Wicomico, Nanticoke, and Choptank Rivers. There are only one or two anglers on each eight-hour trip, so you will have the river and instruction, if needed, to yourself. Offered year-round.

GOLF

Berlin

The Bay Club (410-641-4081; 1-800-BAY-CLUB; www.thebayclub.com), 9122 Libertytown Rd. Thirty-six holes. There is a choice of two courses, both with par 72.

Eagle's Landing (410-213-7277; 1-800-283-3846; www.eagleslandinggolf.com), 12367 Eagle's Landing Rd. Dr. Michael Hurdzan designed Ocean City's municipal 18-hole course with a par 72 and a length of 6,163 feet. The first certified Audubon sanctuary in Maryland; *Golf Digest* magazine rated it one of the state's top 10 courses.

Ocean City Golf Club (410-641-1779; 1-800-442-3570; www.oceancitygolfclub.com), 11401 Country Club Dr. Two courses, one seaside and the other with marshes along Newport Bay.

"WHAT'S THAT?"

The boats with the tall booms and apparatuses that you see in the Ocean City Harbor dredge for clams in the waters around the resort area. Most of the catch is sent to Texas, where Campbell's Soup turns it into canned clam chowder.

CLAM-DREDGING BOATS IN OCEAN CITY HARBOR

River Run (410-641-7200; 1-800-733-RRUN; www.riverrungolf.com), 11605 Masters Lane. On this Gary Player Signature Course, the first nine holes bring to mind Scottish links, while the last nine are set among natural marshes.

Rum Pointe Seaside Golf Links (410-629-1414; 1-888-809-4653; www.rumpointe.com), 7000 Rum Pointe Lane. This par 72 course, designed by Pete and P. B. Dye, overlooks Sinepuxent Bay and Assateague Island.

Bishopville

The Links at Lighthouse Sound (410-352-5767; 1-888-55-HILLS; www.lighthousesound .com), 12723 St. Martin's Neck Rd. One of the closest courses to Ocean City, it has views of the resort area's skyline. Par 72 with a 73.3 rating.

MINIATURE GOLF ✐ **Lost Galaxy Golf** (410-524-4FUN; www.planetmaze .com), 33rd St. and Coastal Hwy., Ocean City. Miniature golf with an outer-space theme featuring spaceships, meteors, fire, and fog. Laser tag and the largest indoor maze in Maryland are also at this location.

✐ **Old Pro Golf** (410-524-2645, main phone number; www.oldprogolf.com). Old Pro has six miniature-golf courses throughout Ocean City. People appeared to have

GOLF VACATIONS

Ocean City has become a golfer's destination, with more than a dozen courses nearby. Contact **Ocean City Golf Getaway** (410-213-7050; 1-800-462-4653; www.oceancity golf.com), 9935 Stephen Decatur Hwy., Unit 141, to help you decide which ones to play—and to arrange special package deals with hotels and restaurants. **Ocean City Golf Groups** (1-888-465-3477; www.ocgolf groups.com), 2200 Baltimore Ave., provides the same type of service.

the most fun at the Lost Civilization theme at 23rd St. and at the indoor Under Sea course at 68th St.

❧ Lost Treasure Golf (410-250-5678; www.losttreasuregolf.com), 140th St. and Coastal Hwy., Ocean City. Caves, waterfalls, and ancient ruins.

HORSE RACING Ocean Downs (410-641-0600; www.oceandowns.com), intersection of US 50 and MD 589 (4 miles west of Ocean City). Has live harness racing during the summer months. You can watch indoors from the Pacers Restaurant or on video screens in the clubhouse. However, to really get into it, you should cheer your choice on by being trackside where swiftly running hooves go by just a few feet away. Simulcast wagering is available seven days a week, as is the opportunity to feed hundreds of slot machines or play table games all year long.

HORSEBACK RIDING *❧* **Holly Ridge Farm** (410-835-2596; www.hollyridgefarm .com), 36609 Purnell Crossing Rd., Libertytown. $50–60; reservations required. Located about 30 minutes from Ocean City. Reservations required. Guided trail rides in the woods using either an English or western saddle. Includes a short instruction session and background on wildlife that may be seen.

KAYAKING AND CANOEING A brochure available from visitors centers (see *Guidance*) provides a brief overview and map of the **EA Vaughn Kayak and Canoe Trail** that begins at Taylors Landing, circles around Mills Island, and ends next to George Island Landing. If you did just the open water portion in Chincoteague Bay, it would be 6 miles, but for those who are looking for protected waters, there are many more miles of tidal creeks, marshlands, and forests to discover. Birdlife can be spectacular, with paddlers having a chance to observe bald eagles, ospreys, owls, and a plethora of shore birds and waterfowl, along with hawks, falcons, and harriers. Brochures are also available for water trails in **Sinepuxent Bay, Pomoke River,** and **Nassawango Creek.**

Several inns and B&Bs have banded together to form the **Inn-to-Inn Canoe Trail** (www .inntours.com) along the Pocomoke River. Tours are two or more days long, and everything is included: canoes, shuttles, three meals a day, and evening accommodations. All you have to do is paddle leisurely along the river enjoying the scenery and wildlife, knowing that soft beds await you. I can't imagine a better way to get to know the interior lands of the Eastern Shore. The **Cedars B&B** (410-632-2165; www.thecedarsbb.com), 107 W. Federal St., Snow Hill, makes the arrangements. The **Pocomoke River Canoe Co.** (410-632-3971; www .pocomokerivercanoe.com), 312 N. Washington St., Snow Hill, not only provides livery service for the inn-to-inn trips, but also provides shuttle service and rents canoes and kayaks for those wanting to explore the river on their own.

Ayers Creek Adventures (443-513-0889; 1-888-602-6288; www.ayerscreekadventures .com), 8628 Grey Fox Ln., Berlin. One of the most authentic ecotours I've taken. So many times I have gone on what has been billed as an ecotour, but turns out to be a trip carelessly put together by a commercial operator with a part-time guide who looks upon this as just a job to get done. However, Steven Taylor grew up on Ayers Creek and he and his wife, Suzy, intimately know and care about its environment. On the Ayers Creek Forested Wetland Kayak Tour I took with Suzy, she provided wonderful running commentary about the animals, birdlife, plants, and natural cycles of the area and how humans have had both beneficial and harmful effects. I also liked how, without calling attention to it, she was conscious of when I needed to take a break from paddling, and we would merely slow down or stop and talk about something. Several different tours are offered at reasonable prices. Kayak and canoe rentals are also available. Pass up that speedboat tour in Ocean City and spend your time and money here.

KITE FLYING Kite Loft (410-289-7855; 1-800-682-5483; www.kiteloft.com), 511 Boardwalk, Ocean City. In addition to selling all manner of kites, the Kite Loft provides free lessons to those who purchase a stunt kite. If you invest the multiple amount of dollars for one of these flying craft, take advantage of this offer so that you will learn how to assemble, fly, and care for it correctly and safely.

PERSONAL WATERCRAFT RENTALS (JET SKIS) Action Watercraft (302-537-6500; 1-800-2GETWET; www.actionmarine.org), 142nd St. Marina, Ocean City.

Action Watersports, Ltd. (410-524-4769; www.actionwatersportsoc.com), 106 52nd St., Ocean City.

Odyssea Watersports (410-723-4227; www.odysseawatersports.com), 50th St. and Coastal Hwy., Ocean City.

Inlet Sea-Doos (410-289-1488; http://oceancityjetskirental.com), 710 S. Philadelphia Ave., Ocean City.

SKATING Roller skating is permitted on the boardwalk in Ocean City, but hours vary greatly according to the season, so check the posted signs. Be aware that skateboards and scooters are prohibited at all times.

Downtown Recreation Complex (410-289-BOWL; www.oceanbowl.com), Third St. and St. Louis Ave., Ocean City. Open daily during the summer. Within this city park is the Ocean Bowl Skate Park, the country's oldest operating municipal skate park and open to skateboarders and in-line skaters Facilities include a bowl, a half-pipe, ramps, and a concrete streets area. The admission fee is $12; more on the weekend.

TENNIS Public courts are located at Third St. and the bay; 61st St. bayside; 94th St.; and 136th St. in Ocean City.

WALKING TOURS Ocean City. A walking-tour brochure describing some of the older structures and sites along the southern end of the Ocean City boardwalk and the downtown area is available from the convention and visitors bureau. It's nice to learn the stories behind the Violets Are Blue House, the Tarry-A-While, and St. Mary's of the Sea Catholic Church.

Berlin. The **Historic District of Berlin** contains structures from the 1790s to the early 20th century, and a walking-tour brochure available in the town offices (10 William St.) will direct you to the most historically and architecturally significant. Be sure to seek out the **Burley House** and its narrow brick chimneys atop a steep gable roof.

Snow Hill. The *Snow Hill Walking Tour* brochure points out more than 50 historically or architecturally important structures within the town limits. Available from the Worcester County Tourism Office.

✸ Green Space

BEACHES All 10 miles of the **Ocean City** beach are free and open to the public 6 AM–10 PM. Beach Patrol members are on duty during the summer from 10 AM–5:30 PM.

&. Access points to the beach for the physically challenged are identified by blue signs along Coastal Hwy.

There are patrolled beaches in both the state park and national seashore on **Assateague Island** that are much less crowded than those in Ocean City. If you want a primitive beach experience, just walk a few hundred yards away from these designated areas, and there is a good possibility of having the sand and surf all to yourself.

PONIES SHARE THE BEACH WITH SUNBATHERS ON ASSATEAGUE ISLAND.

A small strip of beach in the settlement of **Public Landing** is open to the general public, yet very few people ever take advantage of it.

PARKS ☙ **Little Salisbury Park,** 94th St. bayside, Ocean City. In addition to some tennis courts, the park has a dog playground so that Fido and Fifi, who are prohibited on the beach during the warmer months, will have a place to run and socialize with others of their kind. Two separate runs keep the big dogs from overwhelming the smaller ones. Information on the required permit may be obtained by calling 410-250-0175.

Northside Park, 125th St. and the bay, Ocean City. The park's 58 acres, including a paved walking path, fishing piers, and playgrounds for the kids, are situated at the northern end of town on the bayside and enable you to escape the noise and congestion of the rest of the resort area.

Sunset Park, S. Division St. and the bay, Ocean City. Rarely visited except when being used to present concerts, the park's native plants and the railroad architecture employed by the few structures make for an eye-appealing place to escape the crowds of the boardwalk a couple of blocks away.

Pocomoke River State Park (410-632-2566; www.dnr.state.md.us/publiclands/eastern /pocomokeriver.asp), 461 Worcester Hwy., Snow Hill. Canoeing, swimming, hiking, fishing, and two campgrounds.

WALKS **Herring Creek Nature Trail** (410-632-2144), Keyset Point Rd., West Ocean City. An easy-to-get-to escape from the resort area. The 1-mile loop trail passes by a pond and creek, through forested wetlands, and onto a small pine island with picnic tables. Interpretive signs provide background information about the environment.

Coming back from the trail on MD 90, make a stop at the **Isle of Wight Nature Park,** a 12-acre facility within a 223-acre wildlife management area. A 150-foot, handicapped-accessible interpretive walkway provides views of Ocean City and a chance to come into intimate contact with the wetlands.

Assateague Island. Within **Assateague State Park** and **Assateague Island National Seashore** are miles of unspoiled beaches on which to walk. Three short interpretive trails—**Life of the Dunes, Life of the Marsh,** and **Life of the Forest**—are close to the National Seashore Campground. Those wanting a longer hike should consult *50 Hikes in Maryland*

(Countryman Press), which describes a two-day backpacking trip along the beach.

HIKING ✈ About a 30-mile drive from Ocean City, the 1-mile circuit **Bald Cypress Nature Trail** in the Milburn Landing area of **Pocomoke River State Park** is the place to take the kids after they have had enough of sun, surf, and sand and are badgering you about what to do next. The easy walk takes you by a few small swamps and underneath dozens of bald cypress trees, oddities within the world of trees. They are coniferous, meaning they develop cones like pines, firs, and hemlocks—all trees with evergreen needles. Yet while they may look like needles, the leaves of the bald cypress drop off as the weather turns colder, just as those on deciduous trees do. In addition, even though it is called a cypress, the bald cypress is actually a member of the redwood family. It is also a tree more common to the swamps of the South, just barely able to survive here at its very northern limits on the Eastern Shore.

THE ASSATEAGUE LIFE OF THE MARSH TRAIL

✳ Lodging
MOTELS AND HOTELS

Ocean City, 21842
Atlantic Hotel (410-289-9111; 1-800-3-ATLANTIC; www.atlantichotelocmd.com), Wicomico St. and the boardwalk. There are no swimming pools, Jacuzzis, fitness rooms, or private balconies here. If you can accept this, you will enjoy staying in one of the oldest hotels in Ocean City, with its sundeck overlooking the beach, six-over-six sash windows, and historic lobby. Do not come here looking for opulence, but do take advantage of the low rates. Owned by the same family since 1922. $170–230.

♿ **Crystal Beach Hotel** (410-289-7165; 1-866-232-2421; www.crystalbeachhotel.com), 25th St. and the boardwalk. All rooms are efficiencies and have private balconies—some with a side view, some with ocean view. It's your vacation, so spend the few extra dollars and enjoy an ocean-view room. $199–259.

♿ **Dunes Manor Hotel** (410-289-1100; 1-800-523-2888; www.dunesmanor.com), 2800 Baltimore Ave. The only hotel in the city with all its rooms facing the ocean. Invoking the grandeur of 19th-century seaside resorts, the Dunes Manor is furnished with antiques and decorated in a Victorian theme. The suites are exceptionally large. Without being pretentious, everything in the hotel is done with a touch of class. Only one block north of the boardwalk. Indoor/outdoor pool. $254–409. See *Dining Out* for the hotel's restaurant, the Victorian Room.

OCEAN VIEWS IN OCEAN CITY
If you want to see the ocean, ask for a room on the third floor or above if your lodgings are north of 27th Street. The beach's sand dune blocks the views from the first, and often second, floor in this area.

PEOPLE-WATCHING ALONG THE OCEAN CITY BOARDWALK

🏄 ♿ **Dunes Motel** (410-289-4414; www
.ocdunes.com), 2700 Baltimore Ave.
Owned by the same people as Dunes
Manor, this is my sister's family's choice
when they come to Ocean City. It is reasonably priced and caters to families (Disney
Channel on TV and a kids' wading pool). It
is on the very north end of the boardwalk,
which does not have the commercial activity and crowds found on the southern end.
Ocean view, pool view, and efficiencies
available. $209–299.

♿ **Hilton Suites Oceanfront** (410-289-
6444; 1-866-729-3200; www.oceancity
hilton.com), 32nd St. Almost a mirror
image of the Holiday Inn Hotel and Suites,
the Hilton has all of the same amenities,
but everything is a little bit more plush and
swanky. The restaurant, 32 Palm (see *Dining Out*), has a nice ambience and prices
that are in line with the single night's rate of
$519.

🏄 ♿ **Holiday Inn Hotel and Suites** (1-
866-627-8483; www.ocsuites.com), 1701
Atlantic Ave. An all-luxury-suite hotel
directly on the ocean with Jacuzzi tubs and
private balconies. Two elevated swimming
pools overlooking the beach and a children's activity pool. $469–479.

🏄 ♿ **Holiday Inn Oceanfront** (410-524-
1600; 1-800-837-3588; www.ocmdhotels
.com/holidayinn), 6600 Coastal Hwy.
Indoor/outdoor pools with baby pools.

Oceanfront, ocean-view, and garden-view
rooms and suites. Free children's summer-
time activities. $299–369. See *Dining Out*
for Reflections, the hotel's restaurant.

♿ **Princess Royale Family Resort and
Condominiums** (410-524-7777; 1-800-4-
ROYALE; www.princessroyale.com), 9100
Coastal Hwy. One of the city's largest all-
suite facilities. Oceanfront, ocean-view, and
one- to three-room suites overlooking the
Olympic-size pool and atrium are available.
$299–389.

INNS

Berlin, 21811
Atlantic Hotel (410-641-3589; www
.atlantichotel.com), 2 N. Main St. The
Atlantic Hotel was built in 1895 and has
been faithfully maintained with its Victorian
features. The impressive staircase adds a bit
of grandeur to the small entranceway. I
liked watching Berlin's life unfold from the
windows of my second-floor front room,
while another visit in one of the back rooms
was a quiet one removed from the bustle of
Main Street. Private bath, air-conditioning,
television, and phone are in each room;
deluxe rooms can accommodate up to five
people. Each of the 16 rooms is furnished
with antiques and period pieces; marble fixtures, terry toweling, and soft robes bring to
mind the luxuries of yesteryear. Richard
Gere stayed here during the filming of *The*

Runaway Bride. $155–300. See *Dining Out* for the hotel's restaurant.

Ocean City, 21842
♿ **Lighthouse Club Hotel** (410-524-5500; 1-855-432-4377; www.fagers.com), 56th St. On-The-Bay. The custom-made Lawrence Peabody furniture and water views give this lighthouse-shaped inn the feel of a Caribbean resort. Certainly one of the most luxurious and romantic spots in Ocean City, with a balcony, marble bath, whirlpool Jacuzzi, terry robes, and refrigerator in each suite. Even if you don't get a bay-view room, you can still enjoy a view of herons, geese, and ducks wandering around the inland marsh. To keep up with its growing clientele, the management opened **The Edge at the Lighthouse,** a hotel next door with the same amenities. All of this is part of the Fager's Island Restaurant/ Lighthouse Club Hotel complex (see *Dining Out*). $275–475.

Snow Hill, 21863
🐾 ⚲ ♿ **River House Inn** (410-632-2722; http://riverhouseinn.com), 210 E. Market St. The East and West rooms in the 1860 Gothic Revival house (which was showing some of its age last time I visited) are large and bright, and a screened-in porch overlooks the lawn, which slopes down to the Pocomoke River. The 1834 cottage houses two suites, while there are private accommodations in the 1890 cottage. My favorite spot is the upstairs suite in the Waterfront Cottage. Not only can you enjoy the river from the 28-foot-long porch, but when you retire at night, the clouds painted on the bedroom ceiling provide a serene atmosphere to lull you to sleep. Furnishings in the older structures fit the period, while the décor of newer rooms is modern. The inn is a member of the Inn-to-Inn Canoe Trail (see *To Do*). Children and pets are welcome. All rooms have air-conditioning and private bath. $160–325.

BED & BREAKFASTS
Berlin, 21811
⚲ **Holland House B&B** (410-641-1956; www.hollandhousebandb.com), 5 Bay St. Jan and Jim Quick have been operating their B&B for well over a decade and have its operation down to a T. They both have outside jobs, but you would never know it. One or the other will serve you breakfast, and it seems that they are always around when a guest has a question. (They are a great repository of knowledge on where to eat or what to do in the area.) The Holland House was a doctor's residence at the turn of the 20th century, and the size of the rooms and the décor reflect the physician's middle-income status. Many guests enjoy coffee and the morning paper on the front porch. An outside shower enables you to wash off beach sand before dressing for dinner. Children are welcome, which adds to the family atmosphere. $125–140.

Ocean City, 21842
🦢 **Atlantic House B&B** (410-289-2333; www.atlantichouse.com), 510 N. Baltimore Ave. The front porch with an ocean view, a homestyle breakfast buffet, and outdoor hot tub are all compelling reasons to stay in the 1920s Victorian home. It is one of the most convenient and lower-cost places to stay right on the boardwalk. The oceanside rooms let you watch the sunrise, while the bayside rooms catch the sunset's glow. $195–245.

Inn on the Ocean (410-289-8894; 1-877-466-6662; www.innontheocean.com), 1001 Atlantic Ave. The city's only other B&B is also located on the boardwalk. All six rooms have private bath, TV, and air-conditioning. The Veranda Room opens directly onto the wraparound porch (where breakfast is often served), while my favorite, the Oceana Room, has a private balcony overlooking the ocean. Bicycles, beach equipment, and afternoon refreshments are complimentary. $275–395.

Pocomoke City, 21851
⚲ **Littleton's Bed & Breakfast** (410-957-1645; www.littletonsbandb.com), 407 Second St. Constructed with a second empire Victorian design and built by local merchant Thomas Little Clarke in the 1860s, the home is now listed on the National Register of Historic Places. With lovingly landscaped yards, and an organic garden whose bounty is incorporated into the full

breakfasts served to guests in the formal dining room, the B&B is located just a few blocks from Pocomoke City's attractions and riverfront. The hosts are knowledgeable about the area's outdoor activities and will have bicycles and canoes available on request. They also welcome long-distance bicyclists and kayakers who may be on a journey without an automobile; give them notice, and they will pick you up and even drive you around for shopping and dining if their schedule permits. After a day of outdoor activities, the porch swing or a soak in the large claw-foot bathtub are the places to relax. Well-behaved children welcomed. $95–135.

Snow Hill, 21863

The Cedars B&B (410-632-2165; www.thecedarsbb.com), 107 W. Federal St. The restored 1850s home (showing a bit of its age the last time I stayed here) retains the horse-hair plaster and some of the original lighting and fireplace covers. Much of the furniture is of the period. The three guest rooms all have their own bath (check out the 6-foot claw tub in the Johnson Room). Looking through the guest book I found numerous raves about the four-course breakfasts, many of which incorporate the herbs and vegetables grown in the B&B's garden. The porch also looked like a nice place to enjoy a good book. The proprietors also make the arrangements for the Inn-to-Inn Canoe Trail tours (see *To Do*). $180.

🐾 🛶 **The Mansion House** (410-632-3189; www.mansionhousebnb.com), 4436 Bayside Rd., Public Landing. There are two things I remember about the Mansion House: sunrise bathing the entire house, with its golden glow reflected off the waters of Chincoteague Bay, and an abundance of fireplaces. Not only does each guest room have a working fireplace, but there are also fireplaces on each end of the living room. The 1800s building has lots of common space, including a swing on the upstairs porch, in which to relax after a swim in the bay or a walk along the beach. Children and pets permitted with prior notification; additional small fee. $160.

VACATION RENTALS If you plan to spend a week or more in Ocean City, you will probably save quite a few dollars by renting a cottage, house, or condominium. Among the agencies handling these properties are **Long & Foster** (1-800-843-2322; www.lfvacations.com), **Ocean City Weekly Rentals** (1-800-851-8909; www.ocwr.com), and **Coldwell Banker** (1-800-633-1000; www.cbvacations.com).

CAMPING

Berlin, 21811—Assateague Island

Assateague State Park (410-641-2120; 1-888-432-2267; www.dnr.state.md.us/publiclands/eastern/assateague.asp), 7307 Stephen Decatur Hwy. Apr. 1–Oct. 31. More than 300 sites are situated among the sand dunes; almost 40 have hookups. Bathhouse and concession building.

Assateague Island National Seashore (410-641-3030; www.nps.gov/asis), 7206 National Seashore Lane. The National Park Service operates two campgrounds—one near the ocean, the other next to the bay—that offer more of a rustic experience than the other sites listed here. There are no hookups and only chemical toilets and cold showers. Some sites are open year-round. Primitive backcountry sites are available to those willing to walk anywhere from 4 to 11 miles. *50 Hikes in Maryland* (Countryman Press) describes the hike in detail.

Ocean City, 21842

🐾 🛶 **Frontier Town** (410-641-0880; 1-800-228-5590; www.frontiertown.com), on MD 611 south of Ocean City. Only a 10-minute drive from Ocean City, this 500-site campground is part of the Frontier Town Western Theme Park complex. There are tons of activities for the kids, a free shuttle to the beach, free access to the large water slide park, a choice of primitive or deluxe sites, and even some trailers and cabins for rent. The cost of the primitive sites is a bargain given all the extras guests are entitled to.

Snow Hill, 21863

Pocomoke River State Park (410-632-2566; www.dnr.state.md.us/publiclands

/eastern/pocomokeriver.asp), 3461 Worcester Hwy. The **Shad Landing Campground** (off US 113) has a swimming pool, marina, camp store, hook-ups, a dump station, and a playground.

🐾 Also within the park, the **Milburn Landing Campground** (off MD 364) is a bit more primitive, but it does permit pets and has rustic mini cabins.

Whaleyville, 21872

🐾 ✍ **Fort Whaley Campground** (1-888-322-7717; www.fortwhaley.com), 11224 Dale Rd. A companion campground to Frontier Town (see above), it has primitive and deluxe sites. Free admission to the miniature-golf course and Frontier Town's Water Park.

✳ Where to Eat
DINING OUT
Berlin
Drummer's Café (410-641-3589; www.atlantichotel.com), 2 N. Main St. Within the Atlantic Hotel's (see *Lodging*) same room that has served meals to customers for more than one hundred years, the owners of Fager's Island Restaurant in Ocean City have elevated traditional restaurant offerings to fine dining entrées. Fresh fish is offered four different ways, the New York strip is herb-and-bleu-cheese crusted, and the chicken breasts are covered with mushrooms, prosciutto, tomato, and Marsala wine. $16.95-33.95.

Ocean City
✍ ♿ **Fager's Island Restaurant** (410-524-5500; www.fagers.com), 60th St. on the bay. Open every day, all year, Fager's brings daylight hours to a close with the *1812 Overture*. The music starts about five minutes before sunset and ends at the exact moment the sun drops out of view. Meals, either indoors or on the deck, can start with corn and crab fritters with vodka cocktail sauce and basil pesto aioli, progress to bronzed salmon or prime rib with shaved horseradish, and end with an Italian coffee (amaretto, Galliano, and whipped cream, topped with blue curaçao). Fager's is part

of the Lighthouse Club Hotel complex. Expect to spend $25-38 for the main course.

✍ ♿ **Fresco's** (410-524-8202; www.ocfrescos.com), 8203 Coastal Hwy. The quality of the evening entrées makes this the resort town's obvious choice for Italian food. Forget the usual spaghetti and meatballs or lasagna; think more along the lines of penne with crabmeat or chicken Sorrentino. The Tuscan Fiochhi (pasta purses stuffed with cheese and pear with roasted red peppers and pine nuts) is one of the signature dishes, while the veal and lobster tail sautéed with shallots and wild mushrooms, deglazed with champagne, and finished with butter and cream is an exceedingly rich indulgence. Sunsets over the bay cast a reddish glow through the restaurant's picture windows. Fresco's was endorsed by a fellow B&B guest, a visitor from Florence, Italy, no less. $20-35.

Galaxy 66 Bar and Grille (410-723-6762; www.galaxy66barandgrille.com), 6601 Coastal Hwy. I was worried when I learned Ocean City native John Trader, owner of Liquid Assets, had sold the Galaxy. There was no need; the new owners have kept the same chef, and the menu continues to be one of the more innovative and delicious in the city. Everything is right on the mark here, from the décor in the dining area to

TALBOT STREET PIER IN OCEAN CITY

the mosaic sinks in the restrooms. The chef and owners collaborate to create items such as lamb lollipops; crabcakes with chipolte lime basmati rice, mint pesto, and crisp fielle brick; and pistachio encrusted catfish. The menu is ever evolving. Portions are large for a fine-dining establishment, so leave room for the elegantly delightful angel food cake. Lunch items $11–14; dinner entrées $20–40. One of my favorite Ocean City restaurants; it takes on a nightclub atmosphere late at night, especially on the rooftop bar.

&. **Harrison's Harbor Watch** (410-289-5121; www.harborwatchrestaurant.com), South Boardwalk overlooking the Ocean City Inlet. The pleasant view of the Inlet and Assateague Island complements the seafood dishes that are prepared fresh daily. Also on the menu are homemade pastas, breads, and muffins. Has one of the area's most outstanding raw bars. $24–49.

❀ **The Hobbit Restaurant** (410-524-8100; www.thehobbitrestaurant.com), 101 81st St. The Hobbit has been under the same ownership and management since it opened in 1977, decades before the 2001 *Lord of the Rings* movie was even thought about. It moved to the Rivendell Condominiums and now only has a few figurines and paintings depicting characters from J. R. R. Tolkien's fantasy masterpiece decorating the walls. The former location was a favorite of Newt Gingrich and other Baltimore and Washington, DC, politicos and celebrities. Serving only dinner in a formal atmosphere; menu prices run $24–38. Nice sunset views.

❀ **Liquid Assets** (410-524-7037; www.la94.com), 9301 Coastal Hwy. Ocean City native John Trader operated his wine shop for close to two decades before adding a bar and dining options within the shop. This is currently my favorite Ocean City restaurant; the menu, with Italian, Spanish, and Eastern European influences, changes often to take advantage of the freshest local organic items available, so each visit is a new culinary adventure. John and his staff have come up with such delectable items as a shellfish and corn chowder; mahimahi served with lime jus, jalapeños, tomatoes,

and cilantro; and an ale marinated flank steak served with red potatoes, bacon, and grilled corn on the cob. A cheese menu (with each of the two dozen cheeses described in detail) complements the 1,500 different wine choices. $16–28. Sides are extra and served with fresh fruit and mini toast.

❀ **Palm 32** (410-289-2525; www.ocean cityhilton.com), 32nd St. Inside the Hilton Hotel (see *Lodging*), the offerings of Palm 32 reflect a Caribbean cuisine with a few traditional Eastern Shore entrées. It's an elegant atmosphere, with prices to match. Sadly, there is no ocean view. $25–35.

❀ &. **Reflections** (410-524-5252; www.ocmdhotels.com), 67th St. oceanfront. One of the most upscale and formal dining experiences in the city. The small fountain and low, golden lighting make it a place couples come to for a romantic setting. The everchanging Continental menu has tableside flambé cooking, along with variations on seafood, pasta, and steak from $20 to $35. My early-bird special (5–6 PM) filet mignon was charbroiled to my liking and covered with bordelaise sauce. Inside the Holiday Inn.

❀ &. **Victorian Room** (410-289-1100; www.dunesmanor.com), 28th St. and the oceanfront. Located in the Dunes Manor Hotel. American cuisine with items from the sea and the land. $18.95–27.95.

EATING OUT

Berlin

The Globe (410-641-0784; www.globe theater.com), 12 Broad St. Open for lunch and dinner daily; Sunday brunch. Located within the redesigned historic Old Globe Theater, which started showing movies in the 1910s, the Globe serves fare not often found in this part of the Eastern Shore. The gourmet sandwiches are as tasty as they are healthful, and evening entrées have included Saltimbuca, seafood Florentine, and petite filets atop portobello mushrooms. Acoustic jazz, folk, classical, and rock music are presented almost every night. Talent ranges from local to international. The bulk of the audiences come from the surrounding area, so this is the place to mingle with the natives. Entrées $18–35; sandwiches $7–12.

☙ **Raynes Reef Luncheonette** (410-641-2131; www.raynesreef.com), 10 N. Main St. Open for breakfast and extended lunch (well after 6 PM); closed Sun. Mike Queen grew up in Berlin and, during his high school years, worked at the luncheonette, whose building has been a restaurant of some kind or another since 1901. Upon becoming the owner, he remodeled the luncheonette to bring it back to its appearance of the mid-1900s, with a wood floor, lunch counter with stools, and wooden booths. The menu consists of salads and hot and cold sandwiches; the Battleship, a cheesesteak sandwich on a Kaiser roll, has been a local favorite for decades. Hand-made shakes and ice cream sodas draw in travelers during the warmer months. Almost everything is less than $10, so it's a logical choice when you are looking for a meal without having to spend the bucks.

Ocean City

☙ � **Angler Restaurant** (410-289-7424; www.angleroc.net), Talbot St. and the bay. Breakfast, lunch, and dinner. The Angler gives a free (almost) coastline cruise with every evening meal. You are going to eat dinner anyway, so why not take them up on the offer? The daily catch (market price) can be prepared blackened, amandine, island style, or several other ways. Dinner entrées $18–30.

☙ ☙ ⅼ **Atlantic Stand** (410-289-7203; www.atlanticstand.com), Wicomico St. and the boardwalk. With some dishes less than $4, Atlantic has some of the lowest-cost breakfasts, lunches, and take-out food in the city. The most expensive item is a crab-cake for less than $10. In the same location since 1933.

☙ ⅼ **The Bayside Skillet** (410-524-7950; www.baysideskillet.com), 77th St. and the bay. The place for out-of-the-ordinary breakfasts. Choose a hot fudge sundae or peach melba crêpe, a seafood frittata (crab, shrimp, and scallops with marinara sauce), or pan-fried potatoes sautéed with bacon, onions, mushrooms, and cheddar cheese. I

ate about two-thirds of my Spanish omelet and did not eat again until late in the evening. Expect to spend $9–19 at this place, which is easily recognized by its bright pink exterior and lines of people waiting to get in from early morning on. Lunch and dinner are also served.

☙ ⅼ **BJ's on the Water** (410-524-7575; www.bjsonthewater.com), 75th St. on the bay. Open daily for lunch and dinner, with the entire menu available all day. Restaurants tend to come and go quickly in beach areas, but BJ's has been around, and under the same ownership, since 1979. Seafood, obtained as locally as possible, is the focus of the menu, and the flounder is recognized as a specialty. (I enjoyed mine, as it is pan fried in peanut oil, giving a light flavor rather than a heavy deep-fried taste.) Picture windows overlook a marshy inlet of the bay, permitting you to watch the ducks go tail-up in search of the corn BJ's feeds them each day at 1 PM. Entrées $16.95–24.95.

☙ **Bull on the Beach** (410-524-2455; www.bullonthebeachoc.com), 94th St. Although seafood and a raw bar are available, most customers come here for the hand-cut, aged, midwestern steaks seasoned and cooked on an open pit along with the beef for the BBQ sandwiches. Extensive selection of beers and cocktails. $15.95–19.95.

Crazy 8's (410-524-5050; www.eatat8s .com), 35th St. After surfing America's West Coast, the Virgin Islands, and Australia, Eugene Stiltner decided to stay put in Ocean City for a while and he and his wife, Jennifer, offer one of Ocean City's best lunch places with (well-stuffed) wraps, paninis, sandwiches, and fresh-made salads. Whatever you order, be sure to accompany it with the fresh-squeezed lemonade, fresh fruit ice teas, or watermelon drink. $7.95-10.95.

☙ **de Lazy Lizard** (410-289-1122; www .oclazylizard.com), 305 N. 1st St. Come here for the outside seating next to the bay, the cool crush drinks, and the opportunity to rent a Jet Ski or go parasailing. It's pretty much always a Caribbean party atmosphere, with bar food offerings and a few steak and seafood entrées. $10-30.

The Dough Roller (www.doughroller oc.com). There are four locations in Ocean City: S. Division St. and the boardwalk (410-289-3501); Third St. and the boardwalk (410-289-2599); 41st St. and Coastal Hwy. (410-524-9254); 70th St. and Coastal Hwy. (410-524-7981). My sister, by far one of the most severe of pizza critics, says Dough Rollers is the best "fast-food pizza" in the city. Eat in or pick up only; no deliveries.

The General's Kitchen (410-723-0477), 74th St. and Coastal Hwy. Open daily for breakfast and lunch. Like Layton's, the General's Kitchen has been around for many years and serves breakfast at any time during business hours. Prices are very reasonable; nothing was over $9 the last time I visited. An item that is becoming increasingly harder to find, creamed chipped beef, is the house specialty.

Layton's (410-289-6635), 16th St. and Philadelphia Ave. Open for breakfast and lunch daily. Layton's has been owned by the same family since they started baking Dip-n-Donuts in the 1950s (still available). It has a bit of a diner atmosphere, but one that has a nicely painted ocean mural. Breakfast is now served all day, while lunch consists primarily of sandwiches and a few salads. The all-you-can-eat breakfast buffet has people lining up on the street in the early morning. Most items less than $10.

Malia's Café (443-664-2420; www.malias cafeoceancity.com), 1800 Baltimore Ave. Open for breakfast and lunch from Mar.–Nov. It's next to impossible to find healthy food along the boardwalk, so take just a dozen steps off it to find fresh-made hummus and tuna salad, along with veggie roll-ups and an avocado and cheese sandwich. There are also many meat sandwiches and seafood items along with an inventive cheesesteak sandwich. With bright, cheery murals and a shaded patio, this is my pick as the best place to eat lunch without having to leave the beach area. $3.95–10.95.

Melvin's Steak House & Saloon (410-289-7554; www.melvinssteakhouse.com), 25 Philadelphia Ave. Open for dinner daily. After visiting Melvin's Steakhouse as a teenager, Keith Melvin (no relation) dreamed about one day owning the business. The dream came true in 2006, and Keith kept on the same chef who had been there for more than 30 years. It's a fairly simple menu—four kinds of steaks, fried and grilled chicken, BBQ, and seafood. The décor, which has been adopted by national steak house chains, has been pleasing customers since the 1950s. $10–27.

& Phillips Crab House and Seafood Festival Buffet (410-289-6821; www .phillipsfoods.com), 21st St. and Philadelphia Ave. It seems that every ocean resort area in America now has the obligatory all-you-can-eat seafood buffet restaurants, and Ocean City is no exception. With decades of knowledge in the commercial fishing industry, Phillips is the best of the lot and is one of the few still offering steamed crabs on the buffet. Arrive around 4 PM to save a couple of dollars on the approximately $30 charge. Kids and regular menus available.

Sahara Café (410-289-5080; on facebook), 1901 N. Baltimore Ave. Open for breakfast and lunch during the usual tourist season. I've only had breakfast here, so I can't advise you on the lunch offerings, but breakfast was prepared well, served quick, and with ample portions. Creamed chipped beef, sausage gravy, and eggs Benedict are some of the most popular items. If you're willing to pay for it, the crab and chedder omelette is a standout. This place is always crowded for breakfast. $4.95–11.95.

& Seacrets Bar and Restaurant (410-524-4900; www.seacrets.com), 49th St. and the bay. Seacrets capitalizes on its reggae theme by providing 14 indoor and open-air bars. Most of the items on the menu, such as veggie, tuna salad, and spicy chicken sandwiches, or ribs and red snapper platters, have a bit of Jamaican heritage to them. Eat under palm trees or lounge on rafts in the water and have your food brought to you. There is live entertainment year-round, but when bands come to play at

the height of the season, this place hops so much you might think you've walked into an MTV spring break party. Entrées $10–29.

§ **The Shark** (410-641-3589; www.oc shark.com), 12942 Sunset Ave. The Shark's menu is printed daily because the offerings are based on what the nearby fishing captains can provide and what local, fresh produce is available. Items are identified if they are vegetarian, vegan, or gluten-free. It's a varied and inventive menu that has featured everything from blackened fish tacos to crabcakes with crawfish and andouille sausage remoulade to duck meatballs in duck confit with triple cream brie and a balsamic reduction. I enjoyed watching the working boats coming and going just a few feet from the restaurant's picture windows. $14–33.

Pocomoke City

§ **Riverside Grill** (410-957-0622; on facebook), 2 Riverside Dr. Open for lunch and dinner daily. The real draw is the view of the Pocomoke River from the outside deck or the large picture windows from inside. (It gets exciting when the nearby drawbridge opens to allow boat traffic to pass through.) The American style menu has an emphasis on burgers, sandwiches, and seafood. My shrimp salad sandwich was piled high. Most items not much more than $10.

CRABS

Berlin

§ **Assateague Crab House** (410-641-4330; on facebook), MD 611. The post office address is Berlin, but you will find this restaurant on your way to Assateague Island, just south of the MD 611/MD 376 intersection. This is a typical crab house, so the décor is minimal, but the price on the crabcake sandwich served with french fries is certainly reasonable. All-you-can-eat crabs and shrimp available at market prices.

Ocean City

&. **Bahama Mamas** (410-289-0291; www .bahamamamasocmd.com), 221 Wicomico St. The outside deck overlooking Assa-

teague Island is the appropriate place to be cracking open jumbo steamed blue crabs (market price)—obtained fresh from the restaurant's affiliated seafood outlet market just a few miles up the beach. Happy hour 4–7 PM.

§ **Captain's Galley II** (410-213-2525; www.captainsgalley2.com), 12817 Harbor Rd., West Ocean City. Fresh seafood purchased directly from the docks. It's great fun to sit on the outside deck overlooking the harbor and crack open steamed crabs by the dozen (market price).

§ &. **Crab Alley** (410-213-7800; www.crab alleyoc.com), 9703 Golf Course Rd., West Ocean City. If you don't mind driving back onto the mainland, you will probably find some of the freshest steamed blue crabs here. They serve other seafood (such as tuna steak and a seafood platter) when available fresh. Kids' menu has cheeseburgers, hot dogs, and crab balls. Entrées $17.95–market price.

§ **Higgins Crab House** (410-289-2581; www.higginscrabhouse.com), 31st St. and Coastal Hwy. The Higgins Family has been purchasing crabs and other seafood directly from watermen and waterwomen for more than four decades, so they know a thing or two about what to look for and how to serve it. The menu contains many different platters and a large variety of all-you-can-eat crab and seafood offerings. $15.95–34.95

BREWERY **Burley Oak Brewing Company** (443-513-4647; www.burley oak.com), 10016 Old Ocean Blvd., Berlin. The ales, porters, stouts, and more are brewed with locally grown hops, barleys, and other ingredients. Lots of live music and other entertainment every week, with free brewery tours at 3 on Saturday and Sunday.

COFFEE BAR **Berlin Coffee House** (410-629-1073; on facebook), 17 Jefferson St., Berlin. A cozy atmosphere with local artists' works on the walls and a shelf of books and items for customers to use while sipping the coffees and teas or eating sandwiches and baked goodies.

Berlin

Cupcakes in Bloom (410-641-9020), 120 Main St. Shawnee Weber Berzonski has taken one of her passions and turned it into the family-operated Cupcakes in Bloom. Close to two dozen flavors are always on the menu, with special combinations offered seasonally. The shop and its goodies have been featured on the Food Networks' *Cupcake Wars.*

Ocean City

✿ **Candy Kitchen** (1-800-60-FUDGE; www.candykitchen.com), 5301 Coastal Hwy. Ocean City's saltwater taffy connection for more than 50 years has multiple kitchens located throughout the resort area. Also offers homemade fudge and hand-dipped chocolates.

✿ ♿ **Dumser's Dairyland Drive-In** (410-524-1588; www.beach-net.com/dumsers), 49th St. and Coastal Hwy. Dumser's has been serving subs, burgers, and fries in Ocean City since 1939, but the real attraction is the ice cream made on the premises that is sold within a few hours of manufacture. The Hawaiian delight—cherries, pineapples, and bananas in vanilla ice cream—is one of the best sellers. A three-dip super sundae ($6.95) could easily fill up two hungry kids.

Fractured Prune, The Donut Shop (www.fracturedprune.com). Four locations: 127th St. (410-250-4400); 81st St. (410-524-4688); 28th St. (410-289-1134); 9636 Stephen Decatur Hwy., West Ocean City (410-213-9899). Be prepared to wait in a long line at these shops. They serve one of the best-selling goodies in the area, yellow cake donuts made from scratch and cooked just as you order them. Best part? You get to choose from an abundance of toppings and glazes, so you are the creative genius behind your own donut. Don't be put off by the name; it has nothing to do with prunes. It refers to 19th-century Prunella Shriek, who owned the land the original shop is located on, and who was an avid sportswoman—but often sustained broken bones, leading friends to call her The Frac-

tured Prune. The business is turning into a franchise, so you may find one close to your home one day.

WINERY Costa Ventosa Winery (410-352-9867; www.costaventosa.com), 9031 Whaleyville Rd., Whaleyville. Open Fri., Sat., and Sun. The first vines of Costa Ventosa (Windy Coast in Italian) were planted in 2006, the first bottling was in 2009, and by 2012 the winery was winning awards. Owners Kathryn and Jack are happy to provide a tour (time permitting) of the vineyard and winery, providing information on such things as how they pick the grapes, test for sugar, and how they came to be vintners.

WINE TASTING Maryland Wine Bar (410-629-1022; on facebook), 103 N. Main St., Berlin. Open Mon.–Sat. The first of its kind in Maryland, the wine bar offers a rotating selection (usually 50 or more) of Maryland-produced wines. It's a fun and festive atmosphere, with the owner's knowledge helping you choose wines to your liking. Finger foods and small plates compliment the libations.

✳ Entertainment

MUSIC The Globe Theater (410-641-0784; ww.globetheater.com), 12 Broad St., Berlin. See *Eating Out.*

NIGHTLIFE Caribbean Bar and Grill (410-289-0837; www.ocmdhotels.com /plimplaza/thecaribbean.html), Second St. and the boardwalk, Ocean City. Live funk, reggae, or jazz bands nightly.

The OC Jamboree (410-213-7581; www .ocjam.com), MD 611 and Marjan Lane, West Ocean City. Open all year, the Jamboree tries to appeal to families with its Opryland/Branson-type variety musical entertainment.

Shenanigan's Irish Pub (410-289-7181; www.ocshenanigans.com), Fourth St. and the boardwalk, Ocean City. Irish entertainment almost every night during the oceanfront deck during the summer season.

Also see **Seacrets Bar and Grill** in *Eating Out*.

✻ Selective Shopping

ANTIQUES

Pocomoke City
A 2nd Time Around (410-957-1586; on facebook), 153 Market St. With what it labels as repurposed items, the shop has collectibles, jewelry, records, books, and a host of thrift items.

Berlin
Stuart's Antiques (410-641-0435), Pitts St. It would take a full afternoon to look over all the furniture, glass figures and animals, estate jewelry, china, and silverware crammed into this shop.

Town Center Antiques. A gallery-type shop with over 125 antiques dealers; two Berlin locations: 1 N. Main St. (410-629-1895) and 113 N. Main St. (410-629-1595).

✻ **Toy Town Antiques** (410-641-9370; www.tophatz.com/toytown), 110 N. Main St. Is it an antiques shop? A children's toy store? A museum? With model trains, vintage Barbie dolls, wind-up figurines, metal advertising signs, pressed steel and cast iron toys, and old coins, it's a bit of each one and you could spend an hour or more just looking through the items.

ART GALLERIES

Berlin
J. J. Fish Studio and Fine Arts Gallery (410-641-4805; www.jjfishstudio.com), 14 N. Main St. The back of the shop is the studio where husband and wife John and Judy Fisher create their jewelry and metalwork; the gallery contains the works of selected artists and craftspersons whom the couple has met during their appearances at shows and other galleries throughout the county.

Water's Edge Gallery (410-641-9119; www.watersedgeberlin.com), 2 S. Main St. The gallery exhibits monthly fine-art shows by regional artists.

Worcester County Arts Council (410-641-0809; www.worcestercountyartscouncil.org), 6 Jefferson St. Closed Sat. The council's small retail shop is an outlet for a variety of local artists and craftspeople. This is a chance to bring home something that has not been mass produced.

Ocean City
The Art League of Ocean City (410-524-9433; www.artleagueofoceancity.org), temporarily housed in the former bank building at 94th St. Shopping Plaza while a new headquarters is being built, call for current information. Closed Mon. Monthly exhibits of works primarily by members and other local artists.

Ocean Gallery World Center (410-289-5300; www.oceangallery.com), Second St. and the boardwalk. There is no mistaking this building, as its exterior is a most amazing hodgepodge of pieces of other buildings from around the world that fans of the gallery have donated to it. The inside is just as convoluted. There are thousands works of art, some by well-known painters, others of ambiguous origin and quality, stacked one against the other over four different floors. The experience is worth the visit. While taking a lighthearted look at art, you just may find a hidden masterpiece.

Snow Hill
American Art Gallery (410-632-0278; www.americanartmaryland.com), 211 N. Washington St. A nice blend of emerging and well-known artists, both regional and internationally recognized.

Bishop's Stock (410-632-3555; www.bishopsstock.com), 202 W. Green St. A true fine art shop (with prices to match) with some of the best artists from Maryland and nearby states. Fine wines, too.

USED BOOKS

Ocean City
Bookshelf Etc. (410-524-2949), 8006 Coastal Hwy. Three small rooms full of books in one of the few still-standing buildings that was once a private home on Coastal Hwy.

The Bookstore at Bayside Plaza (410-250-1385), 13719 Coastal Hwy. It's small, but there is an extensive selection of hardbacks and paperbacks.

SPECIAL SHOPS

Berlin
Ta-Da (410-641-4430; www.berlintada.com), 18 and 27 N. Main St. Patty Falck markets a diverse collection of handpainted furniture and glassware. Many locals come in to get her customized vases as wedding gifts.

Ocean City
Donald's Duck Shoppe and Gallery (410-524-9177; 1-877-623-8257; www.donaldsduckshoppe.com), 11515 Coastal Hwy. New items that arrive almost daily include unique decoys and gift items with an emphasis on those pertaining to the coast, ocean, and Eastern Shore.

⚓ The Kite Loft. With two locations in Ocean City: Fifth St. and the boardwalk (410-289-6852); 131st St. and Coastal Hwy. (410-250-4970). Box, wind, diamond, airplane, bird shaped, you name it; this shop has more—and different kinds—of kites than anywhere else in Maryland. Prices range from single to almost triple digits.

OUTLETS Ocean City Factory Outlets (1-800-625-6696; www.ocfactoryoutlets.com), Ocean Gateway (US 50) and Golf Course Rd., West Ocean City. Includes outlets for Bass, Carter's for Kids, Tommy Hilfiger, Izod, Dress Barn, and more than 30 other manufacturers.

FARMER'S MARKETS Berlin. Located at N. Main St. Held Wed. and Fri. from 1 PM till sold out, May–Oct.

Ocean City. Located at the Phillips Restaurant on 142nd St. and Coastal Hwy. Open Sun. early May–early Oct.; Tues. late June–early Sept.; Thurs. early June–early Sept.

Pocomoke City. Apr.–Nov., find fresh produce and other farmer's market items, along with a flea market on Fri. and Sat. mornings, at Market St. next to Cypress Park.

PICK-YOUR-OWN FARMS Milton's Produce (410-632-2633), 6230 Worcester Hwy., Newark. A variety of fruits and vegetables is available for picking, 7–7, during their seasons.

✴ Special Events

January: **Nautical and Wildlife Art Festival; North American Craft Show** (410-524-9177). Both held in the convention center, 40th St., Ocean City.

March: **St. Patrick's Day Parade** (410-289-6156). From 61st St. to 44th St., Ocean City. Some say this has become the East Coast's third largest St. Patrick's Day celebration.

March or April: **Easter Arts and Crafts and Kids Fair** (www.oceanpromotions.info), convention center, Ocean City. Egg hunts, clowns, storytellers, and the Easter Bunny. **Ward World Championship Wildfowl Carving Competition** (410-742-4988), convention center, Ocean City. Not to be missed by those who have the slightest interest in decoy art. The largest and, without a doubt, the most prestigious competition of wildfowl art. More than 150 exhibitors and artists.

May: **Springfest** (410-250-0125), Inlet Parking Area, Ocean City. A four-day arts and crafts festival under big-top tents.

June: **Art's Alive** (410-250-0125; www.ococean.com), Northside Park, Ocean City. More than 100 artists displaying and selling their works, along with free music and educational children's programs. **Strawberry Day** (410-632-2032), Furnace Town, Snow Hill. Lots of food created from strawberries; contests and tastings.

July: **Annual Ocean City Tuna Tournament** (410-213-1121; www.octunatournament.com), Ocean City Fishing Center. **Greek Festival** (410-524-0990), convention center, Ocean City. Greek food and goodies, dancing, and entertainment. **Penning of the Ponies** (757-336-6161), Chincoteague Island, nearby in Virginia (see the sidebar on 38). Watch the ponies swim across the channel from Assateague Island

THE WILD PONIES OF ASSATEAGUE ISLAND

to Chincoteague Island. Draws extremely large crowds.

August: **White Marlin Open** (410-289-9229; www.whitemarlinopen.com), Ocean City. Offshore fishing competition for white and blue marlin, tuna, and shark. This is not a small-time event; prize money totals well over $1 million. **Worcester County Fair** (410-632-1972), Furnace Town, Snow Hill.

September: **Berlin Fiddler's Convention** (410-641-4775), downtown Berlin. **Sunfest** (410-250-0125), Inlet Parking Area, Ocean City. Autumn's equivalent of the Springfest. Includes the **Kite Festival,** considered by

many to be America's largest gathering of kite fliers. Competitions and aerial exhibits.

October: **Endless Summer Cruisin'** (410-798-6304), Inlet Parking Area, Ocean City. A hot rod show with more than 1,500 classics, muscle cars, and more. Entertainment, vendors, and a parade.

November–early January: **Winterfest of Lights** (410-250-0125; www.ococean.com), Ocean City. Holiday lights and animated displays throughout the city. In addition, there are over 800,000 lights at Northside Park (410-250-0125), where you can ride the Winterfest Express through a mile of animated ornaments.

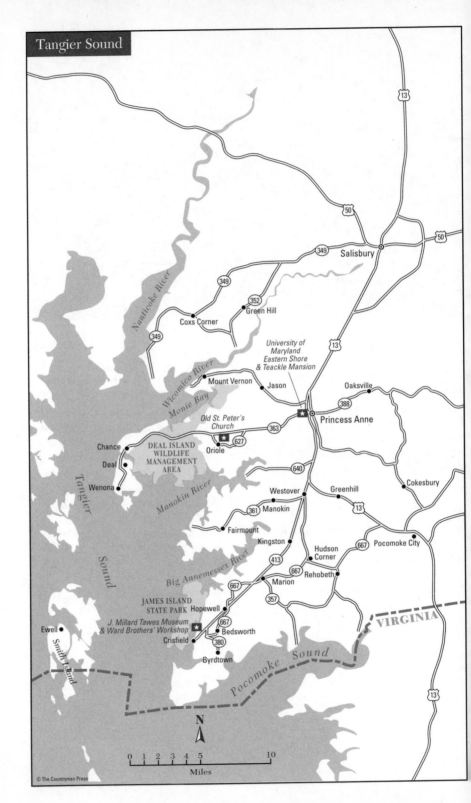

Tangier Sound

© The Countryman Press

N

0 1 2 3 4 5   10
Miles

TANGIER SOUND AREA
CRISFIELD AND PRINCESS ANNE

In *Beautiful Swimmers*, William W. Warner aptly describes Crisfield as "A town built upon oyster shells, millions of tons of it." And he is right, both figuratively and literally.

When large beds of oysters were discovered in Tangier Sound in the mid-1800s, John W. Crisfield recognized the importance of the find. He brought the railroad from Salisbury so that the oysters could be economically transported to the important markets of the Northeast. In order to bring the tracks right to the water's edge, the land was artificially extended upon a base of compacted oyster shells.

In its heyday, Crisfield's population numbered well over 10,000, and more sailing ships were registered here than in any other port in the country. Close to 150 seafood-processing plants, many of them also built upon oyster shells, clustered around the water. Agricultural packinghouses and a sewing industry also moved into the area to take advantage of the railroad.

When the oysters began to play out, the watermen turned their attention to blue crabs and other seafood. Even though the bay's bounty has declined in recent years and housing developments have changed the look of the waterfront, Crisfield remains essentially a working town—and this is the reason to visit. Observing the activity on the city dock could occupy you for a full day. Ferries come and go to Smith Island, tons of seafood are unloaded, and sportfishermen head out with hopes high. Do not expect fancy shops, gourmet food, or theme parks, but the opportunity to observe an industrious way of life.

Princess Anne was chartered in 1733 and became the Somerset County seat in 1742. Until the turn of the 20th century, large ships were able to sail up the Manokin River, bringing growth and prosperity. Many of the town's historic mansions and homes, most notably Teackle Mansion, have been well preserved and make a walking tour of the city (brochure available from Somerset County Tourism; see *Guidance*) worthwhile, while the University of Maryland–Eastern Shore attracts visitors with its cultural events.

COMMUNITIES The small fishing villages of **Deal** and **Wenona** on Deal Island are worth driving through just to catch a glimpse of a lifestyle that may be on its way out.

GUIDANCE **Somerset County Tourism** (www.visitsomerset.com) maintains offices at 11440 Ocean Hwy., Princess Anne, 21853 (410-651-2968; 1-800-521-9189) and at 1003 W. Main St., Crisfield, 21817 (410-968-1543).

GETTING THERE *By car:* **US 13** is the route that will bring you into the area, with **MD 413** going south to Crisfield.

By bus: **Greyhound** (1-800-231-2222; www.greyhound.com) makes a stop at the Student Center at the University of Maryland–Eastern Shore in Princess Anne.

GETTING AROUND The local bus service, **Shore Transit** (443-260-2300; www.shore transit.org), has a route that enables you to reach most of the major towns in the area.

MEDICAL EMERGENCY McCready Health Services maintains a full-service hospital in Crisfield (410-968-1200; www.mccreadyfoundation.org).

✳ To See

COLLEGES Founded as the Delaware Conference Academy in 1886, the **University of Maryland–Eastern Shore** (410-651-2200; www.umes.edu) in Princess Anne is the cultural hub of the area. Its library contains more than 150,000 books, and diverse programs are presented in the **Ella Fitzgerald Performing Arts Center.** The 700-acre campus can be a quiet place for an afternoon's walk.

MUSEUMS J. **Millard Tawes Museum** (410-968-2501; www.crisfieldheritagefoundation .org), Somers Cove Marina, Crisfield. Small admission charge. Mon.–Sat. 10–4, Sun. 10–2 during the usual tourist season. Please note that times and days have been known to change. Donations accepted. J. Millard Tawes was a native of Crisfield and Maryland's 54th governor. In addition to paying homage to his life, the museum chronicles the history of the area, from Native Americans to how the catch of the watermen gradually moved from oysters to crabs. The decoys of the Ward Brothers, models of various boats that worked Tangier Sound, and a mural that provides a sweeping overview of Chesapeake Bay chronology make the museum worth the small price of admission.

HISTORIC HOMES Teackle Mansion (410-651-2238; www.teacklemansion.org), 11736 Mansion St., Princess Anne. Small admission charge. Thurs., Sat., and Sun. 1–3, Apr. through early Dec. Donations accepted. The home of Littleton Teackle, prominent educator, banker, and statesman, is so large it took from 1802 to 1819 to complete. Its center has a Flemish-bond brick facade and decorative plasterwork above the door and first-floor windows. The adherence to Federal-style architecture, with its strict sense of symmetry, is as amusing as it is amazing. The house is furnished in period pieces (very few from the Teackle family), and tour guides point out the family Bible, prints by artists Teackle met in England, banknotes, and a "Report of the State's Bank."

TEACKLE MANSION, PRINCESS ANNE

HISTORIC SITES Ward Brothers' Workshop, Crisfield. Crisfield natives Steve and Lem Ward are generally acknowledged as being the ones who elevated decoy carving into an art form. Their workshop, which was rapidly deteriorating, has been stabilized, but not glamorized. Wood chips from the brothers' work remain on the floor, their ripped vinyl chairs have not been replaced, and even the color of the walls remains the same. This is one of the few historic places in which you get a real feel for what went on inside. This is a highly recommended stop, but you must contact the J. Millard Tawes Museum (see *Museums*) to gain access.

HISTORIC CHURCHES Within the **Asbury United Methodist Church** (410-968-0540; www.goldsboroughsmarine.com/asbury) in Crisfield is a painting of Daniel in the lion's den done by Lem Ward. However, he did not like the way it turned out, so he signed it as having been done by "Balkuaves."

The old **St. Peter's Church** (410-651-2612) in Oriole was founded in 1782, and the congregation is still going strong.

The original congregation of the **Metropolitan United Methodist Church** (410-651-0530; 30522 E. Broad St., Princess Anne) consisted entirely of slaves. The present building was erected in the late 1800s on property that once served as a slave auction block.

GUIDED TOURS The **Port of Crisfield Escorted Walking Tour** is sponsored by the J. Millard Tawes Museum (see *Museums*) and takes you through the historical port areas of town.

✳ To Do

BICYCLING **Adrenaline High** (410-749-2886; www.adrenalinehigh.com). Stan Shedaker has more than 20 years' experience planning and leading group trips and, along with his wife, Rachael, operates a touring company that puts together customized bicycle and kayak tours in and around Somerset County. Tours include some equipment, shuttles, accommodations, and meals.

BIRDING Woodlands, bay shoreline, and brackish marshes are the reason that **Deal Island Wildlife Management Area** (410-543-8223; http://dnr.maryland.gov/wildlife/publiclands/eastern/dealisland.asp; MD 363 west of Princess Anne) has such a diversity of birdlife: bald eagles, short-eared owls, tundra swans, marsh wrens, black rails, the rare peregrine falcon, and Maryland's only nesting population of black-necked stilts.

FISHING **Tangier Sound** has some of the best fishing on the bay, with flounder, striped bass, drum, trout, croaker, and perch being the catch for sportfishermen. Among the many charter-boat captains operating out of Crisfield are **Keith Ward** (410-968-0074; www.crisfield.com/prim) and **Perry Brown** (410-726-6564). **Captains Joe and John Asanovich** (410-957-2562; www.barbaraannfishing.com) operate headboats that leave at 7 AM daily during the usual tourist months from the Somers Cove Marina, Crisfield.

FISHING FROM THE PIER IN CRISFIELD

Somerset County Tourism (see *Guidance*) can provide you with a list of additional charter captains operating in and around Tangier Sound.

GOLF ⚑ **Great Hope Golf Course** (410-651-5900; 1-800-537-8009; www.greathopegolf .com), 8380 Crisfield Hwy., Westover. Closed only on Christmas Day. Five sets of tees at each hole allow you to pick your challenge on the 7,049-yard golf course designed by Dr. Michael Hurzdan. A children's discount is available.

HIKING See *Green Space.*

KAYAKING AND CANOEING **Crisfield Kayak and Canoe Rentals** (410-968-0333; www.crisfieldkayaking.com), 65-C Richardson Ave., Crisfield. Kayak and canoe rentals, by the hour or day, enable you to explore Tangier Sound, Nassawango Creek, the Pocomoke River, or Smith Island. A rarity on the Eastern Shore, they can arrange for backcountry paddle/camping trips. Bicycle rentals, too.

Also see **Adrenaline High** under *Bicycling.*

❊ Green Space

BEACHES **Brick Kiln Beach** is small, may have jellyfish floating about, and is close to the high-rise town houses, but it does provide a chance to swim in the bay in Crisfield.

Located at the northern end of **Deal Island** is a nice, almost-never-used public beach stretching for over 1,000 feet of soft sand. Great place to watch the sunset. It's also a favorite haunt of sea glass hunters.

Also see *Parks.*

DEAL ISLAND'S LIGHTLY USED PUBLIC BEACH

GARDENS The **Boxwood Garden** at the corner of Somerset Ave. and Washington St. in Princess Anne dates from the mid-1800s.

PARKS **Janes Island State Park** (410-968-1565; www.dnr.state.md.us/public lands/eastern/janesisland.asp), 26280 Alfred Lawson Dr., Crisfield. The park is divided into two areas, the 300-acre Hodson Memorial Area on the mainland and, separated from it by the Daugherty Creek Canal, Janes Island itself. Within the memorial area are a marina with boat-launch capabilities, a campground with modern amenities, picnic areas, and rental cabins. Although this area has two hiking trails, each a mile in length, it is the 3,000-acre island that is most worth spending your foot-travel time upon.

Except for a small boat dock and some ruins of a former fishing village on its southern end, Janes Island is completely undeveloped. Bordered by Tangier Sound, it is the quintessential Chesapeake Bay island, with a landscape barely above sea level. You will find windswept beaches, salt marshes, ponds, low-growing vegetation, and an assortment of creatures that exist only in this type of environment. To come here is to be brought back in time, to what many of the islands looked like when Capt. John Smith made his famous exploration of the bay in the 1600s.

✳ Lodging

MOTELS AND HOTELS

Princess Anne, 21853

Richard A. Henson Center (410-651-8100; http://wwwcf.umes.edu/henson), on the University of Maryland–Eastern Shore campus. Students enrolled in the university's hospitality program make up a large part of the staff, so not only are you getting a lower-cost place to stay, but you're helping young people gain experience. In addition, all of the attractions of the university—plays, concerts, art gallery, and lectures—are at your fingertips. The guest rooms are typical of those of a mid-priced hotel, with a microwave, refrigerator, and high-speed Internet connection. $85–100.

BED & BREAKFASTS

Crisfield, 21817

My Fair Lady B&B (410-968-0352; www.myfairladybandb.com), 38 W. Main St. A stay at My Fair Lady provides a glimpse of the opulence and prosperity of Crisfield's seafood boom around the turn of the 20th century. Relax on the wraparound sunporch or explore the three-story octagonal tower before retiring to one of four period-decorated guest rooms or a third-floor suite. Rate includes tax and a full breakfast. $150–380.

Princess Anne, 21853

Alexander House Booklovers Bed & Breakfast (410-651-5195; www.booklovers bnb.com), 30535 Linden Ave. The entire B&B has a literary theme, with books placed everywhere and artwork and furnishings reflecting the literary world. Each of the three guest rooms is devoted to an individual author, including one of my favorites, Robert Louis Stevenson. The Langston Hughes room celebrates the Harlem Renaissance movement, and there is even an audio recording of the author reading his own words. The claw-foot tub in the Jane Austen room is large enough to do some relaxing soaking. No phones or TVs in the rooms allow quiet contemplation, a bar and snacks are always available, and wicker furniture on the porch lets you sit and talk with other guests or say hi to passersby. $125–160.

Hayman House (410-621-5004; www.the haymanhouse.com), 30491 Prince William St. On a quiet side street just one block from the Teackle Mansion, Hayman House is the perfect spot to stay for parents visiting their student-children at the nearby University of Maryland–Eastern Shore. The Victorian parlor with its cranberry-tiled fireplace is a gathering place for quiet conversations, and the carved woodwork and oak floors add a warmth to the interior. Morning coffee is best appreciated on the porch. Choice of private or shared bath. $100–145.

Somerset House (410-651-4451; www .somersethousemd.com), 30556 Washington St. Many of the original features, including the floors, remain in this 1852 home, where the hosts often serve breakfast in the backyard boxwood gardens. The B&B is actually two houses that have been joined together, and this leads to some interesting characteristics, such as having to step down into one of the bathrooms. Antique furnishings add to the historic ambience, as does the 150-foot ginkgo tree given to the home's original owner, John Crisfield, by Henry Clay. $160.

VACATION HOME

Dames Quarter, 21821

The Farm House Vacation Retreat (410-784-2179; www.thefarm-house.com), 11359 Hodson White Rd. It's just a short drive from the services of Princess Anne, but the Farm House provides a quiet, peaceful respite from city life within a few miles of Deal Island. A modernized 1800s home, it has six bedrooms (each with its own bath), a full kitchen, and laundry facilities, so it's great for a family vacation or corporate retreat. The owner is enthusiastic about things to do in the area and can direct you to places to enjoy hiking, biking, kayaking, crabbing, fishing, etc. on your own or will arrange for local guides who can share their knowledge with you. I thoroughly enjoyed my evening sitting on the screened porch (smugly happy that the insects couldn't get to me) and watching a deer and her fawn graze on the large lawn. The house is nicely furnished—and is one of the most spotless vacation homes I have ever stayed in. (The glass door was so clean, and therefore so transparent, that I walked into it.) Weekends are $350 a night; a full week is $1,700.

CAMPING

Crisfield, 21817
Janes Island State Park (410-968-1565; www.dnr.state.md.us/publiclands/eastern /janesisland.asp), 26280 Alfred Lawson Dr. The state park's campground has sites on the shoreline overlooking the water and the island. Rental cabins also overlooking the water are often reserved a year in advance. For a more rugged experience, you could camp in one of the four primitive sites that are located on the island and accessible only by boat.

Westover, 21871
☃ **Lake Somerset Family Campground** (410-957-9897; www.lakesomerset.com), 8658 Lake Somerset Lane. Caters primarily to those with an RV. You'll find hookups, a general store, metered propane, miniature golf, a swimming pool, boat rentals, a 5-acre fishing pond, and rental cabins and trailers. Pets permitted on some sites.

✳ Where to Eat

DINING OUT ♨ **Watermen's Inn** (410-968-2119; www.crisfield.com/watermens), 901 W. Main St., Crisfield. Closed Mon.—Wed. Breakfast only on Sun. Chef Brian Julian and partner Kathy Berezoski both have degrees in culinary arts from Johnson and Wales University in Rhode Island, and they must have studied well. Brian only

uses fresh local seafood and organically grown produce in his cooking, so the menu changes often. Featured at one time or another have been baked flounder stuffed with feta cheese and spinach and smothered with hollandaise sauce (one of the best flounder meals I've had on the Eastern Shore), and a seafood sampler with soft-shell crab, flounder, shrimp scampi, oysters, and mini crabcake. Save room for Kathy's inventive desserts. Breakfast and lunch also served. Do not be misled by the modest exterior; dinner is a fine-dining experience. Entrées $15.95–24.95.

EATING OUT

Chance
Lucky's Last Chance General Store and Paradise Grill (410-784-2722), 23724 Deal Island Rd. Open daily. If you are exploring Deal Island, this is it—the only place to have a meal. However, don't despair. Despite an unassuming exterior and the fact that you enter through the convenience store part of the business, you can enjoy seafood within hours of it being caught in the bay, especially if you happen to be here when oysters are on the menu. They're served fried, on the half shell, as toppings on pizza, or maybe as oysters Rockefeller with fresh spinach.

The clientele is very local, so don't be alarmed when conversation stops and all eyes turn to you when you walk through the door—you'll soon be welcomed into the fold.

Crisfield
Circle Inn Restaurant (410-968-1969), 4012 Crisfield Hwy. Serves breakfast, lunch, and dinner. This is where the locals come for low-cost home cooking. A full breakfast can be had for less than $6, while the most expensive dinner is less than $20.

Gordon's Confectionery (410-968-0566), 931 W. Main St. This is the place to come if you want to soak up the local color. It opens at 4 AM to serve the watermen and is known for its coffee, old-fashioned fountain service, and a drink called a Zip (primarily chocolate or strawberry milk served over crushed ice). The ever-present group of guys in the back never tires of discussing fishing or politics.

Princess Anne

Peaky's (410-651-1950), 30361 Mt. Vernon Rd. Serves breakfast, lunch, and dinner. Known for their fried chicken ($7.95). Many of the lunch and dinner items, such as broiled flounder ($12.99) or pork chops ($12.99), are the same price at both lunch and dinner.

China Chef (410-651-5768), 12087 Somerset Ave. Open for lunch and dinner. The China Chef has the usual menu for Chinese restaurants, but for something different order the ooey, gooey spareribs.

Spike's Pub and Subs (410-651-9124), 30264 Mt. Vernon Rd. This is the local bar, but it does make a variety of good (and filling) subs, and the prices can't be beat: $6–11.

Westover

Caddy Shack (410-651-5900), 8380 Crisfield Hwy. Located within the Great Hope Golf Course, Caddy Shack offers a range of reasonably priced soups, salads, and sandwiches from $5.95 to $10.95.

CRABS

Crisfield

Captain Tyler's Crabhouse (410-968-1131; www.smithislandcruises.com/crisfield-dining-and-seafood), 923 Spruce St. Housed within a large cinder block building, Captain Tyler's steamed blue crabs, oysters, clams, shrimp, and more are served on the outside patio overlooking the water.

The Crab Place (410-968-2222; www.crabplace.com), 504 Maryland Ave. The restaurant outlet for one of the largest online purveyors of Maryland crabs and other seafood has a large screened porch with a concrete floor for casual dining of all-you-can-eat steamed crabs (available and priced according to market conditions). The hush puppies are fried to a nice, deep crunch.

Princess Anne

♿ **Beach to Bay Seafood** (410-651-5400; www.beachtobayseafood.com), 12138 Carol Ln. A family-run enterprise, Beach to Bay is primarily a carryout place, but a few tables with vinyl tablecloths let you enjoy the seafood immediately after being cooked. In addition to steamed and soft-shell crabs (in-season), there are many combination platters and sandwiches to choose from. Unexpectedly, the homemade desserts, especially the brownies, are worth saving room for.

Also see *Soft-Shell Crabs to Go.*

SOFT-SHELL CRABS TO GO

Linton's Seafood (410-968-0127; www.lintonsseafood.com), 4500 Crisfield Hwy., Crisfield. Steamed crabs, crabmeat, fresh seafood, and crabcakes for dine in or take out.

Southern Connection Seafood (410-968-3367; www.crabsandseafood.com), Seventh St., Crisfield. In addition to packaging live or frozen soft-shell crabs for you to travel with, these friendly folks will take you on a tour of the factory to learn more about crabs.

COFFEE BAR **Get'n Grounded** (410-621-5040; www.getngrounded.com), 12302 Somerset Ave., Princess Anne. Closed Sun. Located in a small strip mall next to US 13, so you don't have to take a major detour off the main highway to enjoy a cup (drive-through for even faster service). However, you may want to linger over the fair trade coffee inside the large, bright, and modern place with many seats and large chairs focused on the large screen TV. A small menu with soups, sandwiches, and baked goods (including Smith Island cake). Free wi-fi and live music on the weekend.

SNACKS AND GOODIES

Crisfield

Ice Cream Gallery (410-968-0809), 5 Goodsell Alley. Daily 11–9:30. The Gallery's

> "You have to think like a crab if you want to catch a crab."
> —Charles Bradshaw of Southern Connection Seafood

deck overlooking Tangier Sound is the place to enjoy the sunset after a meal at one of the local restaurants.

Princess Anne

Sno Biz/Shave Ice (410-651-4548), 12100 Carol Lane. Closed Sun. Good for a cool, sweet treat on a hot day.

✳ Selective Shopping

ANTIQUES Choice Antiques, Gifts, & Books (410-651-2238; www.somerset choiceantiques.org), 11765 Somerset Ave., Princess Anne. Everything in the antique shop of the Somerset County Historical Society is on consignment so you never know what you'll find. While looking through glassware, artwork, furniture, silverware, jewelry, and furniture during my last visit, I also came across a fossilized mammoth's tooth, a mounted bug collection, and a mortician's body cooling bed. How can one justify not stopping by here?

ART GALLERIES ♿ Burton Ave. Gallery (410-986-2787), 26430 Burton Ave., Crisfield. The outlet for the artwork of members of the local Somerset County Arts Council.

PICK-YOUR-OWN PRODUCE FARMS Vessey's Orchards (410-957-1454; on facebook), Rehobeth Rd., Rehobeth. Beginning in July, you can pick squash, tomatoes, peaches, apples, and pumpkins during their respective seasons.

WINERY Great Shoals Winery (410-742-6667; www.greatshoals.com), 26431 Mason Webster Rd., Princess Anne. Finding this place will determine if you are a true Eastern Shore explorer. The mailing address may be Princess Anne, but it is far from town (check the Web site or call for directions) in a small cluster of homes on the shoreline. It will be just a tiny sign that will direct you onto what looks like a residential driveway, which it is. The winery and the tasting room (just a piece of cardboard placed atop cases of wine) are located in what was once a two-room outbuilding. Vintner Matt Cimino produces only sparkling wines made from Maryland- and Delaware-grown fruits and pomegranates (naturalized from Smith Island) grown in the winery's side yard. This is an experience like you will have at no other winery.

✳ Special Events

April: **Annual Daffodil Show** (410-651-0556), Princess Anne. More than 400 blooms and arrangements are on display at the Teackle Mansion.

May: **Annual 1800s Festival** (410-651-3945), Fairmont Academy, Upper Fairmont. An 1800s classroom, old-fashioned spelling bee, food, crafts, and music. **Annual Soft Shell Spring Fair** (410-968-1125), Crisfield. Food, crafts, entertainment, and lots of crab.

July: **Annual J. Millard Tawes Crab and Clam Bake** (410-968-2500; 1-800-782-3913), Somers Cove Marina, Crisfield. All-you-can-eat crabs, clams, fish, corn, and more. Tickets must be purchased in advance. **Somerset County Fair** (410-651-2341), Civic Center, Princess Anne.

August: **Skipjack Races & Festival** (410-784-2785), Deal Island. The blessing of the fleet and the races are the main events, along with a car show, arts and crafts, and a parade.

September: **Annual National Hard Crab Derby and Fair** (410-968-2500), Somers Cove Marina, Crisfield. Lots of fun with crab races, boat-racing and boat-docking contests, crab-picking contests, arts and crafts, much seafood, and live entertainment.

October: **Olde Princess Anne Days** (410-651-2238), Princess Anne. Historic home and garden tours, Revolutionary War encampment, period crafts, music, and kids' activities. **Annual Native American Heritage Festival and Powwow** (410-623-2660), Bending Water Park Living Village, Marion.

SMITH ISLAND

Defining the western edge of Tangier Sound and existing in the heart of the Chesapeake Bay—12 miles from Crisfield—is a world unto itself, tiny Smith Island (see the map on page 62). The island is 8 miles long and 4 miles wide, and its highest point is only a few feet above high tide; much of the acreage is marshland. The island was sighted by Capt. John Smith and settled by Cornish fishermen in the 1600s, and some of the island's inhabitants retain the Elizabethan accents and idioms of their ancestors, which have developed into what some refer to as Tidewater English. Many still make their living from the waters of the bay, heading out early in the morning from the island's many marshy channels. Crab-shedding shanties built upon stilts rise near the water's edge, resulting in its unofficial title: "soft-shell crab capital of the world."

The island is actually a conglomeration of islands separated by creeks, canals, marshes, and inlets. The towns of **Ewell** and **Rhodes Point** are connected by a roadway, but tiny **Tylerton** can be reached only by boat.

Visitors are usually day-trippers who ferry over to Ewell to stay on the island for a few hours, have a meal, and take a quick self-guided walking tour reading the interpretive plaques placed along the roadways.

The best way to really appreciate the island's uniqueness, however, is to spend the night. After other tourists have gone, overnight visitors can share unhurried conversations with residents, take a walk along the waterfront, or just enjoy the sunset spreading a reddish glow across the marshlands. Spring—when the blossoms of pomegranate, fig, pear, and mimosa trees color the scenery and perfume the air—is a great time to visit. Be sure to look in the stores for fig preserves and pomegranate jellies made by island residents in their homes.

GUIDANCE The **Smith Island Visitor's Center** (410-425-3351; www.smithisland.org), 20846 Caleb Jones Rd., Ewell, 21824, provides information once you are on the island. Before going, you might want to contact **Somerset County Tourism** (410-651-2968; 1-800-521-9189; www.visitsomerset.com) at 11440 Ocean Hwy., Princess Anne, 21853.

If you want to really understand the history and the people of the island before you arrive, read the book *An Island Out of Time*. Author Tom Horton spent three years on Smith Island, and his book is an eloquent and sensitive study.

GETTING THERE **Smith Island Cruises** (410-425-2771; www.smithislandcruises.com) leaves from the Somers Cove Marina for a lightly narrated cruise at 12:30 daily, arrives at Smith Island about 1:10, and leaves at 4 sharp.

The *Island Belle II* (410-425-4422) is the island's mail boat and follows the same schedule. Hauling passengers as well as the mail, it leaves from the Crisfield city dock.

PREPARING TO LEAVE FOR SMITH ISLAND

The *Captain Jason I* (410-425-5931) departs the Crisfield city dock and follows the same schedule. More a working boat than a tourist boat, it is the one many of the islanders use. Expect to share space with furniture, dog food, cases of paper towels, and other items. The gossip you overhear makes up for the lack of narration.

The *Captain Jason II* (410-425-4471) also leaves at the same time, but takes passengers to Tylerton, enabling you to visit a place that the vast majority of travelers miss.

GETTING AROUND Bicycles and golf carts can be rented at the ice cream stand beside the **Bayside Inn** (410-425-2771; www.smithislandcruises.com), 4065 Smith Island Rd., Ewell. As an alternative, you can bring your own bike on one of the boats (see *Getting There*) by paying a small freight fee.

PUBLIC RESTROOMS Public comfort stations are found inside the Smith Island Visitor's Center.

✳ To See

MUSEUMS ♿ **Smith Island Visitor's Center Cultural Museum** (410-425-3351; www.smithisland.org), 20846 Caleb Jones Rd., Ewell. Small admission charge. Open daily noon–4, Apr.–Nov. Sometimes open during the off-season. Murals, interactive displays, full-sized workboats, and occasional live interpreters make this the first place to stop to learn more about your Smith Island visit. The time line puts things in perspective and shows how the vagaries of the seafood harvest have affected the islanders.

✳ To Do

BICYCLING Bicycles can be rented at the ice cream stand beside the **Bayside Inn** (410-425-2771; www.smithislandcruises.com), 4065 Smith Island Rd., Ewell. In addition to riding around Ewell, take the 1-mile road through salt marshes and over a wooden bridge to Rhodes Point.

FISHING **Chesapeake Fishing Adventures** (410-968-0175), Tylerton. There is a choice of trolling the creeks and marshes of Smith Island in the spring in search of rockfish or going

out into the deeper waters of the bay for flounder, bluefish, drum, and others. CFA will also
arrange lodging if you wish to spend the night on the island.

KAYAKING AND CANOEING More than half a dozen marked routes make up the **Smith Island Water Trails.** If you were to travel each one of the routes, you would cover close to 20 miles and have the opportunity to pass through narrow, winding marsh guts, catch egrets and eagles nesting in shoreline trees, see goats grazing on an island across from Smith Island's main town, or do some early-morning casting for rockfish. Because it takes such an effort for travelers to reach Smith Island, this may possibly be the most lightly used set of water trails in the state—certainly a boon for those who like to paddle in solitude. A brochure is available from Somerset County Tourism or at www.paddlesmithisland.com.

WALKING TOURS The best way to experience Smith Island is by foot, and a small brochure available from the visitors center in Ewell describes the sights you will see in the island's three small towns.

✳ Lodging

BED & BREAKFASTS

Ewell, 21824

❧ **Smith Island Inn** (410-425-2058; www.smithislandinn.com), 20947 Caleb Jones Rd. Although updated, the Smith Island Inn retains much of the feel of its 1800s origins (including the listing pine floors), but offers modern beds and linens. All of the rooms have private baths and are furnished with period antiques. Well-behaved children are welcome. $125–150.

Susan's on Smith Island (410-425-2403; www.susansonsmithisland.com), 20759 Caleb Jones Rd. Stay here and live like an islander. Owner Susan Evans is a thirteenth generation Smith Islander and maintains this simple waterfront home as if an island family was still living here. Ask for the upstairs front room so that you can watch the work boats head out in the morning and return in the evening. If that room is taken, you may still enjoy the scenery from the enclosed front porch. Rooms are small but clean and each has an air conditioner. Kayaks and bicycles are available for guest use. $100–125.

Tylerton, 21866

❧ **Inn of Silent Music** (410-425-3541; www.innofsilentmusic.com), 2955 Tylerton Rd. Apr. to mid-Nov. The only place to stay in Tylerton and accessible only by the *Captain Jason II* (see *Getting There*), the inn has three rooms with private bath. The entire house overlooks the bay, but the upstairs Drum Point Room has the best water views. Canoes, bicycles, and charter boats are available for sight-seeing. Be sure to spend some time in Green House. Akin to a tree house, it overlooks Glennan Marsh and Tangier Sound and is a great place to while away an afternoon in peace and solitude. The seafood and/or vegetarian dinners the inn offers have become legend among former guests. Well-behaved children over 12 years are welcome. $115–135.

✳ Where to Eat

EATING OUT

Ewell

Bayside Inn (410-425-2771; www.smith islandcruises.com), 4065 Smith Island Rd. The Bayside Inn has picture windows overlooking the town dock and is the place most tourists eat lunch, with platters starting at $14.99.

Ruke's Seafood Deck (410-425-2311), 20840 Caleb Jones Rd. Be adventurous and pass up the tourist environment of the Bayside Inn in favor of Ruke's, the local restaurant of choice. If you don't mind the rather dull and dingy décor of this grocery/general store, you can dine on sandwiches, french fries, or crab cakes made from local crabs on a screened porch overlooking the marsh. Better yet, sit inside with everyone else and overhear conversations about who is dating whom at the high school, how the seafood harvest is going, or the latest prank played by one islander on another.

✴ Selective Shopping

SPECIAL SHOPS **Bayside Gifts** (410-425-2771), 4065 Smith Island Rd., Ewell. The shop, a part of the Bayside Inn (see *Eating Out*), has a nautical theme with decoys, gifts, and books on Smith Island and the bay area.

&. **Smith Island Visitor's Center Cultural Museum,** (410-425-3351; www.smithisland.org), 20846 Caleb Jones Rd.,

Ewell. The museum's gift shop stocks a number of locally made items and handicrafts.

Smith Island Baking Company (410-425-2253; www.smithislandcake.com), Ewell. These multi-layered cakes originated hundreds of years ago when baked for dredgers who went onto the water for months at a time; the vast amounts of sugar in the layers of fudge frosting helped to preserve the cakes. Named Maryland's state cake in 2008. Visit the bakery to witness these diabetes-inducing concoctions being produced for shipment around the world.

SALISBURY

S alisbury has been the economic and cultural center of the lower Eastern Shore since its establishment in 1732. Large boats coming up the Wicomico River from the bay were the first to bring trade to the city. Because Salisbury is at the intersection of several railroads, rail lines later figured prominently. Finally, easy access via modern highways brought more commerce to the city. Agriculture has always been important to the area, but today's city owes much to Frank Perdue, whose poultry business is a dominant economic engine.

Devastating fires in 1860 and 1868 almost destroyed the town. As a result, much of Salisbury looks like other modern American cities, with undistinguished strip malls, convenience stores, and fast-food shops. However, pockets of loveliness remain, such as the main downtown area (now a pedestrian mall), the campus of Salisbury University, and the historic district of Newtown, with six blocks of magnificent Victorian homes. The park along the South Prong Wicomico River is a quiet place within the city and contains the well-managed Salisbury Zoological Park.

The arts and cultural offerings are sophisticated in this metropolitan area of close to 100,000 inhabitants. Salisbury has its own symphony orchestra, a minor-league baseball team, and a number of museums, while presentations at Salisbury University range from local stage productions to international guest lecturers.

GUIDANCE A modern and spacious welcome center operated by the **Wicomico County Convention and Visitors Bureau** (410-548-4914; 1-800-332-8687; www.wicomicotourism .org), 8480 Ocean Hwy., Delmar, 21875, is located north of Salisbury on US 13. This is more than just a place to obtain information. It is located next to an attractive, large pond and within the greenery of **Leonard's Mill Park,** which has public restrooms, picnic facilities, a short walking trail, and boat-launching capabilities.

GETTING THERE *By air:* The **Salisbury/Ocean City Airport** (410-548-4827; www .flysbyairport.com), 5485 Airport Terminal Rd., is the second largest airport in the state, averaging close to 150,000 passengers a year. It is currently serviced by regularly scheduled flights via US Airways (1-800-428-4322).

By car: **US 50** and **US 13** intersect in Salisbury and provide access to all points north, south, east, and west. Traffic becomes heavy on US 50 during the summer months as vacationers head to and from Ocean City.

By bus: **Greyhound** (1-800-231-2222; www.greyhound.com) has a station in Salisbury.

GETTING AROUND *By taxi:* **Bailey's Taxi** (410-546-4025; accepts credit cards), **North End Taxi** (410-546-1477) and **Salisbury Taxi** (410-742-6666).

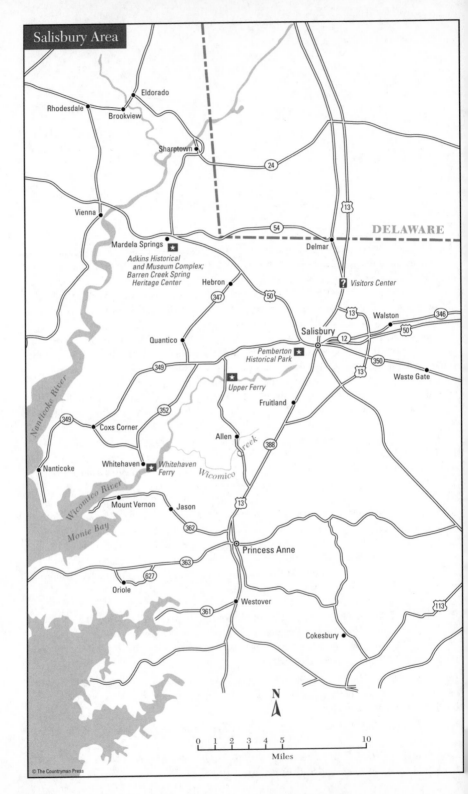

Salisbury Area

Eldorado

Rhodesdale

Brookview

Sharptown

24

Vienna

13

Mardela Springs

Adkins Historical
and Museum Complex;
Barren Creek Spring
Heritage Center

Delmar

DELAWARE

54

Hebron

347

50

Visitors Center

13

Walston

346

Quantico

Salisbury

12

50

Pemberton
Historical Park

349

13

350

Upper Ferry

Waste Gate

352

Fruitland

349

Coxs Corner

Allen

Creek

388

Nanticoke River

Whitehaven

Whitehaven
Ferry

Nanticoke

Wicomico

Wicomico River

Mount Vernon

Jason

13

Monie Bay

362

Princess Anne

363

627

Oriole

Westover

113

361

Cokesbury

N

0 1 2 3 4 5   10

Miles

© The Countryman Press

WICOMICO COUNTY CONVENTION AND VISITORS BUREAU IN LEONARD'S MILL PARK

By bus: The local bus service, **Shore Transit** (443-260-2300; www.shoretransit.org), reaches into every sector of the city and the university. Additional routes make it possible to ride to a number of outlying areas such as Princess Anne, Mount Vernon, Crisfield, Berlin, Ocean City, and Cambridge.

MEDICAL EMERGENCY **Peninsula Regional Medical Center** (410-546-6400; www.peninsula.org), 100 E. Carroll St., Salisbury.

✳ To See

COLLEGES **Salisbury University** (410-543-6000; 1-888-543-0184; www.salisbury.edu), Camden and West College Aves., Salisbury. Tours of the 125-acre campus, which has been declared a national arboretum and called the most beautiful in Maryland, begin every Mon., Wed., and Fri. at 1:30 at the Admissions House. The campus contains more than 2,100 plant species, pieces of outdoor art, and notable works of architecture. The university is home to the Salisbury Symphony Orchestra, SU Theatre, and several galleries, and has a range of lectures and activities open to the public.

ADKINS HISTORICAL & MUSEUM
COMPLEX'S ONE-ROOM SCHOOLHOUSE

MUSEUMS

Mardela Springs
Adkins Historical & Museum Complex (410-677-4740; www.adkinsmuseum.com), Brattan St. Open only by appointment; donations accepted. When putting this book together, a decision was made to leave

out places that are not readily accessible to the public. However, this complex of more than a half dozen buildings has done such a good job of preserving the past (especially on a very limited budget) that it would have been a disservice to leave it out. The 1857 one-room schoolhouse was used until the 1960s, as was the Bratton-Taylor general store. Both display items that provide insight into how they operated. Other buildings contain pieces from yesteryear, including the machine that bottled Mardela Springs water. Also, look for the very ornate discharge proclamation of a soldier from the Confederate army.

Barren Creek Spring Heritage Center and Museum (410-742-9122; www.barrencreek heritage.org). Open 10–2, Sat.–Sun. from Apr.–Oct. So much is packed into this little building that used to be a general store. The Westside Historical Society has 30 permanent exhibits depicting life from the earliest days into the 1900s. Items from nearby mills, timbering activities, shipbuilding, and farming paint a picture of the industries in the area, while clothing, home appliances, and baseball (once a big activity on the Eastern Shore) provide insight into everyday life. You are free to wander on your own or ask the docent to give you a guided tour (if the museum is not busy).

Salisbury

♿ **Eastern Shore Baseball Hall of Fame Museum** (410-546-4444; www.esbhalloffame .org), 6400 Hobbs Rd. Open during Delmarva Shorebirds (see *Entertainment—Sports*) home games; donations accepted. Located on the ground floor of the Perdue Stadium, the one-room museum pays homage to the Delmarva Peninsula's boys of summer, be they professional or amateur. Baseball gloves, bats, uniforms, trophies, and more bring back the glory days of these young men so that their skills may not be forgotten. One of the most interesting items is a player's contract from 1942. It is only one page long and shows that his entire salary was all of $100 a month.

Ward Museum of Wildlife Art (410-742-4988; www.wardmuseum.org), 909 South Schumaker Dr. Open daily. Small admission fee. The $5.5 million Ward Museum, named for decoy carvers Lem and Steve Ward, opened in 1992. Its 4,000 objects interpret the history and development of decoy carving, from early Native American pieces to the present day. An excellent display shows how specialized decoys were developed for the different North American flyways, while another examines various Eastern Shore hunting methods. The re-creation of Lem and Steve Ward's workshop is an accurate portrayal of their Crisfield business. Do not miss the Championship Gallery, which contains winners from past Ward carving competitions held annually in Ocean City. The detail, beauty, and artistry of these pieces is nothing short of spectacular. One of Elmer Crowell's decoys sold for $319,000. The museum's building is a work of art in itself.

Also see **Ward Brothers' Workshop** under *To See* in "Tangier Sound Area."

HISTORIC HOMES Poplar Hill Mansion (410-749-1776; www.poplarhill mansion.org), 117 E. Elizabeth St., Salisbury. Guided tours on first and third

THE DRIFTER

I'm just an old has been decoy,
No ribbons have I won.
My sides and head are full of shot,
From many a blazing gun.
My home has been by the river,
Just drifting along with the tide.
No roof have I had for a shelter,
No place where I could abide.
I've rocked to winter's wild fury.
I've drifted, and drifted, and drifted,
For tides never cease to run.
I was picked up by some foolcollector,
Who put me up here on a shelf.
But my place is out on the River,
Where I can be by myself.
I want to go back to the shoreline,
Where flying clouds hang thick and low,
And get the touch of rain drops,
And the velvety touch of snow.

—Steve Ward, 1971

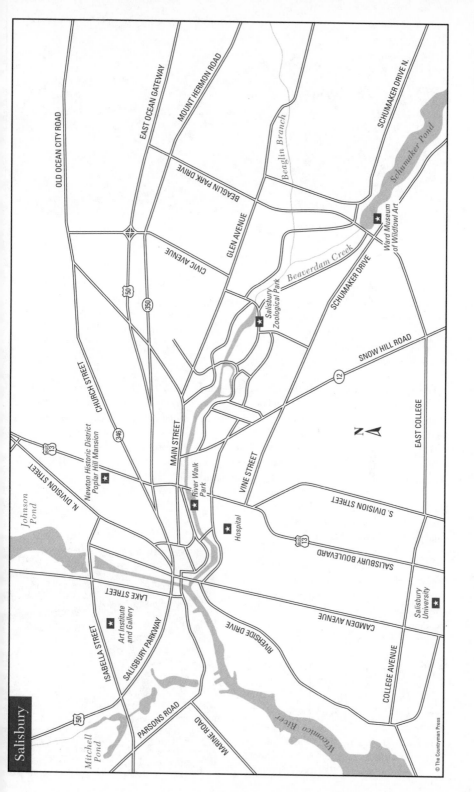

Salisbury

OLD OCEAN CITY ROAD

EAST OCEAN GATEWAY

MOUNT HERMON ROAD

BEAGLIN PARK DRIVE

SCHUMAKER DRIVE N.

Beaglin Branch

Schumaker Pond

GLEN AVENUE

CIVIC AVENUE

Beaverdam Creek

Ward Museum of Wildfowl Art

Salisbury Zoological Park

SCHUMAKER DRIVE

SNOW HILL ROAD

12

EAST COLLEGE

N

CHURCH STREET

346

MAIN STREET

VINE STREET

S. DIVISION STREET

Newton Historic District
Poplar Hill Mansion

River Walk Park

Hospital

13

SALISBURY BOULEVARD

N. DIVISION STREET

Johnson Pond

13

LAKE STREET

ISABELLA STREET

Art Institute and Gallery

SALISBURY PARKWAY

RIVERSIDE DRIVE

CAMDEN AVENUE

Salisbury University

COLLEGE AVENUE

Mitchell Pond

50

PARSONS ROAD

MARINE ROAD

Wicomico River

50

350

PEMBERTON HISTORICAL PARK

Sundays of every month; appointment recommended. Donations accepted. The oldest house in Salisbury (circa 1805) is the logical starting or stopping point for a walking tour of the **Newtown Historic District** (see *To Do*). Even if you can't get inside to enjoy the period antiques and original brass hardware on the woodwork, the transitional Georgian-style building—with bull's-eye windows, dentil molding, and a second-story Palladian window—is worth walking by.

HISTORIC SITES **Pemberton Historical Park** (410-548-4900; www.pembertonpark .org), Pemberton Dr., Salisbury. Small entrance fees are charged for the house and museum. A short drive from downtown Salisbury, this county-operated park includes **Pemberton Hall** (410-742-1741; www.pembertonhall.org), the home of Isaac and Anne Handy, built in 1741. The Flemish-bond brickwork house still contains the original interior wood paneling. Guided tours are given Sun., May–Sept., but call to make sure someone is there. Handy was a shipowner and captain, merchant, farmer, and justice of the peace, and raised grains, tobacco, and flax on his plantation. The park also includes a re-created 18th-century barn with rotating displays of local history, orchards with dwarf variety apples of the kind that would have been grown in the 1700s, a few picnic tables, and almost 5 miles of nature trails that wind onto Bell Island in the Wicomico River. Side-by-side gardens compare 18th-century crops with those of today. Special events range from canoe trips to maple-sugaring demonstrations to living-history weekends.

A BISON IN THE SALISBURY ZOO

ZOO ✐ &. **Salisbury Zoo** (410-548-3188; www.salisburyzoo.org), 750 S. Park Dr., Salisbury. Open daily—and parking and admission are free! The Salisbury Zoo is one of the prettiest in the Mid-Atlantic region, set within an old pine forest and beside the South Prong Wicomico River. Even though it has 400 examples of 100 species found within the Western Hemisphere, it is not overwhelming like some zoos. Expect to devote a couple of hours to observing animals such as American alligators, Central American black-handed spider monkeys, jaguars, capybaras, and the only bear native to South America, the endangered spectacled bear from the Andes Mountains. The pathways are nearly level, so walking is easy and accessible to everyone. Do not miss this place.

✳ To Do

BICYCLING The **Wicomico County Convention and Visitors Bureau** has developed an excellent set of maps and descriptions that detail dozens of rides from a few miles to over 100 miles. Short ones are within the Salisbury area, while others reach to Ocean City, Assateague Island, and Crisfield. A local favorite makes use of the Upper Ferry across the Wicomico River.

The **Salisbury University Bicycle Club** (Campus Box 3046, Salisbury, 21801; www.orgs .salisbury.edu/cycling) welcomes guest riders on their outings.

BIRDING The **Ward Museum of Wildlife Art**, 909 S. Schumaker Dr., and **Salisbury Zoo** (see *To See* for both), 750 S. Park Dr., are both located in Salisbury along the Salisbury Urban Greenway next to the South Prong Wicomico River. Cedar waxwings, hummingbirds, woodpeckers, and nuthatches are often seen in the zoo. Schumaker Pond in front of the museum attracts ducks, wigeon, and swans. Scarlet tanagers often breed on-site.

Open meadows, woodlands, and streambanks attract a variety of birdlife to **Pemberton Historical Park** (see *To See*).

FAMILY ACTIVITIES **Crown Sports Center** (410-742-6000; www.crownsports center.com), 28410 Crown Rd., Fruitland. Within a large metal building, your kids will enjoy the video arcade, climbing wall, and laser tag room. The center also has facilities for team sports that many of the local children take advantage of. Next door is the **Crown Skating Center** (443-736-7652; www.crownskating.com).

FERRIES The **Whitehaven Ferry** (410-873-2862), off MD 352 in Whitehaven, lays claim to being the oldest ferry in continuous operation in the United States. (A ferry in New Jersey is older but has not been in continuous use.) Connected to a fixed line, the ferry's journey across the Wicomico River lasts less than five minutes but offers some of the most free fun you can have on the Eastern Shore. Operates year-round during daylight hours.

The **Upper Ferry** (410-749-2892), off MD 349 in Upper Ferry, crosses the Wicomico River less than 10 miles west of Salisbury. Like the Whitehaven Ferry (see above), it, too, is free and has the same schedule.

ALONG THE SALISBURY URBAN GREENWAY

Delmar

Woodcreek Golf Links (410-896-3000), 9080 Executive Club Dr., Delmar. Opened to the public in 2001, it has town houses for sale around the links.

Salisbury

Horse Bridge (410-543-4446), 32418 Mt. Hermon Rd. Open year-round. Ponds, waste bunkers, and drainage ditches make this a challenging course.

Nutters Crossing Golf Course (410-860-4653; www.nutterscrossing.com), 30281 Southampton Bridge Rd. Eight water hazards and more than 50 bunkers will test your skill.

HIKING **Pemberton Historical Park** (410-548-4900; www.pembertonpark.org), Pemberton Dr., Salisbury. The park has almost 5 miles of trails that wind through bottomland forests along the Wicomico River and deliver you to Bell Island and the site of docks that were once used to load the plantation's crops onto ships.

SWIMMING **Cherry Beach** is a 0.3-mile-long beach along the Nanticoke River in the small town of Sharptown. Access is free, and there are picnic tables and a playground.

The free public beach at **Roaring Point** has to be one of the Eastern Shore's best-kept secrets. I walked up and down its full length of about a half mile on a beautiful summer afternoon and saw only three other people. I could spend an entire vacation here and be quite happy. Although the vegetation is different, the setting of the Roaring Point beach reminded me of the deserted and isolated beaches found on some of the Caribbean's most scenic islands. The oddly and interestingly shaped driftwood that washes up on the sand is another eye-pleasing aspect.

TENNIS A long list of courts located in and around Salisbury can be obtained by contacting the **Wicomico County Department of Recreation and Parks** (410-548-4900; www.wicomicorecandparks.org), 500 Glen Ave., Salisbury, 21804.

WALKING TOURS A brochure describing a *Walking Tour of Downtown Salisbury* is available from the Wicomico County Convention and Visitors Bureau. Fires in the late 1800s destroyed much of

WHITEHAVEN FERRY

STROLLING ALONG ROARING POINT BEACH

the city, so most of the architecture reflects a later period. The Masonic Temple stands next to the Victorian Court House. The old firehouse and the Brewington Building are two other standouts. Many of the buildings line the Pedestrian Plaza.

The *Newtown Walking Tour* pamphlet is also available from the bureau. The neighborhood of Newtown was built after the fires and has now become the oldest part of town. The Victorian homes found here are magnificent and well taken care of. So many of them would make great B&Bs, but ordinances prohibit such an enterprise.

✳ Lodging

MOTELS AND HOTELS

Delmar, 21875

Holiday Inn Express (410-896-9633; www.hiexpress.com), 30232 Lighthouse Square Dr. Just south of the Delaware/Maryland line, the hotel is adjacent to US 13 and close to the Wicomico County Convention and Visitors Bureau. Amenities include complimentary hot breakfast, wi-fi, outdoor pool, fitness center, and guest laundry. $160–190.

Salisbury, 21801

❦ **Best Western** (410-546-1300; www.bestwesternmaryland.com), 1735 N. Salisbury Blvd. On US Business 13 and close to the mall and movie theater. Free exercise room, continental breakfast, and local calls. Pets permitted for extra fee. $120–140. The rates drop by almost 50 percent in the off-season.

❦ **Comfort Inn** (410-543-4666; www.comfortinnsalisbury.com), 2701 N. Salisbury Blvd. Free continental breakfast, pets permitted, and some two-bedroom suites. $149–159.

Hampton Inn (410-334-3080; www.hamptoninnsalisbury.com), 121 E. Naylor Rd. Amenities include an in-door pool and exercise room. Some guest rooms have whirlpool baths. $110–150.

Holiday Inn (1-800-546-4400; www.holidayinn.com), 300 S. Salisbury Blvd. About as centrally located as you can get, the motel is in the downtown district and has a heated indoor pool. Its spacious rooms overlook the River Walk Park and pedestrian plaza. Complimentary Salisbury airport shuttle. $150–260.

Sleep Inn (410-572-5516; www.sleepinn.com), 406 Punkin Court, 21804. Convenient to US 50. Free continental breakfast and local calls. $145–195.

BED & BREAKFASTS

Whitehaven, 21856

❦ ❦ **Whitehaven Hotel B&B** (410-873-3099; 1-877-233-8203; www.whitehaven hotel.com), 2685 Whitehaven Rd. The owners have restored this early-1800s hotel, to which they welcome you with a glass of wine at 5 every evening. Overlooking the marshes and waters of the Wicomico River, all seven rooms have private baths, and the place is outfitted so well with period furniture that I felt as if I had stepped onto a set for a movie. I had a quiet walk around town (all of Whitehaven is on the National Register of Historic Places), took the Whitehaven Ferry across the river, and read a book beside the glow of the fireplace in the living room. It is impossible to find a quieter place in the Salisbury area to spend the night. Next visit, I intend to come in summer so I can make use of the screened second-story porch to watch the sunset. Children and pets are permitted, and kayaks and bicycles are complimentary for guest use. The host can also arrange a yacht dinner cruise on the river for you. In addition, don't neglect to look at the old photographs on the wall from the days when Whitehaven was a bustling port. $110–150.

CAMPING

Delmar, 21875

❦ **Woodlawn Family Camping** (410-896-2979), 1209 Walnut St. Mar. 15–Oct. 31. One of the smallest, but lowest-cost, private campgrounds on the Eastern Shore. Free showers. Pets permitted on a leash.

Nanticoke, 21840

🏕 Roaring Point Campground (410-873-2553), Nanticoke Wharf Rd. Apr. 1–Nov. 1. There are lots of amenities at this campground, which sits next to the wide mouth of the Nanticoke River: boat rentals, a sandy beach, horseshoes, hayrides, basketball, a coin laundry, and live country music on some weekends. Crabs, rockfish, flounder, perch, and more are caught from the 35-foot pier. Pets permitted on a leash.

✳ Where to Eat

DINING OUT

Salisbury

♪ ♿ **Market Street Inn** (410-742-4145; www.marketstreetinnsalisbury.com), 130 W. Market St. Open daily for lunch and dinner, Sun. brunch. Dinner reservations suggested. Occupying a much reworked and redefined building that was constructed as a fish market in 1941, the Market Street Inn offers, as their advertisements say, a "casu-ally upscale dining experience." The American-influence menu constantly changing, and specials reflect what meats and seafood are available fresh each day. Applewood smoking adds a pleasing aroma and flavor to prime pork tenderloins, a sweet honey barbecue sauce coats the grilled chicken kabobs, and the lump crabcakes are accompanied by salsa fresco and caper aioli. The restaurant's location along the banks of the Wicomico River, along with its outside dining and floating dock, makes for a scenic dining occasion. With an emphasis on those from California, the wine list has received awards from *Wine Spectator* and *Wine Enthusiast*. The pub is a popular local watering spot. $19–34.

SoBo's Wine Bistro (410-219-1117; www.soboswinebistro.com), 1015 Eastern Shore Dr. Owned and operated by the same people who run the Red Roost (see *Eating Out*), SoBo's has a cultivated décor and a menu that is printed daily to take advantage of what is available fresh. Dishes have

DO NOT MISS DINING HERE
Restaurant 213 (410-677-4880; www.restaurant213.com), 213 N. Fruitland Blvd., Fruitland. Open for dinner Tues.–Sun. After graduating from Johnson and Wales culinary school, owner Jim Hughes, at the age of 22, became America's youngest executive chef. He was also the second inductee into the Culinary Hall of Fame (Emeril Lagasse was first) and spent a number of years as the personal chef for a Middle Eastern royal family. After practicing his art with an international hospitality company and overseeing the establishment of the University of Maryland's culinary school, he opened Restaurant 213, and we are so lucky he did.

All items on the menu, which has French, Italian, and other global influences, are prepared fresh. And I do mean fresh—how many restaurants located in a business district on a busy four-lane highway have their own on-site vegetable gardens? Everything here is so right on the mark, from the amuse-bouche served to whet your appetite to the fresh-fruit-infused intermezzo sorbet. On my last visit, I started with the chilled crab salad in a tropical fruit coulis (which was a new and delightful way to prepare crab) and moved on to the crispy sea bass served with shrimp and pipenade in a saffron-mussel broth. Save room for one of the desserts, such as the Carnival—a sinfully rich concoction of homemade caramel poured over vanilla ice cream and walnuts atop the best funnel cake you'll ever have.

The wine list, which contains more than 280 selections, priced from $20 to $2,500, has won awards from Wine Enthusiast and Wine Spectator. Chef Hughes is most proud of his DiRoNa Award, given to only about 200 restaurants in the entire United States/Canada/Mexico/Caribbean region. In my opinion, Restaurant 213 deserves all of its accolades and brings a sophistication to an area that is lacking in such gastronomical pleasures. Entrées $25–40.

included pork chop, caramelized sea scallops, and a sea salt and brown sugar cured salmon Oscar. There are always daily special offerings of a pasta, panini, and burger for lunch. All of the wines are from the New World, and the staff takes pleasure in helping to decide which one to choose. $19–28.

EATING OUT
Hebron
Hebron Diner (410-749-9955), 201 S. Main St. Hearty country cooking. $5.95–17.

Pittsville
Pittsville Dinette (410-835-2541), 34200 Old Ocean City Rd. Plain, but good, traditional Eastern Shore food. $5–18.

✍ ↻ **Station 7 Restaurant** (410-835-3577; www.station7restaurant.com), 7456 Gumboro Rd. Lunch and dinner daily. Because it is located about a mile off US 50 east of Salisbury, many people are unaware of Station 7. Todd and Carroll Wampler have restored the town's 1929 volunteer fire station, and many pieces of firefighting memorabilia have been incorporated into the decor, such as firefighters' helmets serving as lamp shades. Todd had the help of local firefighters in naming some of his dishes, and much of the fare is what you might expect to find in a fire hall. Big burgers, overstuffed sandwiches, and nachos slathered with firehouse chili are on the menu, but, because Todd is a Johnson and Wales culinary school graduate, unexpected items like fettuccine with sun-dried tomatoes, artichoke hearts, zucchini, and squash with a roasted garlic basil butter have been offered, but are no longer on the daily menu. A barbecue sauce gleaned from his restaurant days in Charleston, South Carolina, finds its way onto a number of other items. *Insider's tip:* Things get really crowded here when firefighters from around the country arrive in droves during nearby Ocean City's Firefighters Week in June. Entrées $12.99–28.99.

Salisbury
✍ **Brew River Restaurant and Bar** (410-677-6757; www.brewriver.com), 502 W. Main St. The atmosphere and food remind me of an Applebee's or T.G.I. Friday's. The scenery is nice, as the restaurant sits at the end of River Walk Park on the Wicomico River; lots of seating on the outside deck. BBQ ribs (half rack, $17.99) are a favorite. The seafood selection is extensive; shrimp (from $16.99), scallops ($21.99), flounder (from $17.99), crab (market price), and a seafood medley ($24.99). Children's menu.

✍ **Cactus Taverna** (410-548-1254; www.cactustaverna.com), 2420 N. Salisbury Blvd. This restaurant is the end store of a small strip mall, so there isn't a lot of atmosphere, but the quality of the Mexican, South American, and Mediterranean dishes makes up for it. The shrimp Cancún with raspberry sauce ($16.95) is a house favorite, as is the lamb shank roasted in a Spanish red sauce ($17.95). The huge plate of paella ($19.95) I ordered brought back delectable memories of travels to Spain. Lots of appetizers, vegetarian selections, Mexican specialties, and a children's menu could keep you coming back often. Low-key live entertainment some evenings.

Dayton's (410-548-2272), 909 Snow Hill Dr. The breakfast place of choice; low-cost meals. $5–15.

✍ ↻ **The Fountains Steak Salisbury Restaurant** (410-749-5445; www.fountainsinc.com), 1800 Sweetbay Dr. The Fountains draws on the vast kitchen facilities and resources of its affiliated wedding and conference center to offer lunch and dinner to the public daily. Most items are authentically made (the Caesar dressing actually has anchovies in it) and produced daily. The menu changes seasonally but always features many seafood dishes, along with beef, pork, and fowl. Outside seating lets diners enjoy the lush greenery of a landscaped lawn. The décor and setting would qualify this as a *Dining Out* restaurant, yet the prices are more in line with those in the *Eating Out* category. $13–24.

Goin' Nuts Café (410-860-1164; on facebook), 947 Mt. Hermon Rd. As the name implies, the atmosphere makes this a fun place to eat. More than 20 sandwiches to choose from. Entrées are also extensive: vegetable stir-fry, curried honey shrimp, and Thai-seasoned seafood. A signature item is the City Slicker Chicken—mozzarella and prosciutto on chicken breast simmered in a garlic cream sauce. $5.95–19.95.

Lombardi's (410-749-0522; www.lombardi pizza.com), 315 Civic Ave., Twilley Centre. Offers a typical Italian menu of pasta, *strombolis*, and subs. The pizza is the best item, as it is cooked in a stone oven. The cannoli come from Little Italy in Baltimore. $4.50–15.

Yum! Café (410-546-3559; www.yumfresh cafe.com), 501 W. Main St. Open for breakfast and lunch; closed Mon.–Tues. Dana Simson serves about the freshest, locally grown food (much of it from her garden during the summer season) in the Salisbury area. Just about everything is made in-house, including the baked goods and ice creams and sorbets. (The peach in the gelato I had came from her tree.) The melted brie and turkey sandwich with jalapeño/raspberry jam is a customer favorite. Dana's art adorns the walls (see *Crafts*) and adds to the trendy/fashionable feel of this place. My choice for lunch whenever I'm in Salisbury. $8–10.

CRABS

Whitehaven

& **The Red Roost** (410-546-5443; www .theredroost.com), 2670 Clara Rd. Although it does not sit right on the water, the Red Roost is a classic Eastern Shore crab house. The roof is tin, long wooden tables are covered in brown paper tablecloths, and bushel baskets serve as lamp shades. The all-you-can-eat steamed crab special (market price) brings the locals in by droves, but another favorite, which I tried and really enjoyed, is the chicken cordon bleu ($19.95) with lump crabmeat. The Sampler ($23.99) gives you about everything: crab, shrimp, snow crab, and chicken. Portions are large, and desserts are homemade. Be sure to pick up a pamphlet to learn the restaurant's colorful history.

TAKE-OUT Plaza Deli (410-749-0611), Plaza Gallery Building, downtown Salisbury. Fresh-baked breads, breakfast and lunch sandwiches, coffee, and special desserts.

COFFEE BARS Common Grounds (443-736-4598; www.sbycommongrounds .com), 701 E. Naylor Mill Rd., Salisbury. Open daily. Local art adorns the walls and there is live entertainment Fri. and Sat. evenings. Serves fair trade coffee and is a certified green restaurant.

Rise Up Coffee (410-202-2500; www.rise upcoffee.com), 529 Riverside Dr., Salisbury. The coffee is good enough that this small establishment gets quite crowded early in the morning as people line up for their caffeine fix.

✳ Entertainment

FILM Regal Cinema Centre (410-543-0902; www.regmovies.com), 2312 N. Salisbury Blvd., Salisbury, shows first-run movies.

MUSIC Making use of performance facilities at Salisbury University in Salisbury, the **Salisbury Symphony Orchestra** (410-548-5587; www.salisbury.edu/sso) has a full set of concerts scheduled each year.

THEATERS Although the **SU Theatre** (410-543-6000; www.salisbury.edu/theatre anddance) is affiliated with Salisbury University in Salisbury, the cast of most productions is composed of students, faculty, and community members.

SPORTS The **Delmarva Shorebirds** (410-219-3112; www.milb.com/index.jsp ?sid=t548), 6400 Hobbs Rd., Perdue Stadium, Salisbury, are the Class A affiliates of the Baltimore Orioles. Thanks to the wealth of poultry king Frank Perdue, the stadium they play in is one of the plushest you will find of any minor-league team. Admission cost, though, is still a pittance compared with that in the majors. A great way to spend a summer evening.

✳ Selective Shopping

ANTIQUES Holly Ridge (410-742-4392), 1411 S. Salisbury Blvd., Salisbury. A large selection of 18th- and 19th-century items.

Park and Flea (410-603-3930; www.park andflea.com), on US Business 13 between US 50 and Main St., Salisbury. Held each Sat. and Sun., the Park and Flea is flea marketing, antiques shopping, and people-watching all combined into one major attraction on a large downtown parking lot.

Parker Place (410-860-1263; on face-book), 234 W. Main St., Salisbury. Three floors of antiques.

Season's Best Antiques and Collectibles (410-860-8988; www.seasonsbestantiques .com), 104 Poplar Hill Ave., Salisbury. More than 40 dealers under one roof. I saw quite a number of very collectible items, especially some nice Eastern Shore memorabilia.

ART GALLERIES Art Institute and Gallery (410-546-4748; www.aiandg.org), 212 W. Main St., Gallery Building on Downtown Plaza, Salisbury. Changing exhibits of original works by local and regional artists. Sponsors classes, field trips, and free film programs. As an interesting aside, the walls outside the gallery are adorned with old photos of Salisbury.

The **Atrium Gallery** and the University Gallery at Salisbury University, Salisbury, feature the works of students and profes-sors, and traveling exhibits.

BOOKSTORES Henrietta's Attic (410-546-3700; www.henriettasattic.com), 205 Maryland Ave., Salisbury. In addition to antiques and collectibles, Henrietta's has a selection of used books and offers to locate out-of-print books for you.

Market Street Books (410-219-3210), 146 W. Market St., Salisbury. A great collection of used and out-of-print books of interest to adults and children.

CRAFTS Chesapeake East Handmade Ceramics (410-546-1534; 1-800-320-7829; www.chesapeakeeast.com), 501 W. Main St., Salisbury. Dana Simson (one of those people that you wonder, "How does she

have the time to do all of this?") creates original and bright designs, which she incorporates onto ceramic bowls, plates, pitchers, vases, drawer pulls, and more. A multitalented artist, she creates stationery items, décor products, and gift books; writes the award-winning children's "Leg-endbook" series; and publishes the *CHESAPEAKEeast Calendar Guide*. I thought this would be just another pottery shop, but Ms. Simson's works are refresh-ingly new and different. Also, ask for the brochure that describes the building's extraordinary past. Amazingly, she also runs and does the cooking for the adjacent Yum! Café (see *Eating Out*).

SPECIAL SHOPS Country House and Country Village (410-749-1959; www.thecountryhouse.com), 805 E. Main St., Salisbury. Claims to be "the Largest Country Store in the East." With 23,000 square feet of display space for ever-changing merchandise, they may be right.

MALLS The Centre at Salisbury (410-548-1600; www.centreatsalisbury.com), 2300 N. Salisbury Blvd., Salisbury. Contains many of the usual national chains found in most malls.

FARMER'S MARKET Salisbury. Located on the city parking lot on the cor-ner of US 13 and Market St. Sat. 8–1, and on Wed. 3–6 at the Center at Salisbury mall from Apr.–Nov.

PICK-YOUR-OWN PRODUCE FARMS

Eden
Garden of Eden Orchards (410-546-0081), 4380 Upper Ferry Rd. Retail stand and pick-your-own fruits.

Parsonsburg
Strawberry Fields Forever (410-835-8586), 4820 Powell School Rd. Strawberries for the picking from mid-May through mid-June.

Salisbury

Peach Blossom Farm (410-742-6545), 27616 Little Lane. A retail stand, and pick-your-own blackberries.

BREWERY Evolution Craft Brewing Company (443-260-2337; www.evolution craftbrewing.com), 201 E. Vine St., Salisbury. Tasting room open daily, adjoining Public House restaurant open for dinner on weekdays and lunch and dinner on weekends. Reservations are required for the 30- to 40-minute extensive tours given on a private basis. If the axiom is that it takes good water to make good beer, then Evolution is located in the right place. The factory sits directly above the aquifer used in producing its roster of ales, porters, IPAs, pilsners, stouts, and more.

WINERY & **Bordeleau Vineyards & Winery** (410-677-3334; www.bordeleau wine.com), 3155 Noble Farm Rd., Eden. Open for tastings Sat. and Sun. Tom Shelton, a successful poultry businessman, planted his first grapes in 1999 and bottled his first wine in 2006. He had about 20 acres of vines when I last visited and did not have to purchase any grapes from outside sources. He intends to keep it this way so that he can control all of the minor details of the varietals, such as Merlot and Cabernet Sauvignon, that he produces and ages in American and European oak barrels. The tasting room and winery are scenically located along Wicomico Creek, where concerts and special dinners are held throughout the year.

✳ Special Events

Contact the **Wicomico County Convention and Visitors Bureau** for more information on all of these events.

April: **Pork In The Park** (410-548-4911; 1-800-322-TOUR; www.porkinthepark.org), Winterplace Park, Salisbury. The National Bar-b-que Cook-off has food, music, children's activities, and crafts, as well as the culinary competition.

May: **Salisbury Festival,** Salisbury. Entertainment, triathlon, carnival, children's activities, and lots of food.

June: **Seaside Memorial Horse Show,** Equestrian Center, Winterplace Park, Salisbury.

July: **Sunday Night Concerts,** City Park, Salisbury. Free concerts by the Community Band each Sunday evening in July.

September: **Pemberton Colonial Fair,** Pemberton Historical Park, Salisbury. Music, games, sports, crafts, demonstrations, food, and other activities of the 18th century.

October: **Autumn Wine Festival** (410-548-4911; 1-800-322-TOUR; www.autumn winefestival.org), Pemberton Historical Park, Salisbury. More than 15 wineries participate, along with arts and crafts, food, and entertainment. **Chesapeake Wildlife Showcase,** Ward Museum of Wildlife Art, Salisbury. Auctions and sales of antique wildlife decoys.

November: **Salisbury Kennel Club Dog Show,** Salisbury. Competition and judging.

BORDELEAU VINEYARDS & WINERY

CAMBRIDGE AND VICINITY

Cambridge's location on the southern bank of the wide Choptank River makes its setting one of the prettiest on the Eastern Shore. Author James Michener has praised its maritime heritage, shaded streets, and lovingly cared-for homes. A walk down High Street (with a brochure from the Dorchester County Department of Tourism) brings you past one beautiful Victorian home after another, while the public park and wharf at street's end give a sweeping vista of the river.

Despite Cambridge's waterfront location, agriculture was the area's first important business. By the mid-1800s, lumber and flour mills were established, which in turn led to the building of ships to transport goods. The late 1800s saw a rise in oyster harvesting. Local lore claims skipjacks were so tightly packed in Cambridge Creek Harbor that you could walk completely across it on their decks.

Seafood and other packinghouses came to the fore in the early 1900s and, despite some decline, still dot Cambridge's landscape. Visitors of today find a community that is waking up to its appeal to the outside world. Museums, boat trips, and outdoor adventures on the water and land are bringing in increasing numbers of tourists. The opening of the Hyatt Regency Chesapeake Bay Golf Resort Spa and Marina in 2002 provided Cambridge with the area's first destination resort.

COMMUNITIES **Church Creek** received its name from Old Trinity Church, the oldest Episcopal church in continuous use in the United States. The community is believed to have been in existence as early as the late 1600s.

On the banks of the Nanticoke River, **Vienna,** one of Maryland's oldest settlements, was settled by 1669. Once a thriving port, its size diminished as main roadways passed it by. A number of its earliest structures still exist, including a number of homes dating from the mid-1700s to early 1800s. A brochure available from the **Visitors Center at Sailwinds Park** describes a walking tour of the now quiet town.

Hurlock began as a railroad station and is now the second largest town in Dorchester County. The train station has been restored and hosts occasional train trips.

Taylors Island is a traditional waterman's village. Marinas, docks, and activity around the water are the reasons to visit.

Hooper Island, another waterman's settlement, is actually three islands and is even more removed from the mainstream than Taylors Island. The community quietly goes about harvesting and processing thousands of pounds of catch from the bay annually.

A brochure available from the **Dorchester County Department of Tourism** points out the historic aspects of **East New Market,** a town whose four entrances are each marked by a church. The entire town is on the National Register of Historic Places.

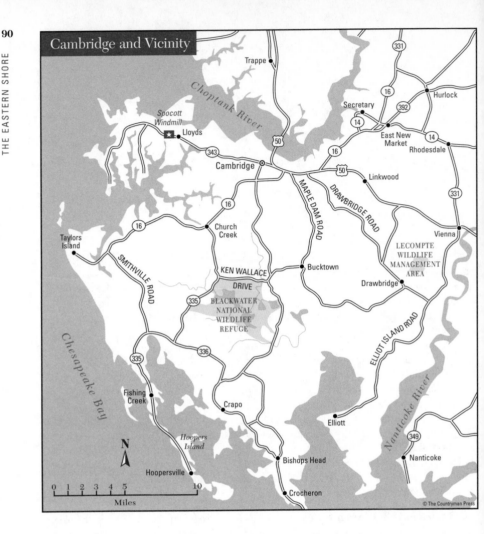

Cambridge and Vicinity

Trappe

Spocott Windmill
Lloyds

Choptank River

Secretary
East New Market
Rhodesdale
Cambridge
Linkwood
Vienna
Church Creek
Taylors Island
SMITHVILLE ROAD
KEN WALLACE DRIVE
Bucktown
LECOMPTE WILDLIFE MANAGEMENT AREA
Drawbridge
BLACKWATER NATIONAL WILDLIFE REFUGE
MAPLE DAM ROAD
DRAWBRIDGE ROAD
ELLIOT ISLAND ROAD
Chesapeake Bay
Fishing Creek
Crapo
Elliott
Hoopers Island
Bishops Head
Nanticoke
Hoopersville
Nanticoke River
Crocheron

N

0 1 2 3 4 5   10
Miles

© The Countryman Press

GUIDANCE ♿ Overlooking the Choptank River beside US 50, the **Visitors Center at Sailwinds Park** and the **Dorchester County Department of Tourism** (410-228-1000; 1-800-522-8687; www.tourdorchester.org), 2 Rose Hill Pl., Cambridge, 21613, have one of the most scenic settings of any welcome center in the state. A gigantic Teflon-coated fiberglass sail makes the spot even more dramatic, while a whimsical outdoor sculpture provides additional charm. There's also a short boardwalk trail to the river and a handicapped-accessible playground. Inside the visitors center are some museum-quality and interactive displays that provide a very good introduction to Dorchester County and its human and natural history, including a quick but comprehensive overview of the Underground Railroad.

GETTING THERE *By car:* **US 50** bisects the region with a north–south orientation.

> **FROM A DISPLAY IN THE VISITORS CENTER AT SAILWINDS PARK**
> "You can make a small fortune workin' on the water, providin' you start out with a big fortune."
>
> —Anonymous waterman

THE OUTDOOR SCULPTURE AT SAILWINDS PARK AND VISITOR CENTER ON THE CHOPTANK RIVER

SAILBOATS IN THE CAMBRIDGE HARBOR MARINA

By air: You can fly your own plane into **Cambridge Dorchester Airport** (410-228-4571), 5223 Bucktown Rd., Cambridge. Otherwise, the closest commercial airport is **Salisbury/Ocean City Airport** (410-548-4827; www.flysbyairport.com) in Salisbury.

By water: If you own or rent a boat, the Choptank River provides easy access from the Chesapeake Bay. A number of marinas in Cambridge have transient slips.

GETTING AROUND Other than **US 50,** which nearly becomes bumper-to-bumper with Ocean City traffic on summer weekends, the roadways in this area are lightly traveled and provide pleasant, unhurried driving experiences.

By taxi: **Elliot's Cab** (410-221-8855).

By bus: The **Maryland Upper Shore Transit** (410-221-1910; www.mustbus.org) routes include Cambridge and part of the surrounding countryside. If you wish to go farther afield, **Shore Transit** (443-260-2300; www.shoretransit.org) can take you to most places on the lower Eastern Shore, including Salisbury and Ocean City.

PUBLIC RESTROOMS Restrooms available to anyone are at the Visitors Center at Sailwinds Park (410-228-1000; 1-800-522-8687; www.tourdorchester.org), 2 Rose Hill Pl., Cambridge.

MEDICAL EMERGENCY Dorchester General Hospital (410-228-5511; www.shorehealth.org), 300 Byrn St., Cambridge.

✴ To See

MUSEUMS The **Dorchester County Historical Society** (410-228-7953; www.dorchesterhistory.org), 1003 Greenway Dr., Cambridge, oversees the **Meredith House, Robbins Heritage Center, Neild Museum and the Herb Garden,** and **Goldsborough Stable** within a small complex along a residential street. Tues.–Sat. 10–4. Items in each building reflect the history of the area and include Native American artifacts, a McCormick reaper, and household items from the 18th, 19th, and 20th centuries.

Harriet Tubman Museum (410-228-0401; www.harriettubmanorganization.org), 424 Race St., Cambridge. Open Tues.–Fri.

10–3, Sat.12–4. All volunteer operated; donations accepted. The small museum shares stories of Harriet Tubman, who led scores of slaves to freedom along the Underground Railroad. Of the several videos available for viewing, possibly the most interesting, though designed for children, is the animated one that follows her life from the time she ran away to when she returned to rescue her parents. A brochure is available that describes a self-guiding driving tour that includes several sites significant in her life and for the Underground Railroad. However, a better way to gain insight is to take the **REI Heritage Tours** (410-820-8350; www.the-rock-newsmagazine.com/harriet.tubman.tours.html) that have a knowledgeable guide accompany you to the sites of her childhood, her first public act of rebellion, and other locations that are historically significant. Such an inspiring person and story should not be missed. The tour may also provide insight and background on African American experiences around the Dorchester area. Just gaining a different perspective on what went on in the town's historic homes makes the tour worthwhile.

Richardson Maritime Museum (410-221-1871; www.richardsonmuseum.org), 401 High St., Cambridge. Wed. and Sun. 1–4, Sat. 10–4; closed Wed. Nov.–Feb. Dedicated to the boatbuilders of the Eastern Shore, the museum's exhibits include dozens of wooden scale models (some are spectacular in detail), a mural depicting Cambridge in the early 1900s, and boatbuilding implements. Of particular interest are the works of local master builder Jim Richardson. All of this is housed in what is believed to be the oldest bank building in town. *Note:* As this book went to press, work was progressing on construction of the massive **Richardson Maritime Complex** into which the museum will move. Other portions of the complex will include the Ruark Boatworks (see *Other Sites*), a heritage center large enough to house entire boats complete with masts and rigging, a boatbuilding school, research center, and more. If plans work out, this will be a destination not to be missed.

HISTORIC CHURCHES Christ Church (410-228-3161), Historic High St., Cambridge. Erected in 1693, it is an outstanding example of American Gothic Revival architecture. Gaze upward to see the interesting gargoyles on the tower. The cemetery contains the graves of Revolutionary and Civil War heroes and five Maryland governors.

Bazzel Church (410-228-0401), Bestpitch Ferry Rd., about 1 mile south of Greenbrier Rd. (which is about 12 miles south of Cambridge). This small wooden structure is where Harriet Tubman's family worshiped in the mid-1800s.

St. Mary, Star of the Sea (410-397-3417; www.staroftheseaghf.org), on MD 335 on the way to Hooper Island. The second oldest Catholic church on Maryland's Eastern Shore.

Old Trinity Church (410-228-2940; www.oldtrinity.net), 1716 Taylors Island Rd., Church Creek. Built in the late 1600s, this is the oldest Episcopal church in continuous use in the United States. The floor tiles, altar table, and exterior brick walls are original.

OTHER SITES Bucktown Village Store (410-901-9255; www.blackwaterpaddleand pedal.com), 4303 Bucktown Rd., Cambridge. Mon.–Sat. 9–4, but hours change seasonally; call ahead. Now the departure place for Blackwater Paddle and Pedal Adventures (see *Kayaking and Canoeing*), this is the site of young Harriet Tubman's first public act of defiance in which an overseer fractured her skull while she attempted to stop the whipping of a fellow enslaved man. The store contains many items of the day, and one of the owners of the outdoors outfitter, Susan Meredith, is so well-versed in the history that the company provides guided Underground Railroad tours by automobile, bicycle, or kayak.

Choptank River Lighthouse (410-330-8016; www.choptankriverlighthouse.org), Long Wharf Park, Cambridge. Open daily 9–6, Apr.–Oct. Donations accepted. A replica of the six-sided screwpile lighthouse that operated on the Choptank River at the mouth of the Tred Avon River from 1921–1964. Exhibits depict the lighthouse's history and that of the Choptank River. The wharf and the lighthouse are nice places to be to greet the sunrise.

THE CHOPTANK RIVER LIGHTHOUSE REPLICA

Ruark Boatworks (410-221-8844; www.richardsonmuseum.org), 103 Hayward St., Cambridge. Inside a huge building (with many recycled parts) that is part of the Richardson Maritime Complex (see *Museums*), volunteers labor away at building new wooden boats or restoring older ones that would have otherwise seen the graveyard. Do not expect to see museum-like displays; this is an active facility with tools, parts, and other items of the trade spread about. Volunteers are usually working on Mon., Wed., and Fri. 9–2. It's best to call ahead of time, but no matter who happens to be there, he or she will be happy to show you around. This is a real treat for those interested in wooden boats.

Spocott Windmill, MD 343, 7 miles west of Cambridge (www.spocottwindmill.org). Daily 9–5. Free admission. No, you are not in Holland! Taking on a different kind of project, master boatbuilder James B. Richardson designed and crafted the fully operating English-style post windmill, which can be turned in any direction to face prevailing winds. This is such a novelty that you have to stop by. Even if a docent is not present, you can still look inside at gears and millstones. Also on-site is the Tenant House of Adeline and Columbus Wheatly, who worked on Spocott Farm from 1880 to 1930, blacksmith shop, and a historic one-room schoolhouse.

GUIDED TOURS Walking Tour of **Historic High Street** (410-901-1000;

THE SPOCOTT WINDMILL CAN BE ROTATED TO FACE ANY DIRECTION.

www.cambridgemd.org) meets at 301 Gay St., Cambridge, every Sat. at 10 (weather permitting) Apr.–Oct. Small fee charged; reservations not required, but appreciated. Sponsored by the West End Citizens Association, the tour's costumed guides provide insight into the lives of residents of the 1700s and 1800s who lived on High St., named one of the most beautiful streets in America by novelist James Michener. There's some juicy gossip behind those grand Victorian homes.

SCENIC DRIVES A marked route, the **Cambridge Scenic Drive,** is 1.5 miles long and takes you from High St. to Maple Ave. along the Choptank River. Some of the residential homes along the tree-shaded streets are nearly as beautiful as the water views.

✳ To Do

BICYCLING The **Dorchester County Department of Tourism** (see *Guidance*) in Cambridge prints a map pamphlet with more than 100 miles of cycle routes within the immediate area. The scenery is great, and the flat terrain, paved roads, and light traffic are bonuses. Places to eat are identified on the maps. See *Kayaking and Canoeing* for guided bicycle tours.

BIRDING According to the *Birdwatcher's Guide to Delmarva,* **Blackwater National Wildlife Refuge** (see *Green Space*), 12 miles south of Cambridge, is the best place on the Eastern Shore to see bald eagles; it has the largest nesting population on the East Coast north of Florida. There is also the possibility of seeing golden eagles and scores of other bird species.

The **LeCompte Wildlife Management Area** (410-376-3236; www.dnr.state.md.us/wildlife /publiclands/eastern/lecompte.asp) near Vienna rewards visitors with species most often found in upland forests and shrubby areas. Also be on the lookout for the endangered Delmarva fox squirrel.

The **Municipal Basin** on the Choptank River in Cambridge is a great place to watch visiting waterfowl from fall to early spring.

If the above places do not present enough birding opportunities for you, obtain the *Birding in the Heart of Chesapeake Country* brochure from the Visitors Center at Sailwinds Park. It details a number of short driving trails throughout Dorchester County that provide the chance to see indigo buntings, hummingbirds, tundra swans, finches, woodpeckers, warblers, stilts, and other species in a variety of settings, such as forests, fields, marshes, and open water.

BOAT EXCURSIONS

Cambridge

Nathan of Dorchester (410-228-7141; www.skipjack-nathan.org), docked at Long Wharf at the foot of High St. Cruise times vary; call for schedule. The skipjack was built and is sailed by volunteers whose enthusiasm surpasses that found on many commercial boat rides. Learn a thorough history of the bay, skipjacks, oystering, charts, crabs, and boatbuilding. Observe the raising and lowering of the sail, and rake for oysters. *The* boat trip to take on the Eastern Shore if you have time for only one.

THE SKIPJACK WAY OF LIFE
Skipjacks became so popular because they were one of the easiest boats to build, and many a waterman spent his off-season building a boat of his own. By tradition, the owner of the boat received one-third of the catch, and the crew would have to split the rest, with the captain receiving two shares. So the captain came out way ahead if he was also the boat's owner.

NATHAN OF DORCHESTER

Choptank River Queen and the **Dorothy & Megan** (410-943-4775; www.dorothy megan.com), 6304 Suicide Bridge Rd. Call for schedule. Sight-seeing and lunch and dinner cruises aboard an authentic early-20th-century paddle-wheeler.

FISHING No license is required to fish from **Long Wharf** at the end of High St. in Cambridge.

CHARTER FISHING Among the many charter boats in the area are **Big Rig Charters** (410-310-1600; www.bigrigcharters .com), 30360 Cods Point Rd., Trappe; **Sawyer Charters** (410-397-3743; www .sawyercharters.com), 1345 Hooper Island Rd., Church Creek; and **Tide Runner Fishing Charters** (410-397-3474; www.captmikemurphy.com), P.O. Box 55, Fishing Creek, 21634.

GOLF Tee times are not necessary in order to play **Linkwood** (410-221-8700), 3715 Linkwood Dr., Linkwood, a public 18-hole course with 10 par 4s and eight par 3s. None of the holes are less than 100 yards.

Also see *Lodging—Resort*.

KAYAKING AND CANOEING A guide to canoe and kayak launches, boat ramps, and facilities is available from the Dorchester County Department of Tourism. An excellent map identifies hundreds of miles of paddleable waterways.

One of the companies that will take you on a guided trip in these waters is **'Peake Paddle Tours** (410-924-5290; www.paddletours.com; located close to Blackwater National Wildlife Refuge), which will also provide you with instructions and safety pointers before starting out. Moving along at an easy paddling, leisurely pace, most trips last four to five hours. All necessary equipment is provided, but you could save a few dollars by bringing your own kayak.

Blackwater Paddle and Pedal Adventures (410-901-9225; www.blackwater paddleandpedal.com), 4202 Bucktown Rd., Cambridge and within the Hyatt Regency Resort. Offers a myriad of outdoor adventures, including full-day and half-day guided kayaking and bicycling trips, with some outings combining both sports. They've been known to provide shuttles (time permitting) for those who have their own equipment, and have even organized hiking trips.

SWIMMING ✐ **Dorchester County Public Pool** (410-221-8535), Virginia Ave., Cambridge. Memorial Day–Labor Day.

FISHING THE CHOPTANK RIVER FROM LONG WHARF IN CAMBRIDGE

TENNIS James Busick Tennis Courts, Glasgow St., Cambridge. Secretary Park, Linden Ave., Secretary. Public tennis courts.

✳ Green Space

GARDENS Harriet Tubman Memorial Garden, US 50 by Washington St., Cambridge. Interpretive signs, landscaped gardens, and a mural are a tribute to the Underground Railroad's "Moses of Her People."

PARKS Great Marsh Park (410-228-2040; www.choosecambridge.com), Somerset Ave., Cambridge. There are picnic tables, short walking paths, a playground, fishing, and a boat ramp on a bit of land jutting into the Choptank River.

WALKS See *Wildlife Refuges.*

WILDLIFE REFUGES Blackwater National Wildlife Refuge (410-228-2677; www .blackwater.fws.gov), 2145 Key Wallace Dr., about 12 miles south of Cambridge. Just about every Marylander knows that in late fall and early winter, the refuge is the place to observe hundreds, even thousands, of migratory waterfowl, especially Canada geese. An important resting and wintering spot for birds that travel the Great Atlantic Flyway from Canada to the Gulf of Mexico, the 28,000-acre area is composed primarily of tidal marshes, evergreen and deciduous forests, freshwater ponds and impoundments, and some cropland. Taking the 5-mile scenic **Wildlife Drive,** walking the short but rewarding trails, bird-watching, and paddling upon multiple miles of flatwater are the favored activities here.

✳ Lodging

RESORT

Cambridge, 21613

♨ **Hyatt Regency** (410-901-1234; www .chesapeakebay.hyatt.com), 100 Heron Blvd. The Hyatt is the area's first destination resort and is being touted as an economic savior. On 342 acres beside the Choptank River are 400 rooms, a golf course, a 150-slip marina with boat rentals and cruises, a spa, five restaurants, indoor and outdoor pools with slides, and children's activities. Many different package rates available.

BED & BREAKFASTS

Cambridge, 21613

Cambridge House B&B (410-221-7700; www.cambridgehousebandb.com), 112 High St. All of the guest rooms in the grand 1830s Queen Anne–style sea captain's mansion have a private bath and electric fireplace (so you can enjoy the look of a fire even in summer). Two of the upstairs rooms overlook the backyard garden and lily ponds, as does the hot tub on the back porch. A full three-course breakfast is served, after which it is only a couple of blocks of walking to enjoy fishing in the Choptank River from the town's public Long Wharf or shopping in the historic downtown district. $165–225.

Kindred Spirits Cottage Retreat & Family Massage (410-221-7575; www .kindredspiritscottageretreat.com), 102 Hiawatha Rd. Sandra Pomeroy has transformed a former garage and workshop into a large one-room guest cottage and small spa. When I asked her what was the impetus, she said that she wanted a place where people could get the full benefits of her massages (see below) by being able to relax in the cottage afterward and not have to abruptly get in a car and drive off. Located a few hundred feet from the Choptank River on a quiet side street and within an easy walk of downtown Cambridge. Refrigerator, microwave, hot plate, Jacuzzi, and a shaded patio with a partial water view. A healthy continental breakfast is delivered to you in the morning. $175.

LODGECLIFFE ON THE CHOPTANK

Within a small room designed for relaxation, Sandra offers Swedish and deep tissue massages, detox soaks, dry body brushing, sugar/salt body scrubs, algae mud body wraps, and facial clay masques. Possibly the best thing about having your spa treatments here is, if you make arrangements to stay in her guest cottage, you can continue relaxing by simply walking out of one door and into another.

Lodgecliffe on the Choptank (1-866-273-3830; www.lodgecliffe.com), 103 Choptank Terrace. Built in 1898 on a bluff with an expansive view of the Choptank River, Lodgecliffe provides pink sunsets over the water, fishing at its doorstep, good birdwatching from the lawn or screened porch, and a tranquil atmosphere to recharge your inner self. Opened to guests in 1986, this was Dorchester County's first B&B and currently offers three guest rooms (each with private bath). Less than a five-minute drive from downtown Cambridge. $180–200.

Mill Street Inn B&B (410-901-9144; www.millstinn.com), 114 Mill St. It took the hosts of the Mill Street Inn more than a year to restore their home, which now features three guest rooms (each with private bath) furnished with antiques and reproductions appropriate to the house's Victorian origins. The original yellow pine floors are still intact on the second floor, and a claw-foot bathtub (and a shower) await those who check into the Edward Room.

The Cambridge Suite, with its alcoved sitting room, invites you to relax and do nothing more strenuous than read a good book. A gourmet breakfast is served in the morning on fine china and silver. $179–229.

Victoria Gardens Inn (410-901-2292; www.victoriagardensinn.com), 101 Oakley St. Built around 1890 and turned into a B&B in 2007, Victoria Gardens is a nice place to sit on one of the porches (with fans to provide a cool breeze) and watch people stroll about the quiet residential neighborhood. The winding staircase in the entrance leads to the guest rooms, each with private bath, while guests can congregate in the drawing room or library. $200.

East New Market, 21631

♂ **Marvels on the Creek B&B** (410-943-4723; www.marvelsonthecreek.com), 6230 Beverly Rd. I like the B&Bs that I stay in to be in quiet, rural settings and this one fits the bill. With almost no neighbors in sight, it sits on the bank of Cabin Creek, its front porch overlooking a dock (where boaters can tie up to stay in the B&B) and the tranquil water of the stream. Guests have use of a canoe and can fish for crab, perch, and catfish from the pier. The long lawn has witnessed many weddings, and terry robes will wrap you in luxury after a soak in the outdoor hot tub or whirlpool tub in your room's bath. $145.

THE MARVELS ON THE CREEK B&B PATIO

Taylors Island, 21669

The Island House B&B (410-228-2184), 513 Taylors Island Rd. The Island House is the place to stay if you truly want to observe the rural and waterman's way of life on the Eastern Shore. Directly across from the Island Grille (see *Eating Out*), where it seems half of the island's population stops in daily, you can sit on the screened porch and watch boats come and go from the marina across the street. This is also the place to stay if you're looking to get on the water with your own kayak or canoe, as a boat launch is also across the street, providing you with access to miles of paddling on creeks and around Taylors Island. Roadways are narrow but lightly traveled, so bring your bike, too. Admittedly, the Island House is not for everyone. It reminds me of an old boardinghouse you might see in a 1930s movie, the three guest rooms are sparsely furnished, and everyone shares the same bath. However, rooms are just clean enough, the host is friendly (and has lots of local knowledge), and the $55 rate gives you a low-cost place to sleep after a day of pedaling and paddling.

Vienna, 21869

❧ **The Tavern House B&B** (410-376-3347; www.tavernhouse.com), 111 Water St. The Tavern House is one of the oldest structures on the Eastern Shore, predating 1800 and overlooking the Nanticoke River. Harvey and Elise Altergott have restored its colonial countenance. A somewhat plain exterior disguises the simple elegance of the interior. Numerous fireplaces, carved woodwork, authentic colors, and white lime, sand, and hair plaster evoke yesteryear. Rooms, with shared baths, are in period decor. The best parts of my stay, though, were the great conversations with Harvey and Elise during evening refreshments and breakfast. $105.

✳ Where to Eat

DINING OUT

Cambridge

Bistro Poplar (410-228-4884; www.bistropoplar.com), 535 Poplar St. Owner/ chef Ian Campbell grew up in Dorchester County, attended the Culinary Institute of America, and worked in a number places before returning home to open Bistro Poplar. Drawing upon the tradition of the Picardy region of France, the menu changes often based upon what fresh items are available locally. My appetizer of fried green tomatoes with a crab and potato hash was a great way to open the meal that moved on to monkfish Provençal with tomatoes, mushrooms, and capers and ended with a pear/cherry turnover with cinnamon anglaise—all made fresh in-house. Currently my favorite Cambridge-area restaurant. $18–32.

Canvasback Restaurant and Irish Pub (410-221-5177), 420 Race St. Tony and Marion Thomas have taken an old storefront and turned it into one of the region's best dining experiences. Lunch is a casual affair, with sandwiches, salads, pasta, and pizza. Dinner entrées change frequently and are clever variations on familiar themes. Undeniably good when I visited was the fried pecan-coated soft-shell crab served with whiskey-lemon butter. Then there was lobster ravioli and chicken scaloppine stuffed with crabmeat and cheese. $23–30.

Hurlock

Suicide Bridge Restaurant (410-943-4689; www.suicidebridge.com), 6304 Suicide Bridge Rd. (*Note:* The mailing address is Hurlock, but the restaurant is actually located closer to Secretary.) The region's special-occasion restaurant, it has picture windows and a deck overlooking Cabin Creek. Nautical charts on the tabletops, wood paneling, and a stone fireplace add to the chimerical atmosphere. A local native, owner Dave Hickerson has been in the seafood business for more than two decades, so dishes such as Chesapeake rockfish ($18.95) and crab imperial ($24.95) reflect his experience. Daily specials are an extra value. The restaurant's name reflects true incidents; ask for the explanation.

EATING OUT

Cambridge

Cambridge Diner (410-228-8898), 2924 Old US 50. Open 24 hours every day. Good diner food, with a menu that is seven pages long. Breakfast starts at around $4 and sandwiches at $4. Entrées ($8.95–25.95) include Italian specialties, seafood, steaks, chops, and just about everything in between.

Jimmy and Sook's (443-225-4115; www.jimmieandsooks.com), 527 Poplar St. When Amanda Bramble announced she was opening a restaurant in the same building that her mother and grandmother had worked in, members of the community pitched in to help her get the place ready. It's a local favorite with more than a dozen beers on tap, many of them regional, and live music on the weekends. Seafood, especially crab, figures heavy on the menu, which also has some nice appetizers and sandwiches. Crab soup is also worth trying. $16.99–24.99.

❖ **Snappers Waterfront Cafe** (410-228-0112; www.snapperswaterfrontcafe.com), 112 Commerce St. Crabcakes (market price) and other seafood (from $17.99). The Crab Skins, potato skins stuffed with crab and cheese, are worth the $12.99 price. Large picture windows provide a view of Cambridge Creek Harbor. Becomes a busy local watering hole on summer and weekend evenings.

Taylors Island
Island Grille (410-228-9094), 514 Taylors Island Rd. Open for breakfast, lunch, and dinner; closed Sun. This is it if you are on Taylors Island and want to eat out. Even though it's a humble place with vinyl tables, it has some nice items created by one of the owners who grew up on the island. Locals talk about the burgers, the restaurant hand-cuts the steaks, and the Island Grille stir fry is a surprise to find in such an out-of-the-way place. There are nightly specials, and the desserts, often simple things like chocolate or pineapple cake, are homemade. Lunch and dinner items have a range of $6.50–16.95.

CRABS *❖* **Ocean Odyssey** (410-228-8633; www.toddseafood.com), US 50, Cambridge. The Todd family has been in business since 1947, at first producing and

marketing crabmeat, and later opening this restaurant, which still receives its seafood from the family's packing plant, where only Chesapeake Bay blue crab is used. The location of this family-friendly establishment makes it an easy place to stop when you are driving around the area—or can't wait until you get to Ocean City to enjoy some fresh seafood. $18–29.

❖ **Portside** (410-228-9007), 210 Trenton St., Cambridge. A characteristically casual seafood restaurant with wooden tables and vinyl-covered booths. The outside deck is beside Cambridge Creek. Steamed crabs (market price) are, of course, a favorite. The shrimp scampi with pasta I sampled was hot and spicy, while my companion liked the teriyaki tuna steak. Sandwiches, salads, and a host of calorie-laden appetizers.

SNACKS AND GOODIES Bay Country Bakery (410-228-9111; www.baycountrybakery.com), 2951 Ocean Gateway (US 50), Cambridge. For more than three decades, the Bay Country Bakery has been a popular place for pastries, cookies, pies, cakes, and fresh breads. It's so popular that you should expect to wait in line during the early-morning rush. America may run on Dunkin,' but you'll be much more satisfied if you come here for your morning doughnut and coffee.

✱ Entertainment
Sailwinds Park in Cambridge is the site of concerts, plays, festivals, carnivals, community events, and more. Contact the Dorchester County Department of Tourism (see *Guidance*) for a schedule of events.

✱ Selective Shopping
ANTIQUES Bay Country Antiques (410-228-5296; www.baycountryantiques.com), 415 Dorchester Ave., Cambridge. High quality antiques.

Country Store Gallery (443-521-8171), 412 Race St., Cambridge. The small store, once a country store more than one hundred years ago, is jam-packed with glassware, pottery, toys, and furniture. Most

SAILWINDS PARK, CAMBRIDGE

notable are the old medical equipment, collection of miniatures, old advertising signs, and the reproductions of original trade signs by owner/artist Kevin Davidson.

Heirloom Antiques Gallery (410-228-8445), 419 Academy St., Cambridge. A cooperative for several dealers of furniture, pottery, clocks, jewelry, and other antique items.

Just Yesterdays (443-225-6963; www.just yesterdays.com), 317 High St., Cambridge. Artisan and children's jewelry, vintage home décor and furniture, and a little bit of just about everything else.

Packing House Antiques (410-221-8544), 411 Dorchester Ave., Cambridge. More than 135 dealers under one roof.

ART GALLERIES Dorchester Center for the Arts (410-228-7782), 321 High St., Cambridge. Ever-changing gallery exhibits of local artists and craftspeople. Paintings, pottery, baskets, quilts, sculptures, books, and more for sale in the gift shop. Sponsors concerts, plays, and lectures.

BOOKSTORE Never on Tuesday Book Store (410-228-8329), 527 Poplar St., Cambridge. Open daily Memorial Day–Labor Day; closed on Tues. rest of the year. With a nice selection of local and regional books, and many novels written by Chesapeake Bay authors, Never on Tuesday

fills a bit of the void that is left by the dearth of bookstores on the Eastern Shore. There is also a small section of used books and a few nice gift items, along with free wi-fi.

SPECIAL SHOPS Bay Country Shop (410-221-0700; www.baycountryshop.com), 2709 Ocean Gateway (US 50), Cambridge. A nice mix of quality clothing, books, gifts, and artwork by local and regional artists and craftspeople. The wildlife decoys, boat models, and paintings are worth seeing, even if you don't intend to purchase anything.

Craig's Drug Store (410-228-3322), 409 Race St., Cambridge. Of interest because it has been serving the community since 1867. Also has a small gift shop.

Joie de Vivre (410-228-7000), 410 Race St., Cambridge. Artist-owner Joy Staniforth has assembled an impressive diversity of local and international artists. You will find jewelry, wall hangings, and a range of paintings and sculpture. In the back of the building is the Race Street Gallery, with a juried exhibition of 20 regional artists. Not just another run-of-the-mill store; there are some unique and distinctive items here.

FARMER'S MARKET Cambridge Farmer's Market (www.cambridgemain street.com), Long Wharf Park, Cambridge.

Thurs. 3–6, May–Oct. One of the very few farmer's markets that are accessible by boat.

PICK-YOUR-OWN PRODUCE

FARM ✿ **Emily's Produce** (410-228-3512; 443-521-0789; www.emilysproduce .com), 2206 Church Creek Rd., Cambridge. Owned and operated by the Jackson family, Emily's Produce was named for a newborn daughter in 1999. In spring, you can pick your own strawberries. Return in the fall to choose your own pumpkin off the vine and have fun negotiating the corn maze. Come here at other times to purchase locally grown fresh produce and homemade desserts. A children's play area will keep youngsters entertained while adults go about choosing what to take home.

WINERY **Layton's Chance Vineyard & Winery** (410-228-1205; www.laytonschance .com), 4225 New Bridge Rd., Vienna. Open daily with tours at 1–3 year-round. The 1,800-acre farm that contains the 14 acres of vines has been in the Layton family for several generations. The 40-minute tour takes you to the vineyard to learn the hard work it takes to harvest and process the grapes. Local art is for sale in the gift shop/tasting room, which is kid friendly with coloring books and other activities. The watermelon wine is a seasonal hit.

✳ Special Events

February: **National Outdoor Show** (410-397-8535; www.nationaloutdoorshow.org), Golden Hill. Muskrat skinning, trap setting, oyster shucking, exhibits, and competitions.

March: **Eagle Festival** (410-228-2677; www.fws.gov/blackwater), family-friendly event with eagle prowls, falcon demonstrations, kids activities.

Harriet Tubman Day (410-228-3106), Elk Lodge on Pine St., Cambridge. Annual event celebrating the life of Ms. Tubman. Includes dinner and tours of her birthplace.

April: **Spocott Windmill Day** (www .spocottwindmill.org). The windmill will be running and grinding grain.

May: **Antique Aircraft Fly-In** (410-228-1899), Cambridge. Antique planes from across the country arrive for judging and exhibits at the Dorchester Heritage Museum. **Annual Flower Fair** (410-228-1424), Cambridge. Outdoor festival with seedlings, flowers, hanging baskets, arts and crafts for sale. Also lots of food, such as oyster fritters, crabcakes, and homemade ice cream, cakes, and candies. **Beckwith Strawberry Festival** (410-228-7807), Cambridge. Strawberries and large flea market.

July: **Annual Power Boat Regatta** (410-228-7920). Races and information booth. Great Marsh Park, Cambridge. **Taste of Cambridge & Crab Cook-Off** (www .cambridgemainstreet.com). Biggest event of the year in downtown Cambridge. Sample crab dishes, watch crab-picking, watermelon-eating, hula hoop contests, and more at this street festival.

August: **Seafood Feast-I-Val** (www .seafoodfeastival.com), Cambridge. All-you-can-eat seafood fest.

September: **Nause-Waiwah Band of Indians Native American Festival** (410-376-3889), baseball field, Vienna. **Dorchester Arts Showcase** (410-228-7782), High St., Cambridge.

October: **Nanticoke River Jamboree** (www.restorehandsell.org), Vienna. Exhibits and demonstrations by regional environmental and historic groups, native plant sale, reenactors, and kayaking and biking events.

December: **Christmas Garden of Trains** (410-22-4220), all month in the Cambridge Rescue Company fire hall, Cambridge. Cambridge-Dorchester Christmas Parade (www.christmasparade.org), Cambridge. One of the state's largest nighttime Christmas parades.

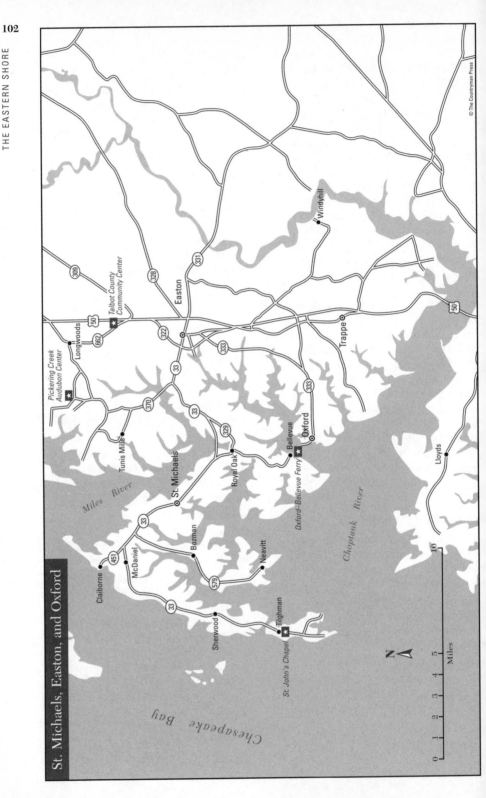

St. Michaels, Easton, and Oxford

© The Countryman Press

ST. MICHAELS, EASTON, AND OXFORD

My wife, a native Annapolitan, can remember in the not-too-distant past when St. Michaels was a quiet Eastern Shore waterman's village with just a couple of stores and restaurants. Then recreational boaters on the Chesapeake Bay started sailing up the Miles River and discovered the pleasures of eating steamed crabs at the Crab Claw Restaurant. Other establishments soon followed, and St. Michaels is now a trendy destination with dozens of upscale shops, boutiques, B&Bs, antiques stores, numerous festivals focusing on boating and/or the bay, and some of the finest restaurants in Maryland. The Chesapeake Bay Maritime Museum, with exhibits indoors and out, has become a must-see stop.

Many visitors still come by water, but the automobile traffic is also so great that driving the few blocks of the business district is a slow proposition on nice weekends throughout the year.

All of this activity in St. Michaels has begun to spill over into Easton, just a few miles away. Entrepreneurs have recently opened quality boutiques and galleries, and innovative chefs are creating an abundance of delicious dining choices for townspeople and the increasing numbers of tourists. Retirees and other emigrants are coming here to live and creating a lively atmosphere for the arts, as evidenced by the restoration of the historic Avalon Theater and the quality of works to be found in the Academy Art Museum.

Easton had its beginnings in 1682 when the Third Haven Friends Meeting House (now the oldest religious frame structure in the United States) was erected. Organized as a town in 1788, its significance grew so quickly after the Revolutionary War that it was dubbed the Capital of the Eastern Shore. In ensuing years, it was home to the first newspaper, first bank, first gas plant, and first steamboat connections to Baltimore. A walking tour takes in several buildings dating back to the 1800s.

Bordered on three sides by water, Oxford was once Maryland's largest port, with tobacco and slaves from the West Indies being two of the most important commodities exchanged by companies based in England. The Revolutionary War, and the increasing importance of Baltimore as a port, struck a blow to the town. After the Civil War, oystering, crabbing, and fish processing and packing became the mainstays of commerce, but the town has never

THE TOWN THAT FOOLED THE BRITISH

On August 10, 1813, residents of St. Michaels learned that British barges planned to attack the town. They tricked the naval forces by hanging lanterns in the masts of ships and in the tops of trees (and blacking out any other lights), causing the cannons to overshoot the town. The ruse was so effective that only one house was hit by a cannonball.

regained its busy prominence. Which is probably fine with its citizens of today, and is certainly okay with travelers who find a quiet village with tree-lined streets, a few shops, several restaurants and lodging choices, and the Oxford–Bellevue Ferry across the Tred Avon River.

A side trip not to be overlooked is the short drive from St. Michaels to Tilghman Island. A slender strip of land surrounded by water, the island is home to the largest remaining commercial fleet of skipjacks in the world, sailing the water for oysters, crabs, and other seafood. Sportfishermen come here for charter boats, while other visitors come for the quiet scenery and good restaurants.

TAKE A BREAK
Take a break from walking or driving around Oxford: Sit on a bench under one of the shade trees in the town park as a cool breeze fans through and gaze out upon the peaceful scene of the Tred Avon River flowing by.

GUIDANCE The **Talbot County Office of Tourism** (410-770-8000; www.tourtalbot.org) is located at 11 S. Harrison St. in Easton.

There is a small information shed with brochures at the corner of N. Talbot and Mill Sts. in **St. Michaels,** brochures in the Oxford Community Center at 200 Oxford Rd., and a booth with brochures at the entrance to **Tilghman Island.**

GETTING THERE *By air:* The closest airports with commercial service would be either **Baltimore/Washington International Thurgood Marshall Airport** (1-800-I-FLY-BWI; www.bwiairport.com) near Baltimore, or the **Salisbury/Ocean City Airport** (410-548-4827; www.flysbyairport.com) in Salisbury. **Bayrunner Shuttle Service** (410-822-5444; www.bayrunners.com) provides a land transportation service between BWI and Easton.

By car: The **Bay Bridge** near Annapolis provides access from the west. **US 50** is the main route through the area; **MD 33** takes you to St. Michaels and Tilghman Island. **MD 322** and **MD 333** lead to Oxford.

By bus: **Greyhound** (1-800-231-2222; www.greyhound.com) services its station at 9543 Ocean Gateway (US 50) in Easton.

GETTING AROUND *By taxi:* **Bay Country** (410-770-9030) and **Scotty's** (410-822-1475) are based in Easton.

PARKING Parking in St. Michaels is free on the street, but good luck finding a spot on the weekends. A **free town parking lot** is located on the corner of N. Talbot and Mill Sts.

PUBLIC RESTROOMS In **Oxford,** you can find restrooms at the Oxford–Bellevue Ferry dock, at the parking lot near the end of the Strand, in the public library on N. Morris St., in Causeway Park located on Oxford Rd. (MD 333), and in the town hall.

MEDICAL EMERGENCY **Memorial Hospital** (410-822-1000; www.shorehealth.org), 219 S. Washington St., Easton. Part of the Shore Health System.

✳ To See
MUSEUMS
Easton
Historical Society Museum (410-822-0773; www.hstc.org), 25 S. Washington St. Wed.–Fri. 10–4, May–Dec.; Thurs.–Sat. 10–4, Jan.–Apr. Free; small admission fee for the house tour. The museum contains more than 40,000 artifacts, documents, and photographs pertaining to

local history. The items pertaining to the history of African Americans, the original deeds of property transfers, and an unusual portrait of Richard Hughlett caught my attention.

The guided "Tour of Three Centuries" takes you through the Federal-period Neall House (circa 1810), Joseph's Cottage (circa 1790), and the Ending of Controversie—a reconstruction from the 1600s. The garden, with one hundred boxwoods, is a quiet spot and open to anyone. A self-guiding tour map of historic sites in Easton is also available free of charge.

THE HOOPER STRAIGHT LIGHTHOUSE AT THE CHESAPEAKE BAY MARITIME MUSEUM

Oxford

Oxford Museum (410-226-0191; www .oxfordmuseum.org), 100 N. Morris St. Among the many items of local history is the oldest known log canoe still in existence, the "Glide," built in 1864. Also look for original papers on indentured servants, and photos of students from the nearby Maryland Military and Naval Academy who revolted against the strict discipline of the late 1800s.

St. Michaels

☙ **Chesapeake Bay Maritime Museum** (410-745-2916; www.cbmm.org), Mill St. Open daily. $13 adults, $10 seniors, $6 children. Possibly the finest maritime museum in the Mid-Atlantic; expect to devote a couple of hours. With some open-air displays, the story is told of the bay, the life of the watermen, and the region's history of fishing and hunting. The short film about oystering is very interesting, and don't overlook the opportunity to walk through the restored 1879 **Hooper Straight Lighthouse.** Several hands-on activities for the kids, and the museum store is a great stop, too (see *Selective Shopping*).

St. Michaels Museum at St. Mary's Square (410-745-9561; www.stmichaelsmuseum.org), Mullberry St. Sat. and Sun. 10–4, Apr.–Oct. A small museum that showcases the St. Michaels of the 1800s. Also publishes an excellent walking tour of historic St. Michaels pamphlet that details more than several dozen sites.

HISTORIC CHURCHES

Easton

Third Haven Meeting House (410-822-0293; www.thirdhaven.org), 405 S. Washington St. Built in 1682 by the Religious Society of Friends (Quakers), this is the oldest frame religious building in continuous use in the United States. You are welcome to walk the grounds (no pets, please) and go into the building, which has no heat, electricity, or water. The wooden shutters are closed to separate men and women for business meetings, but the sexes worship together. The adjacent brick building was built in 1880 and is used in winter.

THIRD HAVEN MEETING HOUSE

Christ Church (410-822-2677; www.christchurcheaston.org), 111 S. Harrison St. This early-English-style church was built in the 1840s and features a tower and spire.

Tilghman Island

St. John's Chapel. Constructed in 1891 of lumber transported by skipjack from North Carolina.

✳ To Do

BICYCLING The **Talbot County Office of Tourism** (see *Guidance*) has maps of lightly traveled routes perfect for cycling.

Easton

Bike Doctor (410-820-9107; www.bikedoctoreast.com), 210 Marlboro Ave. Open daily. Repairs and sales of new bicycles.

Easton Cycle and Sport (410-822-7433; www.eastoncycleandsport.com), 723 Goldsborough St. Open daily. Rentals of bicycles, and single, double, and sail kayaks. They will deliver to you if you do a multiday rental.

St. Michaels

St. Michaels Marina (410-745-2400; www.stmichaelsmarina.com), 305 Mulberry St.; the **St. Michaels Harbour Inn Marina & Spa** (see *Lodging*); and **Tricycle and Run** (410-745-3826; www.tricycleandrun.com), 929 S. Talbot St., where you can rent bikes for the day.

Tilghman Island

Tilghman Island Marina (410-886-2500; www.tilghmanmarina.com), 6140 Mariners Court. Bicycle, kayak, and boat rentals by the hour, half day, or day.

BIRDING See **Pickering Creek Audubon Center** under *Hiking*.

BOAT EXCURSIONS

St. Michaels

&. *Patriot* (410-745-3100; www.patriotcruises.com), Maritime Museum dock. Cruises on weekends at 11, 12:30, 2:30, and 4; 12:30 and 2:30 on weekdays; operates Mar.–Nov. $25 adults, $22 seniors, $12.50 children, $5 three years old and younger. One-hour narrated tours of the St. Michaels area and the Miles River.

PATRIOT LEAVING ST. MICHAELS HARBOR

🐾 **The St. Michaels Harbor Shuttle** (410-745-2198), town dock at Mulberry St. The boat leaves every 30 minutes. A 25-minute overview of St. Michaels Harbor. Pets permitted.

Tilghman Island

🚣 ♿ ***Express Royale*** (1-888-312-7847; www.docksidexpress.com), 21604 Chicken Point Rd. Call for reservations, as schedule and fees vary. The recycled U.S. Navy utility boat takes passengers on two-hour environmental tours, 90-minute champagne sunset tours, or custom tours of your choice. It was on this boat that I learned about crabbing with a trot line and how, at one time, one of the nearby islands was used as a place to commercially raise black cats for their fur (it's quite the interesting story; ask one of the crew if they fail to relate it to you).

Before or after your boat ride, have one of the crew take you through the **Phillips Wharf Environmental Center** (410-886-9200; www.pwec.org), where you and the kids will learn about the life cycle of the blue crab, put your hands in a tank to touch a horseshoe crab or some other sea creature, and find out just how important the Chesapeake Bay is. The center is really just an old one-room crab shanty next to where the *Express Royale* docks, but this just means you can learn a lot in a short period of time. No fee; donations accepted.

M/V *Sharps Island* (410-886-2215; 1-800-690-5080; www.chesapeakelights.com), departs from Bay Hundred Restaurant. It offers a variety of **Lighthouse Tours** that take in as many as 10 lighthouses. You choose how long you want to be out and how many lighthouses you would like to go by. With all of the interest in the lighthouses of the Chesapeake Bay, it's amazing to me that this is one of the few boats that specializes in this kind of guided tour. Also see *Sailing*.

FERRY **Oxford–Bellevue Ferry** (410-745-9023; www.oxfordbellevueferry.com). Closed Dec., Jan., and Feb.; $11 one way (car and passenger); $18 round trip (car and passenger); other vehicle passengers are $1 per person. The ferry makes it easy to complete a circular driving tour of Easton, Oxford, and St. Michaels by making a crossing of the Tred Avon River about every 20 minutes—as traffic demands. Established in 1863, it is the oldest privately owned ferry in the United States. You are permitted to get out of your car and enjoy the scenery as you traverse the wide expanse of the river.

BOAT RENTALS **Tilghman Island Marina** (see *Bicycling*), Tilghman Island. Bicycle, kayak, and boat rentals by the hour, half day, or day.

BOWLING 🎳 **Good Time Charlie's Bowling** (410-822-3426; www.eastonbowl .com), 101 Marlboro Ave., Easton. With 24 lanes, Good Time Charlie's is decorated to return you to the days of the 1950s, but it also has free wi-fi, so you can multitask by trying to get a strike and searching the Web all at the same time. Young children will be happy to have the rails put up so that every one of their turns does not end up as a gutter ball.

FAMILY ACTIVITIES 🎿 **Talbot County Community Center** (410-770-8050), 10028 Ocean Gateway (US 50), Easton. The spot to go for in-line and ice skating, and to try your hand at curling.

COMING INTO OXFORD ON THE OXFORD–BELLEVUE FERRY

FISHING On Tilghman Island, **Captains Buddy Harrison and Buddy Harrison Jr.** (410-886-2121; www.chesapeakehouse.com) are continuing the traditions of their ancestors of more than one hundred years ago by being a one-stop shop for anglers. The **Harrison House** furnishes the lodging, while a restaurant provides the sustenance. The Harrisons offer the largest sportfishing fleet on the bay and accommodate groups large or small. The Harrison House lounge is the place to gather for evening drinks and entertainment. The Harrisons' good fishing reputation ranges far beyond the Eastern Shore. Many package deals available.

In search of rockfish, Spanish mackerel, croaker, bluefish, sea trout, and more, other charter and headboats also operate out of Tilghman Island and St. Michaels. The **Talbot County Office of Tourism** (see *Guidance*) in Easton can supply you with a list of competent captains.

GOLF

Easton

Hog Neck (410-822-6079; www.hogneck.com), 10142 Old Cordova Rd. *Golf Digest* rated this par 72 course as one of the top 25 public courses in the country.

Easton Club (410-820-9100; 1-800-277-9800; www.eastonclub.com), 28449 Clubhouse Rd. The par 72 course has over 6,700 yards and great water views.

St. Michaels

Harbourtowne Golf Resort and Conference Center (see *Lodging*). With views of the Chesapeake Bay, this Pete Dye–designed course offers ponds, walls, railroad ties, and protected greens.

HIKING **Pickering Creek Audubon Center** (410-822-4903; www.pickeringcreek.org), 11450 Audubon Ln., Easton. The center's nature trail begins in a hardwood forest, crosses several bogs, and ends next to a demonstration garden. You can walk the gravel road back to your car instead of retracing your steps on the trail. This is an easy round-trip walk to possibly see hawks, warblers, woodpeckers, owls, thrushes, and bluebirds. Also see *Green Space* for more information about the center.

Although almost too short to be considered a hike, the **St. Michaels Walking Trail** provides a break from the bustling retail shops, passing through fields, woods, by houses, and across a covered bridge over a scenic creek and wetlands.

HORSEBACK RIDING **Country Comfort Farm** (410-745-3160; www.countrycomfort arm.com), 23720 St. Michaels Rd., St. Michaels. Indoor and outdoor arenas, and 70 acres for trail rides with experienced guides and horses.

KAYAKING AND CANOEING **Tuckahoe Creek** near Tuckahoe State Park (see "Around the Bay Bridge and Kent Island") in Queen Anne has well over 10 miles of water bordered by farmlands and forested swamps. The book *Hiking, Cycling, and Canoeing in Maryland*, by Bryan Mac Kay, gives an excellent description of the route and what to watch for.

A brochure describing the **Tilghman Island Water Trail** is available from the Talbot County Office of Tourism (see *Guidance*). The brochure has maps detailing 10 suggested paddling routes around and near the island that permit you to explore the area and maybe see crabs; schools of fish; oyster reefs; swans, geese, gulls, and other birdlife; and observe the watermen going about their business of harvesting the bounty of the Chesapeake Bay. The routes, which are not marked and require a degree of skill and caution, are a great way to spend a morning, afternoon, or full day on the water, but be alert to wind direction and speed, tides, and sudden changes in the weather.

THE *LADY PATTY* ON TILGHMAN ISLAND

St. Michaels Harbour Inn Marina (see *Lodging*), St. Michaels, rents canoes and kayaks by the hour or day.

Tilghman Island Marina (see *Bicycling*), Tilghman Island. Bicycle, kayak, and boat rentals by the hour, half day, or day. See *Bicycling* for additional kayak rentals.

SAILING *Lady Patty* (1-800-979-3370; www.ladypatty.com), Knapps Narrows Marina, Tilghman Island. Champagne sunset cruises; call for schedule. The two-hour sunset sails on this 35-foot bronze and teak Bay Ketch are not billed as ecotours, but I learned more about the bay, pound nets, ospreys, and environmental issues than on most nature-oriented boat trips I've taken. The champagne, the sunset, and Captain Jeff Mathias's tales of the *Lady Patty*'s engaging history will remain in my mind for a long time.

Rebecca T. Ruark (410-829-3976; www.skipjack.org), Dogwood Harbor, Tilghman Island. Built in 1886, this is the oldest skipjack to still be sailing. Capt. Wade Murphy, with more than 40 years of oystering experience, gives two-hour cruises on which you can hoist the sail, steer the boat, dredge for oysters, or throw a line. Walk-ons accepted, but it is best to make a reservation.

Salena II (410-726-9400; www.sailselina.com), N. Harbor Rd. at the Harbor Inn, St. Michaels. Scheduled two-hour sails during the usual tourist months, $65; other trips available. Captain Iris Clarke grew up on the 1926 *Salena II,* a sailing vessel known as a cat boat—it's half as wide as it is long and has a longer boom and mast than other boats its size. During my time on the boat, Captain Iris kept up a running animated conversation, imparting her wisdom about the boat, sailing, and many of the problems facing the health of the Chesapeake Bay. Passengers are limited to only six, so you will have the captain's full attention (and not feel cramped as I have been on other sailboats). In my opinion, *Salena II* is one of the prettiest vessels offering trips in St. Michaels.

SPECIAL CLASSES Sign up for a flight lesson at Easton Airport (410-770-8055; www .eastonairport.com) with **Easton Aviation** (410-822-8181; www.eastonaviation.com), Easton.

✳ Green Space

PARKS See "Around the Bay Bridge and Kent Island."

NATURE PRESERVES ✍ **Pickering Creek Audubon Center,** (410-822-4903; www .pickeringcreek.org), 11450 Audubon Ln., Easton. Open daily. Free admission. There's a lot to do on the 400 acres of forests, marshes, wetlands, and shoreline. Hiking on several nature trails, a canoe launch onto the creek, 150 species of birds to watch, a tool museum, and a wonderful Children's Imagination Garden. Canoe trips, birdwatching walks, lectures, and other programs are offered on a scheduled basis (some fees may apply). This is an oasis in an area where very little land is open to the public for outdoor pursuits.

WALKING TOURS By appointment (410-886-2643; 1-888-312-7847; www.cruisinthebay .com) you can accompany a costumed interpreter on either a **Historic** or **Ghost Tour** of St. Michaels to learn about the history, lifestyle, and paranormal happenings that have taken place in the small bayside village.

WALKS See *Nature Preserves.*

✳ Lodging

RESORT

St. Michaels, 21663

& & **Harbourtowne Golf Resort and Conference Center** (410-745-9066; 1-800-446-9066; www.harbourtowne.com), MD 33 at Martingham Dr. More than 100 standard motel-type rooms at the water's edge of the Chesapeake Bay, each with private balcony and some with fireplace or wood-burning stove. The draws here are the views, bicycling, an outdoor pool, several restaurants, a Pete Dye–designed golf course, and the 153 acres of open space. Very family-friendly; breakfast buffet included. $209–290.

MOTELS AND HOTELS

St. Michaels, 21663

& **St. Michaels Harbour Inn, Marina and Spa** (410-745-9001; 1-800-955-9001; www.harbourinn.com), 101 N. Harbor Rd. Luxury waterfront suites and rooms, many with classy bathrooms and extra features. Outside pool and waterfront spa. $209–329.

INNS

Easton, 21601

Bartlett Pear Inn (410-770-3300; www .bartlettpearinn.com), 28 S. Harrison St., Easton. The downstairs restaurant (see *Dining Out*) may be the domain of her chef husband Jordon, but the inn rooms upstairs are where Alice Lloyd reigns supreme. Each of the seven rooms, named for various species of pears, reflect her skill as a decorator. The Bosc Pear Suite is painted in light tones to take advantage of the sun pouring through the floor-to-ceiling windows, pastels cover the walls of the Concorde Pear Room, and a soaking tub in the Green Anjou Room is just the thing after a long day of sightseeing. Speaking of such,

the inn is conveniently located within a few steps of Easton's many art galleries and quality clothing boutiques. And remember, all you have to do is walk down a flight of stairs to enjoy Jordon's fine cuisine. $169–229.

& & **Tidewater Inn** (410-822-1300; 1-800-237-8775; www.tidewaterinn.com), 101 E. Dover St. The Tidewater is in the heart of town and, although built in 1949, reflects the Eastern Shore's earlier period. Mahogany doors, 18th-century reproductions, and open fireplaces. A favorite place for gentlemen sport hunters, it has a rustic elegance about it. Pay the few extra dollars to stay away from the smaller rooms, as most of the rooms are ample sized and decorated nicely. $189–295.

Oxford, 21654

& **Oxford Inn** (410-226-5220; www.oxford inn.net), 506 S. Morris St. The 1880s inn receives rave reviews from former guests. Most of the 11 rooms have private baths and sparse, yet pleasing country furnishings. The third-floor Tavern Hall Room has four window seats with views of Town Creek, yet the lower-cost Chesapeake Room on the second floor provides the same view. $130–190.

& & **Robert Morris Inn** (410-226-5111; www.robertmorrisinn.com), Morris St. Apr.–Nov.; weekends only, Dec.–Mar. Within view of the Tred Avon River, the inn was built in the early 1700s by ship's carpenters. The 16 rooms have elegant country furnishings such as four-poster beds. Private baths. Some have side water-view balconies. $175–240. James Michener proclaimed the restaurant's crabcakes to be a 9.2 on a scale of 10.

Sandaway (1-888-726-3292; www.sandaway .com), 103 W. Strand St. Open mid-Apr.–

mid-Nov. The first thing I thought about as I pulled into the driveway was, "I could while away many an hour sitting under that spreading sycamore tree, just watching the sailboats ply the wide waters of the Tred Avon and Choptank Rivers." The original part of the inn was built in the 1870s, but even the more modern buildings retain the grace and stylishness of a bygone era. There are too many choices of rooms to enumerate here, but be sure to spend the few extra dollars to receive a water-view room. My favorite room is the Waterfront Tred Avon 102, where you could stay in bed or sit on the screened porch to enjoy the view. $170–300.

Royal Oak, 21662

✍ ⅍ **The Oaks** (410-745-5053; www.the-oaks.com), MD 329 at Acorn Lane. Built in 1748, the Oaks retains its original exterior appearance but has been remodeled with modern amenities on the inside. Rooms look onto either Oak Creek or the formal gardens. Room 27 has its own deck near the water and a fireplace. $190–395.

St. Michaels, 21663

⅍ **Five Gables Inn and Spa** (410-745-0100; 1-866-278-9601; www.fivegables.com), 209 N. Talbot St. All of the 20 rooms have private baths, whirlpool tubs, and gas log fireplaces. Besides being in the middle of town and close to all the activity, the inn offers another enticement: a spa with herbal bath treatments, massages, facials, and body polishes. The setting is elegant, yet quite casual. Many different packages available. $260–425; about $100 less during the week.

⅍ **The Inn at Perry Cabin** (410-745-2200; 1-800-722-2949; www.perrycabin.com), 308 Watkins Lane. A part of the worldwide chain of exclusive Orient-Express properties, the Inn at Perry Cabin became even more exclusive and luxurious with a $15 million renovation and expansion in 2002. The 19th-century mansion now has 82 rooms and suites on 25 acres, and more lavish amenities than ever. The stay is magnificent and the food world-class, but it is not a place for those who must ask how much. Rates from $330 to over $570.

✍ ⅍ **Wades Point Inn** (410-745-2500; 1-888-923-3466; www.wadespoint.com), Wades Point Rd. Chickens in the yard let you know that you will be staying in country comfort. Located on 120 acres, the inn was built in 1819 on a point of land jutting into the bay. Water-view rooms, screened porches overlooking the water, balconies, and a 1-mile nature trail let you enjoy the setting. Children welcome, but no facilities for very young infants. $160–260.

Tilghman Island, 21671

Tilghman Island Inn (410-886-2141; 1-800-866-2141; www.tilghmanislandinn.com), Coopertown Rd. Closed Jan. Spacious and modern rooms and suites with views of the Narrows. Continental breakfast included, and there is an excellent restaurant on the premises (see *Dining Out*). $250–300.

BED & BREAKFASTS

Easton, 21601

The Bishop's House (410-820-7290; 1-800-223-7290; www.bishopshouse.com), 214 Goldsborough St. This 1860s Victorian home is romantically furnished in period pieces and is located within the town's historic district. Sit on the wraparound porch and watch the world go by. All rooms have private bath. Bicycle rentals for guests. $185–195.

Inn at 202 Dover (410-819-8007; 1-866-450-7600; www.innat202dover.com), 202 Dover St. The furnishings and artwork in each of the four guest suites live up to the elegance hinted at when you first gaze upon this massive (and fully restored) Victorian-era mansion. Additional artwork throughout the house, a coffee and sherry bar, and a wraparound porch, along with a garden full of plants appropriate to the era, further enhance the quality of your stay. The real reason to stay, though, is that it is only a matter of walking downstairs to enjoy the fabulous food served at the inn's restaurant (see *Dining Out*). $289–500.

Oxford, 21654

🐾 **Combsberry** (410-226-5353; www.combsberry.net), 4837 Evergreen Rd. A

0.5-mile tree-lined driveway brings you into the 10-acre estate of Combsberry, built in 1730 along Island Creek. Luxury, quiet, and beauty are the emphases. The Waterfront Room in the Manor House has the best view, while the Garden Room looks onto the Victorian Gardens, which are lit at night. Four luxury cottages (the Oxford Cottage is pet-friendly, with a fenced-in area) provide privacy but still let you interact with other guests on the grounds or during breakfast. The house's architecture, the luxurious furnishings, the perfectly cared-for grounds, the hammock on the lawn, and the creek make for a grand place to stay. $250–395.

✂ **Ruffled Duck Inn** (410-226-5496; www.ruffleduckinn.com), 110 N. Morris St. The restored 1850s home features 10-foot ceilings, wide planked pine floors, a porch to sit on in the summer, and a nice fireplace in the living room for cool winter evenings. The three guest rooms have private baths, and a bicycle is available for guest use. A full three-course gourmet breakfast is included in the rate of $150; well-behaved children over the age of 10 permitted.

St. Michaels, 21663

Bay Cottage (410-745-9369; 1-888-558-8008; www.baycottage.com), 24640 Yacht Club Rd. Close to town, but on secluded property, the cottage has six guest rooms and is located on a quiet point of land with water views. $185–195.

Dr. Dodson House B&B (410-745-3691; www.drdodsonhouse.com), 200 Cherry St. The upstairs porch is great for people watching as the 1799 former tavern sits about halfway between St. Michaels's busy Talbot St. and the harbor. Lately the B&B has become known for its lavish breakfasts that have included such delectables as banana pecan waffles, Grand Marnier blueberry cheese blintzes, and berry sorbet. The courtyard garden is the place to relax after such a meal. $250–275.

♿ **Kemp House Inn** (410-745-3323; www.kemphouseinn.com), 412 S. Talbot St. Carved mantels, beaded baseboards, and a central-hall staircase hark back to 1807,

when the Federal-style Kemp House was built. The rooms are decorated with period pieces such as four-poster rope beds and Queen Anne tables. Close to the center of activity in town. $165–275.

♿ **The Parsonage Inn** (410-745-8383; www.parsonage-inn.com), 210 N. Talbot St. On the main street in town, the Parsonage Inn was built in 1883, and the furnishings in its eight guest rooms reflect the period. The host serves up breakfasts of stuffed French toast, egg casseroles, and Belgian waffles. $155–215.

Tarr House Bed & Breakfast Inn (410-745-2175; www.tarrhouse.com), 109 Green St. The small home with a shake roof is actually two houses, one built in the 1700s and the other in the 1800s. There are only two guest rooms, meaning you will receive the attention of and be pampered by the hosts. They also enjoy pointing out some the building's historical eccentricities, like the three little steps and short doorway that must be negotiated to get to the rooms in the 1700s part of the house. It's in a desirable location, within sight of the harbor and only a short block away from the shops and other attractions in St. Michaels. $215–225.

Two Swan Inn (410-745-2929; www.twoswaninn.com), foot of Carpenter St. Right at the water's edge, with a small lawn in front. Built in 1790, it retains the original pine floors, and all rooms have private

TARR HOUSE BED & BREAKFAST INN

baths. The first-floor front room overlooks the water, and upon the walls are official duck stamp prints. The upstairs room on the left has an heirloom bed from the Du Pont family and a sunrise view. $220.

Victoriana Inn (410-745-3368; 1-888-316-1282; www.victorianainn.com), 205 Cherry St. Within sight of the Maritime Museum, the Ionic-columned porch of this 1865 home overlooks the excitement of the harbor. The Tilghman Room and the Junior Suite also have views onto the water. A parlor and sunporch are nice spots for quiet conversation or reading. Complimentary wine, tea, and hors d'oeuvres on weekends. $239–359.

Tilghman Island, 21671

🐾 ⚹ **Black Walnut Point Inn** (410-886-2452; www.blackwalnutpoint.com), Black Walnut Rd. At the very southern tip of Tilghman Island, the inn is located within a 57-acre wildlife refuge and bordered on three sides by water. All the rooms in the main house have water views, while a baby grand piano fits in with the downstairs decor. For privacy, I liked the Choptank North Cottage, which lets you stay in bed and watch the sunrise. Hammocks in the yard, a swimming pool, and tennis courts. $120–225.

Lazyjack Inn (410-886-2215; 1-800-690-5080; www.lazyjackinn.com), 5907 Tilghman Island Rd. Two suites and two rooms with views of Dogwood Harbor or the inn's gardens. I like that you can lie in bed and watch the water spread out before you almost all of the way to Cambridge. The setting also allows you to watch the sailing fleet leave in the morning and return at sunset. $189–289.

COTTAGES

St. Michaels, 21663

🐾 ⚹ **Cygnet Cottage** (410-745-2929; www.twoswaninn.com), 201 Carpenter St. Run by the folks at Two Swan Inn, the cottage has two and a half bedrooms. There is nothing fancy here, the furnishings are simple, but there is a fireplace, and it's a good arrangement if you have children, pets, or a group of up to five. The rate starts at $225

for two and goes up to $595 for five; it drops the longer you stay.

CAMPING See *Green Space* in "Around the Bay Bridge and Kent Island."

✳ Where to Eat
DINING OUT
Easton
Peacock Restaurant at Inn at 202 Dover (410-819-8007; 1-866-450-7600; www.innat202dover.com), 202 Dover St. Meals are adventures in luxurious settings at this establishment, located within an elegant B&B (see *Bed & Breakfasts*). The menu claims to reflect the best of American cuisine with sautéed Amish chicken, apple glazed seared duck breast, and butter poached Maine lobster having been featured at various times. $25–35.

⚹ **Mason's** (410-822-3204; www.masonsgourmet.com), 22 S. Harrison St. Open for lunch and dinner. Mason's began as a gift and chocolate shop more than 40 years ago and has grown to become a restaurant of such renown that politicos such as Dick Cheney and Donald Rumsfeld, along with Hollywood celebrities Owen Wilson and Vince Vaughn, dine here. Still under family ownership, the restaurant's menu draws from international cuisines flavored by Chesapeake Bay traditions and locally available produce. Meals are prepared to order, so don't come here if in a hurry; come to enjoy a meal worth waiting for. Also, order the country soup, still made from the original recipe Mrs. Mason learned from her mother in Italy. $25–30.

⚹ **Out of the Fire** (410-770-4777; www.outofthefire.com), 22 Goldsborough St. Open for lunch and dinner; closed Sun. Reservations recommended. My appetizer of California champagne grapes and blue cheese complemented a medley of lettuce greens. There were so many vegetables in the risotto primavera that it had a different taste with each bite. Chocolate hazelnut gelato ended the meal perfectly. Other dishes include Caribbean spiced pork, wild mushroom penne, and pizzas cooked in a wood-burning stone oven. Bright murals and works of local artists make this a fun place. Entrées $19–26.

♿ **Hunters' Tavern** (410-822-1300; www .tidewaterinn.com), Harrison and Dover Sts. When new owners took over the Tidewater Inn (see *Lodging*), they revamped the inn's restaurant menu. Prices are on the upscale side (a ground beef burger is over $12), but there are some interesting items here. On the menu when last visited were BBQ quail, chicken Oscar, and clams chardonnay. I am glad to see that the inn's traditional Maryland snapping turtle soup, which has been served here for more than 60 years, is still on the menu. Gas fireplaces make sitting outside on cool evenings inviting. Entrées $24–49.

🍽 ♿ **Scossa Restaurant & Lounge** (410-822-2202; www.scossarestaurant.com), 8 N. Washington St. Open for lunch and dinner; closed Mon. Hailing from a small town in Italy, and arriving in America by way of culinary studies in his younger years before becoming chef to a prominent international family, Giancarlo Tondin has raised the bar for Italian cooking in Easton. The menu includes traditional Italian dishes from across the country, but they bear a bit of regional twist gleaned from his time working in restaurants in Venice. Maryland's hunting heritage creeps into the menu in winter, when you may find offerings of duck, quail, or pheasant. It's the little things that make the difference, like using locally grown cantaloupe in the gazpacho, or making the crunchy breadsticks, pastas, and desserts fresh each day. I left here with a wonderfully fresh taste in my mouth and a resolve to return as soon as possible. Modern contemporary atmosphere; on nice days the doors are folded back to give you an unobstructed view of the spreading evergreen trees in the courtyard across the street. $17–40.

Oxford

Latitude 38 (410-226-5303; www.latitude 38.org), 26342 Oxford Rd. The distinct dishes make this a local favorite. The appe-

Bartlett Pear Inn (410-770-3300; www.bartlettpearinn.com), 28 S. Harrison St., Easton. Open for dinner Wed.–Sun. The story of the Bartlett Pear Inn reads like a sweeping epic romance novel interlaced with the creation of a successful business. When Alice Bartlett and Jordon Lloyd, natives of Easton, married at a young age, she took his surname, but he promised her that someday he would find a way to honor her maiden name. After graduating from the International Culinary Academy of Pittsburgh, Jason helped establish a number of four- and five-star restaurants in major markets like New York, Florida, and Washington, DC. Returning to their hometown to raise a family, the couple opened a business of their own. The Bartlett Pear Inn is the fulfillment of his promise to her. Alice is the innkeeper (see *Inns*), while Jordon's culinary skills have won the restaurant many accolades.

You can also add my praises to the chef. My meal started with a cold peach-melon soup that was delectable. When I decided to combine a couple of items from the menu, Jason said the truffle butter glaze he normally paired with the inn-made tagliatelle noodles would not go well with the halibut I also wanted. So, he prepared a creamy sauce that complemented, but did not overpower, the white, meaty texture and flavor of the fish. The philo dough of the berry Napoleon was delicately thin, yet full of the taste you want in a pastry. You may not find these items available because the menu changes often based upon what is available fresh from nearby local suppliers; I feel I can safely say you will be satisfied with just about anything that is offered when you happen to dine.

A nice menu option is to choose the "Pear Plates," which permit you to choose four courses for less than $25. In addition, I'm not a cocktail drinker, but the restaurant is becoming increasingly known for its extraordinary mixed drinks.

The Bartlett Pear Inn is currently my favorite Easton restaurant. Entrées $18–30.

tizer to try is the polenta-fried soft-shell crab with melon salsa and prosciutto-wrapped greens. Where else can you have grilled wahoo on white bean hummus served with jicama and nectarine salad and roasted jalapeño corn *mole?* Other meat, seafood, and chicken dishes are just as unusual. Bistro atmosphere with a small fireplace. $14.95–22.95; half entrées are available at almost half the cost.

Pope's Tavern at the Oxford Inn (410-226-5220; www.oxfordinn.net), 506 S. Morris St. With dining inside or on the porch, the ambience of the 1880s inn adds to the overall pleasure of having a meal here. The menu changes seasonally, and you're likely to find anything from breast of duck to crispy shrimp. The swordfish I had was moist and tender, served with a tasty black bean and pineapple relish. The cucumber, dill, and avocado dish was a nice way to start dinner on a warm summer evening. Nice wine list. $22–32.

Tilghman Island

& **Tilghman Island Inn** (410-886-2141; www.tilghmanislandinn.com), Coopertown Rd. The picture windows and outside deck provide views of Knapps Narrows. Executive chef David McCallum's dishes have been winning awards and accolades for the inn since the late 1980s. The black-eyed pea cakes with tomato salsa is one of his signature appetizers. The rockfish Norfolk I had was a thick fillet smothered by crab, prosciutto, sherry, and succotash. Pasta, paella, beef, duck, and more are served with similar flair. $19–35.

EATING OUT

Easton

The Fountain at Hill's (410-822-9751), 30 E. Dover St. Open for breakfast and lunch; closed Sun. Located in the back of Hill's Drug Store, the Fountain recalls the days when nearly every pharmacy had a small dining counter. This is the place to come for a low-cost ($6 or less) breakfast or a tasty lunch sandwich ($3–9). There are only a few tables, so be prepared to wait to be seated, especially on busy summer weekends.

Lazy Lunch (410-770-3447; www.thelazy lunch.com), behind 28 Washington St. Open for lunch and dinner Mon.–Fri. A nice choice for a quick lunch of a sandwich, soup, or salad. The bonus is the bread, which is made fresh on the premises daily and there are a number of gluten-free offerings.

St. Michaels

Ava's Pizzaria & Wine Bar (410-745-3081; www.avaspizzeria.com), 409 S. Talbot St. Ava's was packed when I stopped by for lunch, every table inside and outside as well as all bar stools taken. It's understandable. All sauces, dough, and cheese (the mozzarella is delicious and creamy!) are made in-house, while wasabi oysters, bleu cheese and bacon mussels, and Gruyere and balsamic reduction veggie panini add interesting options to the gourmet pizzas. Making mint mojitoes kept the bartender busy the entire time I was there. Extensive wine and beer selections. $10–17.

✔ **Marcoritaville** (410-745-5557; www .marcosbar.com), 105 N. Talbot St. I had enjoyed the meals served by Mark Chew at Bay Hundred restaurant on Tilghman Island, so I was disappointed to learn he had sold it. However, I was heartened on my most recent visit in St. Michaels to find Marcoritaville, his latest venture. Although located on the busy main street, the patio with large, colorful umbrellas calls to mind waterfront dining. The menu reflects the owner's international culinary experience with American, European, and Asian influences. Eastern shore cuisine is not forgotten, and my softshell crab (from nearby Tilghman Island) was lightly fried, allowing the tastes to come through. The bar is known for serving inventive and diverse drinks. $16–27.

& **Town Dock Restaurant** (410-745-5577; 1-800-884-0103; www.towndockrestaurant .com), 125 Mulberry St. Yes, you can get steamed crabs (market price) here, but the menu also has some items not often found at a seafood or crab house, such as étouffée, BBQ ribs, cioppino, and tournedos of beef. $21–30.

Tilghman Island

✒ & **Bay Hundred** (410-886-2126; www .bayhundredrestaurant.net), 6178 Tilghman Island Rd. Breakfast, lunch, and dinner. The picture windows and outdoor deck overlook the boat activity of Knapps Narrows. Sandwiches, beef, chicken, and seafood fresh from the bay. The crabcakes are made with a nice blend of spices and come with imperial sauce. $16.95–26.95. Ask about the history of the restaurant's name.

CRABS ✒ & **The Crab Claw** (410-745-2900; www.thecrabclaw.com), on the waterfront, St. Michaels. Open daily 11–10, Mar.–Nov. This place could almost be credited with turning St. Michaels into a tourist town—and establishing what an Eastern Shore crab house should look like. Pleasure boaters and sailors have been pulling up to its dock since 1965 to feast upon bushels of fresh-steamed crabs (market price) on the outside deck. Oysters on the half shell and steamed cherrystone clams are also popular. Entrées start at about $15.

✒ & **St. Michaels Crab and Steak House** (410-745-3737; www.stmichaels crabhouse.com), 305 Mulberry St., St. Michaels. Owner-chef Eric Rosen turns out a crab dip that is a superb, melt-in-your-mouth appetizer, while his crab balls are, refreshingly, broiled and not fried. Steamed crabs (market price) are available by the dozen or half dozen. I have sampled several different entrées here and was well satisfied with all of them ($12.95–26.95). The 1830s former oyster-shucking house on the waterfront makes this an appropriate setting for the restaurant.

TAKE-OUT

Easton

Captain's Ketch Seafood (410-820-7177; 1-800-318-4749; www.captainsketchseafood .com), 316 Glebe Rd. Fresh seafood packed for take-home, travel, or shipment.

Piazza Italian Market (410-820-8281; www.piazzaitalianmarket.com), 218 N. Washington St. An eclectic Italian grocery with take-out items such as sandwiches, sal-ads, and main dishes for those nights you might want to eat in your room.

Earth Origins (410-822-4852; www.earth originsmarket.com), 108 Marlboro Rd. A gourmet supermarket with organic produce, fresh breads and pastries, sushi bar, juices, and espresso.

St. Michaels

Big Al's Seafood Market (410-745-3151), 302 N. Talbot St. Steamed crabs and other fresh seafood are available from a counter in the back of this small convenience store.

COFFEE BARS

Easton

☙ & **Red Hen Coffee House & Café** (410-692-3662; www.redhencoffee.com), 5 Goldsborough St. Coffees, teas, shakes, pastries, candies, salads, and sandwiches. The shop does a brisk breakfast and lunch business. The adjoining **Nightcat** has live entertainment in the evening. Internet access also.

St. Michaels

Blue Crab Coffee Co. (410-745-4155; www.bluecrabcoffee.com), 211 N. Talbot St. Full-service espresso bar and other specialty coffees. Pastries and desserts.

SNACKS AND GOODIES

Easton

Amish Country Farmers Market (410-822-8989; www.amishcountryfarmers market.com), 101 Marlboro Ave. You could gain quite a few pounds just sampling the goodies and food offered in this multibusiness establishment. **Fishers Pastries** features a variety of homemade baked goods, including lemon bars and a rich blueberry crème pie. **Miller's** makes fudge and chocolate-dipped strawberries. **The Little Bulk Food Store** features dried fruits, nuts, pretzels, chips, and more. For something slightly more wholesome, go to **Country Cheese & Salads** or the **Soup and Salad Corner**.

& **Old Towne Creamery** (410-820-5223; www.otcreamery.com), 9B Goldsborough

St. Ice cream, frozen yogurt, shakes, sundaes, and Italian ices.

Oxford

Scottish Highland Creamery (410-924-6298; www.scottishhighlandcreamery.com), 314 Tilghman St. On an out-of-the-way street in the off-the-beaten-path town of Oxford, Victor Barlow attracts droves of people to his tiny establishment. Growing up in Edinburgh, Scotland, above an Italian ice cream shop, he learned the secrets of making a superior gelato. Using only the finest local milk, cream, and fruits, he has created over 600 flavors. Some are quite eccentric, such as cucumber, bacon, oyster, or red hot pepper, but usually you will find the more refreshing flavors like chocolate chip, vanilla, cherry, and one of the most delicious lemon sorbets your tongue will ever lick.

✳ Entertainment

FILM Premier Cinema (410-822-9950; www.cambridgecinemas.com), Tred Avon Square, Easton. First-run movies.

Also see *Theaters* for vintage and nonmainstream films.

THEATERS Avalon Theatre (410-822-7299; www.avalontheatre.com), Dover and Harrison Sts., Easton. A wide range of plays, symphonies, variety shows, musicals, dance, movies, and arts is presented within this historic art deco theater. Worth a peek inside even if you are not attending a function.

✳ Selective Shopping
ANTIQUES

Easton

There are so many antiques shops in Easton that it would be impossible to list them all in this book. A shopping guide available from the Talbot County Office of Tourism lists a large percentage of them.

Tharpe Antiques (410-820-7525; www.hstc.org), 30 S. Washington St. A consignment shop operated in the late-1800s Mary

Jenkins House by the Talbot County Historical Society.

St. Michaels

Nancy's Nostalgia Antiques (410-745-9771), 408 S. Talbot St. Nancy's has been a purveyor of antiques since 1990.

ART GALLERIES

Easton

Academy Art Museum (410-822-2787; www.academyartmuseum.org), 106 South St. Small admission fee. By far one of the best local arts councils in Maryland. They sponsor lecture series, dances, music, theater events, and a host of classes for children and adults. In addition to national touring exhibits, the museum offers changing displays that showcase the talents of local artists—and the quality is above what you often find through an arts council.

Cottage Studio & Gallery (410-822-1199; www.cottagestudioandgallery.com), 19 Goldsborough St. The studio of sterling silver and copper jewelry makers John and Maryetta Dynan also offers the works of other Eastern Shore artists working in a vast array of media.

Grafton Galleries (410-822-8922; www.graftonarts.com), 32 E. Dover St. A working gallery and studio with works by national and regional artists.

Laura Reed Howell Gallery (410-267-6496; www.laurahowell.com), 1 Mill Pl. Painting in oil, acrylic, and watercolor, Howell's landscapes evoke the spirit of the *plein aire* school of art.

✐ **South Street Art Gallery** (410-770-8350; www.southstreetartgallery.com), 5 South St. Works of local and national artists—and a children's gallery room.

Troika Gallery (410-770-9190; www.troikagallery.com), 9 S. Harrison St. Laura Era, Dorothy F. Newland, and Jennifer Heyd Wharton present their works and those of other artists.

The Witte Gallery (410-690-4866; www.thewittegallery.com), 5 N. Harrison St. Fine art.

Royal Oak

The Gallery By the River (410-745-4303; www.ctw-tapestry.com), 5592 Poplar Ln. The works offered here are chosen by Ulrika Leander on her visits throughout America and Europe. While those are certainly interesting enough, the real reason to stop here is to witness Leander's magnificent handwoven cotton and wool tapestries. This is a true master artist at work creating one of a kind tour de forces.

St. Michaels

Artisans of the World (410-745-6040; www.artisansoftheworld.net), 203 N. Talbot St. The owner of the two-story shop travels the world in his off-season searching for exciting items not found in many other shops. He also says he keeps a stock that is 50 percent international, 25 percent national, and 25 percent local. A most interesting place to wander around.

Artiste Locale & Frivolous Fibers (410-745-6580; www.frivolousfibers.com), 112 N. Talbot St. The works of some talented regional artists are on display. Pay close attention to the pottery and the woodwork—they are done especially well. The Frivolous Fibers part of the shop has some locally dyed yarns and other knitting supplies.

The Gregorio Gallery (410-745-0927; 1-866-418-0927; www.gregoriogallery.com), 104 N. Talbot St. The photography displayed in Gregorio Gallery was some of the most stunning I saw in all of St. Michaels.

BOOKSTORES

Easton

News Center (410-822-7212), 218 N. Talbot St. Newspapers, magazines, and the area's largest bookstore.

Oxford

Mystery Loves Company (410-226-0010; www.mysterylovescompany.com), 202 S. Morris St. A century-old brick building, which has been a bank and a post office (ask to see the dip in the floor from so many people standing in line!), houses several small rooms of mysteries, as well as some best-sellers, children's books, and those with a local interest.

St. Michaels

Chesapeake Bay Maritime Museum Store (410-745-2916; www.cbmm.org), Mill St. One of the best and largest collections of maritime and local books and authors to be found on the Eastern Shore. There are also quality selections of children's toys, nautical items, and artwork. (Also see *To See.*)

Tilghman Island

Crawfords Nautical Books (410-886-2230; www.crawfordsnautical.com), Tilghman Island Rd. Open Sat. and Sun., Apr.–Dec. Just like Mystery Loves Company, Crawfords is located in a former bank building. Inside you will find more than 12,000 new, used, and rare books, all with some kind of nautical, ocean, bay, or "watery" theme.

USED BOOKS

Trappe

Unicorn Book Shop (410-476-3838; www.unicornbookshop.com), US 50. Rare and secondhand books bought and sold. Maps, too.

SPECIAL SHOPS

Easton

✿ **Cracker Jacks** (410-822-7716), 7 S. Washington St. Children's books and some engaging toys.

St. Michaels

✿ **The Calico Toys and Games Gallery and Toy Store** (410-745-5370; www.calicotoysandgames.com), 212 Talbot St. The name says it all.

✿ **The Candleberry Shoppe** (410-745-2420; www.candleberryshoppe.com), 105 S. Talbot St. A gift shop with some novel nautically themed toys and games for children (and maybe for you, too).

Chesapeake Trading Co. (410-745-9797), 102 S. Talbot St. A few books, a few CDs, clothing, and an espresso bar.

Flamingo Flats (410-745-2053; 1-800-HOT-8841; www.flamingoflats.com), 100 Talbot St. More than 900 hot sauces, 600 mustards, 200 BBQ sauces, 75 salsas, 50 kinds of olives, and 800 cookbooks. Throw in cigars, pastas, Maryland souvenirs, Haitian art, and 300 flamingos in hundreds of different poses and you have a one-of-a-kind store.

❦ Flying Fred's Gifts for Pets (410-745-9601; www.flyingfreds.com), 202 N. Talbot St. There is always a bowl of water on the front porch for your canine companion, and many items inside, including gourmet baked treats and *Bowser Beer.* I like their slogan: "Come spoil man's best friend."

Galerie Française (410-745-6329; www.judithsummers.com), 211 N. Talbot St. A bit unexpected on the Eastern Shore—vintage French posters and antique furniture from Provence.

Simpatico (410-745-0345; www.simpatico stmichaels.com), 104 Railroad Ave. The owners of Simpatico travel to Italy to personally meet the artists that produce the quality items they offer in their store, including ceramics, linens, food, Pinocchio toys, and Murano glass.

What's This? What's That? (410-745-6699), 207 S. Talbot St. Not the average gift shop. Yes, there are some things you will find in other places, but there is also a nice array of eco-friendly handmade items imported from foreign lands.

FARMER'S MARKETS Easton **Farmer's Market** (410-822-0065; www.eastonmd.org), N. Harrison St. Open on Sat. during the season (which varies from year to year).

St. Michaels Freshfarm Market (www.freshfarmmarkets.org), Muskrat Park. A producers-only market held each Sat. from mid-Apr. to mid-Oct.

WINERY **St. Michaels Winery** (410-745-0808; www.st-michaels-winery.com), 605 S. Talbot St., St. Michaels. One of the most popular tasting rooms—because it is located in tourist-busy St. Michaels—the winery crafts its wines from its own decades-old vineyard located in nearby Wye Mills (supplemented with grapes from other regional and national growers). One of the other reasons it is busy is that it's open daily all year.

✳ Special Events

May: **Historic Homes and Gardens Tours** (410-770-8000), St. Michaels. Takes place every other year. **Wine Fest at St. Michaels** (www.winefestatstmichaels.com), St. Michaels. Wines, foods, crafts.

June: **Eastern Shore Chamber Music Festival** (410-819-0380). Various venues

WINDOW-SHOPPING IN ST. MICHAELS

throughout the area. **Boat Bumm's International Cardboard Boat Races** (410-820-4104), Oxford. Build a boat and enter the race, or just see which boats stay afloat. **Antique and Classic Boat Festival** (410-745-2916), St. Michaels. A rendezvous of more than 100 antique boats and automobiles.

July: **Talbot County Fair** (410-822-8007), Talbot County Fairgrounds, Easton. **Crab Days** (410-745-2916), St. Michaels. Possibly the largest celebration of the blue crab on the Eastern Shore. Crab races, crabbing demonstrations, and lots of crab to eat. **Plein Air Competition & Arts Festival** (410-822-7297; www.pleinair-easton.com), Easton. Regional and national artists compete for thousands of dollars in prize money. There are also lectures and workshops.

October: **Arts Marketplace** (410-822-2787), Easton. **Tilghman Island Day** (410-866-2677), Tilghman Island. Boat races, oyster-shucking and crab-picking contests, music, and food. **Oxford Day** (www.oxfordday.org), Oxford. Thousands come for the parade, food, marine animal exhibits, dog show, music, and more.

November: **Waterfowl Festival** (410-822-4567; www.waterfowlfest.org), Easton. Attracts close to 20,000 visitors. Wildlife arts, duck-calling contests, music, lots of kids' activities, demonstrations. Proceeds benefit Atlantic Flyway migratory bird projects. **Festival of Trees** (410-819-FEST), held at the Tidewater Inn and the Academy Art Museum, Easton. **Oyster Fest** (410-745-2916), St. Michaels. Learn how oysters are caught, shucked, and eaten.

December: **Christmas in St. Michaels** (1-888-465-5428), St. Michaels. House tours, parade, Santa, concerts, and activities throughout town.

AROUND THE BAY BRIDGE AND KENT ISLAND

The completion of the Bay Bridge, which connects Annapolis with Kent Island, in 1952 opened the Eastern Shore to a rush of travelers and new residents (sometimes referred to as "come here-ers" by older Eastern Shore citizens). In a way, history was just repeating itself, as the island had been in the vanguard several centuries before.

A narrow strip of land that juts far into the waters of the upper Chesapeake Bay, Kent Island was the first place to be settled on the Eastern Shore. Soon after William Claiborne established a fort on its western edge in 1631, the fertile soils of the island were being used to raise tobacco, the most important cash crop of the day. Additional settlers pushed their way inland, establishing large plantations that, around the time of the American Revolution, began to switch over to grain crops and dairy farming. When steam-powered boats made the rapid transit of goods possible, oystering, crabbing, and other commercial fishing became viable occupational choices.

Even today there are several large packinghouses clustered around Kent Narrows, and watermen still ply the bay and inlets, capturing large amounts of blue crabs and soft-shell clams. (It is said that the clams grow three times faster in the bay than they do in the North Atlantic.) With its access to the large populations of Annapolis, Baltimore, and Washington, DC, the area has become a center of activity for pleasure sailors and sportfishermen.

Farther inland, and bordering Delaware, is the decidedly more rural land of Caroline County, whose slower pace of life (still with all modern amenities) is its primary draw. Bicycling on the quiet two lane roads is a great way to experience the area (contact the Caroline Office of Tourism—see *Guidance*—for a bicycle routes map), while dining in the non–chain restaurants will bring you in contact with local culinary celebrities. There's also a large arts community and an amazingly active historical society for such a lightly populated area.

COMMUNITIES Little is left of the early days on the main part of Kent Island. The communities have been swallowed by modern-day America, and about all that is visible from US 50/301 are strip malls, restaurants, and motels. However, get off the four-lane and you will discover little gems, such as **Stevensville.** Developing out of a couple of farms owned by James and Charles Stevens in 1850, the town began to grow, as it was the center of the steamboat trade of the late 1800s. The arrival of the railroad made the town thrive even more, but growth came to an end when rail service stopped in the mid-1900s and the main highway bypassed the town.

Today Stevensville is a small town worthy of a short and easy walking tour. Many of its older buildings are in remarkably good shape, and its historic district was placed on the National

121

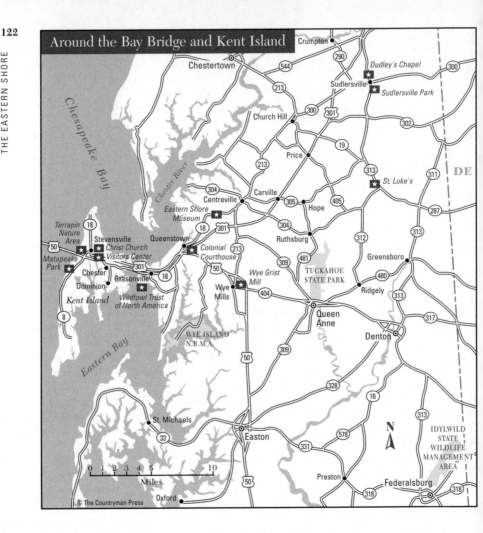

Around the Bay Bridge and Kent Island

Register of Historic Places in 1986. An artists' colony began to develop in the 1990s, and numerous studio-galleries and a couple of nice restaurants have opened and blended in well with the town's character.

Within **Queenstown** is the oldest continuously used courthouse in the state. As with Stevensville, this small village is worth a visit to walk through its historic streets.

A mill has been operating at **Wye Mills** from at least the late 1600s, making it the Eastern Shore's (and maybe even Maryland's) oldest frame gristmill. A small community consisting of blacksmiths, farmers, merchants, and schools, shops, and churches grew up around the mill.

As settlers moved farther inland from the bay, citizens needed a more centrally located county seat, so the legislature moved it from Queenstown to **Centreville** in 1782. A walking tour (brochure available from Queen Anne's County Office of Tourism; see *Guidance*) takes you by many of the buildings still standing from those early days. Styles range from early Federal to late Victorian, providing an architectural view of the town's development. A nice diversion from the city streets is the Nature Walk along the south bank of the Corsica River.

Church Hill is home to St. Luke's Episcopal Church and the Church Hill Theatre, a cultural treasure for the Upper Eastern Shore.

Many people know **Sudlersville** for it famous son, baseball great Jimmy Foxx. He hit 58 home runs in 1932 while playing for the Philadelphia Athletics, and the town erected a life-sized bronze statue of the Baseball Hall of Fame member in 1997.

Reflecting the rural nature of the area around it, **Preston**'s largest structures are a grain elevator and storage silos.

Ridgely was slated to be one of America's first planned communities before the Baltimore Land Association went bankrupt and the town gradually developed into the small community it is today.

Denton, the capital and commercial center of Caroline County, was established in the early 1770s and its Museum of Rural Life provides glimpses of the many phases of the

THE OLD RAILROAD STATION IN HISTORIC STEVENSVILLE

town's progress to today. It's currently home to several of the county's nicest restaurants and a small but notable art gallery.

Federalsburg has embraced its history with the Federalsburg Area Heritage Museum and Exeter, a restored 1808 two-story miller's home. **Idylwild Wildlife Management Area** and **Marshyhope Creek Greenway and Trail** highlight the outdoors.

GUIDANCE ✐ The **Queen Anne's County Office of Tourism** (410-604-2100; 1-888-400-RSVP; www.qac.org), 425 Piney Narrows Rd., Chester, 21619, has a visitors center just a few miles east of the Bay Bridge and is accessed from US 50 Exit 41. Also known as the **Chesapeake Heritage and Visitors Center,** it has interactive displays that are informative for adults, but they are geared toward teaching children about the natural and human history of the Chesapeake Bay and the Eastern Shore; it also has a local arts gallery. A lookout tower provides views of the bay and inlets, and a 530-foot boardwalk takes walkers onto the wetlands and trails of Ferry Point Park.

THE BOARDWALK AND SURROUNDINGS AT THE CHESAPEAKE HERITAGE AND VISITORS CENTER

Along the shore of the upper reaches of the Choptank River is the ♿ **Caroline Office of Tourism** (401-479-0655; www.tour caroline.com) and the **Choptank River Heritage Center** (free) at 10219 River Landing Rd., Denton. The building, the turn-of-the-20th-century Joppa Steamboat Wharf Terminal, was used not only as a warehouse but also for the abundant passenger traffic that rode schooners and steamboats up and down the river for business and pleasure. Displays include a replica of an early 20th century steamboat works, information concerning the many fish canneries that once lined the river, and photos that help visualize those busy days.

A state information center is located inside **Premium Outlets** (410-827-8699; www .primeoutlets.com), at the split of US 50 and US 301 N. in Queenstown.

GETTING THERE *By car:* **US 50/301** crosses the bay just east of Annapolis, making this route the gateway to the Eastern Shore. For travelers from Philadelphia, New York, and other points in the Northeast, US 301 is the most efficient and easy route into the area.

By air: The nearest airport with scheduled flights is **Baltimore/Washington International Thurgood Marshall Airport** (1-800-I-FLY-BWI; www.bwiairport.com) between Baltimore and Annapolis. Locally, the **Bay Bridge Airport** (410-643-4364; www.qac.org) in Stevensville is available for those with their own planes.

By bus: **Annapolis Transit** (410-263-7964; www.ci.annapolis.md.us) provides commuter service to Annapolis, Baltimore, and Washington, DC. Contact **Queen Anne's County Office of Tourism** for a copy of the very complicated schedule.

GETTING AROUND *By car:* Within a few miles of crossing the Bay Bridge, US 50/301 splits. **US 301** heads to the northeast on its way to Wilmington, Delaware, and passes through the dairy farms and croplands of Queen Anne's and Kent Counties. (**MD 213** is a smaller, less traveled route that turns to the west toward Chestertown.) **US 50** drops to the south and then turns to the east, providing the quickest route to Salisbury and the Ocean City area.

By bus: **County Ride** (410-758-2357), 104 Powell St., Centreville, has routes throughout Kent Island and connections with Grasonville, Queenstown, and Centreville.

By taxi: **Dart Cab** (410-643-2466).

PUBLIC RESTROOMS Public restrooms can be found at Queen Anne's County Office of Tourism in Chester, Premium Outlets in Queenstown, at the Matapeake Trail and Pier in Stevensville, and in the Caroline Office of Tourism in Denton.

MEDICAL EMERGENCY Around Kent Island, the closest hospital is in Annapolis: **Anne Arundel Medical Center** (410-481-1000; www.aahs.org), 2001 Medical Pkwy. The hospital operates an urgent-care facility (1-888-909-9729) at 1630 Main St. in Chester.

The **Queen Anne's Emergency Center** (410-827-3900; www.qaemergencycenter.org/) is located at 115 Shoreway Dr. in Queenstown.

For emergencies in the northern part of this area, go to **Chester River Hospital Center** (410-778-3300; www.chesterriverhealth.org), 100 Brown St. in Chestertown.

✳ To See
MUSEUMS
Centreville
Museum of Eastern Shore Life (410-758-8641; www.historicqac.org), 126 Dulin Clark Rd., Centreville. Sat. and Sun. 1–4, Apr.–Oct. Free admission. A collection of tools, implements, and other items from bygone times.

Denton
Museum of Rural Life (410-479-2055; www.carolinehistory.org), 16 N. Second St. Open Fri.–Sun. Donations accepted. It's always amazing to me what a county historical society is able to accomplish. Within this museum is an entire original log cabin of a subsistence farmer, moved and rebuilt here by the society. There are also portions of a middle-class farmer's home, that of a wealthy planter, and the 1819 home of a successful merchant.

Docents will lead you on a guided tour, so be sure to take a look at the "window" showing the home's interior construction and ask for the story about the whipping post.

Federalsburg

& **Federalsburg Area Heritage Museum** (www.historicfederalsburg.org). The museum, which was just beginning to open to the public when I visited, was once a service garage for Model-T Fords. With just the first of the planned exhibits in place, there were good displays about the ocean pearl products (a little known Maryland industry) and a wall of the sand blocks that had been made in the area. Nearby is **Exeter** at 408 Old Denton Rd. The 1808 two-story had just recently been acquired by the Federalsburg Historical Society when I visited, but there are plans to renovate the building that at one time had been the home of the owners who operated the mills that were located across the street along Marshyhope Creek's fall line. A short trail (not currently maintained) leads to the creek and mill site.

HISTORIC SITES **Colonial Courthouse** (410-827-7646; www.historicqac.org), MD 18 and Del Rhodes Ave., Queenstown. Open Mon.–Fri. The first courthouse built in Queen Anne's County, the circa-1708 structure was restored in the late 1900s using most of the original studs, diagonal braces, and doorjambs and headers. A simple one-room wooden building, it is furnished with authentic reproductions. Interestingly, the gavel is made from one of the building's original beams. The attached brick building was added as a kitchen sometime in the mid-1800s.

HISTORIC CHURCHES

Church Hill
St. Luke's Episcopal Church (410-556-6644; www.stlukesandstandrews.org), 401 Main St., was constructed in 1732 and is believed to be the oldest intact brick church in the state. In an example of how important tobacco was in colonial days, the congregation did not pay for the church with money, but with 140,000 pounds of tobacco.

Stevensville
Christ Church (410-643-5921; www.christchurchkentisland.org/), 117 E. Main St. This Gothic church, with its steep slate roof and stone foundation, was constructed—using wooden pegs instead of nails—in 1880. The oldest established congregation in the state, founded in 1631, worshiped here until it moved to a location south of US 50.

Sudlersville
Dudley's Chapel (410-928-3406; www.historicqac.org), Benton Corner Rd. Constructed in the late 1700s, this brick structure is the oldest Methodist church still standing in the United States. The first Native American Methodist minister, Freeborn Garrettson, preached here.

OTHER SITES

Preston
Linchester Mill & Hog Island School (410-786-2549), 3390 Linchester Rd. Open on select Fri. and Sat. You really need to stop here if you have a fondness for historical mills. The main part of the mill was built in 1824, but what makes it so important are the three inventions of miller Oliver Evans. Throughout the mill you will see his innovative elevators, chutes, and conveyor belts with an Archimedes screw that helped bring about America's automated mills. The structure also has a roller mill and cork cracker. Also on site is the 1879 schoolhouse, restored to its earliest look.

& **Outstanding Dreams Farm** (410-673-2002; www.outstandingdreamsfarm.com), 24480 Pinetown Rd. Call or e-mail to arrange a tour; free for individuals or families. Outstanding Dreams is a family-run alpaca farm and the tour will bring you up close with these gentle creatures (who are good with children), and help you learn why their wool is so soft and the

> **Orrell's Maryland Beaten Biscuits** (443-454-4367; 410-822-2065; www.orrellsmbb.com), about 1.5 miles south of Wye Mills on MD 622—watch for the sign. There is no storefront here; just knock on the kitchen door. Open Tues. and Wed.; call ahead to arrange a quick tour. The phrase "a throwback to another time" has never been as appropriate as when describing this place. Beaten-biscuit making is at least three hundred years old, dating from when leavening was hard to come by. The dough was beaten with a hammer—for at least 30 minutes—to get it to rise. Using a rolling machine to take the place of beating, the Orrell family has been selling the biscuits since the 1930s. After the dough has been rolled, five women (several have been with Orrell's for decades), sitting around an old vinyl table, hand-form each biscuit. Cooked in an oven—not a commercial one, but like the one you have in your kitchen—the biscuits are crunchy, but chewy inside. A place with a lot of character that should not be missed.

difference between llamas and alpacas. The farm store has items made from animals on the farm and some fair trade alpaca items from Peru.

Wye Mills

Wye Grist Mill (410-827-3850; www.oldwyemill.org), just a few hundred feet south of the MD 662/MD 213 intersection. Open Fri.–Sun. from mid-Apr. through early Nov.; sometimes during the week. Small donation requested. With flour being shipped to Europe, South America, and the West Indies, the late 1700s were the halcyon days for wheat on the Eastern Shore. The Wye Grist Mill is a bit of that time still in existence. A small museum contains many items from the miller's trade, and when all of the gears, millstone, and wheel are in motion, you will be amazed at how little water is required to operate it.

✳ To Do

BICYCLING Island Bike and Paddle (1-877-545-2925; www.islandbikeandpaddle.com), Wells River Rd., Grasonville. Stop here to rent bikes so that you can ride the Cross Island and Kent South trails (see *Walks*). Helmets and trail maps are provided, along with information about other places to visit on the island. Kayaks are also rented.

BOAT EXCURSIONS

Chester

Kent Narrows Boat Rides (410-353-0054; 410-212-4070; www.kentnarrowsboatrides.com), headquartered in Castle Harbor Marina. In operation May–Oct.; call for reservations (at least a day ahead is best). One of the most reasonably priced boat tour operators in this area, the captains of these two 25- or 26-foot boats can take you on scenic and/or sunset cruises around Kent Narrows or as far away as Rock Hall or St. Michaels. My trip aboard the *Jessie Grace* with Capt. Ted Schultz provided a bit of history, along with a lot of scenery and Chesapeake Bay birdlife.

Grasonville

✵ **Grabacrab Charters** (410-758-1837; www.grabacrabcharters.com), 433 Kent Narrows Way at Harris Crab House. This is an outing for as many as 26 passengers and designed for the whole family, with crabbing for the kids. The cruise includes a feast of crab dip, shrimp, corn, and crabs. Reservations required.

Stevensville

B & B Yacht Charters (410-643-1529), 206 Holly Court. The 40-foot sloop *Captiva* takes passengers onto the Chesapeake Bay for three- and six-hour sailing cruises. Also weekend and weeklong chartered trips.

THE KENT NARROWS BRIDGES AS SEEN FROM THE DECK OF THE *JESSIE GRACE*

FISHING

Grasonville

Tuna the Tide (410-827-5635; www.exploredelmarva.com), 404 Greenwood Creek Lane. You will probably have a somewhat nice and quiet trip as the *Tuna of the Tide* accommodates only six people for fishing and/or sight-seeing charters.

Stevensville

& **Matapeake Pier** (410-974-2149), about 3 miles south of US 50 on MD 8. The 900-foot handicapped-accessible pier is open for public fishing 24 hours a day.

Pocomoke Pier, located at the southern end of MD 8. Open for fishing and crabbing sunrise to sunset, May–Oct.

Captain's Pride Charters (410-758-3107; www.captainspridecharters.net), Kentmoor Marina. Whether you troll for blues or chum for stripers, Captain Joey provides all of the bait and tackle you need at no additional charge.

Southern Belle Charters (410-643-1932; www.southernbellecharters.com), Kentmorr Marina. The *Southern Belle* takes anglers out for rockfish Apr.–Dec. and for bluefish, sea trout, flounder, croaker, and more during other seasons. The 450-horsepower boat can accommodate more than two dozen people and is also available for sight-seeing cruises.

Also contact the **Queen Anne's County Office of Tourism** for a listing of other licensed charter-boat captains.

GOLF

Queenstown

Queenstown Harbor Links (1-800-827-5257; www.qhgolf.com), 310 Links Lane. Two courses. The 18 holes on the River Course are often within view of the Chester River, while the scenery along the other 18-hole course centers upon a series of lakes.

Stevensville

Blue Heron (410-643-5721), 101 Queen's Colony High Rd. Operated by Queen Anne's County Parks and Recreation, and open 7 AM–dusk, the course is open to the public on a first-come, first-served basis.

HIKING   See *Walks* and *Parks.*

KAYAKING AND CANOEING The Choptank and Tuckahoe Rivers Water Trail is a 60-mile route that runs along the narrow, cypress-tree-lined Tuckahoe River and the more open waters of the Choptank River. An excellent guide to this trip—which provides not only route descriptions but also access points, interpretive information, and cultural aspects along the way—can be obtained from the **Caroline Office of Tourism.**

An excellent pamphlet, *Kent Island Water Trails,* is available from the Queen Anne's County Office of Tourism (see *Guidance*) and details six different routes in the waters around the island, most ranging 2 to 3 miles in length. The *Cabin Creek Trail* encompasses a trip on Marshy Creek and Prospect Bay, both of which border the Chesapeake Bay Environmental Center (see *Nature Preserves*), providing a paddle along the least developed shores around Kent Island.

✇ **Adventure Crafters** (1-888-529-2563; www.adventurecrafters.com), 600 Discovery Ln., Queenstown. Usually operating daily Apr.–Thanksgiving; reservations strongly advised. With emphasis on safety and helping you learn how to paddle as efficiently as possible, Robert Scrhack takes individuals or groups out onto the Chesapeake Bay and surrounding waters to explore the beauties of Eastern Shore locales such as Wye Island, Salt House Cove, or the Eastern Neck Wildlife Refuge. Three-hour tours are about $60 for adults, $50 for children 10–14 years of age; free for those 6–9 years old who are permitted to ride in a tandem kayak with a parent. Robert will also arrange full-day custom and private tours, along with classes to improve your paddling skills. Also available are two- to six-hour cruises aboard a 37-foot sloop, where all you have to do is sit back and let the crew take care of the sailing.

Island Bike and Paddle (1-877-545-2925; www.islandbikeandpaddle.com), Wells River Rd., Grasonville. Sales and service of bicycles, kayaks, and stand-up paddles. They also provide lessons and half-day and full-day guided paddle tours.

TENNIS Public courts can be found in **Mowbray Park** on MD 8 south of Stevensville, **Grasonville Park** on Perry's Corner Road in Grasonville, **Roundtop Park** on Roundtop Road in Chester Harbor, and **Love Point Park** on Old Love Point Road in Stevensville.

✳ Green Space

BEACHES See **Matapeake Trail and Pier** under *Parks.*

NATURE PRESERVES

Federalsburg
Idylwild Wildlife Management Area (410-376-3236; www.dnr.state.md.us/wildlife/publiclands/eastern/idylwild.asp), Houston Branch Rd. (MD 306), Federalsburg. As with most wildlife management areas (be aware that hunting is the primary reason for the management area), 3,800-acre Idylwild is the place to go if you want to escape crowds and enjoy nature in relative solitude (most use is by local equestrians). Almost 30 miles of trails (some well-defined old roads, others narrow and unmaintained pathways) wander through hardwood and pine forests, open meadows maintained for wildlife habitat, and along scenic Marshyhope Creek where you may spot a beaver or two. Harriet Tubman and other conductors of the Underground Railroad followed Marshyhope Creek northward in their efforts to help escaping slaves gain their freedom.

Grasonville
✇ **Chesapeake Bay Environmental Center** (410-827-6694; www.bayrestoration.org), 600 Discovery Lane—US 50 and 301 Exit 43B or Exit 44A. Open 9–5. Small admission fee. The 500-acre headquarters of the Wildfowl Trust of North America. I have always been rewarded with something during my walks on the 4 miles of trails: trumpeter swans coming in for a

landing on one of the ponds, an osprey swooping down to grasp a fish in its talons, a black snake warming itself in the sun. There are also canoeing opportunities, kids' exhibits and programs, an enclosed aviary, and special events.

Queenstown

Wye Island Natural Resource Management Area (410-827-7577; www.dnr.state.md.us /publiclands/eastern/wyeisland.asp), 632 Wye Island Rd. Open sunrise–sunset. When Wye Island was threatened with development, many people objected. To prevent future such attempts and to preserve the nature of the locale, the state purchased most of it in the mid-1970s. Because of the foresight of others, a visit here gives you the chance to explore an island that has been used for agricultural purposes for three centuries. The Department of Natural Resources administers the approximately 2,450 acres and still manages them for agricultural uses. There are about 30 miles of shoreline, while virgin stands of timber serve as habitat for the endangered Delmarva fox squirrel. Several short pathways wander through fields, meadows, and woodlands to views of the Chesapeake Bay. If you feel like exploring beyond the trails, you are also permitted to walk the grassy buffer strips between cultivated fields and woodlands.

Ridgely

& **Adkins Arboretum** (410-634-2847; www.adkinsarboretum.org), 12610 Eveland Rd. Daily 10–4. Small admission fee. Many arboretums are artificially created places, but much of the Adkins Arboretum, a part of Tuckahoe State Park, has been left in its natural state. Walking trails, many with informational signs, and service roads wind through the 400 acres of wooded swamps, upland forest, created meadows, and ornamental plantings. The visitors center has maps and information about guided tours. Service roads and some trails could easily be negotiated in a wheelchair.

PARKS

Denton

& **Martinak State Park** (410-820-1688; www.dnr.state.md.us/publiclands /eastern/martinak.asp), 137 Deep Shore Rd. Mid-Mar. through mid-Nov. Most people come to Martinak to take advantage of the boating on the Choptank River and Watts Creek. The 60-site campground has flush toilets and a dump station.

A VIEW FROM THE TRAIL ON WYE ISLAND

Queen Anne

Tuckahoe State Park (410-820-1668; www.dnr.maryland.gov/publiclands /eastern/tuckahoe.asp), 13070 Crouse Mill Rd. About 20 miles east of Wye Mills, and bordered by tranquil wooded swamplands, Tuckahoe Creek forms the dividing line between Queen Anne's and Caroline Counties. Just as it has done with many of its other streams and rivers, the state has wisely protected much of this riparian habitat by establishing 3,700-acre Tuckahoe State Park. Within this tract is a campground with modern facilities, a 60-acre lake providing fishing and canoeing opportunities (canoe rentals available), a ball field, an archery range, and two picnic areas. Naturalist programs are available through spring and summer. All of this is centered in the northern section of the park, which leaves the southern portion—where several pathways wander—undeveloped and natural.

TUCKAHOE LAKE IN TUCKAHOE STATE PARK

Stevensville

🐾 **Island Dog Park** (410-758-0835; www.parksnrec.org), 200 White Pine Lane. When your dog has had enough of being cooped up in the car or tethered to a leash, bring her to the Island Dog Park to romp. Two separate fenced areas keep larger dogs from overwhelming the smaller ones.

🐾 ♿ **Matapeake Trail and Pier** (410-758-0835; www.qac.org), on MD 8 south of US 50 Exit 37. Open dawn–dusk. A small area on the bay operated by Queen Anne's County Parks and Recreation. There is a free public beach (it was the first one in the area), boat ramp, picnic area, fishing pier, and two short pathways—one of them designated as a dog trail. The interesting building that is used for rented events was the depot for the ferry that operated from 1936–1952.

♿ **Terrapin Park Nature Area** (410-758-0835; www.parksnrec.org), 191 Log Canoe Circle. Open dawn–dusk. A nearly level trail winds through meadows, wetlands, and forest on its way to tidal pools and an isolated sandy beach along the bay with a view of the Bay Bridge. A nice place to escape to, and especially quiet during the week. Also a small picnic area and portable restroom facilities.

WALKS ♿ **Cross Island Trail** (410-758-0835; www.parksnrec.org), Stevenville–Kent Narrows. Open dawn–dusk. Completed in 2001, this is one of the nicest things to happen to Kent Island in years. The paved pathway, open to walkers, cyclists, skaters, and wheelchairs, is nearly 6 miles long. Starting at the Terrapin Park Nature Area (see *Parks*) next to the bay, it passes through farmland, small forested areas, meadows, marshes, and beside US 50 to come to an end overlooking Kent Narrows. Access to restrooms, dining, lodging, and the **Chesapeake Heritage and Visitors Center** makes this a great resource that is a part of the American Discovery Trail, which crosses the United States from the Atlantic to the Pacific.

Not quite as scenic, and staying close to MD 8, which it parallels, the **Kent Island South Trail** runs for 8 miles from Matapeake State Park near US 50 to the Pocomoke Pier. It's sometimes in the woods, but most often it is out in the open passing meadows and coming close to private homes. Good for some exercise if you are on this part of the island.

If the above routes are too crowded for you, drive inland to the 2.5-mile (more planned) paved and graveled **Marshyhope Creek and Greenway Trail** in Federalsburg. Used almost exclusively by locals, the paved route runs along its namesake creek, crossing footbridges over wetlands that have been created for erosion control. There is also a fishing dock and canoe launch along the route.

✳ Lodging

MOTELS AND HOTELS

Grasonville, 21638

❦ **Best Western** (410-827-6767; www .bestwesternmaryland.com), 3101 Main St. Nice water views are what set this Best Western apart from the many others in this international chain. Also, this establishment is pet-friendly. $199–219.

⅄ **Hilton Garden Inn Kent Island** (410-827-3877; www.kentisland.stayhgi.com), 3206 Main St. If you are the type that enjoys water views and nice sunsets but don't want to stay in a B&B, consider the Hilton Garden, which overlooks Kent Narrows and the Chesapeake Bay. Those traveling on business should appreciate 24-hour access to computers and printers, along with a fitness facility. $159–209.

⅄ **Holiday Inn Express** (410-827-4454; www.holidaykentisland.com), 1020 Kent Narrows Rd. I'm surprised that the hotel's Web site barely mentions the wonderful bit of waterfront land it sits on with views of the Chester River and Chesapeake Bay (be sure to ask for a water-view room). The pool, tables, and small dock are great places to spend time outside. Business center and complimentary breakfast. $215–225.

❦ **Sleep Inn** (410-827-5555; www .sleepinn.com), 101 VFW Ave. Agreeable rooms with refrigerators, ironing boards, and oversized showers. Continental breakfast, free local calls, and a free scoop of ice cream in the evening. $169–209.

INNS

Stevensville, 21666

❦ **Kent Manor Inn and Restaurant** (410-643-5757; www.kentmanor.com), 500 Kent Manor Dr. This country manor house (circa 1820) has been added onto, providing the inn with 24 guest rooms. It would

be hard to tell which are original, as each room has been constructed and decorated in keeping with the feel of country elegance. All rooms have a private bath, and many feature a fireplace with an Italian marble mantel. The inn's 226 acres invite investigation by the provided bikes and paddleboats, or along the quiet lanes. Many special events and packages available. The restaurant (see *Dining Out*) has a fabulous reputation. $225–275.

BED & BREAKFASTS

Federalsburg, 21632

Idylwild Farm B&B (410-754-9141; www.idylwildfarm.com), 27203 Chipmans Ln. With the house set in the middle of open fields, the views from the two guest rooms take in the large acreages of corn, soybeans, and other products along with that vast amount of Eastern Shore sky. You are welcome to bring your horses (facilities are provided) and take them to nearby public areas for trail rides. $150.

HILTON GARDEN INN KENT ISLAND

Stevensville, 21666

ᕳ Maria's Love Point Bed & Breakfast (410-643-5054; www.bbonline.com/md /mariaslovepoint.com), 1710 Love Point Rd. Lined by a soybean field on one side and a hedgerow on the other, a 0.75-mile driveway delivers you to the striking modern home of Ed and Maria Peffly sitting on 20 acres overlooking the Chester River/Kent Narrows area of the Chesapeake Bay. The couple designed the home, and there's an abundance of public gathering spaces, from the water-view second-floor deck with its two spiral staircases descending to the swimming pool and hot tub, to the quiet library room, to the downstairs bar with a large HD television. There's also a fitness room, pool table, and 850 feet of shoreline from which to dip your toes in the bay. With all of this room to roam, there are only a couple of guest rooms, so you are sure to have some good private conversations with gregarious Ed or soft-spoken Maria. All of this luxury and personal attention, along with a rate of $205, makes this one of the Eastern Shore's most attractive B&Bs.

C A M P I N G Holiday Park (410-482-6797, 1-800-992-6691; www.holidaypark .com), 14620 Drapers Mill Rd., Greensboro. Under the shade of many trees, but located very close together, more than 250 sites with electric and water hook-ups, CATV channels, wi-fi, and more. A number of the sites are located next to the western bank of the narrow headwaters of the Choptank River, providing easy access for fishing or paddling. This is a family-oriented place with numerous planned activities, a swimming pool, and rules ensuring civil behavior. Located less than an hour from Atlantic Ocean beaches.

Also see *Parks.*

✳ Where to Eat

DINING OUT

Denton

Harry's on the Green (410-479-1919; www.harrysonthegreen.com), 4 S. First St.,

Denton. For decades, first in Greensboro and then in Denton, Harry Wyre has been officiating over the front of the restaurant while his wife Jeri has been turning out American cuisine influenced by their travels throughout France. Specials are offered, but the menu contains many items that customers have come to care for and request that they always be available. The orange roughy I had was heavily encrusted with crushed pistachios; the people at the next table shared a brace of roasted quail filled with pate and an entrée of crepes filled with scallops, shrimp, and haddock in a mornay sauce. An extensive wine selection and house-made desserts help make this a special occasion or celebration place. Entrées $25–36.

Stevensville

Kent Manor Inn and Restaurant (410-643-5757), 500 Kent Manor Dr. Reservations required; open only on certain days. Within the setting of four Victorian dining rooms with working fireplaces, Kent Manor offers the area's finest dining. Forgoing other delicious appetizers, start your meal with the lemon pepper calamari dusted with Asiago cheese and served on spicy roasted tomato coulis and chive aioli. You could order crabcakes (market price), twin lobster tails, or wild mushroom chicken penne for dinner. A signature dish is crispy skin rockfish, a fillet of pan-seared wild rockfish served over lobster pureed potatoes, baby rainbow Swiss chard, and topped with fresh pineapple and mango salsa. All I can say is yum! $19–32.

Rustico (410-643-9444; www.rustico online.com), 401 Love Point Rd. Drawing upon the cooking styles of his hometown Naples, Gino Romano provides a menu steeped in the traditions of southern Italy and adapted to make use of local resources. It was obvious by the taste and texture that the buffalo mozzarella on my caprese was made in-house (although I was disappointed with having received only four tiny little leaves of basil with the dish). The marinara in the penne vesuviana had a fresh taste and just the right amount of spices. Based on overheard conversations, the diners at the next table thoroughly enjoyed their seafood and beef selections. Also, Italian wine lovers, rejoice! I counted 90 different wines from Italy among the more than 250 on the list. Entrées $15–30. A four-course menu is offered for $35.

EATING OUT

Denton
The Lily Pad Café (410-479-0700; www .lilypadcafe.net), 104 S. Second St. Open for lunch Mon.–Fri. You may mistake this place for a church as it was originally constructed in 1883 as a schoolhouse built in the Gothic Revival style. With some new twists and combinations, a nice variety of sandwiches and salads are served inside the spacious room with wooden floors. A couple of examples: The Country Apple has ham and apple with apple butter, lettuce, white cheddar, and dijionaise on a butter croissant. The Santa Fe Wrap contains a spring mix, black beans, corn, sweet peppers, avocado, tomatoes, red onion, cheddar, and chipotle mayonnaise. Desserts are homemade; the chocolate cookie is so rich that it almost has the texture of a brownie. $8–10.

Market Street Public House (410-479-4720; www.publichouseonline.com), 200 Market St. With Guinness, Harp, Smithwicke, and Magners on tap and more than two dozen bottled beers, you know this place is serious about providing you some great tasting ales, lagers, and pilsners. Also known for the fish and chips—big enough that two could easily share and still maybe have some left over. Shepherd's pie and Irish stew are also on the menu, along with burgers, wraps, and some seafood entrées. Musical entertainment on the weekend. Entrées $9–18.

Grasonville
Annie's (410-827-7103; www.annies.biz), 500 Kent Narrows Way (US 50/301 Exit 42). At the marina in Kent Narrows, Annie's serves steaks, seafood, and Italian dishes. Entrées $19.99–39.99.

Bridges on Kent Narrows (410-827-0282; www.bridgesrestaurant.com), 321

Wells Cove Rd. There is no doubt that the building that houses Bridges is more upscale than its neighboring waterfront restaurants. (Check out the spectacular wine bottle sculpture of a chandelier.) The menu concentrates on seafood, but again has a distinct personality of its own. The rockfish I had was served with whole grain mustard BBQ, tasso ham, grits, and wilted spinach with roasted corn hollandaise. Designer pizzas, an array of appealing side dishes, and some interesting sandwiches make this the place to visit when you want a festive waterfront atmosphere, but want something more than just a crabcake. $26–33.

☙ ♿ **Fisherman's Inn** (410-827-8807; www.fishermansinn.com), 3116 Kent Narrows Way S. Open daily for lunch and dinner; Sun. brunch. Way back in 1930, decades before the Bay Bridge was constructed and Kent Island became a travel destination, 30-seat Fisherman's Inn was opened in conjunction with a small grocery. It now seats hundreds. If you can't get a water-view seat, ask for one that looks out upon the landscaped garden. Four hundred antique oyster plates and a model train running overhead from one dining room to another add something to look at and talk about. Seafood comes fresh from the adjacent Fisherman's Seafood (see *Seafood Take-Out*). The folks at the table next to me couldn't seem to stop commenting about how good the crab dip served in a bread bowl was. $17–30.

☙ **Holly's** (410-827-8711; www.hollys rest.com), US 50 and Jackson Creek Rd. In business since 1955, Holly's serves home-cooked breakfasts, lunches, and dinners and is the kind of place that everyone ends up at eventually. The Shoreman's Breakfast contains pancakes, eggs, bacon, and sausage. The Shore Special is three pieces of fried chicken and a crabcake. Sandwiches, soups, and homemade ice cream. $12.95–23.95. The children's menu has a choice of almost a dozen items.

☙ **The Narrows Restaurant** (410-827-8113; www.thenarrowsrestaurant.com), 3023 Kent Narrows Way S. Open for lunch and dinner daily; Sun. brunch. A number of locals steered me to the Narrows, in business since 1983, when I inquired about Kent Island's best crabcakes. I certainly was not disappointed when I had one for lunch. The same people said to be sure to sample the mildly spicy gazpacho, available during the warmer months, or the cream of crab during the winter. However, crab is not the only thing. There are other tasty sounding things on the menu, such as Dijon crusted rack of New Zealand lamb, a Cabernet demiglaze beef tenderloin served atop a potato pancake, or a smoked salmon Napoleon. The narrow deck, with heating and air-conditioning, sits directly over the water, so you can watch the boating activity taking place just a few feet away. $23.95–38.95; light dinners available for $15–20.

Ridgely

Ridgely Pharmacy Soda Fountain and Ice Cream Parlor (410-634-1221; www .ridgelypharmacy.net), 7 West Belle St. Open for breakfast, lunch, and dinner Mon.–Sat.; breakfast and lunch only on Sun. Located within a modern building, but with the feel of an old-fashioned soda fountain complete with vinyl-covered stools at a long counter, this is the place to enjoy a hand-dipped milk shake, sundae, or banana split. It's also one of the few places to dine in the immediate area, so maybe also stop in for a BLT, fresh-made chicken salad, or a turkey club sandwich. Ice cream starts at about $2, sandwiches range from $3–5.

Stevensville

Hemingway's (410-604-0999; www .hemingwaysbaybridge.com), 357 Pier One Rd. (US 50/301 Exit 37). Open for lunch and dinner. With one of the most spectacular water views (of the bay and Bay Bridge) of any restaurant on Kent Island, you can sit either in the climate-controlled interior and enjoy the vista through the huge windows or sit outside on an elevated deck or on the patio a few scant feet from the water. Great place to be for sunset. The emphasis is, of course, on seafood, with rockfish, crab, scallops, and salmon featured prominently. Lunch is a little pricey

with sandwiches ranging from $11–17, but consider it the cost of admission for that grand view. Entrées $17–40.

✇ ⅓ **Kentmorr Restaurant** (410-643-2263; www.kentmorr.com), 910 Kentmorr Rd. (US 50/301 Exit 37, south 5 miles on MD 8). Casual dining with a deck and picture windows overlooking the Chesapeake Bay and Kentmorr Harbor Marina. The tuna salad with chunks of fresh fish filled me up for lunch. Dinner selections include flounder, rib-eye steak, and half a rack of ribs with chicken breast. Entrées $18.99–30.99.

✇ ⅓ **R's Americantina** (410-643-7700; www.rsamericantina.com), 410 Thompson Creek Mall. Open for lunch and dinner daily. Known locally as the place to come for margaritas, R's Americantina is a mix of Mexican and American foods, with the burritos, tacos, and other items you would expect to find in such an establishment. I have only dined here once, but I can report that the vegetables in my fajitas were nicely seasoned and crunchy, not overcooked to a limpness and blandness often found in other restaurants. You can have lunch for less than $10, and most dinner dishes are under $23.

CRABS ✇ **Harris Crab House** (410-827-9500; www.harriscrabhouse.com), 433 Kent Narrows Way (US 50/301 Exit 42), Grasonville. The Harris family has been purchasing seafood directly from watermen since 1941 and opened their oystering-paraphernalia-decorated restaurant in 1981. Because it is impossible to find seafood any fresher, it draws many people over the Bay Bridge to devour dozens of steamed and soft-shell crabs (market price) cooked in the Harrises' own hand-tossed spices. The Seafood Basket, with five items and corn, is $38. Rockfish stuffed with crab imperial is $27; other seafood, meat, and chicken entrées $14–29. The Harris family also works with the Chesapeake Bay Foundation and the Oyster Recovery Project to study ways to preserve the waters their restaurant overlooks.

Also see Seafood Take-Out.

SEAFOOD TAKE-OUT Fisherman's Seafood and Crab Deck (410-827-7323; www.crabdeck.com/seafood_market.htm), 3116 Kent Narrows Way S., Grasonville. All items are cleaned and steamed or packed in ice at no extra charge. With a deck that has a party atmosphere right on the water, the restaurant serves a variety of fresh seafood from $21–28.

Hunter's Seafood (410-827-8923), MD 18 and Station Lane, Grasonville. Steamed crabs by the dozen or the bushel. Hunter's also has a complete line of other seafood.

SNACKS AND GOODIES Oh My Chocolate (443-257-1111; www.ohmy chocolate.com), 600A Abruzzi Dr., Chester. Oh my is right. It's just a small shop in a strip mall, but the wonderful variety of handmade chocolates (all natural, by the way) will keep you returning time and again. This place has also elevated the standard for caramel apples—you will never settle for one from any other place again.

✳ Entertainment
NIGHTLIFE
Grasonville
♈ **Fisherman's Crab Deck** (410-827-6666; www.crabdeck.com/crab_deck.htm), 3036 Kent Narrows Way S. Cocktails and live bands on the weekend.

RED EYE'S DOCK BAR

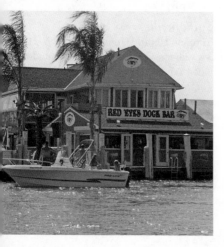

♈ **Red Eye's Dock Bar** (410-827-EYES; www.redeyedockbar.com), 428 Kent Narrows Way N. Open year-round for lunch and dinner. Bright colors, rock 'n' roll music, a full selection of alcoholic beverages, and big crowds make for a definite party atmosphere. Things get even louder and wilder during the summer bikini contests.

THEATERS Church Hill Theatre (410-758-1331; on facebook), 103 Walnut St., Church Hill. Music, plays, films, workshops, and other cultural events are presented inside this art deco theater by professional and amateur groups. Call for schedule.

✳ Selective Shopping
ANTIQUES
Crumpton
Dixon's Furniture (410-928-3006), Dudley Corner Rd. In addition to having an almost incomprehensible amount of antiques, Dixon's holds auctions every Wed. beginning at 9 AM.

Historic Stevensville
Stevensville Antiques (410-643-9533; www.stevensvilleantiques.net), 105 Market Ct. Several dealers of antiques and other collectibles.

Queenstown
J. R.'s (410-827-0555; www.jrsantiques .com), US 301. Open daily. The outlet for a number of dealers.

ART GALLERIES
Centreville
Queen Anne's County Arts Council (410-758-2520; www.arts4u.info), 206 Commerce St. Changing displays of local artisans and craftspeople. Classes, workshops, concerts, lectures, and more.

Denton
The Foundry Gallery & Gifts (410-479-1009; www.carolinearts.org), 401 Market St. Closed Sun.–Mon. The home of the Caroline Council of Arts is housed within the building of a mid-1800s foundry. It will take you a while to wander through the many

rooms of stained glass, fiber arts, paintings, photographs, ceramics, and more. It will take even longer if plans to rehabilitate a number of nearby buildings that will house working artists have come to fruition by time you visit here.

Historic Stevensville

Artists at Work (410-604-1230; www .chesapeakeartleague.org), 109 Cockey Ln. Within the few blocks of Historic Stevensville is a very active artists' colony operating out of a number of outlets and shops. Stop here first, not only to look over the works of several of those artists, but also to talk with gallery owner/artist Jeanne S. Noble so that she can point you in the right direction for other places to browse through.

Kent Island Federation of Art (410-643-7424; www.kifa.us), 405 Main St. Tues.–Fri. 1–4, Sun. noon–4. In addition to featuring works of local artists in its gallery, the federation sponsors art sales, museum exhibits, and dinner-theater bus trips.

My Little Studio & Island Arts (410-604-0721; www.kentislandart.com), 321 Love Point Rd. Closed Mon. It's always enjoyable to walk into galleries such as this. You never know what piece of work will catch your eye or new artist you may discover. Joan McWilliams, who works in paints, pastels, jewelry, and wire in her store's studio, has assembled a nice array of artists, most of whom live on the Eastern Shore.

CRAFTS The Glassburg (410-643-5021), Historic Stevensville. Stroll in and watch stained glass being made and displayed in the studio-gallery.

Paul Reed Smith Guitars (410-643-9970; www.prsguitars.com), 380 Log Canoe Circle, Historic Stevensville. The manufacturing home for the well-known brand of electric guitars. Factory tours are given by reservation Mon.–Wed. at 4.

SPECIAL SHOPS ✍ **Ye Olde Church House** (410-643-6227), 426 Love Point Rd., Stevensville. Fri.–Sun. 10–6. More than just an antiques shop located in a former church. Owner Janet Denny also offers

18th-century crafts items such as hand-spun yarn, handmade soap, herbal vinegars, and dried-flower arrangements. There are also some sheep and goats for children to feed.

OUTLETS Premium Outlets (410-827-8699; www.premiumoutlets.com), at the split of US 50 and 301 N., Queenstown. Outlets for Bass, Liz Claiborne, Brooks Brothers, L. L. Bean, Old Navy, Geoffrey Beene, Pfaltzgraff, and other nationally recognized brands.

PICK-YOUR-OWN PRODUCE FARMS

Centreville

Erickson's Farm (410-758-1655), 171 Strawberry Ln. U-pick strawberries in-season.

Stevensville

✍ **Kent Fort Farm** (410-643-1650), 10 miles south of US 50 via MD 8 to Kent Point Rd. Mid-Apr. through Oct., Tues.–Sun. Berries, fruit, and pumpkins. Also the site of the annual **Peach Festival** in August, with a petting zoo, hay- and pony-cart rides, face painting, and homemade peach ice cream.

Sudlersville

G. H. Godfrey Farms (410-438-3501), 130 Blueberry Ln. Strawberries (mid-May through mid-June) and blueberries (late June through late July).

WINERIES

Sudlersville

Tilmans Island Winery (443-480-5021; www.tilmonswine.com), 755 Millington Rd. Open Sat. Welcome to the one-man winery. There's a small demonstration vineyard that owner Don Tilman will take you through to describe the process of taking care of grapes, but almost all of his fruit is purchased from vineyards within a 20-mile radius. He does all of the work himself—and even corks each bottle with a hand corking device. The tasting room is all of two seats big. A different experience from visiting an acres-encompassing vineyard with a banquet hall tasting room.

Church Hill

Cassinelli Winery & Vineyards (410-556-6825; www.cassinelliwinery.com), 3830 Church Hill Rd. Fri.–Sun. Al Cassinelli is the overseer of a major operation—10,000 grapevines and 1,000 fruit trees growing on a 110-acre farm, more than 20,000 bottles of wine that has matured in French oak barrels, and tours for the public that go into the vineyard to learn the vintner's art. According to Cassinelli, "It's the vines that are the art" of winemaking. He's so attuned to his vines and the soil in which they grow that he can tell by taste where in his vineyard a particular grape grew.

✳ Special Events

March: **Annual Artists of the Chesapeake Art Auction** (410-758-2520), Chesapeake College, Wye Mills.

April: **Tuckahoe Easter Egg Hunt** (410-820-1668), Tuckahoe State Park, Queen Anne. The Eastern Shore's largest Easter egg hunt. **Spring Festival** (410-758-1419), Centreville. Tractor pulls and other activities; also quilting, weaving, chair caning, and other crafts.

May: **Annual Open-Judged Art Show** (410-643-7424), Stevensville. **Annual Bay Bridge Walk** (1-877-BAY-SPAN). The one day of the year when people are permitted to walk across the 4.3-mile span. Strollers and wheelchairs allowed. A big event on both sides of the bay that attracts close to 50,000 people. My wife was the first person to walk across the bridge and back during the first bridge walk several decades ago. **Waterfowl Weekend** (410-643-7226), Chesapeake Bay Environmental Center, Grasonville. Carving competition, exhibits, food, and vendors inside the 500-acre preserve. **Kent Island Days** (410-643-5969), Stevensville. Commemorating the 1631 founding of the island's settlement with historic displays, entertainment, food, crafts, and an 18th-century encampment.

June: **Waterman's Festival** (410-604-2100), Grasonville. Celebrates the waterman's livelihood with docking and anchor-throwing contests, crab races, children's activities, food, and entertainment. **Annual Tuckahoe Triathlon** (410-820-1668), Tuckahoe State Park. A 10-mile bike ride, 2-mile run, and 1-mile canoe course. **Wheat Harvest Fair** (410-822-1910), Wye Mills. A festival celebrating the ways of the past. Oxcart rides, blacksmiths, woodworkers, candle makers, and more. Colonial and Civil War reenactments.

July: **Annual Fireman's Carnival** (410-604-0650), Kent Island. Held annually for more than six decades.

August: **Queen Anne's County Fair** (410-758-0267), Centreville. **Annual Peach Festival** (410-643-1650) at Kent Fort Farm in Stevensville. **Caroline-Dorchester County Fair** (www.caroline-dorchester countyfair.org), Denton. **Wheat Threshing Steam & Gas Engine Show** (www .threshermen.org), Federalsburg. Antique equipment, tractor games, parades, and live entertainment.

September: **Annual Rockfish Tournament** (410-643-8530), Kentmorr Harbor Marina, Stevensville. **Wetlands Fest** (410-827-6694), Chesapeake Bay Environmental Center, Grasonville. Games, exhibits, live-animal programs, hiking, and bird-watching.

October: **Annual Country Fair** (410-758-0620), Gunston Day School, Centreville. Children's games, dog show, baked goods, and more.

December: **Heck with the Malls!** (410-758-2520), Centreville. This annual event provides an alternative to mall shopping for mass-produced goods. The crafts show and townwide open house feature crafts, artists' tables, and opportunities to meet the creative talents.

CHESTERTOWN AND ROCK HALL

The word *quaint* is found so often in travel books that I resist using it. However, in the case of Chestertown I must break my hesitancy. For *quaint* is certainly the right word to describe a place with an Italianate-style courthouse, a hotel that has managed to hang on to its early-20th-century attractiveness, and one after another of stately and well-maintained Victorian homes. The downtown has not been abandoned, turned over to national chain stores, or relegated to parking buildings. Rather, you will find small, independently owned shops, businesses, and restaurants lining laid-brick sidewalks.

There are so many buildings of historic and architectural significance that it takes six columns of a walking-tour brochure (available from the Kent County Office of Tourism and Economic Development—see *Guidance*) to briefly describe them. The town is also home to a college, but not one of those huge universities that takes over the character of a place. Washington College has barely more than 1,300 students and blends in so well because much of its campus is a maintained arboretum.

The Chester River does not figure in economic importance, as it did several centuries ago when Chestertown was a Royal Port of Entry and later the center of an agricultural and seafood area shipping its wares by steamboat. Although watermen still pursue catches within its waters, it is now a stream of pleasure for recreational boaters and sailors—or just plain beautiful scenery when viewed from the town dock or the riverside Wilmer Park.

Rock Hall is one of the few places on the Eastern Shore that has been able to hit a balance in preserving its traditional watermen's way of life while providing the amenities and attractions travelers want and need. In fact, you can observe this balance every day during summer when visitors gather in Rock Hall Harbor about 5 PM to watch the watermen unload their daily catches. Less than an hour later, the crowd moves over to the Harbor Shack's dock to witness the charter boats bring in the sportfishermen's trophies of the day.

A small watermen's museum provides a glimpse of what it once took to survive this rugged occupation, while a drugstore is a reminder of what many small towns in America were like in the early 1900s.

As befits a town bordered on three sides by water, Rock Hall has numerous marinas catering to recreational boaters, dozens of charter-boat captains, and sailing-excursion operators. The many waterfront restaurants serve up the fresh catches of the day.

COMMUNITIES **Betterton** was a thriving beach resort in the days of steamboat travel. Although visitors are now far fewer in number, its small beach remains the only place in the Chesapeake Bay that you can swim without fear of brushing up against a sea nettle (jellyfish).

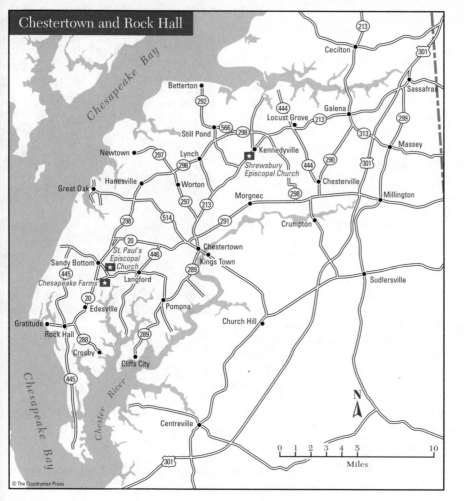

The site of a silver mine before the War of 1812, **Galena** is a small crossroads town with a number of antiques shops and stores. Its dogwood-tree-lined streets come aglow with pink and white blossoms in spring.

GUIDANCE The **Kent County Visitors Center** (410-778-9737) is located at 122 N. Cross St. in Chestertown and is open daily. The **Kent County Office of Tourism and Economic Development** (410-778-0416; www.kentcounty.com) has an office at 400 High St., Chestertown, 21620.

GETTING THERE *By car:* **US 301** crosses in a north–south direction in the eastern part of the area, while the smaller **MD 213** swings to the west to pass through Chestertown.

By air: The nearest and largest airport with scheduled flights is **Baltimore/Washington International Thurgood Marshall Airport** (1-800-I-FLY-BWI; www.bwiairport.com), located between Baltimore and Annapolis.

By water: If you have your own boat, the Chesapeake Bay, of course, is the way to get to the area; the Chester and Sassafras Rivers give you access to inland waters.

GETTING AROUND *By car:* **US 301** and **MD 213** are the major thoroughfares. However, **MD 298** parallels MD 213 several miles to the north, has much less traffic, and passes through some beautiful countryside. **MD 20** is the major link between Chestertown and Rock Hall.

By tram: The **Blue Crab Crawler** (443-282-5092) and **Osprey Flyer** (443-282-5058). General information on www.rock hallmd.com. It's a fun ride, as its passengers are a good mix of locals and visitors. $1 per person per ride or a season pass for $35 per household, slip holder, or visitor. Schedule varies by the season.

A CHESTERTOWN SIDEWALK

PARKING There are three lots in Chestertown, two accessed from Cannon St. and one in Wilmer Park, in which you can park for free seven days a week. The meters along the streets have a two-hour limit but are free from Thanksgiving to New Year's Day.

PUBLIC RESTROOMS The public is free to use the restrooms in Chestertown's library on High St., the courthouse on Cross St., the Kent County Visitors Center, and the town hall at the corner of Cross St. and Maple Ave.

MEDICAL EMERGENCY **Chester River Hospital Center** (410-778-3300; www .chesterriverhealth.org), 100 Brown St., Chestertown.

✹ To See

COLLEGES **Washington College** (410-778-2800; www.washcoll.edu), 300 Washington Ave., Chestertown. Washington College was founded in 1782, making it the first college chartered after the founding of the United States, the oldest in Maryland, and the 10th oldest in the country. It is named for George Washington, who visited the institution in 1784. A walk on campus takes you through the **Virginia Gent Decker Arboretum** and by several buildings dating from the early 1800s. Lectures, exhibits, and other entertainment are presented in the **Gibson Performing Arts Center.**

MUSEUMS

Chestertown
Geddes-Piper House (410-778-3499; www.kentcountyhistory.org), 101 Church Alley. Small admission fee; children under 10 free. Sat. 1–4 May–Oct. and Tues.–Fri. 10–4 all year. The only 18th-century home in Chestertown open to the public on a regular basis. Guided tours bring you to each room of the house to appreciate the slate fireplaces, original kitchen utensils in the basement, and changing exhibits reflecting the region's history. The Victorian room

with a number of quilts, the children's room with a dollhouse, and the fan collection make
for interesting examinations.

Kennedyville

Kent Museum (410-778-9737), 13675 Turner's Creek Rd. Open first and third Sat. of each
month noon–3; donations accepted. Two large metal farm buildings house a collection of
agricultural equipment donated by local people. There are wagons from yesteryear, the first
tractor to bear the John Deere name, a couple of large threshers, and household items from
the late 1800s. One of the more interesting displays contains a number of fabric figurines
handmade by Betty Stirling. A 0.5-mile nature trail runs from the museum though the woods
to an overlook of Turner's Creek.

Rock Hall

Waterman's Museum (410-778-6697; www.havenharbour.com), 20880 Rock Hall Ave. Free
admission. If the museum is not open, you can obtain the key from the Haven Harbor
Marina's Ditty Bag shop next door. Exhibits on oystering, crabbing, and fishing, with carvings
and a reproduction of a shanty house. It's a small museum, but that makes it easy to see
everything; many items donated by local watermen.

Tolchester Beach Revisited (410-778-5347; www.rockhallmd.com), 21341 Virginia Ave.
Sat. and Sun. 11–3; closed Jan.–Feb. A small museum put together by Bill Betts, containing
memorabilia from the Tolchester Beach Amusement Park, which was a popular resort from
1877 to the mid-1900s.

HISTORIC CHURCHES

Chestertown

St. Paul's Episcopal Church (410-778-1540; www.stpaulkent.org), 7579 Sandy Bottom Rd.,
accessed from MD 20 between Chestertown and Rock Hall. The parish was established in
1693. The present building, with a semicircular apse and Flemish-bond brickwork, dates
from 1713, making it one of the oldest continuously used churches in the state. Wander
around the 19-acre churchyard shaded by boxwood trees, and you will find the final resting
place of actress Tallulah Bankhead.

Emmanuel Episcopal Church (410-778-3477; www.emmanuelchesterparish.org), Cross
St. and Park Row. Built in 1767, the large, two-story nave measures 66 feet by 44 feet. Also
take note of the Tiffany window on the south wall, and the bell tower, which was added in
1905.

Kennedyville

Shrewsbury Episcopal Church (540-
0348-5944; www.shrewsburyparish.org),
MD 213. Completed in 1832, this building
was constructed using bricks from one of
the earlier churches built on this site in
1722. The churchyard dates from the Revolutionary War and contains the graves of
veterans from all U.S. wars. Of particular
note is the grave of Revolutionary War hero
Brig. Gen. John Cadwalader.

SCENIC DRIVES Chesapeake
Farms (410-778-8400; www2.dupont
.com/Production_Agriculture/en_US
/knowledge_center/ChesapeakeFarms

AGRICULTURAL EQUIPMENT DISPLAYED AT
THE KENT MUSEUM

.html), 7319 Remington Dr. (off MD 20 between Chestertown and Rock Hall), Chestertown. Open during daylight hours, mid-Apr. to Oct. 10. Free admission. A brochure, available in a box along the drive, is keyed to different signed stops along the way on this 3,300-acre farm. From it you will learn how the ponds, fields, hedgerows, and forests are designed to develop, evaluate, and demonstrate agricultural and wildlife management techniques. It should easily take less than an hour if you stop to read everything (you must stay in your car), but it is still a worthwhile drive if you just want to enjoy the scenery.

A section of Maryland's first **National Scenic Byway** follows portions of MD 20, MD 213, and MD 445.

Also see the **Eastern Neck Wildlife Refuge** sidebar on page 143.

✳ To Do

BICYCLING Maps of a number of bicycle tours in Kent County using lightly traveled roads are available from the **Kent County Office of Tourism and Economic Development** and the **Kent County Visitors Center.**

Chestertown

Chester River Outfitters (410-778-6940; www.chesterriverbikeandpaddle.com), 210 South Cross St. Bicycle, kayak, and other boat rentals in addition to sales, service, and tours.

BOAT CHARTERS Gratitude Yachting Center (410-639-7111; www.gratitude yachting.com), 5990 Lawton Ave., Rock Hall. Boats of varying shapes and sizes are available for charter by the day or week. Since you are your own captain and crew, you must provide some evidence of your sailing proficiency.

FISHING CHARTERS As seems natural for an area close to so much water, there are many captains who take sportfishermen out onto the bay and local rivers. In Rock Hall, among the many are **Capt. Bob Ritchie** (410-639-7063; www.fishfearus.com), **Capt. Jimmy Price** (410-708-6076; www.fishhunt.net), **Capt. Larry Simns** (410-639-2966; www .dawnii.com), and **Capt. Greg Jetton** (410-639-7127; www.gunsmokecharters.com).

The Kent County Office of Tourism and Economic Development can provide a listing of many other Coast Guard–certified charter operators. The amount of fishing time and fees vary greatly, so be sure to check specifically how long your trip is, what is provided, and the total costs.

HORSEBACK RIDING ✍ **Kent Equestrian Center** (410-778-1881; www.kent equestrian.com), Morgnec Rd., Chestertown. Trail rides, pony rides, and hayrides.

KAYAKING AND CANOEING ✍ **Chester River Kayak Adventures** (410-639-2001; www.crkayakadventures.com), 5758 Main St., Rock Hall. In operation Apr.–Thanksgiving. These folks not only provide kayak lessons but also lead guided tours upon the local waters for individuals or groups. The half-day tour is $50, or $40 for children; the full-day tour is $90, or $75 for children; and the sunset trip is $40, or $32 for children. The ecotours always include at least one beach walk. It would be wise to make reservations to ensure your time and place. Sales and rentals are also available, along with packages enabling you to stay in one of the company's B&Bs.

SAILING Blue Crab Chesapeake Charters (410-708-1803; www.bluecrabcharters .com), docked at the foot of Sharp St., Rock Hall. Capt. Mark Einstein takes up to six passengers out on the *Crab Imperial* into the open Chesapeake Bay for 90-minute cruises. The sunset cruises are the most popular.

SAILING LESSONS Maryland School of Sailing and Seamanship (410-639-7030; www.mdschool.com), 22978 McKinleyville Rd., Rock Hall. From Basic Sailing through Ocean Touring Courses, the school can turn any landlubber into an old salt in just a few lessons. Students can become certified by the American Sailing Association. All classes last at least a few days; fees vary. You can take your classes on the bay or travel to exotic locations, such as the Caribbean, with the school.

SWIMMING ✑ The swimming pools in small county-operated parks in Millington, Worton, and Rock Hall are open to the public Memorial Day–Labor Day.

Eastern Neck National Wildlife Refuge (410-639-7056; www.fws.gov/northeast/eastern neck), 1730 Eastern Neck Rd., Rock Hall. Open year-round. From October through mid-March, thousands of migratory waterfowl winter in the Chesapeake Bay region, many of them on this 2,285-acre refuge. The most common species that have been documented here include as many as 20,000 Canada geese, more than 7,000 tundra swans, over 15,000 canvasback ducks, and an assortment of thousands of others—such as mallards, wigeons, pintails, and buffleheads. Seen throughout much of the year are great blue herons, great and snowy egrets, turkey vultures, ospreys, and bald eagles. In addition, close to 250 other species—ranging from common bluebirds and chickadees to rarely observed peregrine falcons and American woodcocks—have been identified.

Why else should you come here? How about a couple of short trails where you might see white-tailed deer, diamondback terrapins, muskrats, beavers, red foxes, eastern gray squirrels, and the endangered Delmarva fox squirrel? Or sift your hands through mounds of huge shells of oysters shucked by Native Americans more than a millennium ago. Then again, you could come to the refuge just for the quiet beauty of a typical Chesapeake Bay landscape of marshes, croplands, loblolly forests, and grass fields surrounded by sun-speckled water.

Getting to Eastern Neck National Wildlife Refuge can be an enjoyable outing in itself—the federal and state governments consider the drive to be so picturesque that it has been designated as part of Maryland's only **National Scenic Byway.** The island can be reached by leaving MD 213 in Chestertown and driving southward on MD 20 for nearly 13 miles to Rock Hall. Turn left onto MD 445 and cross the bridge onto the island 6 miles later.

A BOARDWALK STRETCHES OVER THE MARSH AT EASTERN NECK NWR.

TENNIS Public courts in Worton are available on a first-come, first-served basis in Worton Park.

✳ Green Space

ARBORETUMS **Virginia Gent Decker Arboretum** (410-778-7726; 1-800-422-1782, ext. 7726; www.arboretum.washcoll.edu), Washington College campus, Chestertown. The arboretum was established in 1996 and is based upon the model found at George Washington's Mount Vernon. Building upon the existing trees and shrubs, the college is continually adding to their number and diversity. Although many of the plants are marked by identifying labels, your experience will be enhanced if you pick up an arboretum brochure in Dunning Hall off Campus Ave.

BEACHES **Rock Hall**'s small beach has great sunsets framed by the Bay Bridge to the southwest.

A 3.2-acre sandy beach in **Betterton** is the only swimming area on all of the Chesapeake Bay side of the Eastern Shore that is free of stinging jellyfish. There is also a fishing jetty, boat ramp, and bathhouse. Lifeguards are on duty on Sat. and Sun. during the usual swimming season, but even then the number of people is rather light.

NATURE PRESERVES **Sassafras River Natural Resource Management Area** (410-820-1668; www.dnr.state.md.us/publiclands/eastern/sassafras.asp), on MD 448 about 3 miles north of Kennedyville. Open sunrise–sunset. This area contains close to 1,000 acres of farmland, marshes, forests, beaches, and tidal pools whose access is limited to those on foot, bicycle, or horseback. Expect to see lots of waterfowl, deer, beaver, and maybe a bald eagle. The adjoining Turner's Creek is a recreation area with a public boat ramp, fishing, and picnic facilities. If time permits, do not miss the historic tree grove and farm museum.

PARKS **Wilmer Park** is Chestertown's waterfront park on the Chester River and is just one block from the historic district.

WALKS The *Walking Tour of Historic Chestertown* pamphlet (available from the Chesapeake Heritage and Visitors Center—see *Guidance*) provides historic notes as well as architectural details on two dozen buildings and sites.

✳ Lodging

MOTELS AND HOTELS

Chestertown, 21620

The Imperial Hotel (410-778-500; 1-800-295-0014; www.imperialchestertown.com), 208 High St. Built in 1903, the Imperial has been renovated to give it modern amenities but retain its earlier charm. Its double verandas—one on the first floor, the other on the second—are inviting spots to sit and watch the world go by. All of the deluxe guest rooms ($150) have a private bath and are decorated with period furnishings. The Parlor Suite ($190) occupies the entire third floor and has its own veranda. (Also see *Dining Out.*)

INNS

Chestertown, 21620

🐾 ♫ **Brampton Inn** (410-778-1860; 1-866-305-1860; www.bramptoninn.com), 25227 Chestertown Rd. The Brampton Inn is only five minutes from Chestertown, but its 20 acres of gardens and forest provide a quiet and secluded setting. There is a lot of luxury packed into a stay at this place, which was once operated as a peach plantation and whose owner was the largest slave owner in the area. All of the large guest rooms have operating fireplaces, many offer a whirlpool tub, and all guests have privileges at the nearby country club. Of the rooms in the

BRAMPTON INN

Manor House, I enjoyed the Blue Room the most, as it is bright and sunny, and its second-floor location lets you watch the wildlife go by in the treetops. There is always an array of delicious homemade cookies available, and you could while away many hours on the porch looking at the centuries-old trees and enjoying the breezes of the overhead fans. The several guest cottages are even more deluxe, with flat-screen TVs, large soaking tubs, and private screened porches. Children over 12 are permitted, as are pets (in one of the cottages; hefty additional fee). Rooms in the Manor House are $200–270; cottages $290–430.

Georgetown, 21930

Kitty Knight House (410-648-5200; www .kittyknight.com), 14028 Augustine Herman Hwy. (US 301). In 1813, when the British were torching many Eastern Shore towns, Kitty Knight convinced them to spare the two houses (one was the home of an invalid friend) that now make up the inn, with 11 guest rooms, and restaurant (see *Dining Out*). Some overlook the activity of the harbor on the Sassafras River; all have private bath. Room 1 is the largest; it has its original pine floors and a private deck. Room 5 may be smaller, but it still has a water view and a lower rate. Breakfast in the restaurant is included. $115–180.

Rock Hall, 21661

☘ **Black Duck Inn** (410-708-9222; www .blackduckinn-rockhall.com), 21096 Chesa-

peake Ave. Built by a waterman, Captain Carter, more than one hundred years ago, the inn has a welcoming homey atmosphere with the screened porch and three of the guest rooms having views of the harbor. The Brice Room, where pets are permitted has its own entrance. A dock is available for those who arrive by boat. The Loft is a one bedroom apartment for those who desire more privacy. $130–165.

High Tide Inn (410-778-6697; www.the hightideinn.com), 20828 Rock Hall Ave. Operated by Haven Harbor Marina, the original waterman's home has been modernized, with the kitchen available for guest use. All five of the guest bedrooms have a nautical theme and down comforters, with the downstairs Buckey Room being large and bright. The upstairs Winifred and Maybelle rooms share a bath. Guests have access to the marina's amenities including free use of kayaks, bicycles, and a swimming pool. $110–160.

The Inn at Osprey Point (410-639-2194; www.ospreypoint.com), 20786 Rock Hall Ave. It almost looks like a modern-day hotel when you drive up, but each of the seven guest rooms is nicely decorated. Some overlook the water and marina, while others have a view of the woods. $150–290. The inn's restaurant (see *Dining Out*) draws people from many miles around. Also operated by the marina, **The Annex at Gratitude Marina** is located within a working marina, so don't expect the prettiest of grounds, but once you get on the porch or inside one of The Annex's rooms, you will have views of the Chesapeake Bay (sunsets are pretty spectacular from here). I really enjoyed having lots of room to spread out in my spacious and nicely decorated room.

☘ ✍ **Tallulahs** (410-639-2596; www .tallulahsonmain.com), 5750 Main St. Hosts Barry E. Barr and Jim Messesmith have refurbished this historic late-1800s building, which has been a hotel, inn, or boardinghouse for decades. A good spot for families or those having an extended stay in the area. Each efficiency room (named for significant things in Tallulah Bankhead's life) has a private bath, fully equipped kitchen, and television. Suites include a bedroom, living room, and kitchen. The deck on the second floor is a nice play to lounge, enjoy the scent of magnolia tree blossoms, and cool off with the breezes coming from the bay. Children and pets permitted. $135–155.

BED & BREAKFASTS

Chestertown, 21620

Great Oak Manor (410-778-5943; 1-800-504-3098; www.greatoakmd.com), 10568 Cliff Rd. Constructed in the 1930s, this manor house, surrounded by 12 acres, has the mien of an older Georgian mansion. Lots of common areas, a wonderful library with many good books, a grand staircase, and a private beach on the Chesapeake Bay. All guest rooms have a private bath and are appropriately decorated. $190–315.

❧ **The Inn at Mitchell House** (410-778-6500; www.innatmitchellhouse.com), 8796 Maryland Pkwy. An oft-returning guest told me that he has been coming to this B&B for so long that he has watched the hosts' children go from basically the cradle to college and beyond. Through the years, Jim and Tracy Stone have learned what their guests are looking for and are still happy to provide a relaxing place for travelers. Located in the country a few miles from Chestertown, their home was built in two parts; one around 1735 and the other in 1825. All five guest rooms have private bath, and a one-bedroom guest cottage has a nice fireplace and a private deck. All guests have access to the private beach and facilities of the Tolchester Marina on the Chesapeake Bay. $109–149; cottage $250.

❧ **Lauretum Inn** (410-778-3236; 1-800-742-3236; www.lauretuminn.com), 945 High St. Constructed in 1881 and listed on the National Register of Historic Places, Lauretum sits on a 6-acre tree-covered knoll on the outskirts of town. All rooms have a private bath, and there are a couple of suites ($130–160). Well-behaved children are welcome, and those under 10 are free.

Simply Bed and Bread (410-778-4359; www.simplybedandbread.com), 208 Mount Vernon Ave. Staying here is just like visiting mom and dad. Cheryl and David Hoopes raised their family in this home, family pictures adorn the walls, and the two guest rooms are the ones in which their daughters grew up. Cheryl has stocked a butler's pantry full of things you may have forgotten, including an extra sweatshirt, and the bathrooms have nice touches like homemade soap. Just like mom, Cheryl will not let you ever get hungry, from bountiful breakfasts (she calls one with omelets and homemade cinnamon rolls along with several other items a "continental" breakfast) to homemade snacks available any hour of the day. The location is just a few minutes' walk from just about everything in Chestertown. $149.

White Swan Tavern Bed & Breakfast (410-778-2300; www.whiteswantavern .com), 231 High St. There is a true sense of history to this B&B. Located within the commercial district of town, it dates from the mid-1700s and is furnished with period pieces. It also retains most of the original flooring, window jambs, and trim. All of the four guest rooms and two suites have interesting histories and features. The T. W. Eliason Victorian Suite is on the second floor and has many little twists and turns taking you through the two bedrooms and large parlor. The Thomas Lovegrove Kitchen Room retains the original brick floor and open-beam ceiling. The Thomas Peacock Room is the smallest, but I felt that its canopy double bed and window overlooking the backyard garden gave it the most character. There may be history, but modern conveniences aren't lacking. Each room has its own bath, afternoon tea is served daily, and you stay comfortable with central heating and air-conditioning. As the host told me, "The tavern has seen the world from quill pen to wireless Internet." $150–250.

❧ **Widow's Walk** (410-778-6455; 1-888-778-6455; www.chestertown.com/widow), 402 High St. Built around 1877, the Victorian Widow's Walk is named for the lookout on its roof on which fishermen's wives would stand looking for their husbands to come home from the bay or sea. Innkeepers Bob and Sue Lathroum have made the home a genial place to stay by placing family treasures among the antique furnishings. All three suites have a sitting area and private bath; the two upstairs rooms share a bath. Its central location makes it easy to walk just about anywhere in Chestertown. $120–165.

Galena, 21635
Carousel Horse B&B (410-648-5476; www.carrouselhorsebnb.com), 145 N. Main St. Built by a physician in the 1880s, the home recalls a time when gracious living was the rage. The hosts have retained many of the house's best features, including several sitting rooms, one with a piano, and a screened porch. All guest rooms have private bath. The quiet town of Galena belies its location just 1 mile from the Sassafras River and proximity to large cities just an hour or so drive from the colonial style home. $105–120.

Kennedyville, 21645
Crow Farmstay B&B and Vineyard (410-648-5687; www.crowfarmmd.com), 12441 Vansants Rd. Experience true Eastern Shore farm life. Roy Crow, who grew up on the 365-acre farm (in fact, one of the guest rooms was his boyhood room), along with his wife Judy, offers three guest rooms in the 1847 farmhouse. Each of the rooms

A VIEW OF THE POOL AT CROW FARMSTAY B&B AND VINEYARD

is furnished with family heirlooms and has a private bath. My room overlooked the barn; the Pasture View, naturally, overlooks the farm's expanse; and the Vineyard View takes in the rows of grapes. The bountiful breakfast includes many items from the farm including fresh eggs, smoked ham, and homegrown tomatoes. Enjoy a walk on the grounds, swim in the outdoor pool, or sip one of the wines under the shade of a willow tree. Better yet, get up early in the morning to help with the farm chores. My time here was way too short. $145.

Rock Hall, 21611
Bay Breeze Inn (410-639-2061; www.baybreezinn.com), 5758 Main St. Centrally located in the downtown business district, the home's two front rooms overlook Main St., and the back room has a view of the backyard with its small fish pond. The upstairs suite is all wood and has angles that made me feel like I was in a sailboat cabin. If you want more privacy, opt for the Carriage House and interesting wooden cupola. The inn is operated by the owners of Chesapeake River Kayak Adventures (see *Kayaking and Canoeing*), and they offer a number of kayaking/B&B package deals. $95–150; Carriage House $150.

🐾 ✍ **Inn at Huntingfield Creek** (410-639-7779; www.huntingfield.com), 4928 Eastern Neck Rd. Good reasons to decide to stay here: 70 acres on which to roam; a short pathway through field and forest to a dock overlooking Huntingfield Creek; wildflower gardens surrounding an in-ground pool; a rich wood library full of good books and complimentary drinks; a grand piano on which to keep up your practicing while away from home. All guest rooms have private bath and are decorated with their own themes, and the cottages, set among fields of sunflowers, have Jacuzzis and two-sided fireplaces. The hosts understand what it is to pamper you and use the expertise from a catering business to prepare sumptuous breakfasts. Children and pets are permitted, too. $195–215.

✍ **Moonlight Bay and Marina** (410-639-2660; www.moonlightbayinn.com), 6002

Lawton Ave. Each of the five rooms in the Main Inn has a private bath and a view of the Chesapeake Bay. The Garden Moon Room and Blue Moon Room are the ones that caught my fancy. The West Wing, built in 1997, is even closer to the water and offers five rooms decorated in a Victorian Queen Anne style, each with its own whirlpool tub. Rooms 8 and 9 have the most spectacular views, and a private beach is available for guest use. $160–200.

☀ ✿ Spring Cove Manor (410-639-2061; www.springcovemanor.com), 21060 Spring Cove Rd. Less than 1 mile from town and sitting on 8 acres, this renovated farm home's front porch overlooks Spring Cove. This is a good choice for those who like to kayak, as you can launch right from the 200-foot waterfront. It's also a good choice if you are taking a tour with Chester River Kayak Adventures, as they own the manor and offer a number of package deals for kayaking and lodging with them. $130–160. A separate cottage can accommodate up to five people and rents for $320.

COTTAGES & VACATION RENTALS

Chestertown, 21620

Historic in-Town House (410-778-4526; www.vrbo.com), 407 High St. The 1760 (back of the house) and 1840 (front of the house) home has been so updated that it meets LEED standards, but kept many of the original elements including the wooden floors and original "wavy" glass. The three bedrooms can accommodate up to seven guests, while everything you need to live well for a week is provided. $2,200 a week; weekends are sometimes available on request.

Rock Hall, 21611

Tallulah's on the Beach (410-639-2596; www.tallulahsonmain.com), 5783 Beach Rd. Nothing fancy here—modern furniture in a mid-1900s-style small cottage. But it can accommodate four adults, has spectacular views of Chesapeake Bay sunsets, and is across the street from Rock Hall Beach. Available for $300 a night or $1,500 a week.

✳ Where to Eat

DINING OUT

Chestertown

Blue Heron Café (410-778-0188; www.blueheroncafe.com), 236 Cannon St. Open for lunch and dinner, Mon.–Sat. After running restaurants in New York and California, and the Byard House for the Du Pont family in Chesapeake City, Paul Hanley opened his own place in Chestertown. Building upon local seafood and produce, his recipes let the tastes come through while leaving your mouth feeling refreshed and clean. The smoked salmon is a good appetizer for dinner but is large enough to be served as a lunch entrée. The lump crab frittata is also great for lunch, but if you come here for dinner, do not overlook the cioppino. This stew is packed with lobster, mussels, clams, shrimp, crab, and finfish in an herb and tomato broth. Meat entrées include veal sweetbreads and grilled bavette steak. Dinner entrées $20–30.

✿ Fish Whistle (410-788-3566; www.fishandwhistle.com), 98 Cannon St. Open for lunch and dinner daily. A popular place with the pleasure boaters, as there is free use of a slip for diners, and the bar menu is served until midnight. Although this place has the feel of typical waterside crab house, the menu features some unexpected items, with just about everything made from scratch. Summer offerings have included pan-seared duck breast with mango, lime, and chili jus, and an herb crusted rack of lamb with mushroom risotto. The cucumber and mint soup I started my meal with was very refreshing. Desserts are made in-house. Live music, karaoke, and DJs. Entrées $19–28.

Harbor House Restaurant (410-778-0669; www.harborhousewcm.com), Buck Neck Rd. at Worton Harbor. Dinner only; closed Mon. Out in the boonies, a cinder-block building and a gravel parking lot cluttered with old boats mask some of the Eastern Shore's finest dining. The chef is a graduate of the Culinary Institute of America.

A BUSY LUNCHTIME AT THE FISH WHISTLE

Meals begin with baked breads ranging from dinner rolls to cranberry bread to chocolate bread. The crab imperial is by far the most delicious, and different, that I've had. Huge lumps of crab are baked atop a flavorful and light sauce. The menu changes daily, but representative entrées include filet mignon, rubbed spareribs, and scallops served with a crispy casino and bacon topping. The crabcakes are all crab with just a light seasoning. Once you've had the homemade tiramisu, you will never again order what the Olive Garden serves up as authentic. $23–36.

Imperial Hotel (410-778-5000; www.imperialchestertown.com), 208 High St. Open for lunch and dinner Tues.–Sat. and Sun. brunch. Quality food in turn-of-the-20th-century elegance. Start with the oyster potpie or sautéed crabcake and move on to the veal schnitzel or the lollipop lamb chop. $18–34.

Georgetown
Kitty Knight House (410-648-5200; www.kittyknight.com), 14028 Augustine Herman Hwy. (US 301). One of big draws here is the commanding view of the Sassafras River. One of the other draws is the variety of items that have shown up on the menu.

Depending on when you dine, you may have a choice of seafood jambalaya, baked flounder roulade, chicken Gruyère, a chicken and oysters potpie, or a pork osso buco and chicken breast grilled with a peach-honey barbecue sauce. $15–30. Live music on the awning-covered deck Fri. and Sat. nights, with more laid-back acoustic music presented Sun. afternoon.

Rock Hall
Osprey Point Restaurant (410-639-2762; www.ospreypoint.com), 20786 Rock Hall Ave. Open for dinner Wed.–Sat. Closed Jan. A warm and romantic colonial atmosphere seems like the right setting for the restaurant's traditional dishes, enhanced for modern palates. Oysters Osprey, with prosciutto, crab, spinach, and sherry sauce, is the signature appetizer. The fillet of beef is topped with a Madeira–wild mushroom demiglaze. Duck breast, rockfish with a bourbon maple butter sauce, and crabcakes are other entrée choices. Expect to spend about $25–33 per entrée.

EATING OUT
Chestertown
Evergrain Bread Company (410-778-3333; www.evergrainbreadco.com), 203

High St. Open Tues.–Sat. 6:30–5, Sun. 8–2. Young entrepreneurship is alive and well in Chestertown. Doug Rae built a brick oven in his backyard and at age 14 began selling artisan bread to his fellow students at school. The breads and pastries he serves are in the best of the European tradition (using flour and butter that may be imported just to get the right tastes and textures). His training at Johnson and Wales Culinary School and time in Paris has served him well in creating nice entrées to complement the baked goods, including a most refreshing watermelon gazpacho that I had for lunch. Currently my favorite Chestertown *Eating Out* restaurant. $6–12.

Ellen's (410-810-1992), 205 Spring Ave. Open 6–2 Mon.–Wed. and Sat.; 6–8 on Tues. and Fri.; 6–1 on Sun. The local breakfast spot. Ham and cheese omelet with home fries is only $4.05, while two pancakes are less than $3. Lunch is sandwiches from $2.50, and dinner is home-cooked items such as pork chops and fried chicken.

Uncle Charlie's Bistro (410-778-3663; www.unclecharliesbistro.com), 843-B High St. Open daily for lunch and dinner. Chuck Ministero named his restaurant after his favorite uncle who emigrated from Europe in the 1900s. Meals employ as much local meats and produce as possible, while the ice cream and desserts are made in-house. The Maryland Crab vegetable soup is the way to start a meal, while the crab ravioli with fresh tomatoes, basil garlic, olives, and feta cheese pleased my palette. Try the orange-chipotle glazed ribs if you are not a seafood lover. $16.99–23.99.

Rock Hall

Bay Wolf (410-639-2000), Rock Hall Ave. Open for lunch and dinner. It is unexpected to run into an Austrian/Eastern Shore restaurant in tiny Rock Hall. Dine like you are in the Alps with Wiener schnitzel, Schweinsbraten, and apple strudel. Or return to the Chesapeake Bay with more local dishes such as crab-imperial-stuffed flounder or the broiled seafood combo with a whole lobster, crabcake, shrimp, and scallops. Most entrées in the $19.95–29.95 range.

The Dockside Café (410-708-9222; www .blackduckinn-rockhall.com), 21906 Chesapeake Ave. Open Sat.–Sun. Everything is made fresh, with as many local ingredients as possible, including some from the garden next to the café. The breakfast pizza is the most popular item. Most items are $10–15 or less.

Ford's Seafood Restaurant (410-639-2032), 6262 Rock Hall Rd. After many years in the wholesale business shipping clams and operating an oyster-shucking house, Nevitte and Sharon Ford opened their restaurant on the approach into town. The menu contains sandwiches, soups, and full dinners. The seafood is caught daily and includes rockfish, flounder, and a sampler with a crabcake, a fish fillet, and fried oysters. Live entertainment on Fri. and Sat. evenings. The recipes for the crabcakes, crab imperial, and crab bisque are Sharon's. Entrées $18.95–27.95.

Pasta Plus (410-639-7916), 21356 Rock Hall Ave. Open for breakfast, lunch, and dinner. If you want to hear some tall (and maybe some true) tales, come here early in the morning when the watermen stop by for breakfast. Lunch and dinner are what you would expect from a place with the name like Pasta Plus, although there are some surprises like homemade meatloaf and stewed tomatoes. $5.50–12.

Swan Point Inn (410-639-2500; www.rock hallmd.com/swanpointinn), Coleman Rd. and Rock Hall Ave. Open for lunch and dinner. There is no doubt the appetizer to have is the Angels on Horseback—broiled bacon-wrapped shrimp laced with horse-radish and served with homemade dipping sauce. Three choices of veal entrées, several other meat dishes, and local seafood prepared a variety of ways are included on the dinner menu. $18.95–27.85.

Also see **Harbor Shack** in *Nightlife*.

CRABS J & J Seafood (410-639-2325), 21459 Rock Hall Ave. Open daily. Starting out as just a seafood shop, J & J has added a small dining room where you can order crabs—or their famous (and huge) crab pretzel. Popular local dining place.

♪ Waterman's Crab House (410-639-2261; www.watermanscrabhouse.com), at the foot of Sharp St., Rock Hall. Recreational boaters come here to enjoy mounds of steamed blue crabs by the dozen or the bushel (market price). Tues. and Thurs. nights feature all-you-can-eat crabs (market price). Waterman's is also known for its full rack of ribs and ice cream drinks, such as the Mudslide: ice cream, Kahlúa, and vodka. Live entertainment on the waterfront deck on Fri. and Sat. nights and Sun. afternoon. Entrées $15–29.

TAKE-OUT

Chestertown

Chestertown Natural Foods (410-778-1677; www.chestertownnaturalfoods.biz), 303 Cannon St. One of the few natural foods and products stores on the Eastern Shore.

COFFEE BARS

Chestertown

Play It Again Sam (410-778-2688), 108 S. Cross St. All espresso drinks are made with double shots. Teas, sandwiches, and lots of baked goodies are other reasons to visit.

Rock Hall

Java Rock (410-639-9909), Sharp and Main Sts. With outdoor seating in the center of town, Java Rock adds a bit of a cosmopolitan atmosphere to small-town Rock Hall. In addition to the expected espressos, lattes, and cafe au laits, there are some nice sandwiches, soups, and baked goods. Free wi-fi access; there is a small fee to use the house computers. A small gift and wine section fill nooks and crannies.

SNACKS AND GOODIES

Chestertown

Stam Drugs and Soda Fountain (410-778-3030; www.stamdrugsmd.com), 215 High St. How's this for longevity? Stam Colin started this business in 1886 (it moved to its current location in the early 1900s). With an old-fashioned fountain that still uses the "soda jerk" equipment, it serves just about any kind of soda you can think of (you're welcome to mix and match any of the flavors, including vanilla, cherry, chocolate, strawberry, lemon, and lime). Milk shakes, floats, and more have built a loyal local following.

Rock Hall

Durding's Store (410-778-7957; www.sailingemporium.com/durdings), Main and Sharp Sts. Open daily. Enjoy myriad ice cream concoctions while you sit at the marble counter in this authentic 1930s shop. The stainless-steel fountain is original. In step with modern times, Durding's also offers fat-free and sugar-free ice creams.

Also see **Evergrain Bread Company** in *Eating Out.*

✳ Entertainment

FILM

Chestertown

Chester Theatres (410-778-2227; www.kentcounty.com/events/movies.htm), Washington Square. First-run movies.

Washington College (410-778-2800; www.washcoll.edu). The college's many different clubs, disciplines, and the Office of Campus Events sponsor several film series, festivals, and programs throughout the year, many of them with topics not found anywhere other than a college campus.

MUSIC **Gibson Performing Arts Center** (410-778-2800; www.washcoll.edu), Washington College campus, Chestertown. Concerts, plays, lectures, and more are presented.

NIGHTLIFE

Rock Hall

✿ ♪ Harbor Shack (410-639-9996; www.harborshack.net), 20895 Bayside Ave. Open daily for lunch and dinner; closed Mon. and Tues. in winter. In addition to having crowds show up for their weekend waterside live entertainment, they also have a full menu of local dishes. The deck is next to the water, making this a great spot to watch the commercial, charter, and pleasure boats constantly come and go. The deck

HARBOR SHACK

is also dog-friendly, with a bowl of water always available.

Also see **Fish Whistle** in *Dining Out* and **Waterman's Crab House** under *Where to Eat—Crabs*.

✳ Selective Shopping
ANTIQUES

Chestertown
Chestertown Antique and Furniture Center (410-778-5777; www.chestertown antiqueandfurniturecenter.com), 1 mile south of town on MD 213. Old and new furniture sold under the same roof.

Galena
Firehouse Antique Center (410-648-5639), Main St. A multidealer shop.

Rock Hall
Fishbones Antiques (410-639-9172), 21326 Sharp St. A multidealer shop that also displays the works of local and regional artists.

ART GALLERIES

Chestertown
Chester RiverArt (410-778-6300; www .chestertownriverarts.org), 315 High St. Closed Mon.–Tues. Home of the **Chestertown Arts League.** Formed shortly after World War II, the league provides classes

for those who want to learn arts and crafts as well as exhibits of local talent. Changing exhibits of local and regional works.

The Finishing Touch Gallery (410-778-5292; www.finishingtouchshop.com), 311 High St. Featured artists, limited edition historic prints, duck stamp prints, and other higher-quality items.

Washington College's Tawes Gallery (410-778-2800; www.washcoll.edu), Washington College campus. Ever-changing exhibits of local and student artists, and some nationally touring programs.

Rock Hall
Rock Hall Gallery (410-639-2494), 5764 Main St. Closed Tues. Specialties include furniture, acrylics, glass, textiles, jewelry, woodcraft, pottery, pastels, watercolor and photography.

USED BOOKS

Chestertown
Book Plate (410-778-4167; www.book plate.biz), 112 S. Cross St., Chestertown. Although it looks like a small store from the outside, Book Plate has several large rooms of fine used books, first editions, and quite a few signed volumes. There is also a small section devoted to some interesting handpainted pottery items from Spain and Jerusalem.

Chestertown Old Book Company (410-810-3880; www.chestertownoldbookco .com), 113 S. Cross St. One of the best antiquarian book stores around, with 16th century manuscripts to modern day first editions. The will also repair your prized leather- or cloth-bound books.

Chestertown Used Bookstore (410-778-5777; www.chestertownusedbookstore .com), 1 mile south of Chestertown on MD 213. Located inside the Chestertown Antique and Furniture Center, it claims to have more than 80,000 used books.

SPECIAL SHOP Smilin' Jakes (410-639-7280; www.smilinjakescasualapparel .blogspot.com), 5745 Main St., Rock Hall. I usually don't list apparel stores in this book, but, hey, you're on vacation, and Smilin' Jakes has just the kind of quality casual Hawaiian and Caribbean style of clothing you should be wearing. There's also a nice selection of CDs featuring music from the islands, and you can even pick up a dancing hula doll for your car's dashboard.

FARMER'S MARKETS Chestertown Farmer's Market. In Fountain Park on Sat. 9–noon, Apr.–Dec.

Galena Farmer's Market. Open year-round Thurs.–Sat. at Dogwood Plaza on N. Main St.

Rock Hall Farmer's Market. Open Sat. from 9–12 on Main St.

WINERY See **Crow Farmstay B&B and Vineyard** in *Bed & Breakfasts.*

✳ Special Events

March–April: **Annual Juried Show Chestertown Arts League** (410-778-3224), Chestertown. The event, featuring local and regional artists, has been held for more than 65 years.

May: **Annual Chestertown Tea Party** (410-778-0416), Chestertown. Celebrates May 23, 1774, when local residents boarded

the *Geddes* and dumped its load of tea into the Chester River.

June: **Rockfish Tournament** (410-639-7611), Rock Hall.

July: **July 4th Sassafras Boat Parade** (410-648-5510), Georgetown Harbor, Georgetown. Fireworks and a parade of decorated boats. **Kent County Fair** (410-778-1661), Kent Agricultural Center, Tolchester.

August: **Betterton Beach Day and Parade** (410-348-5239), Betterton. **Pirates and Wenches Fantasy Weekend** (410-935-3491; www.rockhallpirates.com). Sea shanties, decorated dinghy flotilla and race, beach party, pirate's ball, treasure hunts, costume contests, live entertainment, and mayhem.

September: **Art in the Park** (410-778-0416), the sale of works by artists and craftspeople.

October: **Chester River Wildlife Exhibition and Sale** (410-778-0416), Chestertown. Decoy carving, duck- and goose-calling contests, retrieving contests, live raptor exhibit, entertainment, food, and nature and wildlife films and slide programs. **Heritage House Tour** (410-778-3499), Chestertown. A glimpse into some of the town's most historic structures. **Rock Hall Fall Fest** (410-778-0416), Rock Hall. Arts and crafts, music, foods, a Kid's Kourt of children's activities, oyster-shucking contest, and boat show.

November: **Downrigging** (410-778-0416), Chestertown. Traditional sailing vessels from around the Chesapeake will visit Chestertown to help the schooner *Sultana* celebrate the close of her season under sail. **Artworks Studio Tour** (410-778-6300), Chestertown. An event with a self-guided tour of more than two dozen Kent County artists.

December: **Rock Hall Boat Parade** (410-639-7611), Rock Hall. A procession of lighted boats accompany Santa into town.

AT THE HEAD OF THE BAY

CHESAPEAKE CITY, ELKTON, AND NORTH EAST

I t is said that life on the Eastern Shore is determined by the water around it. At the head of the bay, where the Eastern Shore meets mainland Maryland, the land itself is defined by water.

Along its western edge is the wide Susquehanna River, delivering the water it has collected during its long journey from humble beginnings near Cooperstown, New York. At its mouth, where it empties into the bay, are the Susquehanna Flats, shallow waters that attract nearly 90 percent of the waterfowl traveling the Atlantic Flyway. The unique style and heritage of the hunters attracted to these flats more than one hundred years ago are preserved in the Upper Bay Museum in North East.

The Chesapeake Bay rings the area with miles of shoreline, while the land at the southern edge is cut by not just one, but three, waterways: the Sassafras and Bohemia Rivers and the Chesapeake & Delaware (C&D) Canal.

As early as the mid-1600s, Augustine Herman proposed a canal that would reduce water travel by nearly 300 miles between Philadelphia and Baltimore. More than a century passed before surveys were done, and it was not until 1829 that the canal was completed. Today it is the third busiest canal in the world, permitting oceangoing vessels easy passage to the bay as well as providing scores of pleasure boaters a protected and scenic passage along the Intracoastal Waterway.

As for the land in the area, the Kentucky bluegrass has nothing on this gently rolling, coastal plain. Some of the largest and most prestigious horse farms in the country have produced a succession of thoroughbred and standardbred champions. Even if the names Kelso, Northern Dancer, Bet Twice, Barbaro, and Two Punch mean nothing to you, you can still enjoy a ride through the countryside. Miles of wooden fences wrap around acres of lush, green fields, accented by the flying manes and rippled haunches of galloping future champions.

COMMUNITIES The history and fortunes of **Chesapeake City** are tied to the C&D Canal. As construction on the canal progressed, the town sprang up as a place to house workers and supply needed materials. For a while, the canal actually supplied the construction material for the town, as many of its buildings were built from the lumber of dismantled "Susquehanna Arks" that had come across the Chesapeake Bay but were too large to pass through the locks. Chesapeake City's importance as a port faded once the federal government purchased the canal, widened and deepened it, and removed the locks in the early

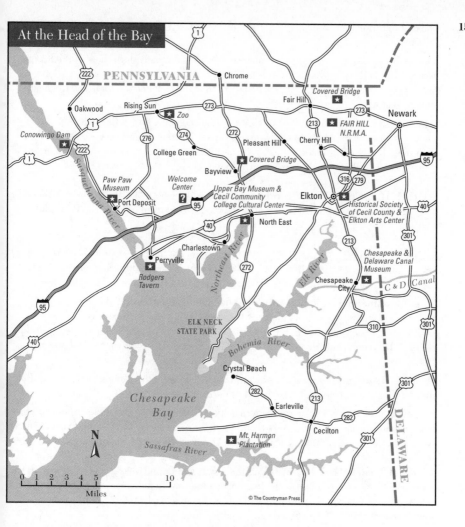

At the Head of the Bay

20th century. Its growth was even more stunted when the construction of the arched bridge on MD 213, which soars 135 feet above the canal, enabled traffic to bypass the town.

Yet it is still one of the most picturesque spots in the area. Many of its buildings date from the early 1800s, and the view of traffic upon the wide waters of the canal makes for a stunning backdrop from the small but active "downtown" area. The Chesapeake and Delaware Canal Museum provides an accounting of the canal's and the town's history, while several good restaurants and an abundance of B&Bs are reason enough to visit.

The origin of **North East** (its motto is, "Not just a direction . . . it's a destination") is also tied to water. In this case, it is the Northeast River, which supplied the needs of several early mills and an ironworks. Most of its buildings are from the late 1800s and early 1900s, and many of them still stand in the busy business district—along with antiques stores, restaurants serving regional foods, and interesting shops—on Main Street. The *Strolling Guide* (available from Cecil County Tourism) provides background on a number of the buildings.

Built upon a narrow strip of land between the Susquehanna River and towering cliffs, the entire town of **Port Deposit** is on the National Register of Historic Places. Many of its buildings are constructed from granite quarried from the cliffs; their history is revealed in a walking-tour brochure available from the Paw Paw Museum in town or from Cecil County Tourism.

Perryville gained importance in colonial days, as it sits on the eastern shore of the Susquehanna River and became a stopover for travelers taking the ferry across the river. George Washington was just one of the many people passing through here on their way to Philadelphia or Baltimore.

Elkton, with a population of close to 15,000, is the economic hub of the area. Some of its earliest structures remain to remind you of the past, although they have become mixed in with the office buildings, storefronts, and strip malls of modern America. The local historical society and art gallery are definitely worth stopping for.

GUIDANCE **Cecil County Tourism** (410-996-6290; 1-800-CECIL-95; www.seececil .org), 68 Heather Ln., Suite 43, Perryville, 21903. Located in an office in the Perryville Outlet.

GETTING THERE *By car:* **I-95** is the main route into the region, providing easy access from Baltimore and the rest of Maryland, and from Delaware and Philadelphia. **MD 213** is the quickest roadway for those arriving from the southern portion of the Eastern Shore.

By air: **Baltimore/Washington International Thurgood Marshall Airport** (1-800-I-FLY-BWI; www.bwiairport.com), located between Baltimore and Annapolis, is about an hour's drive to the southwest of the Chesapeake City area. Located to the northeast, **Philadelphia International Airport** (215-937-6937; www.phl.org) is also about an hour's drive away.

By train: **MARC** (1-800-325-RAIL; www.mta.maryland.gov), the commuter train from Baltimore, makes its final stop at Perryville on its northeastern run.

By water: If you own a boat or are chartering one, the Chesapeake Bay is the obvious way to come from mainland Maryland. Also, the Chesapeake & Delaware Canal is a part of the Intracoastal Waterway and provides access from the Delaware River and other points to the east.

GETTING AROUND *By car:* **I-95** is the way to get around quickly, but using **US 40** will give you a chance to see more of the towns along the way. Lightly traveled **US 222** and **US 1** run through the more rural northern portions of the area, while **MD 213** takes you into the southern region to the C&D Canal and Sassafras River.

By taxi: **North East Taxi** (410-287-8828) is headquartered in North East. Joe's Taxi Service (410-392-8070) operates out of Elkton.

PARKING Municipal parking lots in North East are located off Main St. between West St. and Wallace Ave. Municipal parking lots are also available in Elkton and Port Deposit.

PUBLIC RESTROOMS In **Chesapeake City,** a public restroom is located beside the Franklin Hall building on Bohemia Ave.

In **North East,** restrooms can be found in the North East Community Park off Walnut St. at the southern end of town and next to the town hall on Main St.

MEDICAL EMERGENCY **Union Hospital of Cecil County** (410-328-4000; www .uhcc.com), 106 Bow St., Elkton, is a full-service facility with an emergency room.

✳ To See

COVERED BRIDGES Spanning a waterway within the Fair Hill Natural Resources Management Area in Fair Hill is the **Big Elk Creek Covered Bridge.** An interesting tid-

THE BIG ELK CREEK COVERED BRIDGE

bit: Construction cost for the bridge in the 1860s was $1,165; its 1992 renovation came in at an amazing $152,000.

About 3 miles north of North East on MD 272 is the 1860 **Gilpin Falls Covered Bridge.** The arches of this 119-foot bridge—the longest covered bridge still standing in the state—are made from single timbers that were gradually warped into shape by balancing them on a pivot and pulling down on each end with cables and restraints.

MUSEUMS

Chesapeake City

Chesapeake and Delaware Canal Museum (410-885-5621), Second St. and Bethel Rd. Mon.–Sat. Free admission. Exhibits, displays, and models provide a glimpse into the canal's past. One of the models is of the James Adams Floating Theater, which worked the C&D Canal and was the inspiration for the musical *Showboat*. (Yes, *Showboat* took place on the Mississippi, but it was this boat that piqued the composer's imagination.) A computer screen shows the location of ships—in real time—as they travel the canal. Also on museum grounds is a replica of the Bethel Bridge Lighthouse—and sweeping vistas of the canal.

Elkton

Historical Society of Cecil County (410-398-1790; www.cchistory.org), 135 E. Main St. Mon. 10–4, Tues. 6 PM–8:30 PM, Thurs. 10–4, and the fourth Sat. of each month 10–2. Free admission, but donations accepted. Housed in a former bank building (circa 1830), the society maintains exhibits relating to colonial furnishings, Victorian dollhouses, a country store, an early American kitchen, and a log house. Of particular note is the Sheriff John F. DeWitt Military Museum. What started out as a personal collection has grown into a room full of military uniforms, weapons, medical military equipment, and more dating from the Civil War to the present.

North East

Upper Bay Museum (410-287-5909), Walnut St. at the North East Community Park. Wed.–Sun. 11–3, but hours and days have been variable. Housed within two large buildings, the museum has a collection of materials reflecting the history of commercial and recreational hunting and fishing on the upper Chesapeake Bay. The size of the decoy collection is impressive when you realize the museum is sponsored and maintained by the local Cecil-Harford Hunters Association. The punt guns, sculling oars, and sink boxes (ask if you don't know what these are—they're interesting) sketch a vivid picture of the heady age of bay waterfowl hunting.

Port Deposit

Paw Paw Museum (410-738-4480), 98 N. Main St. Open 1–5 on the second and fourth Sun. of the month, May–Oct. Items relating to the history of Port Deposit include letters from Civil War soldiers and photographs of the town in the 19th and 20th centuries. Ask for the story about the signature quilt, which came into being as punishment for "acting up in church."

THE SUSQUEHANNA RIVER AS SEEN FROM RODGERS TAVERN IN PERRYVILLE

HISTORIC SITES Rodgers Tavern (410-642-6066), 259 Broad St., Perryville. Hours vary; call for times. George Washington, Marquis de Lafayette, Thomas Jefferson, and James Madison are just a few of the luminaries to make a stop at Rodgers Tavern. Built in the early 17th century, it served passengers using the ferry to get across the wide mouth of the Susquehanna River. Guided tours take you through the lightly furnished basement tavern, first-floor parlor and office, and second-floor sleeping accommodations. George Washington truly did sleep here! The view from the lawn is spectacular.

GUIDED TOURS Chesapeake Horse Country Tours (410-287-2290; 1-800-874-4558), 135 S. Main St., North East. Offered for two to seven people by reservation Mon.–Sat. Wayne Hill has put together a tour that provides an overview of life, in his words, "at the peak of the Chesapeake." After a walking tour of Chesapeake City, a guided driving trip (in your vehicle) explores Maryland's largest land preserve, which encompasses many of

HISTORIC HOME

Mount Harmon Plantation (410-275-8819), Mount Harmon Rd. (off Grove Neck Rd. [MD 282]), Earleville. Tues.–Sun. 10–3, May–Sept. Small admission fee. In 1963, Mrs. Harry Clark Boden IV purchased the early-1700s tobacco plantation home of her ancestors. She had it restored (which included installing beautifully hand-painted Chinese wallpaper) and furnished with American, English, Irish, and Scottish antiques of the period.

A 2-mile tree-lined drive brings you to the three-story, five-bay brick manor house. Tour guides point out the Italian marble fireplaces (the screens kept sparks and fire off ladies' dresses), the master-of-the-hunt chair, and the wooden panels along the staircase. The furnishings and artwork are some of the nicest I've seen. Make sure you see the portrait of Lady Arabella Stuart. It reminds me of a modern holograph: The image changes depending on the angle it is viewed from—but it was painted in the 1500s! (Also quite remarkable are the extraordinarily ornate bathrooms installed in the mid-1900s.) Tours also take in the plantation kitchen and the tobacco prize house. A "prize" is a large wooden screw used to compress tobacco into half its volume for more efficient shipment.

Afterward, you are free to wander around the plantation's 200 acres, enjoying the formal boxwood and wisteria gardens or following maintained pathways along fields, forests, and creeks (ask for a trail brochure). The entire plantation is a nature preserve that protects several rare species of plants.

This is an example of historic preservation at its best.

THINGS TO LOOK FORWARD TO

Principio Iron Works (410-642-2358), Perryville, and **Elk Landing** (410-651-9213; www.elk landing.org), Elkton, are being developed as historic sites. The Iron Works were most active before the Revolutionary War, but production continued into the 1900s. Although not in the best of shape, the manor house, furnace, and some outbuildings remain.

THE MANOR HOUSE AT PRINCIPIO IRON WORKS

At the confluence of Little Elk and Big Elk Creeks, Elk Landing played a role in the colonies' earliest transportation corridor. There are big plans for both of these places, including living-history demonstrations. Check with Cecil County Tourism to find out what is available while you are in the area.

the horse farms in the area. In addition to enjoying the scenery, you will learn of the Du Pont family's role in reviving the horse industry here, travel through their Bohemia Stables Farm, and make a stop at the grave of Kelso, a champion stallion who was Horse of the Year an unprecedented five times. Upon his gravestone are the words WHERE HE GALLOPS, THE EARTH SINGS.

Z O O ✍ **The Zoo at Plumpton Park** (410-658-6850; www.plumptonparkzoo.org), 1416 Telegraph Rd. (MD 273), Rising Sun. Hours and days vary by the season. Adults $10.95; over 60, $8.95; children 3–11, $6.95; younger than 3 free. This small zoo had its beginnings as a haven for injured animals. Since then, it has accepted exotic and endangered species

THE BOHEMIA STABLES OF WOODSTOCK FARM NEAR CHESAPEAKE CITY

confiscated by U.S. Customs, and animals no longer wanted or on loan from other zoos. Because of this, there is no real theme to the park, but you do get the chance to see more than 250 animals from around the world. There are also picnic facilities, a children's playground, and a nature trail.

✳ To Do

AUTO RACING **Cecil County Dragway** (410-287-9105), 1573 Theodore Rd., Rising Sun. Mar.–Nov., you can listen to the roar of engines as various vehicles head down the 0.25-mile track in Federal Mogul Points, rocket, and street races.

BOAT EXCURSIONS

Chesapeake City

Miss Clare Cruises (410-885-5088; www.missclarecruises.com), 64 Front St. Scheduled one- and two-hour cruises Sat. and Sun. May–Oct. Reservations are required during the week. The sight-seeing cruises are nice enough, but because Capt. Ralph H. Hazel Jr. is a fifth-generation Chesapeake City resident who worked the water for decades on his custom-built Chesapeake deadrise, try to take one of the historic cruises. You will learn more of the local C&D Canal and town history, along with what it's like to try to make a living on the water, than if you spent months doing research in a library.

BOAT RENTALS

Charlestown

North East River Marina (410-287-5298), 724 Water St. The same family who runs the marina rents kayaks, pontoon boats, and a small motorized fishing boat. Rentals are by the hour (two-hour minimum), half day, day, and week. The kayak rental rates were quite reasonable the last time I stopped by.

CASINO

⚥ **Hollywood Casino** (410-378-8500; www.hollywoodcasinoperryville.com), 1201 Chesapeake Overlook. You can play a variety of table games or feed more than a thousand slot machines from soon after the sun rises all of the way to the wee hours of the morning. I'm not much of a gambler, but as you have seen throughout this book, I do like to eat, and the Celebrity Bar and Grill has some of the nicest casino food I've come across. Using fresh and local items, there are new variations on old standards including a crab mac and cheese and rockfish "Oscar." Interestingly, the gift shop is not the usual kind found in a casino—it actually has some nice Maryland-themed items. Also, sports fans take note: The plethora of large flat screens guarantee you will never miss a game.

GOLF

Elkton

Bittersweet (410-392-4099; www.bittersweetgolfcourse.com), 1190 Augustine Herman Hwy. (MD 213). Championship 18-hole course with clubhouse and pro shop.

Elkton Club at Patriot's Glen (410-392-9552; 1-800-616-1776; www.patriotsglen.com), 300 Patriots. One of the newer courses in the area, it has a par 72.

North East and Rising Sun

Chesapeake Bay Golf Club North East (410-287-0200; www.chesapeakegolf.com), 1500 Chesapeake Club Dr., and **Chesapeake Bay Golf Club Rising Sun** (410-658-4343; www.chesapeakegolf.com/risingsun.html). These two 18-hole courses are under the same management and are only 6 miles apart. The North East course is a bit more rolling and wooded than the Rising Sun course. Discounts are given if you play both of them. The food at Knicker's Grille (at the North East course) is of higher quality than that found at many other golf clubs.

Perryville

Furnace Bay (410-642-6816; www.furnacebaygolf.com), 79 Chesapeake View Rd. Opened in 2000, the 18-hole public course has some reasonable fees, especially if you are a senior or under 15.

HIKING **Elk Neck State Park** (410-287-5333), 4395 Turkey Point Rd., North East. Upland forests just a short distance away from the shorelines of the Chesapeake Bay and Elk River provide some of the most diverse environments found in a park on the Eastern Shore, and the best way to explore them is via the park's pathways.

The easy 1.5-mile **Red Trail** passes through a forest of beech; tulip poplar; and red, white, and chestnut oak. A hike along the 1-mile **Green Trail** overlooks a small lake and a marsh. The 2-mile **Black Trail** provides access to the shoreline of the Elk River, where you can take a swim (at your own risk—no guards). The white-blazed **Thackery Swamp Self-Guiding Nature Trail** is only 0.75 mile long, with an interpretive booklet available at the camper registration office.

The trail I enjoy most is the 2-mile **Blue Trail,** which passes through field and forest on its way to the **Turkey Point Lighthouse** and a 100-foot-high cliff overlooking the Chesapeake Bay and Elk River. There is absolutely no better way to greet a new dawn than to be sitting on one of the benches next to the lighthouse and watching the source of Earth's warmth rise inch by inch into the eastern sky.

Also see **Fair Hill Natural Resources Management Area** under *Green Space.*

HORSEBACK RIDING **Fair Hill Stables** (410-620-3883; www.fairwindsstables .com), accessed from Entrance 3 in Fair Hill State Park on MD 273, Fair Hill. Operated by Ted and JoAnn Dawson, hosts of Fairwinds Farm. Guided one-hour trail rides ($30) through the woods and fields of Fair Hill Natural Resources Management Area. Pony rides by reservation. The Dawsons also offer riding lessons, and carriage and hayrides. Fair Hill Stables is where Barbaro trained.

SPECIAL CLASSES **Horizon Photography Workshops and Gallery** (410-885-2433; www.horizonworkshops.com), 98 Bohemia Ave., Chesapeake City. Drawing upon his more than two decades of experience as a commercial photographer, Steve Gottlieb established his photography workshop business as an alternative to the usual weeklong events that are offered by most other workshops. Within these two- to three-day sessions, Steve and his instructors provide a vast amount of information, with the emphasis on participants shooting in

EARLY MORNING AT TURKEY POINT LIGHTHOUSE

the field and obtaining immediate feedback on their work. The maximum class size is 12 to assure personal attention. A large number of the workshops use locations in and around the Eastern Shore, while some are offered in places such as the coast of Maine and the Black Hills of South Dakota. A partial list of Steve's students reads like a Who's Who in the world of photography.

SUMMER CAMPS ✿ **Sandy Hill Camp** (410-287-5554; www.sandyhillcamp.com), 3380 Turkey Point Rd., North East. June–Aug. This residential camp for boys and girls 8–16 years of age is located on 216 acres overlooking the Chesapeake Bay. There are weekend and weeklong sessions of equestrian activities, sailing, sports, English for international travel, a counselor-in-training program, and traditional camp activities. Eight campers and two counselors share a rustic cabin.

✳ Green Space

BEACHES **Crystal Beach** (410-275-8083), Earleville. Admission fee. A small, sandy public beach located along the Elk River at the end of MD 282.

PARKS

Elkton
Fair Hill Natural Resources Management Area (410-398-1246), 300 Tawes Dr. Open sunrise–sunset. At 5,613 acres, this is one of the largest pieces of public land on the Eastern Shore. Approximately 20 miles of very well-maintained and well-identified trails, open to hikers, bicyclists, and horseback riders, wander through woods and fields and across many water runs. An additional 80 miles of pathways are also available to be used. A very popular place for the local equestrian community. Facilities include the Fair Hill Training Center for racehorses, and a turf course, where steeplechase and flat races are held.

North East
Elk Neck State Park (410-287-5333), 4395 Turkey Point Rd. In addition to a network of hiking trails, the state park offers picnic areas, a boat launch (bring your own vessel or rent

A CARRIAGE RIDE WITH FAIR HILL STABLES

one), fishing, a naturalist program, rental cabins, and a campground with bathhouses. Bordered by the Elk River and the Chesapeake Bay, it is a place of grand sunrises and sunsets.

WALKS The shoreline **Riverwalk** in Port Deposit is a part of the proposed Lower Susquehanna Heritage Greenway, which will include multiple miles of trail along both sides of the Susquehanna River.

✳ Lodging

MOTELS AND HOTELS
North East, 21901
☙ **Comfort Inn Suites** (410-287-7100; 1-800-631-3803; www.comfortinn.com), 1 Center Dr. (MD 272 at I-95 Exit 100). Spacious rooms, each with microwave, refrigerator, and free local calls. Indoor pool, whirlpool, spa, fitness room, and deluxe continental breakfast. A short drive to North East, Elk Neck State Park, Elkton, and outlet shopping. One of the more pleasant motels I've stayed in. Pets permitted with deposit. $99–149.

Best Western North East Inn (410-287-5450; www.bestwestern.com), 39 Elwoods Rd. at I-95 Exit 100. Large rooms, refrigerator, microwave, free wi-fi, coffee/tea maker, free local calls under 30 minutes, deluxe continental breakfast, heated indoor pool, business center, and fitness center. $79.99—$119.99.

BED & BREAKFASTS
Chesapeake City, 21915
♪ & **Blue Max Inn** (410-885-2781; www.bluemaxinn.com), 300 Bohemia Ave. Less than two blocks from the waterfront and main business area. The large porch invites guests to just sit and watch small-town life unfold as they listen to the sounds of the grand player piano coming from the living room. There are seven guest rooms; I liked the rich blue color of the Randall Room with its own balcony. The Lindsey Room on the first floor is handicapped accessible. Owner Christine Mullen serves a large breakfast in the solarium or the fireside dining room—and then provides afternoon tea and cookies. Children 10 and over welcome. $130–255.

If you are wondering about the name, it comes from a former occupant, Jack

Hunter, who wrote *The Blue Max*. A bestseller, the book was adapted as a major motion picture.

♪ **Inn at the Canal** (410-885-5995; www.innatthecanal.com), 104 Bohemia Ave. The inn is located in the heart of Chesapeake City. The hosts greet you upon arrival to their 1870s Victorian-Gothic home with refreshments, and a full gourmet breakfast is served in the morning, prepared by innkeeper Bob Roethke, a Culinary Institute of America trained chef. Each of the seven guest rooms has its own decorating theme and private bath. Far from minding the few wooden steps I had to go down to get to the bathroom in my room, I felt that it just added another historical and unique aspect to my stay. My after-dinner lounging was done on the front porch, watching the boats on the C&D Canal. Children over 10 may be welcome; call to make arrangements. $100–225.

& **Ship Watch Inn** (410-885-5300; www.shipwatchinn.com), 410 First St. All eight suites in this 1920s waterfront inn have private whirlpool bath and private balcony. Room 5 is the largest, but my choice would be Room 6 because you can see the water without even having to sit up in bed. Room 2 is handicapped accessible. A nice touch is the binoculars to watch the boats on the canal. $145–245.

Elk Mills, 21920
& **Elk Forge B&B Inn and Retreat** (410-392-9007; 1-877-ELK-FORGE; www.elkforge.com), 807 Elk Mills Rd. An intriguing place whose core is a centuries-old home, but whose additions, while modern, provide very pleasant and interesting guest rooms (each with a private bath). Harry and LeAnn Lenderman engaged artists Jeanette Robison and Vitale Sem to paint pictures in

Sinking Springs Herb Farm (410-398-5566; www.sinkingsprings.com), enter from 843 Elk Forest Rd., Elkton. A visit to the Sinking Springs Herb Farm is like stepping into a chapter of Jethro Kloss's *Back to Eden*. There is a little bit of New Age mixed in with a lot of just good old country living. Ann and Bill Stubbs's Wellness Retreats focus on stress, health issues, nutrition, and gardening, and include yoga, massage therapy, regression hypnosis, and more. You do not have to participate in a retreat to enjoy a stay in the small and rustic, but cozy, Garden Cottage B&B ($110) or to make arrangements for a family-style lunch with Ann and Bill in their 1700s home. The quiche, bread, and vegetables (all with fresh herbs) I had were a welcome taste of delicious home-cooked food after I'd been on the road for a long time.

Within a couple of outbuildings are a gift shop offering the Stubbs's herbs and dried-flower arrangements. Walking trails wander around the herb and flower gardens and throughout the farm's 130 acres. Be sure to stop and pay homage to the huge sycamore tree next to the house. It was already full grown when Shakespeare was but a teenager.

each room. Robison created one in a 1920s art deco style and painted angels floating on clouds in one of the hallways. Sem's works are more classical, such as the stunning action scene depicting George Washington at the Battle of Brandywine.

The solarium, which overlooks the yard and woodlands and contains a stained-glass window from a Pennsylvania church, is so big that a large water fountain is dwarfed inside it. LeAnn's breakfasts, served in the solarium, have portions to match the size of the room. The many miles of pathways within Fair Hill Natural Resources Management Area can be accessed directly from the side yard.

LeAnn also operates a spa and tea room within Elk Forge that is just one more reason to stay in this most relaxing, inviting, and unique B&B. There are many thoughtful amenities for business travelers, too. $115–239.

North East, 21901

☙ **Fairwinds Farm** (410-658-8187; www .fairwindsstables.com), 41 Tailwinds Ln. Children over eight are welcome. This has the feel of what B&Bs started out as. You share the Victorian farmhouse with a family—Ted and JoAnn Dawson and any of their children that happen to be visiting at the time. Of two guest rooms, I liked the Blue Room, with its bed in a recessed alcove. A good place to relax and enjoy the quiet beauty of a 50-acre working farm. You

may bring your own horses and stable them overnight in the 17-stall barn. The Dawsons also own the Fair Hill Stables. In fact, some of their horses were featured in Oprah Winfrey's film *Beloved*—and JoAnn has been an actress in such films as *Twelve Monkeys* and *The Sixth Sense*. $90.

☙ **North Bay** (410-287-5948; www.north bayinc.com), 9 Sunset Dr. Four contemporary, antiques-accented guest rooms (one with private bath) on the headwaters of the bay. The Captain's and Harbor rooms have their own water views. $65–125.

COTTAGES

Chesapeake City, 21915
The Old Wharf Cottage (410-885-5040; 1-877-582-4049; www.bayardhouse.com), 10 Bohemia Ave. You cannot get any closer to the water than in this small cottage, administered by the Bayard House next door. At the very edge of the land, it has served as an icehouse, tailor shop, and cargo-storage place. It is in the center of activity in town, so expect to have many passersby. $160; discounted rates for multiple-night stays.

VACATION RENTALS

North East, 21901
Elk Neck State Park (1-888-432-2267; www.dnr.state.md.us/publiclands/central/elk neck.asp), 4395 Turkey Point Rd. Rental cabins are available from the first weekend

in May through the second weekend in Oct. Some are equipped with electricity, refrigerator, stove, and running water; others are more rustic, with just electricity. Both types make use of a central bathhouse and are popular, so make reservations as soon as possible. $60.

CAMPING

Elkton, 21921

Woodlands Camping Resort (410-398-4414; www.woodlandcampresort.com), 265 Starkey Ln. A semi-private, family-oriented camping resort with a couple of rental cabins and transient sites. Swimming pool and many planned activities. As with most places such as this, sites are located close together.

❦ For a more rustic experience, check into the campground at **Elk Neck State Park** (see *Hiking*). Pets on a leash are permitted in certain sites.

✳ Where to Eat

DINING OUT

Charlestown

& **The Wellwood** (410-287-6666; www .wellwoodclub.com), 523 Water St. Open for lunch and dinner. The Wellwood was established as a gentlemen's club in the late 1800s and has played host to some of America's significant movers and shakers, including presidents, members of congress, governors, and other political figures. If the waitstaff are not real busy, you may be able to get a short guided tour of the establishment, enabling you take a look at a lamp donated to the club by Calvin Coolidge, decoys owned by Grover Cleveland, and a carved eagle from Teddy Roosevelt.

Of course, the food is why you want to come here, and the menu features well-prepared traditional Maryland items, such as crab-stuffed shrimp and fillet Chesapeake, alongside some items I have not come across often. The pan-seared Atlantic salmon I had was oh so moist and tender, but what made it a real standout was that it was broiled with a raspberry glaze and topped with wild berries and Brie. The din-

ers at the table next to me were sharing dishes of scallops with tomatoes, garlic, shallots, basil, and white wine, along with pork chops covered by bourbon candied apples and walnuts, and bowls of chicken, crab, and corn chowder. Entrées $14–32.

The Wellwood's **River Shack,** located next door, has a bar atmosphere and serves lighter fare to guests, who can choose to sit outside on the constructed sandy beach. No charge for boaters to tie up at the adjacent marina and eat at either restaurant.

Chesapeake City

Bayard House (410-885-5040; www.bayard house.com), 11 Bohemia Ave. Open for lunch and dinner. Some of the most pleasurable dining in the area is found in this structure, built decades before the construction of the C&D Canal. Once a private home, it has been a restaurant or tavern since 1829 and was restored in 1985. Its ambience, quality of food, and sweeping water vista make it a favorite special-occasion restaurant.

The award-winning Maryland crab soup is spicy without being hot and is full of crab. One of the most popular entrées, the Anaheim peppers are stuffed with lobster, crabmeat, and shrimp and baked with green chile salsa and cheddar cheese. They are simply luscious. Even side dishes are prepared with thought. The au gratin potatoes are made rich and creamy by adding sour cream, cheddar cheese, chives, and smoked bacon.

Other entrées include salmon with watercress and artichokes and broiled crabcakes. Especially indulgent are the twin filets mignons, one topped with a crabcake, the other with a lobster cake. If with a group, try the petits fours for dessert. Each of you will get to try a variety of flavors, textures, and tastes. Entrées $19–29.

Chesapeake Inn (410-885-2040; www .chesapeakeinn.com), 605 Second St. Open for lunch and dinner. Upscale waterfront dining with a bit of a Mediterranean flavor to the menu. Popular items are the crab ravioli, and the encrusted ahi tuna with candied walnuts over a pineapple risotto with coconut cream sauce. I made a full lunch out of the seafood quesadilla. Entrées $18–34.

North East

Steak & Main (410-287-3512), 107 S. Main St. Open for lunch and dinner. Although the menu's emphasis is on beef, there is a full page of oyster dishes and a variety of seafood offerings. With a casual atmosphere (the two tables in the window alcoves are the coveted seats), the restaurant has an extensive wine list, full bar offerings, and light lunch sandwiches and salads that are also available at dinner time. Entrées $24–33, with a couple of extra-special surf-and-turf items going for close to $100.

Port Deposit

✒ **Back Fin Blues** (410-378-2722; www .backfinblues.com), 19 S. Main St. Closed Mon.–Tues.; reservations suggested, especially Fri. and Sat. With a back deck overlooking the wide mouth of the Susquehanna River, Back Fin Blues is one of the places than has led to a surge of quality dining in Port Deposit. There is an emphasis on seafood (my rockfish with garlic buerre blanc and grilled zucchini was quite nice), but there are also steaks, veal, and pasta. On my next visit I intend to make a meal of the great-sounding starters, such as roasted red pepper crab soup, lobster bisque, and calamari Provencal. $25–38.

Union Hotel (410-378-3503; www.union hotel-restaurant.com), 1282 Susquehanna Rd. Open for lunch and dinner. Closed Mon. The hotel was built of hemlock logs around 1783 to cater to the needs of travelers on the Susquehanna Canal. Janet Dooling has been overseeing the restaurant for more than 20 years, serving soups, salads, sandwiches, and light entrées for lunch. I was here with three others, and we all agreed on the watercress and spinach quiche. Dinner is a bit more formal and hearty. Sambuca shrimp and scallops is popular, as is the grilled rack of lamb. A couple of dishes reflect the hotel's earlier days: sautéed veal liver with bacon and onions and maple-mustard pork loin. Dinner entrées $15–49.

EATING OUT

Chesapeake City

Yacht Club Restaurant (410-885-2267; www.yachtclubrestaurant.com), 225 Bohemia Ave. Open for lunch and dinner. Chef Gary Klunk has no formal training, yet most of the Yacht Club's savory offerings are his recipes. It was hard deciding which appetizer to try: the escargot over a pastry puff, sautéed spinach, and hazelnut butter, or the crab and corn chowder. The gazpacho with lump crab I settled on did not disappoint. The chicken Chesapeake was rubbed in Old Bay seasoning and topped with crabmeat in a luscious cream sauce—a nice variation on an old standard. Sandwiches are served at lunch, and seafood, meat, and pasta dishes at dinner.

I liked the waiters' attentive but nonintrusive service, as well as the old photos of Chesapeake City on the walls. Gary and co-owner Cheri Wilson did such a good job of renovating that you would never imagine you are eating in a former hardware store. $16.95–34.95.

Elkton

Baker's Restaurant (410-398-2435; www .bakersrestaurant.net), 1075 Augustine Herman Hwy. Open for lunch and dinner; closed Tues. Rob Matthew's grandmother opened Baker's in 1958 and he has kept many of her entrées and recipes on the menu, including the chicken and hand-rolled dumplings, which is the weekly Thursday special. (The portion is so large that it could easily be shared by two.) Other items from grandma's cookbook are the coleslaw and rice pudding. However, there are also some entrées you won't find at a traditional family restaurant, such as pecan crusted talipia and shepherds's pie. Desserts are all homemade. $7.99–14.99.

Lyon's Luncheonette (410-398-2820), 107 E. Main St. In this day of large chain pharmacies, it's nice to see a business that has been, and still is, thriving since 1896. Within the drug store is a traditional fountain that serves breakfast (the most expensive item is about $5) and lunch sandwiches (can't beat the grilled cheese for $2.95).

SUPERIOR DINING IN A 1700S INN

Fair Hill Inn (410-398-4187; www.fairhillinn.com), at the intersection of MD 213 and MD 273 north of Elkton. Open for dinner Wed.–Sat. Reservations strongly recommended. Inside a restored mid-1700s inn with many original fixtures remaining, such as the huge stone fireplace, chefs/owners Phil Pyle Jr. and Brian Shaw have created one of Maryland's most exceptional dining establishments. Not content to use as many locally available fresh items as possible, they have established a garden of their own, which means just about all of the herbs, tomatoes, squash, carrots, and other vegetables that will be a part of your meal were picked just a short time before you arrived for dinner. They also cut and cure all meats on the premises, and almost every item you eat will be made by them and their staff. This means going so far as to creating their own mustards or canning vegetables from the garden to be used later in the year. The last time I visited, they had planted hops and grape vines so that they could produce their own beer and wine. The dining area is actually four rooms, and they limit guests to only 12 per hour, so you are assured of receiving personal service from the waitstaff and the kitchen.

All of this attention to detail translates into an experience you will remember for a long time. The menu changes monthly, and Phil told me that once one of the innovative dishes he and Brian create is gone, it will never be prepared again—meaning each your visits will be a new adventure. On the menu one June were pork tenderloins covered in a wildflower-glazed BBQ sauce; tuna tartare mixed with ginger, shallots, fennel, and avocado; lemon sole asparagus wrapped in the restaurant's homemade two-year-old prosciutto; and a selection of cheeses from around the world (according to Phil, the selection depends on the "worldwide milking cycle"). The dessert I had was made with cherries picked from an orchard less than 2 miles away, and my dining companion whimpered in ecstasy with every bite of the lemon-infused pastry she lingered over. A list of more than five hundred wines from around the world ensures that you will find the perfect pairing.

Because Fair Hill Inn offers a seven-course tasting menu that costs scores of dollars (you won't be disappointed if you decide to go for it), the restaurant has been unfairly saddled with a local reputation of being expensive. Entrées are $25–30, quite reasonable for an experience that will stay with you long after your meal is done. Do not pass up the chance to dine here.

THE CHEF SHOWS OFF THE FAIR HILL INN GARDEN.

Also, how long has it been since you've had someone hand mix you a real cherry Coke, with cherry and cola syrups? The hand dipped milk shakes and sundaes are also yummy throwbacks to another time.

North East

Nauti-Goose (410-287-7880; www.nauti goosesaloon.com), 200 Cherry St. Closed Tues. With a deck overlooking the Northeast River, the Nauti-Goose is a favorite of Chesapeake Bay boaters who can tie up at the restaurant's dock. Crabcakes are featured prominently (try the ones with key lime buerre blanc) as is much seafood, like the grilled shrimp taco or lobster mac and cheese. Get the combo ($33.95) if you can't decide on one type of seafood. Most meals are $11.95–32.95.

Pier One (410-287-6599), 1 N. Main St. Pam and Vinny Cirino have been operating this popular diner-style place since the late 1990s. Like most diners, it has an extensive menu of sandwiches, pastas, meats, and seafoods. $13.95–27.95.

Perryville

Tiffine's Bistro (410-642-6299; www .tiffinescatering.com), Perryville Outlet Center. Incongruously located within the outlet mall, Tiffine's had not been open long when I had a delectable lunch consisting of a sampler of the many Greek-influenced items created by Tiffine Bouloubassis. The menu also features burgers, sandwiches, and other American, Italian, and Mediterranean items. My hope is that the business is able to survive the initial shakedown period that all restaurants go through—and is able to move to a location more suitable to the quality of its food. $8–19.

Port Deposit

Joe's Grog House (410-287-4764), 26 S. Main St. Yes, Joe's looks like a neighborhood bar from the outside—and it is a crowded and friendly place to grab a drink—but do not be misled to believe that's all it is. Cajun and southwest cuisines influence much of the menu of steaks, BBQ, sandwiches, and other entrées. These folks make their own salsa (some of the best

I've had), breads, and tortillas, along with, almost unheard of in places like this, doing their own smoking of the meats. The setting within the old Falls Hotel is also quite interesting, so be sure to get someone to relate the history of this place and its granite stone walls. $10–30.

CRABS ✔ **Woody's Crab House** (410-287-3541; www.woodyscrabhouse.com), 29 S. Main St., North East. Open for lunch and dinner. A classic Maryland crab house with brown paper tablecloths and a concrete floor (on which you are expected to throw the shells from the complimentary peanuts served with every meal). Steamed crabs in Woody's own spice blend (market price) are the obvious choice, but people also come here for the steamed sack of 50 shrimp or big bucket of littleneck clams. My dining mate and I couldn't decide, so we ordered the Net Buster, with enough lobster, crabcake, crab imperial, two varieties of shrimp, clams, and fresh fish to satisfy us both. A crowded, noisy, and fun atmosphere. Entrées $15.95–35.95.

COFFEE BAR Beans, Leaves, Etc. (410-287-8033), 33 S. Main St., North East. Coffees, teas, and gourmet foods.

SNACKS AND GOODIES

Chesapeake City

Canal Creamery (410-885-3314), 9 Bohemia Ave. With outdoor seating right on the waterfront, this is the best spot for homemade ice cream on a hot afternoon or as an after-dinner treat. Also serves light lunch and dinner items.

Rising Sun

✔ **Kilby Cream** (410-658-8874; www.kilby cream.net), 129 Strohmaier Ln. The Kilby family, who has been dairy farming in Maryland for more than a century, invites guests to their farm, where kids can visit calves, cavort about on the farm-theme playground, or work their way through the corn maze in the fall. However, you really want to visit here so that you can choose one of their many flavors of homemade, and farm fresh, ice creams. Worth a visit to the country.

✳ Entertainment

THEATERS **Cecil Community College Cultural Center** (410-287-1037; www .communityculturalcenter.org), I-95 Exit 100, North East. Dance, music, and theatrical productions are presented here. The local Covered Bridge Theatre Company does at least three presentations annually, two of which are musicals.

✳ Selective Shopping

ANTIQUES **5 and 10 Antique Market** (410-287-8318), 115 S. Main St., North East. Eighty dealers housed within a former hotel (which was also a five-and-dime store).

North Chesapeake Antique Mall (410-287-3938), 2288 Pulaski Hwy., North East. Another multidealer shop, this one is on US 40 north of town.

ART GALLERIES
Chesapeake City
Kevin Quinlan Photography (1-800-330-3127; www.kevinquinlanphotography.com), 210 George St. Like many photographers, Mr. Quinlan's bread and butter comes from being a wedding photographer, but a few moments of wandering around his studio will enlighten you as to his expertise as a chronicler of nature.

Neil's Artwork (410-885-5094), 226 George St. Neil's works focus on the scenery of the upper Chesapeake Bay.

Elkton
Art Space on Main (410-620-2464; www .artspaceonmainmd.com), 138 W. Main St. The gallery and boutique that displays the works of members of Art Space may just inspire you to try your own hand at pottery. Within 20 minutes of sitting down at the wheel, I had been guided through the process of creating a bowl—that actually looked liked and would function as a bowl!

Elkton Arts Center (410-392-5740; www .cecilcountyartscouncil.org), 135 E. Main St. Open Mon.–Fri. and the first and fourth

Sat. of the month. The home of the extremely active Cecil County Arts Council, Elkton Arts Center's calendar of events includes changing exhibits of regional artists and craftspeople, classes, concerts, dance recitals, readings, lectures, and more.

The Palette and The Page (410-398-3636; www.thepaletteandthepage.com), 120 E. Main St. More than two dozen local and regional artists and authors (a nice twist on the traditional art cooperative) are featured here. Expect to see some exceptional pieces of jewelry, paintings, photography, textiles, pottery, and more. There is also a selection of gently used books. In keeping with the business's mission to bring the arts to the public, it also sponsors live music events.

USED BOOKS **Bookseller's Antiques** (410-287-8652), 35 S. Main St., North East. Used books and old papers.

CRAFTS **England's Colony on the Bay** (410-287-5575), 505 S. Main St., North East. There are many touristy items in here, but be sure to stop in to take a look at the decoys and birds carved by local artisans.

SPECIAL SHOPS
Chesapeake City
Back Creek General Store (410-885-5377), 100 Bohemia Ave. It is worth it to step into this shop, which has been restored to its 1800s makeup with original shelving and glass cabinets.

Elkton
Trains, Planes, and Automobiles (410-620-5595; www.trainsplanesandautos.com), 124 W. Main St. For those just starting out, or for the serious hobbyist, this little store is packed with model trains, miniature cars, track, airplanes, and numismatic supplies.

Terra Joy (443-480-5417; www.terrajoy ediblelandscapes.com), 19 N. Main St. Anyone with the slightest awareness of plants, the environment, or landscaping will love this place. With plants and artwork (avant-garde sculpture, garden furniture, flags, etc.) placed in eye-pleasing arrangements throughout the property, the owners have the goal of teaching the world about edible landscaping. Even if you're traveling and not really looking to buy a plant at the moment, stop here to take in the beauty of the fruit trees, bushes, edible vines, and berries. I wish this business much luck and hope that they are able to create many converts.

North East

Day Basket Factory (410-287-6100; www .daybasketfactory.com), 714 S. Main St. Although no longer owned by the Day family, the factory is still making baskets in the same manner it has since 1876. Each piece of local white oak is split and woven by hand into utilitarian and ornamental baskets. If the craftspeople are at work, ask to take a quick tour, and you will see why these baskets, which have only copper and brass fittings—not steel—put those marketed by Longaberger to shame. Day baskets are also guaranteed for life.

England's Colony on the Bay (410-287-5575), 505 S. Main St. The items that Carol England chooses for her store are often exceptional or different and she has a real interest in promoting the works of regional artists. One of the two places I would direct you to purchase a souvenir of your travels in this part of Maryland. I'm not very partial to Christmas shops, but the one that is in the back of this store has so many interesting, well-decorated, and colorful Christmas music boxes and skillfully hand-painted ornaments that I spent more time here than I had expected.

Kathy's Corner Shop (410-287-2333; www.kathyscornershop.com), 100 S. Main St. Not your typical gift shop full of mass-produced items. Almost everything in here is made regionally by talented artists or craftspersons. (I hope they are still carrying the sandcast leaves when you stop in.) The other place that I recommend you go if you want to bring home a memento from your North East visit.

Where Butterflies Bloom (410-287-2975), 24 S. Main St. Closed Tues.–Wed. A small gift shop with some interesting items such as Himalayan crystal salt lamps (pur-ported to provide powerful negative ion benefits), colorful and fragrant handmade soaps, and collectible figurines.

OUTLET Perryville Outlets (410-378-5758; www.perryvilleoutletcenter.com), I-95 Exit 93, Perryville. Includes the outlet shops of Nike, L'eggs, Van Heusen, OshKosh B'Gosh, Book Cellar, and other nationally known names.

PICK-YOUR-OWN PRODUCE FARMS *ℰ* **Milburn Orchards** (410-398-1349; www.milburnorchards.com), 1495 Appleton Rd. (MD 316), Elkton. The orchards have been in the Milburn family for more than one hundred years, and the Milburns have learned a few things about growing and marketing produce. Their U-pick selections include cherries in early summer, peaches in midsummer, and apples in early fall. Lots of fun kids activities throughout the season, with a playground, petting zoo, and barnyard animals. Hayrides, crafts shows, corn maze, and other activities in fall. The farm market (open July 5 through the last Saturday in January) sells not only produce but also some delicious home-baked goodies.

Walnut Springs Farm (410-398-3451; www.strawberryfarm.com), Blue Ball Rd., Elkton. U-pick fruits and seasonal events.

FARMER'S MARKET Detwiler Farm Market (410-392-5179), 235 Lancaster Point Rd., Elkton. In the countryside south of Elkton, Detwiler's sells produce grown in neighboring Lancaster County, PA. In the Amish tradition of that area they also sell fresh baked goods, including shoofly and whoopee pies.

WINERY Dove Valley Winery (410-658-8388; www.dovevalleywine.com), 645 Harrington Rd., Rising Sun. Open Thurs.–Sun. When the Dove Valley's owners purchased this property they found many wild grapevines, prompting them to investigate if the soil was conducive to becoming a vineyard. The answer is obvious, as all of the wines are made exclusively from grapes grown on-site, a rarity for Maryland wineries. The large pine tasting room is a pleasant place to sample wares, which are produced in French and American oak barrels. During the winter, the winery offers tastings directly from the barrels.

✳ Special Events

May: **Spring Fling** (410-642-6066), Rodgers Tavern, 259 Broad St., Perryville. Entertainment, crafts, food, and exhibits. **Highland Gathering** (410-885-2005), Fair Hill Race Track, Fair Hill. A gathering of the clans for dance, piping, drumming, sheepdog demonstrations, and food. **Artists' Open Studio Tour** (410-392-5740; www.cecilcountyartscouncil.org), Elkton. A driving tour takes you to more than 20 artists' studios, so you may view paintings, sculptures, pottery, weaving, wood turning, and more.

June–July: **Summer Music in the Park** (410-392-5740), Pell Gardens, Chesapeake City. Free outdoor concerts ranging from bluegrass to rock 'n' roll. Sun. at 6 PM.

June: **Annual Mid-Atlantic Chevelle Show** (410-879-7893), Community Park, North East. Scores of Chevelles from 1964 to 1987. **Canal Day** (410-885-3132), Chesapeake City. A street festival with arts, crafts, food, and music.

July: **Cecil County Fair** (410-392-3440; www.cecilcountyfair.org), Fair Hill Fairgrounds, Fair Hill.

September: **Annual Juried Exhibition** (410-392-5740), Elkton Arts Center, 135 E. Main St., Elkton. Works by regional artists. **Yesterdays** (410-287-5801). North East celebrates its heritage with street entertainment, demonstrations, children's activities, crafts, music, and an evening ghost walk.

October: **Festival in the Country** (410-755-6065), Fair Hill Natural Resources Management Area, 376 Fair Hill Dr., Fair Hill. International-level equestrian championships and dog agility trials. **Upper Bay Decoy Show** (410-287-5600), VFW Post 6027, North East. Decoy and wildlife carving displays, demonstrations, and competitions.

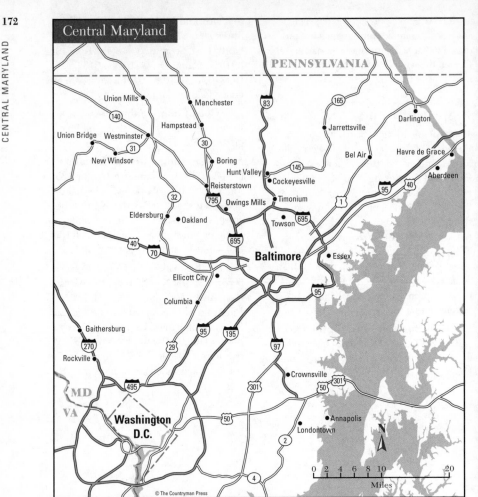

Central Maryland

PENNSYLVANIA

Union Mills
Manchester
83
165
Darlington
140
Hampstead
Jarrettsville
Union Bridge   Westminster
31
30
Bel Air
Havre de Grace
New Windsor
Boring
Hunt Valley
145
Aberdeen
Reisterstown
Cockeyesville
95
40
32
795
Owings Mills
Timonium
1
Eldersburg
Oakland
Towson
695
40   70
695
Baltimore   Essex
70
Ellicott City
95
Columbia
Gaithersburg
95
195
270
29
97
Rockville
MD
495
301
Crownsville
301
VA
Washington
D.C.
50
301
50
Annapolis
Londontown
2
N

0 2 4 6 8 10   20
Miles
4
© The Countryman Press

Central Maryland 2

HARFORD COUNTY
Havre de Grace, Aberdeen, and Bel Air

NORTH OF BALTIMORE
Owings Mills, Hunt Valley, Westminster,
and Taneytown

BALTIMORE

WEST OF BALTIMORE
Ellicott City and Columbia

ANNAPOLIS AND VICINITY

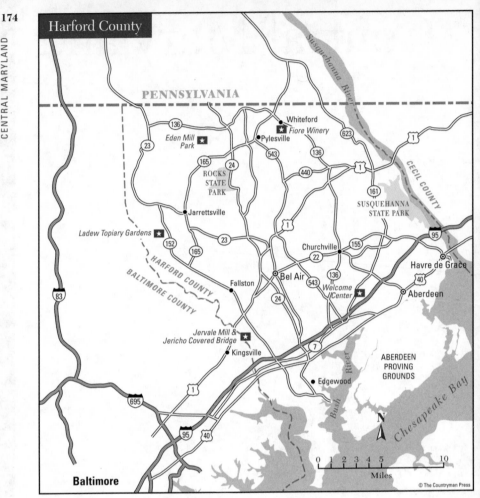

Harford County

PENNSYLVANIA

Susquehanna River

136
Whiteford
Fiore Winery
623
1
Eden Mill
Park
Pylesville
23
165
24
543
136
440
1
ROCKS
STATE
PARK
161
CECIL COUNTY
SUSQUEHANNA
STATE PARK
Jarrettsville
95
Ladew Topiary Gardens
152
23
Churchville
155
165
22
Havre de Grace
HARFORD COUNTY
Fallston
Bel Air
136
40
BALTIMORE COUNTY
543
Welcome
Center
Aberdeen
83
24
Jervale Mill &
Jericho Covered Bridge
7
ABERDEEN
PROVING
GROUNDS
Kingsville
Bush River
695
Edgewood
Chesapeake Bay
1
N
95
40
0 1 2 3 4 5   10
Miles
Baltimore
© The Countryman Press

HARFORD COUNTY
HAVRE DE GRACE, ABERDEEN, AND BEL AIR

Harford County is a place of transition. Its southern portion lies on the Coastal Plain, with the low, flat type of terrain and access to the Chesapeake Bay most often associated with the Eastern Shore. Yet north of I-95, the land rises quickly to the Piedmont Plateau, a landscape of rolling hills and deep gorges created by swiftly moving streams and waterfalls.

Water used to play a more important part in citizens' livelihoods than it does today. During the 1800s, the Susquehanna & Tidewater Canal carried timber, wheat, coal, and other products from Wrightsville, Pennsylvania, to Havre de Grace, but use of the canal declined with the coming of the railroads. Some of the best waterfowl hunting in the world was along the Susquehanna Flats, where the Susquehanna River meets the Chesapeake Bay. Many local residents became commercial hunters, and many more catered to the thousands of sport hunters who flocked to the area. The decline in waterfowl populations and necessary strict regulations brought that way of life to an end in the 1960s.

Like all metropolitan areas, Baltimore is ever expanding, and Harford County started becoming one of its bedroom communities around the 1970s. In fact, a large percentage of the population is now employed in the Baltimore metro area or is engaged in meeting the needs of those who are. It only takes a short drive on a country road to see how quickly living in housing developments is becoming the norm.

Yet a quick drive, especially into the northern and eastern reaches of the county, will also reveal that much of the beauty of the land survives. Susquehanna and Rocks state parks preserve thousands of acres along waterways, and large farms still provide large, pleasing-to-the-eye, open spaces.

Havre de Grace's location next to the water would have, by itself, ensured that it was the county's most scenic town. Although high-rise housing now lines its waterfront, it has managed to become a 21st-century travel destination without damaging its earlier architecture and small-town atmosphere. Elegant Victorian homes line Union Avenue, waterfront parks abound, and independent businesses—not national chains—still occupy the downtown area.

Havre de Grace has dubbed itself the Decoy Capital of the World, and its Decoy Museum goes a long way in substantiating that claim. The Susquehanna Museum at the Lockhouse chronicles the days when the town was the southern terminus for the Susquehanna & Tidewater Canal, while the Maritime Museum tells the story of the waters around the town. A favorite activity of residents and visitors alike is the simple joy of walking the Promenade, a boardwalk along the shoreline.

COMMUNITIES **Aberdeen** was originally called Hall's Cross Roads but was renamed when the Wilmington & Baltimore Railroad's first station manager asked that it be changed to the name of his hometown in Scotland. It was an important transshipment center but truly began to grow after the establishment of the military's Aberdeen Proving Grounds in 1917. Aberdeen's best-known site celebrates the town's favorite son, baseball legend Cal Ripken Jr.

Bel Air is the county seat, which, in addition to its administrative functions, primarily serves as a retail hub for the thousands of homes and housing developments that began to ring around it in the late 20th century. The nearby community college has an active Center for Cultural Arts, and the Ma and Pa Railroad Trail provides a pleasant diversion from urban activity.

GUIDANCE **Harford County Tourism** (410-638-3059; 1-888-544-GO95; www.harford md.com) has an office at 220 S. Main St., Bel Air, 21014. Information specific to the Havre de Grace area can be obtained through the **Havre de Grace Office of Tourism and Visitors Center** (410-939-2100; 1-800-851-7756; www.hdgtourism.com), 450 Pennington Ave., Havre de Grace, 21078. If you stop in, be sure to take a look at the excellent exhibit portraying events that took place locally during the War of 1812.

A state visitors center, the **Maryland House Travel Center** (410-272-0176) is on I-95 between Exits 80 and 85 and can provide information on the local area as well as the entire state.

GETTING THERE *By car:* **I-95** is the main route into the region, providing easy access from Baltimore and the rest of Maryland, and from Delaware and Philadelphia.

By air: **Baltimore/Washington International Thurgood Marshall Airport** (1-800-I-FLY-BWI; www.bwiairport.com), located between Baltimore and Annapolis, is less than an hour's drive to the southwest. Located to the northeast, **Philadelphia International Airport** (215-937-6937; www.phl.org) is a bit more than an hour's drive away.

By train: As a part of its Washington, DC–New York route, **AMTRAK** (1-800-USA-RAIL; www.amtrak.com) has a station in Aberdeen and makes a stop there. **MARC** (1-800-325-RAIL; www.mta.maryland.gov), the **commuter train** from Baltimore, makes stops in Edgewood and Aberdeen.

By water: If you own a boat, or are chartering one, the Chesapeake Bay is the obvious way to arrive. Also, the Chesapeake & Delaware Canal is a part of the Intracoastal Waterway and provides access from the Delaware River and other points to the east.

GETTING AROUND *By car:* **I-95** is the way to get around quickly. **US 40** is also a four-lane highway, but it has a tendency to bring you by the faded parts of the county. **US 1** runs through the more rural, central portions of the area, while **MD 136** in the very northern part of the county is a designated **State Scenic Byway.**

By bus: **Harford County Transportation Services** (410-612-1621; www.harfordtransit.org) has several bus routes that operate in towns along the I-95/US 40 corridor, and one that runs into Bel Air.

By taxi: In Havre de Grace, you can call **Montville Taxi** (410-939-0900). **Victory Cabs** (410-272-0880) operates out of Aberdeen.

PARKING In Havre de Grace, parking lots are located near the water at the foot of Franklin St., in town at the corner of N. Union and Pennington Aves., and at the Havre de Grace Yacht Basin next to Millard E. Tydings Memorial Park.

PUBLIC RESTROOMS   In Havre de Grace, you can find public restrooms in Millard E. Tydings Memorial Park along the southern end of the Promenade, and in small Hutchins Memorial Park at the foot of Congress Ave. near the center of town.

MEDICAL EMERGENCY **Harford Memorial Hospital** (443-843-5000; www.uchs .org), 501 S. Union St., Havre de Grace.

Upper Chesapeake Medical Center (443-643-1000; www.uchs.org), 500 Upper Chesapeake Dr., Bel Air.

✳ To See

COLLEGES **Harford Community College** (443-412-2000; www.harford.edu), 401 Thomas Run Rd., Bel Air. Most community colleges go about their business of providing an education but are not known for their cultural arts offerings to the local community. Not the case here. The **Center for Cultural Arts** is very active in presenting concerts, plays, musicals, dance theater, and a changing gallery of works of art.

COVERED BRIDGES See Jerusalem Mill under *Historic Sites.*

MUSEUMS

Aberdeen

U.S. Army Ordnance Museum (410-278-3602; www.ordmusfound.org), Maryland and Aberdeen Blvds., on the Aberdeen Proving Grounds. A photo ID is required to gain admission to the military installation. Open daily 10–4:45; the outside exhibits are open during daylight hours. Free admission. There were major changes taking place at this museum as this book went to press (so call ahead). Just about everything that had been exhibited was moved to another location, but according to a press release, new exhibits will include American, German, and British tanks; Italian tank destroyers; Jeeps; a display about the Lunar Roving Vehicle that was tested here; and the bazooka that was developed here.

Bel Air

Hays House Museum (410-838-1213; www.harfordhistory.net), 324 Kenmore Ave. Sun. 1–4. Small admission fee. Provides a glimpse into the daily life of an upper class family in the late 1700s and early 1800s. Retains many original architectural details, such as the staircase, mantels, woodwork, and shutters, along with period furnishings.

Havre de Grace

Havre de Grace Decoy Museum (410-939-3739; www.decoymuseum.com), 215 Giles St. Open daily. Small admission fee. The excellence and quantity of decoys here rivals that of the larger Ward Museum of Wildlife Art in Salisbury on the Eastern Shore (see "Salisbury"). The exhibits include working decoys (hand carved and factory produced), decorative decoys, and those made by local, but nationally known, craftspeople. Do not overlook the superb diorama of a decoy carver's shop or the upstairs picture windows' sweeping view of the bay.

Susquehanna Museum at the Lock House (410-939-5780; www.thelockhousemuseum .org), Erie and Conesto Sts. Fri. and Sun. 1–5, Apr.–early Nov. Donations accepted. The Susquehanna & Tidewater Canal provided a water transportation system between Philadelphia and Baltimore from the early 1800s to 1900. Although much has changed at this site, which was the canal's southern terminus, you can still get a feel for the early days by walking along a short section of the towpath and across the pivot bridge. Volunteers take visitors into the lock house furnished with Victorian-period reproductions. The 1782 survey map of the town also helps bring things into perspective.

Havre de Grace Maritime Museum (410-939-4800; www.hdgmaritimemuseum.org), 100 Lafayette St. Open daily June–Aug.; Sat., Mon., Wed., Fri. Sept.–May. Donations accepted. One of the nicer cultural assets in Havre de Grace, the Maritime Museum preserves the heritage of the area with artifacts, photographs, and memorabilia.

Steppingstone Museum (410-939-2299; www.steppingstonemuseum.org), 461 Quaker Bottom Rd. (accessed from I-95 Exit 89). Open Sat. and Sun. May–Sept. Small admission fee; free for children under 12. A stone farmhouse and several outbuildings preserve and demonstrate the 1880–1920 rural lifestyle and crafts of the region. (Also see *To Do—Special Classes.*)

HISTORIC SITES

Havre de Grace

Rock Run Grist Mill, in Susquehanna State Park, north of Havre de Grace. Located next to the Susquehanna River, the Rock Run Grist Mill was built by John Stump in 1794. It still works, and grinding demonstrations are presented on a scheduled basis. The building to the left of the parking area is the Jersey Toll House, built for the toll collector of the Susquehanna River Bridge, which was destroyed by ice floes in 1856. It is now the information center for the park. To get a better understanding of the mill and its heyday, pick up the historic walking-tour brochure from the information center. On the easy 45-minute journey you will learn how the mill operated and pass by the springhouse, the miller's home, and the stone Rock Run House.

Kingsville

Jerusalem Mill (410-877-3560; www.jerusalemmill.org), 2813 Jerusalem Rd. (off MD 152). Open Sat. and Sun. 1–4, with living-history demonstrations on some Sat. and Sun. Donations accepted. The Friends of Jerusalem Mills have restored the 18th-century mill and several other buildings that were a part of a Quaker settlement that prospered for two centuries. A

ROCK RUN GRISTMILL

GARDENS

✿ Ladew Topiary Gardens (410-557-9570; www.ladewgardens.com), 3535 Jarretsville Pike, Monkton. Mon.–Fri. 10–4, Sat.–Sun. 10:30–5, Apr.–Oct. Admission to the gardens and nature walk is $10 adults, $8 seniors/students, and $2 children. Admission for the gardens, nature walk, and a guided tour of the house is $13 adults, $11 seniors/students, and $5 children.

Expect to spend several hours to appreciate all that is here. In fact, bring your lunch or eat in the Ladew Café and devote half a day to walking, relaxing, and enjoying the gardens' 22 acres and house.

Between 1929 and 1971, Henry S. Ladew developed 15 gardens, each with a different theme, form, and color. Among them are the Woodland Garden (the first to bloom in spring), the Berry Garden (designed to be bright and colorful in winter and to provide forage for birds), and the Yellow Garden (with its variety of yellow blossoms throughout the season). I found that as I walked from one to the other, the landscaping created angles of vegetation that were pleasing to the eye and drew me along in anticipation of what was around the next bend.

The centerpiece, of course, is the Topiary Garden, with its sculpted unicorn, sea horses, Churchill's top hat and victory sign, birds in flight, and more. Very young children will enjoy the animal sculptures, while older teens will appreciate the work and talent that went into creating them.

The Manor House is also a tribute to Ladew's vision. It was nothing more than a farmhouse when he purchased it in 1929. It is now a place of such architectural character and lavishness, tempered with an eye toward quality, that one of its rooms, the Oval Library, is included in the book *100 Most Beautiful Rooms in America*.

FANCIFUL SHRUBBERY AT LADEW TOPIARY GARDENS IN MONKTON

small museum, and living-history demonstrations presented from time to time, provide background information. The circa-1865 **Jericho Covered Bridge** is nearby and was an important part of the community.

HISTORIC CHURCH Calvary United Methodist Church (410-734-6920), 1321 Calvary Rd., Churchville. The oldest continuously operating original Methodist church on Maryland's western shore, it still has many of its 1821 features—including the slave gallery.

LIGHTHOUSE Concord Point Lighthouse (410-939-0768; www.concordpoint lighthouse.org), Concord and Lafayette Sts., Havre de Grace. Sat. and Sun. 1–5, Apr.–Oct. No admission fee; donations accepted. Built of nearby Port Deposit granite in 1827, this is one of the oldest continuously operating lighthouses in the United States, and possibly the oldest in Maryland. Other than its electric light, it has been restored, with lighthouse-keeper furnishings and other accoutrements, to appear as it did in the 19th century. Being at the end of the Promenade and overlook-

CONCORD POINT LIGHTHOUSE

ing the point where the Susquehanna River meets the Chesapeake Bay, this is a great spot to sit, walk, or picnic even if the lighthouse is not open. Across the street is the historic home of John O'Neil, keeper of the lighthouse.

✳ To Do

BOAT EXCURSIONS Lantern Queen (410-939-1468; www.lanternqueen.com), docked in Hutchins Park, Havre de Grace A true paddle-wheeler, the *Lantern Queen* began

THE *LANTERN QUEEN*

its cruising life in South Dakota and moved on to Florida and Philadelphia before coming to Havre de Grace. Its schedule varies by the season, but there is usually at least one evening dinner cruise on the Susquehanna River a week Mar.–Oct. There is a bit of narration about history and the sights the boat passes, but this usually takes place during dinner, and the sound of diners' conversations drown out what is coming from the speaker. However, that doesn't really matter; the scenery and excitement of being on a replica of a Mississippi paddle-wheeler are reward enough.

SKIPJACK *MARTHA LEWIS* MOORED IN HAVRE DE GRACE

Oldtown Parasail (410-688-2397; www.oldtownparasail.com), 211 Congress Ave. Kind of a one-stop shop for things aquatic, these folks offer scenic boat excursions, parasail trips (for singles or couples), and kayak rentals.

Skipjack Martha Lewis (410-939-4078; www.skipjackmarthalewis.org), at the Concord Point Lighthouse, Concord and Lafayette Sts., Havre de Grace. The *Martha Lewis*, owned by the Chesapeake Heritage Conservancy and one of the last remaining oyster dredge boats, offers 75-minute Discovery Cruises to the public. Cruises depart on Sat. and Sun., mid-May–mid-Oct. Reservations are not needed, but be mindful that the sailboat is limited to 28–30 passengers.

BOWLING Bowl Harford Lanes (410-272-3555; www.bowlharfordlanes.com), 20 Custis St., Aberdeen.

GOLF

Havre de Grace

Bulle Rock (410-939-8887; 1-888-285-5375; www.bullerockgolf.com), 320 Bleinheim Lane. Bulle Rock is a Pete Dye course that opened in the late 1990s to favorable reviews from numerous golfing magazines.

MINIATURE GOLF *&* **Churchville Golf and Baseball** (410-879-5357; www.church villegolf.com), 3040 Churchville Rd., Churchville. Batting cages, arcade, and miniature golf.

HIKING A 20-mile section of the 190-mile **Mason-Dixon Trail System,** which branches off the **Appalachian Trail (AT)** in Cumberland County, Pennsylvania, passes through Harford County and Susquehanna State Park (see below). Some of it follows roadways, yet it is a scenic hike with a number of views of the Susquehanna River. More information can be obtained from www.masondixontrail.org.

As it comes through the county, the Mason-Dixon Trail System shares its footpath with a portion of the **Lower Susquehanna Heritage Greenway,** a proposed system of trails that will include multiple miles of pathways along both sides of the Susquehanna River. Approximately 10 miles of the trail that run from Havre de Grace to Susquehanna State Park (see below) have been marked and are easy to follow. The Lower Susquehanna Heritage Greenway, Inc. (410-475-2482; www.hitourtrails.com), 4948 Conowingo Rd., Darlington, 21304, can provide maps and up-to-date information.

THE SUSQUEHANNA RIVER AS VIEWED FROM SUSQUEHANNA STATE PARK

Susquehanna State Park (410-557-7994; www.dnr.state.md.us/publiclands/central
/susquehanna.asp), north of Havre de Grace along the Susquehanna River on Stafford and
Rock Run Rds. The waters of the Susquehanna River rise in Otsego County, New York, and
flow for more than 400 miles to empty into the head of the Chesapeake Bay, close to where
the river separates central Maryland from the Eastern Shore. Protecting a portion of the
river's drainage just before it meets the bay is 3,600-acre Susquehanna State Park.

A network of approximately 15 miles of pathways enables you to explore this varied topography of riverside vegetation, heavy forest cover, lightly flowing brooks, rock outcrops with
grandstand views of the river, and interesting history (see *Historic Sites*). In addition, the
park offers a campground with rental cabins, restrooms and hot showers, a picnic area, boat-
launch facility, and evening interpretive programs.

Rocks State Park (410-557-7994; www.dnr.state.md.us/publiclands/central/rocks.asp), 3318
Rocks Chrome Hill Rd., Jarretsville. Deer Creek has cut a gorge into the Piedmont Plateau,
creating a rugged scenery of large boulders, interesting rock formations, and steep cliffs. The
park's trail system winds through the irregular landscape, going down to the creek and up to
the heights. Don't miss the route to the **King and Queen's Seat.** These rock outcrops, close
to 200 feet above the creek, look down onto some pretty dramatic views.

Located nearby, and administered by the state park, are **Hidden Valley Natural Area** with
additional trails, and **Kilgore Falls** at **Falling Branch,** the state's second highest vertical
waterfall.

Also see *Parks* and *Walks.*

SAILING BaySail (410-939-2869; www.baysail.net), 100 Bourbon St., Tidewater Marina,
Havre de Grace. BaySail is a one-stop sailing shop. Their school, which offers courses for
beginners on up to bareboat-charter certification, is certified by the American Sailing Association. Once you gain a bit of proficiency, you can set out on your own cruise with a charter
boat rented by the half day, day, or week—or buy a boat of your own from BaySail. If you

don't have the time to gain the needed expertise, just ask them to include a captain with your charter boat.

SPECIAL CLASSES **Steppingstone Museum** (410-939-2299; www.steppingstone museum.org), 461 Quaker Bottom Rd. (accessed from I-95 Exit 89), Havre de Grace. The museum sponsors historical crafts workshops in early spring, usually in May. (Also see *Museums.*)

SWIMMING Deer Creek passes through **Rocks State Park** in Jarretsville and is a popular swimming and tubing stream. Be aware that you are on your own; there are no lifeguards.

TENNIS Courts open to the public are located in a number of the parks operated by the Harford County Department of Parks and Recreation. Among the many are **Francis Silver Park** on Shuresville Rd., **Churchville Recreation Complex, Forest Hill Recreation Complex,** and **Norrisville Recreation Complex.** Indoor tennis is available in at the **Emmorton Recreation and Tennis Center** in Bel Air. More information can be obtained by calling 410-638-3572.

✳ Green Space

PARKS ✐ ᕦ **Eden Mill Park and Nature Center** (410-836-3050; www.edenmill.org), 1617 Eden Mill Rd., Pylesville. The nature center, located in an old mill building, is one of the most impressive I have seen in a county-operated park. Lots of good displays for the kids and a very active volunteer group that presents programs on a wide variety of topics. The park's trail system is well thought out. In just 2 miles, it can take hikers through a variety of environments along Deer Creek, into small meadows, and over a low ridge. There are also several public canoe-launch sites; one is handicapped accessible.

WALKS **The Promenade** in Havre de Grace is a 0.5-mile boardwalk along the waterfront with interpretive signs explaining the natural and human history of the area. Because it starts at **Millard E. Tydings Memorial Park,** goes by the **Decoy** and **Maritime museums,** and ends at the **Concord Point Lighthouse,** it is a convenient way to see the sites without having to drive. Looking out upon the Chesapeake Bay, it is also a great place to be for sunrise and sunset. This is surely one of the nicest gifts the citizens of Havre de Grace have given themselves and visitors to enhance the quality of town life.

Also in Havre de Grace is the **North Park Loop Trail**, a 1.5-mile pathway that begins near the Susquehanna Museum at the Lock House and through woods and meadow at the very mouth of the Susquehanna River at the head of the bay. A brochure available at the Lock House provides interpretive information keyed to number spots along the way.

The Ma and Pa Trail (www.mapatrail.org) in Bel Air follows an easy, nearly level old railroad grade through the town of Bel Air and out into the countryside. Several miles are usable now; when completed, it will total 7 miles in length.

✳ Lodging
MOTELS AND HOTELS
Aberdeen, 21001
🐾 ᕦ **Clarion Hotel Aberdeen** (410-273-6300; www.clarionaberdeen.com), 980 Hospitality Way. Located just off I-95, the hotel has a fitness center, seasonal outdoor pool,

and a business center. Pets are permitted, and each room has a refrigerator and microwave. $139–199.

Edgewood, 21040
🐾 **Best Western** (410-679-9700; www .bestwestern.com), 1709 Edgewood Rd.

(accessed from I-95 Exit 77). Exercise room, pool, and pets permitted. $89–99.

♪ ₺ **Ramada** (410-679-0770; www.ramada .com), 1700 Van Bibber Rd. (accessed from I-95 Exit 77). Within easy driving distance of many area attractions. Lots of extras, including complimentary deluxe continental breakfast, HBO, in-room coffeemakers, and an outdoor pool. Children 18 and under stay free. $85–150.

INNS

Havre de Grace, 21078

🦞 **Chipparelli's** (410-939-5440; www .chipparellishdg.com), 400 N. Union Ave. The Old Chesapeake Hotel, dating from the late 1800s, offers three suites, all with private bath. The Chesapeake Suite has marble in the bathroom and a Jacuzzi. Lunch or dinner is a simple matter of walking down the steps to Ken's Steak and Rib House (see *Dining Out*). The size of the rooms and their elegant furnishings are a good deal for the price. $119–129.

♪ **Vandiver Inn** (410-939-5200; 1-800-245-1665; www.vandiverinn.com), 301 S. Union Ave. Built in 1886 by Murray Vandiver as a wedding gift to his wife, Annie. The opulence of the house reflects his political career, which included serving in the Maryland House of Delegates, as state treasurer, as mayor of Havre de Grace, and an appointment to the IRS by President Cleveland. The chandelier and stained glass in the parlor are original, as are many items in the eight large guest rooms. The two houses next door to the inn have eight rooms available to guests. Children welcome. $129–159.

BED & BREAKFASTS

Havre de Grace, 21078

Currier House (410-939-7886; 1-800-827-2889; www.currier-bb.com), 800 S. Market St. In 1996, Jane Currier Belbot opened a B&B in the late 1700s house that has been in her family since 1861. She has been in business so long now that she told me, "I have so many regular guests now that it's like old friends are always coming to visit."

I truly felt more like I was visiting someone's home than I did in any other establishment in Harford County. The house is decorated with heirlooms, family furniture, original Currier and Ives lithographs, and photos of ancestors and the glory days of Havre de Grace. All four guest rooms have a private bath, and two of them have a balcony overlooking a grand magnolia tree, the Concord Point Lighthouse, and the bay. I was especially taken by the milieu of the Crawford Room's cedarwood-lined bathroom. The full watermen's breakfast includes oysters and Maryland stewed tomatoes (in-season). $110–135.

La Clé D'or (410-939-9562; 1-888-HUG-GUEST; www.lacledorguesthouse.com), 226 N. Union Ave. This place should have a motto something like, "Live in opulence for a while without spending a fortune." The 1868 home is loaded with gorgeous antiques and has 17 Strauss crystal chandeliers. The guest rooms are decorated with their own theme. Breakfast is served on a variety of fine china accompanied by gold utensils, the brick-walled garden is entered through a wrought-iron gate, and the outdoor Jacuzzi is large enough to handle a party of 10. Refreshments and a cookie jar are always available. $140–160.

♪ **Spencer Silver Mansion** (410-939-1485; 1-800-780-1485; www.spencersilver mansion.com), 200 S. Union Ave. Children welcome. One of the most beautifully restored Victorian mansions I've seen. Guest rooms are lavishly furnished with oak and mahogany antiques of the period; a stone two-story carriage house is available for those wishing privacy. $90–130.

COTTAGE

Havre de Grace, 21078

White House Guest House (443-553-7609; www.whitehouseofhavredegrace .com), 412 Green St. Less than a half a block from Havre de Grace's retail district, the White House is a good choice for a couple wanting a bedroom and a kitchen close to most of the town's restaurants, shops, waterfront, and other attractions. It's a small house that has been modernized, but

SPENCER SILVER MANSION

retains much of its original charm, including the hardwood floors. A continental breakfast, including goodies from Goll's Bakery, is provided each morning. $125.

CAMPING **Bar Harbor RV Park & Marina** (410-679-0880; 1-800-351-CAMP; www.barharborrvpark.com), 4228 Birch Ave. Not far from I-95 and about 30 minutes from Baltimore, the campground is located next to the water at the head of the Chesapeake Bay. As the name implies, it caters to RV travelers who don't mind being packed in closely side-by-side. Full hook-ups, TV, pool, and a few other amenities.

Also see **Susquehanna State Park** under *Hiking.*

✳ Where to Eat

DINING OUT

Havre de Grace

Chipparelli's (410-939-5440; www.chipparellishdg.com), 400 N. Union Ave. Chipparelli's in housed within the old 1893 Chesapeake Hotel building (where Al Capone once dined). If you have dined at Chipparelli's of Little Italy in Baltimore, you know what you are about to experience. My meal included Maryland crab soup and gnocchi Bolognese. Full picture windows look out on the street and the upstairs offers guest rooms (see *Inns*). $13–20.

Laurrapin (410-939-4956; www.laurrapin.com), 209 N. Washington St. Open for lunch and dinner. This is my kind of place. A large percentage of the furnishings, from the tables to the artwork on the walls, is from the owners' artist friends. The owners and chef are from the area, and they use as much locally grown organic and free-range meats as possible. This means the menu and daily specials change often, but that's okay, because the quality of the northern California–influenced Chesapeake Bay dishes doesn't. My Maryland crab gazpacho was nice and refreshing, and the vegetarian muffuletta was big enough that it could have served two people. Dinner selections have included lamb shank osso buco, meat loaf wrapped in bacon with caramelized onions, and wild caught salmon on a bed of California spinach. This restaurant is well worth spending the $15–27 for a dinner entrée.

✐ **MacGregor's** (410-939-3003; www.macgregorsrestaurant.com), 331 St. John St. Open for lunch and dinner. Seafood is the definite specialty of this restaurant, which has a casually elegant atmosphere. Crabcakes (market price), stuffed flounder, shrimp, and the Dijon herb breadcrumb –encrusted rockfish make use of the local catch. The older portion of the restaurant is inside a former bank building, while the newer glass-enclosed section provides memorable views of the Susquehanna River. The tavern serves light fare and has live entertainment on the weekends. Entrées $18.99–28.99.

Note to film and history buffs: The Mac-Gregor name comes from owner Daniel Lee, a direct descendant of Rob Roy MacGregor.

✐ **Tidewater Grille** (410-939-3313; www.thetidewatergrille.com), 300 Franklin St.

Open for lunch and dinner. The dining room and two outside decks overlook the Susquehanna River. Seafood, much of it mixed with pasta, occupies at least half of the menu, with chicken, beef, and chops making up the rest of the entrées. Meat lovers will enjoy the Tidewater Mixed Grille with a petite fillet, breast of chicken, loin lamb chop, and andouille sausage. $16–28.95. Lighter fare, with a little lower prices, is available in the bar/lounge area.

EATING OUT

Aberdeen

Durango's Southwestern Grille (410-273-6300; www.clarionaberdeen.com), 980 Hospitality Way. As it is located inside the Clarion Hotel, Durango's makes it easy to have breakfast, lunch, or dinner without having to drive very far if you are staying at the hotel. It's quite a varied menu, from Maryland crabcakes to south of the border tacos, quesadillas, and enchiladas. $8.99–22.99.

✿ **Japan House** (410-272-7878), 984 Beards Hill Rd. Open for lunch and dinner. Fresh sushi and sashimi are what bring diners in. Items from the teppanyaki grill, such as salmon and sesame chicken, are also popular. $13.95–20.95.

The New Ideal Diner (410-272-1880), US 40. Open for breakfast (served all day), lunch, and dinner. Established in 1931. The present structure is the restaurant's fourth dining car in the same location. The gleaming stainless-steel and green-enamel striped car was manufactured by Jerry O'Mahony, Inc., and transported to the site in four sections in 1952. A very popular local favorite, it is always crowded for breakfast and lunch. Dinner selections include seafood, meats, and pasta. $8.45–19.95.

✿ **Olive Tree** (410-575-7773; www.mary landitalianrestaurant.net), 1005 Beards Hill Rd. Open for lunch and dinner. Since the pasta is made fresh before your eyes inside the glass "pasta booth," it only makes sense to order a dish containing one of its many forms. Choose a pasta entrée by itself or accompanied with crab, chicken, or beef. $9.95–19.

Havre de Grace

✿ **The Bayou Restaurant** (410-939-3565; www.bayourestaurant.net), 927 Pulaski Hwy. (US 40). Open for lunch and dinner. You know that family-owned restaurant near you that has been around for decades and that everyone in town patronizes from time to time? Well, this is Havre de Grace's version. Expect friendly service and honest home cooking. All of the soups, breads, and pies are made from scratch. The seafood combo of flounder, crabcake, oysters, shrimp, and scallops is available broiled or fried. A filling, healthful, and low-cost entrée is the vegetarian fettuccine. Many choices of beef, veal, poultry, and other seafood entrées fill the menu. $8.50–27.95.

COFFEE BAR Java by the Bay (410-939-0227), 118 N. Washington St., Havre de Grace. Coffees and teas by the cup or the pound. Lots of goodies to choose from, such as a bagel, muffin, or Danish, to go with your drink.

SNACKS AND GOODIES Bomboy's (410-939-2924; www.bomboyscandy.com), 329 Market St., Havre de Grace. Closed Mon. The chocolate candies created at Bomboy's, available by the piece or the pound, are made fresh daily using old family recipes. Fresh fudge and sugar-free chocolates are also available. If candy is not your fancy, **Bomboy's Homemade Ice Cream** is directly across the street.

Golls Bakery (410-939-2556; www.golls bakery.com), 234 N. Washington St., Havre de Grace. A true old-fashioned bakery that has been a family-operated business since 1930. Fresh made breads, doughnuts, cookies, and, maybe best of all, a wide variety of individual-sized pies.

✳ Entertainment

FILM Regal Bel Air Cinema (410-569-8276; www.regalmovies.com), 409 Constant Friendship Blvd., Abingdon. One of the places to see movies in the local area. The other is **Flagship Cinemas** (410-734-9275; www.flagshipcinemas.com), 2408 Churchville Rd., Churchville.

✳ Selective Shopping

ANTIQUES

Havre de Grace

There are so many antiques shops clustered along St. John St., N. Union Ave., and N. Washington St. in Havre de Grace that the area has come to be known as **Antique Row**. One of the standouts is **Seneca Cannery Antiques** (410-942-0701; www .antiquesinhavredegrace.com/seneca), 210 St. John St. With two floors and 20,000 square feet of space, you never know what treasure you may find displayed by multiple dealers. The building is a historical antique itself, having been built in the (possibly) early 1800s. The original interior and exterior walls are still visible, as well as the post and beam support structure.

Bahoukas Collectables and Muzeum (410-942-1290; www.bahoukas.com), 408 N. Union Ave. An interesting place to wander around, although it's so packed you'll have a hard time making it through the aisles of pottery, furniture, sports memorabilia, beer signs, dolls, figurines, vintage toys, and some of the more interesting life-sized wooden caricatures you'll ever come across.

Bayside Antiques (410-939-9397), 232 N. Washington St. An antiques mall with a number of dealers offering upscale merchandise.

ART GALLERIES The Picture Show

Art Gallery (410-939-0738), 301 St. John St., Havre de Grace. Features Chesapeake Bay sculpture and artwork.

Riverview Gallery (410-939-6401), 224 N. Washington St., Havre de Grace. A small gallery with paintings, sculpture, pottery, and photographs.

USED-BOOK STORES Washington

Street Books (410-939-6215; www .washingtonstreetbooks.com), 131 N. Washington St., Havre de Grace. Wed.–Mon. noon–6. More than 35,000 used, rare, and out-of-print books, along with a large offering of comic books (many collectibles) and a small selection of new books.

Courtyard Book Shop (410-939-5150), 313 St. John St., Havre de Grace. Open every day. A selection of used and antiquarian books.

SPECIAL SHOPS

Havre de Grace

Doodads (410-939-8003; www.doodads .us), 308 St. John St. Doodads is a global fair trade gallery, meaning that the products in the shop are made by workers around the world earning at least their home country's minimum wage. In addition, the producers are encouraged to manage and use local resources in a sustainable way. If you're going to buy a memento to bring home, why not do it here?

✐ **Just for Fun** (443-502-2798; www.just forfunmd.com), 464 Franklin St. New and old comics along with sports cards, novelty items, and a great selection of very collectible figurines.

Simply Art & Gift Gallery (410-939-6129; www.simplyart.vpweb.com), 456 Franklin St. More gift shop than art gallery, the store does offer the interesting artwork of owner and self-taught artist Stephen G. Formalt and other regional artists.

Vincenti Decoys (410-734-7709; www .vincentidecoys.com), 353 Penningtonton Ave. The retail outlet of the decoy-carving couple Pat and Jeannie Vincenti displays and sells their working and decorative decoys, as well as decoy carving supplies and the works of other artists in various media. Drive the short distance to their Churchville studio (410-734-6238; 303 West Ln.) to see this couple's creative process in person.

FARMER'S MARKETS Havre de

Grace Farmer's Market. You can find seasonal offerings at the market on Pennington Ave. 9–noon, May–mid-Nov.

Bel Air Farmer's Market. Produce stands are set up at 2 S. Bond St. on Sat. 7–11, mid-Apr.–mid-Nov.

Edgewood Farmer's Market. You can purchase the bounty of the seasons in Edgewood in the lot across from the

MARC station on Thurs. 3–6, May–mid-Nov.

PICK-YOUR-OWN PRODUCE FARMS ✔ Applewood Farm (410-836-1140; www.applewoodfarm.org), 4425 Prospect Rd., Whiteford. You can pick your own pumpkins, gourds, and mums during Sept. and Oct. Special events during the year include a petting zoo, hayrides, a maze, and train displays.

WINERY Fiore Winery (410-879-4007; www.fiorewinery.com), 3026 Whiteford Rd. (MD 136), Pylesville. Open for tours and tastings Mon.–Sat. 10–5 and Sun. noon–5. Vintner Mike Fiore was born in Calabria, Italy, and grew up in a family whose experience in winemaking goes back more than four hundred years. Coming to this sloping hillside in northern Harford County, he planted his first grapes in 1977. Besides the tour and the tastings, you are also permitted to enjoy the scenery and the vineyards. Fiore sponsors several annual fun events, such as its well-attended jazz and arts festival.

✳ Special Events

May: **Annual Decoy and Wildlife Art Festival** (410-939-3739; www.decoymuseum.com). For three days in May, Havre de Grace hosts one of the largest and longest-running festivals to honor decoy carving and other forms of wildlife art. **ArtQuest** (410-638-5974), Bel Air. Food and live entertainment accompany the works of local professional and amateur artists.

June: **Annual Evening of Wine and Jazz** (410-939-5780), Susquehanna Museum, Havre de Grace. **Celtic Festival** (410-939-2299), Steppingstone Museum, Havre de Grace. A full day of pipe-band music, sheep herding and shearing, spinning and weaving, and lots of Celtic food and fashions.

July: **Harford County Farm Fair** (410-838-8663; www.farmfair.org), Bel Air.

August: **Annual Arts and Crafts Show** (410-939-9342), Millard E. Tydings Memorial Park, Havre de Grace. For more than four decades, the local chapter of Soroptimist International has been sponsoring this two-day event. Arts, crafts, food, demonstrations, and music. **Pirate Pub Crawl** (410-939-2100; www.thelockhousemuseum.org), Havre de Grace. **Seafood Festival** (410-939-1525; www.hdgseafoodfest.org), Millard E. Tydings Memorial Park, Havre de Grace. More than 20 vendors serving a variety of foods, with many incorporating local seafood. Arts and crafts and free live entertainment.

September: **Annual Duck Fair** (410-939-3739), Havre de Grace. Wildlife artists and carvers, retriever demonstrations, and many children's activities.

September and October: **Haunted History and Ghost Tours** (410-939-1811), Havre de Grace. Fri. and Sat. evenings through Oct.

December: **Candlelight Tour** (410-939-3947), Havre de Grace. A yearly event in which businesses, churches, B&Bs, and historic homes open their doors to visitors.

NORTH OF BALTIMORE
OWINGS MILLS, HUNT VALLEY, WESTMINSTER, AND TANEYTOWN

B altimore's neighbors to the north, especially those within 15 miles or so of the I-695 beltway, are becoming ensnared in the city's sprawl. Long strings of strip malls, fast-food restaurants, and convenience stores meld into one another. It's hard to tell where some towns, such as Pikesville, Owings Mills, Towson, Lutherville, and Timonium, begin or end.

This does not mean you should overlook these places in your quest to explore the best that Maryland has to offer. Just off the beltway in Towson is Hampton, the first property to be accepted into the National Park Service system on architectural, and not necessarily historic, merit in 1948. The Fire Museum of Maryland in Lutherville, with more than 60 vehicles dating from the early 1800s, has one of the largest collections of its kind in the country. The last remaining serpentine grasslands in the state, Soldier's Delight National Environmental Area, are located just outside Owings Mills, while more than ¼ of all of Maryland's horse farms occupy large amounts of acreage between I-83 and MD 140/MD 30.

Also providing quick escapes from the density of Baltimore are Oregon Ridge, a regional park whose pathways provide impressive views of Hunt Valley, and the North Central Railroad Trail, with a level route stretching for 20 miles from the Pennsylvania border to Cockeysville. More than 100 miles of trails snake around the varied terrain of 17,000-acre Gunpowder Falls State Park.

Farther afield, and a bit to the west, Carroll County has vast amounts of land devoted to agricultural purposes. A drive on just about any of its two-lane roadways yields a scenery of rolling meadows freckled by grazing cattle and poultry farms. All of those open fields means the county is also the least forested, but places like Piney Run and Hashawha parks help preserve large stands of mature trees for present and future generations.

Substantial population growth in the last few decades has not robbed the communities of their small-town personalities. On the outskirts of Westminster, the county seat, MD 140 is lined with big-box discount stores and shopping centers, yet the historic district around Main Street remains packed with structures from the 1800s, many mom-and-pop businesses, and a 1920s Art Deco theater—home of the local arts council.

Nearby Taneytown (pronounced *tawneytown*), most scenically reached via MD 832 instead of MD 140, is the county's oldest town. George Washington visited the Adam Good Tavern in 1791, when a sign above it read: A DAMN GOOD INN, ENTERTAINMENT FOR MAN AND BEAST. Undoubtedly much more upscale, the Antrim 1844 Inn takes in today's travelers.

Mount Airy has always been a place along America's busiest transportation routes. First, it was the Old National Pike in the early 1700s, then the Baltimore & Ohio Railroad in the

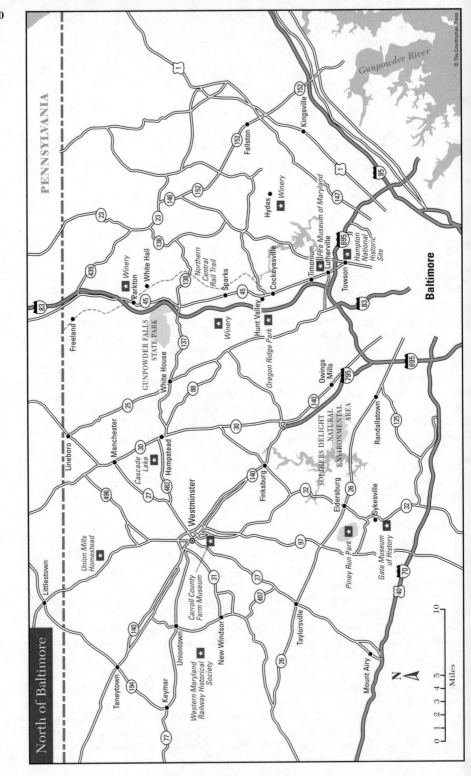

North of Baltimore

© The Countryman Press

1800s, and US 40 in the early 1900s. High-speed motorists on I-70 now tend to zip by, missing its antiques shops and nearby wineries.

An interesting chapter in Sykesville's history is Betsy Syke's wedlock to Napoleon Bonaparte's brother, Jerome. Napoleon was against the marriage and refused to allow Betsy to enter France, and she never saw Jerome again. The town is one of the many old railroad towns in Maryland that thrived when the trains came through but withered away once they left. The train station now houses a restaurant whose live folk and jazz entertainment attracts many locals and Baltimoreans on the weekend.

Uniontown has no such commercial establishments; its claim to fame is its historic district, with a diversity of 18th-, 19th-, and 20th-century structures. An easy walking tour of 20 minutes will take you past an abundance of architectural delights decorated by cupolas, cornices, dormers, and hipped roofs.

GUIDANCE The **Carroll County Visitors Center** (410-848-1388; 1-800-272-1933; www.carrollcountytourism.org) shares space with the Historical Society of Carroll County and is located at 210 E. Main St., Westminster, 21157.

The Baltimore County Conference and Visitors Bureau (410-887-2849; www.enjoy baltimorecounty.com) is at 400 Washington Ave., Towson, 21204.

GETTING THERE *By car:* **I-83** heads directly north of Baltimore after it branches off the **Baltimore Beltway (I-695)** at Exit 24 near Lutherville. The largest percentage of listings and attractions in this section are located in Carroll County, which can be reached by taking **I-795** from Baltimore and then continuing along **MD 140.**

By air: **Baltimore/Washington International Thurgood Marshall Airport** (1-800-I-FLY-BWI; www.bwiairport.com), located between Baltimore and Annapolis, is about an hour's drive to the southeast.

GETTING AROUND *By car:* Traffic along any of the roads within 15 miles of the **Baltimore Beltway (I-695)** is extremely heavy during the morning and evening rush hours. There are not any good alternatives, so just turn on the radio and accept it. During the middle of the day, **I-83** becomes a fairly rapid way to head directly north into Baltimore County. The situation is much better in Carroll County. **MD 140** is a good four-lane highway that becomes a two-lane country road north of Westminster. Other roads are lightly traveled during the middle part of the day.

By rail: The **Central Light Rail Line** (410-832-1200, ext. 3990), the commuter train service out of Baltimore, basically parallels I-83 and makes stops at Lutherville, Timonium Business Park, and Timonium. Trains run about every 15 minutes and operate until 11 PM; 7 PM on Sun. The **MARC** rail service (1-800-325-RAIL; www.mta.maryland.gov) makes stops in Owings Mills and Hunt Valley.

By taxi: One phone number—410-486-4000—puts you in contact with taxicabs based in Owings Mills, Reistertown, and Pikesville.

PARKING In Westminster, parking meters are free after 5 PM and all day Sat. and Sun.

MEDICAL EMERGENCY **St. Joseph Medical Center** (410-337-1000; www.sjmcmd .org), 7601 Osler Dr., Towson.

Northwest Hospital Center (410-521-2200; www.lifebridgehealth.org), 5401 Old Court Rd., Randallstown.

Carroll Hospital Center (410-848-3000; www.carrollhospitalcenter.org), 200 Memorial Ave., Westminster.

✳ To See

COLLEGES **McDaniel College** (410-848-7000; www.mcdaniel.edu), Westminster. A liberal arts college, McDaniel has been educating students for more than 150 years. It could also be considered one of the cultural engines for the area with its **Esther Prangley Rice Gallery** and various vocal and instrumental groups, lectures open to the public, and its sponsorship of **Common Ground on the Hill.**

MUSEUMS

Freeland

& **Morris Meadows Historic Preservation Museum** (1-800-643-7056; www.morris meadows.us/museum.htm), 1523 Freeland Rd. Associated with the Morris Meadows Campground (see *Lodging*); you may need to go to the campground to get someone to open the museum. Old tractors, dolls, farm machinery, and displays of a schoolhouse, general store, kitchen, and gristmill. The sheer volume of items becomes even more impressive when you realize it is the private collection of Clive and Virginia Morris.

Lutherville

✔ & **Fire Museum of Maryland** (410-321-7500; www.firemuseummd.org), 1301 York Rd. (accessed from I-695 Exit 26B). Wed.–Sat., June–Aug.; Sat. only, Sept.–Dec. and May. Adults $12; seniors and firefighters $10; children 3–18 get in for $5. Presents the history of firefighting from the colonial days to the present. Children especially enjoy sitting in the 1938 fire engine driver's seat.

Middle River

Glenn L. Martin Maryland Aviation Museum (410-682-6122; www.marylandaviation museum.org), located in Hangar 5 of the Martin State Airport, which is east of Essex off MD 150. Wed.–Sat. 11–3; photo ID may be required to pass through guard gate. Very small admission fee. The small museum is dedicated to providing the history of the company founded by Glenn L. Martin (and then merged with Lockheed). This is the corporation that developed such famous jets as the F-16, Nighthawk, and Thunderbird. I found the wooden models most interesting, along with a display of astronauts who grew up in Maryland and a discussion of the nearby NASA Goddard Space Center. You always learn some interesting tidbit of history when visiting a museum like this, and I found out that human flight first occurred in the Western Hemisphere in 1784 when Peter Carnes took off in a balloon from a field near Baltimore.

WOODEN MODELS ON DISPLAY AT THE GLENN L. MARTIN MARYLAND AVIATION MUSEUM

Sykesville

Gate House Museum of History (410-549-5150; www.sykesville.net/gatehouse), 7283 Cooper Dr. Thur.–Fri. 1–5; Sun. 1–4. Donations accepted. A small collection of objects from the town's history.

Union Bridge

Western Maryland Railway Historical Society (410-775-0150; www.western marylandrhs.com), Union Bridge Station (MD 75). Sun. 1–4. Housed in the 1902 station is a collection of artifacts and memorabilia from the 125-year history of the Western Maryland Railroad.

UNION MILLS HOMESTEAD

Westminster

Historical Society of Carroll County (410-848-6494; http://hscc.carr.org), 210 E. Main St. The society's Shriver-Weybright Exhibition Gallery displays items from its 25,000-item permanent collection illustrating the history of the county. The exhibits include a large collection of tall clocks and works by famous sculptor William Henry Rinehart. The Sherman-Fisher-Spellman House next door has been restored to look as it would have when the first owners lived in the house from 1807–1842. Be sure to ask the docent to show you the clever auto-closing door hinges.

Union Mills Homestead (410-848-2288; www.unionmills.org), 3311 Littlestown Pike (about 7 miles north of Westminster on MD 97). Tues.–Fri. 10–4, and Sat. and Sun. noon–4, June–Aug. Weekends only in May and Sept., noon–4. Small admission fee. Because all of the furniture and artifacts in this 1797 clapboard farmhouse belonged to the Shriver family, visitors get a true picture of what life was like when the Shrivers lived here. Things that caught my eye were the letter to David Shriver from Thomas Jefferson, the 1863 Steinway piano, and an original WANTED poster for runaway slaves. The gristmill, built with bricks made on the property, still works. Guided tours are given of the house and mill.

HISTORIC HOMES **Hampton National Historic Site** (410-823-1309; www.nps.gov /hamp), 535 Hampton Ln. (just a few moments' drive from I-695 Exit 27B), Towson. Open daily 9–5. Hampton was the largest house in the country when constructed in the late 1700s.

✤ ⅙ **Carroll County Farm Museum** (410-386-3880; 1-800-654-4645; www.carrollcountyfarm museum.org), 500 S. Center St., Westminster. Apr.–Oct. Small admission fee. Was I ever mistaken when I thought all I would see was a few old farm implements! This 140-acre complex does contain a few of those, but it provides a much broader picture of 1800s farm life with its completely furnished farmhouse, wagon shed, kitchen, smokehouse, and springhouse. Artisans within the living-history center practice the crafts of yesteryear that would have supplied the farm with many of its necessary items. Be sure to walk over to the barnyard full of chickens, cows, turkeys, pigs, horses, goats, and lambs. Bring a picnic lunch and plan to spend a few hours. This is one of the best re-created farms I have ever seen—especially in light of the small amount of change it costs to get in.

HAMPTON NATIONAL HISTORIC SITE

Guided tours take you through this grand house, which is furnished almost exclusively with items that belonged to the six generations of the Ridgely family. Afterward, walk over the rest of the grounds to the family cemetery, slave quarters, dairy house, and gardens.

SELF-GUIDED TOURS Carroll County Visitors Center (410-848-1388; 1-800-272-1933; www.carrollcountytourism.org), 210 E. Main St., Westminster. They have put together a number of walking-tour brochures for Westminster, Uniontown, and other nearby sites. For a fun time, pick up the one for the ghost walk through Westminster. There are also driving-tour pamphlets to the Civil War sites and one that takes you to places important to the birth of American Methodism.

✳ To Do

BICYCLING Race Pace (410-876-3001; www.racepacebicycles.com), 459 Westminster Blvd., Westminster. If you are riding around in the area and your bike develops a problem, these folks have a complete center that services all makes and models.

ROAD BIKING CARROLL COUNTY

A brochure available from the Carroll County Visitors Center details 10 rides throughout the county. Conceived by a group of local cyclists, the outings range from 8 miles to 33 miles and take in scenic farmlands, lightly traveled country roads, and small towns. Three are designed to bring you past ice cream shops, some go by historic sites, and others enable you to leave the bike for a while and take to a hiking trail. All of the rides are circular, so you always return to the starting point, where you are permitted to park your car.

I like the 15-mile **Westminster South Route,** which not only delivers me to Hoffman's Ice Cream Shop but also enables an exploration of the **Carroll County Farm Museum** (see the sidebar on page 193). Then there is the 30-mile **Taneytown Tour,** with lots of great scenery and diversions. Open meadows are often dotted with deer, small Pipe Creek bubbles beside the road, and the coffee shop at the corner of MD 140 and MD 194 serves some nice fresh pastries.

CIVIL WAR   The rolling terrain of this area north of Baltimore saw a lot of troop movement and battle activity during the Civil War, especially when Robert E. Lee was trying to gain a foothold in Northern territory. That movement was, of course, halted at Gettysburg in the summer of 1863. Brochures available from the **Carroll County Visitors Center** map out a couple of driving tours to the site of a cavalry skirmish that took place in Westminster and other places that played a part in the Gettysburg drama.

FAMILY ACTIVITIES ⚓ **Cascade Lake** (410-374-9111; www.cascadelake.com), 3000 Snydersburg Rd., Hampstead. Open Mon.–Fri. 10–6; Sat.–Sun. and holidays 10–7; the season is usually from around Memorial Day through close to Labor Day. This 6-acre spring-fed lake has a gently sloping sandy bottom and a large roped-off swimming area watched over by certified lifeguards. The kiddie area has a number of fun things to do and is wellguarded. There are several water slides, floating rafts, and a high-dive platform. Within the 25-acre property are fishing and boating areas (boat rentals), picnic tables, a playground, and a hiking trail. Popular with local families.

GOLF

Finksburg

River Downs Golf Club (410-526-2000; www.riverdownsgolf.com), 1900 River Downs Dr. A par 72 Arthur Hills–designed course on very rolling, wooded countryside.

Timonium

Fox Hollow (410-887-7735), 1 Cardigan Rd. A scenic and open course that is considered to be friendly to beginning golfers. Fees are lower here than at many other courses in the area.

Westminster

Wakefield Valley (410-876-6662; www.wakefieldvalley.com), 1000 Fenby Farm Rd. Three 9-hole courses make up Wakefield Valley's 27 holes. The Green Course has long par fives, and the White Course covers hilly terrain. Combined, the courses have the second highest slope rating in the state.

McDaniel College Golf Course (410-848-7667; www.mcdanielathletics.com/information /facilities/golf). This 9-hole course was built on the college campus in 1935 by students and faculty and is one of the oldest courses in the county. Open to the public; students, faculty, and staff play for free.

White Hall

Greystone (410-887-1945), 2115 White Hall Rd., less than 10 minutes from I-83 Exit 31. An abundance of tall trees and other vegetation, ponds, and wetlands add a challenge to this Joe Lee–designed course.

MINIATURE GOLF ⚓ **Four Seasons Sports Complex** (410-239-3366; www.4seasons sportscomplex.com), 2710 Hampstead-Mexico Rd., Hampstead. There are fast-pitch baseball and slow-pitch softball batting cages in addition to the 18-hole Play-A-Round Miniature Golf Course.

HIKING

Kingsville

Gunpowder Falls State Park (410-592-2897; www.dnr.state.md.us/publiclands/central /gunpowder.asp), 2813 Jerusalem Rd. Cool, shaded spots by a small swimming hole. Wildflower and pine fragrances wafting through the air. Owl hoots breaking the stillness of early evening. Muskrat and raccoon paw prints stamped into soft mud. Hazy silhouettes of deer foraging in the morning mist.

These are not descriptions of things you must travel to western Maryland to enjoy, but rather some of the delights to be found in Gunpowder Falls State Park, located a short drive from Baltimore. More than 100 miles of trails wander through the park's 17,000 acres, which are divided among four areas that are separated from one another. *50 Hikes in Maryland* (Countryman Press) describes a hike in each area.

Owings Mills

Soldier's Delight National Environmental Area (410-461-5005; www.dnr.state.md.us /publiclands/central/soldiersdelight.asp), 5100 Deer Park Rd. Looking at the types of vegetation in Maryland today, it may be hard to imagine that grasslands once spread across tens of thousands of acres of this landscape. Prior to colonial settlement, much of Baltimore and Harford Counties, and adjacent counties in Pennsylvania, were covered by open spaces not unlike the prairies found in the Midwest. At 2,000 acres, Soldier's Delight preserves the largest remaining serpentine grasslands in the state. A network of trails lets you explore the area to enjoy the open scenery and wide skyscape, and to find interesting plants and flowers, such as the sandplain gerardia and fringed gentian.

HORSEBACK RIDING Brochures and maps available from the **Carroll County Department of Parks and Recreation** (410-386-2103; http://ccgovernment.carr.org/ccg /recpark/rec-coun.asp), 300 S. Center St., Westminster, 21157, point out the many miles of trails and locations in the county available to equestrians.

KAYAKING AND CANOEING **Ultimate Watersports** (410-335-5352; www.ultimate watersports.com), located at the Hammerman Area of Gunpowder Falls State Park, White Marsh. Open daily June–Aug., on the weekends May and Sept. (sometimes into Oct.). The owner of Ultimate Watersports learned how to windsurf in college and found that he

Northern Central Railroad Trail (administered by Gunpowder Falls State Park; see *Hiking*). The northernmost parking area for this trail is on MD 108 at Freeland, and the southern terminus is on Ashland Rd. in the Ashland Village housing development off MD 45 in Hunt Valley. The Rails-to-Trails Conservancy, the association generally recognized as spearheading the nationwide movement to convert abandoned railroad rights-of-way into trails, was formally organized in 1986. Nearly a decade before that, though, the state of Maryland, Baltimore County, and a group of local citizens were already laying the groundwork for the Northern Central Railroad Trail.

From 1838 to 1972, the Northern Central Railroad connected Baltimore with York, Pennsylvania, providing a major link for small communities along the way. Union troops made use of the railroad during the Civil War, and Abraham Lincoln traveled it on his way to deliver his famous Gettysburg Address. The construction of the interstates—and the resulting increase in truck and automobile transportation—marked the railroad's decline. Floods from Hurricane Agnes in 1972 dealt the final blow by washing out trestles and miles of track.

Never far from civilization, yet with long stretches of detachment from the humanized world, this 20-mile route is a great place to introduce someone to the joys of outdoor walking, without subjecting them to the rigors, and fear, of a harsh or isolated terrain. The pathway is level, and road crossings are fairly frequent if the need for help should happen to arise. In addition, public restrooms are situated at seven sites, with drinking water available beside three of the road crossings. The historic aspects of the railroad are an added bonus. This is a multiuse trail, also open to bicyclists and equestrians, so always walk to the right and avoid walking two abreast. Pets must be on a leash.

LEARNING TO WINDSURF WITH ULTIMATE WATERSPORTS

enjoyed being on the Chesapeake Bay so much that he wanted to share his excitement with others. Now in operation for more than two decades, the business offers instruction for windsurfing, kayaking, canoeing, and sailing. They also will take you on guided nature, history, sunset, and full-moon kayak tours. It's your choice of open water (you should probably have a bit of kayaking experience) or quiet stream water (anyone can do these excursions). All of the trips are designed to be done at a leisurely pace. If you want to do some sailing, take one of the Hobie Cat tours. If you want to do things on your own, Ultimate Watersports also rents their equipment.

SAILING See *Kayaking and Canoeing*.

SKIING, CROSS-COUNTRY See *Green Space*.

TENNIS Six of the parks in Carroll County have courts that are open to the public. Call 410-386-2103 for locations and availability.

WINDSURFING See *Kayaking and Canoeing*.

✳ Green Space
PARKS
Cockeysville
🐾 **Oregon Ridge** (410-887-1815; www
.oregonridge.org), 13555 Beaver Dam Rd. Oregon Ridge is an excellent model of a county or regional park that has been able to meet many of the diverse recreational needs of a growing local population, yet still keep the vast majority of the land undisturbed. Within the park's 1,036 acres are tennis courts, picnic areas, a dinner theater and lodge, an outdoor stage (the summer home for the Baltimore Symphony Orchestra), a swimming lake and sandy beach, and a bathhouse and snack bar. A network of marked pathways meanders through the undeveloped part of the park, rising to the main forested ridgeline and descending into a narrow creek valley. The nature center, with exhibits relating to local natural and human history, sponsors one of the best and most active interpretive programs available anywhere in Maryland— pick up a schedule and take part in an activity. Pets permitted on leashes.

Sykesville
🐾 𝒪 ♿ **Piney Run Park** (410-795-5165; http://ccgovernment.carr.org/ccg/recpark /pineyrun), 30 Martz Rd. Apr. 1–Oct. 31, 6

PINEY RUN PARK

AM–sunset. Small vehicle entrance fee. Nov.–Mar. visitors may park outside the gate, hike the trails, fish from the banks, and visit the nature center.

In addition to fishing and boating opportunities on the 300-acre lake, there is a network of trails on the surrounding 500 acres. One of the trails is open to mountain bikers and another to equestrians; all trails are open for cross-country skiing in winter. If your time is short, follow the **Field Trail,** as it will lead you into a variety of environments in only ⅜ of a mile. Canoes, sailboats, rowboats, kayaks, and electric-powered fishing boats are available for rent during the season. The nature center has several small exhibits and offers a host of programs for children and adults. Pets on leashes are permitted.

Union Bridge

& The small **Little Pipe Creek Park** has a short 0.5-mile trail that makes a nice spot to explore meadows and wetlands populated by variety of birds. Among the many I spotted on just one visit were cedar waxwings, flycatchers, orioles, redwing blackbirds, woodpeckers, mockingbirds, swallows, swifts, goldfinches, and more.

Westminster

🐾 ⚥ & **Hashawha Environmental Center** (410-386-3560; http://ccgovernment.carr.org /ccg/recpark/hashawha/), 300 John Owings Rd., Westminster. Open sunrise–sunset. So much land is devoted to agricultural purposes (and lately housing developments) that Carroll County is the least forested county in the state. Knowing that may help you to appreciate even more so the woodlands that the pathways of Hashawha wander through. The trails are open to hikers, bikers, and cross-country skiers; one is handicapped accessible. **Bear Branch Nature Center** (410-848-2517), inside the park, has a number of interpretive displays and sponsors a variety of outings and programs on- and off-site.

✳ Lodging

MOTELS AND HOTELS

Westminster, 21157
The Boston Inn (410-848-9095; www .thebostoninn.com), 533 Baltimore Blvd. The size of the well-kept and clean rooms is exactly what you would expect from a motel built in the mid-1900s, and the rates are hard to beat. For $70–80, you get an outdoor swimming pool, guest laundry facilities, a modest continental breakfast, and a room with an LCD TV and DVD player (movie rentals available), Internet access, microwave, and a refrigerator.

INNS

Taneytown, 21787
⚥ & **Antrim 1844** (410-756-6812; 1-800-858-1844; www.antrim1844.com), 30 Trevanion Rd. It is almost hard to grasp that small Taneytown contains one of the most celebrated inns in all of America. The constant attention to details, lavish furnishings, and impeccable service are rarely found in such a perfect combination. The 40 guest rooms and suites are furnished with canopy feather bed, fireplace and/or Jacuzzi (my room had a pedestal Jacuzzi, a bidet, and a private balcony), and antiques appropriate to the inn's antebellum history.

Everything has been arranged to be pleasing to the eye, even the 23 acres of grounds. The gardens are reminiscent of those found in European estates, the croquet lawn is

ONE OF MANY RELAXING SPOTS ON THE 23 ACRES OF ANTRIUM 1844

HILLTOP HIDEAWAY B&B

perfectly manicured, and the swimming pool and its gazebo are surrounded by hedgerows. The quality of the restaurant's meals (see *Dining Out*) matches that of the inn. $295–400.

BED & BREAKFASTS

Hampstead, 20174

Hilltop Hideaway B&B (410-374-0440; www.hampsteadhideaway.com), 2525 Hanover Pike. Built with a B&B in mind, the Hilltop Hideaway (which really does sit high atop a knoll) offers many wonderful modern amenities, such as a huge game room and a separate theater room with overstuffed and comfy leather seats. Each of the two suites features Sleep Number beds, refrigerator, TV, fireplace, and a double Jacuzzi. My favorite place was the porch, where I would watch the sun set over the green fields and woodlands to the west. A most relaxing place to stay. $125.

New Windsor, 21776

Atlee House Bed & Breakfast (410-871-9119; www.atleehousebb.com), 120 Water St. Family portraits hanging throughout the 1800s house add a homey feel to this B&B. Situated on a nicely landscaped and cared-for corner lot close to the local fairgrounds and town park, it offers two guest rooms and a suite, each with its own private bath. It may not be as large as the suite, but the Atlee Room is the one I liked the most, especially its bathroom with hand-painted wall art and glass-enclosed shower. The front porch is the place to have evening

conversations and watch the neighborhood kids at play. $145–175.

❧ **Yellow Turtle Inn** (410-635-3000; www.yellowturtleinn.net), 111 Springdale Ave. Several years ago, Joan Bradford had a dream about opening an inn. She became convinced it was her destiny when, a few days later, someone else said they, too, had had a dream about her and an inn—and the inn looked exactly the same in both dreams.

Sitting on 3 acres, the 1800s house is decorated in an amazing amount of Victorian furnishings and items. Each guest room is unique: The Windsor Vineyard Room has a curved wall, there is a mural in the Mary Cole Room, and the Queen's Chambers has a bed constructed of tree branches.

The grounds include an interesting seven-circuit meditation labyrinth. If a full-body massage and herbal tea are not enough to relax you, the view of the 100-acre preserved farmland from the wraparound porch surely will. $105–180.

Sykesville, 21784

🐾 **The Inn at Norwood** (410-549-7868; www.innatnorwood.com), 7514 Norwood Ave. Built in 1906 and located in a residential neighborhood of Sykesville, the inn has four guest rooms in the main house, a cottage, and the spacious loft room above a garage. All of the rooms are large, nicely decorated, and come with their own air-conditioning, cable TV, and two-person Jacuzzi. I felt like I was in the lap of luxury during my stay in the Loft Room. I had lots

ATLEE HOUSE BED & BREAKFAST

of room to roam about, the Jacuzzi was relaxing after a long day of travel (the provided rubber duck was a nice touch), and the refrigerator kept my beverages nice and cold. One of the parlors in the main house is filled with a collection of antique coin-operated arcade games, and you can spend hours reliving how people used to entertain themselves before the advent of computer games. Small pets are permitted. $145–225.

CAMPING

Freeland, 21053
Morris Meadows (410-329-6636; 1-800-643-7056; www.morrismeadows.us), 1523 Freeland Rd. (located just a couple of minutes' drive from I-83 Exit 36). The campground is on land that has been in the Morris family since 1793; the original deed, written on goatskin, is on display in the registration lobby. This is a mini family resort with tent and RV sites, rental cabins, a swimming pool, miniature golf, fishing, and the most extensive list of planned activities (Apr.–Oct.) I've ever seen in a commercial campground. (Also see *Museums*.)

Woodbine, 21797
⚲ **Ramblin' Pines Campground** (410-795-5161; 1-800-550-8733; www.ramblin pinescampground.com), 801 Hoods Mill Rd. (3 miles from I-70 Exit 76). As much a destination resort as it is a campground. Besides RV (with full hook-ups) and tent sites, there's a swimming pool, a playground, a miniature golf course, hiking trails, and planned activities such as hayrides, bingo, and live entertainment. Sites are somewhat close together, but the property is rambling and spread out. Cabins and trailers available for rent.

✳ Where to Eat
DINING OUT
Silver Run
Bud's at Silver Run (410-346-6816; www .budsatsilverrun.com), 4115 Littlestown Pike. This is one of those places you should not judge from its exterior; I thought it was a biker bar when I pulled into the parking

lot. With works by local artists adorning the walls of an 1870s farmhouse, Bud's is the place for an elegant yet casual dining experience. After more than three decades of stints throughout the United States and the Virgin Islands, owner/chef Ken Lurie has settled here—and we are the beneficiaries. My companion and I shared appetizers of crab and goat cheese cheesecake (sublime!) and local Italian sausage, spinach, and bell peppers with freshly grated parmesan cheese over locally ground grits. The equally innovative entrées, such as Magret duck and leg/thigh confit served with zesty strawberry BBQ sauce or seared day-boat sea scallops over mango-ginger sauce served with herbed quinoa let you know that you, too, misjudged this place when you first arrived. $18.95–33.95.

Sykesville
Baldwin's Station Restaurant (410-795-1041; http://baldwinsstation.com), 7618 Main St. Things can get pretty exciting when a train goes zipping by just 10 feet away from this restored railroad station. That's okay, though, as it just adds to the ambience, especially if you are seated in the main room that retains its original brick walls. The menu changes often because its emphasis is on seafood, and the owners insist on serving only what is freshly available. The same goes for the meat offerings (which are delivered daily from Fell's Point in Baltimore) and the wine list. Live entertainment is presented on a regular basis, the bar in a separate room is a local favorite, and the outside deck overlooks the river. Most entrées are $22–39.

Taneytown
♿ **Antrim 1844's Smokehouse Restaurant** (410-756-6812; 1-800-858-1844; www.antrim1844.com), 30 Trevanion Rd. Open for dinner. Reservations are mandatory. *The* place to go to really celebrate a special occasion. The six-course prix fixe ($68.50 per person) dinner is determined each evening by renowned chef Michael Gettier from a menu of regional cuisine accented with a French flair. Hors d'oeuvres delivered to you in the parlor by a butler, a

wine list with more than one thousand selections, large fireplaces, and a warm-hued brick floor complement the experience.

Westminster

🍷 ✦ **Paradiso Ristorante** (410-876-1421; www.paradiso-westminster.com), 20 Distillery Dr. Open for lunch and dinner. Salvatore and June Romeo serve traditional Italian dishes in what was once the dryer house for a distillery. The large windows allow the sun to light the attractive atmosphere. The cheese tortellini rose, with mushrooms, sun-dried tomatoes, and prosciutto, is a taste I will always remember. My dining partner raved about her veal medallions sautéed in cognac sauce with mushrooms and spinach. The service, setting, and quality make the prices a bargain. Entrées $13–27.

EATING OUT

Mount Airy

Brick Ridge (301-829-8191; www.brick ridge.com), 6212 Ridge Rd. Hours vary slightly each day, but it is open for dinner daily except Mon.; Sun. brunch 11–2. The menu changes often at the Brick Ridge, as the culinary team strives to provide contemporary cuisine from every state in America. A sample of a dinner menu includes filé gumbo, horseradish-encrusted beef, and Porterman's pie, a slight variation on shepherd's pie. The restaurant's building began its life in the late 1800s as a school for children from the ages of 6 to 20 years. $18–28.

Westminster

🍷 ✦ **Baugher's** (410-848-7413; www .baughers.com), 289 W. Main St. Extension (junction of MD 31 and MD 32). Open for breakfast, lunch, and dinner. You know this place—it has vinyl chairs and Formica tabletops, serves home-cooking-style food, and attracts everybody in town. The prices on the breakfast plates ($3.85–6) and lunch sandwiches ($3.50–8) may make you think you have entered a time warp. And where else can you get four pieces of fried chicken, two vegetables, a roll, and a beverage for less than $10? Similar entrées run

$7.95–16.95. Save room for homemade ice cream or a slice of pie.

Ma Baugher began selling pies and other baked goods to supplement a meager income during the Depression. The operation today includes more than 1,000 acres of farmland, a packinghouse, fields of produce, a farm stand, and the restaurant.

✦ **Harry's Main Street Grille** (410-848-7080), 65 W. Main St. Harry's has a full breakfast, lunch, and dinner menu, but its real claim to fame are the Coney Island–style hot dogs ($1.95) covered with chili, mustard, and onions. Soups, salads, and other sandwiches are served for lunch. I stopped by for dinner, as the grill is also known for baby back ribs that are marinated for seven days, simmered for hours, and char-grilled with Harry's BBQ sauce. The half rack ($10.95) filled me up, but you could also order a full rack ($14.95). Other options for dinner are pastas, seafood, beef, and 8-ounce burgers. $4.95–20.95.

✦ **Johanssons** (410-876-0101; www .johanssonsdininghouse.com), 4 W. Main St. Open daily for lunch and dinner. Johanssons makes its own beers, and the aroma of the brewing process spreads throughout the restaurant. The Honest Ale was to my liking, flavorful but not heavy. I decided on something light for lunch—the vegetable turnover; the shell would do any pastry chef proud. Various forms of seafood, meats, and chicken are offered for dinner. $13.95–27.95. Ask for a window seat to watch the traffic go by on MD 27. **The Down Under Bar and Grill** downstairs is a festive place with billiard tables, a game room, and live entertainment on the weekend.

Maggie's Restaurant and Pub (410-848-1441; www.maggieswestminster.com), 310 E. Green St. Maggie's has been in business for approximately four decades, so the owner and the longtime chef must be doing something right. From the name and the building's exterior, I expected typical bar food, but was wrong. Everything is made from scratch, and my prime rib sandwich was not sliced meat, but a huge piece of prime rib accompanied by freshly shaved horseradish. Other surprises were a nice gazpacho, a savory quiche, and a seafood cassolette. Daily specials are designed to take advantage of what is fresh for the day, and there is always some kind of "sale," such as half-price drinks or a reduced rate for your entire bill. $16.99–28.99.

♪ **O'Lordans Irish Pub** (410-876-0000; www.olordansirishpub.com), 14 Liberty St. Open for lunch and dinner; closed Mon. So many times I go to a place that calls itself an Irish pub, and there is very little, if anything, Irish about the place or the menu. Not true here, as the menu contains some classic Irish dishes. I really enjoyed my lunch of bangers and mash, and my dining companion said her shepherd's pie was really good. Other offerings have included corned beef, lamb stew, and fish-and-chips. The rest of the menu items also contain a nod to Irish roots. There's a hearty vegetable terrine, mussels poached in Magner's, Guinness-marinated chicken, and an offering of assorted Irish cheeses with fruit chutney and flatbread. Entrées $12.95–26.95.

Rafael's (410-840-1919; www.rafaels restaurant.com), 32 W. Main St. Open daily for breakfast, lunch, and dinner. A pleasant place that, in addition to a usual menu of sandwiches and entrées with meat, serves a number of healthy vegetable dishes. Start with the marinated artichoke salad, and then do the veggie-filled crêpes ($14.50) for dinner. Entrées $13.99–23.99.

CRABS

Westminster
Gary and Dell's Crab House (410-346-7652; www.garyanddellscrabhouse.com), 2820 Littlestown Pike. Like all crab houses, Gary and Dell's serves steamed crabs by the dozen (market price), but the real deal here is the all-you-can-eat crab special for only $28.95. And you are permitted to eat for three hours if you wish! I hope it is still offered when you stop by. Sandwiches,

other seafood, and meats round out the menu. $6–27.95.

TAKE-OUT Giulianova Groceria (410-876-7425; http://www.brothersun.biz), 11 E. Main St., Westminster. The grocery part of the store carries everything you could want to make your own Italian meal. If you don't feel like cooking, you can always order a hoagie, hot entrée, or Italian-style soup to go. Don't miss getting a cannoli for dessert—the pastry shell is not stuffed until you order it.

COFFEE BAR CUP Tea Bar Café (410-848-7622; www.cupteabar.com), 7 E. Main St., Westminster. With some items prepared by its sister business, Gypsy's Tea Room, the café offers breakfast and lunch—and live music on occasion.

MICROBREWERY Johanssons (410-876-0101; www.johanssonsdininghouse .com), 4 W. Main St., Westminster. Johanssons brews its own beers within its historic 1800s restaurant (see *Eating Out*). There are always at least five different brews to choose from at any time.

SNACKS AND GOODIES Baugher's (410-848-7413; www.baughers.com), 289 W. Main St. Extension (junction of MD 31 and MD 32), Westminster. Baugher's makes homemade pies (47 different kinds) and ice cream (20 flavors), both available for eat-in or take-out. Ask them to heat a piece of pie and top it with ice cream, and you will be in sweets heaven. (Also see *Eating Out*.)

Heinz Bakery (410-848-0808), 42 W. Main St., Westminster. This family-owned bakery, turning out soft, creamy doughnuts, pastries, and breads, has been a downtown mainstay for many years.

Hoffman's Home Made Ice Cream (410-857-0824; www.hoffmansicecream .com), 934 Washington Rd., Westminster. Open until 10 PM every day. Jeff, Linda, and Lori Hoffman use the same recipes that their grandfather used when he started making ice cream in 1947. There are at least 30 different flavors available daily.

Starry Night Bakery & Coffee House (410-871-9131; www.starrynightbakery .com), 140 Village Rd., Westminster. The place to enjoy a cup of coffee and some nice baked goods like an éclair, cupcake, or cannoli. Light breakfast and lunch items also available.

Treat Shop & Chocolate Factory (410-848-0028; www.treatshopfactory.com), 15 S. Cranberry Rd., Westminster. Open daily. The Treat Shop has been making fresh candy and fudge daily in Westminster for close to 50 years. It is almost impossible to walk by without being drawn in by all the delicious creations displayed in the window.

✳ Entertainment
FILM
Hunt Valley
Hoyts Hunt Valley Cinema (410-329-9800; www.regmovies.com), 11511 McCormick Rd. Mainstream films.

Owings Mills
Loews Valley Center (410-363-4194; www.amctheatres.com), 9616 Reisterstown Rd., and **AMC Owing Mills 17** (443-394-0060; www.amctheatres.com), 10100 Mill Run Circle. Both show first-run movies.

Westminster
Regal Cinemas (410-857-1410) 400 N. Center St. Located in Town Mall of Westminster.

White Marsh
Loews White Marsh (410-933-9428; www .amctheatres.com), 8141 Honeygo Blvd. Another spot to see movies.

MUSIC **Common Ground on the Hill** (410-857-2771; www.commongroundon thehill.com), McDaniel College campus, Westminster. The organization takes its name from its mission, which is to promote learning experiences for artists, musicians, and craftspeople while searching for a common ground among ethnic, gender, and

racial groups. Sponsors workshops and the annual Common Ground on the Hill Festival during summer.

✳ Selective Shopping
ANTIQUES
Mount Airy
Westminster
Sidetracked Antiques and Design (410-875-4455), 10 E. Main St. The store combines two of the owner's passions—antiques (18th- and 19th-century furniture, paintings, Oriental rugs) and estate jewelry—with a selection of fine wines inside an early-19th-century building.

& **Westminster Antique Mall** (410-857-4044; www.westminsterantiquemall.com), 433 Hahn Rd. Dealers have filled more than 200 booths and showcases with merchandise.

ART GALLERIES **Ain't That a Frame/Gallery 99** (410-876-3096; www .aintthataframe.com), 99 W. Main St., Westminster. A large art gallery, antiques shop, and custom framing store.

& **Carroll Arts Center** (410-848-7272; www.carr.org/arts), 91 W. Main St., Westminster. Within a refurbished 1928 art deco movie house, this is much more than just an art gallery displaying changing exhibits. The theater is the setting for films, concerts, lectures, theatrical productions, and recitals. Classes in all of the various arts are available.

Esther Prangley Rice Gallery (410-857-2595; www.mcdaniel.edu), Peterson Hall, McDaniel College campus, Westminster. The gallery is the site of changing exhibits in a variety of media from students, professors, and local and national artists. There is also the continuous display of the Albert and Eva Blum Collection of Art from Five Continents.

Off Track Art (410-259-6403; www.off trackart.org), 11 Liberty St., Westminster. A cooperative of about 10 artists, the gallery is ever-changing with works by guest artists, as well the members who work in a variety of media, including photography, silk, basketry, metalwork, and more. One of the artists, Kevin Dayhoff, is there on most days the shop is open and, if so, conversations with him will surely keep you entertained. Occupying the room next door is the award-winning work of Robert Lewis at **Carousel Stained Glass** (410-596-6110).

The Shop at Cockey's (410-848-6494; www.theshopatcockeys.org), 216 E. Main St., Westminster. The museum store and book shop of the Carroll County Historical Society offers the works of local and regional artists and craftspersons. I'm sometimes disappointed by the quality of items in places such as this, but not here. I think you will agree that the pottery, baskets, beadwork, jewelry, fiber arts, batik, watercolors, and woodwork are of a little higher standard.

BOOKSTORES A Likely Story Bookstore (410-795-1718; www.sykesville books.com), 7566 Main St., Sykesville. New and used books.

SPECIAL SHOP Electicity (240-409-4863; www.electicity.com), 13 John St., Westminster. I wasn't sure how to categorize Electicity. It could easily go under *Art Galleries* for its offerings of interesting (and different) artwork, or under *Bookstores* for the many new and used books that are carried, including a nice selection of local authors. But I put it here because you can also browse for DVD movies and music CDs, in addition to attending live performances and workshops.

Gypsy's Tea Room (410-857-0058; www .gypsystearoom.com), 111 Stoner Ave., Westminster. Afternoon tea with scones by reservation Tues.–Sat. 11–4.

The Maryland Store (410-751-2050; www .themarylandstore.com), 2200 Sykesville Rd., Westminster. Located in the country within the former 1891 Deer Park Chapel, The Maryland Store has one of the most complete collections of Maryland-oriented and/or Maryland-made items I've come across. The store grew out of the owners' travels, during which they were able to purchase quality items from the locales they were visiting, but were unable to obtain the same type of quality products once they returned home. Even many of their display cases are made in Maryland. Be sure to stop by if in search of a Maryland souvenir of distinction.

FARMER'S MARKETS

Hampstead
The **Hampstead Farmers Market** (420-239-8110; www.townofhampstead.us) has seasonal produce May–Oct. on Sat. 8–12 at 1341 N. Main St.

Mount Airy
Crafts and entertainment, along with the usual market items, may be found May–Sept. on Wed. 3:30–6 at the **Mount Airy Main Street Farmers Market** (301-829-1983; www.mountairymainstreet.org) in the municipal parking lot.

SERRV Gift Shop (410-635-8711; www.serrv.org), 500 Main St. (MD 31), New Windsor. This nonprofit organization, started by the Church of the Brethren in the late 1940s, buys crafts at fair prices from more than 30 countries and the United States. These purchases help to provide a small bit of security for hundreds of those who are otherwise underprivileged. The items here are not only of high quality but would be hard to find anywhere else: textiles, pottery, furniture, candles, musical instruments, wood carvings, jewelry, and much more. If you're going to buy a gift or something for yourself, why not get it here and put money into the hands of a person instead of a faceless multinational corporation? A highly recommended stop; the peaceful setting on a knoll overlooking the countryside will do your soul some good, too. Mail-order catalogs available.

Taneytown

There is also entertainment June–Sept. on Sat. 9–12 in the Memorial Park at the **Taneytown Farmers Market** (443-918-8100).

Westminster

&. **Carroll County Farmer's Market** (410-848-7748; www.carrollcountyfarmers market.com) operates from mid-June through early Sept. in the Agricultural Center at 700 Agriculture Center Dr. on Sat. 8–1; additional farm products can be found at the Downtown Westminster Farmers Market, Conaway parking lot (Railroad Ave. and Emerald Hill Ln.), 8–noon on Sat., from May–Nov. Both are handicapped accessible.

PICK-YOUR-OWN PRODUCE FARMS

New Windsor

✧ **Shady Hill Farm and Orchard** (410-875-0572), 2001 New Windsor Rd. (MD 31). A variety of apples become ripe from mid-Sept. through Oct. The orchard has 600 dwarf and semidwarf trees, so it's a perfect outing for young children. There are also free hayrides on Sunday for pick-your-own customers.

Westminster

✧ **Baugher's** (410-848-5541; www .baughers.com), 1236 Baugher Rd. The season begins in late May with strawberries

and peas. Cherries come in late June and early July. Pumpkins can be picked Sat.– Sun. in Oct., when hayrides will take you to and from the patch. The kids will enjoy the variety of animals in the petting zoo, which is open throughout the season. (Also see *Eating Out.*)

WINERIES

Detour

Detour Winery (410-775-0220; www .detourwinery.com), 7933 Forest & Stream Club Rd. Open for tastings Thurs.-Sun.; call ahead to arrange an extensive tour of the grounds. I visited Detour Winery soon after Dann and Beth Tamminga had bottled their first wines from their 35 acres of vines in 2012 and, yet, their wines had already received 24 medals. However, they have even more ambitious plans and, if they come to fruition, Detour will become one of the first truly family-friendly destination wineries. Plans include hiking trails throughout the scenic property, a fishing pond, swimming lake (complete with sandy beach), zip lines, ball fields, and more.

Hydes

Boordy Vineyards (410-592-5015; www .boordy.com), 12820 Long Green Pike. Open for tastings and sales Mon.–Sat. 10–5, Sun. 1–5. Tours at 2 and 3:30 daily. Maryland's oldest winery was established in 1945. The vines you see were planted in the

BAUGHER'S RESTAURANT AND PRODUCE STAND IN WESTMINSTER

1960s, and the winery began bottling in the 1980s. The 19th-century fieldstone barn is a pleasant atmosphere for tastings and serves as the focal point for the winery's many annual events.

Manchester

Cygnus Wine Cellars (410-374-6395; www.cygnuswinecellars), 3130 Long Ln. Tours, tastings, and sales on Sat. and Sun. noon–5. Sparkling and red and white table wines.

Parkton

Woodhall Wine Cellars (410-357-8644; www.woodhallwinecellars.com), 17912 York Rd. Tours, tastings, and sales are available Tues.–Sun. noon–5. Woodhall was started by three amateur winemakers in 1983 and moved to its present scenic location next to the Gunpowder River in 1995. The largest percentage of grapes comes from outside sources.

Sparks

Basignani Winery (410-472-0703; www.basignani.com), 15722 Fall Rd. Wed.–Sat. 11:30–5:30 and Sun. noon–6. Bertero Basignani was an amateur winemaker for 15 years before establishing his own winery in 1986. His low-key operation employs traditional cellar methods and produces about 5,000 gallons a year from grapes that are estate-grown and estate-bottled.

BOORDY VINEYARDS IN HYDES

Westminster

Serpent Ridge Vineyard (410-848-6511; www.serpentridge.com), 2962 Nicodemus Rd. Open Sat. and Sun. Amateur winemakers Greg and Karen Lambrecht originally planted 3 acres of vines for their own use, but soon got their winemakers' certifications and their business has taken off. It's a small operation that involves family and friends helping with the harvest and bottling the wine by hand. Mixing Old World techniques with modern ones, the winery employs flex tanks and old planks to process the wine. The tasting room includes a small gift shop featuring local artwork.

✳ Special Events

Year-round: **Movie Night** (410-848-7272). Sponsored by the Carroll Arts Center in Westminster on the fourth Fri. of each month.

January: **Central Maryland Farm Toy Show** (410-848-2735), Agriculture Center, Westminster. Take a look at the items throughout the day and make a bid for them during the evening auction.

February: **Stop, Swap, and Save Bicycle Swap Meet** (www.stopswapandsave.com), Agriculture Center, Westminster. The state's largest bicycle show, where you may obtain new and used parts, accessories, and complete bicycles.

March: **Maple Sugarin' Festival** (410-848-9040), Hashawha Environmental Center, Westminster. A day of maple syrup demonstrations, taste testing, kid's activities, and country crafts. **Annual Toy Show and Sale** (443-277-6204), Taneytown. New and antique farm and collectible toys for sale. **Random House Book Fair** (410-386-8155), Carroll Community College, Westminster. Book signings by authors, silent auctions of signed and first-edition books, workshops, and children's stories.

April: **Annual Flower and Plant Market** (410-848-2288), Union Mills Homestead, 3311 Littlestown Pike, Westminster. Food. Fee for tours of the house and mill.

May: **Westminster Flower and Jazz Festival** (410-848-9393), E. Main St., Westminster. Plants, crafts, music, and food. **Annual Taneytown Fishing Derby** (410-751-1100; www.taneytown.org), Robert Mill Park, Taneytown. For ages 3–14 with prizes awarded for age groups and fish size.

June: **Deer Creek Fiddlers' Convention** (410-857-2771), Carroll County Farm Museum, Westminster. A competition of bluegrass musicians with awards, crafts, and farmhouse tours. **Annual Barbershop Show** (410-795-5050; www.oldone statesmen.org), Westminster. Patriotic songs in four-part harmony.

July: **Carroll County 4-H and FFA Fair** (410-386-3247), Carroll County Agricultural Center, Westminster. **Annual Ice Cream Sundae Social** (410-848-2288), Union Mills Homestead, Westminster. Lots of fun for the kids, with face painting, pony rides, a clown, and tours of the mill.

August: **Annual Car Show** (410-751-0506), Taneytown. A gathering of antique, rod, and custom cars and trucks. There is also lots of food, music, raffles, and games.

August–September: **Maryland State Fair** (410-252-0200), State Fair Grounds, Timonium. **Annual Old-fashioned Corn Roast Festival** (410-848-2288; www.unionmills .org), Union Mills Homestead, Westminster. Traditional foods, along with all the roasted corn you can eat. Tours of the homestead and mill.

September: **Maryland Wine Festival** (410-386-3880; 1-800-654-4645), Carroll County Farm Museum, Westminster. The largest celebration of the fruit of the vine in the state. Thousands attend for the tastings, wine seminars, crafts, food, and strolling entertainers.

October: **Fall Festival** (410-795-8959), Sykesville. A banquet of arts, crafts, food, and entertainment in a small-town atmosphere. **Fall Harvest Days** (410-876-2667), Carroll County Farm Museum, Westminster. Bring the kids and yourself for scarecrow making, wagon rides, puppet shows, country food and crafts, and—the best of all—the milk mustache contest.

November: **Mistletoe Mart** (410-848-3251), Church of the Ascension, Westminster. Juried arts and crafts featuring pottery, stained glass, jewelry, baskets and gifts. Café, country store, hourly door prizes, silent auction, and quilt raffle.

&. *November-December:* **Festival of Wreaths** (410-848-7272), 91 W. Main St., Westminster. The annual display and silent auction of more than one hundred handmade theme wreaths that benefits the Carroll Arts Center.

BALTIMORE

Baltimore grew from a small tobacco-producing community to a major shipping center in less than one hundred years. By the mid-1700s, it was exporting flour, grains, iron, tobacco, and produce, and importing sugar, molasses, rum, slaves, and manufactured goods. It came into true prominence during the Revolutionary War, when members of the Continental Congress met in the city for two months after signing the Declaration of Independence.

Privateers, sailing in sleek clipper ships built in the city's harbors, took advantage of the turmoil to prey upon British merchant ships. Within a few years, they had made off with booty estimated at more than a million English pounds. They infuriated the British once more by resuming the practice during the War of 1812. Detained upon an English ship, Francis Scott Key watched Great Britain's forces exact revenge by bombarding the harbor area throughout the early morning of September 14, 1814. When the sun's first rays illuminated the large flag flying over Fort McHenry, signifying that the fort and city had held, Key was inspired to write what would become the U.S. national anthem.

It was primarily settlers from Germany and the British Isles, along with their African slaves, who first shaped the city, but soon immigrants from other parts of the world began to arrive. Italians, Russians, Ukrainians, Poles, and Lithuanians poured in, attracted by Baltimore's flourishing shipbuilding and shipping industries, transportation services, and cannery factories. In the last few decades, the majority of newcomers have been Hispanic, Caribbean, and Near Eastern in origin. The many cultural backgrounds are celebrated with a series of ethnic festivals throughout the summer months.

Just as the city's population is composed of diverse groups of people, so too are its neighborhoods. Many still reflect the origins of their inhabitants, while others possess a personality and atmosphere all their own.

Inner Harbor was the focus of an intense revitalization program that began in the late 1970s. What was once a place of decaying factories and warehouses is now a vibrant showplace attracting thousands daily. Water taxis cross the water, taking commuters and visitors all around the harbor. There is almost always some kind of outside entertainment going on, and the Harborplace pavilions are full of shops and restaurants. The strikingly triangular-shaped National Aquarium in Baltimore is topped by glass pyramids and contains more than 11,000 species of marine life. Tours of the USS *Constellation*, the last all-sail vessel built by the U.S. Navy, and other historic ships tie into the harbor's past seafaring life.

Along the eastern edge of Inner Harbor is the Power Plant, a huge brick building the city obtained from the Baltimore Gas and Electric Company in 1977. It now houses a large Barnes & Noble bookstore and a Hard Rock Café, and has proven to be a magnet for the harbor area. Reflected in the water are the soaring, modern, high-rise steel and glass structures of a number of national hotel and motel chains.

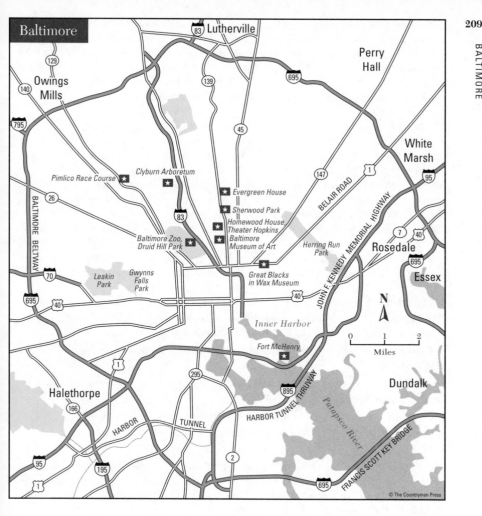

I'm convinced you gain weight just by breathing in the aromas that waft through the 12 blocks of Little Italy. Dozens of restaurants, some quite formal and others very casual, line the streets and employ and expand the culinary arts that have made Italian food a world favorite. Take a walk through the neighborhood, and you may feel like you've been transported to the Old Country. Good-natured, accent-flavored arguments arise from the games of bocce ball.

Fell's Point was established as a shipbuilding center in 1730, making it Baltimore's first port and one of the country's oldest waterfront communities. It soon developed a rough and rowdy reputation as sailors came ashore for rest and relaxation. Many of the rather seedy buildings were condemned to make way for an interstate in the late 1960s. However, locals banded together, defeated the idea, and embarked upon a revitalization program. Their efforts have been more or less successful, as the best way to describe the area would be "shabby chic." Hip restaurants, live theaters, and upscale lodging spots are interspersed among coffeehouses and shops that sport bohemian atmospheres. By the way, so that you won't be marked as an outsider, you need to pronounce Thames (Street) just as it is spelled, not as they say it in London.

Jubilant citizens went to one of the highest points in their city to mark Maryland's ratification of the U.S. Constitution in 1788 with celebrations and fireworks; it's been referred to as Federal Hill ever after. A park upon the promontory provides one of the best views of the city. The area was settled by blue-collar workers and still retains much of that feel, as many of the homes are two-story row houses. The Baltimore Museum of Industry, the innovative American Visionary Art Museum, an assortment of antiques shops, and a variety of restaurants are reasons to visit.

Mount Vernon, laid out in 1831, was once the most in-vogue address in town. The movers and shakers of Baltimore's politics and businesses took up residence in many of the largest homes and row houses. With their money came an array of cultural diversions, including the Walters Art Museum, Peabody Conservatory of Music, Lyric Opera House, and, later, Joseph Meyerhoff Symphony Hall. Charles Street, known as "Restaurant Row," is packed with culinary offerings from what seems like every nation in the world. The street also leads to the neighborhood's central point, the Washington Monument. A climb up the 228 steps will help work off some of the calories consumed for lunch. Baltimoreans claim that the structure, which was conceived in 1809 and completed in 1829, is the first one that was dedicated to the Father of Our Country. However, the citizens of Boonsboro, Maryland, completed their Washington Monument in 1827 and assert that theirs was the first.

GUIDANCE Information about all of Baltimore can be obtained from the **Baltimore Area Convention and Visitors Association** (410-659-7300; 1-877-BALTIMORE; www .baltimore.org) at 100 Light St., 12th Floor, Baltimore, 21202.

Located on the waterfront in Inner Harbor is the **Baltimore Visitors Center** (1-877-BALTIMORE).

The **Fell's Point Visitors Center** (410-675-6750; www.preservationsociety.com) at 812 S. Ann St., Baltimore, 21213, is open daily 10–4.

The **Mount Vernon Cultural District, Inc.** (410-244-1030; www.mvcd.org), at 217 N. Charles St., 21201, does a good job in highlighting what many people think is the city's cultural center.

The *Destination Planning Guide* will help you plan your trip, while *Baltimore's African American Heritage and Attractions* is a guide to the city's African American attractions. Both publications can be obtained from the **Baltimore Area Convention and Visitors Association** or the **Baltimore Area Visitors Center.**

The *City Paper,* available free from newspaper boxes, provides a lot of art, dining, and entertainment information as well as an alternative view of the city.

GETTING THERE *By car:* Like the spokes on a pinwheel, interstate highways come into Baltimore from many different directions. **I-95** is the major East Coast highway that runs from Florida to Maine and is the way people driving from the northeast (Philadelphia, Pennsylvania, New York City) or the southwest (Washington, DC, and Richmond, Virginia) will probably arrive. (The **Baltimore–Washington Parkway** is a slightly more scenic alternate from DC.)

I-83 comes in from due north and ends near Inner Harbor. Travelers from the west (Frederick, Maryland, and Pittsburgh, Pennsylvania) will find that **I-70** is the most direct route. **I-795** connects the suburbs of the northwest with the city, while **I-97** is the fastest way from Annapolis and the Eastern Shore.

By air: **Baltimore/Washington International Thurgood Marshall Airport** (1-800-I-FLY-BWI; www.bwiairport.com) is just about 10 miles south of Baltimore and has interstate, MARC and AMTRAK (see *By train,* below), and limousine connections with the city.

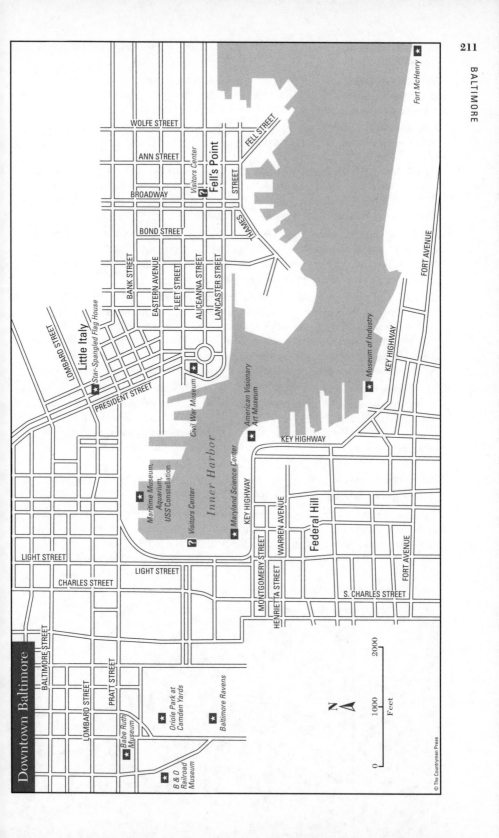

Downtown Baltimore

Fort McHenry

WOLFE STREET

ANN STREET

BROADWAY

BOND STREET

FELL STREET

Visitors Center

Fell's Point

STREET

THAMES

BANK STREET

EASTERN AVENUE

FLEET STREET

ALICEANNA STREET

LANCASTER STREET

FORT AVENUE

LOMBARD STREET

Little Italy

Star-Spangled Flag House

PRESIDENT STREET

Civil War Museum

Museum of Industry

KEY HIGHWAY

American Visionary
Art Museum

Inner Harbor

Maritime Museum,
Aquarium,
USS Constellation

Visitors Center

Maryland Science Center

KEY HIGHWAY

KEY HIGHWAY

WARREN AVENUE

Federal Hill

FORT AVENUE

LIGHT STREET

CHARLES STREET

LIGHT STREET

MONTGOMERY STREET

HENRIETTA STREET

S. CHARLES STREET

BALTIMORE STREET

LOMBARD STREET

PRATT STREET

Oriole Park at
Camden Yards

Baltimore Ravens

Babe Ruth
Museum

B & O
Railroad
Museum

N

2000

1000

0

Feet

© The Countryman Press

By bus: **Greyhound** (1-800-231-2222; www.greyhound.com) will deliver you to several locations in Baltimore.

By train: **AMTRAK** (1-800-USA-RAIL; www.amtrak.com) at Penn Station (410-231-2222), at the intersection of I-83 and N. Charles St., is close to the University of Baltimore and has received a major face-lift in the last few years.

MARC (1-800-325-RAIL; www.mta.maryland.gov) provides commuter rail service between Washington, DC, and Baltimore on weekdays.

GETTING AROUND *By car:* **I-695 (Baltimore Beltway)** encircles the city, giving access to each of its neighborhoods and suburbs. Going into Mount Vernon, Inner Harbor, and Federal Hill, **Charles St.** completely intersects the city in a north-south direction. **US 40** goes through the city in a west-to-east orientation.

Like all big cities, Baltimore has a traffic problem during rush hours, but it is surprisingly easy to get around during other times of the day. This is especially true in the downtown/Inner Harbor area—as long as you pay attention to the many one-way streets. Luckily, street and directional signs are plentiful and well placed.

By bus, by subway, and by rail: The **Mass Transit Authority** (MTA) (410-539-5000; 1-800-543-9809; www.mta.maryland.gov) operates bus, subway, and rail lines that reach into every nook and cranny of the city, and many nearby areas and counties, making it possible to leave your hotel, go to dinner, and then attend the theater without having to drive. Maps and timetables can be obtained at the visitors center in Inner Harbor or by calling MTA. A daily pass is available that is good on any MTA system; exact fare is required to ride the bus.

The **Charm City Circulator** (410-350-0456; www.charmcitycirculator.com) is a free (!) bus service that has a number of routes that will deliver you to places throughout the Inner Harbor, Federal Hill, Fells Point, Fort McHenry, and Mount Vernon, as well as the campuses of Johns Hopkins and the University of Maryland. The buses run on a frequent schedule, but be aware that, because they are free, they may often be so full that you may not be able to get on.

By taxi: The companies servicing the city are **Yellow Cab** (410-685-1212), **Diamond Cab** (410-947-3333), and **Arrow Cab** (410-484-4111).

By water: Among the most fun, and certainly most scenic, ways to reach many sites along Baltimore's waterfronts are the water shuttles and taxis. Coming to each stop at about 15-minute intervals (40 minutes off-season), they will take you to Inner Harbor, Fell's Point, Canton, Federal Hill, and Fort McHenry. You also get ever-changing views of the city from

THE FUN (AND FASTEST) WAY TO GET AROUND INNER HARBOR

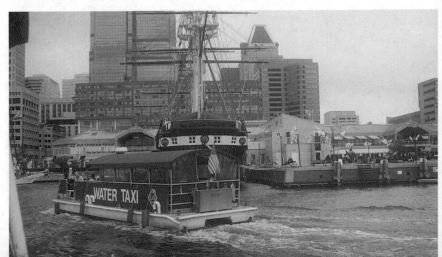

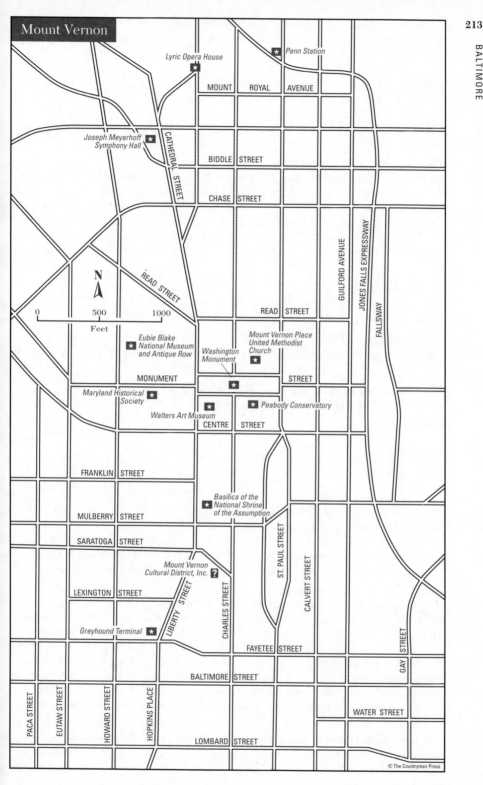

Mount Vernon

Lyric Opera House

Penn Station

MOUNT ROYAL AVENUE

Joseph Meyerhoff
Symphony Hall

CATHEDRAL STREET

BIDDLE STREET

CHASE STREET

GUILFORD AVENUE

JONES FALLS EXPRESSWAY

FALLSWAY

N

0   500   1000

Feet

READ STREET

READ STREET

Eubie Blake
National Museum
and Antique Row

Washington
Monument

Mount Vernon Place
United Methodist
Church

MONUMENT STREET

Maryland Historical
Society

Walters Art Museum

Peabody Conservatory

CENTRE STREET

FRANKLIN STREET

Basilica of the
National Shrine
of the Assumption

MULBERRY STREET

ST. PAUL STREET

SARATOGA STREET

Mount Vernon
Cultural District, Inc.

LEXINGTON STREET

LIBERTY STREET

CHARLES STREET

CALVERT STREET

Greyhound Terminal

FAYETEE STREET

GAY STREET

BALTIMORE STREET

PACA STREET

EUTAW STREET

HOWARD STREET

HOPKINS PLACE

WATER STREET

LOMBARD STREET

© The Countryman Press

the water, something many visitors miss. **Baltimore Water Taxi** (410-563-3901; 1-800-658-8947; www.thewatertaxi.com) is the city's original water service ($12 adults, $6 children 10 and under, for an all-day, unlimited-use pass).

PUBLIC RESTROOMS In the downtown/Inner Harbor area, restrooms can be found in the Pratt St. and Light St. pavilions.

MEDICAL EMERGENCY Baltimore has more than a dozen hospitals with emergency rooms. Among them are:

Downtown/Inner Harbor
University of Maryland Medical Center (410-328-8667; www.umm.edu), 22 S. Greene St. The state's largest hospital. On the corner of Baltimore and Greene Sts., about seven blocks west of Inner Harbor. **Mercy Hospital** (410-332-9000; www.mdmercy.com), 345 St. Paul Place—at the corner of Saratoga and Light Sts. About seven blocks north of Inner Harbor. **Johns Hopkins Hospital** (410-955-5000; www.hopkinsmedicine.org), 600 N. Wolfe St. Located near the intersection of Orleans St. and Broadway about 2 miles northeast of Inner Harbor.

Mount Vernon
Maryland General Hospital (410-225-8100; www.marylandgeneral.org), 827 Linden Ave. On the western edge of Mount Vernon next to Madison St.

Northern part of the city
Good Samaritan Hospital (410-532-4040), 5601 Loch Raven Blvd. About 3 miles south of I-695 Exit 29.

Northwestern part of the city (Park Heights)
Sinai Hospital (410-601-9000; www.lifebridgehealth.org), 2401 Belvedere Ave. Accessed from I-83 Exit 10.

✳ To See
MUSEUMS

Downtown/Inner Harbor
Baltimore Civil War Museum (410-385-5188; http://civilwarbaltimore.com), 601 President St. Open daily; small admission fee. Inside the old President Street Depot, which served rail customers from the mid-1800s to the mid-1900s, the Maryland Historical Society presents the role Baltimore played in the Civil War and the Underground Railroad. It is a small museum; an available cassette will take you on a 10-minute guided tour if your time is limited.

🔹 ♿ **Maryland Science Center, Davis Planetarium, and IMAX Movie Theater** (410-685-5225; www.mdsci.org), 601 Light St. Open daily during usual tourist season; closed Mon. other seasons. Adults $16.95; seniors $15.95; children 3–12 are $13.95; IMAX is an extra fee. There is much to keep you and the children involved and learning for hours. Three floors with hundreds of interactive exhibits and hands-on displays relating to the bay, mathematics, energy, space, and other scientific discoveries. Pay whatever it costs to see a movie in the five-story IMAX theater, especially if the presentation is in 3-D. The IMAX 3-D films pull the images off the screen and put you in the middle of the action—the experience is unforgettable.

🔹 ♿ **Babe Ruth Museum and Birthplace** (410-727-1539; www.baberuthmuseum.com), 216 Emory St. Open daily 10–5. Small admission fee. The Sultan of Swat was born in this humble home in 1895 and went on to become baseball's greatest player (without the controversial steroid use of today's players). Tours take you through the home and its collection of memorabilia.

✍ ♿ **Sports Legends at Camden Yards** (410-727-1539, ext. 3011; www.baberuthmuseum .com), north end of the Camden Yards complex. Open daily. Small admission fee. This $16 million attraction was opened in 2005 to house the memorabilia collection that had become too large for the Babe Ruth Museum to contain. The 22,000-square-foot structure has exhibits relating to Babe Ruth, Johnny Unitas, Maryland Terrapins, Baltimore Orioles and Colts, and the city's Negro Leagues.

Note: You can save a few dollars by purchasing the combination ticket if you plan to visit both the Babe Ruth Museum and Sports Legends.

✍ ↑ **Geppi's Entertainment Museum** (410-625-7060; www.geppismuseum.com), 310 W. Camden St., at the north end of the Camden Yards complex. Open Tues.–Sun. 10–6. Adults $10; seniors $9; students $7; children 4 and under are free. What started out as a personal collection has grown into an entire museum full of pop culture icons and toys. Each room in the museum centers on a certain period, starting with the simple toys of the late 1700s to the complicated electronic entertainment systems of today. Each generation of visitors will have happy memories rekindled with displays of the Katzenjammer Kids, Disney characters, Howdy Doody, Superman, the Beatles, Star Wars, and more.

↑ **Reginald F. Lewis Museum of Maryland African American History & Culture** (443-263-1800; www.rflewismuseum.org), 830 E. Pratt St. Open Wed.–Sun. Small admission fee. With a striking architectural style, both inside and out, the museum contains three primary galleries. In one, exhibits detail how skills brought from Africa shaped the lives of those brought to America. Interactive displays let you try your hand at these skills. The other galleries explore African American families and communities and their creative spirits. An ambitious schedule of special exhibits and public programs could keep you coming back many times for new experiences.

✍ ↑ **The Samuel D. Harris National Museum of Dentistry** (410-706-0600; www.dental museum.org), 31 S. Greene St. Open Wed.–Sun. Small admission fee. It's a good bet your first reaction to this was, "A museum of dentistry? How boring!" Overcome that judgment, and you're in for a couple of hours of engaging exhibits and interactive displays. If you grew

---

✍ ♿ ↑ **National Aquarium in Baltimore** (410-576-3800; www.aqua.org), 501 E. Pratt St., downtown/Inner Harbor. Open 9–8 daily in July and Aug.; 10–5 Sat.–Thurs. and 10–8 Fri., Nov.–Feb.; 9–5 Sat.–Thurs. and 9–8 Fri., Mar.–June and Sept.–Oct. Adults $29.95; seniors $26.95; children 3–11 are $20.95.

I admit to being somewhat of a skinflint when it comes to paying admission charges, but I urge you to pay whatever they are asking to experience the National Aquarium. I've never been anywhere that does a better job of displaying the underwater world with live specimens and then explaining it with vivid exhibits.

A gently sloping walkway takes you along one tank after another, letting you linger as long as you want to observe the more than 11,000 creatures housed in the seven-story structure. There are sharks, dolphins, sea horses, frogs, eels, piranhas, stingrays, and turtles. The kids will love the touch tank and the dolphin show within the 1.2-million-gallon water-tank theater.

Be aware that baby strollers are not permitted and that long lines can form early in the day, especially during the summer months and in fall when school classrooms fill the aquarium with hundreds of kids. Allow a minimum of two to three hours to experience it all. I felt rushed even when I spent more than three hours there—and that was before the aquarium had completed an expansion that nearly doubled its size.

up in the mid-1900s, old toothpaste commercials and cartoon-character toothbrushes will bring back memories, while your kids can play-act being a dentist or practice flossing on a giant set of plastic teeth, and everyone can become a CSI investigator helping to identify victims through dental charts and radiographs. The museum also has George Washington's denture set, so you can find out once and for all if the country's first president wore wooden teeth.

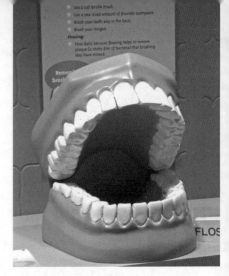

THE SAMUEL D. HARRIS NATIONAL MUSEUM OF DENTISTRY

Federal Hill

⚓ **Baltimore Museum of Industry** (410-727-4808; www.thebmi.org), 1415 Key Hwy. (between Federal Hill proper and Fort McHenry). Open Tues.–Sun. Adults $12; seniors $9; and children over six are $7. Hands-on exhibits revisit the Industrial Revolution's impact on Baltimore, the bay, and the rest of Maryland. Includes the **Museum of Incandescent Lighting,** with more than 50,000 lightbulbs and related objects, such as some of Thomas Edison's earliest experimental bulbs.

American Visionary Art Museum (410-244-1900; www.avam.org), 800 Key Hwy. Closed Mon. Adults $15.95; seniors $13.95; and children over six are $9.95. The museum showcases the talents of innovative, self-taught artists, so the works you see here are almost always different, often unique, and probably found nowhere else.

Fell's Point

⚓ ♿ ⛵ **Frederick Douglass–Isaac Myers Maritime Park Museum** (410-685-0295; www.douglassmyers.org), 1417 Thames St. Open Mon.–Fri. Small admission fee. Located within the oldest standing industrial building along Baltimore's harbor, the museum tells the story of African Americans living in Fell's Point during the late 1800s and early 1900s, and focuses on the lives of two of the neighborhood's most noted residents. There are items from the lives of Douglass, an orator, and Myers, who established the country's first black owned and operated shipyard. How his successful business rose above the discriminations of the time is an interesting story. Hands-on exhibits, which let visitors caulk a ship's hull and lift a

⛵ ♿ **Baltimore Museum of Art** (410-396-1700; www.artbma.org), N. Charles and 31st Sts. (3 miles north of Inner Harbor), Uptown. Opens at 11 AM Wed.–Sun. Admission is free; a few special exhibits during the year may require an admission fee. Everything about the museum requires a superlative: As the state's largest art museum, it houses more than 100,000 objects that range from the ancient to the contemporary. The museum has one of the broadest Andy Warhol and other modern artists' collections; multiple galleries devoted to European masters such as Raphael and Rodin; art of Africa, Asia, the Americas, and Oceania; an American wing with paintings, furniture, and more from the 1700s to the present; and one of the country's most expansive outdoor sculpture gardens.

The Cone Sisters' collection of more than 500 works of art is considered to be one of the most important in the world. Because of them, you are able to appreciate the talents of Matisse, Picasso, Gauguin, van Gogh, Renoir, Cézanne, and others. Even the building is a work of art, having been designed by John Russell Pope, designer of the National Gallery of Art in Washington, DC.

heavy barrel with the aid of pulleys, and a demonstration on building a ship's skeletal hulk are fun and enlightening for both children and adults. Don't forget to walk along the waterfront Promenade, taking in the sights of the busy harbor and of the impressive sculptures placed along the way.

Mount Vernon

🎨 ♿ **Walters Art Museum** (410-547-9000; www.thewalters.org), 600 N. Charles St. Closed Mon. and Tues. Free admission to the permanent collection. The Walters contains 55 centuries of art displayed in a manageable way. With just one or two visits, you can experience much of its Egyptian, Roman, Greek, Etruscan, and ancient Near East collection. A renovation has made the exhibit spaces flow into one another, enhancing what each has to offer. The free admission is quite unexpected, especially when compared with the high admission costs of other art museums—many of which are not even close to being on par with the Walters.

Maryland Historical Society (410-685-3750; www.mdhs.org), 201 W. Monument St. Closed Mon. and Tues. Small admission fee. The original manuscript of the "Star-Spangled Banner" is probably the most famous of the 5 million objects in the society's collection. You will also find furniture, costumes, uniforms, and more that relate to the state's past. The gift shop has many handmade items.

Eubie Blake National Jazz Institute and Cultural Center (410-225-3130; www.eubie blake.org), 847 N. Howard St. Open Wed.–Sat. Honors the life and music of this jazz great and Baltimore native. Also highlights others, such as Cab Calloway and Billie Holiday, who were also from Baltimore. Changing exhibits focus on many aspects pertinent to the city's African American community.

North of Mount Vernon

National Great Blacks in Wax Museum (410-563-3404; www.greatblacksinwax.org), 1601–3 E. North Ave. (about 3 miles north of Inner Harbor). Closed Mon. Adults $12; seniors, students, and children 12–17 are $11; children 2–11 are $10. The country's first and only wax museum of African American history has more than one hundred lifesized figures. A replica of a slave ship is also featured.

FREDERICK DOUGLASS–ISSAC MYERS MARITIME PARK MUSEUM

Washington Village/Pigtown

🚂 **B&O Railroad Museum** (410-752-2490; www.borail.org), 901 W. Pratt St. (10 blocks from Inner Harbor). Open daily 10–5. Adults $16; seniors $14; children 3–12 are $10. Free parking. The huge 1844 brick-and-glass 22-sided polygon roundhouse is a familiar landmark to Baltimoreans and the largest circular industrial building in the world. You don't have to be a train buff to appreciate the spectacular 40-acre collection of locomotives, railcars, models, and artifacts, which is purported to be the most comprehensive collection of railroad artifacts in the Western Hemisphere. The kids' (and your) imaginations will bring the glory days back to life when you actually get to board some of the engines and walk through the cars.

SAVE A FEW DOLLARS

Harbor Pass (1-877-BALTIMORE; www.baltimore.org) provides admission to the **National Aquarium in Baltimore, the Maryland Science Center,** and the **Top of the World Observation Level** on the World Trade Center. It also provides admission to your choice of a few other attractions, such as **Port Discovery** or **Sports Legends at Camden Yards.** The pass is good for three days and can be purchased over the phone, online, or from the Baltimore Visitors Center in Inner Harbor. Adults $49.95; children 3–12 are $35.95.

HISTORIC SHIPS Historic Ships in Baltimore (410-539-1797; www.historicships .org), 301 E. Pratt St., downtown/Inner Harbor. Open daily. Adults $18; seniors $15; children 6–14 years old $7; children 5 and under are free. There is a smaller fee to visit just one or two ships. There are no real walls to this museum, as it consists of four ships docked about a block from one another. The U.S. submarine *Torsk* was the last ship to sink an enemy boat in World War II, the *Taney* is the only ship still afloat that was in Pearl Harbor, and the *Chesapeake* served as a lightship for more than 29 years. The real standout is the USS *Constellation.* Handheld audio devices take you on a guided tour of the 1854 ship, the last all-sail vessel built by the U.S. Navy. I liked learning about the history and operation of the ship, but most amazing was the number of levels below the main deck. Tickets also give you admission to the **Sevenfoot Knoll Lighthouse,** the oldest screw-pile lighthouse in the state.

HISTORIC HOMES

Little Italy
The Flag House and Star-Spangled Banner Museum (410-837-1793; www.flaghouse .org), 844 E. Pratt St. Tues.–Sat. 10–4. Free parking. Small admission fee. The 1793 home, furnished in Federal-period antiques, was the home of Mary Pickersgill, who sewed by hand the flag that inspired Francis Scott Key's famous poem. The museum next door chronicles the War of 1812.

THE USS *CONSTELLATION* IN INNER HARBOR

SEVENFOOT KNOLL LIGHTHOUSE IN INNER HARBOR

Uptown

Evergreen House (410-516-0341; www.museums.jhu.edu/evergreen), 4545 N. Charles St. Open daily (except Mon.) to 4 PM; tours offered on the hour. Small admission fee. Surrounded by 26 acres, the Italianate Evergreen House was built in 1840, and its 48 rooms are filled with decorative arts, antiques, and Tiffany glass. The house and grounds have been restored to reflect the time when Ambassador John Garrett's family resided here, from 1878 to 1942.

Homewood House (410-516-5589; www.museums.jhu.edu/homewood), 3400 N. Charles St. Open to 4 PM; tours on the hour. Closed Mon. Small admission fee. The Federal-architecture 1801 house was a wedding gift from Charles Carroll to his son and is now on the campus of Johns Hopkins University. Many of the pieces in the home belonged to the Carroll family. Be sure to visit the brick outhouse, which has graffiti from when the house served as a boys' school.

Southwest

⊤ **Mount Clare Museum House** (410-837-3262; www.mountclare.org), 1500 Washington Blvd. Open Thurs.–Sun. 11–4. Small admission fee. There's a lot to take in during the 45-minute guided tours (they begin on the hour, with the last tour starting at 3). Sitting atop a knoll within Carroll Park, the 1760 colonial Georgian house was the home of one of Maryland's first senators, Charles Carroll. The house also became the state's first house museum in 1917, and has been open to the public since then. Many things impressed me here: Close to 80 percent of the furnishings are the Carroll family's; all of the portraits are family members; the house contains the oldest bathtub and sewing sampler in Maryland; and the overall architecture of

INTERIOR OF THE *TORSK*

MOUNT CLARE MUSEUM HOUSE

the building. Most impressive, though, is that the docents do not shy away from discussing the family's careless treatment of their slaves and iron workers.

HISTORIC SITES ✦ **Fort McHenry** (410-962-4290; www.nps.gov/fomc), 2400 E. Fort Ave. Open daily; small admission fee. After witnessing 25 hours of vehement bombardment by the British, the flag flying over this fort on the morning of September 14, 1814, inspired Francis Scott Key to pen the "Star-Spangled Banner." Star-shaped Fort McHenry has been restored to its pre–Civil War appearance with cannons, barracks, and jail cells. Be sure to watch the presentation in the visitors center, and remember that the place is a great spot to watch ships going in and out of the harbor.

HISTORIC CHURCHES **Basilica of the National Shrine of the Assumption** (410-727-3565; www.baltimorebasilica.org), Cathedral and Mulberry Sts., Mount Vernon. The 1821 basilica was the first Roman Catholic cathedral built in America and was designed by Benjamin Henry Latrobe, the architect of the U.S. Capitol. Many consider it to be one of the best neoclassical structures in the world. Guided tours are provided (usually) three times a day Mon.–Sat. and noon on Sun.

FORT MCHENRY

Mount Vernon Place United Methodist Church (410-685-5290; www.mvpumc.org), 10 E. Mount Vernon Place, Mount Vernon. The ornately carved interior of the 1874 church contains an organ with 3,287 pipes and a labyrinth nearly a mile long. The green serpentine and gray stone church is on the site where Francis Scott Key died in 1843.

FORT MCHENRY DURING DEFENDER'S DAY
CELEBRATIONS

GUIDED TOURS Baltimore Trolley Tours (410-254-8687; http://baltimore trolley.com), depending on the season, the tours depart from the National Aquarium in Baltimore or Baltimore Visitors Center on Light St. Adults $24.95, children 2–10 years old $14.95; children younger than 2 are free. The ticket includes an all-day pass for the Baltimore Water Taxi (see *Getting Around*). The 90-minute tours aboard a bus trolley with narration will acquaint you with almost two dozen of the city's best attractions. It's a good way to see the city, and to help you decide which places you will want to visit later, but I also enjoyed learning little tidbits of information that would have been hard to come by anywhere else. Things such as how textiles played an important role in the city's history, that many of the restaurants in Little Italy were started during the Great Depression as a way to supplement incomes and that the food was served in a family's own dining room, and that Baltimore lays claim to having America's first Catholic cathedral—and the first indoor mall.

African American Cultural Tours (410-727-0755; www.angelfire.com/retr02/aact) and **Renaissance Productions and Tours** (410-728-3837) conduct tours highlighting contributions, landmarks, institutions, and individuals of significance to African Americans.

OBSERVATION POINT Top of the World Observation Level (410-837-8439; www.viewbaltimore.org), 401 Pratt St., downtown/Inner Harbor. Days and hours change with the seasons, but generally open Sun.–Wed. Small admission fee. Located on the 27th floor of the

AN AERIAL VIEW OF FORT MCHENRY

TOP OF THE WORLD VIEW OVER THE HARBOR

World Trade Center, the world's tallest pentagonal building (423 feet above the harbor), designed by architect I. M. Pei. The observation level has expansive windows that provide vistas onto the Inner Harbor, the surrounding city, and the Chesapeake Bay. Guides provide information and facts about the city and surrounding area. A great place to be as the sun sets and the harbor's waters reflect its golden glow and those of the thousands of electric lights that brighten Baltimore at night. The observation level also has rotating art, history, and cultural exhibits and events.

TOP OF THE WORLD VIEW OVER BALTIMORE

ZOO ✄ ♿ **The Maryland Zoo in Baltimore** (410-396-7102; www.marylandzoo.org), Druid Hill Park, Uptown (accessible from I-83 Exit 7). Open daily. Free parking. Adults $16.50; seniors $13.50; children 2–11 are $11.50. Admission is a little less on weekdays. Opened in 1867, this is the third oldest zoo in the country and home to more than two thousand animals from six continents. There are the exotic species such as polar bears, lions, and leopards, as well as the locally familiar turtles, barnyard animals, and owls. This is a very child-friendly place, as most of the exhibits are arranged so that even the smallest of visitors can see the animals. Lots of special events for children, too.

✳ To Do

BICYCLING Bicycle trails wend their way through the green landscape of **Herring Run Park** (see *Green Space*).

✄ **Light St. Cycles** (410-685-2234; www.lightstcycles.com), 1124 Light St., Federal

LESSER FLAMINGOS AT THE MARYLAND
ZOO IN BALTIMORE

Hill. A bicycle may just be the best way to tour the downtown/Inner Harbor/Federal Hill area, and these folks will rent you one for an hour or a day.

BIRDING See *Nature Preserves.*

BOAT EXCURSIONS

Fell's Point
⚓ **Urban Pirates** (410-327-8378; www .urbanpirates.com), Ann St. Pier. $20; children under 3 are $10. It seems that every tourist destination close to a body of water is now offering a pirate adventure. Of course, the reason is that the adventure is really popular with the kids. Who can resist dressing up like a pirate, fighting enemies with a water cannon, and discovering hidden treasures? *Arrr!*

Inner Harbor
Cruises on the Bay (410-268-7601; 1-800-569-9622; http://cruisesonthebay.com), departs from the City Dock. A division of Watermark, this company provides a number of day and evening cruises in and around the Inner Harbor and the bay on the *Annapolitan II,* which has a climate controlled lower deck and open upper deck. The 45-minute Inner Harbor cruise (adults $17, children 3–11 years old $6, and 2 and younger free) I have taken has a running narration that provides information on the sites the cruise goes by, such as Federal Hill, Fells Point, the USS *Constellation,* and Fort McHenry. The most memorable moment was when the boat floated by the Domino Sugar factory and the air became permeated with an exceedingly sweet smell.

Harbor Cruises (1-866-845-7245; www.spiritcruises.com), 561 Light St. (close to the Maryland Science Center). Offers daily lunch, dinner, sightseeing, and evening cruises on three different boats. Departure times, costs, and itineraries vary widely, so call to obtain the latest information.

BOAT RENTALS ⚓ **S J Koch Electric Boat Rentals** (443-433-2129; www .experiencetheduffyboat.com), 300 2nd St. Boats of various shapes and sizes are available for rent so that you can explore the harbor on your own.

FAMILY ACTIVITIES ⚓ ♿ **Port Discovery** (410-727-8120; www.portdiscovery .com), 35 Market Pl., downtown/Inner Harbor. Open daily during the summer; schedule changes for other seasons. Adults and children $13.95. The kids will just think they're having fun deciphering hieroglyphics, piecing together clues, or crossing the

THE URBAN PIRATES EN ROUTE TO PLUNDER

rope bridge, but Walt Disney's Imagineers designed the activities for children 6–12 to teach goal setting, problem solving, and creative thinking. Allow one to two hours.

✂ ⸙ ⌕ **Ripley's Believe It or Not Odditorium, 4D Moving Theater, and Mirror Maze** (443-615-7878; www.ripleys .com/baltimore), 301 Light St. Open daily. Adults for one attraction $17.99, two attractions $22.99, three attractions $27.99; children 4–12 years old for one attraction $11.99, two attractions $14.99, three attractions $17.99. The Odditorium is full of many of the wild and bizarre items on which the Ripley's reputation was built. The 4D Moving Theater, with motion seats, shows a variety of adrenaline-producing movies, and it may take you quite a while to negotiate the 2,000 square feet of the Mirror Maze. It has close to one hundred mirrors leading on a circuitous route of dead-ends and hidden corners, all while lights are flashing and loud music is playing.

Also see *Zoo*.

RIPLEY'S BELIEVE IT OR NOT ODDITORIUM

FISHING **Captain Don Marani** (410-342-2004; www.captdoncharters.com), 1001 Fell St., Fell's Point. Captain Don heads into the bay from Henderson's Wharf Marina in search of rockfish, bluefish, croaker, spot, and more. Charters range from $260 (two hours) to $550 (full day).

GOLF There are five courses within the municipal boundary of Baltimore. Information on all five can be obtained by calling 410-444-4933 or visiting www.bmgcgolf.com.

HORSE RACING ⌕ **Pimlico Race Course** (410-542-9400; www.preakness.com), Hayward and Winner Aves., Mount Washington (northwestern part of the city). Pimlico is home to the second jewel in thoroughbred racing's Triple Crown, the Preakness Stake. The Preakness is run annually on the third weekend in May, but you can attend other races here throughout the warmer months of the year.

WALKING TOURS **Frederick Douglass Walking Tour** (443-983-7974). The guided walk travels to sites involved with enslaved Africans, free blacks, runaways, and that Frederick Douglass called home.

The Fell's Point Preservation Society (410-675-6750; www.preservationsociety.com), 812 S. Ann St. Fell's Point sponsors a number of **Fell's Point Walking Tours,** including a garden tour, immigration tour, secrets of the seaport tour, and one that provides a glimpse into the seaport's tavern life.

The Mount Vernon Cultural District, Inc. (see *Guidance*), Mount Vernon. Has several brochures describing different walks throughout the neighborhood, taking in the cultural, historic, and retail aspects of each.

✳ Green Space

GARDENS **Sherwood Park** (410-323-7982), Stratford Rd., Guilford (northeastern part of the city). Open dawn–dusk daily. Free admission. It is small, but loaded with azaleas, boxwoods, cherries, dogwoods, magnolias, and wisterias. The most spectacular time to visit is late Apr.–early May, when the 80,000 tulips are in bloom.

NATURE PRESERVES & **Clyburn Arboretum** (410-367-2217; www.clyburn association.org), 4915 Greenspring Ave., Mount Washington (northwestern part of the city). Grounds generally open during daylight hours; closed Mon.; mansion and museum open Tues.–Fri. 8–3. Free admission. Signs identify hundreds of plants and trees throughout the 170 acres. There are marked trails, a garden of senses for the physically impaired, and a number of flower gardens. The 1888 Clyburn Mansion contains a commendable nature museum.

This is one of the Baltimore Bird Club's favorite sites. Great horned owls are year-round residents, and a variety of thrushes and warblers pass through during migrations. Come here in midspring and you'll see (or at least hear) sparrows, scarlet tanagers, finches, and yellow-bellied sapsuckers.

PARKS ✿ **Druid Hill Park** (410-396-7900; http://bcrp.baltimorecity.gov/parks), Druid Park Lake Dr., Hampden (accessed from I-83 Exits 7 and 8). One of the largest urban parks in America, Druid Hill was set aside as public space in 1688. Tennis courts, a public swimming pool, and lots of picnic tables. The main draws are the large amount of open ground on which to wander and several points overlooking various parts of the city. Pets permitted on a leash.

✿ **Herring Run Park** (410-396-7900), Belair-Edison (northeastern part of the city). A linear urban park along the waters of Herring Run. A few picnic tables and several streamside trails make this green space a neighborhood escape. Parking is available at Sinclair Lane and Harford and Belair Rds. Pets permitted on a leash.

✿ **Gwynns Falls–Leakin Parks** (410-396-7900; http://bcrp.baltimorecity.gov/parks), Edmonson Village (western part of the city). Officially they are separate parks, but they are side by side and their pathways connect. Altogether they provide more than 1,200 acres of preserved land within the city limits. One trail follows the route of an old millrace along Gwynns Falls, while others wind through the deep cleft created by Dead Run. Pets permitted on a leash.

ALONG THE WATERFRONT PROMENADE IN INNER HARBOR

WALKS The **Waterfront Promenade** in the downtown/Inner Harbor area runs for more than 7 miles, taking in the best that the waterfront has to offer. By starting at one end, you could walk through Canton, Little Italy, Inner Harbor, and Federal Hill, and end up at Fort McHenry.

✱ Lodging

RESORT

Stevenson, 21153

Gramercy Mansion B&B (410-486-2405; 1-800-553-3404; www.gramercymansion.com), 1400 Greenspring Rd. It calls itself a B&B, but with a swimming pool, a tennis court, formal and herb gardens, an organic farm, and trails winding through its 45 acres, I call it a resort. Guest rooms in the antiques-furnished, fireplace-rich 1902 Tudor-style mansion house range from spacious three-room suites with whirlpool tubs and private sunporches to basic rooms with shared bath. The basic "back-hall" rooms are a real deal, as they are less than half the cost of other rooms. Because all the amenities were still available to me, I didn't feel like I was missing a thing. $160–375.

MOTELS AND HOTELS

Downtown/Inner Harbor, 21202

Baltimore Marriott Waterfront (410-385-3000; www.marriotthotels.com), 700 Aliceanna St. Most of the Marriott's more than 700 rooms on 32 floors have views of the water. Indoor pool, exercise room. $299–394.

♿ **Days Inn** (410-576-1000; 1-800-DAYS-INN; www.daysinnerharbor.com), 100 Hopkins Pl. Just across the street from the Baltimore Convention Center and almost next door to Camden Yards, the Days Inn is also just a couple of blocks away from all of the Inner Harbor's attractions. With an outdoor pool, exercise center, business center, concierge and valet services, and large rooms, this has to be one of the most deluxe locations of the Days Inn chain. Its rate of $209 and above is also a bargain considering its location.

♿ **Hilton Baltimore and Convention Center** (443-573-8700; http://www3.hilton.com), 401 W. Pratt St. A massive hotel with close to 800 rooms and 60,000 square feet of meeting space. Fitness and business centers, plush furnishings and amenities in the guest rooms and suites, swimming pool, concierge and valet services, and even currency exchange. $249 and up.

Hyatt Regency (410-528-1234; 1-800-233-1234; www.baltimore.hyatt.com), 300 Light St. The gleaming glass-and-steel Hyatt towers over Inner Harbor, reflecting the water, sky, and surrounding buildings. Amenities include an extensive health club, a recreation deck with jogging track, a putting green, tennis courts, and almost 500 guest rooms with great views. Concierge service. Parking fee. $199–299.

♿ **Pier 5 Hotel** (410-539-2000; www.harbormagic.com), 711 Eastern Ave. The Pier 5 is one of Baltimore's few boutique hotels—its art deco style is a splash of colors—and it is the only Inner Harbor hotel situated right next to the water. This permits you to walk to all of Inner Harbor's attractions without having to cross any busy streets.

Staff is gracious and very attentive to your needs, but the more than 60 spacious rooms let you attain large-hotel anonymity if you wish. Some rooms have water views, while others have views of the city; my room had both, as it overlooked the harbor and National Aquarium. Terry-cloth robes permitted me to lounge in comfort, while nightly turndown service let me know someone cared. Parking fee. Pets permitted; must be brought into the hotel in a travel crate. $249–349; many packages

PIER 5 HOTEL IN INNER HARBOR

NIGHT VIEW FROM THE RENAISSANCE BALTIMORE HARBORPLACE

available. (Also see McCormick and Schmick's under *Dining Out.*)

✿ ⅙ **Renaissance Baltimore Harborplace** (410-547-1200; 1-800-HOTELS-1; www.renaissancehotels.com), 202 E. Pratt St. Another towering steel-and-glass structure overlooking the harbor, the Renaissance has more than 600 rooms. Connected to the Gallery Mall, it has a swimming pool and exercise room. Children under 18 stay free in the same room with parent. Some rooms don't have a water view, so pay the extra few dollars to ensure you have one; it would be a shame to be here and overlook the backs of other buildings instead of the harbor. Parking fee. $309–399; some suites are available, ranging $600–3,500.

Sheraton Inner Harbor (410-962-8300; www.sheraton.com/innerharbor), 300 S. Charles St. Its location is perfect for families with dedicated sports fans and other members who would rather shop or see the sights. It is located just one block from Inner Harbor, two blocks from the Orioles' Camden Yards, and a few more blocks from the Ravens' stadium. Some rooms have water views; amenities include pool and fitness room. Free on-site parking. $190–449.

✿ ⅙ **Tremont Plaza Hotel** (410-685-7777; www.tremontsuitehotels.com), 222 St. Paul Place. Located about halfway between Inner Harbor and Mount Vernon. Italian marble and mahogany add a touch

of distinction to the lobby. All of the more than 200 guest accommodations are suites with separate living and sleeping rooms and fully equipped kitchens. Parking fee; pets permitted with extra fee. $179–259.

Mount Vernon, 21201

✿ **Hostelling International Baltimore** (410-576-8800; www.baltimorehostel.org), 17 W. Mulberry St. The atmosphere is typical hostel—somewhat simple (and donated) furnishings, bunk beds in dorm rooms, shared baths, and an old mansion that shows some signs of wear. However, you also get the use of a nicely equipped kitchen and a computer, and the opportunity to meet travelers from all over the

HARBOR VIEW FROM THE RENAISSANCE BALTIMORE HARBORPLACE

world (English was a second language for 7 out of 10 guests who wrote in the register the last time I stopped by). In addition, the nightly fee of about $30 a person (Hostelling International membership is not required) is outrageously inexpensive to have accommodations within walking distance of dozens of Baltimore's best attractions. Unlike many hostels, there is no lockout and no curfew, and some private rooms are available.

Note: Many more hotels and motels are located near the Baltimore/Washington International Thurgood Marshall Airport and almost every exit along the I-695 beltway. Among the lower-cost national chains are **Days Inn** (1-800-544-8313; www.days inn.com), **Comfort Inn** (1-800-228-5150; www.comfortinn.com), **Red Roof Inn** (1-800-RED-ROOF; www.redroof.com), **Courtyard by Marriott** (1-888-236-2427; www.courtyard.com), and **Microtel** (410-865-7500; www.microtelinn.com). The **Homestead Village Guest Studios** (410-691-2500), 939 International Dr., with low-cost studio efficiencies, is close to the airport.

INNS

Canton, 21224

✐ **Inn at 2920** (410-342-4450; 1-877-774-2920; www.theinnat2920.com), 2920 Elliott St. The inn's late-1800s building has been many things during its lifetime, including a tavern and a brothel. The current owners have done a nice job of blending the old (brick walls are exposed and wood trim has been retained) with modern amenities and furnishings. Unlike many inns and B&Bs that are so cluttered you are afraid to move around, the eye-pleasing furnishings here leave you with a feeling of spaciousness and luxury. Well-behaved children 13 years and older are permitted, and there is free on-street parking. It's only one block away from the lively nightlife establishments of Canton, so it's an easy walk to enjoy a drink or a meal, but remember that the partying sometimes spills out onto the street below the inn on the weekends. $195–230.

Fell's Point, 21231

🐾 ✐ ♿ **The Admiral Fell Inn** (410-522-7380; www.admiralfell.com), 888 S. Broadway. The European-style Admiral Fell Inn's main building originally served as a seamen's hostel. Today guests sip complimentary coffee or tea next to the lobby's fireplace or retire to rooms decorated with Federal-period furnishings. My room had a canopy pencil-post bed and overlooked the fading VOTE AGAINST PROHIBITION sign painted on the building next door. Specialty rooms and suites have deep dormers, original wood floors, Jacuzzis, and balconies. A complimentary house breakfast is included. Dogs permitted with extra fee; free parking nearby. $219–300.

🍴 ✐ ♿ **Inn at Henderson's Wharf** (410-522-7777; 1-800-292-4667; www.hendersons wharf.com), 1000 Fell St. The inn was originally constructed in 1893 as a tobacco warehouse. Many of the large guest rooms retain the original 3-foot-thick brick walls, providing a warm radiance. Some rooms overlook the water; others face the cobble-stoned inner courtyard. Continental breakfast included. A good value when compared with the hotels in Inner Harbor. $199–239.

BED & BREAKFASTS

Butchers Hill, 21231

Blue Door on Baltimore (410-732-0191; www.bluedoorbaltimore.com), 2023 E. Baltimore St. Although this row house was built in 1907, it has been refurbished into a modern B&B whose three guest suites all have king beds, balconies, and private baths featuring a shower and a tub. If you're a tech savvy person, you'll enjoy staying here as the host has guaranteed that you won't need to suffer electronics withdrawal no matter what device you are addicted to: free wi-fi is always available; clock radios have phone and MP3 docks; chargers for all kinds of devices are available for your use; 140 channels are on the satellite television; you can connect to the Internet in your room via Apple TV (even if you didn't bring your device with you); and you can connect to the B&B's printer via your smart phone, laptop, or Internet mobile device. Continental breakfast served weekdays; full breakfast on the weekends. $139–175.

Camden Yards, 21230

Rachel's Dowry (410-752-0805; www .rachaelsdowrybedandbreakfast.com), 637 Washington Blvd. This 18th-century Federal-style home is a most elegant place to stay during a visit to Baltimore, and it's just a short walk to the attractions of the Inner Harbor, Camden Yards, and the convention center. The furnishings are period antiques, each guest room or suite has a private bath with a large shower or soaking tub, the staircase has little nooks on each landing that invite you to linger and take in the appealing surroundings, and the breakfast always includes local and organic produce. I enjoyed being in the Ella Virginia Suite on the third floor looking into the upper limbs of stately trees and down onto the nicely landscaped front yard gardens. I also like that the hosts have incorporated as much green technology into the house as possible. $150–230.

Federal Hill, 21230

Scarborough Fair (410-837-0010; www .scarborough-fair.com), 801 S. Charles St. This is the place to stay if you want to be close to Inner Harbor (it is only two blocks away) but don't want the impersonal service of a hotel. The B&B offers six period-and/or reproduction-furnished guest rooms in the 1801 home; each has a private bath, and four have working fireplace. Free off-street parking. $235–259.

Fell's Point, 21231

⚓ ♿ **Celie's** (410-522-2323; 1-800-432-0184; www.celieswaterfront.com), 1714 Thames St. There are seven guest rooms in this large row house (long and narrow like most of Baltimore's row houses). Some have fireplaces, others whirlpool tubs; all have a TV and video player. The ground-floor room has its own private courtyard and is handicapped accessible. Walk up the steps to the roof deck for a small view of the harbor. Children over 10 are welcome. $149–299.

⚓ **Abercrombie** (410-244-7227; www .abacrombieinn.com), 58 W. Biddle St. This 1880s row house is conveniently located in Mount Vernon, close to many of Baltimore's cultural offerings. The 12 guest rooms have private bath, while guests meet and greet one another in the parlor on the first floor. Well-mannered children over 10 are welcome. $85–135.

Aunt Rebecca's B&B (410-625-1007; www.auntrebeccasbnb.com), 106 E. Preston St. Within their 1870s brownstone town house, Becky and Joe Pitta offer three large (12-foot ceilings) guest rooms furnished in Victorian style. Each room has individually controlled air-conditioning, and the bathrooms retain the original claw-foot tubs for relaxing soaks. Off-street parking available. $135–150.

♿ **4 East Madison Inn** (410-605-2020; www.4eastmadisoninn.com), 4 E. Madison St. 4 East Madison provides a glimpse into life in Baltimore during the mid-1800s, when the structure was built. Bay windows, mahogany doors, marble fireplaces,

4 EAST MADISON INN

tiger-striped flooring, and a stained-glass skylight harken back to the time when Dr. William Stevenson Baer, a pioneering orthopedic surgeon at the Johns Hopkins School of Medicine, lived here. Modern luxuries, such as 600-count cotton sheets, private baths, individual heating and cooling controls, and high-speed Internet access, along with free off-street parking, are further enticements to stay in this well-kept boutique hotel. The small garden patio is an attractive retreat from the hustle and bustle of the nearby Mt. Vernon business and dining district. $185–250.

✱ Where to Eat

DINING OUT

Downtown/Inner Harbor

& **Charleston** (410-332-7373; www .charlestonrestaurant.com), 1000 Lancaster St. (between Inner Harbor and Fell's Point). Open for dinner 5:30–10 Mon.–Sat. Reservations strongly advised. Considered by many to be one of Baltimore's finest dining experiences. Chef Cindy Wolf prepares a daily changing selection of American cuisine with bits of Southern and French influences. Recent menus have included pan-roasted salmon dusted with marcona almonds and served with cauliflower and chervil beurre blanc, and grilled pork tenderloin with butternut squash, andouille sausage risotto, and local apple cider reduction. The prix fixe menu with a choice of several courses starts at $89; with wines to match each course, $139. The wine list contains hundreds of bottles, with the top price of almost $5,000.

& **Fogo de Chão** (410-528-9292; www .fogodechao.com), 600 E. Pratt St., #102. Open for lunch Mon.–Fri., daily for dinner. Meat lovers take notice. Drawing on the history of *gauchos* (cowboys) in southern Brazil (where this international chain is based), who cooked their meals over open flames while in the field, Fogo de Chão serves more than a dozen meats, including beef, chicken, and pork, which are offered by servers dressed as *gauchos*. You are given two cards: One summons the *gauchos*

to your table, and they'll keep serving you until you put up the stop card. It's an interesting experience, and the salad bar is the most bountiful one you'll probably ever come across. If $50 sounds like too much for dinner, come for lunch, as the same menu is offered for about $30.

& **McCormick and Schmick's** (410-234-1300; www.mccormickandschmicks.com), 711 Eastern Ave. (in the Pier 5 Hotel) at Inner Harbor. Open for lunch and dinner daily. Walls of dark wood, stained glass, and a mahogany bar embellish the view of the harbor. This Portland, Oregon–based chain came to Baltimore in 1998 with a changing menu featuring more than 30 varieties of fish from both of America's oceans. There can be as many as 10 different appetizers on the half shell, and the menu tells you where the fish came from that day. Wanting to stay somewhat local, I had the mackerel, from New Jersey, grilled with tomatoes and capers. Entrées $17–32.

Fell's Point

& **The Black Olive** (410-276-7141; www .theblackolive.com), 814 S. Bond St. Open for dinner daily. Dimitris, Pauline, and Stellos Spiliadis use only organic produce, milk products, flour, and sugar in their Greek restaurant. The fish offerings, such as arctic char, sea bream, and Dover sole, arrive fresh from around the world and are filleted tableside. Lamb, veal, and several vegetarian selections are also prepared with care. Entrées $29–48; small plates available.

& **Kali's Court** (410-276-4700; www.kalis court.com), 1606 Thames St. Open for dinner daily. Like the Black Olive (see above), Kali's offers fish from around the world. Many dishes, like the Australian swordfish and the bouillabaisse, are cooked in a brick oven for a bit of a different taste. Appetizers range from the brick-oven oysters to lacquered octopus with spinach and feta. Most dishes are $30–36.

Adjacent to Kali's Court is **Kali's Mezze** (410-563-7600; www.kalismezze.com), serving an upscale menu of tabouleh, fattoush, grape leaves, baba ghanoush, and other traditional Greek dishes. Most items are reasonably priced at $4.50–10.95.

&. **Pierpoint** (410-675-2080; www
.pierpointrestaurant.com), 1822 Aliceanna
St. Open Tues.–Sun. Chef-owner Nancy
Longo has been attracting customers into
her small space since the late 1980s. The
smoked crabcakes (market price) established her reputation as someone who does
things differently. The BBQ duck egg rolls,
corn-fried oysters, and Maryland-style cioppino are just a few other examples. $18–27.

Little Italy

&. ✪ **Aldo's** (410-727-0700; www.aldositaly
.com), 306 S. High St. Open daily for dinner. Possibly the poshest place to dine in
Little Italy. Reservations strongly advised;
couples desiring the most romantic setting
should ask to be placed in the "plaza." Definitely one of the best Italian restaurants in
the state—I knew I was in for something
special when the salad was the best thing I
had tasted all week; ditto the colossal lump
crab cocktail (that had been sautéed in
wine). Then came the main course, whose
veal was so tender I cut it with my fork.
Thanks to the chef using granulated sugar
instead of powdered, my dessert, a delicious cannoli, was lighter and tastier than
most I have had. This is a place not to be
missed. Entrées range from $20–50, with
most around $25.

Da Mimmo Ristorante (410-727-6876;
www.damimmo.com), 217 S. High St. Open
for lunch and dinner daily. Reservations
strongly advised. Low lights, candles on the
table, and a tuxedoed waitstaff in a 200-
year-old building—the idyllic setting to
savor Chef Masood's irreproachable prepa-
rations. The pasta fagioli was like my
mother's, while the taste of the gnocchi alla
Napolitana almost made me believe my
Italian grandfather had come back to life.
An order of veal chops could serve a small
army, as could the filet mignon alla Rossini.
As a bonus, Da Mimmo is the only restaurant in Little Italy with its own parking lot.
$20–39.

&. **Dalesio's** (410-539-1965; www.dalesios
.com), 829 Eastern Ave. Dalesio's forte is
northern Italian cuisine, which, by its
nature, has a bit of a French character to it.
The frutti di mare all Mediterranea is

shrimp and scallops with mushrooms in a
creamy Marsala sauce. Not quite as heavy is
the capellini al Carciofi, with artichoke
hearts, tomatoes, and a touch of Chianti.
Veal, chicken, and duck dishes $17–29.

🍲 **La Scala** (410-783-9209; www.lascala
dining.com), 1012 Eastern Ave. Italian
cooking that is inspired by the whole country and not just one region. Open daily for
dinner. The prices on the pasta dishes, such
as the capellini al pomodoro, are great deals
at $14.95–21.95. Chicken, veal, beef, and
seafood entrées are only slightly higher.

&. ✪ **La Tavola** (410-685-1859; www.la
-tavola.com), 248 Albemarle St. Open for
lunch and dinner daily. Chef-owner Carlo
Vignotto grew up working in his parents'
and grandparents' beachside restaurants in
a small village near Venice and spent a
number of years in other European establishments before bringing his culinary
expertise to Baltimore's Little Italy. His
menu contains traditional dishes with some
delightful twists (my pasta with raisins, nut-
meg, and cinnamon was a refreshing blend
of flavors). All bread, pasta, and desserts are
handmade every morning, and the extensive list of daily specials depends on what
Chef Carlo is able to find fresh when he
goes to market every morning. The rockfish
cheeks (with a crablike texture) I had were
caught in the bay just a couple of hours
before being served. The waitstaff are helpful and knowledgeable, and I even enjoyed
the dinner music being played. Dine here
and you are sure to have a good experience.
Entrées $16–30.

Mount Vernon

&. **Tio Pepe** (443-863-8808; www.tiopepe
baltimore.com), 10 E. Franklin St. Open
for lunch Mon.–Fri., dinner daily; hours
vary slightly each day. Note: This is not a
place to show up in casual dress; reservations strongly recommended. The dining
rooms in which Tio Pepe serves its authentic Spanish food are in one of Baltimore's
famous row houses. Black bean is the soup
to go with. The veal chops in black truffle
sauce are truly decadent, while the paella
for two could probably feed four. Entrées
$19–50.

Patterson Park

Bistro Rx (410-276-0820; http://bistro
rx.net), 2901 E. Baltimore St. Open Sun.
for brunch and daily for dinner. Hip. Chic.
Sophisticated. Relaxed. Call it whatever you
want, Bistro Rx is a popular upscale neighborhood dining establishment whose entrée
items will sound familiar to you, but are
prepared in such a way as to stand out from
what you have had in other places. I ate
every morsel of my cornmeal crusted cod
with crawfish étouffée and my dining companion smiled with every bite of the chorizo
and crab mac and cheese. The offerings
seem to be ever-changing, so you'll want to
keep coming back. I like that the menu
provides a three- or four-word description
of each wine and that there are always at
least seven beers on tap. $16–24, with sides
a few dollars more. Desserts are made in-
house and worth the calories.

EATING OUT

Downtown/Inner Harbor

& **Attman's** (410-563-2666; www.attmans
deli.com), 1019 E. Lombard St. Open daily
for breakfast and late lunch; closes at 6:30
Mon.–Sat. and 5 on Sun. In the same location and serving a taste of New York deli
sandwiches since 1915. Reubens, pastrami,
kosher hot dogs, cream cheese and lox on a
bagel, liverwurst, and combination sandwiches. They even have rice and bread
puddings for dessert—and free parking, a
plus in this part of Baltimore. $7–15.

Mo's Seafood (410-837-8600; www
.mosseafood.com), 219 S. President St.
Mo's has been around for decades and,
while my crabcake was tasty and huge, this
place just had the feeling of being tired.
Décor and atmosphere felt tired, service
felt tired, and my dining companion left
more than half her order of mahimahi on
the plate. At $19.99–45.99 it's quite pricey
for the atmosphere and quality.

& & **Hard Rock Café** (410-347-7625;
www.hardrock.com), 601 E. Pratt St. (in the
Power Plant). The Baltimore location of the
international café chain serves traditional
American food (burgers, steak, and pasta)
amid a profusion of rock 'n' roll memorabilia. Entrées $10–27.

THE HARD ROCK CAFÉ IN INNER HARBOR

Federal Hill

&. **Blue Agave** (410-576-3938; www.blue
agaverestaurant.com), 1032 Light St. Open
daily for lunch and dinner. The Blue Agave
brought authentic food from the heart of
Mexico and Baja peninsula to Federal Hill
several years ago. Don't look for bland fajitas
or chimichangas. Instead, try the mahimahi
Veracruzana with sauce made from tomatoes, poblano chile, lime, olive, garlic, and
oregano. Or maybe the quail stuffed with
huitlacoche (often called Mexico's truffle)
and served with green chile and sautéed
spaghetti squash. Three different house-
made salsas come with the complimentary
tortilla chips. Other entrées $13–28.

& &. **Mother's Federal Hill Grille** (410-
244-8686; www.mothersgrille.com), 1113 S.
Charles St. Open for breakfast, lunch, and
dinner daily. Brothers Dave and Adam
Rather took an old bakery and turned it
into a local gathering spot. Crabcakes and
other seafood are favorites, but don't overlook the ribs, tuna wrap, or Mediterranean
pasta. A number of bottled microbrews and
homemade ice cream are other reasons
people like Mother's. $8.99–26.95.

Little Italy

& &. **Chiapparelli's** (410-837-0309; www
.chiapparellis.com), 237 S. High St. Open
daily for lunch and dinner. Serving southern
Italian cooking since the 1940s. Many people come just for the house salad (served
with each entrée), which is topped by
Chiapparelli's dressing of garlic, oregano,
Parmesan cheese, eggs, and pepperoncini.
Pastas, chicken, veal, beef, and seafood
dishes available. $16–28.

Mount Vernon

&. **Sascha's 527** (410-539-8880; www
.saschas.com), 527 N. Charles St. Closed
Sun. Sascha's has grown from a lunch-
delivery-only service to serving cafeteria-
style for lunch and employing a waitstaff at
dinner. With a hip and upbeat personality
and world-inspired dishes, it has some of
the most refreshing foods I've encountered.
How about shredded duck and apple
ragout over an apple onion pancake for
lunch? Instead of french fries (which are

also available), get the portobello fries with
peach ketchup and gingered soy. Big sandwiches, a host of salads and veggie offerings, daily plate specials, and designer
pizettes will make you want to come back
again. Entrées $17–26; tasting plates about
half the price.

Sofi's Crepes (727-7732; www.sofiscrepes
.com), 1723 N. Charles St. Open for lunch
and dinner Thurs.–Sun., dinner only Mon.–
Wed. Sofi's offers an almost staggering variety of crêpes. When I'm looking for something filling, I usually order the mozzarella,
basil, tomato, and olive oil crêpe for lunch,
but when the mood for something sweet
hits, I go with a caramel, chocolate, and
nuts or a banana and homemade butter-
scotch crêpe. Most crepes are $6–8.

Woman's Industrial Exchange (410-685-
4388; www.womansindustrialexchange.org),
333 N. Charles St. Open Mon.–Fri. 11–3
for lunch. You will spend money eating out
anyway, so let it do some good at this nonprofit group (see *Special Shops*). The prices
are reasonable; sandwiches are usually less
than $10 (the taste and quality of my
chicken salad sandwich confirmed why this
is the establishment's most-ordered item)
and full entrées $10–15. Finish the meal
with a strawberry, chocolate, and vanilla
crème brulee ($6) or any other of the
house-made desserts.

Uptown

& &. **Gertrude's** (410-889-3399; www
.gertrudesbaltimore.com), 10 Art Museum
Dr. Open for lunch and dinner Tues.–Sun.
The setting could certainly not be any more
aesthetically pleasing, as Gertrude's is
located inside the Baltimore Museum of
Art. However, many people come just for
the flavorful Chesapeake-style food. Lots of
seafood dishes, such as herb-encrusted
rockfish (market price), crabmeat quiche,
and gumbo with six different seafoods and
andouille sausage. There are also "platters
from the land" and several veggie offerings.
The panini smothered in peppers, onion,
field greens, caponata, and fresh mozzarella
I had was an outstanding blend of tastes.
Entrées $17–28.

CRABS

Canton

Ƨ **Bo Brooks** (410-558-0202; www.bo brooks.com), 2780 Lighthouse Point. (inside the Baltimore Marine Center). Open daily for lunch and dinner. There have been several owners since Mr. Brooks began his business in the 1940s, but steamed crabs (market price) have remained a constant. The latest owner has expanded and updated the menu to include a crab quesadilla, other seafood, and sandwiches. Most dinner items are $15–29.

TAKE-OUT Neo Viccino (410-347-0349; www.viccino.com), 1317 N. Charles St., Mount Vernon. It is only a carry-out, but you'll get some of the city's best pizza. Try the Pizza Viccino, and you may never want another kind. Salads, pasta, and huge calzones. $7–19.

COFFEE BARS

Fell's Point

The Daily Grind (410-558-0399), 1720 Thames St. A local hot spot that attracts the bohemian/shabby-chic local crowd. At times it is next to impossible to get in, but the coffee is good enough that you should try.

MICROBREWERIES

Downtown/Inner Harbor

Pratt Street Ale House (410-244-8900; www.prattstreetalehouse.com), 206 W. Pratt St. Open daily. The menu is typical bar fare—burgers, sandwiches, pizzas, and a few entrées—but you really come here for the selection of English-style Oliver ales.

Halethorpe

Clipper City Brewing Company (410-247-7822; www.clippercitybeer.com), 4615 Hollins Ferry Rd. This is not a restaurant, but a true brewery that offers factory tours on selected days (schedule is on the Web site). They brew everything from American-style lager to ales and wheat beers, and a selection of bottle conditioned beverages. At one time distribution was limited to

Maryland, Washington, DC, and Virginia, but it's now found throughout much of the eastern United States. Of course, you can always stop by the brewery to pick up a case or two.

SNACKS AND GOODIES

Downtown/Inner Harbor

Cheesecake Factory (410-234-3990; www.thecheesecakefactory.com), 201 E. Pratt St. (inside the Pratt St. Pavilion). Yes, this national chain has a full menu, but the desserts are the real reason to visit. The thick slices of cheesecake are available in more than 30 varieties. The espresso drinks are a good complement.

Fell's Point

Maggie Moo's Ice Cream (410-342-8399; www.maggiemoos.com), 821 S. Broadway. The ice cream is made fresh daily in the shop.

Mount Vernon

The Peanut Shoppe (410-685-3731; www.bonniespeanutshoppe.com), 212 N. Charles St. This business has been roasting nuts in their shop for more than three-quarters of a century! Many good candy selections, too.

Little Italy

Ġ **Vaccaro's** (410-685-4905; www.vaccaros pastry.com), 222 Albemarle St. Some of the best Italian sweets to be found in the eastern United States. The tiramisu melts in your mouth, the cream in the éclairs is surely rich enough to clog your arteries after two bites, and the cannoli are stuffed to order. To really indulge, have your pastry topped with a dip of gelato.

✳ Entertainment

FILM Ġ **Charles Theater** (410-727-3456; www.thecharles.com), 1711 N. Charles St., Charles Village (a few blocks north of Penn Station). This neighborhood theater is the place to go to see the foreign, art, independent, and documentary films that never seem to make it to the cineplexes.

& The Senator (www.thesenatortheatre.com), 5904 York Rd., Homeland (northern part of the city). The 1939 Senator shows first-run movies in its opulent art deco atmosphere and has been named one of the top movie theaters in the country. Please note: The Senator was closed and undergoing renovation as this book went to press.

MUSIC & **Baltimore Concert Opera** (443-445-0226; www.baltimoreconcertopera.com), 11 W. Mount Vernon Place. Think of it as a no-frills opera. You get the complete libretto, the operatic singing, and at least one musical instrument, but no costumes, stage sets, or acting. An interesting concept that lets you experience the opera without spending a whole lot of money.

& Baltimore Symphony Orchestra (410-783-8000; www.baltimoresymphony.org), Joseph Meyerhoff Symphony Hall, 1212 Cathedral St., Mount Vernon. A wide variety of classical, pops, and family entertainment is presented throughout the year in the near-perfect symphony hall.

& Peabody Conservatory of Music (410-234-4500; www.peabody.jhu.edu), 1 E. Mount Vernon Place, Mount Vernon. Operas, symphonies, and recitals performed by student and guest artists. Many of the performances are free.

NIGHTLIFE

Downtown/Inner Harbor
Ⓨ **Howl at the Moon** (410-783-5111; www.howlatthemoon.com), 34 Market Place. Claims to be "the World's Best Dueling Piano Rock-and-Roll" bar.

Fell's Point
Ⓨ **The Horse You Came In On Saloon** (410-327-8111; www.thehorsebaltimore.com), 1626 Thames St. It says it was established in 1775, which would make it the country's oldest saloon. The saloon has a bit of an English pub atmosphere. Local live music is presented nightly.

Latin Palace (410-522-6700; www.latinpalace.com), 509 Broadway. Closed Mon. Learn the merengue or salsa as you dance

the night away to Latin and international music.

THEATERS

Downtown/Inner Harbor
Hippodrome Theatre at the France-Merrick Performing Arts Center (410-837-7400; www.france-merrickpac.com), 12 N. Eutaw St. Now restored to its original 1914 appearance, the historic vaudeville theater has more than 2,000 seats from which to enjoy productions of Broadway shows such as *Mamma Mia, The Lion King,* and *The Phantom of the Opera.*

Fell's Point
& The Vagabond Players (410-563-9135; www.vagabondplayers.org), 806 S. Broadway. All of the actors and stagehands are volunteers, but this does not stop them from presenting professional-caliber theater. Productions have included *Prelude to a Kiss, Inherit the Wind,* and *Blood Brothers.*

Mount Vernon
CENTERSTAGE (410-332-0033; www.centerstage.org), 700 N. Calvert St. The **State Theater of Maryland** mounts productions ranging from Broadway hits to works by new artists. Previous presentations have included *A Raisin in the Sun, Three Tall Women,* and *The Pajama Game.* The season usually runs Oct.–June.

Uptown
& Theater Hopkins (410-516-5153; www.krieger.jhu.edu), the Merrick Barn at Johns Hopkins University. An ever-changing and entertaining schedule of major American, British, and Irish plays is presented in the 1804 brick barn.

SPORTS & **1st Mariner Arena** (410-347-2020; www.baltimorearena.com), 201 W. Baltimore St. Home for the Baltimore Blast (410-732-5278; www.baltimoreblast.com), members of the Major Indoor Soccer League.

ℰ & Baltimore Ravens (410-986-5225; www.baltimoreravens.com), 1101 Russell St. (M&T Bank Stadium). The Browns changed their name to the Ravens to honor Edgar Allan Poe when they moved from Cleveland to Baltimore in the mid-1990s. Their stadium is a luxurious place compared with the old Memorial Stadium—and ticket prices reflect the cost to build it.

♪ ⚿ **Oriole Park at Camden Yards** (410-685-9800; www.theorioles.com), 333 W. Camden St. (about six blocks west of Inner Harbor). The American League Baltimore Orioles have been playing in Baltimore since 1954 and in Camden Yards since it was built in the early 1990s. All of the seats in the stadium provide a clear view of the action, and, amazingly in this day and age, bleacher seats are still a bargain.

✳ Selective Shopping

ANTIQUES

Federal Hill
Antique Center at Federal Hill (410-625-0182), 1220 Key Hwy. Open daily. More than 25 dealers display their wares in room settings instead of the usual large warehouse atmosphere.

Fell's Point
There are close to 30 antiques dealers within a few blocks of one another in Fell's

THE SHOPS AT FELL'S POINT

Point, so just about everything imaginable is available. I found artwork, lamps, furniture, handcrafted pieces from around the world, architectural items, memorabilia, and more. A map and brochure of the shops is available from the **Fell's Point Antique Dealers' Association** (410-675-4776). The association can also supply information about the **Antique Market** held on the second Sunday of every month Apr.–Oct.

Mount Vernon
The 700 and 800 blocks of Howard St. are known as Baltimore's **Antique Row**. There are close to 40 shops that, very appropriately, are located in somewhat revitalized antique buildings. A brochure available from the Mount Vernon Cultural District, Inc., describes what each shop has to offer.

ART GALLERIES

Downtown/Inner Harbor
Maryland Art Place (410-962-8565; www.mdartplace.org), 8 Market Pl., Suite 100. Open Tues.–Sat. The nonprofit organization shows a wide variety of ever-changing exhibits in an area superbly designed to showcase artwork in its best light. This is a quality place made all the more outstanding for the fact that there is no admission fee.

Art Gallery of Fell's Point (410-327-1272; www.fellspointgallery.org), 1716 Thames St. Open daily. A cooperative of more than 40 artists working in a variety of media.

BOOKSTORES With the proliferation of e-book readers and online shopping, brick and mortar bookstores are disappearing at an alarming rate and could almost be considered an endangered species. That's why it's nice to see that quite a number still populate, and thrive in, Baltimore. Each has carved out a niche of its own and provides a gathering place within its own neighborhood. Be sure to visit and reawaken the joy that can only come from browsing rows and rows of books and physically holding one in your hands.

Abell

Normals (410-243-6888; www.normals .com), 425 E. 31st. St. Open daily. Like Red Emma's (see below), Normal's is collectively owned and operated, but here the emphasis is on used books and vinyl record albums (although there are also a few newer items). Having been around for decades, the place has become a cultural institution in Baltimore and once you visit this alternative-style business you'll see why. Their devotion to obscure music and small presses and magazines (ever heard of *In These Times, Signal to Noise, Fifth Estate,* or *Reason?*) is to be commended and patronized.

Cross Country

The Ivy Bookshop (410-377-2966; www .theivybookshop.com), 6080 Falls Rd. Open daily. Within a small shopping mall, this is what non-chain, independent bookstores used to be, and should be, like. Bright, open, and full of new books, with little clutter or extraneous other bits of merchandise. The last time I visited, the staff was cheerful and helpful, pointing out some of their favorite new books, along with listening to the likes and wants of the customers. The manager expressed an opinion that I hold to be true, "You can order a book online. You can only find a book in a bookstore."

TIM MCFADDEN AT WORK

East Baltimore

McFadden Art Glass (410-631-6039; www.mcfaddenartglass.com), 6800 Eastern Ave. Tim McFadden studied glass blowing at Salisbury State University, and his enthusiasm for the medium shows through in the products he produces. I grew up in West Virginia, a state known for the artistry of its glass blowers, and I think that Tim's pieces show a quality and creativeness not found in pieces by people who have been working in glass years before Tim was even born. Stop by here to see his work, and, if time permits, he may make you your own piece of art glass. I predict a bright future for this talented artist.

Federal Hill

Montage Gallery (410-752-1125), 925 S. Charles St. Tues.–Sat. Monthly exhibits of artwork from recognized and new regional, national, and international artists.

Tradestone Gallery (410-602-9899; www.tradestonegallery.com), 803 Light St. Closed Mon. Offers paintings of Russian artists and other items—such as nesting dolls and painted eggs—of Russian origin.

Downtown/Inner Harbor

Barnes & Noble (410-385-1709; www
.barnesandnoble.com), 601 E. Pratt St. (in
the Power Plant). Yes, this is the chain
store, but its location in Inner Harbor
makes it very convenient. It is also one of
the largest and busiest in the chain.

Federal Hill

The Book Escape (410-504-1902; www
.thebookescape.com), 805 Light St. Somehow I have missed ever visiting this shop,
but acquaintances say I need to check out
their thousands of new and used books. You
probably should, too. They have another
location at 10 N. Calvert St. (410-504-1902)
in the downtown/Inner Harbor area.

Mount Vernon

☞ **Drusilla's Books** (410-728-6363; www
.drusillasbooks.com), 809 N. Howard St.
Tues.–Sat. A place to bring back childhood
reading memories, as Drusilla's specializes
in children's and illustrated books, both old
and rare.

Read Street Books (410-669-4103;
http://74.112.205.100/~readstre), 229
West Read St. It's small and most of its
stock is used books, with a few new books
for sale, but it's still a great place to grab a
cup of coffee and soak in the bookstore
atmosphere.

Red Emma's Bookstore Coffeehouse
(410-230-0450; www.redemmas.org), 800
St. Paul St. (As this book went to press,
the shop planned to relocate to the North
Avenue Market on W. North Ave.) Red
Emma's is a "collectively owned and
operated infoshop" whose members
belong to different committees that
decide which books and magazines, along
with organic and natural foods and
drinks, that the endeavor will offer to the
public. As the manager told me, "We specialize in politics and philosophy, but do
also carry many bestsellers. Just don't
expect to find Danielle Steel here." Sponsors many events, such as book readings
and live entertainment. Reminiscent of
the bookstore/coffeehouses that once
flourished in New York City's Greenwich
Village.

Wyndhurst

☞ **The Children's Bookstore** (410-532-
2000; www.thecbstore.com), 737 Deepdene
Rd. Closed Sun. On a quiet tree-lined side
street, this bright and open shop has something for children from their baby years to
the older teen years. I eavesdropped on a
great conversation with a young teen saying
she was looking for a new series of books to
read and, after learning just exactly what
type of fantasy the reader liked, the clerk
steered her to several different choices. You
won't get this kind of service when you go
browsing on the Internet.

SPECIAL SHOPS

Fell's Point

Ten Thousand Villages (410-342-5568;
www.tenthousandvillages.com), 1621
Thames St. This is the local outlet for the
international nonprofit organization by the
same name that purchases fairly traded
handicrafts from around the world. A number of unique items.

Mount Vernon

Woman's Industrial Exchange (410-685-
4388; www.womansindustrialexchange.org),
333 N. Charles St. The nonprofit exchange
was established in 1880 to benefit finan-
cially ailing women by providing a place to
sell their handcrafted goods. The purpose is
still the same, except some of the items are
now produced by men. The quality items
you find here may not be available anywhere else—and the money you spend
helps others. Also see *Eating Out*.

FARMER'S MARKETS **Baltimore
Farmer's Market** (410-752-8632),
Saratoga St. (between Holiday and Gay
Sts.), downtown/Inner Harbor. You will find
thousands of people shopping for fresh pro-
duce 8–noon on Sunday morning June–
Dec. Lots of parking space underneath
I-83.

Waverly Street Farmer's Market (www
.32ndstreetmarket.org), 400 block of E.
32nd St., Charles Village. This place almost
becomes a street fair every Sat., 7–noon,
throughout the year, as people come out to

eat goodies and watch the entertainment in addition to buying produce.

✳ Special Events

Late February and/or March: **American Craft Council Craft Show** (1-877-BAL-TIMORE; http://shows.craftcouncil.org), Baltimore Convention Center, 1 W. Pratt St. Usually features more than eight hundred craftspeople from across the country. All artists are selected through a jury process, so the quality of work and originality are excellent.

April: **Baltimore Waterfront Festival** (1-888-BALTIMORE). A free four-day festival with maritime exhibits, vendors, activities, contests, and live music.

May: **Film Festival** (1-877-BALTIMORE), various locations. A week of lectures, screenings, and events that highlight the city's contributions to the movies. **The Preakness Celebration** (410-837-3030) is held in different places. The running of the Preakness race is preceded by a week of events including a parade, a hot-air balloon race, the Pee Wee Preakness, boat races, and a concert.

June: **LatinoFest** (410-563-3160; www.latinofest.org), Patterson Park, downtown. A celebration of Latino heritage.

July: **African American Heritage Festival** (410-244-8861; www.africanamerican festival.net). The festival is so large (usually attracting close to 400,000 people over the three-day event) that it takes place in Camden Yards and the M & T Bank Stadium. **Artscape** (410-752-8632; www.artscape .org), Mount Royal (in the northern part of the city). Thought to be the largest arts festival in the country.

July–August: **Little Italy Open-Air Film Festival** (1-877-BALTIMORE), Little Italy. If you saw *Cinema Paradiso*, you will love this festival, which projects movies onto an outdoor screen every Fri. at 9 PM.

September: **Book Festival** (410-752-8632; www.baltimorebookfestival.com), various locations in Mount Vernon. The annual event includes author readings and signings, children's writers and storytellers, and book vendors. **Ukrainian Festival and Carnival** (410-682-3800), Patterson Park, downtown. Dances, songs, and Ukrainian Easter eggs and crafts.

October: **Annual Fun Festival** (410-675-6750; www.preservationsociety.com), Fell's Point. Food, drink, dancing, and a plethora of local bands. **Annual Chocolate Festival** (410-685-6169; www.lexingtonmarket .com), Lexington Market. The city's bakeries and confectioners come together to present a bewildering array of chocolate treats, from truffles to cakes to coated fruits.

November–December: **Zoo Lights** (410-366-LION; www.baltimorezoo.org), Baltimore Zoo. Annual display of more than 750,000 lights. Active and passive light sculptures and displays.

WEST OF BALTIMORE
ELLICOTT CITY AND COLUMBIA

Three Quaker brothers, John, Andrew, and Joseph Ellicott, traveled from their Pennsylvania home and settled along the banks of the Patapsco River in the 1770s. Deeper and stronger than it is today, the river provided the power needed for the brothers' mill to grind wheat produced by local farmers. The town, known as Ellicott City (first called Ellicott Mills), that grew up around their business soon became the largest flour-milling center in the American colonies. Although it gave life to the settlement, the Patapsco River has been a harsh benefactor, periodically flooding nearly the entire town. Markers on the railroad bridge show the dates of the floods and how high the water has reached.

The country's first railroad terminal was built in Ellicott City in 1831, to service the first 13 miles of track laid in America. Soon afterward, Andrew Jackson became the first president to ride a train, taking it from the city into Baltimore. The station is now a museum, providing insight into the past.

In fact, much of the town, now bypassed by four-lane US 40, is like a museum. Buildings within the historic district have been well preserved. Some of today's restaurants were former mills, and shops along Main Street are filled with antiques that would have suited the town's glory days. Tongue Row, a small specialty-shop area off Main Street, was once owned by Ann Tonge as rental property. Local tradition says the spelling of its name changed because so many "miller's wives would lean out of windows to gossip with one another."

Columbia's birth as one of America's first planned communities in 1966 was conceived and directed by developer James Rouse. He envisioned a city that would give residents a sense of belonging by having a variety of houses set up in small communities, with each clustered around its own neighborhood social center. The city would provide a large portion of its own jobs, shopping, health care, education, cultural resources and activities, and recreation. Commercial and industrial development would be balanced by permanently designated parks and green spaces.

For the most part, his dream has retained its original ideas. Columbia is now a city of about 100,000 residents (with average family income well over $80,000) living in a number of designated villages. Cultural venues abound, from art classes and exhibits at several community centers to the city's own orchestra, a professional theater troupe, and an endless procession of festivals, celebrations, and free concerts and movies. More than 5,300 acres (well over one-third of the city's land) have been set aside for parks, playgrounds, and natural areas, and close to 88 miles of walking and biking trails provide alternatives to getting around by automobile.

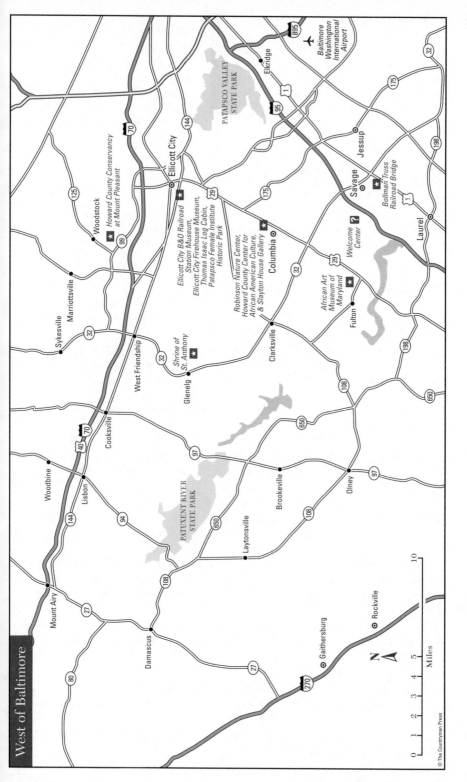

West of Baltimore

PATAPSCO VALLEY STATE PARK

PATUXENT RIVER STATE PARK

Baltimore Washington International Airport

Elkridge

Jessup

Savage

Bollman Truss Railroad Bridge

Laurel

Welcome Center

Columbia

African Art Museum of Maryland

Fulton

Robinson Nature Center, Howard County Center for African American Culture, & Slayton House Gallery

Clarksville

Ellicott City B&O Railroad Station Museum, Ellicott City Firehouse Museum, Thomas Isaac Log Cabin, Patapsco Female Institute Historic Park

Ellicott City

Howard County Conservancy at Mount Pleasant

Woodstock

Marriottsville

Sykesville

West Friendship

Shrine of St. Anthony

Glenelg

Cooksville

Brookeville

Olney

Laytonsville

Woodbine

Lisbon

Mount Airy

Damascus

Gaithersburg

Rockville

N

Miles

0 1 2 3 4 5 10

© The Countryman Press

COMMUNITIES The Patapsco River was a major means of transportation during our nation's early history, and trade vessels would ply its waters to the bustling port town of **Elkridge.** Now much shallower—due to erosion and siltation—the river is no longer a busy thoroughfare but a quiet waterway protected by long and narrow Patapsco Valley State Park. The town's fortunes have followed those of the river, and despite some recent housing development around it, its stately Victorian homes give it an air of a slow-moving small town.

FEATURED ON FILM

Kim Stanley and Lloyd Bridges ventured to Ellicott City to act in the 1957 movie *The Goddess*. The area around the small town starred in 1990's *Cry-Baby*, the 1999 horror movie *The Blair Witch Project*, and TV shows *The Simple Life* and *Homicide: Life on the Street*.

Savage grew up around its namesake textile mill, which operated from the early 1800s to the mid-1900s. Many of the modest mill workers' homes are still occupied by today's residents. The mill has been converted to a major antiques, specialty-shop, and artisans' workshops attraction.

GUIDANCE **Howard County Tourism, Inc.** (410-313-1900; 1-800-288-TRIP; www .visithowardcounty.com) is at 8267 Main St., Ellicott City, 21043. In addition to providing the usual tourist information, the facility has a number of displays that provide good historical background about the county.

Maryland **welcome centers** are located on I-95 between Exits 35 and 38. The phone number for the one near Savage is 301-490-1333. You can contact the other, near Laurel, by calling 301-490-2444.

GETTING THERE *By car:* **I-70** cuts across the northern portion of this part of Maryland. It arrives from Baltimore in the east and Frederick in the west. **I-95** and **US 1** run along the area's eastern section, as they connect Baltimore with Washington, DC.

By air: **Baltimore/Washington International Thurgood Marshall Airport** (1-800-I-FLY-BWI; www.bwiairport.com) is about a 20-minute drive from the eastern part of this region.

By rail: **AMTRAK** (1-800-USA-RAIL; www.amtrak.com) makes stops in Baltimore and Washington, DC. Local buses and **MARC** commuter trains (see *Getting Around*) can then deliver you to several points in the Ellicott City–Columbia area.

GETTING AROUND *By car:* **I-70** runs east-west along the north, while **I-95** and **US 1** run north-south in the eastern part of this region. Four-lane **US 29** is the quickest route between Columbia and Ellicott City. **MD 144** is only a two-lane road, but it goes through some of the smaller towns.

By bus: **Howard Transit Service** (410-313-1919; www.howardtransit.com) makes multiple stops in Columbia, Ellicott City, the BWI Thurgood Marshall airport terminal, the MARC/AMTRAK station, and along the US 1 corridor. **MTA** (1-800-543-9809) has buses that will take you into Baltimore and Washington, DC, on a scheduled basis.

By rail: The **MARC** commuter trains (1-800-325-RAIL; www.mta.maryland.gov) make stops in Savage, Jessup, Dorsey, and St. Denis as they run between Baltimore and Washington, DC.

By taxi: **AAA Star Cab** (410-461-7777); **Columbia Cab of Howard County** (410-604-5800; www.columbiacabhowardco.com).

In Ellicott City, parking is free in the municipal lots on the corner of Ellicott Mills Dr. and Main St., on Courthouse Dr. above the main part of the city, and in the Oella Lot located across the Patapsco River. Some of the spaces in the lot behind the tourism office's Welcome Center are free; other spaces have meters. Check the signage for the on-street parking, as some spots have one-hour limits and others have two-hour limits.

MEDICAL EMERGENCY **Howard County General Hospital** (410-740-7890; www .hcgh.org), 5755 Cedar Ln., Columbia.

✳ To See
MUSEUMS
Columbia
❧ **Howard County Center of African American Culture** (410-715-1921; www.hccaac .org), 5434 Vantage Point Rd. Open Tues.–Fri. 10–5, Sat. 12–4. Small admission fee. A dining room, kitchen, and living room are furnished to represent the 19th-century lifestyle of county African Americans. Other exhibits include sports and military memorabilia, hands-on exhibits for children, and an extensive collection of early and contemporary African American artwork, inventions, and musical recordings.

Ellicott City
❧ **Ellicott City B&O Railroad Station Museum** (410-461-1945; www.ecborail.org), 2711 Maryland Ave. Open Wed.–Sun, but hours have been known to vary. Small admission fee. The oldest railroad terminal in America, it was built circa 1830 to accommodate freight service and expanded for passengers in 1856. Amazingly, almost 50 percent of all of the supplies and soldiers that participated in the entire Civil War passed through the town on the railroad.

Exhibits chronicle its history, but there is much more to see and experience here. Costumed interpreters are on hand to answer questions, living-history demonstrations are presented on an irregular basis, and the HO model layout of the railroad from Baltimore to Ellicott City is elaborate and detailed. Special exhibits come and go on a scheduled basis. One of the most entertaining past exhibits chronicled the exploits of Owney, the mascot of the Railway Mail Service. A stray dog who was adopted by postal workers, he rode the trains on top of mailbags. At each stop workers would attach tags to commemorate his visit. He collected more than 1,000 and traveled to far-flung places in the world such as China and Japan.

Firehouse Museum (410-313-5131; www.howardcountymd.gov), Main St. and Church Rd. Open Sat.–Sun. 1–4 Apr.–Nov. Donations accepted. The firehouse was built on an incline above the town to give the firemen "a running start." Artifacts include a horse-drawn hose cart, the original fire-alarm bell that was loud enough to be heard across town, and a whimsical display of toy fire equipment.

Fulton
African Art Museum of Maryland (301-490-6070; www.africanartmuseum.org), 11711 E. Market St. Open Fri.–Sat. and the first Sun. of the month 11–4. Donations accepted. Within its small quarters, the museum presents permanent and changing exhibits of masks, sculptures, textiles, musical instruments, jewelry, baskets, and items of everyday life from the entire African continent. I was especially impressed by the intricacy of work on the gold weights made by the lost-wax method (which may or may not be on display when you arrive).

Ellicott City

Heritage Orientation Center (410-313-5131; www.howardcountymd.gov), 8334 Main St. This was the county's first court records building. It's just a small stone building with a few displays concerning the 18th and 19th century history of Ellicot City and the surrounding area. It will only take you a few minutes to look through it, but it's worth it, especially since you are going to walk right by it if you've parked in the Lot F on Ellicot Mills Dr.

Thomas Isaac Log Cabin (410-313-5131; www.howardcountymd.gov), Main St. and Ellicott Mills Dr. Open Sat.–Sun. 1–4 Apr.–Nov. Donations accepted. Living historians relate the story of the National Road and what life was like in the late 1700s. The cabin is the oldest surviving structure in the city.

& **Patapsco Female Institute Historic Park** (410-313-5131; www.howardcountymd.gov), 3961 Sarah's Ln. Tours Sat.–Sun. at 1:30. Donations accepted. On a hilltop overlooking Ellicott City, the institute opened in 1837 as a finishing school for young women. It was one of the first places in America to teach math and science to women. The building was used for various venues after the school closed in 1891 but eventually fell into ruin.

It is now the site of what is believed to be one of the few stabilized ruins in the country, and elevated walkways lead visitors through the building's shell to imagine what the living quarters, classrooms, and kitchen would have looked like.

Savage

Bollman Truss Railroad Bridge, 8600 Foundry St. (next to Historic Savage Mill; see *Selective Shopping*). This style of wrought-iron and cast-iron semisuspension bridge was once used throughout the United States and Europe. This B&O Railroad bridge from the 1860s is the last of its kind left in the world.

HISTORIC CHURCHES St. Paul's Catholic Church (410-465-1670; www.stpaulec .org), St. Paul St., Ellicott City. The 1830s church was the site of Babe Ruth's first wedding, in 1914.

OTHER SITES Shrine of St. Anthony (410-531-2800; www.shrineofstanthony.org), 12300 Folly Quarter Rd., Ellicott City. Originally, this was part of the 18th-century country estate of Charles Carroll, who was the last living signer of the Declaration of Independence. Folly Quarter is now the site of a Franciscan friary and chapel dedicated to St. Anthony, patron saint of the lost. The public is welcome, and I enjoy visiting the extensive grounds, taking a quiet walk on the meditative nature trails, and appreciating the architecture of the chapel and other buildings.

✳ To Do

BALLOONING Friendship Hot Air Balloon Company (410-442-5566; www .ballooningusa.com), 12465 Barnard Wy., West Friendship. Sunrise and sunset flights over central Maryland.

BICYCLING Columbia Association Welcome Center (410-715-3000; www.columbia association.org), 10221 Wincopin Circle, Columbia. The association publishes a map of the more than 90 miles of biking and hiking trails that wind through natural areas and connect the city's villages with one another. Some of those miles pass through parklands, while many are roadway or sidewalk connectors.

Also see the **Patapsco Valley State Park** sidebar on page 247.

BIRDING Schooley Mill Park (410-313-6130; www.co.ho.md.us), 12975 Hall Shop Rd., Highland. The wetlands, pond, fields, and forests provide some nice birding opportunities. Throughout most of the year you may be able to catch glimpses of pileated, downy, and red-bellied woodpeckers; woodcocks; finches; turkey vultures; bluebirds; and red-shouldered and red-tailed hawks. It's also a good place to catch the spring and fall migrants.

BOAT RENTALS Centennial Park (410-313-7271; www.co.ho.md.us), MD 108, Ellicott City. Visitors can rent small boats May–Aug. and enjoy the park's 52-acre lake.

FAMILY ACTIVITIES

Brookeville

✿ **Sharp's at Waterford Farm** (410-489-2572; www.sharpfarm.com), 4003 Jennings Chapel Rd. Make an autumn visit to this 550-acre farm that has been placed under a conservation easement, and you will be able to take hayrides, pick your own pumpkin, work your way through a corn maze, enjoy fresh apple cider, shop at a country store, learn about agriculture in the farm museum, walk a nature trail, and visit the chickens, pigs, sheep, cows, rabbits, and peacocks.

Ellicott City

✿ **Clark's Elioak Farm** (410-730-4049; www.clarklandfarm.com), 10500 MD 108. Open Tues.–Sun. Apr.–late Sep., daily late Sep.–early Nov. Small admission fee. Maryland baby boomers and those who grew up in the 1970s and 1980s, rejoice! Your childhood memories of visiting the Enchanted Forest no longer have to be just memories. The figures and structures of the make-believe world were left to the harshness of weather and slowly deteriorated after the Enchanted Forest closed. However, thanks to the efforts of the Clark family, who restored and moved many of the attractions to their farm, you—and your children—can once again visit the Three Bears's house, sit in Willie the Whale's mouth, step aboard *Little Toot* the tugboat, or gaze upon Jack and Jill as they tumble down the hill. Located on a working farm, which has been in the Clark family since 1797; there is also a petting zoo where children can get close up to chickens, pigs, sheep, goats, and other barnyard animals. Pony rides, hayrides, educational tours, and special events almost every weekend make this a good

CLARK'S ELIOAK FARM

place to bring the kids—and have them be entertained and educated without being plugged into some kind of electronic device.

GOLF

Elkridge
The Timbers at Troy (410-313-GOLF; www.timbersgolf.com), 6100 Marshalee Dr. The par 72 course has over 6,650 yards from the back tees and is bordered by streams and mature woodlands.

Marriottsville
Waverly Woods (410-313-9182; www.waverlywoods.com), 2100 Warwick Way. The Arthur Hill–designed course follows the natural contours of the land with minimal bunkering. Five sets of tees range from 4,808 yards to 7,024 yards.

West Friendship
Willow Springs (410-442-7700; www.willowspringsgolfcourse.com), 12980 Livestock Rd. Opened in the 1990s and designed by Al Janis. Walk-ons are welcomed and will be accommodated as soon as possible.

Also see **Turf Valley Resort and Conference Center** under *Lodging*.

MINIATURE GOLF See *Family Activities*.

WALKING TOURS **Columbia Association Welcome Center** (410-715-3000; www .columbiaassociation.org), 10221 Wincopin Circle, Columbia. The association publishes a pamphlet describing the sites to be seen along Lake Kittamaqundi. Most interesting are the outdoor sculptures, especially that of Pierre du Fayet.

✳ Green Space

CONSERVANCY **Howard County Conservancy at Mount Pleasant** (410-465-8877; www.hcconservancy.org), 10520 Old Frederick Rd., Woodstock. Grounds and trails open daily dawn–dusk, Environmental Education Center open Wed.–Sat. (closed Sat. in winter). The conservancy has helped protect close to 2,000 acres in Howard County, and the 232-acre Mount Pleasant site (on what was a 300-year-old farm) is the organization's showpiece.

THE ROBINSON NATURE CENTER

About 4 miles of maintained trails (self-guiding interpretive brochures are available on-site) meander over an easy terrain of forest, meadow, and gardens. The Environmental Education Center incorporates many innovative "green" building designs, displays the works of local and regional artists, and hosts a variety of workshops and events. All in all, a great outdoors resource that is only 15 minutes away from busy Columbia.

NATURE CENTER ✐ ° **Robinson Nature Center** (410-313-0400; www .howardcountymd.gov), 6692 Cedar Ln., Columbia. Open Wed.–Sun. Small admission fee. My experiences with nature centers had almost always been disappointing.

HIKING

✧ ♿ **Patapsco Valley State Park** (410-461-5005; www.dnr.state.md.us/publiclands/central /patapsco.asp), 8020 Baltimore National Pike (US 40), Ellicott City. Surprisingly detached from the signs of civilization surrounding it, this park is an exquisitely beautiful area with trails beside tumbling streams and along quiet hillsides. The park is more than 40 miles long and is developed in several separate sections.

The 5-mile **Switchback Trail** (a favorite with mountain bikers) and its numerous side routes in the McKeldin area lead into a wonderfully isolated valley in which the river rolls down picturesque **South Branch Rapids.** Trails in the **Daniels Dam** area (off Old Frederick Rd. in Ellicott City) provide easy miles of walking to discover the ruins of a former river town. About 3 miles of trails wind along the hillside and connect the campground (see *Lodging*) to the river in the Hollofield area.

CASCADE FALLS

Within the Hilton and Avalon– Orange Grove areas are easy trails along the river that are favorites with families with small children, while the routes that wind onto the hillside attract mountain bikers. **Buzzard Rocks** overlooks the river, and **Cascade Falls** tumbles down the hillside. Be aware that the hillside trails in these areas may have few signs, meager markers, rugged terrain, and rough footing. If this isn't to your liking, take the **Grist Mill Trail Extension,** a paved, wheelchair-accessible route that runs from the state park to Ellicott City. Along the way it crosses an impressive cable stay bridge and passes by the world's first fully submerged hydroelectric plant and a number of interpretive signs that help you realize what you are walking by.

So often a "nature center" is a small room with a few stuffed animals, several reference books, and poisonous snake caged in a tiny terrarium. Not so with this place! It's a huge (23,000 square feet) building with extensive, and high quality, exhibits and interpretive information about the history and environment of the area. A boardwalk within the building entertainingly takes you through the simulated (but lifelike) environments of life on the forest floor and what takes place there under the cover of darkness. There are also hands-on displays for the kids, a planetarium, a "living" roof, and a 1-mile trail that gently descends to the Middle Patuxent River.

GARDENS **Mill Stone Park,** Ellicott Mills Dr., Ellicott City. Millstones rescued from the Patapsco River are bordered by a small garden maintained by local volunteers.

PARKS See the **Patapsco Valley State Park** sidebar above.

248

CENTRAL MARYLAND

✴ Lodging

RESORT

Ellicott City, 21042

Turf Valley (410-465-1500; www.turfvalley
.com), 2700 Turf Valley Rd. On land that
was once a thoroughbred farm, the 1,000-
acre resort is family owned, and it shows.
Unlike corporate properties that sometimes
become "tired" looking and have personnel
who are just putting in time, Turf Valley is
well maintained, and all of the employees I
met were friendly and helpful. There are
two 18-hole golf courses to choose from
(one is in the valley for easier play; the little
tougher one works its way through woods
and over small knolls), two restaurants,
more than 200 hotel rooms, several golf vil-
las, indoor and outdoor swimming pools, a
fitness center, business center, and a full
European spa. Most amenities require an
additional fee, but many available packages
can be structured to include them without
any additional fees. $180 and up. The pri-
mary dining spot, Alexandra's, is definitely a
cut above many resort restaurants. Its large
picture windows let you watch golfers testing their skills on the greens as you sample
the lamb, crab, or other offerings. I made a
complete meal out of the delicious fried
tomato sandwich. Entrées are $26–25.

MOTELS AND HOTELS

Columbia, 21045

Hampton Inn (410-997-8555; www
.hamptoninn.com), 8880 Columbia 100
Pkwy. Indoor pool, fitness center, and complimentary deluxe continental breakfast.
The common areas are large and nicely furnished. $119–155.

&. **Sheraton** (410-730-3900; 1-800-638-
2817; www.sheratoncolumbia.com), 10207
Wincopin Circle, 21044. Overlooks 25-acre
Lake Kittamaqundi in Columbia's Town
Center. Fitness room, pool, and in-room
coffee. $129–245.

✴ ✪ &. **Sonesta ES Suites** (410-964-9494;
1-800-238-8000), 8844 Columbia 100 Pkwy.
Designed for extended-stay business travelers, the studio, one-bedroom, and two-
bedroom/two-bath suites also appeal to
families with children. Complimentary
breakfast. $125–200.

Elkridge, 21075

Best Western (410-796-3300; 1-800-528-
1234; www.bestwestern.com), 6755 Dorsey
Rd. (accessed from I-95 Exit 43). Just a few
minutes away from Baltimore/Washington
International Thurgood Marshall Airport.
Fitness center, indoor pool, sauna, and free
morning newspaper. $129–139.

Ellicott City, 21043

✴ &. **Residence Inn by Marriott** (410-
997-7200; 1-800-331-3131; www.residence
inn.com), 4950 Beaver Run. Most of the
guest accommodations are like small apartments. One or two bedrooms, kitchen, and
a separate sitting room. Small pets permitted with a substantial deposit. $109-159.

The Obladi (410-480-1968; www.the
obladi.com), 8060 Main St. My wife and I
thoroughly enjoyed our stay in this boutique hotel/inn operated by diehard Beatles
fans (think about one of the group's most
fanciful songs and you'll know how to say
the name of the hotel). The historic structure was built in 1838, but the owners have
done a wonderful job of juxtaposing the old
with the new. The timber beams and white
plaster walls mix easily with the bright, airy,
and modern atmosphere of the four guest
rooms (each themed for an individual Bea-
tle), with en suite bathrooms, gas fireplaces,
and flat screen TVs. A kitchen and gathering space is available for guest use; do not
miss going onto the patio garden—it again
shows the decorating expertise of the owners. $200 (includes all sales and hotel taxes).

Jessup, 20794

Holiday Inn (410-799-7500; www.hi
columbia.com), 7900 Washington Blvd.
Characteristic Holiday Inn rooms with in-
room coffee and pay-per-view movies.
Swimming pool and coin laundry. $99–190.

Super 8 (410-796-0400), 8094 Washington
Blvd. Nothing fancy, but one of the lowest
rates in a high-rate area. $75–149.

BED & BREAKFASTS

Catonsville, 21228
The Wilderness Bed and Breakfast
(410-744-0590; www.thewilderness.biz), 2
Thistle Rd. The Wilderness, once a palatial
summer mansion for a wealthy Balti-
morean, is now on the National Register of
Historic Places and has been restored to its
turn-of-the-20th-century greatness with an
abundance of antiques and period furnishings and details. However, the three guest
suites, which all have a large bedroom, sitting room, and private bath, are outfitted
with the amenities modern travelers are
accustomed to. The grounds invite walks
through the forest and lawn, where you
may see some of the large variety of birds
that have been sighted here. $140–160.

Columbia, 21044
Columbia Inn at Peralynna (410-715-
4600; 1-877-PERALYNNA; www.peralynna
.com), 10605 Clarksville Pike. Peralynna
Manor caters primarily to extended-stay
corporate travelers but also accepts guests
for single nights if possible. And what a
place to stay. The 14,000-square-foot contemporary manor, located next to a 1,100-
acre farm, has a great room bigger than my
entire home. Guest suites are large, have
private balconies, and are packed with
amenities geared for those on business
trips. Exercise equipment, hot tub, and
food provided to make your own breakfast.
$145–325.

Ellicott City, 21042
Wayside Inn (410-461-4636; www.wayside
innmd.com), 4344 Columbia Rd. The fieldstone inn was built in the late 1700s as a
plantation manor, and local lore claims it
was visited by George Washington and John
Quincy Adams. The three suites and three
guest rooms all have private baths. Flat-
screen TVs and Jacuzzi also available. My
choice would be the Ellicott Room, with
fireplace, sleigh bed, and view of the landscaped backyard. $169–219.

Savage, 20763
Commodore Joshua Barney House
(301-362-1900; 1-800-475-7912; www.joshua
barneyhouse.com), 7912 Savage Guilford
Rd. Cdre. Joshua Barney was the only
American officer to win acclaim in both the
Revolutionary War and the War of 1812.
His 1760s home, listed on the National
Register of Historic Places, now serves as a
gracious B&B, with guest rooms and suites
available (all with private bath). Antiques,
fine art, and a host of amenities make stays
here luxurious, while the 6 landscaped
acres along the Little Patuxent River provide a quiet and restful atmosphere. A
favorite of business travelers. $175–225.

CAMPING

Ellicott City, 24102
❀ ♿ **Patapsco Valley State Park** (410-
461-5005; 1-888-432-CAMP; www.dnr.state
.md.us/publiclands/central/patapsco.asp),
8020 Baltimore National Pike (US 40).
More than 70 RV and tent sites are available in the Hollofield area of the park next
door to Ellicott City. A special loop is
reserved for those with pets. The season
usually runs late Mar.–late Oct.

Woodbine, 21797
Ramblin' Pines (410-795-5161; www
.ramblinpinescampground.com), 801 Hoods
Mill Rd. More than 150 RV sites and about
20 tent sites. A dump station, showers, a
pool, and miniature golf; facilities limited in
winter. Short nature trails wind through the
45 acres.

✳ Where to Eat
DINING OUT
Columbia
Aida Bistro (410-953-0500; www.aida
bistro.com), 6741 Gateway Dr. Open for
lunch Mon.–Fri., dinner Tues.–Sat. You will
regret it if you pass up a meal at Aida. This
business is run by a husband and wife (with
other family members also providing some
help) who have taken recipes from their
Italian heritage and collaborated with their
chef to come up with a wonderful mix of
traditional and progressive dishes. My Italian mother always said that you can tell the
quality of a restaurant by sampling the

marinara sauce, and my plate of homemade pasta smothered by a flavorful and fresh-tasting marinara let me know that other entrées would receive the same kind of thought and care.

Don't just stick with the traditional dishes; try grilled salmon topped with crabmeat or jumbo scallops with goat cheese and roasted squash risotto. The small-plate menu lets you enjoy the fare without consuming a large number of calories, while the prix fixe menu provides a three-course sampling.

Ellicott City, Columbia, and the surrounding environs have some marvelous restaurants; Aida is currently my favorite. Entrées $10.99–26.99.

Café de Paris (410-997-3904; www.cafe depariscolumbia.com), 8808 Centre Park Dr. Eric Rochard serves many of the traditional dishes of his homeland, including *croque monsieur, boeuf bourguignon,* and *escalope de veau,* but has been known to change the menu a bit to suit the requests of his customers. My apprehension as to whether I was going to like this meal as much as those I had in France was laid to rest when a group of French tourists called Eric to their table to serenade him with La Marseillaise and other traditional French tunes to thank him for the meal they had enjoyed. Entrées $16.95–36.95. Arrive before 6 and take advantage of the three-course early-bird special (it was only $19.95 the last time I visited).

Elkridge
᚛ **Elkridge Furnace Inn** (410-379-9336; www.elkridgefurnaceinn.com), 5745 Furnace Ave. Open for lunch Tues.–Fri. 11:30–2; open for dinner Tues.–Fri. 5–9, Sat. 4–10; open Sun. for brunch 10–2, dinner 4–8. Dinner reservations recommended. Meals can be peaceful and relaxing in this 1700s country manor home and restaurant on the banks of the Patapsco River. Chef-owner Dan Wecker changes his French-cuisine menu almost every month. Appetizers have included *gâteau au fromage*—walnut-topped blue cheese and cream cheese cake filled with bacon and house-cured salmon, served with a tomato

relish; entrées might range from fennel and pine nut tortellini to trout fillet and filet de *boeuf.* Entrées $21–35. Small plates and a prix fixe also available.

Ellicott City
Cacao Lane (410-461-1378; www.cacao lane.net), 8066 Main St. Open for lunch and dinner daily. Three historic buildings constructed of locally quarried stone and brick have been joined together to form Cacao Lane, which many people consider to be one of the area's most romantic dining spots. An outside deck is available during the warmer months. The many varieties of steaks are all served with a sauce of some kind, such as brandy crème or Dijon bleu cheese butter. Seafood offerings have included shrimp Santa Cruz and seafood Norfolk. Pasta dishes are also varied and often come mixed with a meat of some kind. Entrées $19–27.

Portelli's (410-720-2330; www.portallisec .com), 8085 Main St. Open daily for lunch and dinner. Within an historic building, the elegant décor of Portelli's sets the stage for fine dining of traditional and innovative Italian dishes, with a few items that would fit into the American fare category. The meats come from the local butchers and, whenever possible, the vegetables are purchased fresh from a stand just a few blocks away. Everyone was way more than satisfied with what they had ordered the last time I dined here with three friends. My seafood *fra diavolo* had just the right amount of spiciness and the tiramisu filling had an almost-cake-frosting consistency. The staff is good at suggesting the wine to go with your meal. $15–25.

᚛ **Tersiguel's** (410-465-4004; www .tersiguels.com), 8293 Main St. Open for lunch Mon.–Sat. 11:30–2:30; lunch Sun. 10:30–2:30; dinner Mon.–Thurs. and Sun. 5–9; dinner Fri. and Sat. 5–10. Dinner reservations recommended. French country fare based upon Fernand and Odette Tersiguel's original home in Brittany. Served in the 1800s home of one of Ellicott City's mayors. The hors d'oeuvres menu takes up a full page; *saumon fumé* is a local favorite. Lamb, steak, duck, chicken, pork, and seafood entrées are well presented. Entrées $29.95–38.95. Daily specials and prix fixe menu also available.

EATING OUT

Columbia

♪ ꜛ **Clyde's** (410-730-2829; www.clydes .com), 10221 Wincopin Circle. Open for lunch and dinner daily. Picture windows overlook Columbia's Lake Kittamaqundi, and the Victorian bar is decorated with circus and travel posters. Sandwiches and light entrées for lunch. I liked the vegetable frittata. Dinner entrées are a bit heavier, with pork chops, BBQ platter, and pan-roasted halibut being some of the favorites. Most dinner items are $15.95–20.95. Extensive wine list.

ꜛ **La Madeleine French Bakery and Café** (410-872-4900; www.lamadeleine .com), 6211 Columbia Crossing. Open for breakfast, lunch, and dinner daily. This national chain sends each new café manager to France to learn the country's ways. Breakfast is light baked goods, lunch is sandwiches and pizza, and dinner has many choices, like goat cheese ravioli and pasta Française. Dinner entrées $10–21.

♨ ꜛ **The Mango Grove** (410-884-3426; www.themangogrove.net), 8865 Stanford Blvd. Open for lunch and dinner daily. Authentic southern Indian vegetarian food served in a plain interior at amazingly low prices. The waitstaff will be happy to explain if you do not know what samosas, *dosas,* and curries are. The most expensive dinner entrée is less than $25.

ꜛ **P. F. Chang's China Bistro** (410-730-5344; www.pfchangs.com), 10300 Little Patuxent Pkwy. (at the Mall in Columbia). Open daily for lunch and dinner. Possibly the most impressive things about this chain are the huge sculptures at its restaurants' entrances. They are interpretations of 11th-century BC sculptures unearthed in China in the 20th century. The menu draws from major regions of the country. The beef à la Szechuan is twice-cooked with celery and carrots; the mu shu pork is served with hoisin sauce and thin pancakes; lemon-

pepper shrimp is stir-fried with chives and bean sprouts. Entrées $8.95–24.95.

Ellicott City

♪ ꜛ **Shanty Grille** (410-465-9660; www .shantygrille.com), 3410 Plumtree Dr. Fresh seafood in its many forms makes up the bulk of the menu, with a few meat items. If you are on a tight budget, go for the shrimp-and-fish combo; if money is no object, then the two New Zealand lobster tails are for you. Most entrées $15.95–27.95. Almost every item in the décor has a story, which is related on the back of the menu.

♪ **Ellicott Mills Brewing Company** (410-313-8141; www.ellicottmillsbrewing.com), 830 Main St. Within one of the city's historic brick buildings, this microbrewery serves up its own ales, lagers, porters, and stouts, along with some nice sandwiches and a few international surprises on the dinner menu. The Louisiana-inspired jambalaya is a local favorite, the *kassler rippchen* is a Bavarian-style pork chop, and the lime-and-cilantro-marinated chicken is dusted with Caribbean jerk seasoning. $15.95–24.95.

ꜛ **La Palapa** (410-465-0070; www.lapalapa grill.com), 8307 Main St. Open daily for lunch and dinner. The fajitas, chimichangas, enchiladas, and tacos are joined on the menu with house specialties such as chili verde; chicken mole; trout grilled with tomatoes, onion, capers, olives, and wine; and a *muy delicioso* vegetarian burrito. Live music on the weekend turns out the crowds for quite the party. Most entrées are $11.95–19.95.

The Trolley Stop (410-465-8546; www .newtrolleystop.com), 6 Oella Ave. Open for breakfast, lunch, and dinner. Yes, the trolley did stop at this tavern constructed in 1833, and the brick walls and exposed beams hark back to the building's earliest days. Lots of soups (the Maryland crab has a definite homemade taste), salads, and sandwiches for lunch. A few entrées are also served for lunch, with more on the dinner menu. The chicken *riggie* with artichoke and shallots is a standout. Other entrées $14.95–20.95.

Jessup

♿ **Frank's 24-Hour Diner** (410-799-8198), 7395 Cedar Ave. and US 1. Nothing fancy here; the name describes it well. Breakfast is always available, so it is the place for when you feel the need for eggs, pancakes, bacon, or sausage. Lunch and dinner are the usual sandwiches and diner entrées. Meat loaf is a specialty. Dinner entrées $9–18.

COFFEE AND TEA Bean Hollow (410-465-0233; www.beanhollowcoffee.com), 8059 Main St., Ellicott City. Open daily. Coffees are roasted on-site and there's a nice selection of snacks and sandwiches.

Tea on the Tiber (410-480-8000; www.teaonthetiber.com), 8081 Main St., Ellicott City. A Victorian tea room that will transport you back to the days of elegant afternoon teas. Open Thu.–Sun. for seatings that include tea and a small meal. Reservations suggested.

Also see **Old Mill Bakery Café** under *Snacks and Goodies.*

SNACKS AND GOODIES

Ellicott City

Old Mill Bakery Café (410-465-2253; www.oldmillbakerycafe.com), 4 Frederick Rd. The espressos, cappuccinos, and lattes are superb complements to the many goodies. The éclairs, danishes, rolls, muffins, and cookies are baked in-house. The gourmet pastries are made by "various chef friends" who bake for Washington, DC, embassies and hotels.

Sweet Cascades (410-750-8422; www.sweetcascades.com), 8167 Main St. Closed Mon. If the bakeries above did not entice you in for some high-calorie foods, maybe Sweet Cascades will be able to tempt you with the Belgian and French chocolates it uses to handmake its many offerings. There are also some frozen goodies and thick milk shakes. Try the PB&J chocolate sandwich for a sweet overload.

✳ Entertainment

FILM Marvelous Movies and More at the Slayton House Gallery (410-730-3987; www.wildelake.org), Wilde Lake Village Green, Columbia. A series of classic movies from the 1920s through the 1950s is presented throughout the year. Most of the films are unavailable in video, and a discussion and dessert bar are held after each showing. A most interesting way to spend an evening.

AMC Columbia (410-423-0510; www.amctheatres.com), 10300 Little Patuxent Pkwy., and **Snowden Square Stadium** (410-872-0676; www.regmovies.com), 9161 Commerce Center Dr., are Columbia's first-run movie houses.

MUSIC Columbia Orchestra (410-465-8777; www.columbiaorchestra.org). The orchestra began life as a small chamber music group in 1978 but grew quickly to include well over 50 members. It now presents a season of full orchestral works and numerous small "candlelight concerts" at various area venues.

Sundays at Three (410-381-3240; www.sundaysatthree.org), Christ Episcopal Church (corner of Oakland Mills and Dobbin rds.), Columbia. Chamber music concerts presented in an intimate setting on selected Sunday afternoons. The audience is invited to mingle with the guest artists after the performances.

THEATERS ♿ Rep Stage (443-518-1500; www.repstage.org), 10901 Little Patuxent Pkwy., Howard Community College, Columbia. The theater offers professional productions at low ticket prices; the troupe has received a multitude of Helen Hayes awards and nominations. Past performances have included O'Neill's *A Moon for the Misbegotten* and Albee's *Three Tall Women.*

Toby's (410-730-8311; 1-800-88-TOBYS; www.tobysdinnertheatre.com), 5900 Symphony Woods Rd., Columbia. Toby's is a dinner theater "in the round" that has presented productions such as the *Wizard of Oz*, *It's a Wonderful Life*, and *Joseph and the Amazing Technicolor Dreamcoat*. Performances are accompanied by live music. Also see **Howard County Arts Council** and **Slayton House Gallery** under *Selective Shopping*.

✳ Selective Shopping

ANTIQUES

Antique Depot (410-750-2674; http://antique-depot-ec.com), 3720 Maryland Ave., Ellicott City. Close to the B&O Railroad Museum. Furniture, vintage clothing, and household items.

Ballindullagh Barn Antiques (410-988-8002; www.bbpineantiques.com), 2410 Woodstream Crt., Ellicott City. European pine and hardwood furniture from the 18th century.

Ellicott City's Country Store (410-465-4482), 8180 Main St., Ellicott City. Open daily. There are four floors of antiques within the historic Walker-Chandler Building, believed to be the country's first duplex.

Taylor's Antique Mall (410-465-4444; www.taylorsantiquemall.com), 8197 Main St., Ellicott City. Open daily. Four floors of possible hidden treasures presented by more than two hundred dealers.

Wagon Wheel Antiques (410-465-7910; www.wagonwheelantiquesandgifts.com), 8061 Tiber Alley, Ellicott City. Be sure to go upstairs to see the 1850s Easton's Funeral Hearse that owner Ed Growl has restored.

ART GALLERIES

Columbia

Slayton House Gallery (410-730-3987; www.wildelake.org), Wilde Lake Village Green. The nonprofit organization provides space for classes, and theatrical and musical performances. Its two galleries have changing exhibits from local artists working in various media.

Ellicott City

Art & Artisan (410-203-9370; www.artandartisan.com), 8020 Main St. Many nice things in a wide variety of media in this shop. Original and limited editions from artists working locally, regionally, and as far away as Guatemala, Poland, Romania, and the Netherlands.

Gallery 44 (410-465-5200; www.gallery44.com), 9469 Baltimore National Pike. Commercial art galleries have a tendency to come and go, but Gallery 44 has been displaying the works of artisans from around the world for close to four decades. Hopefully, the 3,000-square-foot establishment will still be around when you stop by.

Howard County Arts Council (410-313-ARTS; www.hocoarts.org), 8510 High Ridge Rd. The county's arts council offers a gallery for changing exhibits of local and regional artists. Its **Black Box Theatre** provides a venue for emerging groups, and theatrical and musical productions. A great

ENTRANCEWAY TO ART & ARTISAN

place to not only catch locals "in the act" but also see works not found anywhere else.

BOOKSTORES **Daedalus Books** (410-309-2370; www.daedalusbooks.com), 9645 Gerwig Ln., Columbia. Warehouse outlet with most books at least 50 percent off.

USED BOOKS **Gramp's Attic Books** (410-750-9235), 8304 Main St., Ellicott City. Used, old, and rare books in many different categories.

SPECIAL SHOPS

Ellicott City

⚓ **All Time Toys** (410-418-4788; www.alltimetoys.com), 8185 Main St. The name is somewhat of a misnomer, as the vast majority of the offerings are action figures from the movies, television, and comics, and vintage and die-cast toys. A place where the serious collector (the kind that never opens the box) could spend hours and many dollars.

⚓ **Forget-Me-Not Factory** (410-465-7355), 8044 Main St. The building once served as an opera house and vaudeville theater, and is rumored to be where John Wilkes Booth gave his theatrical debut. It is now filled with items such as fairy crowns, bubble wands, wind banners, toys, and other whimsical things of interest to both children and adults. Ask them to let you see where the hillside bedrock was incorporated into the structure when it was originally built.

Hutcraft (410-465-0520; www.hutcraft.com), 8120 Main St. Quality fair trade items from around the world.

Joan Eve Classics and Collectibles (410-750-1210; http://joaneve.net), 8018 Main St. It may initially feel like you've walked into a gift shop, but you'll soon see this place contains many (possibly unique) things you may have never seen before. Be on the lookout for interesting copper items, vintage jewelry and clothing, and china and porcelain figurines.

⚓ **Mumbles and Squeaks** (410-750-2803; www.mumblesandsqueaks.com), 8133 Main

St. The small building once housed a Chinese laundry but is now packed from floor to ceiling with toys.

⚓ **Precious Gifts** (410-461-6813; 1-800-461-6813; www.preciousgifts.com), 8225 Main St. An expansive, almost overwhelming, offering of thousands of figurines, ranging from the well-known Disney and Hummel classics to the whimsical porcelains that are exclusive to Precious Gifts. Collectors could spend hours here.

🐾 **Work Play Bark** (410-750-9663; www.workplaybark.com), 8104 Main St. Treat your pooch to some gourmet goodies, and let him play with the new toy you buy him, maybe sleep in a new bed, or have him parade around in some hotsy-totsy upscale doggy attire.

Savage

Historic Savage Mill (1-800-788-MILL; www.savagemill.com), 8600 Foundry St. One of the most interesting venues for a shopping center you will ever visit. The mill operated as a weaving business from 1822 to 1947, and its 200,000 square feet are now home to more than 50 specialty shops (primarily antiques or art shops) with more than 250 dealers. Part of the amusement in visiting here is negotiating the maze of convoluted great rooms, halls, and stairways to discover a nearly hidden treasure store or an artist painting a life-sized portrait. The **Bollman Truss Railroad Bridge** is next to the mill.

PICK-YOUR-OWN PRODUCE FARMS

Glenelg

Triadelphia Lake View Farm (410-489-4460; www.tlvtreefarm.com), 15155 Triadelphia Mill Rd. Pick your own vegetables from mid-July through September.

Woodbine

⚓ ♿ **Larriland Farm** (410-442-2605; 301-854-6110; www.pickyourown.com), 2415 Woodbine Rd. (MD 94). The Moore family invites people to pick a very wide variety of fruits and vegetables from midspring into fall. October activities include hayrides and a straw maze. Choose and cut your own tree at Christmastime.

❋ Special Events

April–November: **Ghost Tours** (410-313-1900; www.visithowardcounty.com), Ellicott City. On select weekends, guides tell true tales of hauntings in the city. The stories are all collected from the local residents and, unlike most ghost tours, focus on more modern paranormal activities instead of those that happened many years ago.

May: **Maryland Sheep and Wool Festival** (410-531-3647; www.sheepandwool .com), fairgrounds, West Friendship. Nationally known festival with sheepdog demonstrations, shearing, spinning and weaving, arts and crafts, and more than 1,000 woolly animals. **Wine in the Woods** (410-313-PARK; www.wineinthewoods .com), Merriweather Post Pavilion, Columbia. Samples of Maryland's wines, foods, and arts and crafts.

June: **Columbia Festival of the Arts** (410-715-3044; www.columbiafestival.com), various locations in Columbia. A two-week celebration with entertainers, children's activities, and arts and crafts.

June–September: **Summer Lakefront Festival** (410-715-3000), Columbia. Music, movies, and other events every night of the week.

July: **Paint It: Ellicott City, A Juried Plein Air Paint-Out** (www.hocoarts.org), Ellicott City.

August: **Howard County Fair** (410-442-1022; www.howardcountyfair.com), fairgrounds, West Friendship.

September: **Maryland State Quarter Horse Show** (410-747-0363), fairgrounds, West Friendship. **Annual Farm Heritage Days** (410-489-2345), Howard County Living Farm Museum. Vintage farm equipment, antique cars and trucks, wagon rides, music, and crafts.

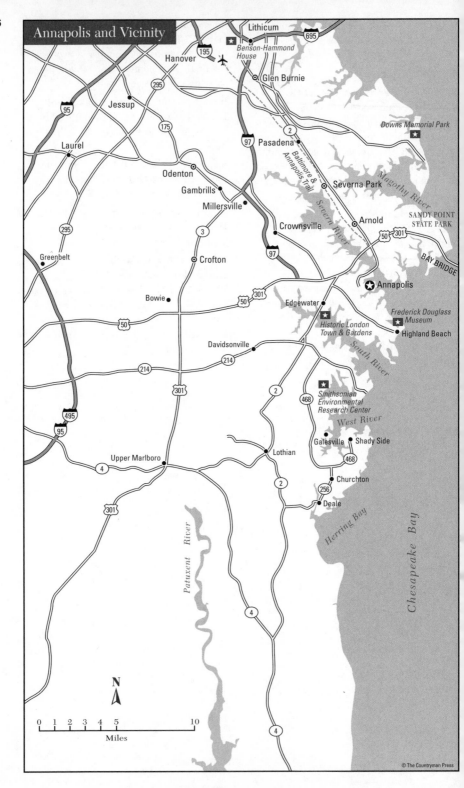

Annapolis and Vicinity

ANNAPOLIS AND VICINITY

Annapolis has come to be a special place for me. It is where my wife was born and raised, and we have spent many a blithe hour or day revisiting the places of her memories. She has brought me to the woods where she and her friends would ride bikes and transport themselves to their imaginary worlds of cowboys and Indians, knights in shining armor, and the jungles of Tarzan. I have seen her favorite swimming hole, the high school she graduated from, her old family home, and the preferred haunts of her teenage years.

Although the town she grew up in has changed—former cow fields are now shopping malls, housing developments have replaced woodlands, and four-lane highways reach into previously isolated locales—much has remained the same.

The waterfront has been the focal point of activity since 1649, when a group of Puritans wandered northward from Virginia in search of religious tolerance. Within a year, their settlement along the Severn River was part of the new Anne Arundel County, named for the wife of Cecil Calvert, second Lord Baltimore. Around 1695, the town became the capital of the Maryland colony and was renamed Annapolis in honor of Princess Anne, heiress in the British monarchy.

The protected harbor soon enabled the city to become a major international shipping center, with goods flowing to and from England, Africa's west coast, and the West Indies. Prosperous merchants built their Georgian-style town houses just a block or two from the water. A stroll in the area will take you through what the federal government proclaims is "the greatest concentration of 18th-century buildings anywhere in America." All four of Maryland's signers of the Declaration of Independence lived here, and three of their homes are open for public tours.

The merchants of today occupy the same storefronts as their predecessors. Except for a few changes for modern serviceability, the buildings look as they did centuries ago, and the brick-lined streets are as narrow as they were in horse-and-buggy days. The plaque dedicated to Kunta Kinte was placed at the waterfront in 1981 and commemorates the day that Alex Haley's ancestor arrived in America aboard a slave ship.

The U.S. Naval Academy was established in the mid-1800s, and its presence almost overshadows everything else in Annapolis. Much of the life in the city revolves around the academy's calendar, and the town becomes loaded with proud parents in late May when midshipmen graduate to become fully commissioned naval officers. There are no professional sports teams in Annapolis, but that doesn't matter, as the academy's football, lacrosse, soccer, and other athletic endeavors provide a full roster for spectators year-round. The academy, and St. John's College—one of the country's oldest—create an atmosphere of culture, sophistication, and artistic endeavor often found lacking in towns of similar size.

The City Dock is no longer crowded with warehouses of goods waiting to be sent to foreign lands. Yet the Naval Academy, recreational boaters, and sailing schools keep the harbor so busy that the town has been dubbed America's Sailing Capital. One of the most pleasant, and absolutely free, things to do in Annapolis is to walk down Main Street and watch the glow of a morning or evening sun light up the water to highlight the scores of sailboats wending their way in and out of the harbor.

COMMUNITIES The **Eastport** neighborhood of Annapolis developed as a farming and maritime community around the time of the Civil War and is now a vibrant residential and dining spot. A walking-tour brochure from the **Annapolis and Anne Arundel County Conference and Visitors Bureau** provides great detail on the neighborhood's colorful background.

The area around **Spa Creek** is a quick walk or water-taxi ride from the City Dock and is full of marinas and popular restaurants.

Highland Beach began as the state's first incorporated African American settlement when the son of Frederick Douglass subdivided 44 acres south of Annapolis. Many of the families that live on this beautiful stretch of land along the Chesapeake Bay are descendants of the original homeowners.

Arnold, Severna Park, Pasadena, Glen Burnie, Linthicum, and other neighborhoods strung along MD 2 serve as bedroom communities for the Washington, DC/Baltimore/Annapolis metro area.

The southern portion of Anne Arundel County, known by the locals as "South County," belies its proximity to such a large population center. Here the small maritime villages of **Galesville, Deale,** and **Shady Side** still go about the business of harvesting the fruits of the Chesapeake Bay. This is the place to go if you want to catch a glimpse of the way life used to be along the bay but don't have time to visit the Eastern Shore.

GUIDANCE Information can be obtained by contacting or stopping by the **Annapolis and Anne Arundel County Conference and Visitors Bureau** (410-280-0445; 1-888-302-2852; www.visitannapolis.org), 26 West St., Annapolis, 21401.

ANNAPOLIS ROW HOUSES

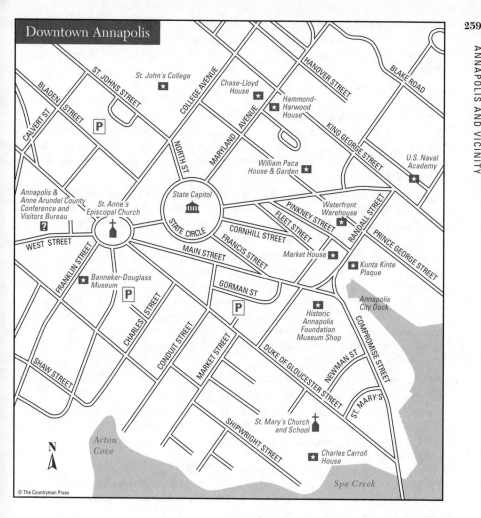

Downtown Annapolis

St. John's College
Chase-Lloyd House
Hammond-Harwood House
William Paca House & Garden
U.S. Naval Academy
Annapolis & Anne Arundel County Conference and Visitors Bureau
St. Anne's Episcopal Church
State Capitol
Waterfront Warehouse
Banneker-Douglass Museum
Market House
Kunta Kinte Plaque
Annapolis City Dock
Historic Annapolis Foundation Museum Shop
St. Mary's Church and School
Charles Carroll House
Acton Cove
Spa Creek

N

© The Countryman Press

There is also a **Visitors Information Kiosk** open seasonally near the harbormaster's office at the City Dock.

The free *What's Up* magazine has articles about life in and around the city and features a calendar of events.

GETTING THERE *By car:* **US 50/301** is the main four-lane highway access to Annapolis and connects the city with Washington, DC, and the Eastern Shore. **I-97** comes southward from Baltimore and connects with US 50/301 just west of Annapolis.

By air: The **Baltimore/Washington International Thurgood Marshall Airport** (1-800-I-FLY-BWI; www.bwiairport.com) is located in the northwestern part of Anne Arundel County and is less than a 30-minute drive from Annapolis. Interstate highways, rail, bus, taxi, and limousine services can transport you just about anywhere you wish to go from the airport.

By bus: **Greyhound** (1-800-231-2222; www.greyhound.com) stops in Annapolis at the Department of Transportation at 308 Chinquapin Round Rd. several times a day. The **Maryland**

Mass Transit Administration (410-539-5000; 1-800-543-9809; www.mtamaryland.com) operates both rail and bus routes that permit you to travel to Annapolis and northern Anne Arundel County from Baltimore, Washington, DC, and the Eastern Shore without having to drive a car.

By rail: See *By bus.*

GETTING AROUND *By car:* The streets within the Annapolis downtown/City Dock area were created in the 17th century for horse-and-buggy travel and have not changed much since then. There are many narrow, one-way streets and traffic circles, so pay attention to the signs and avoid the short rush times in the mornings and evenings. Traffic is tolerable the rest of the day.

The **Governor Ritchie Highway (MD 2)** is the local route between Annapolis and Baltimore, but you will probably make better time using **US 50** and then **I-97**. MD 2 is known as **Solomons Island Road** as it travels south of Annapolis. It is an efficient and scenic way to get into the southern portion of Anne Arundel County.

By bus: **Annapolis Transit** (410-263-7964; www.ci.annapolis.md.us/government) serves the city and much of the surrounding area with regular bus routes that have more than 150 stops. The **City Circulator** (www.annapolis.gov) is a free bus that takes people around the central historic district. It has designated stops along its route, but it will also stop for those who hail it like a taxi. The electric-powered **eCruisers** (443-481-2422; www.ecruisersllc.com) are an environmentally friendly—and fun—way to go just about anywhere you want in downtown Annapolis and Eastport. Give them a call and they'll pick you up at your door. The cost? Just a tip to the driver.

By taxi: **Annapolis Cab** (410-268-0022; 410-268-1323), **Checker** (410-268-3737), **Neet-N-Kleen** (410-320-3374), and **Reliable Cab** (410-268-4714).

By water: Although it does not provide quite the extensive service that its counterparts in Baltimore do, The **Water Taxi** (410-263-0033; http://cruisesonthebay.com) is still a fun and efficient way to get around to many of the waterfront areas—and to do some sightseeing along the way.

PARKING In Annapolis, parking meters are in effect 10 AM–7:30 PM daily and have only a two-hour time limit. You are permitted to park free on residential streets, but again the limit is only two hours. This rule is strictly enforced.

In the downtown area, the **Gotts Court Garage** off Calvert St. or Northwest St., **Knighton Court Garage** on West Street, and the **Hillman Garage** off Main St. provide public parking for an hourly fee. Be sure to get your ticket stamped for a discount if you make a purchase at a participating **Park and Shop** store.

You can avoid the headache of parking downtown by leaving your car at the **Navy–Marine Corps Memorial Stadium** and taking a shuttle into the historic district. Parking is about $5, and the shuttle is about $2 (it is free on the way back).

PUBLIC RESTROOMS In Annapolis, public restrooms are located in the Harbor Masters Building at the City Dock, in the State House on State Circle, and in the Annapolis and Anne Arundel County Conference and Visitors Bureau at 26 West St.

MEDICAL EMERGENCY **Anne Arundel Medical Center** (443-481-1000; www.aahs.org), 2001 Medical Pkwy. (off Jennifer Rd.), Annapolis.

Baltimore/Washington Medical Center (410-787-4000; www.mybwmc.org), 301 Hospital Dr., Glen Burnie.

COLLEGES **St. John's College** (410-263-2371; www.sjca.edu), 60 College Ave., Annapolis. In a city filled with historic sites, St. John's is one of the most historic. It traces its origins all the way back to 1696 with the founding of King William's School. McDowell Hall was built in the mid-1700s for the colonial governor and housed the entire college when given to the school in the 1800s. The exhibits in **Mitchell Art Gallery** (see *Selective Shopping*) are open to the public. Known today for its fine liberal arts education, the school has an unusual curriculum that features the study of "great books of the ages."

Also see **U.S. Naval Academy** under *To See*.

MUSEUMS

Annapolis

 ♿ **Banneker-Douglass Museum** (410-216-6180; www.bdmuseum.com), 84 Franklin St. Tues.–Sat. 10–4. Free admission; donations accepted. The State of Maryland's official repository for African American heritage, the museum maintains a collection of artifacts and photographs relevant to black life in Maryland, along with African and African American art, documents, and rare books. The former Mount Moriah African Methodist Episcopal Church, which houses the museum, is a Victorian Gothic structure worthy of being named a National Historic Landmark in 1973.

Waterfront Warehouse (410-267-7619; www.annapolis.org), 4 Pinkney St. Exhibits within the 1800s warehouse focus upon Maryland's early tobacco trade with Great Britain.

Linthicum

National Electronics Museum (410-765-0230; www.nationalelectronicsmuseum.org), 1745 W. Nursery Rd. Closed Sun. Very small admission fee. Arranged in chronological order, seven galleries take you through the development of communications, radar, underwater, spy, optical, and space electronic equipment. It's hard to believe that this museum can be as extensively put together as it is and still charge no admission fee. You'll get to hear the voice of Guglielmo Marconi, the inventor of the radiotelegraph, and even learn how bar codes on the everyday items you purchase work. One of the things I came away with was how much time and money are spent developing a new technology—and then how quickly it becomes obsolete.

HISTORIC HOMES

Annapolis

 ♿ **Hammond-Harwood House** (410-263-4683; www.hammondharwoodhouse.org), 19 Maryland Ave. Open Tues.–Sun.; last tour begins at 4. Small admission fee. The carved entranceway, large and elegant formal rooms, and grand scale of Matthias Hammond's 1774 home are a testament to his wealth and architect William Buckland's talent. Guided tours take guests throughout the house, furnished with 18th- and 19th-century decorative arts and Peale family portraits. Be sure to go into the gardens to enjoy the boxwoods and to appreciate the house's design and 15-inch-thick walls.

Chase-Lloyd House (410-263-2723), 22 Maryland Ave. Mon.–Sat., Mar.–Dec. Small admission fee. Guided tours of the 1769 Georgian mansion of Samuel Chase, a signer of the Declaration of Independence.

William Paca House and Garden (410-263-5553; www.annapolis.org), 186 Prince George St. Open daily, but hours are limited in Jan. and Feb. House and garden admission is $10 for adults; $9 for seniors; $5 for children 6–17. Fees are less to visit either just the house or just the garden. The restored 1760s Georgian mansion of William Paca, a signer of the Declaration of Independence, contains period furnishings. The garden, a re-creation of the one laid out around 1770, is one of the most relaxing places in the downtown area.

&. **Charles Carroll House** (410-269-1737; www.charlescarrollhouse.com), 107 Duke of Gloucester St. Open most Sat. and Sun. June–Sep. The waterfront home of Charles Carroll, who was the last living signer of the Declaration of Independence and the only Catholic, was built in several stages over the course of one hundred years. The partially restored home has little furniture, but it does retain its original flooring and many drawings from the days when George Washington and General Lafayette were regular visitors.

Highland Beach

Frederick Douglass Museum and Cultural Center (410-268-2956), 3200 Wayman Ave. Small admission fee. Many places that are open only by appointment have been left out of this book, but abolitionist/orator/publisher Frederick Douglass is such an important and inspiring figure in our nation's history that it would have been a disservice to ignore this small home and museum. Douglass's former summer home overlooks a small beach along the bay (with a grand view of the water) and contains a number of items that belonged to him. The impressive woodwork in the modest home is original, while displays and exhibits provide insight into the man, the experiences of other African Americans, and a bit of history on the local community.

Linthicum

Benson-Hammond House (410-768-9518; www.aachs.org), 7101 Aviation Blvd. Sat.–Sun. 11–3. Small admission fee. The Anne Arundel County Historical Society saved this farmhouse from destruction by the expansion of the Baltimore/Washington International Thurgood Marshall Airport in the mid-1970s. Made of clay bricks from the farm, the original four rooms were constructed in the 1820s. Some of the floors are still original, and the period furnishings reflect the times when the Hammond family occupied the house, from the 1880s to the 1940s.

THE FREDERICK DOUGLASS MUSEUM AND CULTURAL CENTER, HIGHLAND BEACH

HISTORIC LONDON TOWN

HISTORIC SITES

Annapolis

Maryland State House (410-974-3400), 91 State Circle, Annapolis. Free brochure provides information for a self-guided tour of the country's oldest continuously used statehouse (adults must show photo ID). The only statehouse to also serve as the nation's capital, it was built between 1772 and 1779 and occupies the highest point in the city. The tour takes you into the Old Senate Chamber where Congress ratified the Treaty of Paris, giving America its independence from Great Britain.

Historic London Town and Gardens (410-222-1919; www.historiclondontown.com), 839 Londontown Rd., Edgewater. The house is closed for tours Jan.–Mar., but the visitors center and gardens are open Mon.–Fri. During the rest of the year, the house is open Wed.–Sun. Please note that hours have been known to change. Admission fee for visitors center, house, and garden $10 adults; $9 seniors; children 7–12 are $5. The fee is less if you wish to tour just the garden or just the house. Whatever you do, take time to look at the exhibits in the visitors center, which start with the history of the Native Americans and move on to provide an overview of colonial life during the 1700s, along with a good description of how archaeology "works." Among the many things I learned were that the colonists were not as isolated from the rest of the world as is often depicted and that just about everyone, including women and children, smoked pipes.

Established along the South River in 1863, London Town was a major tobacco-exporting center by the early 1700s. William Brown—carpenter, ferry master, and tavernkeeper—built his large brick home around 1760. He used convict labor to operate a tavern and inn in part of the house, and a guided tour takes visitors through the restored home, which reflects those days. Ongoing archaeological digs are uncovering more of the history of the town and have resulted in a partial reconstruction of the town that helps you visualize what life was like for the common person from 1720 to 1750. And yes, these small structures that make up the village really were this close to Brown's palatial home. A walk through the extensive gardens, filled with tree peonies, daylilies, cherry trees, bloodroot, trillium, and many shrubs, takes you down to the banks of Almshouse Creek and is the way I like to relax and end my visits here.

HISTORIC CHURCHES **Asbury Methodist Church** (410-268-9500; www.gbgm-umc .org/aumcannapolis), 87 West St., Annapolis. This 1888 Gothic Revival church stands on the site of an earlier 1803 church, which was home to one of the earliest African American congregations in Annapolis.

St. Anne's Episcopal Church (410-267-9335; www.stannes-annapolis.org), Church Circle, Annapolis. The present structure, built in the late 1800s, is the third church to stand on this site. The stained-glass window by Tiffany and Company won first prize for ecclesiastical art in the 1893 World's Fair, and the silver communion service presented to the congregation by King William III in 1695 is still in use.

St. Mary's Church (410-263-2396), 109 Duke of Gloucester St., Annapolis. The Victorian Gothic church dates from the 1860s. Be sure to go inside the rib-vaulted interior to view the wonderfully hand-carved altar screen.

GUIDED TOURS ✔ **Annapolis Segway Tours** (410-280-1577; 1-888-280-1577; www .annapolissegwaytours.com), 131 Prince George St., Annapolis. $50 for one hour, $70 for two hours. Reservations suggested, but walk-ins will be accommodated as possible. No minimum number of people; minimum age is 14. The one- to two-hour tours start with a thorough training session in how to safely ride a Segway and navigate through Annapolis's downtown streets. I found that it was really nice that you were given wireless headsets to listen to the narrator's comments. Not only do you get to hear every word he or she says, but you don't lose time stopping to hear the comments, which include a great deal of historical information. A fun way to see the city—and be the envy of those who are merely walking.

Capital City Colonials (1-800-979-3370; www.capitalcitycolonials.com; www.annapolisfood tours.com). Well versed in the city's history, colonial-garbed guides lead a two-hour walk (adults $17, children 3–12 are $10; a shorter one-hour tour is $12, children $8) through Annapolis's historic district, taking you into places such as the Waterfront Warehouse, St. Anne's Church, and a 1774 mansion. One of this company's most popular outings is the Food and History Tour (adults $55), during which you not only learn about history, but spend time sampling the fare of one restaurant after another. Believe me, you will be full by the time the tour is over.

✔ **Discover Annapolis Trolley Tours** (410-626-6000; www.discoverannapolis.com) depart from the Annapolis and Anne Arundel County Conference and Visitors Bureau at 26 West St., Annapolis. Adults $18; children 11–15 are $9; children 10 and under are $3; preschoolers are free. The one-hour narrated tour of the city in air-conditioned/heated buses runs daily Apr.–Nov. and on most weekends Dec.–Mar.

♿ **U.S. Naval Academy** (410-293-8687; www.navyonline.com), 52 King George St. (entrance is at Gate 1), Annapolis. The grounds and visitors center are open to the public 9–5 (9–4, Jan. and Feb.); the chapel and crypt close at 4. Several tours are given daily, but times vary with the season. The first tour always begins at 10; be aware that it is quite tight to get everything in before closing time if you take the 3 PM tour. Small admission fee. (Anyone 16 and over must show photo ID.) The 338-acre academy along the banks of the Severn River was established in 1845 and is the undergraduate college of the U.S. Navy. There is much to see here, and the best way to do it is to take one of the guided tours that originate at the Armel-Leftwich Visitors Center. You will walk through 33-acre Bancroft Hall to see a typical midshipman's dorm room, the Tripoli Monument (oldest military statue in the United States), Memorial Hall, the Academy Museum, chapel, and the crypt of Revolutionary War

Watermark Cruises and Annapolis Tours (410-268-7600; www.annapolistours.com) depart from 26 West St., Annapolis. Daily, Mar.–Oct.; once only on Sat., Nov.–Mar. Other places at various times and days of the year. Adults $16; children 3–11 are $10. I enjoyed following the colonial-garbed guide, taking in the many historic sites in the city and the U.S. Naval Academy. However, I was most entertained by the guide's explanations of phrases we use in our everyday conversations:

Put your best foot forward: Colonial women enjoyed looking at men's well-developed calves, so a man would stand with one foot in front of the other, which accentuated his calf muscle.

Mind your P's and Q's: Tavern revelers would run a tab; in order not to come up short of money, a barmaid had to keep track of who had drunk how many pints and quarts.

Crack a smile: Beeswax was used as a facial cosmetic, which you would crack if your smile was too large. Also the origin of *Mind your own beeswax.*

Not playing with a full deck: The king put a tax on playing cards, but it only applied to the ace of spades. So people would purchase a deck without that card.

Straitlaced: Respectable ladies would keep their bodices tightly laced. On the other hand, a female who wanted to show a bit of her bosom would not pull the laces quite so tight. She soon became known as a "loose" woman.

Putting on the dog: Affluent members of society would have slippers made out of the family dog's hide and fur after it died.

hero John Paul Jones. If you are here around noon on weekdays during the school year, you will witness the formation of all midshipmen as they march off to lunch.

✴ To Do

BICYCLING Annapolis has been called one of the most walker-friendly cities in the country, but it has not forgotten bicyclists. A 38-mile system of designated bike routes along city streets and grade-separated trails lets you explore on two wheels instead of four. The **City Planning and Zoning Department** (410-263-7961; www.ci.annapolis.md.us) can provide more information. All buses in the city have racks that will hold two bikes; there is no additional charge for this service.

The **Baltimore and Annapolis Trail** is a paved pathway that follows the route of an old railroad bed close to Governor Ritchie Hwy. (MD 2) for more than 13 miles. Although it does pass by busy streets, housing developments, and a mall or two, it can be a nice ride, especially along the least-developed 3 miles closest to Annapolis. The trail begins near the Baltimore/Washington International Thurgood Marshall Airport (where it connects with another paved trail encircling the airport) and ends on MD 2 just as it enters Annapolis. More information and a map can be obtained from the **Anne Arundel County Department of Recreation and Parks** (410-222-6244; www.aacounty.org).

For those who don't quite have the oomph they used to, **Green Pedals** (410-280-5005; www.green-pedals.com) at 105 B Annapolis St. (closed Sun.–Mon) rents, and sells, electric motor assisted bicycles to help you get around.

Also see Quiet Waters Park and Truxton Park under *Parks.*

BOAT EXCURSIONS 🐾 **Watermark Cruises** (410-268-7601; 1-800-569-9622; www .watermarkjourney.com), Slip 20 at the City Dock, Annapolis. Narrated tours of 40 minutes (adults $14; children 3–11 are $6) and 90 minutes (adults $23; children 3–11 are $10) are provided Mar.–Dec. Days and times vary throughout the season, so call for the latest information. A three-hour tour (adults $42; children 3–11 are $20) takes passengers by three of the Chesapeake Bay's famous lighthouses and under the bay bridges. Narrated by a "turn-of-the-century lighthouse keeper." I am most familiar with the lighty narrated (prerecorded) 40-minute tour of the Annapolis Harbor and Spa Creek that goes by the naval academy. A nice way to give legs a rest from exploring the rest of the historic area of Annapolis. Pets (on leash) permitted on all cruises!

$ Pirates Adventure on the Chesapeake (410-263-0002; www.chesapeakepirates.com), 311 3rd St. Sails several times daily during usual tourist months; less frequently other times of the year. $20; children 2 and under $12. Unleash your and your children's inner pirate on a one-hour cruise in the Chesapeake Bay.

$ Schooner Woodwind (410-263-7837; www.schoonerwoodwind.com), 80 Compromise St. (at the Marriott Hotel), Annapolis. Times and rates vary. Most cruises are around $40 for adults and $30 for children under 12. The 74-foot sailboat, beautiful with its mahogany woodwork and chrome trim, offers daily sailing cruises. Most of the trips last about two hours and take in Annapolis harbor, the Naval Academy, and a portion of the Severn River. You can be passive or take a turn at the wheel or hoist the four sails.

Water Taxi (410-263-0033; www.watermarkjourney.com), City Dock, Annapolis. One of the most fun ways to get to and from and explore the harbor, Spa Creek, and Back Creek. Depending on where you want to go, the rate could be as much as $2 a person. Does not run on a scheduled basis, but will pick you up when called.

BOAT RENTALS **South River Boat Rentals** (410-956-9729; www.southriverboatrentals .com), located at Pier 7 Marina, Edgewater. Half-day, daily, overnight, and weekly rentals of a variety of motor- and sailboats. No experience needed. Rates range from $160 for a half day to $1,200 per day.

Also see **Quiet Waters Park** under *Green Space*.

CASINO **Maryland Live! Casino** (410-528-1034; www.marylandlivecasino.com), 7002 Arundel Mills Circle. Located next to the Arundel Mills Mall, the casino is open 24 hours a day, so you can feed the slots at 3 in the morning if you feel the need. Dining options include The Prime Rib, a steakhouse with fireplaces and patio seating, and the Live! Buffet with chefs constantly preparing fresh versions of international dishes from America, Italy, Asia, and other regions. There's some kind of entertainment available almost every evening.

FISHING Charter fishing excursions are offered by a number of outfitters in the Annapolis area. Among the many are:

Annapolis Fishing Unlimited (410-353-8919; www.fishannapolis.com), 301 4th St. Annapolis. This group will take just one person fly-fishing or handle an entire large party wanting to try fishing the bay

.**Bounty Hunter** (410-286-8990; 1-800-322-4039; www.bountyhuntercharter.com), 8076 Windward Key Dr., Chesapeake Beach. Capt. Glenn James takes groups of 6–49 onto the water on the 55-foot *Bounty Hunter.*

Down Time Spotfishing Charters (443-949-8030; www.downtimechaters.com), 1039 Broadview Dr. Annapolis. Full time fishing guides for up to six guests.

GOLF

Arnold

$ Severna Park Golf Center (410-647-8618; www.severnaparkgolf.com), 1257 Governor Ritchie Hwy. A nine-hole course and a driving range with sheltered and heated tees. Miniature golf and batting cages for the kids.

Dwight D. Eisenhower Golf Course (410-571-0973; www.eisenhowergolf.com), Generals Hwy. (MD 178). You will need to reserve your tee time at this public course.

Edgewater

The Golf Club at South River (410-798-5865; www.mdgolf.com), 3451 Solomons Island Rd. The closest private course to Annapolis is set amid a dense forest with dramatic elevation changes on the links.

MINIATURE GOLF See **Severna Park Golf Center** under *Golf.*

KAYAKING AND CANOEING

Kayak Annapolis (443-949-0773; www.kayakannapolistours.com) departs from Truxton Park. The two-hour guided paddle trips near the Annapolis harbor and the U.S. Naval Academy depart three times a day during the season. The one that leaves early in the morning usually has the best chance of seeing birds and other wildlife—and will also be the coolest trip of the day.

Paddle or Pedal (410-271-7007; www.paddleorpedal.com), 600 Quiet Waters Park Rd., Annapolis. As the name says, they will rent you all manner of paddle craft or bicycles. Their guided sunset tours are popular. Located within Quiet Waters Park.

SAILING LESSONS ⚓ **Annapolis Sailing School** (1-800-638-9192; www.annapolis sailing.com), 601 Sixth St., Annapolis. One of the best-respected institutions of sailing knowledge, Annapolis Sailing is also the oldest and largest sailing school in the country. Courses of various duration are designed for basic, cruising, and advanced sailing, and for those interested in preparing for a bareboat charter or coastal navigation and piloting. There are also classes for children 5–15 years aboard 12- to 14-foot sailing dinghies.

Womanship, Inc. (1-800-342-9295; www.womanship.com), 137 Conduit St., Annapolis. Sailing instruction taught by and for women. Their courses are for novice to advanced sailors. I like their motto: "Nobody yells!"

Annapolis Powerboat School (410-267-7205; www.annapolispowerboat.com), 601 Sixth St., Annapolis. Several different hands-on, on-the-water classes are offered. One of the most popular is the five-day instruction course, which cruises around the bay, enabling you to spend evenings at various waterfront inns.

SKATING See **Quiet Waters Park** under *Parks.*

SWIMMING See *Tennis* and **Truxton Park** under *Green Space.*

TENNIS The **Anne Arundel County Recreation and Parks Department** (410-222-7300; www.aacounty.org), 1 Harry S. Truman Pkwy., Annapolis, oversees more than 30 regional parks with tennis courts open to the public on a first-come, first-served basis, and four parks with swimming available to the general public. Contact them for more information.

Also see **Truxton Park** under *Green Space.*

WALKING TOURS Annapolis boasts more than 35 homes and sites of historical significance within a few blocks of one another in the downtown/City Dock area of the city. These sites are described in the *Annapolis and Anne Arundel County Visitors Guide,* which is available from the Annapolis and Anne Arundel County Conference and Visitors Bureau. Pick up a copy and take an easy stroll into the city's past.

✳ **Green Space**

BEACHES See the **Sandy Point State Park** sidebar below.

GARDENS ♿ **Helen Avalynne Tawes Garden** (410-260-8189; www.dnr.state.md.us /publiclands/tawesgarden.asp), next to the Tawes State Office Building on Taylor Ave., Annapolis. Open daily dawn–dusk. Expect to see a number of state employees escaping bureaucratic headaches when you walk through this 6-acre park. One of the nicest free city botanical gardens on the East Coast, it has sections representing Eastern Shore habitats, mountain forestland, and streamside environments. An abundance of birds and small wildlife make their home in the garden.

PARKS

Annapolis

🚣 ♿ **Quiet Waters Park** (410-222-1777; www.aacounty.org), 600 Quiet Waters Park Rd. Open 7 AM–dusk; closed Tues. Small admission fee. This 336-acre park is easily accessed from Bay Ridge Rd. in the Eastport neighborhood of the city and has been called the finest county-operated park in the state. It is bordered by Harness Creek and the South River, so much of the recreational emphasis is on water sports, with a variety of boats for rent from spring through fall. There are also more than 6 miles of hiking/biking trails through wetlands and shoreline, picnic facilities, a visitors center (with two art galleries), a large playground, and even an outdoor ice rink open during the colder months. A great place to make a quick escape from the city traffic and noise.

🚣 **Truxtun Park** (410-263-7958; www.ci.annapolis.md.us), Hilltop Ln. Only 77 acres in size, the park is a city playground with tennis and basketball courts, a swimming pool, bike routes, and picnic facilities. Small fee for swimming.

Pasadena

Downs Memorial Park (410-222-6230; www.aacounty.org), Johns Down Loop. Small parking fee. A small shoreline park that offers biking opportunities, picnicking, interpretive programs, and outdoor concerts.

WALKS 🚣 **Smithsonian Environmental Research Center** (443-482-2200; www.serc.si .edu), 647 Contees Wharf Rd., Edgewater. An easy pathway works its way to a re-created Piscataway Indian village, by dairy farm implements and exhibits about tobacco plantations, and across a marsh. A great escape spot from noisy highways and cities.

🚣 ♿ **Sandy Point State Park** (410-974-2149; www.dnr.state.md.us/publiclands/southern /sandypoint.asp), 800 Revell Hwy. (off US 50/301), Annapolis. Open year-round for day use. Less than 10 miles northeast of Annapolis, the park's beaches (guarded Memorial Day–Labor Day) are considered among the finest along the Chesapeake Bay and are favored by local families. Rowboats and motorboats are available for rent, and close to 5 miles of trails course through woodland and marsh. The varied habitat makes for good bird-watching and, being on the Atlantic Flyway, attracts a large number of migratory waterfowl. Some facilities are handicapped accessible.

Of the more than 4,600 miles of shoreline around the bay, less than 2 percent is accessible to the public; the rest is privately owned—a fact that is almost impossible to accept. Maybe we should utter a word of thanks that the state was wise enough to preserve the open land of Sandy Point in the 1950s.

✳ Lodging
MOTELS AND HOTELS

Downtown and close to downtown, 21401

&. Annapolis Marriott Waterfront Hotel (1-888-773-0786; www.annapolismarriott .com), 80 Compromise St. The Annapolis location of this national chain is the city's only downtown hotel located directly on the water. $379–499.

☀ &. Loews Annapolis Hotel (410-263-7777; 1-800-23-LOEWS; www.loews annapolis.com), 126 West St. One of the closest hotels to the waterfront and the City Dock. Large, luxurious rooms and an attentive staff have enabled the Loews Annapolis to be designated a AAA four-diamond hotel for more than a decade. The common areas are bright and airy. Pets permitted. $179–299; additional parking fee adds about $20 per overnight/day stay.

&. O'Callaghan Hotel Annapolis (410-263-7700; www.ocallaghanhotels-us.com), 174 West St. Located in the downtown area, it is within walking distance of the Naval Academy and City Dock. The convenient location is matched by the attentive service and luxurious style. $139–279; additional parking fee adds about $20 per overnight/day stay.

☀ &. Westin Annapolis Hotel (410-972-4300; www.westin.com), 100 Westgate Circle. The luxury hotel, a couple of blocks farther away from the harbor than the O'Callaghan Hotel Annapolis, has more than 200 rooms and is next door to six restaurants offering quite varied menus. Heated indoor pool, fitness center, spa, and concierge services. Pets permitted. $189–329; additional parking fee.

Note: Many more hotels and motels are located near the Baltimore/Washington International Thurgood Marshall Airport and along many state roads between Annapolis and Baltimore. Among the lower-cost national chains are **Days Inn** (410-224-4317; 1-800-544-8313; www.daysinn .com), **Courtyard by Marriott** (410-266-1555; 1-888-236-2427; www.courtyard

.com), and **Microtel** (410-865-7500; www .microtelinn.com). **The Comfort Suites** (410-691-1000; 1-800-228-5150) at 815 Elkridge Landing Rd. in Linthicum is within a couple of minutes' drive of the airport. $119–199.

INNS

Downtown, 21401

&. Gibson's Lodgings (410-268-5555; 1-877-330-0057; www.gibsonslodgings.com), 110 Prince George St. Features a variety of guest rooms in two historic homes and another structure built in 1988. Close to most of the downtown/City Dock attractions. $129–259.

Historic Inns of Annapolis (410-263-2641; 1-800-847-8882; www.annapolisinns .com.), 58 State Capital Circle. The Historic Inns are actually three inns operated under the same management group. The **Governor Calvert House,** facing the State Capitol, was built in 1727 for the colonial governor. The **Robert Johnson House,** also facing the capitol building, was constructed as a private residence in 1765. The **Maryland Inn,** on State Circle, is the only one of the three that was originally built to cater to travelers. The Treaty of Paris restaurant (see *Dining Out*) downstairs has been serving patrons for more than 200 years. Each inn offers a wide variety of accommodations, with many different amenities. $145–205.

Scotlaur Inn (410-268-5665; www.scotlaur inn.com), 165 Main St. Wallpaper, quilts on metal beds, throw rugs, and windows overlooking the bustle of Main St. give the 10 rooms above Chick and Ruth's Deli (see *Eating Out*) the feel of a neighborhood hotel or tourist home from the turn of the 20th century. Central heating and air-conditioning. $110–125.

Rose Haven, 20714

♂ &. Herrington Harbour Inn (410-741-5100; 1-800-213-9438; www.herrington harbourinn.com), 7149 Lake Shore Dr. Those of you who don't want to drive all of the way to Ocean City to experience sand and water, take note. Sure, it doesn't have a miles-long beach, big waves, or boardwalk amusements, but the inn does have its own little bit of beach on the Chesapeake Bay. The bay here stretches off to the far horizon, so you do have that feeling of an endless body of water. The inn's rooms have the look of a mid-1900s motel, but some are equipped with a hot tub, and the entire place has the feel of a well-run and ecologically minded resort (everything is recycled, the shoreline is covered by native plants, and the adjoining marina has won major environmental awards). In addition to the beach, brick pathways wind through palm trees to a swimming pool and sauna, restaurant, fitness center, playground, and picnic areas. A nice family-friendly place to spend a vacation. $220–600.

BED & BREAKFASTS

Downtown, 21401

1747 Georgian House Bed and Breakfast (410-263-5618; www.georgianhouse .com), 170 Duke of Gloucester St. Closing in on being 300 years old, the B&B has guest rooms named after the signers of the Declaration of Independence. With the elegance appropriate to the home, the house retains the original red pine flooring, working fireplaces, period antique furnishings, and each guest room has a private bath. The thick brick walls (common when the house was built) provide a level of privacy not found in modern homes. The library has a microwave and refrigerator for guest use. The bountiful breakfasts of fresh breads and hot entrées are reason enough to stay here. There is also the masterful decorating of the guest rooms and common areas. $189–225.

✿ 🦜 **Academy Bed and Breakfast** (410-990-1234; www.academybedandbreakfast .com), 134 Prince George St. Sumptuous, luxurious, warm, inviting. These are the words that were in my notebook after visiting the Academy B&B. In one word— classy. All of the guest rooms are large and wonderfully decorated (and incorporate many of the original aspects of the historic home), and each (except the smaller Garden Room) has a steam room and Jacuzzi. Each has its own view, be it of the harbor, the cathedral, state house, or Prince George St. The Garden Room is pet-friendly. Located less than a block to the harbor. $205–310.

HERRINGTON HARBOUR INN'S BEACH ON THE CHESAPEAKE BAY

The Annapolis Inn (410-295-5200; www
.annapolisinn.com), 144 Prince George St.
The hosts have turned the home of Thomas
Jefferson's physician into the modern per-
sonification of pampering and luxury. Crystal chandeliers, etched-glass shower and
pocket doors, sumptuous furniture, cedar
guest closets, and a heatable tumbled-
marble bathroom floor are just a few of
the niceties. Yet they have kept much of
the old, such as original crown moldings
and medallions, and the horse-hair plaster
on the walls. $310–475.

Charles Inn Bed and Breakfast (410-268-
1451; www.charlesinn.com), 74 Charles St.
On what is now a quiet side street, but was
once the main avenue to Annapolis's harbor,
the B&B has three guest rooms of various
sizes and amenities, but each with a private
bath. The two things that come to mind
when I think about the place are the gorgeous hardwood floors throughout the house
and the nicely landscaped backyard perfect
for quiet contemplation and a small dock for
access to the water. Children permitted with
prior notice. Off-street parking. $169–279.

✍ **Chez Amis** (410-263-6631; 1-888-224-
6455; www.chezamis.com), 85 East St. It's a
triangular house! And if you stay here,
you'll get to see what one looks like on the
inside. Chez Amis was a corner grocery
store when the 20th century began and, as
the B&B home of Elly and Joe Tierney,
retains the original Georgia pine floors, tin
ceiling, and an oak display counter. All
rooms have down comforters on the brass
beds, private bath, TV, and a large selection
of movies for the DVD player. Children 10
and over welcome.

I defy you to leave hungry after Elly's
three-course "sweet and savory" breakfasts.
Each meal always starts with a bread (hopefully it will be the Amish friendship bread
or a blueberry coffee cake). In addition, I
have had many versions of yogurts in the
hundreds of B&Bs I've stayed in. There is
no doubt; Chez Amis's was the most delicious. If the morning meal is not enough to
fill you, homemade baked goodies and liquid refreshments are available throughout
the day. $180–260.

✍ **Flag House Inn** (410-280-2721; 1-800-
437-4825; www.flaghouseinn.com), 26 Randall St. The location couldn't be any better.
The City Dock and the main Naval Academy gate are only one block away, and the
B&B has private off-street parking. All six
guest rooms in the restored 1870 Victorian
home have a private bath, TV, and air-
conditioning. There were so many things I
enjoyed about my stay here: the two-sided
fireplace that heated the living and dining
rooms, the front porch to lazily sit on and
watch the rest of Annapolis hurry by, and
Charlotte and Bill Schmickle's large English
breakfast. The guests I shared breakfast
with came from many corners of the globe.
Children over 10 welcome. $200–235.

Gatehouse B&B (410-280-0024; www
.gatehousebb.com), 249 Hanover St. The
Georgian-style B&B overlooks the Naval
Academy and is furnished in period reproductions. Most rooms have a private bath;
all come with fresh flowers to brighten the
day and soft robes for comfortable lounging. Breakfasts are wonderful variations on
old standards, such as cream cheese and ice
cream French toast or Italian-style quiche.
$200–330.

Inn at 30 Maryland (410-263-9797; www
.30maryland.com), 30 Maryland Ave. The
large guest rooms of the regal Queen Anne
Victorian B&B have some nice views of
the historic Chase Lloyd Gardens. If the

ACCOMMODATIONS AT CHEZ AMIS

continental breakfast isn't enough for you, snacks are always out for guests to nibble on any time of the day. $199–269.

Randall House (410-263-4970; www.randallhousebb.com), 30 Randall St. Just a couple of doors down from the Flag House Inn (see above), the Randall House shares the same great location. Each guest room in the mid-1800s house has a private bath; the back room has a deck overlooking the garden. $160–200.

Reynolds Tavern (410-295-0555; www.reynoldstavern.org), 7 Church Circle. Staying in one of the two suites or one guest room of the mid-1700s brick B&B (floors and walls are original) has you located just a two-minute walk from the state house or the attractions and businesses of downtown/harbor Annapolis. You are also only one flight of stairs away from getting to dine in the tavern's superb restaurant, located on the first floor. $220–295.

Royal Folly (410-263-3999; www.royalfolly.com), 65 College Ave. Among the late-1800s building's 14 rooms are five spacious guest suites, each separated from each other so that you will have a good degree of privacy. Some of the suites have fireplaces, others have a hot tub, and some have both. Many of the home's original features still remain, including all of the leaded-glass windows and most of the light fixtures. A good choice for families with students attending St. John's College, as the school is just across the street. $295–425.

THE ENTRANCE TO THE ANNAPOLITAN

Two-O-One (410-268-8053; www.201bb.com), 201 Prince George St. All of the guest quarters in this Georgian home have four-poster beds and are elegantly furnished, but I am particularly smitten by the Crow's Nest Suite on the third floor. There is just something about the large tiles and woodwork in the bathroom that provides a rich and sensuous experience. The large gardens are a nice respite from the noise of the city. Off-street parking. $180–250.

Close to downtown, 21401

✦ **The Annapolitan Bed and Breakfast** (410-990-1234; www.theannapolitan.com), 1313 West St. The Annapolitan has been a guest home of one kind or another for more than a century. Once housing workers who worked on the farm (hard to believe the busy thoroughfare the house is located next to was once a farm!), it now offers five opulently appointed rooms, each with private bath and its own hand-painted landscape on the wall (or ceiling—I like being in bed and looking up at the soaring gulls in the upstairs Beacon Room). The common

THE ANNAPOLITAN DINING ROOM

areas, such as the sitting room with a piano, the dining area with wonderful wooden accessories, wraparound porch, outside bar, and the quality artwork throughout the house, make this a place of distinction. Children permitted. $130–225.

Eastport neighborhood of Annapolis, 21403

♿ **Inn at Horn Point** (410-268-1126; www.innathornpoint.com), 100 Chesapeake Ave. Located in a quiet residential neighborhood just seven blocks from the Annapolis harbor. The hosts who rehabilitated this 1902 home had been in the hospitality business and know a few things about what guests like and want. One thing that was done to ensure a bit of peace and quiet was making the walls three layers thick as well as double thickness for the ceilings. Guests will also appreciate other thoughtful features, such as a claw-foot tub in one of the suites and high-quality linens. $199–309.

Edgewater, 21307

Fisherman's Dock House Boat Rentals (410-541-9544; www.fishermans-dock.com),

FISHERMAN'S DOCK HOUSE BOAT RENTALS

INN AT HORN POINT

1057 Carr's Wharf Rd. As their brochure says, "If for you, funky and quirky translates to inadequate and unsatisfactory," a stay here may not be for you. However, if you can get into the adventure of sleeping on a houseboat that will gently rock you to sleep, was custom built by the owners of this business, and uses composting toilets, then check out their Web site and make a reservation (last-minute deals will save you a few dollars). Free canoes and kayaks are available for guest use. $200; winter rate is $50, but there is no running water.

Lothian, 20711

Butterfly Fields Bed and Breakfast (410-271-1433; www.butterfly-fields.com), 320 Frank Moreland Pl. Butterfly Fields, a retreat to rural land in an area that is increasingly developed, is a working farm that has so many animals, you will see one kind or another when you look out any of the guest rooms. The hosts have done many things to make this an environmentally friendly place and a quiet retreat. Vines drape themselves over the deck, providing passive cooling for the house, and no television in the rooms ensures that your time here will be relaxing. After a full farm breakfast, take a walk in the eye-pleasing and very well-maintained flower gardens. My time here was way too short; I bet you'll feel the same way when you have to leave, too. $175.

Near the South River, 21401

♪ ঙ **Laurel Grove Inn** (443-370-2394; www.laurelgroveinn.net), 2881 S. Haven Rd. Sitting just 50 feet or so above the South River, the modern upscale home, which incorporates lots of rock and stone in its architecture, has three guest rooms and two suites, each with private bath. (Groups may rent the entire house.) All of the rooms have a nice view (or a deck) overlooking the river, where guests are welcome to swim or arrive by boat and tie up at the private dock. $100–185.

VACATION RENTALS Leisure Management, LLC (410-224-3257; www.leisuremanagementllc.com), 617 Ridgely Ave., #1A, Annapolis, 21401. If you will be in the area with a large group or family for an extended period, you might consider contacting these folks, who operate two four-bedroom, two-and-a-half-bath modern houses in the Eastport neighborhood. A group of eight can rent the entire house for $1,600 for a three-day weekend. Weekly and monthly rentals also available.

CAMPING

Lothian, 20711

❅ **Duncan's Family Campground** (410-741-9558; 1-800-222-2086; www.duncansfamilycampground.com), 5381 Sands Rd. Open year-round; limited facilities in winter. Located in the southern part of Anne Arundel County, close to the bay and Patuxent River Park. Free transportation to Washington, DC, metro services. Pool, miniature golf, tent sites. Small pets permitted.

Millersville, 21108

❅ **Capital KOA** (410-923-2771), 768 Cecil Ave. Late Mar.–Nov. 1. This is the closest campground to Annapolis and one of the closest to Washington, DC. Free daily shuttle to DC Transit. Expect the many amenities found in this national chain: pool, dump station, playground. Pets permitted.

✳ Where to Eat

DINING OUT

Annapolis

Reynolds Tavern (410-295-9555; www.reynoldstavern.org), 7 Church Circle. Open daily for lunch and Wed.–Sun for dinner. On the first floor of a building that is believed to have served food to travelers and guests as early as 1747, Reynolds Tavern serves a nice mix of dishes, with the shepherd's pie and bangers and mash fitting in well with its historical aspect, and the Thai salmon, Chilean sea bass, New Zealand rack of lamb, and chicken Chesapeake reflecting the world view of its menu. The menu does keep some items, but it also changes seasonally so that the chef can take advantage of what is freshest at the time. I was here for lunch, and the chicken, bacon, and cheddar sandwich was tasty and filling. Dinner entrées list for $15–30. An afternoon tea is offered, and since it is not the stuffy, high-tea type of service where you have to dress up with white gloves, it's a nice choice for those just getting introduced to the tradition.

Ristorante Piccola Roma (410-268-7898; www.piccolaromaannapolis.com), 200 Main St. Open daily for lunch and dinner. I enjoyed several meals here when Silvana Recine operated this restaurant. All of the dishes were from her recipes, which she had brought from her native Rome, with many adapted to make use of local products. I have not yet dined here since the ownership has changed, but it is my understanding that several of the chefs have stayed on, so it is my hope that at least some of the entrées are prepared in the same manner. I do know the place is gaining a reputation for creating some inventive cocktails. Let me know what you think. $18–32.

Treaty of Paris (410-216-6340; www.historicinnsofannapolis.com), Church Circle and Main St. (inside the Maryland Inn). Nouveau French cuisine served within the gracefully restored inn. A lunch buffet is available, but you will certainly enjoy the food—and appreciate the kitchen's abilities—more if you order from the menu. Entrées $18–28.

Wild Orchid Café (401-268-8009; www .thewildorchidcafe.com), 200 Westgate Circle. With an elegant setting (on the ground floor of an office building), Wild Orchid incorporates a farm-to-table philosophy in its menu. If offered, the best deal is the four course prix fixe for $39 ($59 with wine pairings), especially in light of the fact that to have a side with the $16–29 entrées is an additional $5. The made-in-house bread pudding is big enough the feed three for dessert.

Close to downtown

🏅 ᬓ **Les Folies Brasserie** (410-573-0970; ww.lesfoliesbrasserie.com), 2552 Riva Rd. It sometimes seems like you have to take out a second mortgage to enjoy a meal at a good French restaurant. Not at Les Folies. Here there is a Parisian atmosphere and quality food at rational prices. The recipes of the ever-evolving menu reflect distinct regions of France: Paris, Gascony, Provence, Alsace, Lyon, and others. Expect an appetizer of crabmeat custard with lobster sauce on one visit, and garlic sausage over lentil salad on another. The fish and pasta dishes are some of the most popular entrées, and, of course, you cannot leave without having one of the special desserts. My second favorite Annapolis dining spot. Entrées $18–34.

Eastport neighborhood of Annapolis

Carrol's Creek (410-263-8102; www .carrolscreek.com), 410 Severn Ave. Steaks and other meats are available at this waterfront restaurant, but it would be a mistake not to go for the seafood. The cream of crab soup is thick and rich, but you might also want to try the curried zucchini and shrimp soup. The crabcakes (market price) are delicious, as is the rockfish served over Parmesan polenta. Most entrées run $22–35.

Rockfish (410-267-1800; www.rockfish md.com), 400 Sixth St. Open for lunch and

dinner. Based on the quality of the appetizers that made up lunch for me and my dining companion, dinner at Rockfish should be a satisfying experience. The chef employs as many local and organic items as possible, and the large open restaurant, with an open kitchen, lends itself to savoring the Maryland crab soup or the rockfish scented with rosemary, garlic, and olive oil. Another interesting item that has been on the menu is the shellfish strudel, a puff pastry stuffed with lobster, shrimp, and crab, and served with asparagus, red peppers, and tarragon cream sauce. If you are here with a group of people, start your meal with the Rockfish Shellfish Tower, which includes raw oysters, topneck clams, jumbo shrimp, and a lobster tail. Entrées $17–35.

EATING OUT

Annapolis

Annapolis Gourmet (410-263-6115), 116 Annapolis St. The Leano family has been in the deli business for more than 65 years, so they know a thing or two about making sandwiches, soups, and salads. The chicken salad has become a local tradition. Entrées $7–19.

🍴 **Buddy's Crabs and Ribs** (410-626-1100; www.buddysonline.com), 100 Main St. Open for lunch and dinner daily. A typical crab house, and close to the City Dock. Many people choose the buffet bar, but you will probably be more satisfied with ordering from the menu. Entrées $13.99–47.99.

🍴 ᬓ **Chick and Ruth's Delly** (410-269-6737; www.chickandruths.com), 165 Main St. Open daily for breakfast, lunch, and dinner. Chick and Ruth have been gone for some time now, but their family continues to serve up solid deli and diner food. A long menu complete with 16 kinds of omelets ensures that this is the place to start your day. As a bonus, you can join the staff as they recite the Pledge of Allegiance each morning. Entrées $8.95–24.95.

49 West Coffeehouse (410-626-9796; www.49westcoffeehouse.com), 49 West St. Open daily for breakfast, lunch, and dinner. I thought long and hard on how to describe this place to you. I came up with: It is a funky-chic place that appeals to the sophisticated beatnik/vegetarian/meat eater/ yuppie/coffee lover in all of us. The interior is a quirky blend of an old brick wall on one side, a 1950s dropped acoustic-tile ceiling above, and a plaster wall covered in artwork for sale on the other side.

The menu is as varied. Baked goods, a Belgian waffle, quiche, and egg dishes for breakfast. Sandwiches range from melted ham and cheese to vegetarian burgers with soy cheese. Entrées served after 6 PM include crab scampi over pasta and honey-garlic pork. Everything is well prepared. $8–19.95.

Galway Bay (410-263-8333; www.galway baymd.com), 61–63 Maryland Ave. Open daily for lunch and dinner. Authentic Irish food prepared according to the recipes of owner Michael Galway, who left his native Kilkenny in southeast Ireland in 1986. My potato-leek soup served with hearty baked bread was creamy and tasty, while the seafood pie, crammed with salmon, shrimp, crabmeat, scallops, and clams, was a nice variation on the traditional shepherd's pie. Steak, chicken, and other seafood prepared the Irish way are also available. Bread pudding, rhubarb and strawberry tart, and Irish

whiskey cake are just a few of the desserts. Entrées $15.95–24.95.

McGarvey's Saloon and Oyster Bar (410-263-5700; www.mcgarveys.net), 8 Market Space. Open for lunch and dinner Mon.–Sat.; Sun. brunch at 10. The festive, publike atmosphere and location at the City Dock has made McGarvey's a popular eatery since it opened in 1975. Obviously, oysters prepared many different ways are a specialty, but there is also light fare, sandwiches, and a few entrées such as filet mignon. The rich wood-and-brick interior created a pleasant place to enjoy the fillet béarnaise sandwich I ordered. Entrées to $29.95.

✪ **Middleton Tavern** (410-263-3323; www.middletontavern.com), 2 Market Space. Open daily for lunch and dinner. Traditional American/Maryland cuisine inside the historic tavern on the City Dock. Many seafood items from the raw bar and appetizer menu. Pasta, sandwiches, meats, and seafood entrées. The seafood crêpe with crab, shrimp, and scallops in a brandy sherry crème sauce is a house specialty. Entrées $24.95–37.

Deale

Skipper's Pier (410-867-7110; www .skipperspier.com), 6158 Drum Point Rd. Open daily for lunch and dinner. Its location next to the bay's shoreline has made it a popular destination with recreational boaters for close to four decades. It has a festive and friendly atmosphere to it. (The place was nearly full when I stopped in on a Wed. midafternoon.) The menu is what you would expect—steamed crabs, fresh fish, a selection of steaks and chicken, and a few sandwiches. The little bits of parsley in the crabcakes I ordered added a nice and refreshing taste. Entrées $18.99–25.99.

Eastport neighborhood of Annapolis

✪ **Boatyard Bar and Grill** (410-216-6206; www.boatyardbarandgrill.com), 400 Fourth St. Much local color here, as this is where the area's resident sailors, boaters, fishermen, and boatyard workers hang out. Open daily for lunch and dinner; also serves

CHICK AND RUTH'S DELLY IS A LOCAL INSTITUTION.

SKIPPER'S PIER

breakfast on weekends. The menu has influences from the Chesapeake Bay, Caribbean, and Key West. Dressings and soups are made from scratch. Standouts include crab dishes, conch fritters, jerk chicken, Key West steamed shrimp, and daily specials. Entrées $13–25. Drinks by the pint, a coffee bar, and sandwiches to go.

Davis's Pub (410-468-7432; www.davispub .com), 400 Chester Ave. Open daily for lunch and dinner. This place may have been featured on Food Network's *Diners, Drive Ins, and Dives* and access cable's *Feasty Boys,* but it has retained its down-home neighborhood bar atmosphere where you may be the only nonlocal. Also, it may be a bar, yet the food is well worth coming here. The gazpacho I had was tasty and full of chunky pieces of tomato, onion, cucumber, and green pepper. The famous crab pretzel is huge and the filling goes well with a cold beer. And how many bars do you know of that incorporate vegetables from their own gardens into the menu offerings? This is an off-the-beaten-path kind of place that you want to find. $7.95–16.95.

The Main Ingredient Café (410-626-0388; www.themainingredient.com), 914 Bay Bridge Rd. (at Georgetown Plaza). Open for breakfast, lunch, and dinner. It is in a strip mall, but the sunlight and bright décor can help you overlook that fact. The food will, too; there is a light touch on everything, even the fried onion rings and the Thai chicken quesadilla. Lots of healthy items like applewood-smoked salmon, bruschetta, and three-bean chili. Heartier appetites might go for the fish-and-chips, meat loaf, or pesto shrimp. $16–30.

✪ ✿ **Vin 909** (443-415-9708; www.vin909 .com), 909 Bay Ridge Ave. Owner Alex Manfredonia and chef Justin Moore met while working in restaurants throughout California and have brought their experience back to Alex's native Annapolis—and all who dine here are the lucky recipients of their decision to do so. With an emphasis on Mediterranean cuisine, the menu consists of small plates designed to encourage guests to share. My companion and I enjoyed the wood-chip smoked pizza with a heavenly thin crust (mozzarella made fresh in-house), muffeletta panini, shrimp casoullet, and wild boar meatballs. We started to share a dessert, but one bite of the chocolate pot de crème convinced us that we each wanted one of our own.

Without a doubt, Vin 909 is currently my favorite Annapolis area restaurant. The cuisine is new, fresh, and ever changing and incorporates as many local ingredients as possible. Although I have placed Vin 909 in the *Eating Out* category because of its low prices and casual atmosphere, make no mistake, this is fine dining at its best. $9–25.

Forest Plaza Shopping Center

Jalapeños (410-266-7580; www.jalapenos online.com), 85 Forest Dr. Open for lunch Mon.–Sat.; dinner daily. Gonzalo Fernandez and Alberto Serranco serve up foods from Spain and Mexico, and you can choose items from either or both countries in one meal. A house favorite is the *gambas alajillo*—shrimp sautéed in olive oil, garlic, tomatoes, and dry sherry. Paella, enchiladas, and other entrées $11.95–22.95.

CRABS

Annapolis

✦ **Cantler's Riverside Inn** (410-757-1311; www.cantlers.com), 458 Forest Beach Rd., near Annapolis. Open daily for lunch and dinner. Cantler's own boats bring the seafood in daily, so you know it is fresh. Many B&B owners directed me to this scenic Mill Creek spot when I inquired about the best place in Annapolis for steamed hard-shell crabs (market price). There are also many types of fresh fish and meat entrées to choose from. $10.95–26.95.

Edgewater

Mike's Restaurant and Crab House (410-956-2784; www.mikescrabhouse.com), 3030 Old Riva Rd. Open daily for lunch and dinner. On the South River waterfront, Mike's serves steamed crabs by the dozen or by the bushel (market price). Other seafood available for lunch and dinner ($17.95–29.95). Takes on a festive atmosphere on the outside deck every day in summer and has live music on Fri. night.

COFFEE BARS

Annapolis

City Dock Coffee Company (410-263-9747; www.citydockcafe.com), 71 Maryland Ave. Enjoy a cappuccino as you sit on the window couch watching the rest of Annapo-

lis walk by. There is another location that is actually on the City Dock.

Also see **49 West Coffeehouse** under *Eating Out* and **Hard Bean Café** under *Bookstores.*

SNACKS AND GOODIES *✦* A. L.

Goodies General Store (1-800-898-9701), 112 Main St., Annapolis. They make all of their items—fudge, cookies, peanut brittle, lemonade, and more—from scratch, and you can watch them do it.

Annapolis Ice Cream Company (443-482-3895; www.annapolisicecream.com), 196 Main St., Annapolis. Nothing could be better than a dip or two of super-premium (17 percent butterfat) ice cream after walking around town on a hot summer day. These folks are scrupulous with what is put into their product—no high fructose corn syrup, no artificial flavors, coloring, or preservatives. The fruit flavor comes from fresh fruit, the vanilla is a pure extract, and only fresh brewed coffee is used to make the coffee-flavored ice creams. *The place* to get ice cream in the waterfront area.

Great Harvest Bread Co. (410-268-4662; www.greatharvest.com), 208 Ridgely Ave., Annapolis. Closed Sun. and Mon. The owners and employees are up and working early in the morning to deliver more than a dozen types of baked goodies (the caramel chip scones are great!) by 7 AM and at least two dozen varieties of bread by 9 AM. (Not all are available each day.) Great Harvest grinds its own wheat fresh every day.

✦ **Storm Brothers Ice Cream Factory** (410-263-3376; www.stormbros.com), 130 Dock St., Annapolis. A wide variety of flavors in a family-owned business at the waterfront.

✳ Entertainment

DANCE & **Ballet Theatre of Maryland** (410-263-8289; www.balletmaryland.org), 801 Chase St., Annapolis. The professional troupe's season usually runs from Oct. into Apr. and consists of at least four different programs. The ballet has been offering live music along with its dance performances during a few of its presentations over the last few seasons.

FILM Among others in the area, **Bowtie Theaters of Annapolis** (410-224-1145; www.bowtiecinemas.com), 2474 Solomons Island Rd.; **Cinemark Egyptian** (443-755-8990; www.cinemark.com), 7000 Arundel Mills Circle; and **UA Marley Station** (410-760-3300; www.regmovies.com), 7900 Governor Ritchie Hwy., Glen Burnie, show first-run movies.

MUSIC Annapolis Opera (410-267-8135; www.annapolisopera.org), Maryland Hall for Arts, 801 Chase St., Annapolis. The season runs from Sept. into Apr. There are usually two or three full operas (with electronic English subtitles) and several other concerts during the season. *La Bohème* and *Don Giovanni* are a couple of past productions.

Annapolis Symphony Orchestra (410-269-1132; www.annapolissymphony.org), 801 Chase St., Annapolis. The city's professional music organization offers classical, pops, family, and chamber music presentations throughout the year.

NIGHTLIFE ⛾ **Rams Head Tavern and and Rams Head On Stage** (410-268-4545; www.ramsheadgroup.com), 33 West St., Annapolis. Open daily. You can enjoy a good meal, a Fordham microbrew, and a nationally known act all in the same location. Past performers have included Arlo Guthrie, Livingston Taylor, Richie Havens, José Feliciano, Spyro Gyra, and Leon Redbone. Dinner/show combos are available.

THEATERS Annapolis Summer Garden Theatre (410-268-9212; www.summergarden.com), 143 Compromise St., Annapolis. Comedies and musicals are presented in an outdoor setting Thurs.–Sun. in the evening Memorial Day–Labor Day.

Colonial Players (410-268-7373; www.cplayers.com), 108 East St., Annapolis. This acting troupe's season usually runs from Sept. into Apr. This is a great place to see theatrical works that are well known but not presented that often on stage. Past productions have included *The Trip to Bountiful, Hay Fever,* and *To Gillian on Her 37th Birthday.*

✴ Selective Shopping

ANTIQUES

Blue Crab Antiques (443-949-7055; www.bluecrabantiques.com), 55 Maryland Ave., Annapolis. Closed Mon. Not a "flea market" antiques store. There are some real treasures here, many of them priced in the thousands of dollars.

Bon Vivant (410-263-9651; www.bonvivantantiques.com), 104 Annapolis St., Annapolis. Furniture, glassware, dolls, toys, plus designer pieces by local artists.

ART GALLERIES

Annapolis/downtown/City Dock
Annapolis Marine Art Gallery (410-263-4100; 1-800-410-0727; www.annapolismarineart.com), 110 Dock St. Open daily. Befitting the Sailing Capital of the World, the gallery presents only marine art—paintings, graphics, ship models, scrimshaw, and more—produced by living artists.

ArtFX (410-990-4540; www.artfxgallery.org), 3 Church Circle. Closed Mon. A cooperative venture of approximately 25 artists, so you will find items in just about every medium possible. You can meet a new featured artist on the first Sun. of every month 6–9 PM.

Aurora Gallery (410-263-9150; www.auroragallery.net), 67 Maryland Ave. Changing exhibits by local and regional artisans in a variety of styles and media.

La Petite Galerie (410-268-2425), 39 Maryland Ave. Closed Mon., Tues., and Wed. Works by Chinese, French-Russian, American, and local artists.

Main St. Gallery (410-276-7166; www.mainstreetfineart.com), 216A Main St. A variety of art in all media from local, regional, and national artists. Monthly showings.

Maria's Picture Place (410-263-8282; www.mariaspictureplace.com), 45 Maryland

Ave., Annapolis. Open daily. The shop to go to if you're looking for good quality prints, photography, or artwork of scenes from Annapolis, the naval academy, or the Chesapeake Bay. All artists are from the area.

Maryland Federation of Art Gallery on the Circle (410-268-4566; www.mdfedart .org), 18 State St. Closed Mon. The exhibits in all media by local and regional artists change monthly in the nonprofit organization's gallery. A good place to catch rising or promising artists early in their career.

McBride Gallery (410-267-7077; www .mcbridegallery.com), 215 Main St. Open daily. The city's largest gallery contains seven rooms of landscapes, wildlife paintings, and nautical scenes.

☞ **Mitchell Art Gallery** (410-626-2556; www.sjca.edu), 60 College Ave. Closed Mon. St. John's College's art gallery features changing exhibits of high-quality works in a variety of media. Also sponsors tours, lectures, and children's programs.

BOOKSTORES

Annapolis/downtown/City Dock

Annapolis Bookstore (410-280-2339; www.annapolisbookstore.com), 68 Maryland Ave. New and used books and a café. The business card of this small, but fully stocked, shop says that they "specialize in maritime history, sailing, the classics and anything that strikes our fancy."

Hard Bean Café (410-263-8770), 36 Market Space. Although this is primarily a coffeehouse and café, the walls are lined with close to 10,000 cut-out and discounted books—a place to find a bargain.

U.S. Naval Institute Bookstore (410-293-2108; www.usni.org), Preble Hall, U.S. Naval Academy, 52 King George St. (entrance is at Gate 1). The number of books pertaining to seamanship and naval history, American and worldwide, is just short of phenomenal.

MALLS

Annapolis

Annapolis Harbour Center (410-266-5857; www.annapolisharbourcenter.com),

US 50 Exit 22. Contains a Barnes & Noble bookstore, other national chains, and a multiplex.

Westfield Annapolis (410-266-5432; www.westfield.com), 2002 Annapolis Mall. Located 4 miles from downtown.

Hanover

Arundel Mills (410-540-5110; www .arundelmillsmall.com), at the intersection of I-295 and MD 100 (near the Baltimore/ Washington International Thurgood Marshall Airport). The area's largest mall attracts shoppers from Baltimore, Annapolis, and Washington, DC.

SPECIAL SHOPS

Capital Comics (410-216-9711; www.capitalcomicsmd.com), 207 Main St., Annapolis. You could spend a fortune on the thousands of comics and collectible figurines available here.

Historic Annapolis Foundation Museum Store (410-268-5576; 1-800-639-9153), 77 Main St., Annapolis. This little shop gets my vote as the best place to obtain mementos of your visit to the area. In addition to pottery, jewelry, glassware, and books, the store offers many items that relate to the history of Annapolis.

Ka-Chunk Records (410-571-5047; on facebook), 78 Maryland Ave., Annapolis. Open daily. Those who say that vinyl records have gone the way of the dinosaur need to visit Ka-Chunk Records. Their stock includes more than seven hundred artists in the new vinyl section, along with hundreds of used LPs and even some limited edition screen prints.

♥ **Paws Pet Boutique** (410-263-8683; www.pawsannapolis.com), 64 State Circle, Annapolis. In addition to handmade doggie treats shaped like crabs, there are also selections of handmade toys, leash racks, and jewelry for you and your pet's enjoyment.

Plat du Jour (410-269-1499; www.platdu jour.net), 210 Main St., Annapolis. You would have to travel to Italy or France to find the selection of linens, glassware, ceramics, and artwork that you can purchase here.

FARMER'S MARKETS

Anne Arundel County Farmer's Market (410-570-3646; http://aacofarmersmarket.com), Riva Rd. and Harry S. Truman Pkwy., Annapolis. Apr.–early Dec. Usually on Sat. and Tues. 7–noon. Days and hours may change late in the season.

Deale Farmer's Market (410-570-3646), Deale-Churchton Rd., Deale. Produce dealers bring their wares to the Cedar Grove Methodist Church parking lot in the southern part of Anne Arundel County on Thurs. 4–7, July–Oct.

FRESHFARM Markets (202-362-8889; www.freshfarmmarkets.org), Donner parking lot next to the Annapolis Harbor. Sun. 8–noon. Supports local farmers and producers from Maryland and surrounding states.

Piney Orchard Farmer's Market (410-672-4273; http://pineyorchardfarmersmkt.nova-antiques.com), Stream Valley Rd. (off MD 170), Odenton. Wed. 2–6:30, June–Oct.

Severna Park Farmer's Market (410-841-5770), MD 2 and Jones Station Rd., Severna Park. Look for fresh fruits and vegetables Sat. 8–noon from mid-Apr. through late Nov.

PICK-YOUR-OWN PRODUCE FARMS

Mt. Airy U-Pick (410-798-0838), 832 Mt. Airy Rd., Davidsonville. Planters Jim and Tim Hopkins request that you call first before heading out to choose your own strawberries from mid-May through mid-June.

✳ Special Events

April: **County Fair Craft Show** (410-923-3400; www.aacountyfair.org), fairgrounds, Crownsville. More than one hundred artists and craftspeople show their wares. **Annual Wildlife Art Show and Sale** (301-497-5789), Patuxent Research Refuge, National Wildlife Visitors Center.

May: **Chesapeake Bay Blues Festival** (410-257-7413; www.bayblues.org), Sandy Point State Park.

June: **Annapolis Greek Festival** (410-573-2072; www.annapolisgreekfestival.org), Ss. Constantine and Helen Greek Orthodox Church on Riva Rd, Annapolis. Foods, crafts, and music.

July: **Annapolis Irish Festival** (410-980-7971; www.annapolisirishfestival.com), Fairgrounds, Annapolis. Music, workshops (especially for children), and contests like Best Legs in a Kilt, Most Freckles, and Best Head of Red Hair.

August: **Rotary Crab Feast** (1-800-327-1982; www.annapolisrotary.com), Annapolis. Thought to be the largest crab feast in the world. So many people attend that it is held in the U.S. Navy–Marine Corps Stadium. **Kunta Kinte Celebration** (410-349-0338; www.kuntakinte.org), Annapolis. A two-day celebration of African American history, arts, and entertainment. Children's tent and ethnic foods.

September: **Anne Arundel County Fair** (410-923-3400; www.aacountyfair.org), fairgrounds, Crownsville. **Annual Maryland Seafood Festival** (410-266-3113; www.mdseafoodfestival.com), Sandy Point State Park, Annapolis. Arts and crafts, beach golf, and lots of other family-oriented activities in addition to mounds of Chesapeake Bay seafood prepared various ways. **Drum Corps Associates World Championships** (917-528-9340; www.dcacorps.org), Navy-

---

𝄞 **Maryland Renaissance Festival** (410-266-7304; 1-800-296-7304; www.rennfest.com), on Crownsville Rd. in Crownsville. Held every weekend late Aug.–late Oct. Adults $17–22; seniors $15–19; children 7–15 are $8–10; special prices for multiday visits. Go back in time to 16th-century England and watch knights in armor joust on horseback, eat a turkey leg so big that it would have choked even Henry VIII, and watch comedies and tragedies unfold on 10 theatrical stages. The atmosphere of this festival is one of grand celebration. Visitors, as well as volunteers, show up in period dress and never break character for a moment. Many children's activities and much food and music from those merry old days.

Marine Corps Memorial Stadium, Annapolis. More than 40 drum corps compete in front of 13,000 performers and fans. **Deale Bluegrass Festival and Car Show** (410-867-6707), Herrington Harbor North Marina, Deale.

October: **United States Sailboat Show and United States Powerboat Show** (410-268-8828; www.usboat.com), Annapolis City Dock. These shows run back to back over two weekends and are the country's oldest and largest in-water boat shows. They attract tens of thousands of vendors and enthusiasts from around the world. **Anne Arundel Scottish Highland Games** (410-849-2849), Anne Arundel Fairgrounds, Crownsville. A clans' gathering that includes dancing, piping, fiddling, sheepdog demonstrations, children's games, and livestock exhibitions. A variety of Scottish goods for sale, too. **Fall Crafts Festival** (410-923-3400; www.aacountyfair.org), fairgrounds, Crownsville. More than one hundred crafters, entertainment, flower and pumpkin sales.

November: **Annapolis by Candlelight** (410-267-78146; www.annapolis.org), Annapolis. An annual self-guided tour of private homes and public sites in the city's historic district.

December: **Eastport Yacht Club Lights Parade** (410-263-0415), Annapolis Harbor. The state's oldest lighted boat parade usually has more than 70 lighted boats.

Capital Region 3

LAUREL, COLLEGE PARK, BOWIE,
AND UPPER MARLBORO

SILVER SPRING, BETHESDA,
ROCKVILLE, AND GAITHERSBURG

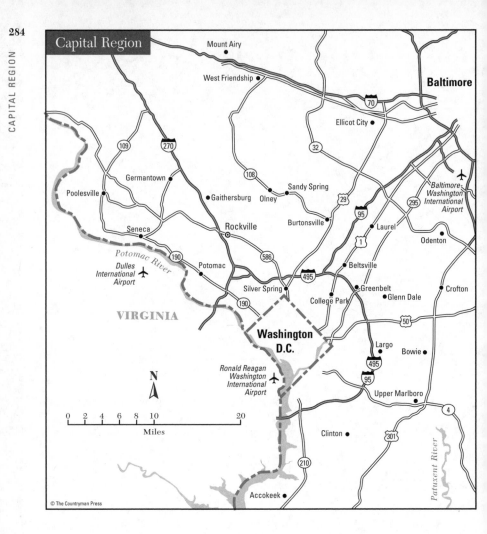

Capital Region

CAPITAL REGION

Getting a handle on just what is available, and where it is located, can be difficult in the Capital Region, that portion of Maryland around Washington, DC. An ever-expanding population, spurred on by ever-increasing federal and state bureaucracies, has transformed the once agrarian landscape. It is now a place of sprawling housing developments, large business parks and office buildings, and scores of malls and other shopping centers. Town lines have blurred, and it is often hard to tell where one ends and another begins.

This can be a good thing for travelers and explorers, however. You are, of course, right next door to Washington, DC, and can make quick forays into the city without having to pay its inflated lodging rates. You also don't have to drive very far to take in most of the Capital Region's museums, galleries, parks, restaurants, shopping areas, and other attractions.

Laurel, College Park, Bowie, and Upper Marlboro

The Laurel Museum
★ Laurel
195
97
29
32
Montpelier
Mansion ★
270
95
1
PATUXENT RESEARCH
REFUGE/NATIONAL
WILDLIFE VISITOR
193
CENTER
Beltsville
NASA/Goddard
Space Flight
3
Greenbelt
Visitor Center
Museum
Dorsey
Chapel
197
Belair Stable
★
★
★
★ Belair Mansion
College Park
564 Glenn Dale
★ Aviation Museum
193
Bowie
Hyattsville
Riverdale
Lanham
50
301
Riversdale
New Carrollton
Mansion Museum ★
50
Washington
Chevery
193
D.C.
★ Andover Hills
Mitchellville
214
202
214
Largo
★ Watkins Regional Park
495
Ronald Reagan
Washington
95
National
Suitland
202
395
Airport
4 Upper Marlboro ⊙
495
95
4
● Oxon Hill
★ Oxon Hill Manor
Surratt House
★ Museum
Clinton
His Lordship's
301
VIRGINIA
Kindness ★
Duvall Tool Museum
★
& Patuxent River Park
★
Merkle Wildlife Sanctuary
Fort ●
Washington
223
5
★ Fort Washington Park
Brandywine
★
Piscataway Park
Accokeek ●
CEDARVILLE
STATE FOREST
210
5
N

0 1 2 3 4 5   10
Miles
301

Patuxent River

Potomac River

© The Countryman Press

© The Countryman Press

LAUREL, COLLEGE PARK, BOWIE, AND UPPER MARLBORO

Laurel was one of the area's first industrial centers. Early in the 1800s, members of a prominent Quaker family, the Snowdens, developed iron mines and furnaces, and operated gristmills and cotton mills. The Laurel Museum helps preserve those times. By the early 1900s, most of these businesses had closed, but due to Laurel's proximity to Washington, DC, the town's population has only continued to grow and is now dominated by shopping centers, restaurants, and other services associated with bedroom communities. Yet, the old downtown area retains a number of buildings and other structures from the early days, and the City of Laurel Walking Tour pamphlet (available from the Prince George's County, Maryland, Conference and Visitor's Bureau, Inc.) points out the 1840 Methodist meeting-house, the first automobile repair garage between Baltimore and Washington, DC (Babe Ruth had his car repaired here), and the oldest row houses still standing in Prince George's County.

Life in College Park focuses upon the University of Maryland, and businesses clustered around the school reflect the liberal lifestyles of the 35,000 students. The university's Clarice Smith Performing Arts Center is a theatrical showplace that provides the town with a cultural event of some kind or another almost every day of the year.

Unbeknown to many of the state's citizens, Bowie is Maryland's fifth largest municipal entity. It quickly grew as a transportation center around two railroad lines that junctioned here soon after the Civil War. Although the city has expanded to encompass 16 square miles, the old part of town has retained its early charms. A brochure detailing a self-guided tour of historic sites is also available from the Prince George's County, Maryland, Conference and Visitor's Bureau.

Although it is the county seat of Prince George County, the municipal boundary of Upper Marlboro is quite small. Once a thriving center of trade for the tobacco grown around it, the town lost some of its prominence when large-scale plantations began to fail and modern highways passed it by. Those roadways did, however, enable scores of housing developments to spring up on former agricultural lands.

For a region with such a dense population, the area has a surprising amount of land set aside for recreational and open-space use. Patuxent Research Refuge encompasses 13,000 acres; 6,000 acres along the Potomac River are preserved by Piscataway Park; and state and regional parks, forests, and preserves ensure that thousands of other acres will escape any future development.

GUIDANCE The **Prince George's County, Maryland, Conference and Visitor's Bureau, Inc.** (301-925-8300; www.visitprincegeorges.com), is located in a modern office building within a business park at 9200 Basil Court, Suite 101, Largo, 20774. There is ample free parking, but you may have to drive around the building to find an open space.

GETTING THERE *By car:* **US 50** cuts across the northern part of this region, arriving from Washington, DC, in the west and continuing to the Eastern Shore in the east. The **Baltimore–Washington Parkway (I-195)** connects those two cities and provides access to the northwestern part of the region. **US 301** crosses the Potomac River on a toll bridge, arriving from Virginia's Northern Neck.

By air: **Ronald Reagan Washington National Airport** (703-417-8000; www.metwash airports.com/reagan/reagan.htm) in northern Virginia and **Baltimore/Washington International Thurgood Marshall Airport** (1-800-I-FLY-BWI; www.bwiairport.com) between Baltimore and Washington are within a 30-minute drive. Both have bus and rail connections that can bring you into this region.

By bus: **Greyhound** (1-800-231-2222; www.greyhound.com) makes stops at the New Carrollton Metro Station, 4700 Garden City Dr., Landover.

By rail: **AMTRAK** (1-800-USA-RAIL; www.amtrak.com) makes a stop in New Carrollton during its New York–Washington, DC, run.

GETTING AROUND *By car:* **I-495 (Capital Beltway), I-195, US 50, US 301,** and **MD 201** are four-lane highways, but expect heavy traffic on all of them throughout most of the daylight hours.

By bus: **MTA** (1-866-743-3682; www.mtamaryland.com) buses connect and make stops in all of the major cities and towns in the region. **The Prince George's County Bus System** (301-324-BUSS) provides service on a more local level, enabling you to visit most of the attractions listed in this region without having to drive to them.

By rail: **MARC** commuter rail service enables you to visit many of the towns in this area, as well as Baltimore and Washington, DC, without the hassle of driving a car. **Metrorail** (202-637-7000; www.wmata.com) provides the same service from Capitol Heights, Cheverly, Landover, New Carrollton, College Park, and a few other sites. (Also see *By bus.*)

MEDICAL EMERGENCY A number of hospitals have the facilities to handle an emergency should one arise:

Greater Laurel Beltsville Hospital (301-725-4300; www.dimensionshealth.org/website /c/lrh), 7300 Van Dusen St., Laurel.

Doctor's Community Hospital (301-552-8118; www.dchweb.org), 8118 Good Luck Rd., Lanham.

Prince George's Hospital Center (301-618-2000; www.dimensionshealth.org/website/c /pghc), 3001 Hospital Dr., Cheverly.

Southern Maryland Hospital Center (301-868-8000; www.medstarsouthernmaryland .org), 7503 Surratts Rd., Clinton.

✳ To See

COLLEGES **University of Maryland** (301-405-1000; www.maryland.edu), College Park. The university began as an agricultural college in the mid-1800s; in 1988 it joined a statewide system that includes numerous other campuses, with a total enrollment of more than 130,000 students. The school offers a full range of graduate and undergraduate courses, but possibly its most interesting facet for a visitor is the **Clarice Smith Performing Arts Cen-**

BOWIE RAILROAD STATION AND HUNTINGTON MUSEUM

ter. Opened in 2001, the $130 million, 318,000-square-foot center has performance halls, galleries, studios, and rehearsal rooms. See *Entertainment* for information on performances presented by the various art disciplines.

MUSEUMS

Bowie

Bowie Railroad Station and Huntington Museum (301-575-2488; www.cityofbowie .org), 8606 Chestnut Ave. Open Tues.–Sun. noon–4. Donations accepted. The town of Bowie grew up at the junction of two rail lines, and a small depot, control tower, and passenger shelter have a few photos and implements from the early days, starting around 1872. Rail fans take note: The station is next to AMTRAK and MARC tracks, and with more than three dozen trains passing by here every day, you can do some great trainspotting. The adjacent small museum, which also serves as the town's welcome center, has a few more photos and items of historical note.

Clinton

Surratt House Museum (301-868-1121; www.surratt.org), 9118 Brandywine Rd. Wed., Thurs., and Fri. 11–3, mid-Jan. through mid-Dec.; Sat. and Sun. noon–4. Small admission fee. Period-dressed guides present a balanced account of the role John and Mary Surratt played in Lincoln's assassination. Their middle-class home was a tavern, post office, inn, and safe house in southern Maryland's Confederate underground. John Wilkes Booth stopped here during his escape from Washington, DC, to retrieve weapons and supplies, and the upstairs bedroom is furnished as it would have been at that time. The museum also sponsors a 12-hour bus trip, the John Wilkes Booth Escape Route Tour, which makes stops at significant sites on his flight through Maryland. Dates, times, and fees vary; call for the latest information.

College Park

✔ **College Park Aviation Museum** (301-864-6029; www.collegeparkaviation museum.com), 1985 Corporal Frank Scott Dr. Open daily; small admission fee. The museum is adjacent to **College Park Airport,** the world's oldest continuously operating airport, and celebrates its many aviation firsts: the first American female passenger, the training of the first military pilots (by Wilbur Wright), the first U.S. Postal Air Mail service, and more. There is a multitude of kid-friendly interactive exhibits and a number of historic aircraft—like the plane Gus McCloud flew over the North Pole. You are even permitted to sit in a Taylorcraft airplane. The upstairs contains changing exhibits and a balcony to view the aircraft from a different angle.

LEARNING HISTORY AT THE SURRATT HOUSE

Greenbelt

&. **Greenbelt Museum** (301-507-6582; www.greenbeltmuseum.org), 10-B Crescent Rd. Sun. 1–5. Free admission. The small museum is actually one of the planned community's original houses (for more information on this community, see Greenbelt Park under *Parks*). It lends insight into the lives of those who lived here when Greenbelt first opened during the Great Depression. The two bedrooms, bath, living room, and kitchen are decorated with the original furniture constructed specifically for the community. Within walking distance is the art deco–style community center, with friezes on the outside wall depicting the preamble to the Constitution and exhibits inside pertaining to life in Greenbelt.

Laurel

Laurel Museum (301-725-7975; www.laurelmuseum.org), Main and Ninth Sts. Wed. and Fri. 10–2; Sun. 1–4. Free admission. The 1830 mill workers' house contains photographs, tools, personal belongings, and other items depicting the town as a thriving mill center in the early 1800s.

Suitland

Airmen Memorial Museum (301-899-8386; 1-800-638-0594; www.hqafsa.org), 5211 Auth Rd. Open Mon.–Fri. Donations accepted. Uniforms, photographs, bombsights, and more highlight the history, bravery, and heroism of airmen from all branches of the U.S. military, from aviation's earliest days to present.

Upper Marlboro

&. **Duvall Tool Museum** (301-627-6074; history.pgparks.com), 16000 Croom Airport Rd., Patuxent River Park. Sun. 1–4. W. Henry Duvall scoured the countryside for more than 50 years, buying old farm, home, and hand tools used during the 1800s. His collection of 1,000 pieces is now housed in this museum.

HISTORIC HOMES

Bowie

&. **Belair Mansion and Stable Museum** (301-809-3089; www.cityofbowie.org), 12207 Tulip Grove Dr. Days and times that this attraction is open seem to change constantly, but it has always been open Sun. 1–4. Donations accepted. Self-guided tours of the 1700s five-part

BELAIR STABLES IN BOWIE

Georgian mansion take in many original pieces of furniture that help interpret its 300-year history.

The largest cucumber tree of its kind in the state (planted in 1820) is located on the terraced grounds leading down to the stables. From the 1930s to the 1950s, this was one of the premier racing stables in the country and was the home of Gallant Fox and Omaha, the only father-and-son horses to win the coveted Triple Crown. Individual stalls contain separate and distinct displays chronicling thoroughbred racing in America.

Clinton

Poplar Hill on His Lordship's Kindness (301-856-0358; www.poplarhillonhlk.com), 7606 Woodyard Rd. Thurs. and Fri. 10–4, Sun. noon–4 Mar.–Dec. Schedule has been known to change; call ahead. Small admission fee for self-guided tour. This National Historic Landmark was named by Col. Henry Darnell in gratitude for the 7,000-acre land grant given to him by Lord Baltimore. The architecture and many features in the house are original; however, it is furnished as it would have been in the 1950s, when the last owners, John and Sarah Walton, lived there.

Laurel

Montpelier Mansion (301-377-7817; http://history.pgparks.com), Muirkirk Rd. and MD 197. Tours given on the hour Sun.–Thurs. noon–3 (at 1 and 2 Jan. and Feb.); please note that this schedule has been known to change frequently. Small admission fee. Guided 60-minute tours take visitors through the late-1700s Georgian home of Thomas and Anne Ridgely Snowden. Furnished with period pieces based upon an 1831 inventory of their belongings. The dining room contains some original family pieces; also on display is the wedding dress of the Snowdens' granddaughter. If not discussed during your tour, ask your guide to show you the secret trapdoor and hidden stairway. Also, lovers of grand old trees should not miss taking a stroll on the grounds.

The **Montpelier Arts Center** (301-377-7800; http://arts.pgparks.com) is adjacent to the mansion. Self-guided tours (daily 10–5) enable visitors to watch sculptors, painters, printmakers, and other craftspeople at work.

Riverdale

Riverdale Mansion (301-864-0420; http://history.pgparks.com), 4811 Riverdale Rd. Sun. noon–4. Small admission fee for a 60-minute guided tour. Open Fri. and Sun. A National Historic Landmark, the five-part, stucco-covered plantation home of George Calvert, grandson of the fifth Lord Baltimore, has been restored and furnished to reflect the early 1800s. The mahogany handrail and some of the furnishings are original, and be sure to ask a docent to provide background on the scenic wallpaper in the study.

MONTPELIER MANSION

Upper Marlboro

Darnell's Chance (301-952-8010; http://history.pgparks.com), 14800 Governor Oden Bowie Dr. Open for guided tours Fri.–Sat noon–4. Small admission fee. Built in 1742 by a successful businessman who married Lettice Lee of the famous Lee family of Virginia. The house has undergone many changes through the years, but it has now been restored to look as it would have in the mid-1700s. The focus of the tours is not so much on the house, but rather to relate and compare Lettice Lee's life with the lives of other women of her day. You'll get glimpses into the upper class, the average citizen, and the enslaved. Ask to be taken to the underground burial vault outside if you guide neglects to. It is one of only two known such vaults in the state.

SITES ALONG THE POTOMAC RIVER There is a succession of protected lands strung along the east bank of the Potomac River. They preserve and interpret bits of history and provide spectacular views across the wide river to Washington, DC, and Alexandria and Mount Vernon in Virginia. They can all be accessed from **MD 210,** and from north to south are:

Oxon Hill

✍ **Oxon Cove Park/Oxon Hill Farm** (301-839-1176; www.nps.gov/oxhi), 6411 Oxon Hill Rd. Free admission and parking. The 512-acre property is operated as a working farm of the late 1950s by the National Park Service. It is a great place for urban children to find out about country life. I've watched entire groups become amazed when a ranger reaches under a cow and squeezes some milk into a pail. Chickens, sheep, and donkeys wander around in pens next to fields of corn, sorghum, and wheat. The farmhouse, barn filled with historic agricultural equipment, and a visitors center help round out the story. The horses stabled here are the ones that pull the White House tree through the streets of Washington, DC, at Christmastime. Short hiking and biking trails wind into fields and woods, and down to the river. Great views of Alexandria, Virginia.

Fort Foote Park, Fort Foote Rd. A small picnic area on the site of a pre–Civil War fort. A few of the old ramparts and guns remain. Nice views across the river.

Fort Washington

Fort Washington Park (301-763-4600; www.nps.gov/fowa), 13661 Fort Washington Rd. Open daily. Small entrance fee per car. You can take a self-guided tour or a ranger-narrated

LEARNING TO MILK A COW AT OXON HILL FARM

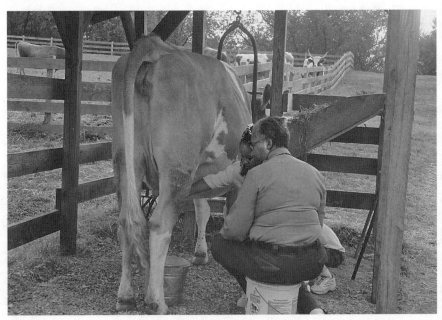

walk (times and dates vary) of the early-1800s fort, built on the site of an earlier one destroyed by the British in the War of 1812. Cannons, ramparts, earthworks, and displays in the visitors center help interpret the fort's important history as the first line of defense of the nation's capital. As a journalist once remarked, "We know our country is safe as long as we see the garrison flag at Fort Washington." Impressive view of Washington, DC.

A COSTUMED DOCENT AT THE NATIONAL COLONIAL FARM

Accokeek

✧ **National Colonial Farm and Piscataway Park** (301-283-2113; www.nps.gov /pisc; www.accokeek.org), 3400 Bryan Point Rd. Tues.–Sun., mid-Mar. through mid-Dec.; open on weekends the rest of the year. Small admission fee. The farm is operated by the nonprofit Accokeek Foundation as a living-history demonstration of a typical 1800s farm owned by a colonial family of modest means. Many of the plants and animals are heritage breeds—meaning they are no longer part of mainstream farming and are in danger of disappearing.

Self-guided tours (or guided tours on weekends) take you by structures and gardens, all built and tended with period practices and implements. A ferryboat (a replica of an 1800s riverboat) crosses the Potomac to Mount Vernon, Virginia, on weekends to provide insight into how the upper classes fared during colonial days. The foundation also sponsors an eco-farm, on which local volunteers work to create organic produce.

The colonial farm is within the 6-mile-long, 4,000-acre **Piscataway Park,** created by the National Park Service to protect the views of Mount Vernon. Numerous trails, some along the Potomac River, meander through the property and provide easy escapes from the modern world.

HISTORIC CHURCHES Dorsey Chapel (240-264-3415; www.pgparks.com), 10704 Brookland Rd., Glen Dale. Open the first and third Sunday of each month. Small admission fee. The small frame meetinghouse-style church was in use by the local African American community throughout most of the 1900s.

OTHER SITES

Greenbelt

✧ ♿ **NASA/Goddard Space Flight Visitors Center** (301-286-8981; www.nasa.gov/centers /goddard), Explorer Rd. Closed Mon. Free admission. Goddard is the center of NASA's spaceflight-tracking activities. There are many presentations, interactive displays, programs, and the opportunity to view the working areas of communications operations, satellite control, and spacecraft construction.

Laurel

✧ **National Wildlife Visitors Center in Patuxent Research Refuge** (301-497-5580; www.fws.gov), 10901 Scarlet Tanager Loop. (Also see the sidebar on page 297.) Open daily. Free admission. The National Wildlife Visitors Center is by far the largest and best facility of its kind that I have ever seen. The quality and quantity of its displays and exhibits outshine many museums for which you pay a fee to visit. Hands-on activities, multimedia presentations, and life-sized dioramas not only portray the natural drama of the refuge but also examine global environmental issues, different habitats around the world, and the behavior of a wide variety of animals. Be sure to allot a few hours to take it all in; what you learn here will add greatly to outings you happen to take anywhere in the natural world.

GUIDED TOURS See Surratt House Museum under *Museums*.

SCENIC DRIVES ✔ **Chesapeake Bay Critical Area Driving Tour** (301-627-6074; www.pgparks.com), 16000 Croom Airport Rd., **Patuxent River Park** (see *Green Space*), Upper Marlboro. Open to automobiles Sun. 10–3; open to walkers and bicycles Sat. Originating at the entrance of the Jug Bay Natural Area of Patuxent River Park, the 4-mile, self-guided drive highlights the natural resources of the river and the Chesapeake Bay. Passing over wetlands on an elevated boardwalk, it has tidal marshes, forests, a 40-foot observation tower with a grand view of the river, and glimpses of wildlife. I think this is one of the best and, since you are driving and not walking, easiest introductions to a variety of the state's environments.

✳ To Do

BICYCLING **Washington, Baltimore, and Annapolis Trail** (301-699-2407; www.pgparks.com). The 5.6-mile trail follows an old electric railroad grade from Glen Dale to the Patuxent River.

ONE OF THE SIX FLAGS ROLLER COASTERS

Anacostia Trails (301-210-3788; www.pgparks.com). A system of trails, multiple miles in length, is open to bikers and hikers along the Anacostia River and a number of its tributaries. Some trails are nicely isolated while others go through urban areas, but they all are pleasant alternatives to driving in this region.

Also see *Scenic Drives, Hiking*, and the **Patuxent Research Refuge** sidebar on page 297.

FAMILY ACTIVITIES

Largo
✔ **Six Flags America Theme and Hurricane Harbor Water Parks** (301-249-1500; www.sixflags.com/america), 13710 Central Ave. Usually open limited days Apr.–May and Sept.–Oct., and daily June–Aug. A one-day ticket is about $60 (advance purchase online gives substantial savings; season passes are only a few dollars more and provide a number of other benefits); the ticket grants admission to both parks. From humble beginnings as a small animal-safari park, Six Flags America has grown to 140 acres (and still owns about 400 acres on which to expand). Live shows, special small-children's

rides in Looney Tunes Movie Town, and at least eight roller coasters, two of which are wooden—the Wild One (relocated in 1986 from Paragon Park in Massachusetts where it had been in operation since 1917) and ROAR, which drops 10 stories and has 20 crossovers. The Superman has a 200-foot crest and reaches 75 miles an hour on its 1.5-mile track. You ride lying down on the Batwing and stand up while hurtling along the 0.5-mile course of the Apocalypse. My wife's favorite, the Joker's Jinx, uses a set of induction motors to create a magnetic wave that propels the cars from 0 to 60 mph in just over three seconds at the very beginning of the ride. Six Flags says that the Mind Eraser was the first of its kind in the world, where your feet dangle as the ride careens around rollovers, dives, sidewinders, and spins, with an inverted loop and corkscrew finale.

Hurricane Harbor is more than the average water park that only has maybe a wave pool and a few long slides. In addition to those attractions, there are a number of innovative rides designed to get you into the water via a number of exciting ways. Riders sit on rafts that drop through a 60-foot-tall water tunnel more than 130 feet long on the Tornado. You'll be riding on inner tubes while descending down the Bahama Blast and the Paradise Plunge/Reef Runner. Leave the tubes behind and use your body to navigate the Hammerhead, a darkness-enclosed slide.

Insiders Tip: There is little shade in the park, so slather on the sunscreen before arriving, and bring a hat and cover-ups. Water fountains seem to be in short supply; bring your own or expect to purchase bottled water or other drinks.

Upper Marlboro

✿ **Watkins Regional Park** (301-249-9220; www.pgparks.com), 301 Watkins Park Dr. The 1,800-acre park provides a great variety of activities for the family. In addition to a small campground and several miles of nature trails, there are tennis courts, a miniature-golf course, and a miniature train that winds through woodlands and by the **Old Maryland Farm.** The farm is a petting zoo that provides the chance to visit livestock, participate in nature activities, and walk through organic gardens. Close to the farm is the **Chesapeake Carousel,** an early-1900s Dentzel carousel with hand-carved animals. All of these attractions are open on various days and times; contact the park office for details.

GOLF

College Park
Paint Branch (301-935-0330; www.pg parks.com), 4690 University Blvd. Like Henson Creek (see below), Paint Branch is a nine-hole course with no advance tee times. Its links are short and flat, and have small greens.

Fort Washington
Henson Creek (301-567-4646; www.pg parks.com), 7200 Sunnyside Lane. The nine-hole course is open to the public with no advance tee times—first come, first served.

Mitchellville
Enterprise Golf Course (301-249-2040; www.pgparks.com), 2802 Enterprise Rd. The par 72 course is constructed on the site of a former dairy farm and is open daily 6:30 AM–dark.

OLD MARYLAND FARM IN WATKINS REGIONAL PARK

Upper Marlboro

Marlton Golf Club (301-856-7566; www.marltongolf.com), 9413 Midland Tpke. Open to the public with bent-grass fairways, water hazards, and many sand bunkers.

MINIATURE GOLF See Watkins Regional Park under *Family Activities.*

HIKING Cedarville State Forest (301-888-1410; www.dnr.state.md.us/publiclands /southern/cedarville.asp), MD 310 and Cedarville Rd., Brandywine. Harboring some of Maryland's rare and endangered species, such as the bald eagle, red-bellied woodpecker, and diamondback terrapin, **Zekiah Swamp** is the state's largest freshwater swamp. Stretching to the southwest for approximately 20 miles, from Cedarville State Forest to the Wicomico River, it is almost a mile wide in some places.

Within the boundary of the state forest, miles of trails cross and parallel headwater streams, where the extra moisture enables the vegetation to become lush and thick. This provides a wonderful feeling of walking along a swamplike environment but without having your boots become mired in several inches of mud and ooze. In addition, the deep forest filters out much of the noise from the outside world, creating a quiet sense of isolation. Trails are also open to mountain bikers and equestrians.

Also see Oxon Cove Park/Oxon Hill Farm and National Colonial Farm and Piscataway Park under *To See; Bicycling;* Merkle Wildlife Sanctuary under *Nature-Watching;* the Patuxent Research Refuge sidebar on page 297; and *Green Space.*

KAYAKING AND CANOEING See Patuxent River Park under *Green Space.*

NATURE-WATCHING Merkle Wildlife Sanctuary (301-888-1410; www.dnr.state .md.us/publiclands/southern/merkle.asp), 11704 Fenno Rd., Upper Marlboro. The center opens at 10 daily; trails are open sunrise–sunset. Rover and Fido must be left at home. Continuing the dream of Edgar Merkle, the 2,000-acre sanctuary provides habitat for Canada geese. Trails go by ponds, wetlands, upland and bottomland forest, cultivated fields, and creeks, which provide a variety of scenery as well as habitats for plants and animals. It takes a six-page pamphlet to catalog all of the birds observed here, while raccoons, rabbits, squirrels, skunks, foxes, and white-tailed deer have been spotted making quick dashes from field to forest. A list of flowers blooming in just one month, July, contains nearly 100 species. Exhibits in the visitors center focus on the goose and local human history. An observation deck with telescopes overlooks Merkle Pond, and an extensive schedule of interpretive programs is offered throughout the year.

RACING Rosecroft (301-567-4500; 1-877-818-WINS; www.rosecroft.com), 6336 Rosecroft Dr., Fort Washington. Admission $3. Free parking. Live harness racing Fri.–Sat. Feb.–June and Nov.–Dec. starting at 6:30 PM.

✳ Green Space

PARKS

Greenbelt

Greenbelt Park (301-344-3948; www.nps.gov/gree), 6565 Greenbelt Rd. (accessed from I-495 Exit 22). It is ironic that a bureaucratic housing project ended up saving the natural environment of Greenbelt Park. The land was acquired in the 1930s by the federal government to be part of Greenbelt, one of a number of model towns within a belt of open space to be developed around the District of Columbia. Although some housing was constructed, the project never progressed as hoped, and the government sold the buildings to a local cooperative. Most of the remaining land became a component of the National Park Service in 1950.

THE BOARDWALK IN PISCATAWAY PARK IN ACCOKEEK MAKES A GREAT OUTDOOR CLASSROOM.

Although the park is bordered by four-lane highways on three sides, its network of more than 8 miles of trails enables you to make a quick escape from urban landscapes to sweet gum trees, blueberry bushes, and small wetlands areas. The park also has a campground and sponsors nature walks and evening programs.

Upper Marlboro

Patuxent River Park (301-627-6074; www.pgparks.com), 16000 Croom Airport Rd. Located along the river after which it was named, the 6,000-acre park contains marshes, swamps, and forests with many miles of trails. Also available are fishing piers, canoe and kayak rentals, and a number of organized hikes, boat excursions, and special events.

Also see **National Colonial Farm and Piscataway Park** under *To See.*

☃ ✇ **Patuxent Research Refuge** (301-497-5580; www.fws.gov), 10901 Scarlet Tanager Lp., Laurel. President Franklin D. Roosevelt established the refuge in 1936, and it has grown from an original 2,670 acres to nearly 13,000 acres. It supports a diversity of wildlife in a typical Maryland landscape of meadow, wetland, and forest habitats. Although the more than two hundred species of birds that are known to be in the refuge at one time or another receive the greatest share of visitors' attention, deer, beavers, squirrels, muskrats, snakes, lizards, turtles, frogs, salamanders, raccoons, rabbits, and mice are also part of the environment.

The refuge is divided into three areas. The **North Tract** offers over 10 miles of roads and trails that are open to hikers, bikers, and horseback riders. The **Central Tract** contains offices and study sites, and is closed to the public. The **South Tract** is probably the most visited portion, with a network of scenic trails (open only to foot travel), two large lakes, and a visitors center. Pets are permitted on the trails but must be leashed. Sadly for those who enjoy early morning or early evening strolls, when wildlife is most active, the South Tract is open to the public only 10–5:30. (The North Tract has longer hours; check at the visitors center.)

✳ Lodging

MOTELS AND HOTELS

Beltsville, 20705

& **Comfort Inn** (301-572-7100; www
.choicehotels.com), 4050 Powder Mill Rd.
(accessed from I-95 Exit 29). Fairly low
rates for being this close to Washington,
DC, and having a swimming pool and
exercise room. Entire inn is smoke-free.
$89–119.

Bowie, 20716

& **Hampton Inn** (301-809-1800; 1-800-
HAMPTON; http://hamptoninn3.hilton
.com), 15202 Major Lansdale Rd. All rooms
have a large desk and chair, in addition to
an iron and a hair dryer. Swimming pool.
Close to Six Flags America. $129–199.

Clinton, 20735

& **Colony South Hotel and Conference
Center** (301-856-4500; www.colonysouth
.com), 7401 Surratts Rd. (accessed from I-
495 Exit 7A). With a Cape Cod–like exterior and lush wooden interior, this place
feels more like a country lodge than a hotel
that is less than 5 miles from Pennsylvania
Ave. and downtown Washington, DC.
Rooms are quite large, there is a full-
service fitness center with indoor pool, and
free shuttle service is provided to and from
Ronald Reagan Washington National Airport in Virginia and a Metro station.
$89–149. (Also see Wayfarer under *Dining
Out.*)

College Park, 20740

& **Marriott Inn and Conference Center**
(301-985-7300; www.marriott.com/wasum),
University Blvd. and Adelphi Rd. Original
paintings and sculptures fill the spacious
public areas and hallways, calling to mind
an upscale resort more than a hotel interior.
Within a few short blocks of the University
of Maryland's Clarice Smith Performing
Arts Center, it has its own fitness room, golf
course, and jogging and walking trails.
$189–249. (See also the Garden Restaurant
under *Dining Out.*)

Largo, 20774

& **Radisson Hotel** (301-773-0700; 1-888-
201-1718; www.radissonhotel.com), 9100

Basil Court (accessed from I-495 Exit 17A).
Large and comfortable lobby and other
public areas, nicely appointed rooms,
heated indoor pool, exercise facility, and
sauna. Within a few minutes' drive of
USAir Arena and downtown Washington,
DC. $139–199.

Oxon Hill, 20745

& **Clarion** (301-749-9400; www.clarion
hotel.com), 6400 Oxon Hill Rd. (accessed
from I-495 Exit 3A). Indoor pool, weight
room, and oversized guest rooms. Very reasonable rates given its close proximity to the
attractions of Washington, DC. $109–179.

Upper Marlboro, 20774

& ☙ **Executive Inn and Suites** (301-627-
3969; http://executiveinnandsuitesmd.com),
2901 Crain Hwy. Nothing fancy here—no
swimming pool or fitness center—but all
rooms do have a refrigerator, coffee maker,
and microwave, and they will let you take
your pet into the room with you (for an
additional fee). A few Jacuzzi rooms available. $89–129.

BED & BREAKFAST

Fort Washington, 20744

Madly Living B&B (301-292-9008; www
.madlyliving.com), 11961 Autumnwood Ln.
Within a quiet residential neighborhood of
modern homes, Candice Camille and
Mariby Corpening have created what they
call "a soul-filled suburban retreat—priced
affordably chic." The four guest suites are
lavishly decorated and each has a private
bath. $159–249.

CAMPING

Brandywine, 20613

☙ **Cedarville State Forest** (301-888-
1410; www.dnr.state.md.us/publiclands
/southern/cedarville.asp), MD 310 and
Cedarville Rd. The wooded camping area,
with a central bathhouse, is open late
Mar.–early Dec. A couple of sites are
reserved for campers with pets.

Clinton, 20735

Cosca Regional Park (301-868-1397;
www.pgparks.com), 11000 Thrift Rd. A

small campground with a central comfort station.

College Park, 20740

🐾 ♿ **Cherry Hill Park** (301-937-7116; www.cherryhillpark.com), 9800 Cherry Hill Rd. The closest RV campground to Washington, DC, its 60 acres have a heated swimming pool, miniature golf, and modern facilities. A dog-walking service is offered, as well as guided tours of the nation's capital. Metro buses also make several stops a day to take visitors into Washington, DC.

Greenbelt, 20770

🐾 **Greenbelt Park** (301-344-3948; www.nps.gov/gree), 6565 Greenbelt Rd. (accessed from I-495 Exit 22). Just 12 miles from the downtown attractions of Washington, DC. The setting of the 174 spaces is a bit more forested than those found in Cherry Hill Park (see above). Other than traffic noise from nearby four-lanes, this is usually a quiet, laid-back experience. Pets permitted.

Upper Marlboro, 20774

Watkins Regional Park (park office 301-249-9220; campground 301-249-6900; www.pgparks.com), 301 Watkins Park Dr. Located next door to Six Flags America, this small campground has just over 30 sites with a restroom/shower facility in the middle of it. Be aware that there are neither hook-ups nor a dump station for RVs.

A CITY RISES BESIDE THE POTOMAC

It has been quite some time since Maryland has seen the development of an entire planned city, such as Greenbelt or Columbia. Located along the southern edge of Washington, DC, close to I-495 and the Woodrow Wilson Bridge that crosses the Potomac River into Virginia, **National Harbor** (www.nationalharbor.com) began to come together in the early 2000s and opened the first of its many businesses and buildings to the public in 2008. Scheduled to take approximately 20 years to complete, the 300-acre city will include hotels, thousands of residential units, one or more major museums, a farmer's market, and a commercial center with scores of upscale shops and offices, along with a few places of entertainment.

Although plans do not appear to include much green space like Greenbelt or Columbia, there will be at least two piers, a marina, a walkway beside the water, some tree-lined promenades in the commercial district—and an amazing amount of public art. Possibly the most notable piece is J. Seward Johnson's *The Awakening,* a colossal sculpture that depicts the arousing of a giant. It is actually five pieces, with the giant's head, hand, an outstretched arm, bent knee, and foot breaking free from the sand beside the Potomac River. *The Beckoning,* two 4,500-pound stainless-steel eagles by artist Albert Paley, rides the wind on 60-foot poles. Other public art includes two stained-glass mosaics and a terrazzo mural depicting local and regional history and scenes.

Among the businesses and attractions that were in place on my last visit were:

♿ **Aloft Hotel** (301-749-9000; www.aloftnationalharbor.com), 156 Waterfront St. Features loftlike accommodations with emphasis on connections and ports for all of your tech gadgets, walk-in showers, and a small kitchen with microwave and refrigerator. For me, however, the best thing was the huge picture window that enabled me to watch the surface of the Potomac River turn a deep crimson red at sunset. There's also a large gathering room with activities that encourage socializing with other guests. $159–279.

♿ **Gaylord National Resort and Convention Center** (301-965-2000; www.gaylord national.com), 201 Waterfront St. Occupies 41 of the city's 300 acres, with approximately 2,000 upscale guest rooms and the largest amount of space of any convention center in the Washington, DC/Baltimore area. Its atrium is so large that two full-sized, two-story replicas of colonial-era homes are dwarfed inside of it. Also within the atrium are a waterfall and fountain that perform nightly light and water shows, a number of shops, and an 18,000-square-foot garden with 1,200 trees and tens of thousands of blooming plants. Restaurants (all upscale, but with a casual dress code) include **Old Hickory Steakhouse and Lounge** (entrées $24–65); **National Pastime Bar and Grill** (sports bar with 30-foot-high definition video wall; many beers and specialty drinks; bar-food-type menu with most items below $25); and **Pienza Italian Market** (Italian offerings in a buffet-style setting; expect to spend at least $30 a person on the buffet).

Other services include a complete spa and business center. The front of the hotel is all glass and looks out upon the expanse of the Potomac River. The glass and the rest of the building absorb so much of the sun's heat that its girders and other infrastructure have rollers and springs on them to allow the building to expand and contract as much as 18 inches a day! Room rates are $300–475.

  ♿ **The Westin** (301-569-3999; www.westin.com/nationalharbor), 171 Waterfront St. Has less than 200 rooms, but it sits right on the waterfront and, because of its smaller size, has a staff that make a point to remember your name. Its restaurant, **Saucity,** has picture windows that are almost level with the Potomac River and, as the name implies, serves its meals (expect to spend about $40 a person, minus drinks or desserts) with at least two sauces, so that your entrée can have as many as four different tastes. Room rates are $150–250.

  Fiorella Pizzareia e Caffé (301-839-1811; www.fiorellapizzeria.com), 152 National Plaza. Fiorella makes pizza the way my Italian aunts always said it should be done—a thin crust so you can taste all of the fresh ingredients and not just gobs of dough. There's more than pizza here, though. The huge portion of lasagna is served "open face," the minestrone soup is made in house, and the daily fresh fish offerings are prepared one of four ways, depending on your preference. $10–30.

  ♿ **McCormick & Schmick's Seafood Restaurant** (301-567-6224; www.mccormickand schmicks.com), 145 National Harbor Plaza. Each location of this national chain has its own chef, who chooses what dishes will be offered based on what fresh fish is flown in twice daily (the

GAYLORD NATIONAL RESORT AND CONVENTION CENTER

menu is printed twice a day to reflect this). As an example, the day I dined, rainbow trout from Idaho, halibut from Alaska, tilapia from Ecuador, and salmon from Canada were on the menu, along with Maryland crabcakes and Gulf shrimp. Steaks, poultry, and pasta are also served. Desserts are made in-house, and my dining companions and I shared the creamy key lime pie and moist (made with pineapple) carrot cake. Entrées $18.95–29.95.

McLoone's Pier House (301-839-0815; www.mcloonespierhousenh.com), 141 National Harbor Plaza. Open daily for lunch and dinner. Starting with a place on the Shrewsbury River waterfront in Sea Bright, New Jersey, musician Tim McLoone has expanded his operations to include a number of places; the restaurant in National Harbor is the first to be located outside of that state. With entrées that change seasonally and specials offered based on availability, the menu has steaks, burgers, and other expected items, but the emphasis is on fresh seafood. The time I was here, the menu featured recipes perfect for summer's hot weather. The manager said the salmon grilled and topped with mandarin oranges, chopped mango, and sunset chili sauce was the most popular dish. Another well-liked entrée was the grilled mahimahi topped with pineapple chutney. I made a meal of two of the small plates—flash-fried rock shrimp tossed with chili slaw and spicy aioli (a wonderful blend of tastes with a light spicy kick) and crab bruschetta. I didn't sample any of the house-made desserts but everything on the tray the server brought tableside looked tempting, especially the key lime pie. Additional draws are the great waterside views from the inside and outside seating, and the (mostly) acoustic live music offered every evening. $18–30.

America! (301-686-0413; www.nationalharbor.com/stores/america), 177 Waterfront St. It doesn't matter if you are a Democrat, Republican, or independent, you can find some serious and not-so-serious items supportive of your political views (whether they be pro or con). Also, a good place to pick up a Maryland or Washington, DC souvenir.

Artcraft (301-567-6616; www.artcraftonline.com), 140 American Wy. A nice addition to the several eclectic shops in National Harbor. Nearly every item (jewelry, clocks, toys, blown glass and glassware, pottery, furniture, outdoor items, rugs, sculpture, wall art, and more) is handmade from artists throughout North America and even the few machine-made articles are nicely created and not often found in other places.

Art Whino (301-567-8210; www.artwhino.com), 173 Waterfront St. Was one of the first galleries to open up at National Harbor and represents more than one hundred artists, most of whom have been categorized as being edgy, urban contemporary, lowbrow, or members of the graffiti movements. Worth a visit, especially if you are unfamiliar with these styles.

Potomac Gourmet Market (301-839-2870; potomacgourmetmarket.com), 180 American Wy. An upscale grocery store with a good selection of wines, cheeses, groceries, and pre-made sandwiches and salads for those times when you don't feeling like going out and just want to spend the evening in your room.

The Potomac River Boat Company (301-684-0580; 1-877-511-2628; www.potomacriverboatco .com). Has two water taxis that run approximately 10 AM–10 PM and cross the Potomac River to Alexandria, Virginia. The round-trip cost of less than $20 a person is a bargain when compared to the several scenic cruises that are also offered. Of those, one of the best is the Mount Vernon Cruise, whose $40 ($20 children) fee includes the cost of admission to George Washington's Mount Vernon in Virginia.

Thai Pavilion (301-749-2033; www.thaipavilionnationalharbor.com), 151 American Wy. Adds one more bit of international flavor to those available in National Harbor.

Tiki and Me (301-839-3911; www.tikiandme.com), 161 Fleet St. Have a pet that you just can't seem to lavish enough attention on? This is the place for you. Apparel, choke-free harnesses, beds, bowls, treats, fine wine (yes, fine wine [alcohol-free] for your pet!), and gourmet treats.

✳ Where to Eat

DINING OUT

Clinton

✒ **Wayfarer** (301-856-4500), 7401 Surratts Rd., inside the Colony South Hotel. Open for breakfast, lunch, and dinner. Consistent with the country-lodge feel of the hotel, the restaurant's décor includes a fireplace and beamed ceilings. The menu focuses on northern Italian dishes such as veal Piccata, chicken Romana, and penne with crabmeat and spinach (market price). A lunch buffet is offered Mon.–Fri. $14–24.

EATING OUT

Beltsville

Kay's Diner (301-595-3002), 10973 Baltimore Ave. Open 6 AM–4 PM. Closed Sun. How can you go wrong when the average price of a complete breakfast is less than $6? Most lunches, such as sandwiches, burgers, and a few entrées, will not cost you more than $9.

Bowie

✒ **Old Bowie Town Grille** (301-464-8800; www.oldbowietowngrille.com), 8604 Chestnut Ave. Open for lunch and dinner; closed Mon. The Irish-style pub has live entertainment almost every evening, and the works of local artists adorn the walls and reception area. Even though it serves the typical bar food, there are actually a number of healthy items on the menu, including a portobello sandwich, fresh fish, and a spinach, blue cheese, and walnut salad. The children's menu is surprisingly varied, too. Entrées $15–28.

College Park

✒ **R. J. Bentley's Filling Station** (301-277-8898; www.rjbentleys.net), 7323 Baltimore Blvd. Open for lunch and dinner. Located within in a 1920s gas station, Bentley's has been a favorite with University of Maryland students and alumni for several decades. Signed jerseys of university athletes who went on to become professionals adorn the walls. The menu features bar food: lots of burgers and sandwiches ($7.95–11.95), with a few chicken, pasta, and steak dinner entrées ($12.95–21.95).

Laurel

✒ **Pasta Plus** (301-498-5100; www.pastaplusrestaurant.com), Central Plaza Shopping Center, 209 Gorman Ave. The name as well as this restaurant's exterior do not do justice to its warm interior and quality of food. The pizzas ($10.95–18.95) have a great taste because they are cooked in a wood-burning stove, and most of the other dishes are delicious because the pasta and sauces are made fresh daily on the premises. Veal and seafood round out the menu. $12–23.

CRABS

Landover Hills

Pop's Seafood and Carry Out (301-459-4141), 7437 Annapolis Rd. You come here for the hard- and soft-shell crabs (market price), not for the atmosphere, but Pop's has been open for more than three decades.

✳ Entertainment

DANCE School of Dance (301-405-ARTS; www.claricesmithcenter.umd.edu), University of Maryland, College Park. The school sponsors performances throughout the school year, many of them by professional troupes, and several student presentations each semester.

FILM All of the following show first-run movies.

Beltsville

AMC Center Park (301-937-0742; www.amctheatres.com), 4001 Powder Mill Rd.

Bowie

Regal Bowie Crossing Stadium (301-262-7433; www.regmovies.com), 15200 Major Lansdale Blvd.

Greenbelt

Old Greenbelt Theater (301-474-9744; www.pandgtheatres.com), 132 Centerway Rd.

MUSIC Maryland Presents (301-405-ARTS; www.claricesmithcenter.umd.edu), University of Maryland, College Park. Maryland Presents is the theatrical arm of the **Clarice Smith Performing Arts Center,** which presents a wide range of programs throughout the year. Performances include solo artists, full orchestras, quartets, popular music, Broadway and theatrical productions, and student and faculty recitals. Since all of the arts disciplines are housed in the center, artists from each discipline often work together on the productions.

THEATERS

Cheverly

&. **Publick Playhouse** (301-277-0312; http://arts.pgparks.com), 5445 Landover Rd. Located just 10 minutes from downtown Washington, DC, the playhouse—a converted 1940s movie theater—presents everything from jazz and gospel to modern dance, and from musical theater to historic drama.

College Park

University of Maryland Department of Theater (301-405-ARTS; www.clarice smithcenter.umd.edu), University of Maryland. Performances have included many Broadway standards, such as *The Music Man*, along with newer works like George F. Walker's *Problem Child*. The productions include members of the school's faculty, students, and local actors—professional and amateur.

SPORTS

Bowie

&? **Bowie Baysox** (301-805-6000; 1-800-956-4004; www.baysox.com), Prince George's Stadium, 4101 North East Crain Hwy. Come watch a possible future Baltimore Oriole as the AA team plays its season Apr.–Sept.

College Park

University of Maryland Terrapins (301-314-7070; www.umterps.com). The university's student teams provide action for spectators in basketball, baseball, soccer, lacrosse, swimming, and other sports.

Landover

Washington Redskins (301-276-7000; www.redskins.com), FedEx Field. The professional NFL team plays its home games in the 83,000-seat FedEx Field.

✳ Selective Shopping

ART GALLERIES **Harmony Hall Regional Center** (301-203-6040; www .pgparks.com), 10701 Livingston Rd., Fort Washington. A converted elementary school provides arts classes and an exhibition gallery.

Also see **Montpelier Mansion** under *To See.*

FARMER'S MARKETS **College Park Farmer's Market** (301-262-8662; www.crs.umd.edu/cms/wellness/farmers market.aspx), 5211 Calvert Rd., College Park. Stands are temporary and quite informal, as everything is set up in a swimming-pool parking lot on Sat., May–Nov. Things crank up at 7 AM and get pretty quiet by noon.

Main St. Farmer's Market (301-808-3078), 15200 Annapolis Rd., Bowie. Start the week with fresh produce by stopping by on Sunday between 9 and 1 during the season of May–Oct.

Prince George's Plaza Farmer's Market (310-627-0977), MD 410, Hyattsville. Strawberries are some of the first things to appear when the season opens in May, while pumpkins close it out in November. Open Tues. 3–6.

USDA Farmer's Market (301-504-1776; 1-800-384-8704), 5601 Sunnyside Ave., Beltsville. This market should offer some of the best fruits and vegetables around, as it is adjacent to the Beltsville Agricultural Research Center. Open Thurs. 10–2, May–Oct.

PICK-YOUR-OWN PRODUCE FARMS

Brandywine

&? **Robin Hill Farm Nursery** (301-888-1849; www.naturalmaryland.com), 15800 Croom Rd. Bring the kids out to choose a pumpkin so that they can carve their own jack-o'-lantern.

Clinton

Cherry Hill Orchard (301-292-4642; www.naturalmaryland.com), 12300 Gallahan Rd. The season starts in mid-May with red raspberries and continues well into fall with other berries, fruits, and a very wide variety of vegetables.

Miller Farms (301-297-5878; www.natural maryland.com), 10140 Piscataway Rd. The strawberries are usually ripe by mid-May; return about a month later to choose and pick your own vegetables.

✳ Special Events

February: **Annual Choreographers' Showcase** (301-405-ARTS), Clarice Smith Performing Arts Center, College Park.

March: **Annual Jewelry, Mineral and Fossil Show and Sale** (301-297-4575), Fort Washington. Also includes the **Family Wildlife Art Festival,** with performances, music, workshops, and kids' activities.

April: **Play Festival** (301-322-0444), Prince George's Community College,

Largo. Annual presentation of new theatrical works and talent from the region.

May: **Spring Festival Horse Show** (301-952-7999), Upper Marlboro. A-rated hunter/jumper horse show. **Montpelier Spring Festival** (301-776-2805), Laurel. Arts and crafts, several stages presenting music and dance, pony rides, and kids' parade. **Harlem Renaissance Festival** (301-918-8418; www.prgeoharlem renaissancefestival.org), Landover. Several stages of music, dance, poetry, and theater, with other activities for all ages. **Marlboro Day and Parade** (301-952-9575), Upper Marlboro. Parade, food, crafts, vendors, and entertainment.

June: **Main St. Antique, Arts, and Craft Show** (301-725-7539), Laurel. Juried show featuring regional artists and antiques dealers. Appraisals and entertainment.

September: **County Fair** (301-579-2598), Equestrian Center, Upper Marlboro.

November–early January: **Winter Festival of Lights** (301-699-2545), Watkins Park, Upper Marlboro.

SILVER SPRING, BETHESDA, ROCKVILLE, AND GAITHERSBURG

Francis Preston Blair was out riding his horse in the mid-1800s when his mount became spooked, throwing him to the ground. With his face in the mud, he noticed he had landed next to a spring, whose mica deposits shone like silver in the bright sunshine. He purchased the land around the water source, built his home, and Silver Spring was born.

Although it is not an incorporated city, its downtown area was a major shopping point in the mid-1900s but lost favor as the 20th century came to a close. A $400 million revitalization program has reversed the trend, and shops, restaurants, and businesses have returned. The National Capital Trolley Museum is just a few miles away and chronicles the days before automobiles ruled the roadways.

Numerous research centers, such as the National Institutes of Health, National Naval Medical Center, National Cancer Institute, and software development and telecommunications firms make Bethesda the state's second largest employment center. The money generated by these enterprises has transformed the city into a sophisticated and trendy place. The shopping district is crowded with some of the most upscale stores—both locally owned and national chains—in the Washington, DC, area.

Bethesda is also a great patron of the arts, especially with its Art in Public Spaces Discovery Trail. A stroll along urban streets and byways will reveal more than 40 indoor and outdoor works of art, and McCrillis Gardens and Gallery presents a changing array of exhibits. The written word is also valued here, evidenced in the number of bookstores selling new and used titles.

Rockville began with the establishment of Owen's Ordinary, an inn and tavern, around 1750. A few years later, in 1774, citizens gathered in another inn, Hungerford's Tavern, to discuss their outrage over Britain's blockade of Boston Harbor and called for a Maryland boycott of trade with England. From those early days, Rockville has become Maryland's second largest city in area, occupying more than 13 square miles.

Much of its history is preserved in the architecture of the downtown area and within the 1800s Beall-Dawson House, open for public tours. F. Scott Fitzgerald, his wife, Zelda, and other family members are buried in the cemetery of nearby St. Mary's Church. Those wishing to escape the urban environment can drive just a few miles to Rock Creek Regional Park along the city's northern border, or Cabin John Regional Park to the south.

Gaithersburg began as a small agrarian community known as Log Town in the mid-1700s. The arrival of the Baltimore & Ohio Railroad in 1873 allowed the farmers to reach a wider market and enabled travelers to escape the summer heat in Washington, DC. These earlier

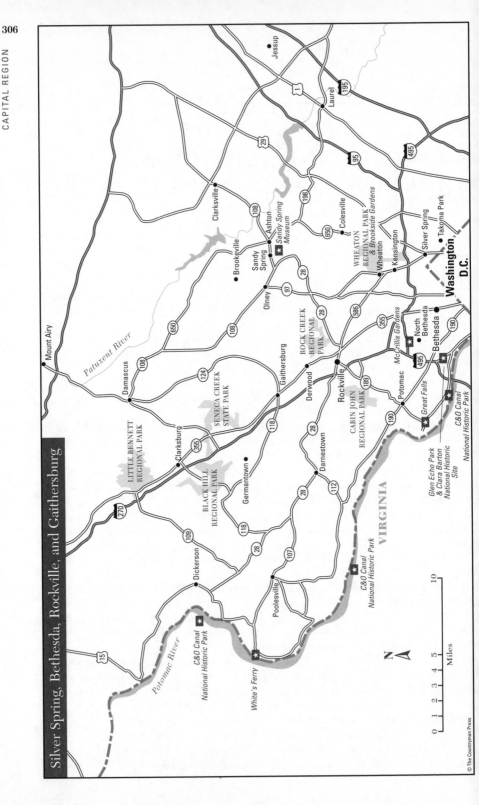

Silver Spring, Bethesda, Rockville, and Gaithersburg

© The Countryman Press

days are recalled in the exhibits of the now restored B&O Railroad Station. The arrival of the interstates, specifically I-270, in the late 20th century put an end to the farming way of life, and the city now functions as a bedroom community for the Washington, DC, metropolitan area.

COMMUNITIES Towns removed just a few miles from the I-270 corridor are also growing but so far have escaped rapid urbanization. **Sandy Spring** was settled by Quakers in 1725, and the Sandy Spring Museum documents its history.

Close to the Potomac River, **Poolesville** was settled in 1783 and retains much of its rural, farming roots. It is believed that **Clarksburg** can trace its roots back to a Native American trading post. Much of the green space that would have surrounded the small Indian settlement has been preserved by Little Bennett Regional Park.

GUIDANCE For information, brochures, and other travel advice, contact the **Conference and Visitors Bureau of Montgomery County, Maryland, Inc.** (240-777-2060; 1-877-798-6904; www.visitmontgomery.com), 111 Rockville Pike, Suite 800, Rockville, 20850.

GETTING THERE *By car:* **I-270** makes an almost arrow-straight run through the middle of the region and connects with **I-70** at Frederick to the northwest and with the **Capital Beltway (I-495),** which encircles Washington, DC, to the southeast. The **Intercounty Connector (ICC)** is a toll highway that connects I-270 in Gaithersburg to I-95 and US 29.

By air: This area is blessed with being serviced by three major airports. The two closest are **Ronald Reagan Washington National Airport** (703-417-8000; www.metwashairports .com/reagan/reagan.htm) and **Washington Dulles International Airport** (703-572-2700; www.metwashairports.com/dulles/dulles.htm) in northern Virginia. Located between Baltimore and Washington, DC, is the **Baltimore/Washington International Thurgood Marshall Airport** (1-800-I-FLY-BWI; www.bwiairport.com).

By rail: **AMTRAK** (1-800-872-7245; www.amtrak.com) makes a stop at the Rockville Metro Station, which means you can arrive here by train from any other place that has AMTRAK connections.

By water: **White's Ferry** (301-349-5200), US 15. The only remaining ferry across the Potomac River permits you to come into Maryland near Poolesville from US 15 just north of Leesburg, Virginia. Although the ferry is a utilitarian boat, the ride across the river can be a scenic and enjoyable one as you watch waterfowl and other birds wing their way above the water. You will also get a chance to look at the river and the Chesapeake & Ohio (C&O) Canal from the same perspective as the folks who took the ferry in the 1800s did. It operates daily 5 AM–11 PM and costs about $5 one way; $8 round trip.

GETTING AROUND *By car:* **I-270** and **I-495 (Capital Beltway)** are the major limited-access highways. The interstates are extremely crowded and slow during morning and evening travel hours as well as at lunchtime; automobile travel on local highways can be frustratingly slow at any time of day. Just accept it, go with the flow, and give yourself twice as much time as you think you need to get to your destination. Here's an insider's tip: It is not always true, but many times **MacArthur Blvd.** and **Clara Barton Pkwy.** along the Potomac River are blessedly free of traffic when other roadways are bumper to bumper.

By bus: The **Metrobus** (202-637-7000; www.wmata.com) system has routes on every major roadway in the region and can also transport you into Washington, DC, and Baltimore.

Ride On (240-777-0311; www6.montgomerycountymd.gov), the Montgomery County bus system, has more than 80 routes with thousands of stops. Its buses also connect with the Metro system to provide transportation throughout the Washington, DC/Baltimore area.

The **Bethesda Circulator** (301-215-6661; www.bethesdatransit.org) has a figure-eight route that takes the trolley through the downtown business and office area. It runs until midnight Mon.–Thurs., and until 2 AM Fri. and Sat.

By rail: The **Metro** (202-637-7000; www.wmata.com) subway rail system operates out of Washington, DC, and makes 13 stops in this region. The line is just a bit east of the I-270 corridor it parallels.

By taxi: Among the many taxi companies operating in and around Silver Spring, Bethesda, Rockville, and Gaithersburg are **Montgomery County Taxicab** (301-762-2001), **Action Taxi** (301-840-1222), **Barwood Cab** (301-984-1900), and **Regency Cab** (301-990-9000).

MEDICAL EMERGENCY **Suburban Hospital** (301-896-3100; www.suburbanhospital .org), 8600 Old Georgetown Rd., Bethesda.

MedStar Montgomery Medical Center (301-774-8882; www.montgomerygeneral.com), 18101 Prince Phillip Dr., Olney (close to Rockville and Gaithersburg).

Shady Grove Adventist Hospital (301-279-6000; www.adventisthealthcare.com), 9901 Medical Center Dr., Rockville.

Holy Cross Hospital (301-754-7000; www.holycrosshealth.org), 1500 Forest Glen Rd., Silver Spring.

✳ To See

MUSEUMS

Bethesda
Dennis and Philip Ratner Museum (301-897-1518; www.ratnermuseum.com), 10001 Old Georgetown Rd. Sun. 10–4:30; Mon.–Thurs. noon–4. Free admission. Provides a visual depiction of the Hebrew Bible through sculpture, drawings, paintings, and other works of art—primarily those of Philip Ratner. Although this is a private museum based upon the scriptures of the Jewish faith, everyone is welcome, the atmosphere is low-key (in other words, no proselytizing like that found in some other religious museums), and the artwork is interesting and worthwhile.

Gaithersburg
Community Museum (301-258-6160; www.gaithersburgmd.gov/museum), 9 S. Summit Ave. Thurs.–Sat. 10–2. Donations accepted. Exhibits inside the restored 1884 B&O Railroad Station chronicle local rail history and the city's movement from a farming community to the present day. The outdoor rail yard has a number of locomotives and other railcars.

Sandy Spring
Sandy Spring Museum (301-774-0022; www.sandyspringmuseum.org), 17901 Bentley Rd. Much to see and do here. The **Farquhar Gallery** features changing traveling exhibits, a guided tour explains the museum's historical aspects and furnishings, and a stables and blacksmith shop reflect the life of earlier times. Musical concerts of various types are presented throughout the year.

Silver Spring
✑ **National Capital Trolley Museum** (301-384-6088; www.dctrolley.org), 1313 Bonifant Rd. Open Sat.–Sun. and other days at various times of the year, but days and hours vary greatly. Small admission fee. *Clickety-clack, clickety-clack.* Take a ride on one of the electric trolley cars that serviced the area for nearly one hundred years to relive the days of screeching wheels and swaying cars. The museum has interactive displays, a model streetcar layout, and dozens of vehicles that serviced the area "from Lincoln to Kennedy."

C&O CANAL NATIONAL HISTORICAL PARK

Around the turn of the 19th century, individual canals afforded access around waterfalls and rapids, providing an easy water route between a young America's eastern coastline and areas west of the Blue Ridge Mountains. Taking a cue from ideas expressed by George Washington and Thomas Jefferson, construction of the Chesapeake & Ohio Canal began on July 4, 1828.

Originally projected to extend 360 miles, the canal never lived up to its investors' dreams. Mounting costs, coupled with other problems, caused financial backers to decide in 1850 that enough was enough, and that Cumberland was the farthest west the canal would be constructed—a distance of 184.5 miles.

Dry spells, floods, winter freezes, and competition from the B&O Railroad (which coincidentally began construction on the very same day) kept the canal from operating at a profit. A tremendous flood in 1924 destroyed so much of the infrastructure that the canal never reopened. Canal owners turned it over to the federal government for $2 million in 1938.

The canal was proclaimed a national monument in 1961 and named a national historical park in 1971. Today the towpath is open to hikers, bikers, and (except for a short section) horseback riders, and camping is permitted at designated sites. The park service has an abundance of informational handout sheets at its **Great Falls Visitors Center** (301-299-3613; www.nps.gov /choh), 11710 MacArthur Blvd., Potomac. Exhibits within the center illustrate the history of the canal, while Mike High's book *The C&O Canal Companion* covers the subject in great detail.

Also see *Hiking.*

HISTORIC HOMES

Glen Echo

Clara Barton National Historic Site (301-320-1410; www.nps.gov/clba), 5801 Oxford Rd. (off MacArthur Blvd.). Open daily. Free admission and parking. Almost before artillery stopped firing and bullets ceased whistling through the air, Clara Barton was on the battlefield attending to the wounds of Civil War soldiers. Guided one-hour tours take you through the home of this founder of the American Red Cross. The 1891 house, which was built along the lines of a Red Cross relief structure, contains many items that once belonged to Barton. Adjacent to Glen Echo Park.

Olney

Oakley Cabin (301-650-4373; www.montgomeryparks.org), 3610 Brookeville Rd. Free guided tours from 12–4 on the second and fourth Sun. of the month Apr.–Oct. Built around 1820, the two-story cabin was once a home to slaves, but, after emancipation, became part of a blossoming African American community and was occupied until the 1970s. The inside of the cabin is furnished to look as it did in the 1800s, with tools and other items that were dug up during archeological studies of the site. Behind the house is a short trail leading to the site of Newlin's Mill along Reddy Branch.

Rockville

Beall-Dawson House (301-762-1492; 301-340-2825; www.montgomeryhistory.org), 103 W. Montgomery Ave. Wed.–Sun. noon–4. Small admission fee. Guided tours provide insight into early-1800s life. Many of the items in the house (such as the pianoforte and the interesting tin bathtub) belonged to the Beall family. Mr. Beall came and went often, so most of the time the house was inhabited and run by women and slaves. Rotating exhibits on the second floor focus on local Rockville history. Located on the lawn is the small **Stonestreet**

Museum of 19th-Century Medicine. The Gothic Revival office was built for Dr. Stonestreet in 1852 and contains many items from his practice.

OTHER SITES

Kensington

The Church of Jesus Christ of Latter Day Saints Washington, DC, Temple Visitors Center (301-587-0144; www.lds.org/placestovisit), 9900 Stoneybrook Dr. The contemporary visitors center has some very interesting and modern displays that provide a good background on the history of the Mormon religion. You are only permitted to take a look around accompanied by a guide, and, depending on which guide you get, you may receive more preaching than just being guided around, which is a shame, especially if you are just interested in learning a bit of history and not being told about the only way to obtain heaven. The temple also displays changing works of art in its gallery and offers secular concerts, plays, and other theatrical events in its plush auditorium.

Rockville

F. Scott Fitzgerald Burial Place (301-428-9702), corner of Rockville Pike (MD 355) and Viers Mill Rd. In what could be interpreted as a summation of the human condition, Fitzgerald wrote in *The Great Gatsby*, "So we beat on, boats against the current, borne back ceaselessly into the past." These words are now engraved upon his St. Mary's Church cemetery tombstone, located at a busy highway intersection next to a Metro rail station. His wife, Zelda Sayre, lies next to him.

✳ To Do

BICYCLING **Capital Crescent Trail** (202-234-4874; www.cctrail.org). The packed-surface rail-trail connects local communities from Georgetown in Washington, DC, to Silver Spring—for a distance of about 11 miles. It does pass through heavily populated areas, but by making use of the C&O Canal, a country club, and a couple of parks, the trail ride can be a pleasant one. One of the highlights is the Delecarlia Tunnel, whose brick-faced portals are a testament to the masons' expertise.

Rock Creek Trail (301-495-2525). This mostly paved route follows Rock Creek for 21 miles from Lake Needwood in Rockville to the heart of Washington, DC. Most of the time it runs through the woods along the creek or passes through the recreation areas of neighborhood parks. Be careful at the many intersections with busy roadways.

Seneca Creek State Park (301-924-2127; www.dnr.state.md.us/publiclands/central/seneca .asp), Gaithersburg. The trailhead parking lot is at 14938 Schaeffer Rd., accessed from MD 118 (Germantown Rd.) south of Gaithersburg. In an out-of-the-way section of Seneca Creek State Park, local citizens have cooperated with authorities and put in many volunteer hours constructing and maintaining a 10-mile network of trails. Hikers, mountain bikers, and horseback riders can freely visit over and over again, watching corn and soybean crops advance from tiny seed sprouts to tall mature plants. The variation from open land to wooded tracts ensures a variety of wildlife, and warblers, vireos, meadowlarks, woodpeckers, vultures, and owls have all been seen visiting or living here.

Also see the **C&O Canal National Historical Park** sidebar on page 309.

BOAT EXCURSIONS ✐ **C&O Canal,** Great Falls. The one-hour rides originate at the Great Falls Visitors Center (301-767-3714; www.nps.gov/archive/choh) and operate Apr.–Oct. Small fee. Take a ride on a mule-drawn boat. Rangers, naturalists, and the mule driver dress in period costume, and the *clip-clop* of the mules along the towpath brings back the canal's former days.

Also see **Rock Creek Regional Park** under *Green Space*.

✔ **Glen Echo Park** (301-492-6282), 7300 MacArthur Blvd., Glen Echo. Open daily. Free admission and parking. It almost feels as if you have walked into the middle of a *Twilight Zone* story: The bumper-car pavilion and the arcade still stand, and the horses of the carousel are freshly painted, but no one is there to operate the rides or entice you to play a game of ring toss.

The land was first developed in 1891 by the National Chautauqua Assembly as a center for the sciences, arts, languages, and literature. The Glen Echo Company, operators of trolleys in the Washington, DC, area, purchased the land and operated the amusement park from 1899 to 1968. The federal government acquired it in 1971, and the park is now used, once again, as a place for cultural pursuits. Classes are conducted on nearly every type of art and craft imaginable; children's theater productions are presented throughout the year—the Puppet Company's are a favorite; and the dances (waltz, big band, contra, square, and popular) in the Spanish Ballroom are attended by hundreds every weekend. The **Discovery Center Children's Museum** is geared for children ages 2–11.

I just enjoy coming here for an early morning walk or a browse through the bookstore and gift shop, and to take a ride on the carousel when it happens to be operating (May–Sept.). Ranger-conducted tours of the carousel are given at 2 PM on Sunday.

THE REFURBISHED CAROUSEL'S ROUND HOUSE

FAMILY ACTIVITIES ✔ Within the **South Germantown Recreational Park** (301-670-4660; www.montgomeryparks.org), 18056 Central Park Circle, Boyds, is a wide variety of activities to engage in with the children. Test your aim at the archery park, the golf driving range, or the miniature golf course. Work up a sweat on the ball fields and soccer fields, and then cool off in the waters of the indoor aquatic center or the Splash Playground. The latter is quite the water park, with a large waterfall, rain trees, a water tunnel, and a water maze that shoots out gallons of water per minute.

Also see *Miniature Golf* and **Dave and Buster's** under *Eating Out*.

GOLF

Ashton

Hampshire Greens (301-476-7999; www.montgomerycountygolf.com), 616 Firestone Dr. Features bent grass all the way from the tee to the green on all 18 holes. Total distance from the tip tees is almost 7,000 feet.

Clarksburg

Little Bennett Golf Course (301-253-1515; www.montgomerycountygolf.com), 25900 Prescott Rd. The par 72 course's hilly terrain offers a challenge as well as nice scenery.

Mount Airy

Rattlewood Golf Course (301-607-9000; www.montgomerycountygolf.com), 13501 Penn Shop Rd. The excellent drainage on this par 72 course makes it the place to go when other courses are too wet to play on.

Olney

Trotter's Glen (301-570-4951; www.trottersglen.com), 16501 Batchellors Forest Rd. Ed Ault designed this par 71 course.

Potomac

Falls Road Golf Course (301-299-5156; www.montgomerycountygolf.com), 10800 Falls Rd. The weekend fee for playing the 18 holes situated around a lake is about $35.

HIKING **Seneca Creek State Park** (301-924-2127 www.dnr.state.md.us/publiclands /central/seneca.asp). Seneca Creek State Park (also see *Bicycling*) provides enough easy trails to make for enjoyable morning or afternoon hikes. The 3.7-mile **Lake Shore Trail** encircles Clopper Lake, passing through fields of wildflowers. **Long Draught Trail** is 2.5 miles long and follows a stream to a wetlands area and onto a laurel-covered hillside. The **Great Seneca** and **Mink Hollow trails** are each 1.25 miles in length and traverse forested slopes and marshlands. The **Old Pond Trail,** only 0.3 mile long, passes by a pond in its last stages of succession. All of these pathways interconnect in some way or another.

C&O Canal, Great Falls (also see the sidebar on page 309). The area around Great Falls has an abundance of hiking trails. One side trail off the main towpath leads to the dramatic scenery of **Great Falls,** where the Potomac River rushes and churns over a series of drops within the narrow confines of the gorge it has etched out of the landscape. Another outing, with only a few short ups and downs, brings you by reminders of gold-mining days and may enlighten you as to just how much wildlife can exist in proximity to large human population centers.

The **Billy Goat Trail** just might have the most awkward and exhausting 1-mile portion of trail in all of Maryland as it climbs over huge boulders and rock outcroppings along the northern bank of the Potomac River.

Also see *Bicycling* and *Parks.*

HORSEBACK RIDING **Wheaton Regional Park** (301-905-3045; www.montgomery parks.org) and **Rock Creek Regional Park** (301-589-9026; www.montgomeryparks.org) provide lessons, recreational riding, and some boarding services throughout the year.

You are also permitted to ride your own horse on the trails of many of the regional parks. Contact the **Montgomery County Department of Parks** (301-495-2507; www.montgomery parks.org), 9500 Brunett Ave., Silver Spring, for the latest information.

Also see the **C&O Canal National Historical Park** sidebar on page 309, and **Seneca Creek State Park** under *Bicycling.*

KAYAKING AND CANOEING Canoes, rowboats, and some paddleboats are available for rent during the warmer months at **Black Hill** (in Boyds) and **Rock Creek** (in Rockville) **regional parks.** Most of the paddling is on small lakes or quiet creeks.

One of America's most scenic waterways, the **Potomac River** provides close to 30 miles— from White's Ferry to Great Falls Park—of delightful canoeing and kayaking for paddlers of all skill levels. Below the Great Falls Visitors Center at **Great Falls** the river reaches its fall line and becomes narrow, swift, and dangerous for anyone but those who possess the most proficient of paddling skills. If you are an expert, however, that stretch of river will give you the thrill of your life, with narrow channels, 90-degree turns, and drops of 22 or more feet.

Anyone attempting to paddle the falls should go with someone who has made a successful run; paddlers are required to register with C&O Canal park rangers in the visitors center before beginning the trip. Have fun—this is a great thrill—but do not take it lightly, as many have lost their lives here.

Canoes for paddling the Potomac River are available for rent by the hour or day at the **White's Ferry store** (301-349-5200; on facebook), White's Ferry. They will also shuttle you and your canoe if you make reservations ahead of time.

NATURE-WATCHING See *Walks*.

SKATING

Gaithersburg
Skate Park in Bohrer Park (310-258-6359; www.gaithersburgmd.gov), 510 S. Frederick Ave. Open daily; children under 10 must be accompanied by an adult. The 12,300-square-foot park is designed for in-line skating and skateboarding. The ramps and boxes are designed to suit all skill levels, while the ground surface is asphalt.

Rockville
Cabin John Regional Park (301-765-8620; www.montgomeryparks.org), 10610 Westlake Dr. The park's enclosed rink provides ice skating well into June.

Rockville Town Square Outdoor Ice Rink (310-545-1999; www.rockvilleiceskating.com). Reminiscent of skating in New York's Times Square. Open in winter only.

Silver Spring
Veterans Plaza Ice Rink (301-588-1221; http://silverspringiceskating.com). Only open in winter.

Wheaton
Rubini Athletic Complex—Ice Skating Rink (301-649-2703; www.montgomeryparks .org), 11710 Orebaugh Ave. Located within Wheaton Regional Park.

SWIMMING The **Montgomery County Department of Recreation** (301-217-6880; www.montgomeryparks.org) operates six public outdoor pools (usually open Memorial Day–Labor Day) and three year-round indoor pools.

Water Park at Bohrer Park (301-258-6445; www.montgomeryparks.org), 510 S. Frederick Ave., Gaithersburg. Open Memorial Day–Labor Day. Small admission fee. The main pool has several different areas, and a double 250-foot water slide twists and turns into the splash pool.

✳ Green Space

GARDENS

Bethesda
McCrillis Gardens and Gallery (301-962-1455; www.montgomeryparks.org), 6910 Greentree Rd. Open daily 10–sunset. The time to visit is between April and mid-June, when the 5 acres are ablaze with azaleas and rhododendrons. The gallery features changing exhibits from area artists.

Wheaton

Brookside Gardens (301-949-8230; www.montgomeryparks.org), 1800 Glenallan Ave. Open daily sunrise–sunset. By far one of the most well-maintained, extensive, and prettiest free-admission gardens I have been privileged to visit. A dozen themed gardens, with plants that bloom from early spring into early winter, allow you to enjoy the beauty of the 50 acres. Sculpted ponds add variety to the scenery, as does the maturing forest around the gardens. This is a don't-miss place, and even if outside temperatures drop too low for you in winter, you can always visit the plants and flowers inside the two conservatories.

PARKS

Boyds

& **Black Hill Regional Park** (301-528-3490; www.montgomeryparks.org), 20930 Lake Ridge Dr. Little Seneca Lake, at 505 acres, is the focal point of the park. You can bring your own electric-powered boat or rent a canoe or rowboat (in-season). Anglers come here for the largemouth bass, tiger muskie, crappie, catfish, and sunfish. A fishing pier is handicapped accessible. A system of more than 13 miles of trails (3 miles are paved and handicapped accessible) enable exploration of the surrounding fields and woodlands. Other features include playgrounds, volleyball courts, and a fitness course.

Clarksburg

Little Bennett Regional Park (301-528-3450; www.montgomeryparks.org), 23701 Frederick Rd. Unlike many other parks located close to large population centers, Little Bennett Regional Park is not overdeveloped with swimming pools, amusement centers, skating rinks, basketball courts, and the like. It does offer a campground with hot showers and a camp store, horseshoe and volleyball areas, and a nature center, yet these facilities are concentrated on just a few acres of its southern edge off MD 355 (and are only available to campers).

BROOKSIDE GARDENS IN WHEATON

The rest of the park has been—more or less—left in its natural state, and 14 miles of trails are available to lead visitors onto 3,700 acres of dense forests, open meadows, narrow hollows, low-rising ridgelines, and small stream valleys lush with vegetation.

Rockville

Rock Creek Regional Park (301-589-9026; www.montgomeryparks.org), 15700 Needwood Lake Circle. Located close to the center of Montgomery County, the park has two distinct sections: The portion around Lake Needwood is quite developed, with an 18-hole golf course, an archery range, picnic shelters, a playground, a snack bar, and a boat shop that rents canoes, rowboats, and paddleboats in-season. There is even a pontoon boat that carries 25 people onto the lake for 20-minute cruises on weekends and holidays throughout the summer season.

In contrast, the section of the park near Lake Frank has been left in a more natural state. A well-designed network of trails goes beside a small pond, comes into contact with several streams and open areas, and swings around the lake. You may be privileged to watch some of the park's inhabitants—such as squirrels, rabbits, white-tailed deer, snakes, frogs, salamanders, raccoons, weasels, foxes, and beavers—go about their daily lives.

WALKS **Woodend Nature Trail** (301-652-9188; www.audubonnaturalist.org), 8940 Jones Mill Rd., Chevy Chase. Woodend is the headquarters of the Audubon Naturalist Society of the Central Atlantic States. The 40-acre property was willed to the society in 1967, and a brochure keyed to stops along the trail describes the wonders of a nature preserve hidden within a major metropolitan area. The walk is easy and should take about 30 minutes. Free guided walks of the trail are given on the third Sat. of each month at 10, and bird-watching and other nature programs are provided on a scheduled basis. Be sure to visit the gift shop for a superb selection of natural-history books.

* Lodging

MOTELS AND HOTELS This area is nearly bereft of B&Bs but is awash with scores of hotels and motels. Any national chain you can think of will have one or more properties here. Some of the standouts that I have stayed in or visited include:

Bethesda, 20814

Bethesda Court Hotel (301-656-2100), 7740 Wisconsin Ave. This boutique hotel has imaginatively appointed rooms and serves a European-style afternoon tea. Exercise room. $99–199.

Gaithersburg, 20879

🐾 ♿ **Holiday Inn** (301-948-8900; 1-800-HOLIDAY; www.holiday-inn.com), 2 Montgomery Village Ave. The many amenities raise the rooms a notch above those typically found in a Holiday Inn. In-room iron and ironing boards, coffeemaker, free movie channel on the TV, and an unusually large amount of work space. Indoor pool and fitness center are also available. $94 and up.

♿ 🐾 **Hyatt House** (301-527-6000; http://gaithersburg.house.hyatt.com), 200 Skidmore Blvd. The one- and two-bedroom suites are large and all have full kitchens and large work desks. Business center, fitness room, outdoor pool, complimentary full breakfast. $109–159. Pets permitted with an additional (and astronomical) fee of $150.

♿ **Springhill Suites by Marriott** (301-987-0900; www.marriott.com), 9715 Washingtonian Blvd. All of the guest accommodations are spacious suites with a sofa bed in the outer room. Fitness center, heated pool, whirlpool, and complimentary continental breakfast. $149–159.

Rockville, 20850

🐾 ♿ **Sleep Inn** (301-948-8000; www.sleepinn.com), 2 Research Court. One of the lowest-cost motels in the region, it has an outdoor swimming pool and free continental breakfast. $109–125.

Silver Spring, 20904

 & **Courtyard by Marriott** (301-680-8500; www.marriott.com), 12521 Prosperity Dr. Spacious rooms and nicely decorated public areas and landscaped courtyard. Pool, whirlpool, and exercise room. Some rooms have a coffeemaker, refrigerator, and microwave. $109 and up.

BED & BREAKFASTS

Boyds, 20841

Pleasant Springs Farm B&B (301-972-3452; www.pleasantspringsfarm.com), 16112 Barnesville Rd. A long, shaded driveway delivers you to the farm and the small 1768 log cabin that is going to be your home for the evening. The host, who hand spins wool from her own flock of sheep, lives in the farmhouse several hundred yards away and delivers your breakfast in a basket each morning, often with some items freshly picked from the garden. The cabin's upstairs bedroom overlooks the dogwood trees and out across the grounds to the small fishing pond, where you are welcome to canoe or fish. There's also a nature trail passing through the woodlands. All in all, a nice, rustic experience. $195.

Brookeville, 20833

 ✍ **Longwood Manor** (301-774-1002; 1-866-774-1002; www.bbonline.com/md/longwood), 2900 DuBarry Lane. Once

PLEASANT SPRINGS FARM B&B

here, you realize that the modern housing development you drove through occupies land that once belonged to the manor house. Situated on 2 of the original 280 acres, the Mount Vernon–like house was the home of Thomas Moore, who had his friend Thomas Jefferson stay with him a number of times.

Hosts Bruce and Lynn Bartlett are proud of their home and love to share its history (ask about its Civil Defense days) and that of the surrounding area. The furnishings reflect its early-1800s origin, and guest accommodations include two suites and a room that can accommodate three people. I enjoyed sitting on the screened porch overlooking the grounds during my stay in the Brookmore Suite, and I look forward to returning in warmer weather to make use of the swimming pool surrounded by century-old trees. Children over 12 are welcome. $95–155.

CAMPING

Clarksburg, 20871

Little Bennett Regional Park (301-972-9222; www.montgomeryparks.org), 23701 Frederick Rd. The campground is located within one of the largest regional parks in the Washington, DC, area and provides access to miles of trails and 3,600 acres of woodlands. Close to 100 tent and RV sites with showers, dump station, and coin laundry.

Rockville, 20850

Cabin John Regional Park (301-765-8620; www.montgomeryparks.org), 7701 Tuckerman Lane. Head to this park for rustic camping at its seven walk-in primitive sites. Water is not available Nov.–Mar. Permits must be obtained in advance by calling 301-495-2525.

Also see **Seneca Creek State Park** under *Bicycling* and *Hiking*.

✳ Where to Eat

DINING OUT

Chevy Chase

 & **La Ferme** (301-986-5255; www.laferme restaurant.com), 7101 Brookeville Rd.

Old Angler's Inn (301-365-2425; www.oldanglersinn.com), 10801 MacArthur Blvd., Potomac. Open for lunch and dinner; closed Mon. Reservations recommended for dinner, when semiformal attire is expected. Old Angler's opened in 1860 to serve C&O Canal travelers and local estate owners. Its popularity with the movers and shakers of the federal government continues to this day, and it is very possible that the person at the next table will be a Washington, DC, politico, an upper-echelon business executive, or a nationally known sports figure.

Olympia Reges, who passed away in 2005, had owned the inn for more than 50 years, and many of its recipes are hers. She did, however, let the kitchen staff be a bit adventurous at lunch, while the offerings at dinner are classic French. Her family continues to operate the restaurant in the same way. Sit on the patio in good weather, or use the spiral staircase to reach the second-floor dining area.

I practically melted into my chair when a bite of the crab porcupine with tarragon hit my taste buds. My dining mate smiled when she sampled her tuna carpaccio. We both smiled as we dined on roast guinea hen with rosemary sauce and the bourride of seafood medley. Other items on the menu sounded equally enticing and ranged $20–45. The menu changes seasonally, so there will always be something new and exciting.

OLD ANGLER'S INN

Open for lunch and dinner Mon.–Sat. except closed for lunch Sat.; brunch only Sun. The traditional French cuisine pairs with an ambience and décor inside an old farmhouse to transport you to the French countryside. Châteaubriand is a house specialty, but many diners claim the fricassee of lobster is the restaurant's pièce de résistance. Prices are very reasonable for a French restaurant. Entrées run $25–36.

Olney
🍴 The Inn at Brookeville Farms
(301-924-6500; www.theinnatbrookeville farms.com), 19501 Georgia Ave. Open for lunch and dinner daily; Sun. brunch and dinner. Occupying the many rooms of a large 1919 house that was the center of a diary farm, The Inn is the place for that special occasion meal (many weddings have taken place on the 35-acre grounds),

complete with period furniture and nice artwork and frescos on the walls. It's also a place for a casual lunch. The bisque I started my lunch with was full of shrimp and bits of corn that added a crunchy sweetness. The brushetta was garnished with an avocado, something I had never had before, but was to my liking. Dinner entrées are what I would describe as upscale/innovative country cooking—with interesting things such as smoked cauliflower, gorgonzola polenta, and carrot-ginger risotto showing up on the dishes. Desserts are made in-house; the bread pudding with buttermilk ice cream and bourbon crème Anglaise is the most popular. Entrées $21–31.

EATING OUT

Gaithersburg

Growlers of Gaithersburg (301-519-9400; www.growlersofgaithersburg.com), 227 E. Diamond Ave. Located in Olde Towne Gaithersburg, this microbrewery always has at least five of its in-house brewed ales and porters available. Although it serves sandwiches and other bar-type foods, the menu offerings are quite extensive and inventive. There's a lamb shank with tomatoes, olives, baby potatoes, and thyme; spinach, egg, and tomato tortellini with herb-pesto cream sauce and chorizo sausage; and your choice of a vegetable, seafood, or meat paella. Even the grilled cheese I had for lunch was much more than a typical sandwich—it was crammed full of four kinds of cheeses and grilled with bacon and tomatoes on a hoagie bun. The collection of hundreds of beer cans lining the walls can keep you occupied while waiting for your order to arrive. Desserts are quite nice, too, like the orange-vanilla flan my dining companion and I split. Almost all entrées are less than $20.

ℰ **O'Donnell's** (301-519-1650; www.odonnellsrestaurants.com), 311 Kentlands Blvd. Open daily for lunch and dinner. Fresh fish is brought in daily. Most dishes are prepared as Tim O'Donnell prepared them when he founded his restaurants in 1922. Raw bar, crabcakes, steaks, pasta, and

chicken. The broiled rockfish with corn, crab aioli, fried green tomatoes, and rice was tasty and nicely presented. And, oh, those rum buns they serve with each meal! They alone make a visit here worth your time. Entrées $19.95–34.95.

Kensington

ℰ **Dave and Buster's** (301-230-5151; www.daveandbusters.com), 11301 Rockville Pike. Open daily for lunch and dinner. Much like an ESPN Zone restaurant, food is almost secondary to entertainment at Dave and Buster's. The business occupies 60,000 square feet on the third floor of the White Flint Mall, and most of it is devoted to video games, billiard tables, and simulated horse and car racing and golf games. Lunch is busy, but evenings truly attract the crowds—families and singles alike.

The six-page menu is full of salads, sandwiches, seafood, steaks, chicken, and pasta. The Jack Daniels BBQ cheeseburger is popular for lunch; expect dinner entrées to be around $18–22. I enjoyed the chicken tortilla soup.

Olney

ℰ **The Tavern** (301-260-0500; www.olneytavern.com), 18200 Georgia Ave. Open daily for breakfast, lunch, and dinner. I have only had breakfast at The Tavern (a bit more upscale than the name implies), but it was so good that this is definitely going to be my area choice for the meal from now on. The entrées are the usual breakfast items, with some other wonderful concoctions like the eggs Chesapeake (with lump crabmeat) and a cheese blintz that will bring a smile to the taste buds. Lunch and dinner run $4.95–21.95, with a two-course early-bird special for $12.95.

Rockville

Addie's (301-881-0081; www.addiesrestaurant.com), 11120 Rockville Pike. Reservations recommended. The modest home converted to a restaurant belies the quality of cuisine here. Here's just a sampling: pork chop with bacon braised cabbage, rutabaga, mustard ale sauce, and pickled apples; hardwood grilled swordfish

with eggplant puree, raisin-pinenut couscous, and chermoula; sautéed trout with
potato gallette, egg salad, smoked trout roe,
and grilled scallions. I was introduced to
bronzino, also known as European seabass,
and enjoyed the way it was prepared to
enhance its delicate flavor. In addition,
more than just saying they support local
agriculture, Addie's lists on the menu the
producers they receive their products from.
Tables are packed tightly together, but this
just enabled the couple at the next table to
lean over to let me know how good the gazpacho was. Entrées $15–29.

First Watch (301-762-0621; www.first
watch.com), 100 Gibbs St. This national
chain has the feel of a California coffee bar,
with gourmet coffees and teas. However, it
offers much more, including omelets, waffles, crêpes, burritos, salads, and sandwiches. The atmosphere invites you to
linger. $3.95–10.95.

Silver Spring
☙ **Crisfield Seafood Restaurant** (301-
589-1306), 8012 Georgia Ave. Open for
lunch and dinner; closed Mon. A local tradition for more than half a century. The
décor is, of course, nautical and the atmosphere relaxed. Seafood dishes include crab-
stuffed flounder and fried oysters. The
creamy seafood bisque is the way to start
your meal. Entrées $15–24.

Wheaton
Ruan Thai Restaurant (301-942-0075;
www.ruanthaiwheaton.com), 11407
Amherst Ave. Open daily for lunch and dinner. Ruan Thai is on an out-of-the-way side
street, in a small strip mall, and, with its
vinyl tablecloths and chairs, almost reminds
you of a Chinese take-out establishment.
Don't be fooled. This is authentic Thai food
(and at reasonable prices). It is a family-
owned business, and everyone who does
the cooking does so based on the matri-
arch's recipes from the home country.
There are many good shrimp dishes, and
fans of hot and spicy should try the *haw
mok talay paw,* a baked seafood combination in a red curry sauce. Entrées
$11.95–15.95.

FILM
Bethesda
The Bethesda Row Cinemas (301-652-
7273), 7235 Woodmont Ave. Presents independent and foreign language cinema.

Gaithersburg
Kentlands Stadium (301-519-6868; http://
kentlandsstadium8.com), 629 Center
Point Way. This is the place to see the
blockbusters.

Silver Spring
AFI Silver Theater (301-495-6700; www
.afi.com/silver), 8633 Colesville Rd.; and
Regal Majestic (301-565-5884; www
.regmovies.com), 900 Ellsworth Dr. are
usually among the first theaters in the area
to show Hollywood's most highly advertised
films.

MUSIC See **Sandy Spring Museum**
under *To See,* **Strathmore Hall** under
Selective Shopping, and **Imagination
Stage** under *Theaters.*

NIGHTLIFE
Bethesda
♈ **Rock Bottom Brewery** (301-652-1311;
www.rockbottom.com), 7900 Norfolk Ave.
Open daily. A full restaurant menu of pizzas, steaks, and meats is served alongside
the microbrewer's own offerings of lagers,
ales, and stouts. Pool tables attract people
during the week, and crowds pour in for
the live music on the weekends.

Silver Spring
Hollywood Ballroom (301-476-7760;
www.hollywoodballroom.com), 2126–38
Industrial Pkwy. Singles and couples show
up Wed.–Sun. to practice and participate in
new and old dance steps on the 7,200-
square-foot floating maple dance floor.

THEATERS
Bethesda
☙ **Imagination Stage** (301-961-6060;
www.imaginationstage.org), 4980 Auburn
Ave. Imagination stage produces plays,

musicals, and other theatrical events for children throughout the year. Free or very low-cost admission.

Olney
The Olney Theatre Center (301-924-3400; www.olneytheatre.org), 2001 Olney–Sandy Spring Rd. One of the two state theaters of Maryland, the Olney is located on 14 acres and has presentations throughout the year. Besides staging 20th-century American classics, it also produces experimental and alternative plays. Past productions have included *Grease!, Candida,* and *Bye Bye Birdie.*

✳ Selective Shopping
ANTIQUES
Gaithersburg
The Emporium of Olde Towne (301-926-9148; www.emporiumofoldetowne.com) and **Olde Towne Antiques** (301-926-9490; on facebook), 223 E. Diamond Ave. Open daily. Side-by-side shops that are so full of antiques and collectibles that the items fill up just about every inch of available space.

Kensington
You could easily spend a full day enjoying the architecture and investigating the treasures to be found in the five-block **Antique Row** in Old Town Kensington. Among the many places to browse are:

Prevention of Blindness Society Antique Shop (301-942-4707; http://kensingtonantiquerow.com/preventionof blindness/index.html), 3716 Howard Ave. All of the money generated from the shop helps the nonprofit society offer free visual screening and testing, eyeglasses, and other services to those who would go without. Shop here and do a good turn all at the same time.

Pritchard's (301-942-1661; http://kensingtonantiquerow.com/pritchards/index.html), 3748 Howard Ave. Stained glass, art deco items, and Mission arts and crafts.

Dianne's Antiques (301-946-4242; http://kensingtonantiquerow.com/dianesantiques

/index.html), 3758 Howard Ave. From Beanie Babies to Victorian furniture.

Kensington Antique Center (301-942-4440), 3760 Howard Ave. More than 10 dealers in one building.

ART GALLERIES
Kensington
Ada Rose Gallery (301-922-0162; www.adahrosegallery.com), 3766 Howard Ave. Changing exhibits and displays from local artists.

North Bethesda
The Mansion at Strathmore Hall (301-530-0540; www.strathmore.org), 10701 Rockville Pike (MD 355). A dozen major exhibits focusing on artists of the area are presented throughout the year in the early-1900s mansion. Classes on various art disciplines are also provided, along with a series of classical, jazz, and popular music programs.

Rockville
VisArts (301-315-8200; www.visartscenter.com), 155 Gibbs St. Upstairs are studios where the center provides classes to budding artists and space for those who are serious about their work (you are often permitted to watch something being created). As the curator told me, "The downstairs gallery is where you may see the works of up-and-coming local and regional artists."

Takoma Park
Gudelsky Gallery (301-649-4454), 10500 Georgia Ave. Located at the Takoma Park/Silver Spring campus of Montgomery College of Art and Design. One goes to the Gudelsky to see tomorrow's art luminaries today. Although there are exhibits by professional artists, some of the most interesting are those from the college's students and faculty.

Also see McCrillis Gardens and Gallery under *Green Space.*

BOOKSTORES **Barnes & Noble** is well represented in Kensington, Bethesda, Gaithersburg, and Rockville.

Also see **Woodend Nature Trail** under *Green Space.*

USED BOOKS

Kensington

All Books Considered (301-929-0036; www.allbooksconsidered.com), 10408 Montgomery Ave. Located at one end of Antique Row, it has an extensive collection of used and rare books.

Rockville

Second Story Books (301-770-0477; www.secondstorybooks.com), 12160 Parklawn Dr. It has more than 86,000 titles in stock, so you are sure to find something to your liking.

SPECIAL SHOPS

G Street Fabrics (301-231-8998; www.gstreetfabrics.com), 5520 Randolph Rd., Rockville. Open daily. The store is known and visited by people from around the country who prize its wide selection of materials and sewing items.

Ten Thousand Villages (301-340-7122; www.tenthousandvillages.com), 107 Gibbs St., Rockville. Fair trade handmade items from Asia, Africa, Latin America, and the Middle East.

FARMER'S MARKETS Gaithersburg Farmer's Market (301-258-6350), at the corner of Fulks Corner Ave. and MD 355. On Thurs. 2–6, June–Oct., make your choice from the offerings.

Silver Spring Farmer's Market (202-362-8889), Ellsworth Dr. between Fenton and Georgia Ave. Lot 3 is the site of crates and boxes full of the bounty of the land for sale Sat. 9–1 Apr.–Dec. and 10–1 Jan.-Mar.

PICK-YOUR-OWN PRODUCE FARMS

Germantown

✔ **Butler's Orchards** (301-972-3299; www.butlersorchard.com), 22200 Davis Mill Rd. A variety of berries is available for picking from late spring through early fall. Call to find out what is in-season when you get ready to go. Butler's also has a pumpkin festival each weekend in October with hayrides, a petting zoo, and entertainment.

✔ **Phillips Farm** (301-540-2364; www.phillipsfarmproduce.com), 13710 Schaeffer Rd. Jean Phillips invites people to the farm from midsummer into autumn to pick hot peppers, nonhybrid varieties of tomatoes, and flowers. Free hayrides to the pumpkin patch during October.

Poolesville

✔ **Homestead Farm** (301-977-3761; www.homestead-farm.net), 15600 Sugarland Rd. Fruits and vegetables available throughout the entire growing and harvesting season. Hayrides every weekend in October, and you can return in December to cut your own Christmas tree.

Silver Spring

✔ **Beacraft's Farm** (301-236-4545; www.naturalmaryland.com), 14722 New Hampshire Ave. (MD 650). Pick strawberries in May and return to choose a pumpkin in October. Weekends in October are quite festive, with a corn maze, a pumpkin patch, and kids' games.

WINERY Sugarloaf Mountain Vineyard (301-605-0130; www.smvwinery.com), 18125 Comus Rd., Dickerson. Open daily June–Oct.; Wed.–Sun. for Nov.–May. In the shadow of its namesake mountain, the vineyard, the closest one in Maryland to Washington, DC, has a little over 17 acres of vines. The year of its first bottling, 2006, the establishment won double gold in an international competition, and each year since has received numerous other awards, including a second double gold. The bright tasting room is within a large, red 1910 barn, with a patio to enjoy on nice-weather days. Owned and operated by three families, the 85-acre farm produces Bordeaux-style wines from its certified French clone grapes. Stop in to taste the Cabernet Sauvignon, Merlot, Cabernet Franc, Malbec, and Petit Verdot. The two whites being produced on my last visit were Chardonnay and Pinot Grigio.

✳ Special Events

February: **Mid-Atlantic Jazz Festival** (888-909-6330), Rockville. Concerts, exhibitors, workshops, and competitions.

March: **Gem and Mineral Show** (301-926-7190), fairgrounds, Gaithersburg. An annual exhibit of minerals, gemstones, and fossils. Demonstrations, workshops, and sales from screened and certified reputable dealers.

April: **Annual Sugarloaf Crafts Festival** (1-800-210-9900), fairgrounds, Gaithersburg. A major festival that attracts more than five hundred artisans and craftspeople from around the country. **Bethesda Literary Festival** (301-215-6660), various sites in downtown Bethesda. Annual event that features nearly 50 literary and cultural artists.

May: **Audubon Nature Fair** (301-652-9188), Woodend, 8940 Jones Mill Rd., Chevy Chase. Annual event of juried arts and crafts, live animals, educational games, and entertainment.

May-September: **Wings of Fancy Butterfly Exhibit** (301-962-1400; www.brookside gardens.org), Brookside Gardens, Wheaton.

June: **Annual Strawberry Festival** (301-774-0022), Sandy Spring Museum, Sandy Spring. Strawberries galore, plus crafts, music, and kids' games.

August: **Montgomery County Fair** (301-926-3100), Agricultural Center, Gaithersburg. The largest county fair in Maryland.

September: **Germantown Octoberfest** (240-777-6821), Town Center, Germantown. **Takoma Park Folk Festival** (301-589-3717), Takoma Park Middle School, Silver Spring. Six stages of music and dance, crafts, and children's activities.

October: **Antique and Classic Car Show** (301-309-3340), Civic Center Park, Rockville. Car show and automobile-related flea market. **F. Scott Fitzgerald Literary Conference** (301-309-9461), Montgomery College, Rockville. Workshops, discussions, and tours.

November: **Railroad-Transportation Artifacts Show and Sale** (703-536-2954), fairgrounds, Gaithersburg. More than six hundred tables of railroad, steamship, bus, and airline memorabilia for sale.

December: **Winter Lights Festival** (301-258-6310), Seneca Creek State Park, Gaithersburg. A 3.5-mile drive through the holiday light show. **Garden of Lights Festival** (301-962-1400; www.brookside gardens.org), Brookside Gardens, Wheaton.

Southern Maryland

4

ALONG THE CHESAPEAKE SHORE
Chesapeake Beach, North Beach,
Prince Frederick, and Solomons

AT THE MOUTH OF THE POTOMAC
St. Mary's City and Leonardtown

ALONG THE POTOMAC SHORE
La Plata, Port Tobacco, and Waldorf

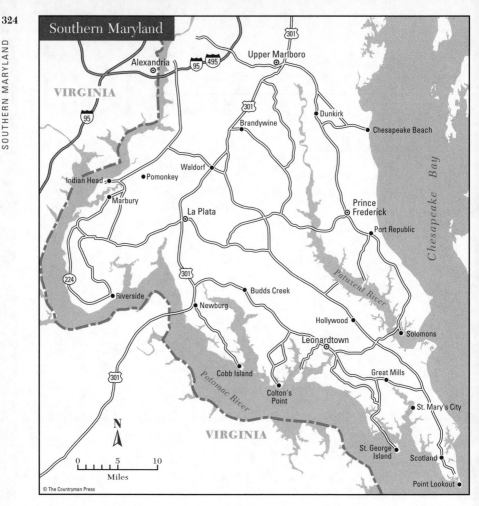

Southern Maryland

301

Upper Marlboro

Alexandria
95 495

VIRGINIA

95

301

Dunkirk

Brandywine

Chesapeake Beach

Waldorf

Indian Head Pomonkey

Marbury

La Plata

Prince
Frederick

Port Republic

Chesapeake Bay

Patuxent River

224

301

Budds Creek

Riverside Newburg

Hollywood

Solomons

Leonardtown

301

Cobb Island

Great Mills

Potomac River

Colton's
Point

St. Mary's City

N

VIRGINIA

St. George
Island Scotland

0   5   10
Miles

© The Countryman Press

Point Lookout

SOUTHERN MARYLAND

A bit off the beaten path, and overshadowed by the Washington, DC/Baltimore metro area, southern Maryland is often ignored as a travel destination by Marylanders and visitors alike. Yet this is where the state had its beginnings when 140 European settlers arrived to found the Maryland Colony in 1634. One of the best-preserved 17th-century town sites in the United States, Historic St. Mary's City is an 800-acre living-history museum on the site of the state's first capital.

History is around every curve in the road. St. Ignatius Church is one of the oldest active Catholic parishes in the country, having served worshipers for more than three centuries. The home of Dr. Samuel Mudd, the physician who treated the broken leg of President Lincoln's assassin, is here, in Waldorf. Several lighthouses from bygone eras are preserved near the shorelines, while it is even possible to scuba dive to the only known World War II rubber-clad German U-boat found within America.

Southern Maryland's lifestyle and low-lying landscape are influenced by the waters of the Chesapeake Bay and those of the Patuxent and Potomac Rivers. Although some of the trappings of the 21st century—such as strip malls and planned communities—are making inroads into the area, many of the old ways remain. In search of flounder, crab, clams, and oysters, many watermen rise before dawn to venture onto the rivers and the bay. Oyster houses and seafood-processing plants along the waterfronts provide employment for those who stay on land.

Numerous tiny towns dot the many miles of shoreline, which, in addition to providing scenic places to rest, can arrange charter excursions for those wanting to cast a line for rockfish or bass. The gently rolling terrain has attracted road bikers for decades, and the local tourist offices have responded by producing a brochure describing various circuit excursions. Finally, no journey into southern Maryland would be complete without a hike to the bay's western shore at Calvert Cliffs State Park to hunt for fossilized shark's teeth.

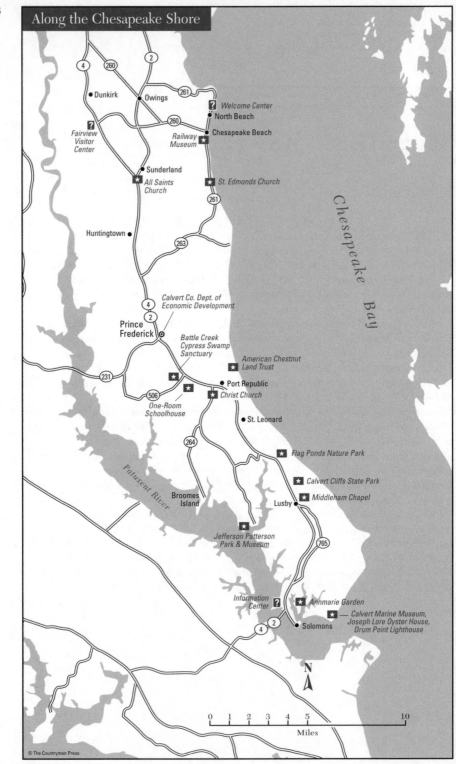

Along the Chesapeake Shore

Dunkirk

Owings

Fairview Visitor Center

Welcome Center
North Beach
Chesapeake Beach
Railway Museum

Sunderland
All Saints Church

St. Edmonds Church

Huntingtown

Chesapeake Bay

Calvert Co. Dept. of Economic Development

Prince Frederick

Battle Creek Cypress Swamp Sanctuary

American Chestnut Land Trust

Port Republic
Christ Church

One-Room Schoolhouse

St. Leonard

Flag Ponds Nature Park

Patuxent River

Calvert Cliffs State Park
Lusby
Middleham Chapel

Broomes Island

Jefferson Patterson Park & Museum

Information Center
Annmarie Garden
Calvert Marine Museum, Joseph Lore Oyster House, Drum Point Lighthouse
Solomons

N

0 1 2 3 4 5   10
Miles

© The Countryman Press

ALONG THE CHESAPEAKE SHORE

CHESAPEAKE BEACH, NORTH BEACH, PRINCE FREDERICK, AND SOLOMONS

Chesapeake Beach began in 1900 as the dream of Colorado railroad baron Otto Mears. By laying railroad tracks from Washington, DC, he hoped to entice people to visit his newly constructed resort town on the western shore of the Chesapeake Bay. For a while his dream was a reality, with scores of people flocking to the amusement park, casino, and hotel along the mile-long boardwalk. Fires, the Great Depression, and easy access to Ocean City on the Eastern Shore brought the dream to an end by the mid-1930s.

Gradually, though, the town has reemerged as a destination spot with a sandy beach, a water park, and several good restaurants.

Due to its proximity to Chesapeake Beach (in fact, it is hard to tell where one town ends and the other begins), the history of North Beach is a parallel of its neighbor's: a rise in tourism in the early 1900s, a decline in the mid-1900s, and revitalization in the late 1900s. A brochure available from the North Beach Welcome Center leads visitors along on a self-guided walking tour of the significant features of the waterfront town. Many people may not take the full tour, but it would be a mistake to overlook the town's boardwalk (now bordered by homes) and beach.

Prince Frederick has been the Calvert County seat since 1725, but little remains of its early days. The British burned it in 1814, and another fire in 1884 completed the job of destroying many other buildings. It remains the hub of county services and has developed into the economic and shopping center of the region.

Solomons has emerged as the area's primary 21st-century destination spot. It was the scenery that first drew me, and many other people, to the small village, located as it is at the wide mouth of the Patuxent River where it meets the Chesapeake Bay. Once here, though, I found many reasons to linger: the excellent exhibits in the Calvert Marine Museum, the Riverwalk boardwalk (from which sunsets are nothing short of spectacular), charter fishing and other boat excursions, and an abundance of B&Bs and restaurants. Nearby, Annmarie Garden and Calvert Cliffs State Park satisfy the need to explore the natural world.

GUIDANCE The **Calvert County, Maryland, Department of Economic Development** (410-535-4583; 1-800-331-9771; www.co.cal.md.us), Courthouse, Prince Frederick, 20678, is full of useful information, and its employees are well versed in what to see and do.

The **Solomons Information Center** (410-326-6027), MD 2/4, Solomons, 20688, sits underneath the Governor Thomas Johnson Memorial Bridge and is staffed by information specialists proud of the area in which they live.

SOLOMONS HARBOR

Along the North Beach boardwalk is a small structure housing the **North Beach Welcome Center** (410-286-3799; www.ci.north-beach.md), 9032 Bay Ave., North Beach, 20714.

At the very northern end of this area is the **Fairview Information Center** (410-257-5381), 8120 Southern Maryland Blvd. (MD 2), Owings, 20736.

GETTING THERE *By air:* The closest two airports with commercially scheduled flights are **Baltimore/Washington International Thurgood Marshall Airport** (1-800-I-FLY-BWI; www.bwiairport.com) near Annapolis and **Ronald Reagan Washington National Airport** (703-417-8000; www.metwashairports.com/reagan/reagan.htm) in northern Virginia.

By car: **MD 4** arrives in the region from the Washington, DC, area, while **MD 2** comes in from the north—allowing access from **US 50/301** near Annapolis and the Eastern Shore. (MD 4 and MD 2 combine into one four-lane roadway north of Huntingtown.) The **Governor Thomas Johnson Memorial Bridge** crosses the Patuxent River at Solomons, bringing travelers into the region from St. Mary's County on **MD 2/4.**

By bus: **Calvert County Public Transportation** (410-535-4268) operates several commuter buses that, on weekdays, could bring you from Washington, DC, to connect with buses continuing on to local sites and towns.

By rail: **AMTRAK** (1-800-USA-RAIL; www.amtrak.com) will deliver you to Washington, DC. From there, you could take one of the commuter buses (see *By bus,* above) into the area.

By water: If you own a boat, or are chartering one, the Chesapeake Bay is the obvious way to arrive. There are many marinas along the shoreline to take care of your needs.

GETTING AROUND *By car:* Four-lane **MD 2/4** runs in a north-south direction through the center of this area. Traffic is only moderately heavy, even during rush hours. The smaller two-lane roadways that reach into the more isolated areas are lightly traveled and are great ways to see the local countryside without feeling harried. **MD 261** through Chesapeake Beach, and **MD 263** to Plum Point, are particularly scenic.

By bus: **Calvert County Public Transportation** (410-535-4268; www.co.cal.md.us) has interconnecting bus routes that reach into nearly every corner of the region. You may have to take a couple of different buses, but you can get to wherever you wish from wherever you are.

The **Beach Trolley** (1-877-777-2708; www.beachtrolleyassociation.org), which operates from Memorial Day to Labor Day, is a convenient way to travel around Chesapeake Beach and North Beach, and as far away as Deale.

By taxi: **Checker Taxi** (240-508-2001), and **Calvert Taxi** in North Beach (410-257-2510) and Prince Frederick (410-535-6272).

PUBLIC RESTROOMS In **North Beach,** restrooms (and shower facilities!) are located in the rear of the Welcome Center on the boardwalk.

In **Solomons,** public restrooms can be found along the boardwalk overlooking the Patuxent River and inside the Solomons Information Center.

MEDICAL EMERGENCY **Calvert Memorial Hospital** (410-535-4000; www.calvert hospital.com), 100 Hospital Rd. (about 1 mile north of town), Prince Frederick.

Dunkirk Medical Center (410-286-7911; www.calverthospital.org), 10845 Town Center Blvd., Dunkirk; and **Solomons Medical Center** (410-394-2800; www.calverthospital.org), 14090 Solomons Island Rd., Solomons, have urgent-care facilities that can handle minor emergencies.

✳ To See
MUSEUMS

Chesapeake Beach
&. **Chesapeake Beach Railway Museum** (410-257-3892; www.cbrm.org), 4155 Mears Ave. (off MD 261). Call ahead as hours vary throughout the year. Free parking and admission.

THE RAILWAY MUSEUM IN CHESAPEAKE BEACH

Exhibits in the 1898 rail station focus on Chesapeake Beach's boardwalk, amusement park, and railroad history.

Port Republic

Port Republic School Number 7 (410-856-1418; www.calvertoneroomschool.org), Broomes Island Rd. Sun. 2–4, May–June. Free. The little one-room schoolhouse served the community for more than one hundred years and is now restored and filled with memorabilia.

⚓ ♿ **Calvert Marine Museum** (410-326-2042; www.calvertmarinemuseum.com), 14200 Solomons Island Rd., Solomons. Open daily 10–5. Small admission fee. It may be smaller in size, but the quality of exhibits and the experience you will have here will easily rival those found in the maritime museum in St. Michaels on the Eastern Shore. Life-sized boats, models, paintings, and wood carvings illustrate the life of the watermen, while fossilized remains and skeletal models of huge sea creatures vividly paint the natural history of the bay and its tributaries. More than 15 **aquariums** contain live specimens of the bay's colorful inhabitants. A **children's Discovery Room** has enough activities to keep even the most rambunctious kid interested and occupied. Outside exhibits include a re-created salt marsh, live river otters splashing about in a native habitat site, and a boat basin with vintage vessels.

Don't leave the museum without climbing through the hatch of the **Drum Point Lighthouse,** one of only three surviving Chesapeake Bay screw-pile, cottage-style lighthouses. Restored to its original appearance and furnished as it would have been in the early 1900s, it is a glimpse into the past.

One-hour cruises around Solomons's harbor and the Patuxent River aboard the *Wm. B. Tennison,* the only Coast Guard–licensed passenger-carrying log-hulled vessel on the bay, originate from the museum's dock (see *To Do*).

The museum also sponsors shuttle-bus trips (daily June–Aug., weekends in May and Sept.) to the **Cove Point Lighthouse,** the oldest continuously operating lighthouse in the state. Built in 1828, it marks one of the narrowest parts of the Chesapeake Bay and helps guide ships into the Patuxent River.

THE DRUM POINT LIGHTHOUSE AT CALVERT MARINE MUSEUM

Solomons

Joseph C. Lore & Sons Oyster House (410-326-2042), 24430 Solomons Island Rd., Solomons. Open daily 10–4:30, June–Aug.; 10–4:30 Sat. and Sun. only in May and Sept. Free admission. The restored 1934 packinghouse chronicles the boom and decline of the area's seafood business. Tools, equipment, and boats illustrate the lifestyle of the watermen.

HISTORIC CHURCHES

Chesapeake Beach

St. Edmonds United Methodist Church (410-535-2506), 3000 Dalrymple Rd. The original church on this site was built of logs and served as a house of worship and a school for the African American community. It burned in 1893.

Huntingtown

Patuxent United Methodist Church (410-535-9819), 3500 Solomons Island Rd. Built by its African American congregation, the original church on this site burned in 1893 and was replaced with the present structure.

Lusby

Middleham Episcopal Chapel (410-326-4948; www.middlehamandstpeters.org), 10210 H. G. Trueman Rd. Built in 1784, this is the oldest religious structure in Calvert County. It is also the oldest cross-shaped church in the state. The bell is the oldest one in Maryland.

Port Republic

Christ Episcopal Church (410-586-0565; www.christchurchcalvert.org), 3100 Broomes Island Rd. The present structure dates from 1772; be sure to take a walk through its garden of biblical plants.

Solomons

St. Peter's Episcopal Church (410-326-4948; www.middlehamandstpeters.org), 14590 Solomons Island Rd. S. The board and batten Victorian Gothic structure with lancet windows was built in 1889 as a comfort church to Middleham Chapel.

Sunderland

All Saints Episcopal Church (410-257-6306; www.allsaints1692.org), at the intersection of MD 4 and MD 2. The Flemish-bond brick church is based upon Georgian ecclesiastical architecture. The baptismal font was imported from England in the early 1700s.

OTHER SITES

St. Leonard

& &. **Jefferson Patterson Park and Museum** (410-586-8501; www.jefpat.org), 10515 Mackall Rd. Wed.–Sun., 10–5, Apr. 15–Oct. 15. Grounds open year-round. Free admission. There is more going on in this park than is at first apparent when you drive in. The museum part of the 544-acre park has a permanent exhibition (12,000 Years in the Chesapeake), a children's discovery room, and historic farm equipment. Several short trails (brochure available in the museum) go through fields and forest and down to the bank of the Patuxent River. Interpreters help visitors make their way through a replica of a Native American village of the 1400s and 1500s, and educational programs are part of the park's schedule throughout the year. Possibly most interesting is the fact that visitors are welcome to take a guided tour (a single person or a group must make an appointment) of the Maryland Archaeological Conservation Laboratory that is geared toward your interests. The tour through the laboratory will introduce you to some of the 7 million (and growing) artifacts housed here. You will also get to witness the many methods employed to conserve these artifacts. On another historical note, the waters bordering the park were the site of the largest naval engagement to ever occur in Maryland (during the War of 1812).

Solomons

Chesapeake Biological Laboratory Visitors Center (410-326-7443; www.umces.edu), Charles St. Tues.–Sun. 10–4, mid-Apr. to early Dec. Free. The small visitors center tells the story of the oldest state-supported marine laboratory on the East Coast. Its mission is to increase knowledge about the ecology and natural history of the bay. Free tours of the entire facility are available on Wed. and Fri. at 2, but you must make arrangements in advance.

✹ To Do

BICYCLING The flat to gently rolling terrain of this region makes it an ideal place to explore by wheel and pedal power. Most of the side roads are lightly traveled, while the main highway, MD 2/42, has moderately heavy traffic but is blessed with paved shoulders.

The Calvert County, Maryland, Department of Economic Development can supply information on several popular and scenic circuit rides. One of the rides is 37 miles long and passes by the beaches at **Chesapeake Beach, North Beach,** and **Breezy Point,** in addition to traversing lightly traveled roads close to the **Patuxent River.** Another, about 15 miles in length, offers the opportunity to get off the bike and do some walking in **Battle Creek Cypress Swamp Sanctuary, Flag Ponds Nature Park, Jefferson Patterson Park and Museum,** and **Calvert Cliffs State Park.** A third circuit ride is less than 3 miles long and takes in most of the small streets and attractions in **Solomons.**

Also see Chesapeake Beach Railway Trail in *Walks.*

BOAT EXCURSIONS

Chesapeake Beach

Mary Lou Too (301-928-3757; www.maryloutoocharters.com), 5510 Cheryl Ln. Capt. Russ Mogel has spent more than four decades on the Chesapeake Bay. So, whether you hire the 46-foot *Mary Lou Too* for a fishing expedition, a scenic trip, or a lighthouse tour, you are sure to gain from his experience and hear some great stories. I was astonished to find out how far away the fish that he tags as part of scientific studies have been found from the Chesapeake Bay. Ask him about it. Captain Russ's two sons also have their captain's license, so there should always be someone available to take you out on the water, early morning or evening, spring through the fall. The boat has a 435-horsepower engine; you will get to your fishing destination quickly.

THOMAS POINT LIGHTHOUSE FROM THE *MARY LOU TOO*

Solomons

✪ ✇ **Solomons Island Heritage Tours** (301-672-35098; www.solomonsisland heritagetours.com). Captains (and married couple) Rachel and Simon Dean are working watermen and provide a number of excursions (for small groups of up to six), including "The War of 1812," "Michener's Chesapeake," and "Lighting Our Way" lighthouse tours.

My "Waterman for a Day" tour on their 40-foot Chesapeake Bay–built *Roughwater* was one of the most authentic experiences I've had on the waters of the bay. They let me try my hand at paten tonging, crab scraping, eel potting (I even got to hold a live eel in my hands; it's not as slimy or as yucky as you think), and oyster dredging. All the while, they kept up a running commentary on the life and problems of a waterman and those of the bay. You may not agree with all of their opinions, but it is certainly interesting to hear how and why their experiences have brought them to their conclusions. I highly recommend spending an hour or two with the Deans.

🦪 *Wm. B. Tennison* (410-326-2042; www.calvertmarinemuseum.com), docked at the Calvert Marine Museum. Cruises Wed. at 2, May–Oct.; there is an additional 12:30 PM cruise in July and Aug. Small admission fee. The lightly narrated one-hour trips aboard this 1899, nine-log, chunk-built bugeye (the oldest licensed passenger-carrying vessel of its kind on the bay) take you along Back Creek and onto the wide mouth of the Patuxent River. It's a nice excursion that gives you a different perspective on the land you sail by. The pure white stucco of Our Lady of the Sea Catholic Church stands out impressively against the scenic background.

BOAT RENTALS Solomons Boat Rental (410-326-4060; www.solomonsboatrental .com), 14406 Old Solomons Island Rd., Solomons. If sailboats, canoes, and pontoon boats are too slow for you, these folks rent 15- and 20-foot powerboats in one-, four-, and eight-hour increments.

Paddle or Pedal (410-991-4268; www.paddleorpedal.com), 4055 Gordon Stinnett Ave, Chesapeake Beach. Offering non-motorized boat and bike rentals including kayaks, canoes, pedal boats and stand-up paddle boats. Kayak lessons.

BOWLING Lord Calvert Bowl (410-535-3560; www.lordcalvertbowling.com), 2275 Solomons Island Rd., Huntingtown. Has 22 lanes.

FAMILY ACTIVITIES

Chesapeake Beach

🏄 **Chesapeake Beach Water Park** (410-257-1404; 301-855-3803; www.chesapeake beachwaterpark.com), 4079 Gordon Stinnett Ave. Open daily after school lets out and closes when school reopens; then on weekends until about Labor Day. Admission is by height: Guests 48 inches or taller are $18; those shorter (and seniors) are $16. County and town residents are admitted at a reduced rate. It may be small by the standards of water parks in major resort areas, but it still has enough features for a full day's worth of fun. Activity pool, kids' pool, seashell and other slides, and free use of tubes.

Prince Frederick

🏄 **R & J's Playpark** (410-535-4522; www.playpark.biz), 900 Sherry Lane. When the children have tired of touring museums

CHESAPEAKE BEACH WATER PARK

or you have had enough of riding in the car with them, R & J's will help alleviate the stress by letting you and them smack some baseballs around in the batting cages or ram into each other with the bumper boats. After everyone calms down, you can play a round of miniature golf.

FISHING The middle part of the Chesapeake Bay is generally considered to have the best variety of fish species. Charter boats usually take sport anglers onto the water in April in search of rockfish, and in late May and early June for black drum and Atlantic croaker. Bottom fishing for spot, trout, and white perch takes place in July. Bluefish and Spanish mackerel make their appearance in August and are joined by schools of gray trout in September. The season is rounded out by the return of the rockfish in October.

This area of Maryland lays claim to having the largest charter-fishing fleet on the Chesapeake Bay. It is certainly true that there are so many charter boats and charter-boat associations, it is impossible to list them here. **The Calvert County, Maryland, Department of Economic Development** can supply you with information on the associations and individual charter companies.

Under the auspices of **Rod 'N Reel** (301-855-8450; www.cbresortspa.com), some boats operate out of Chesapeake Beach, and others through **Bunky's Charter Boats** (410-326-3241; www.bunkyscharterboats.com) in Solomons. Additional sources of charters are the **Charter Boat Fishing Association** (410-760-8242; www.breezypointmarina.com) in Chesapeake Beach and the **Solomons Charter Captains Association** (410-326-2670; www.fishsolomons.com) in Solomons.

GOLF

Dunkirk
& **Twin Shields Golf Club** (410-257-7800; 301-855-8228; www.twinshields.com), 2425 Roarty Rd. Roy and Ray Shields designed the par 70 course with rolling terrain and water hazards on seven of the holes.

Lusby
& **Chesapeake Hills** (410-326-4653; www.chesapeakehills.com), H. G. Trueman Rd. The par 72 course has tree-lined fairways, doglegs, and a varying terrain. The back nine have a number of water hazards.

Owings
& **Mellomar Golf Park** (410-286-8212; www.mellomar.com), 6215 Scaggs Rd. The nine-hole course has water hazards, sand traps, and bent-grass greens.

HIKING **Flag Ponds Nature Park** (410-586-1477; www.calvertparks.org), Flag Ponds Pkwy. (MD 4), Lusby, is just a 10-minute drive north of Calvert Cliffs State Park. Small fee. It is worth visiting while you're in this area. A network of trails courses through a similar environment and can deliver you to another beach for more fossil hunting.

Also see the **American Chestnut Land Trust** sidebar on page 336.

KAYAKING AND CANOEING

Chesapeake Beach
Paddle or Pedal (410-991-4268; www.paddleorpedal.com), 4055 Gordon Stinnett Ave. Offering nonmotorized boat and bike rentals. Enjoy a day of traversing wetlands or the Chesapeake Bay on a variety of boats including kayaks, canoes, pedal boats and stand-up paddle boards. Sunset and sunrise tours, kayak lessons.

Patuxent Adventure Center (410-394-2770; www.paxadventure.com), 13860C Solomons Island Rd. Open daily. Rents single or tandem kayaks for four and eight hours and some quite reasonable rates. Guided group tours are given on Wed. evenings and Sun. mornings. The center also rents bicycles if you wish to take advantage of the back roads and flat to gently rolling terrain in southern Maryland.

✳ Green Space
BEACHES
Chesapeake Beach
Bay Front Park (410-257-2230; www.chesapeake-beach.md.us). There is a fee of $10 for ages 12–54 and $6 for ages 3–11 and 55+ for this small, sandy beach open daily during daylight hours.

♿ **Breezy Point Beach and Campground** (410-535-0259; http://md-calvertcounty.civic plus.com/facilities.aspx), Breezy Point Rd. (off MD 261 about 5 miles south of town). Usually open May–Oct. Small fee; children under two are free. This sandy beach on the Chesapeake Bay is about 2,600 feet long; nets protect the swimming area from jellyfish. Popular with the locals for swimming, picnicking, and crabbing from a 300-foot pier.

The campground (additional fee) has waterfront and water-view tent and RV sites with hookups. May 1–Oct. 1.

North Beach
✐ **North Beach Public Beach** (410-257-9618; 301-855-6681; www.northbeachmd.org). Small fee. The beach and its bordering boardwalk measure just a bit more than 0.5 mile in length. A fishing and crabbing pier is open 24 hours; the beach is open 6 AM–10 PM. Public restrooms and shower facilities are located in the rear of the welcome center. Since there are no large, rolling ocean waves, the beach is the perfect place to let the kids build a sand castle without fear of it (or them) getting washed away. This gets my vote as the best developed beach in Maryland after Ocean City.

Also see *Hiking* and the **Calvert Cliffs State Park** sidebar on page 337.

GARDENS ✐ **Annmarie Sculpture Garden and Arts Center** (410-326-4640; www .annmariegarden.com), Dowell Rd., Solomons. Garden open daily 10–5; Arts Building Tues.–Sun. 10–5. Ages 12+ $3; ages 5–11 $2; seniors 65+ $2; and children 4 and under are

THE NORTH BEACH BOARDWALK

free. The combination sculpture and botanical garden lends itself to quiet contemplations of artwork and appreciation of the beauty found in nature. The 30 acres are divided into display areas with individual works connected by an easy, level path through the woods. Pick up the little guide at the trailhead so that you may learn a little more about the sculptures, some of which may be on loan from other places. The Toddler Tour and Sculpture Scavenger Hunt pamphlets will help hold the little ones' interest. The Arts Building is associated with the Smithsonian, so you know the changing exhibits are going to display some quality art. The gift shop features works of local and regional artists. I thoroughly enjoy this place and urge you to visit; even the entrance gate and the restrooms are works of art.

ANNMARIE SCULPTURE GARDEN

WALKS 🐾 ♿ **Battle Creek Cypress Swamp Sanctuary** (410-535-5327; www.calvert parks.org), Grays Rd., Prince Frederick. Closed Mon. Free. This is a favorite place of mine when I don't have a lot of time to spare but still have a strong urge to return to the natural world. A 0.25-mile boardwalk snakes through the 100-acre sanctuary, allowing me to enjoy the abundant wildlife and stately bald cypress trees—which are at their northernmost natural limit here. Exhibits in the nature center explore the area's mysteries (what purpose do cypress knees serve?) and its natural and cultural history.

♿ **Chesapeake Railway Trail** (410-257-2230; www.chesapeake-beach.md.us), begins behind the Chesapeake Beach Water Park. Part of a rail trail that will eventually pass

NATURE PRESERVE

American Chestnut Land Trust (410-414-3400; 410-586-1570; www.acltweb.org), Scientists Cliffs Rd., Port Republic. Open daily dawn–dusk. Free. Concerned about the detrimental effects Calvert County was experiencing as a result of having the fastest population growth of any county in the Washington, DC, area, a group of farsighted citizens banded together to form the nonprofit American Chestnut Land Trust. So far, the trust has been able to preserve almost 1,000 acres and has accepted the management of 350 acres owned by the state. Along with adjacent land held by the Nature Conservancy, 2,700 acres of fields, forests, marshes, swamps, and streams are no longer threatened by the modern world.

A network of pathways on these lands is open to the general public. Because they are not well known and are located off main roadways, the trails are blissfully underutilized. About the only other people you may see are trust members on a hike or a local neighbor out for a morning walk. Among the natural features are Maryland's only known community of sweet pinesap, a saprophytic plant that somewhat resembles its better-known relative Indian pipe, and Parkers Creek, a brackish tidal stream that flows through the last pristine salt marsh on the bay's western shore.

✒ **Calvert Cliffs State Park** (301-743-7613; www.dnr.state.md.us/publiclands/southern /calvertcliffs.asp), 9500 H. G. Trueman Rd., Lusby. Open daily sunrise–sunset. Impressively rising to heights of more than 100 feet above the water, Calvert Cliffs was formed millions of years ago when southern Maryland was under a shallow sea. More than six hundred species of sea creatures, such as whales, sea cows, porpoises, rays, sharks, seabirds (the size of small airplanes!), crocodiles, mollusks, and reptiles lived in the warm waters.

Since as far back as the 1600s, people have been coming to the base of the cliffs to see what new fossils they would yield. Whale ear bones and skulls, sea cow ribs, crocodile snouts (and fossilized dung), and even peccary scapulas and fossilized pinecones have been uncovered. But it is the thousands of fossilized shark's teeth, some from megalodon (an extinct relative of the great white shark) that have made the cliffs famous and drawn generations of schoolchildren and other visitors to the area.

Today most of the cliffs' 30 miles are privately owned, so you and I are lucky that the state has set aside a short stretch of the shoreline. Here we can walk to the water's edge, study the bay's ecology, search for small paleontological treasures hidden in the sand, or just sit peacefully on the beach. (For visitors' safety, walking on or below the crumbling cliffs is prohibited. To keep the cliffs from deteriorating any faster, visitors are not permitted to dig for fossils on them.) A network of marked trails takes visitors into upland forest, through freshwater and tidal marshlands, and beside slowly flowing creeks. It is about 2 miles (one-way) to the beach.

CALVERT CLIFFS

through a number of counties, this trail utilizes boardwalks in this area to take hikers, bikers, and those in wheelchairs over marshlands and Fishing Creek. It's an easy scenic walk that has interpretive signs providing natural and human history tidbits and provides the possibility of seeing bald eagles and other creatures.

✱ Lodging

MOTELS AND HOTELS

Chesapeake Beach, 20732

& **Chesapeake Beach Resort & Spa** (410-257-5596; 1-866-312-5596; www .chesapeakebeachresortspa.com), 4165 Mears Ave. Sitting directly next to the Chesapeake Bay, the resort's more than 70 rooms have water views, and some deluxe suites have Jacuzzis and fireplaces. There's a heated indoor pool, a fitness center, sauna, and guest laundry. The spa is full service, with massages and body therapies, along with a salon with hair and nail services, and waxing for those who need to tidy up a bit. The waterfront location is the best part of the resort, with direct access to the water and a small fishing pier. $175–425; many package deals available.

Dowell, 20629

& **Hilton Garden Inn Solomons** (410-326-0303; www.solomons.stayhgi.com), 13100 Dowell Rd. Located less than 2 miles from the attractions of Solomons Island, the Hilton has close to 100 guest rooms and a number of suites, and it provides guests with a heated indoor pool, exercise facility, business center, and guest laundry facilities. All rooms have refrigerator, microwave oven, and coffeemaker. $145–169.

Prince Frederick, 20678

& **Springhill Suites by Marriott** (443-968-3000; www.marriott.com/bwipf), 75 Sherry Ln. Set on a side street a nice distance away from the main four-lane highway so that traffic noise is reduced, the hotel offers an indoor pool and whirlpool, fitness center, and a complimentary continental breakfast. All rooms are suites with a work area, a pullout sofa bed, refrigerator, and microwave. $125–149.

Solomons, 20688

& ❦ **Comfort Inn** (410-326-6303; www .choicehotels.com), 255 Lore Rd. Close to the working Beacon Marina, the two-story motel sits close to the water with some rooms that have limited views. Complimentary "deluxe" continental breakfast, microwave and refrigerator in the room, and an outdoor pool and whirlpool. Small pets permitted with an additional fee of $20. $109–139.

& **Holiday Inn Select** (410-326-6311; www.holidayinn.com), 155 Holiday Dr. More than 300 rooms on a 9-acre waterfront property. Health club, outdoor pool, and tennis and volleyball courts. Modern, clean, well kept, and a friendly staff. $139–189.

BED & BREAKFASTS

Huntingtown, 20639

❧ **Open Gates Farm Bed & Breakfast** (301-812-0209; www.opengatesfarm.com), 6525 Huntingtown Rd. With snacks and drinks always available, and a full country breakfast served in the morning, the friendly hosts of this mid-20th-century farmhouse B&B will make sure that you won't go away hungry. You will also receive their full attention as there is only one guest suite, which has a sitting room, full bath, a small library alcove, and a kitchenette. Located at a crossroads in the country, so you get a good feel for life in rural southern Maryland. $159.

Solomons, 20688

& **Back Creek Inn B&B** (410-326-2022; www.backcreekinnbnb.com), Alexander Lane and Calvert St. Former navy wives Lin Cochran and Carol Pennock offer landscaped gardens and a goldfish pond, a hot tub, and water-view rooms in their 1880s waterfront home. All rooms have a private bath. The suites and cottage (with its own whirlpool) are additions that provide a bit more privacy with their own entrances. I was drawn to the Tansy Room, where you can watch the sun rise over the water in autumn. Free bike use for guests. $130–225.

Blue Heron Inn Bed and Breakfast (410-326-2707; www.blueheronbandb.com), 14614 Solomons Island Rd. Everything about the B&B in this columned Charleston colonial home speaks of class. All four guest rooms have tasteful furnishings, private bath, and water views. The suites also have private balconies from which you can watch the comings and goings of the working and pleasure boats in the harbor. Evening wine and hors d'oeuvres, a very special gourmet breakfast, and free use of bicycles included. $179–249.

Solomons Victorian Inn B&B (410-326-4811; www.solomonsvictorianinn.com), 125 Charles St. The 1906 Queen Anne Victorian home overlooks Solomons harbor. All guest rooms and suites have a private bath; my favorite was the third-floor Solomons Sunset Suite. Its nooks and lush woodwork made me feel like I was in the cabin of a sailboat. The Carriage House suites have great harbor views. Breakfast is a grand affair with dishes such as shrimp soufflé or a Brie tarragon croissant. $110–240.

COTTAGES

North Beach

Heron's Rest Guest House (410-741-5056; www.heronsrestcottage.com), 4104 Third St. Small Heron's Rest is only 50 feet from the boardwalk, making it an ideal location for beach lovers. It has been modernized with a sleeping loft (with a view of the bay), flat screen TVs, and small kitchen, but since it was built in the 1940s, it's a way to get the feel of the bygone days of North Beach and Chesapeake Beach. The small front porch is a nice added amenity that lets you do some people watching. This is not a B&B, but the owner does provide you with coupons for Blondie's Bakery nearby. Her artwork adorns the walls. $195.

Seahorse Guest Cottage (410-610-9322; www.seahorseguestcottage.com), 8811 Dayton Ave. Located a few blocks from the beach in a residential neighborhood, the renovated early-20th-century cottage has a living room, bedroom, TVs, sunroom with a daybed, and a small backyard with a deck and gas grill. Like Heron's Rest, Seahorse harkens back to the early days of this area being a popular resort destination when many of the cottages were owner-built. (I'm not sure if Seahorse was, but its listing floors attest to its authenticity of being from the period.) Rates include free pass to the

North Beach town beach and pier. $185; weekly and monthly rates available.

Port Republic, 20676

The Cottages of Governors Run (410-586-2346; 1-877-586-1793; www.bay cottages.com), 2847 Governors Run Rd. Mid-Mar.–Oct. Two cottages are on a low cliff overlooking the Chesapeake Bay, so great sunrises are assured. A third cottage is only 200 feet away. A small beach is only a minute's walk away. Sue and Steve Kullen have refurbished the 1940s vacation homes and stocked them with everything you need, including linens. One cottage sleeps four to six; the others are designed for two to four. Weekly rates are $1,395.

St. Leonard, 20685

♿ **Osprey's Nest Guest Cottage** (443-532-5975; www.homeaway.com), 6040 Bayview Rd. Calling this 3,300-square foot modern home a cottage has to be a major misnomer. There are four bedrooms, three baths, great room, living room, game room, and more. What I liked the most is that, although crowded in by neighboring homes of the community of Long Beach, the "cottage" sits high on the hillside, with soaring views of the sparkling water of Chesapeake Bay below. You can take in the view outdoors from the deck or, if you happen to be the lucky one in the master bedroom, from your bed. The sandy beach is less than a three-minute walk away. Since the house sleeps up to 10, this place is good for large groups at only $450 a night or $2,500 a week. The same owners offer **Jeff's Bed & Fix Your Own Breakfast** across the street at 6027 Bayview Rd. It sleeps 12 and is only $300 a night or $1,400 a week.

CAMPING

St. Leonard, 20685

Patuxent Camp Sites (410-586-9880; www.patuxentcampsitesllc.com), 4764 Williams Wharf Rd. Open year-round, but limited sites and facilities in winter. Waterfront sites with hook-ups, dump stations, and hot showers in the bath facilities. The 100-foot pier is great for fishing or crabbing.

Also see **Breezy Point Beach and Campground** under *Green Space*.

✴ Where to Eat

DINING OUT

Prince Frederick

& **Saphron Restaurant at Old Field Inn** (443-975-7560; www.saphronrestaurant .com), 485 Main St. Open for dinner Tues.–Sat. The winding driveway that goes by manicured lawns delivers you to the 1890s Victorian home and its graciously furnished dining rooms. The owner is from Charleston, South Carolina, and low country cuisine influences the menu. Look for shrimp and grits, gumbo, and fried okra and collard greens to almost always be on the menu. The *swai basi* is an interesting dish of a lightly floured and sautéed catfish fillet with a curry coconut sauce, red rice, and collard greens. Many other standards, such as steaks and pasta, are also available. A nice place to spend a quiet, romantic evening. Entrées $15–27.

Solomons

& **Dry Dock Restaurant** (410-326-4817; www.zahnisers.com/drydock.htm), C St. in Zahniser's Marina. Open daily for dinner only; fewer days in winter. Great view of

Solomons Harbor. The menu changes almost daily and features seafood purchased fresh from local vendors. The day I dined, the chef prepared basil-crusted rockfish with garlic and parsley tossed pasta, jumbo lump crabcakes, Cornish game hen, and cinnamon-crusted oysters . Lots of big chunks of meat in the crab soup. Most entrées are $19–32.

White Sands

& **Vera's Beach Club Restaurant and Marina** (410-586-1182), 1200 White Sands Dr. Vera's extraordinary personality, wardrobe, and decorating style made this a must-see place for decades. Holding court under a reed-and-bamboo ceiling, she wandered among guests bedecked in pearls, woven headband, and Polynesian-style dress, sipping an endless glass of champagne. Vera has passed on, but the restaurant remains, and dinner entrées include beef, poultry, lamb, and seafood. $15.95–25.95.

EATING OUT

Broomes Island

❀ & **Stoney's Seafood House** (410-586-1888; www.stoneysseafoodhouse.com), 3939 Oyster House Rd. Open daily (except Tues.) for lunch and dinner; this is a sea-

STONEY'S SEAFOOD HOUSE

sonal location, so call ahead to be sure it's open. The restaurant is next to the Patuxent River, and to get a real feel of being on the water, ask to be seated on the floating deck. Entrées are made with items purchased from Denton's Seafood next door, so everything is as fresh as it can get. The crabcakes (market price) have received accolades for years, while the Neptune's platter gives you a taste of several items. If you are here in the right season, lunch on one of the softshell crab sandwiches (market price). Most entrées $14.95–29.95. Steamed crabs by the dozen (market price) are served if locally available.

Chesapeake Beach

✄ ఈ **Rod 'N' Reel** (410-257-2735; 1-877-RODNREEL; www.chesapeakebeach resortspa.com), 4160 Mears Ave. Open daily for lunch and dinner, Sat.–Sun. for breakfast. As the name should suggest, and in operation since 1946 (take a look at the old Chesapeake Beach photos on the wall), the emphasis here is on seafood, some of it caught locally. Although I have not had a chance to try them, several people said they enjoyed the crabcakes, and one person told me they thought the lobster was good. The shrimp scampi I had for lunch was satisfying, and the steak ordered by my dining companion was tender. Ask for a window table so that you can watch all of the activity on the water. $18–32.

✄ ఈ **Traders Seafood Steak & Ale** (410-257-6126, www.traders-eagle.com), 8132 Bayside Rd. Open daily for breakfast, lunch, and dinner. The building that Traders is in has been a restaurant of some kind or another since 1956 and its current full name pretty much describes it—seafood, steak, and ale. You'll find that they also serve a good breakfast and a nice breakfast buffet on Sundays. A favorite place of the locals. $11.99–22.99.

Owings

✄ ఈ **Thursday's** (410-286-8695; www .thursdaysrestaurant.com/thursdaysbarand grill), 1751 Horace Ward Rd. Open daily for lunch and dinner. Thursday's is a local watering hole that serves good, solid food. Appetizers and soups are made from

scratch, and prime rib is hand cut and slow roasted. A few seafood dishes and south of the border items are also on the menu. A dozen draft beers complement meals. $11.95–23.95.

Prince Frederick

Mamma Lucia (443-486-4701; mamma luciarestaurant.com), 862 Costley Wy. Open daily for lunch and dinner. Located in a free-standing building within a small shopping mall complex, Mamma Lucia's menu is based on southern Italian cuisine. Pastas are made fresh in-house and portions are large enough that you are more than likely to bring some home for lunch tomorrow. The menu seems to always feature new items, old favorites returning, and daily specials, so you'll have something different to try each time you visit. $12.95–20.95.

Solomons

ఈ **The CD Café** (410-326-3877; www .cdcafe.info), 14350 Solomons Island Rd. Open daily for lunch and dinner. There is a reason people are willing to sometimes wait a long time to get seated at one of the less-than-a-dozen tables here: the place turns out delicious, and for the most part healthful, dishes. The roasted vegetarian sandwich (with house salad; $10.95) I lunched on was full of sweet and flavorful red peppers. The pasta with sun-dried tomatoes, artichoke, feta, and garlic caper sauce ($15.95) I had the next evening was equally satisfying, while my dining mate almost wanted to lick the plate after finishing her pan-roasted salmon ($22.95). Other entrées $8.95–24.95. CD Café is, without a doubt, my choice for Solomons's best taste-bud experience.

Lotus Kitchen and Kim's Key Lime Pies (410-326-8469; www.kimskeylimepies .com), 14618 Solomons Island Rd. Open Wed.–Sun for breakfast, lunch, and dinner. It's often hard to find what at least approaches healthful food, so it's nice to find another place in Solomon's that will treat your body better than a greasy burger and fries. Inside a former home, you find breakfast items like egg, mozzarella, and pesto on toasted ciabatta. Lunch and dinner are mostly sandwiches, such as the chicken wrap with black bean–corn relish, gua-camole, cheddar, and chipotle ranch. Most items $5–9.

⚓ ♿ **Stoney's Kingfishers** (410-394-0236), 14442 Solomons Island Rd. Serves lunch and dinner daily in a casual waterfront atmosphere. A dock is available for those arriving by boat. The menu at this Stoney's includes steaks and other entrées, but since you are next to the Chesapeake Bay, go for one of the well-prepared seafood dishes. The cream of crab soup (market price) may just be the best and creamiest you will find in all Maryland, and the crab imperial is full of backfin crabmeat. Entrées $19–31.

♿ **Stoney's Solomons Pier** (410-326-2424), 14575 Solomons Island Rd. Open daily for lunch and dinner. Located on the pier built in 1919 on the Patuxent River, so it has a great view of its surroundings. It's nice to be here for sunsets or to watch storms roll in across the water. Downstairs hops with local workers enjoying the bar, while upstairs is loud and noisy with families and large groups enjoying the festive atmosphere. Like its sister restaurant in Broomes Island, seafood is the specialty, with a variety of crab dishes (market price), oysters (market price), and crab-imperial-stuffed flounder. Chicken, steak, pasta, and other entrées $14.95–32.95. Rockfish bites are a nice appetizer, and the Angels on Horseback (fried oysters with applewood-smoked bacon on a French roll) is a good lunch sandwich.

CRABS

Chesapeake Beach

♿ **Abner's Crab House** (410-257-3689; 301-855-6705; www.abnerscrabhouse.com), 3748 Harbor Rd. Open daily for lunch and dinner. Overlooks the marsh in Fishing Creek Park. Typical crab house with crab balls, crabcakes, and other fresh catches from the bay. Daily specials and a raw bar. $14.95–market price.

TAKE-OUT

Chesapeake Beach

Tyler's Tackle Shop and Crab House (410-257-6610; www.tylerstackle.com), 8210 Bayside Rd. If you don't have any luck catching something on your own, Tyler's can not only tell (and sell) you what piece of equipment you should have been using, but they can also supply you with the crab, fish, or other seafood you had been hoping you could catch yourself.

Solomons

Captain Smith's Seafood Market (410-326-1134), MD 4/2. Live and steamed crabs, shrimp, seafood, and fresh crabmeat.

MAKE YOUR OWN CRABCAKES

Many restaurants proclaim that their crabcakes are 100 percent meat—so that they won't be accused of using filler—but the traditional Maryland recipe included a few extra ingredients:

1 cup seasoned bread crumbs (Old Bay seasoning)
1 large egg
¼ cup mayonnaise
½ teaspoon salt
¼ teaspoon pepper
1 teaspoon Worcestershire sauce
1 teaspoon dry mustard
1 pound crabmeat
butter or oil for frying

Mix the bread crumbs, egg, mayonnaise, and seasonings together; then mix in the crabmeat. Shape into six cakes. Cook in a frying pan with a bit of oil until well browned on each side. Enjoy.

SNACKS AND GOODIES ✆ Old
Town Candy (410-286-7300), 9122 Bay
Ave., North Beach. Lots of things to satisfy
the sweet tooth. Individual candy bars or
items by the pound.

Sweet Dreams (410-610-3669), 4902 St.
Leonard Rd., St. Leonard. With the feel of
an old-time candy shop, Sweet Dreams has
one of the most extensive offerings of lollipops you are likely to find, from small
suckers to those huge swirly pops that are
so often used as props in Hollywood
movies. There's also an extensive selection
of peppermint sticks and some handcrafted
chocolates.

Sweet Sue's Bake Shop and Coffee Bar
(410-286-8041; www.sweetsues-bakeshop
.com), 9132 Bay Ave., North Beach. Closed
Mon. The owners of Sweet Sue's have an
impressive array of baking credentials. Sue
Dzurec operated a catering and baking
business in Cheverly, Maryland, that
became so well respected that she was
hired to design specialty desserts for the
U.S. Naval Academy's officers' club. Her
daughter, Lauren, is a culinary arts graduate
from Johnson and Wales University, and
together the two provide this part of Maryland with some pleasing baked goods,
custom-designed cakes, and coffees
imported from around the world. The
breakfast specials bring the locals in during
the early morning hours, and some nice
sandwiches are the draw for lunch.

✳ Entertainment
FILM Apex Theatres (410-535-0781;
www.apexcinemas.com), Calvert Village
Mall, Prince Frederick. Shows first-run
movies.

✳ Selective Shopping
ANTIQUES
Dowell
Grandmother's Store Antique Center
(410-326-3366), 13892 Dowell Rd. Open
daily. Inside an old country store are nine
rooms of antiques, books, and other items
available from various vendors. Be sure to

locate the **In the Country** shop to take a
look at the "Lilamericans" figurines hand-
sculpted by the owner-artist.

North Beach
About a dozen antiques dealers, some with
their own storefronts and others in a center
with several other shops, are located on
Bay, Seventh, and Chesapeake Aves. in
North Beach. All are within easy walking
distance of one another.

Nice and Fleazy Antique Center (410-
257-3044); Seventh and Bay Aves. Several
dealers specializing in refurbished oak and
Victorian furniture, clocks, vintage slot
machines, and nautical items.

St. Leonard
The Chesapeake Marketplace (410-586-
3725; 1-800-655-1081; www.chesapeake
marketplace.com), 5015 St. Leonard Rd.
Wed.–Sun. 10–5. More than 80 shops gathered within a 5-acre, former lumberyard
complex. The majority are antiques dealers;
the others have local crafts, gift items,
ceramics, and collectibles.

Solomons
Island Trader Antiques (410-326-3582),
225 Lore Rd. Closed Wed. A mix of furniture, trunks, linens, and old advertising
boxes.

ART GALLERIES
North Beach
ArtWorks @ 7th (410-286-5278; www
.artworksat7th.com), 9131 Bay Ave.
Located on the second floor of the Nice
and Fleazy Antique Center (see *Antiques*),
this is an artist-owned gallery that displays
works in many media, including photography, sculpture, jewelry, and painting.

Prince Frederick
**Calvert County Cultural Arts Council
CalvArt Gallery** (410-535-0302; www
.calvertarts.org), 246 Mirrimac Crt. A small
area displays the works of local council
members.

Solomons
Carmen's Gallery (410-326-2549; www
.carmensgallery.com), 14550 Solomons

Island Rd. Open Thurs.–Sun. This is not a run-of-the-mill local/regional artist gallery. Yes, there are some exceptionally fine artists representing the area, but what you are going to find here are masters from all corners of the earth—Spain, Peru, China, Russia, England, Iran, and, of course, America—who have been exhibited in such esteemed places as the Smithsonian and the Louvre. Price tags of $875–6,000 reflect the renown of those that Carmen has deemed worthy of her gallery. She also offers fine handmade jewelry and wearable art. It's almost an education in art to walk into the place.

USED BOOKS Second Look Books (410-535-6897), 759 Solomons Island Rd. N., Prince Frederick. A huge selection of books, covering just about any topic you can think of, crammed into a small space located in a strip mall. Like most shops of this kind, there are a few hardbacks, but primarily the selection is paperbacks. There's also an offering of audiobooks.

WINERIES
Lusby
Cove Point Winery (410-326-0949; www .covepointwinery.com), 755 Cove Point Rd. Open for tastings Sat.–Sun. Cove Point was Southern Maryland's first winery, but it still qualifies as a microwinery that obtains about half of its grapes from nearby vineyards. Amazingly this nearly one-man operation create dozens of award-winning wines including reds, whites, and fruit blends.

Solomons Island Winery (410-394-1933; www.solomonsislandwinery.com), 515 Garner Ln. No appointment needed Sat.–Sun.; call to visit noon–5 Tues.–Fri. In addition to Bordeaux-style wines aged in Hungarian oak casks, the winery also produces some interesting blends, like Reisling with green apple flavors; blueberry Pinot Noir; and Sauvignon Blanc with kiwi and pear. By the time you visit, the winery should have its expansive and environmentally friendly facilities and tasting room in place.

Owings
Fridays Creek Winery (410-286-WINE; www.fridayscreek.com), 3485 Chaneyville.

Open for tastings Thurs.–Mon. 11–5. Fridays Creek's vines are growing on land that once grew tobacco for some of Maryland's earliest colonists, and the winery's tasting room is located in a barn that was once used to hang and dry that tobacco. The tasting room is an inviting place that makes use of rich walnut and oak woods that were harvested from the property. Upstairs is a gallery displaying the works of local artists. Several thousand gallons of the wines produced come from the winery's own vineyards. In addition to the whites and reds, there is a selection of fruit wines.

Prince Frederick
⚥ **Running Hare Vineyard** (410-414-8486; www.runningharevineyard.com), 150 Adelina Rd. Tastings Wed.–Sun. 1–6 year-round. This is one of those vineyards that has acres of vines stretched across rolling land that is so pleasing for the eye to take in. There are more than 5,000 vines growing on 8 of the property's 300 acres. There's almost always some kind of public event every weekend, and the grounds are often the site of a wedding. All of the vineyard's wines have won awards (some even international), including the dessert wine Chambourcin.

FRIDAYS CREEK WINERY

✳ Special Events

March: **Taste of Solomons** (410-326-9900; www.atasteofsolomons.com), Solomons. A chance to sample the best of culinary delights.

April: **Discovering Archaeology Day** (410-586-8501; www.jefpat.org), Jefferson Patterson Park and Museum, St. Leonard. Demonstrations, tours, and activities for budding archaeologists of any age. **Celtic Festival of Southern Maryland** (443-404-7319; www.ssm.org), St. Leonard. Music, dance, bagpiping, children's games, competitions, storytelling, and all things Celtic.

May: **Annual Herb and Wildflower Show** (410-535-5327), Battle Creek Cypress Swamp Nature Center, Prince Frederick. The sale of herbs and native wildflowers benefits local environmental education programs. **Annual Maritime Festival** (410-326-2042; www.calvert marinemuseum.com), Calvert Marine Museum, Solomons.

June: **Annual African American Family Community Day** (410-535-2730), Jefferson Patterson Park and Museum, St. Leonard. Music, wagon rides, African dancing, kids' activities, crafts, and food. **Tobacco Trail Antique and Classic Car Show** (410-326-4640; www.annmarie garden.org), Solomons. The automobiles are displayed among Annmarie Garden's sculptures, celebrating both as art forms.

July: **American Indian Heritage Day** (410-586-8502), Jefferson Patterson Park and Museum, St. Leonard. Dance, music,

and other visual and performing arts by American Indians from the region. Hands-on basketry, archery, and stone tool making.

August: **Calvert County Jousting Tournament** (410-586-0565), Port Republic. Oldest tournament in Maryland of the state's official sport. Crafts, country supper, and bazaar. **North Beach Bayfest** (301-855-6681), North Beach. Crafts, Maryland food, pony rides and other children's activities, music, and antique cars.

September: **Artsfest** (410-326-4640; www .annmariegarden.org), Annmarie Garden, Solomons. Juried arts and crafts show, with visual and performing arts. **War of 1812 Reenactment and 19th-Century Tavern Night** (410-586-8502), Jefferson Patterson Park and Museum, St. Leonard. Relive the Battle of St. Leonard during the War of 1812. Reenactors stage the land and water aspects of the skirmish. Re-creations of camp life, period crafts, and food. **Calvert County Fair** (410-535-0026; calvert countyfair.com), fairgrounds, Barstow.

November: **Hospice Festival of Trees** (410-535-0892), Patuxent High School, Lusby. Marvelously decorated trees, holiday music, and crafts. Benefits Calvert Hospice.

December–early January: **Garden in Lights** (410-326-4640), Annmarie Garden, Solomons.

December: **Solomons Christmas Walk** (410-326-1950; www.solomons.business .com), Solomons. Annual event with candlelit streets, art, entertainment, bell choirs and carolers, a puppet show, and a boat light parade.

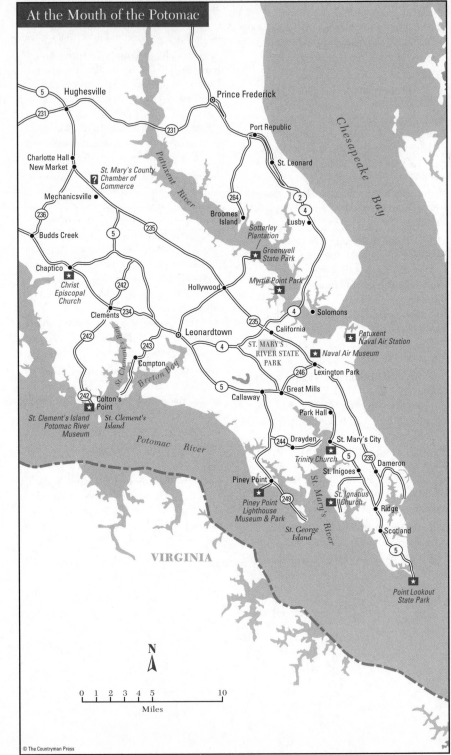

At the Mouth of the Potomac

Hughesville
Charlotte Hall
New Market
Mechanicsville
Budds Creek
Chaptico
Christ
Episcopal
Church
Clements
Compton
Colton's
Point
St. Clement's Island
Potomac River
Museum
St. Clement's
Island

Prince Frederick
Port Republic
St. Leonard
St. Mary's County
Chamber of
Commerce
Broomes
Island
Lusby
Sotterley
Plantation
Greenwell
State Park
Myrtle Point Park
Hollywood
Solomons
Leonardtown
California
Patuxent
Naval Air Station
ST. MARY'S
RIVER STATE
PARK
Naval Air Museum
Lexington Park
Callaway
Great Mills
Park Hall
Drayden
St. Mary's City
Trinity Church
St. Inigoes
Dameron
Piney Point
St. Ignatius
Church
Ridge
Piney Point
Lighthouse
Museum & Park
St. George
Island
Scotland
Point Lookout
State Park

Chesapeake
Bay

Patuxent River

St. Clement's Bay

Breton Bay

Potomac River

VIRGINIA

St. Mary's River

N

0 1 2 3 4 5   10
Miles

© The Countryman Press

AT THE MOUTH OF
THE POTOMAC
ST. MARY'S CITY AND LEONARDTOWN

Maryland's deepest roots grow here, for this is where the colony that eventually became a state was born.

Maryland's story begins in November 1633. Imagine the courage, fortitude—and desperation—it must have taken for close to two hundred British men, women, and children to leave all they had known to venture forth into unclear futures in an unknown land. Longing for a religious tolerance denied to them in their home country, they boarded the Ark and the Dove to face a four-month voyage across the Atlantic Ocean. Sailing into the mouth of the Potomac River, these seekers of a new life landed at St. Clement's Island in March 1634. A large wooden cross was erected in thanks, and they prayerfully celebrated the first Roman Catholic Mass in the English-speaking colonies.

Soon afterward, they moved to a more suitable site for a permanent settlement along the St. Mary's River. Their story, and that of the state's early days, is vividly portrayed and preserved for visitors to experience in 800-acre Historic St. Mary's City.

As to be expected on fertile land bordered by two rivers and the Chesapeake Bay, life in the colony developed around large plantations and seafood harvesting. To some degree, many things remain the same today. Yes, housing developments eat into farmland and strip malls replace tobacco barns, but acres of open meadows still edge quiet country lanes, and new generations of watermen carry on the traditions of their grandparents. And like many American presidents, going all the way back to James Madison, visitors are lured here by the water, the scenery, and a slower pace of life. Montana may be known as Big Sky Country, but to stand on a southern Maryland shoreline surrounded by open fields and gaze to where water meets earth's canopy is to be filled with a sense of immense space.

COMMUNITIES **Leonardtown,** despite being St. Mary's County seat since 1708, still has a population of only slightly more than two thousand people. While retaining a small-town atmosphere—it has a central square bordered by local businesses and the courthouse—it has some of the best upscale restaurants and shops in the region. The *Historic Leonardtown Walking Tour* brochure (available from the St. Mary's County Division of Tourism) takes you by more than 20 of the town's more interesting buildings. A waterfront park with a few interpretive signs adds to the town's appeal.

The area around **Lexington Park** remained a quiet place until the middle of World War II, when a small naval station expanded into the 6,000-acre Patuxent River Naval Air Station.

The federal government developed a housing project outside the station for military personnel, and the city has continued to expand. It is now the economic center of the region and shows all of the signs of rapid modernization, with shopping centers, restaurants, strip malls, and—modest by big-city standards—the heaviest traffic around.

California is basically a suburb of Lexington Park, and its stores and restaurants are the first things people see when they arrive from Solomons across the MD 4/Governor Thomas Johnson Memorial Bridge.

Like a thin finger jutting into the expanse of water created by the confluence of the Potomac and St. Mary's Rivers, **St. George Island** is connected to the mainland by a two-lane bridge. The life you see here is representative of what you would find if you were to drive many of the region's country lanes to small communities at land's end.

Amish families from Pennsylvania began to move onto farmland around **Charlotte Hall** in the mid-1900s, and it is not an uncommon sight to see a horse and buggy moving along at 18th-century speeds on some of the back roads.

GUIDANCE **St. Mary's County Division of Tourism** (301-475-4200; 1-800-327-9023; www.visitstmarysmd.com), 23115 Leonard Hall Dr., Leonardtown, 20650.

The **St. Mary's County Welcome Center** (301-884-7059), 37575 Charlotte Hall Rd, Charlotte Hall, 20622, can also supply you with some information. You should stop by here even if you don't need any information, as the center has some displays that provide wonderful background on the county you are about to visit. This is also the site where, in 1698, the Maryland General Assembly established one of the country's earliest hospitals, next to some springs prized for the exceptional quality of the water. Those springs are still flowing, and a short pathway takes you to them.

ST. CLEMENT'S ISLAND

GETTING THERE *By car:* This is almost a you-have-to-want-to-get-here kind of place. **MD 5/235** is the main highway coming into the area from the north and provides access from Washington, DC, and the interstates. The **MD 4/Governor Thomas Johnson Memorial Bridge** crosses the Patuxent River near California for those coming from Solomons and other points in Calvert County.

By air: The two airports that serve this area with scheduled commercial flights are **Baltimore/Washington International Thurgood Marshall Airport** (1-800-I-FLY-BWI; www.bwiairport.com) near Annapolis and **Ronald Reagan Washington National Airport** (703-417-8000; www.metwashairports.com/reagan/reagan.htm) in northern Virginia.

By water: There are no scheduled boats to bring you into the region, but if you own or are renting one, there are scores of marinas to make your stay easier.

direction through the region. **MD 5** parallels MD 235 a bit to the south, is primarily two-lane, and travels through smaller towns and scenic countryside.

By bus: The **St. Mary's Transit System** (301-475-5100; www.co.saint-marys.md.us) has bus routes that make it possible to get to just about anywhere in the area: Leonardtown, Lexington Park, California, Great Mills, Charlotte Hall, and points in between. Most fares are about $1, but some rural routes are up to $3; exact change required.

By taxi: **Chesapeake Cab** (301-863-1151) in Lexington Park and **Leonardtown Cab** (301-475-9157) in Leonardtown.

MEDICAL EMERGENCY St. Mary's Hospital (301-475-8981; www.stmaryshospitalmd.com), 25500 Point Lookout Rd., Leonardtown.

✳ To See
MUSEUMS
Colton's Point
♿ **St. Clement's Island Museum** (301-769-2222; www.stmarysmd.com/recreate), 38370 Point Breeze Rd. Weekdays 9–5 and weekends noon–5, late Mar.–Sept.; noon–4 Wed.–Sun., Oct.–late Mar. Small admission fee; children 12 and under are free. The displays in the small museum do a good job of telling the story of Maryland's first English settlers. By the time I left here, I knew what prompted them to leave their homeland and the difficulties they faced before and during their ocean voyage. A 20-foot mural celebrates their arrival on St. Clement's Island. Next to the museum is the Little Red Schoolhouse, relocated here after serving the children of Charlotte Hall from 1820 to the 1960s.

The museum sponsors boat tours to the 40-acre island on Sat. and Sun. at 10–2, June–Sept. The water taxi rate is $7 per person and includes admission to the museum. Now a state park, the island has interpretive signs along short pathways that lead to the large cross erected in 1934 to celebrate the 300th anniversary of the settlers' arrival. A replica of the Blackstone Island Lighthouse, which was built in 1851 and destroyed by vandals in the 1950s, was constructed in 2008 and is open to visitors on certain occasions.

Lexington Park
♿ **Patuxent River Naval Air Museum** (301-863-1900; www.paxmuseum.com), MD 235 (next to Gate One of the Patuxent River Naval Air Station). Open 10–5; closed Mon. Free parking and admission. The only museum in the country dedicated to naval aviation research and testing. Outside are a number of historic aircraft, such as an E-2B Hawkeye, F-14 Tomcat, and Grumman A-6 Intruder. The inside exhibits tell of the development of the ejection seat, flight helmet, and the amazingly portable helicopter. One the most fun things is an official naval flight simulator that the public is welcome to operate.

HISTORIC HOMES Tudor Hall (301-475-2467; www.smchistory.org), 41680 Tudor Place, Leonardtown. Wed.–Fri.

THE REPLICA OF THE BLACKSTONE ISLAND LIGHTHOUSE

10–4. Donations accepted. The 1700s Georgian mansion is notable for its inset portico, a new style for its day. The home sat on a 1,000-acre farm and was once owned by members of the Francis Scott Key family. It is now the research repository for the St. Mary's Historical Society. The public is welcome to walk through the house with a member of the society.

✤ **Summerseat Farm** (301-373-6607; www.summerseat.org), 26655 Three Notch Rd. Open first Saturday of the month May–Oct. 10–2. Donation of $10 a car requested. With a history dating back to the late 17th century, Summerseat is a 127-acre working farm with a QueenAnne–style house, outbuildings including meat and dairy houses, barns, and gardens. Summerseat breeds the only publicly accessible herd of American Buffalo in the region. The farm has other heritage farm animals (that the children are welcome to feed), a vineyard, and trails. Tables and a gazebo are available for picnickers.

Public interest really picked up when the SyFy Channel broadcast an episode of *Ghost Hunter* from Summerseat in 2011. So much so that the farm has embraced its haunted reputation and now conducts tours and even has ghost walks with actors portraying the various characters.

HISTORIC SITES

Hollywood
♿ **Sotterley Plantation** (301-373-2280; 1-800-681-0850; www.sotterley.com), on MD 245. Grounds open all year ($3), Tues.–Sun. 10–4; guided house tours (adults $10, seniors $8, children 6–12 years old $5) given Tues.–Sun., May–Oct. Operates as a working plantation of the 1800s. The house's initial construction began in 1717, making it decades older than other famous homes such as Mount Vernon and Monticello. The extensive grounds sit next to the Patuxent River. One of the most interesting sites is the slave quarters of the Hillary Kane family, the only publicly accessible slave cabin in the state. (Greenwell State Park is just a couple of minutes' drive from here; see *To Do*.)

Leonardtown
Old Jail Museum (301-475-2467; www.stmaryshistory.org), 41680 Tudor Pl. The museum is officially open Wed.–Fri. 10–4, but you may need to go to Tudor Hall to find someone to open it for you. A few pieces of furniture and other artifacts depict what the jail would have looked like soon after it was built in the mid-1800s. The jailer's family residence was on the first floor, the small women's cell has a bunk in it, and the larger men's cell is on the top floor. One of the rooms is a tribute to Dr. Philip Jenifer Bean, who served the county from 1914 to 1980. Many of his medical instruments and devices are on display. Also, take a look at the cannon on the museum's front lawn. It is from the *Ark*, one of the ships that brought the first colonists to Maryland in the early 1600s.

HISTORIC CHURCHES

Chaptico
♿ **Christ Episcopal Church** (301-884-3451; www.christepiscopalchaptico.org), MD 238. Constructed in 1736. During the War of 1812, the British dug up graves in the yard and stabled their horses inside the church. Members of the Francis Scott Key family are buried here in a family vault.

Charlotte Hall
Dent Chapel (301-884-8171), Old MD 5. Constructed of granite with a brick belt in 1883, it may be one of the best Victorian Gothic structures in the state.

Compton
St. Francis Xavier Church (301-475-9885; www.stfrancisxavierchurch.org), MD 243. Constructed in 1731, less than 100 years after the first settlers arrived in the area, it is thought to be the oldest Catholic church in continuous use in English-speaking America.

🦐 ⚓ **Historic St. Mary's City** (240-895-4990; 1-800-SMC-1634; www.stmaryscity.org), Rosecroft Rd. (off MD 5). Fri.–Sun. 11–4, Jan.–mid-Mar.; Tues.–Sat. 11–5, Mar.–June; Wed.–Sun. 11–5, June–Sept.; Tues.–Sat. 10–5, Oct.–Nov. Adults $10; students with ID $6; children 6–12 are $3.50.

One of the best-preserved archaeological sites in America and certainly the best representation of a 17th-century colonial town in Maryland. Schedule a minimum of half a day to take in everything on this 800-acre living-history site of Maryland's first permanent English settlement. Self-guided tours (with provided map/brochure) lead you to costumed interpreters (who are some of the best I've met in not breaking character) in the reconstructed Woodland Indian settlement, Godiah Spray Plantation, Farthings's Ordinary, State House, and—most spectacularly—a full-sized reproduction of the *Dove*, one of the ships that transported the settlers across the ocean.

Williamsburg in Virginia may be bigger, yet Historic St. Mary's is a much more manageable place to get a handle on the big picture—and its admission fee is much less.

THE FULL-SIZED REPRODUCTION OF THE
DOVE

Historic St. Mary's City

Trinity Episcopal Church (301-862-4597; www.olg.com/trinitysmcmd), MD 5. Constructed in 1829 with bricks that were salvaged from Maryland's first statehouse, which had been built in 1676.

St. Inigoes

St. Ignatius Church (310-862-4600), Villa Rd. (off MD 5). Constructed in 1785, it is believed to house the oldest active Catholic parish in the country.

LIGHTHOUSES ♿ **Piney Point Lighthouse Museum and Historical Park** (301-994-1471; www.stmarysmd.com/recreate), MD 249 and Lighthouse Rd., Piney Point. Grounds open daily sunrise–sunset; the museum is open Fri.–Mon. noon–5, May–Oct. Small admission fee. Built in 1836, the brick tower Piney Point Lighthouse was Maryland's first permanent lighthouse on the Potomac River and is the only accessible such structure on its original location in southern Maryland. The small museum, once the chief petty officer's garage, tells the story of its construction and operation, and the role of the Coast Guard. A building next door contains a historic vessel collection. Included the last time I visited were a bugeye, skipjack, yawl, log canoe, and a dory.

Piney Point's beautiful scenery and cool breezes have made it a popular recreation spot for many U.S. presidents, beginning with James Madison. A small beach is available for

PINEY POINT LIGHTHOUSE AND MUSEUM

swimming (no lifeguards). Be here as the glow of a rising or setting sun shimmers upon the broad expanse of water, and you will understand why they came.

OTHER SITES **Naval Air Station** (301-757-4814), Lexington Park. The world's premier research, development, testing, and evaluation center for naval aircraft covers 6,000 acres, much of it environmentally and culturally interesting. A pamphlet describing a self-guided tour is available at the entrance gate. *Please note:* Continuing security concerns have led to restrictions on public visitation at military installations; call for the latest information.

United States Colored Troops Memorial Monument (301-737-5447), 21550 Willows Rd., John C. Lancaster Park, Lexington Park. The sculpture of an African American Civil War soldier honors the two USCT soldiers from St. Mary's County, Sgt. James H. Harris and Pvt. William H. Barnes.

✳ To Do

AUTO RACING க. **Maryland International Raceway** (301-884-9833; www.mirdrag .com), MD 234, Budds Creek. Races take place on weekends Mar.–Oct. at the International Hot Rod Association (IHRA) 0.25-mile drag-racing track.

Budds Creek Motocross & Speedway (301-475-2000; www.buddscreek.com), 27963 Budds Creek Rd., Mechanicsville. Features United States Grand Prix and 125/250/500 National events. Many amateur Motocross events and hare scramble races are held throughout the year. This is the Mid-Atlantic Motocross Association's home track. Events held most weekends.

Potomac Speedway (301-884-4200; potomacspeedway.com), 27963 Budds Creek Rd., Mechanicsville. This facility holds 4,000 race fans and features a ⅜-mile clay oval stock car racetrack. Every Friday night 7:30 Mar.–Oct.

BICYCLING More and more bicyclists are discovering the pleasures of riding the lightly traveled roadways of the area. The **St. Mary's County Division of Tourism** can provide information on four popular circuit routes.

One trip is almost 26 miles long and concentrates on the sites to be seen near **St. Clement's Bay** and the **Wicomico** and **Potomac Rivers.** Another is a ride of less than an hour that is more centered upon sights to be seen along the **Patuxent River,** such as **Sotterley Plantation** and **Greenwell State Park.** A third journey is just over 40 miles. Its route includes the waterside along **St. George Island** and **Piney Point Lighthouse.** The fourth ride, at 27.5 miles, is historically interesting, as it brings riders into **Historic St. Mary's City** and **Point Lookout State Park.**

St. Mary's River State Park (301-872-5688; www.dnr.state.md.us/publiclands/southern /stmarysriver.asp), Camp Cosoma Rd. (off MD 5), Great Mills. You may not think of the flat land of southern Maryland as having much terrain for mountain bikers. However, the 9-mile singletrack course, built with mountain bikes in mind, encircles a 250-acre lake and can be a good challenge and a nice ride. Also open to hikers.

Three Notch Trail (301-475-4200; www.co.saint-marys.md.us/recreate). It's always exciting when a new outdoor opportunity arrives in an area, and the 28-mile Three Notch Trail, which follows a former railroad route from Charlotte Hall to New Market, was nearing completion the last time I visited. Although some spots still need to be constructed, hikers and bikers are already enjoying the many miles of paved route that are in place. Interpretive panels along the way highlight the history of the railroad and the land around the trail. The more northern section is interesting for its passage beside Amish farmlands.

Mike's Bikes (301-863-7887; on facebook), 21310-C Great Mills Rd. (at Great Mills Shopping Center), Lexington Park. Closed Sun. They sell skateboards, and also sell and service bicycles.

BIRDING

Hollywood

✿ ⓗ **Greenwell State Park** (301-872-5688; www.dnr.state.md.us/publiclands/southern /greenwell.asp), 25402 Rosedale Manor Ln. Open daily during daylight hours. The many different environments of the park—riparian, wetlands, floodplain, field, and forest—are attractive to a wide variety of feathered creatures. Among the many seen here are great blue heron, bald eagle, osprey, American kestrel, a variety of hawks (primarily red-tailed), and the elusive Swainson's hawk. Barred, great horned, and eastern screech owls are sometimes heard in the early evening, while black vultures soar over the fields—which are home to a bird I see and hear less often than I used to, the bobwhite.

U.S. COLORED TROOPS MEMORIAL MONUMENT

Scotland

Point Lookout State Park (310-872-5688; www.dnr.state.md.us/publiclands/southern /pointlookout.asp), MD 5. Its location on the tip of land at the confluence of the Potomac River and the Chesapeake Bay ensures the park as a great place to experience the migrations along the Great Atlantic Flyway. Watch for northern gannets, brown pelicans, and others.

BOAT EXCURSIONS See **St. Clement's Island Museum** under *To See.*

Clements

⚓ **Bowles Farms and A-Maze-N Place** (301-475-2139; www.bowlesfarms.com), Pincushion Rd. (off MD 234). Sat.–Sun. from Sept.–Oct. Admission fee is $10; children under three are free. A fun way to spend a morning or afternoon. More than 3 miles of trails twist, turn, and befuddle as the maze takes you through 15 acres of tall, living cornstalks. After making your way through the labyrinth (some folks have had to be rescued!), you can reward the kids by wandering over to the petting zoo, taking a hayride, and/or picking out your Halloween pumpkin.

Mechanicsville

⚓ **Forrest Hall Farm Crazy Corn Maze** (301-884-3086; www.forresthallfarm.com), 39136 Avie Lane. Sat.–Sun. from mid-Aug.–Oct. Corn maze, hayrides, farm animals, picnic area, and local produce.

FISHING Fishing in the area starts in late April and continues through December. Charter boats, many providing very personal service by taking only six or fewer passengers, can take you onto the water for rockfish, flounder, sea trout, Spanish mackerel, black sea bass, and more. The **St. Mary's County Division of Tourism** can supply you with a full list of contacts, one of whom is Capt. Phil Langley and the **Fish the Bay Charters** (301-872-4041; 301-904-0935; www.mdcharterfishing.com), 20126 Dove Cove Rd., Dameron. He grew up in St. Mary's County and has decades of experience on the water. The day I went along with him for a scenic tour of Point No Point, Hooper Island, and Point Lookout lighthouses, he showed just a portion of the catch he had helped anglers catch earlier in the day, and it filled several 20-gallon buckets.

Some of the other well-respected captains in the area include:

Capt. Gary Sacks (301-872-5506; www.maricaii.com), Ridge.

Capt. Randy Powers (301-872-9321), Ridge.

Capt. Joe Scrivener (301-994-1525; www.poorboycharter.com), Valley Lee.

NEGOTIATING THE BOWLES FARM CORN MAZE

POINT NO POINT LIGHTHOUSE AS SEEN ON
A TRIP WITH FISH THE BAY CHARTERS

Chaptico

& **Wicomico Shores** (301-884-4601; www
.wicomicoshoresgolfcourse.com), Aviation
Yacht Club Rd. (Wicomico Shores Subdivi-
sion). Open daily. The course is scenically
located next to the Wicomico River and has
many wooded areas with lots of wildlife.
The back tees measure 6,397 feet, and 72
is par.

Leonardtown

& **Breton Bay Golf and Country Club**
(301-475-2300; www.bretonbaygolf.com),
21935 Society Hill Rd. Open daily. The
semiprivate 18-hole course was designed by
J. Porter Gibson and built in 1974. Fairways
have Bermuda grass; the greens are planted
with bent grass. Lakes and other water
come into play.

HIKING 🐾 & **Greenwell State Park**
(301-872-5688; www.dnr.state.md.us
/publiclands/southern/greenwell.asp), 25402
Rosedale Manor Ln., Hollywood. The 600-acre park is on land that was once a part of 4,000-
acre Resurrection Manor. A patchwork of open fields, wetlands, and forests keeps the land
looking much the way it would have in the 17th century, and about 6.5 miles of trails take
visitors out to the far reaches. Most of the routes are easy and level, but if you don't have
time to hike all the pathways, I urge you to at least take the one along the Patuxent River. It
is a particularly pretty outing, and a portion of it is handicapped accessible. All but two of the
trails are also open to bikers and equestrians; pets must be leashed.

Also see **St. Mary's River State Park** and **Three Notch Trail** under *Bicycling* and *Green
Space*.

KAYAKING AND CANOEING The *Water Trail in Western St. Mary's County, Maryland* map (available from the St. Mary's County Division of Tourism, see *Guidance* or www
.visitstmarysmd.com) provides details about the many paddling opportunities in the area. It's
nice that it not only shows the routes of the outings, but also provides a lot of background
information on what you will see along the way.

McIntosh Outfitters (240-577-3971; 240-577-3977), Leonardtown Wharf, Leonardtown.
Some of the most reasonable rates in Maryland for hourly, half-day, and full-day rentals of
kayaks (single and tandem) and canoes. Better yet, take one of their guided tours out onto
the open water and then along one of the area's most scenic creeks. I enjoyed the scenery of
my tour and hope that by the time I return, the outfitters will have worked out the details of
overnight kayaking trips that they were planning to do.

Also see **Patuxent Adventure Center** under *Parks*.

SCUBA DIVING U-1105 Black Panther Historic Ship Preserve (301-994-1471;
www.stmarysmd.com/recreate), Piney Point. The World War II German Black Panther was
the world's first stealth weapon, as its rubber coating made it invisible to sonar equipment.

Captured near the end of the war, it was tested by the U.S. Navy and then intentionally sunk in about 100 feet of water in the Potomac River. Expert recreational divers are permitted to dive to the site after obtaining information from the Piney Point Lighthouse and Museum.

✳ Green Space

BEACHES

California

Myrtle Point Park (301-475-4572; www.stmarysmd.com/recreate), Patuxent Blvd. The small beach and several short trails have a view onto the Patuxent River and its Governor Thomas Johnson Memorial Bridge. No lifeguards.

Dameron

Elm's Beach (301-475-4572; www.stmarysmd.com/recreate), Forest Rd. Free. A county-operated park, Elm's has a nice beach (access open year-round) on the Chesapeake Bay. The bay is so wide here that you could almost convince yourself that you are at an oceanside beach. No lifeguards.

Hollywood

🐾 **Greenwell State Park** (301-872-5688; www.dnr.state.md.us/publiclands/southern /greenwell.asp), 25402 Rosedale Manor Ln. Swimming is permitted from the park's small beach along the Patuxent River. Remember that you are swimming in a river, so there may be a strong current to contend with. No lifeguards.

PARKS 𝄢 **Point Lookout State Park** (310-872-5688; www.dnr.state.md.us/publiclands /southern/pointlookout.asp), MD 5, Scotland. Open daily sunrise–sunset. Small admission fee. The park's location at the mouth of the Potomac River made it a strategic defense point, and it served as a watch post during the Revolutionary War and the War of 1812. During the Civil War, it functioned as a military hospital and prison camp—in which more than 3,000 of the estimated 20,000–50,000 Confederate prisoners died from exposure, starvation, and dis-eases related to poor sanitation. The park's museum (the original photos of prisoners are vivid relics of the past) and nearby ruins of **Fort Lincoln** tell the story.

Also in the park are picnic areas, several short nature trails, and a swimming beach and picnic area. The 1830 **Point Lookout Lighthouse** sits at land's end and is open to the public on the first Sat. of the month Apr.–Nov.

POINT LOOKOUT LIGHTHOUSE

Port of Leonardtown Park and Wharf (301-475-9791; http://leonardtown.somd .com), at the foot of Washington St. It's only a few hundred yards long, but the brick walkway and boardwalk next to Breton Bay and McIntosh Run is a very pleasant place to spend some time. Not only is there the restful scenery of the quiet creek, but inter-pretive signs along the way provide back-ground on what you are seeing and what has taken place here in the past. Be sure to take a look at the beautiful compass rose in the brickwork. **Patuxent Adventure Center** (410-394-2770; www.paxadventure.com) rents canoes and kayaks (on selected days) so that you can get out onto the inviting water.

✳ Lodging

MOTEL

Piney Point, 20674

The Island Inn and Suites and Crab House (301-994-9944; www.stgeorge islandinnandsuites.com), 16810 Piney Point Rd. The Island Inn and Suites is situated on the narrow strip of land between St. George's Creek and the Potomac River, so no matter which side of the building your room is on, you are going to have great views of water. Looking onto the creek, the sunrise will help you greet the day; or if the room faces the Potomac, you'll get to enjoy a restful sunset at the end of the day. All rooms have balconies, TVs, and refrigerator and microwave. Guests have free use of the outdoor grill, kayaks, bicycles, and fishing pier. With the Crab House next door (which has a great interior and the same water views; go check it out) providing meals, refreshments, and a party atmosphere, you may find that you never want to leave the property. $119–159.

INNS

St. Mary's City, 20686

The Inn at Brome-Howard (301-866-0656; www.bromehoward.com), 18281 Rosecroft Rd. Roses on your bed and dresser welcome you to your room in the elegant 19th-century inn. All guest rooms and the suite have a private bath. Come here for beautiful St. Mary's River views, miles of hiking trails connecting with those of Historic St. Mary's City, and free bicycle use. Ask how the house came to sit on this particular piece of land—it is an amazing story. $145–185.

BED & BREAKFASTS

Avenue, 20609

⚓ **Colton's Shipping Point Farm** (310-807-0988; www.coltonshippingpointfarm .com), 39244 Burch Rd. Colton's is the place if you and your small family are looking for a secluded and private getaway. Overlooking the waters of Deep Creek and St. Clements Bay, the modest two-bedroom cottage with a full kitchen sits on a 130-acre

tree farm. In addition to 1 mile of waterfront, guests are permitted to walk the 5 miles of trails that wander through the property that has been in the same family since 1888. $175; additional rates for longer stays.

Colton's Point, 20626

⚓ **Nekadesh Farm Bed and Breakfast Retreat** (301-769-4333; 1-800-934-8094; www.nekadeshfarm.com), 20520 Wellington Crt. Robert and Pennsacola Jefferson have built a lovely modern home on the northern shore of the Potomac River, and guest accommodations permit you to share their home and the grand view across the water to Virginia. The Wilson Suite is where I would spend my time, with its comfortable furnishings and an area to do some work if you just can't leave your job behind. Then again, I'd have to devote some time to sitting on the dock watching boat traffic sail by, or ride one of the B&B's bicycles over to nearby St. Clement's Island Museum. By the way, Robert is an accomplished musician, and you never know what band or celebrity musician you might find spending some time here. $105–135. Children 13 years of age and older are welcome.

Hollywood, 20636

The Victorian Candle Bed & Breakfast (301-373-8800; www.victorian-candle.com),

THE REAR ENTRANCE OF THE INN AT BROME- HOWARD, IN ST. MARY'S CITY

25065 Peregrine Wy. The owner of this modern Victorian-style home built the entire house by himself (ask him the story), and all but one of the seven guest rooms and suites have private entrances. All of the rooms have private bath, television, small refrigerator, and individual heat and air-conditioning. It's also interesting how he and his wife, who is from Sierra Leone, met—be sure to also ask them to tell you this story. Their large family now includes nine children, any number of which may join you for the morning meal. After the lively conversation at the breakfast table, guests may make use of the exercise room or hot tub. The extensive grounds and M. E. Butler Gathering Room are capable of handing 100 people or more for weddings and conferences. $110–160.

Ridge, 20680

Bard's Field B&B (301-872-5989), 15671 Pratt Rd. Host James Pratt grew up in this 1798 small Colonial manor home that overlooks Rawley Bay on the Potomac River. He and his wife, Audrey, refurbished it and offer two large guest rooms that share a bath. The surrounding fields, gardens, and water make for a relaxing stay. Do not leave without having James take you into the basement. It is a virtual museum of items he has collected from days gone by—tools, drills, carpenter's planes, and more. $90. *Please note:* Bard's Field was for sale as this book went to press.

Scotland, 20687

St. Michael's Manor (240-298-3339; www.stmichaels-manor.com), 50200 St. Michael's Manor Way. There are only two guest rooms (with shared bath) in this brick 1805 home sitting alone on 10 waterfront acres, so it has a very homey feel. In addition to cooking a full country breakfast, Nancy and Capt. Joseph Dick set out figs, apples, and fruits freshly picked from their garden. A canoe and a pedal boat are available for guest use; the hammock overlooking the water is relaxing after a dip in the pool. $70–100.

Also see **Slack Winery** under *Winery*.

CAMPING

Callaway, 20620

☙ **Take It Easy Campground** (301-994-0494; 1-877-994-0494; www.takeiteasy campground.com), 45285 Take It Easy Ranch Rd. (off MD 249). Open year-round. There are tent and RV sites with hookups

NEKADESH FARM BED AND BREAKFAST

and a dump station, a swimming pool, and a 7-acre fishing lake on the 200-acre property. Pets permitted.

Leonardtown, 20650

La Grande RV Sales & Camping Resort (301-475-8550; www.lagranderesort.com), MD 5 (south of Leonardtown). There are a few tent sites, but the obvious clientele is the motorized crowd. Hook-ups, a dump station, and RV sales and service.

Ridge, 20680

Seaside View Recreation Park & Campground (301-872-4141; www.seaside-view .com), 48593 Seaside View Rd. Tent and RV sites with hook-ups and a dump station. A restaurant and full-service marina on Jutland Creek are on the premises.

St. George Island, 20674

Camp Merryelande (301-994-1722; www .campmd.com), 15914 Camp Merryelande Rd. Open year-round. Waterfront tent sites overlooking the broad mouth of the Potomac River. A beach and swimming area, crabbing and fishing pier, and laundry. Rental cottages (one to six bedrooms) complete with kitchen, linens, TV, and air-conditioning.

Also see **Point Lookout State Park** under *Green Space*.

✳ Where to Eat

DINING OUT

Lexington Park

The Tides Restaurant (301-852-5303; www.thetidesrestaurant.net), 46580 Expedition Dr. Open for lunch and dinner Mon.– Fri.; dinner only Sat.–Sun. (*Please note:* Hours of operation have been known to change.) One of Lexington's most popular restaurants, often thought of as a special-occasion place, the Tides has an upscale atmosphere, windows that are so heavily tinted that it feels like evening even on the brightest of days, and a reputation for making some killer, and a diverse choice of, martinis (it takes a full page just to list them all). It's hard not to fill up on the house-

made bread before your meal arrives, but resist the temptation so that you can enjoy your entrée of lamb, beef, or seafood. Desserts are also made in-house, and the peach and mango cobbler with homemade ice cream will nicely round out your meal. $12–30.

St. Mary's City, 20686

The Inn at Brome-Howard Brome-Howard Inn (301-866-0656; www.brome-howardinn.com), 18281 Rosecroft Rd. Roses on your bed and dresser welcome you to your room in the elegant 19th-century Brome-Howard Inn. All guest rooms and the suite have a private bath. Come here for beautiful St. Mary's River views, miles of hiking trails connecting with those of Historic St. Mary's City, and free bicycle use, and the opportunity to enjoy a delicious dinner (see *Dining Out*). Ask how the house came to sit on this particular piece of land—it is an amazing story. $145–185.

EATING OUT

California

Lenny's (301-737-0424; www.lennys.net), 23418 Three Notch Rd. Open daily for lunch and dinner. The current chef/owner (a graduate of the Culinary Institute of America) is the son of the original Lenny who started the restaurant in this same location in 1952. While keeping many of the items from those early days, such as fried chicken, creamed spinach, and pot roast, the menu also has such features as jambalaya pasta and lobster. $9.99–29.99.

Hollywood

&. ♪ **Clarke's Landing** (301-373-8468; www.clrestaurant.com), Clarkes Landing Rd. Open daily for lunch and dinner, but closed Mon., Oct.–May. The restaurant overlooks the Patuxent River, so it stands to reason that the seafood is obtained fresh locally. Steamed and soft-shell crabs are a favorite, but Rusty Shriver (the former head chef of Stoney's in Calvert County) also prepares pastas, soups, and hand-cut steaks. Entrées $14–market price.

CLARKE'S LANDING, HOLLYWOOD

Leonardtown

&. **Café des Artistes** (301-997-0500; www
.cafedesartistes.ws), corner of Fenwick and
Washington Sts. Lunch, Tues.–Fri. 11–2;
dinner, Tues.–Sat. 5–9 and Sun. 11–8. Days
and hours subject to change. Such a
delightful place to find in a small town. All
dishes are based upon the French chef's
own recipes. The *croque monsieur* (grilled
ham and Swiss, $8.95) brought back memo-
ries of my travels through the Pyrenees. I
returned for dinner, and the filet mignon in
a puff pastry and green peppercorn sauce
($24.95) transported me to Paris.

And—ooh, la la—the desserts. Be sinful
and have the pastries stuffed with ice cream
and covered by warm dark chocolate
($5.95). Lunch entrées $9.95–15.95; dinner
entrées $19.95–29.95. The real deal is the
three-course prix fixe dinner for $23.95
served on certain nights and Sun.

Kevin Thompson's Corner Kafé (301-
997-1260; eatatkevins.com) 41565
Lawrence Ave. Open for lunch Mon.–Wed.,
lunch and dinner Thurs.–Sat. The plain
exterior does not do justice to the interior
of all wooden walls and ceiling with
exposed beams—and the wooden half-boat
counter. Kevin Thompson started out making crabcakes at his family-owned shop in
Mechanicsville (where he obtains his

seafood, so it's about as fresh as you can
get). Portions are ample and the cake and
brownies are made in-house. It may seem
like a minor thing to highlight, but I
enjoyed the cole slaw here more than most
other places (it's hand cut). Other entrées
worth trying are the rockfish, crabs, oysters,
and gumbo. $12.99–28.99.

Mechanicsville

&. **Bert's 50's Diner** (301-884-3837; http://
berts50sdiner.com), 29760 Three North Rd.
(MD 5). Return to the middle of the 20th
century, with lots of neon lights, memorabilia, and hand-dipped ice cream, malts,
and milk shakes. Blue-plate specials include
meat loaf, hot turkey sandwich, and coun-
try-fried steak. Burgers, subs, pizza, and
fries. Most full meals will cost you less than
$18.

Ridge

Courtney's (301-872-4403), Wynne Rd.
The fading cinder-block exterior and old
1950s paneled interior make this the kind
of place you might pass up if you didn't
know locals congregate here daily for
breakfast, lunch, and dinner. The owner is a
waterman, so the fish is fresh. His wife,
Julia, from the Philippines, does the cooking and provides a bit of a twist to the usual
southern Maryland fare. Crabcake dinner,

as well as a variety of broiled fish, chicken, and T-bone steaks. $9.95–19.95.

Tall Timbers

Chief's—Your Neighborhood Bar (410-994-0772; www.wjdent.com), 44584 Tall Timber Rd. OK, when you pull up to this place you're going to say: Really? I've been sent to this small grocery store (which has been in business since 1927) to have dinner? And then when you walk into the back of the store where the bar/restaurant is, you're going to think the same thing. But once your meal of some kind of seafood (that's my choice, other items are available) arrives, you'll know why this funky spot is in this book. Who knew you could get good oysters Rockefeller in a place like this?! $12–24.

TAKE-OUT **Crabknockers Seafood Market** (301-475-2722), Leonardtown Center, Leonardtown. A convenient location to pick up crabs and other fresh seafood.

Good Earth Natural Foods (301-475-1630; www.goodearthnaturals.com), 41675 Park Ave. Open daily. Good Earth is a grocery store with all natural and organic food and products (many from local sources) to help counteract what you have been consuming during the rest of your vacation.

COFFEE BAR

California

Coffee Quarter (301-866-0106; www.coffeequarter.com) 22576 McArthur Blvd. Closed Sun. Locally owned and offers fresh roasted coffee, espresso drinks, salads, sandwiches, bakery items, and pastries in a bright and roomy atmosphere. (Be sure to take a look at the impressive mural.)

Leonardtown

Brewing Grounds Coffee & Tea (301-475-8040; http://gobrewinggrounds.com), 51658 Fenwick St., Leonardtown. Closed Sun. Sip hot or cold coffees or teas, and dine on baked goods or complete breakfast and lunch items, while you surf the Internet on your notebook computer via the free wi-fi.

✳ Selective Shopping

ANTIQUES & **Maryland Antiques Center** (301-475-1960; http://maryland antiquescenter.com), MD 5 (about ⅛ mile south of the MD 243 intersection), Leonardtown. More than 30 dealers are spread out over 10,000 feet of display area. In addition to the usual antique items, be on the lookout for quality used books, artware, and nautical instruments.

ART GALLERIES

California

Mattedi Gallery (301-866-5477; www.mattedigallery.com), 23415 Three Notch Rd. A small shop inside a strip mall, the framing and gift shop also carries some interesting works by local, regional, and international artists, including P. Buckley Moss and Paul Landry.

Leonardtown

& **North End Gallery** (301-475-3130; www.northendgallery.org), 41652 Fenwick St. A cooperative gallery by local artists working in myriad media, including one of the most modern—digital images. There is a feature exhibit and a reception each month.

USED BOOKS **Fenwick Street Used Books & Music** (301-475-2859; www.fenwickbooks.com), 41655A Fenwick St.,

MAKE YOUR OWN MARYLAND STEAMED CRABS

1 large pot with perforated false bottom

1 cup vinegar

1 cup water

1 dozen live crabs

3 tablespoons salt

2½ tablespoons seafood seasoning (such as Old Bay)

Bring the vinegar and water to a boil and add the live crabs (do not cook dead crabs, which contain bacteria!), sprinkling a mixture of salt and seasoning between each layer. Allow the water to return to a boil, then let the crabs steam for at least 30 minutes.

Leonardtown. You will not only find some used-book treasures in this well-organized shop, but it also has an extensive offering of record albums for those who believe that analog vinyl still sounds better than digital.

CRAFTS

Great Mills

& **Cecil's Old Mill** (301-994-1510), 20853 Indian Bridge Rd. Open Thurs.–Sun., mid-Mar.–Oct.; daily Nov.–Dec. 24. An interesting place: 50 craftspeople create and sell their wares among the gears, cogs, and other machinery of the circa-1900 gristmill and sawmill. Some of the items are—please forgive the pun—just run of the mill, but much of what is displayed is high quality, different, and worth stopping by to see even if you don't intend to buy anything.

Craft Guild Shop of St. Mary's (301-997-1644; www.craftguildshop.com), 26005 Point Lookout Rd. Open Tues.–Sun. The outlet for the talents of more than a dozen local artists and craftspersons.

SPECIAL SHOPS & **Cecil's Country Store** (301-994-9622; www.cecilscountry store.com), Indian Bridge Rd., Great Mills. Across the street from Cecil's Old Mill (see *Crafts*), this place keeps the same hours. It is part antiques shop, part country store. Collectors take note that they have a large selection of retired Village pieces and are the largest dealer of works by Maryland artist Mary Lou Troutman. What sets the place apart for me is that many of the items are displayed inside old dairy cases and iceboxes.

FARMER'S MARKETS

California

California Farmer's Market (301-475-4404), 22180 Three Notch Rd. (MD 235). Sat. 9–1. The season lasts May–Oct.

Charlotte Hall

Farmer's Market and Auction (301-884-3966), MD 5. Open year-round. As much of a flea market as it is a produce stand; there are more than 150 vendors here on Wed. and Sat. 8–5. Also a place to find Amish goods.

North St. Mary's Farmer's Market (301-475-4200, ext.1402), in the library parking lot at the intersection of MD 5 and MD 6. Closed Sun. Fresh produce, along with many products produced by the local Amish community, are available daylight hours May–Oct.

WINERIES

Leonardtown

Port of Leonardtown Winery (310-690-2192; http://portofleonardtownwinery.com), 23190 Newtowne Neck Rd. A cooperative effort between the town of Leonardtown and approximately 20 growers of grapes (it also has 3 acres of vines adjacent to the Leonardtown Park and Wharf). The winery is in a pleasantly refurbished old state highways garage that has been retrofitted with wine production equipment. Tasting and tours of the winery's press, vats, and barrels (French and American oak) are given Wed.–Sun.

Ridge

Slack Winery (301-872-5175; www.slack wine.com), 16040 Woodlawn Ln. Tastings Fri.–Sun. As I came in on the long gravel drive, I decided that, with the late 1700s manor home of Leonard Calvert, first governor of the Maryland Colony, and an absolutely quaint (a word I use very sparingly) cottage/tasting room overlooking the waters of Calvert Creek and the Potomac River, Slack Winery has, without a doubt, some of the most eye-pleasing scenery in southern Maryland. I was also pleasantly surprised to find two kindred spirits here.

Proprietor Maggie O'Brien is a former president of Hollins College and I attended many of the presentations that the college sponsored under her tutelage when I lived nearby in Roanoke, Virginia. Then, while conversing during the tour of the tasting room and manor, I found that her son, who was the one that wanted to start the winery, is a fellow Appalachian Trail 2,000-miler.

The manor, which retains almost all of its original woodwork and many other features, is now a B&B with two suites in the house and five nearby cottages, all with views of the water and surrounding grounds. All of the accommodations have modern amenities and full breakfast is served in the manor. Rates are $170–260.

And, of course, there are the wines. Slack produced its first bottling in 2009, and has gone on to win major national and international awards. Not only did I enjoy sampling several of them, I like the idea that the tasting fee is waived if you purchase a bottle.

✳ Special Events

March: **Maryland Day** (301-769-2222), St. Clement's Island Museum, Colton's Point, and at Historic St. Mary's City. A commemoration of the founding of Maryland. Wreath laying, militia musters, and refreshments.

April: **Piney Point Lighthouse Waterfront Festival** (301-769-2222), Piney Point Lighthouse Museum and Park, Piney Point. Lighthouse tours are the highlight, but there are also maritime exhibits and demonstrations, and children's activities.

May: **Annual Quilt and Needlework Show** (301-373-2280; www.sotterley.org), Sotterley Plantation, Hollywood. Juried exhibition. **Annual Blue and Gray Days** (301-872-5688), Point Lookout State Park. Artillery demonstrations, infantry march, and other living-history activities. Tours of Fort Lincoln. **Maritime Heritage Festival** (240-895-4990; www.stmaryscity.org), Historic St. Mary's City. A celebration of the maritime and nautical heritage of Maryland, with lots of hands-on activities and boats of all kinds on display.

June: **Juneteenth African American Heritage Celebration** (301-475-1861; www.ucaconline.org), Lexington Park. African dance and drumming, singing,

clothing and crafts vendors, and children's activities. **Crab Festival** (301-475-6910), St. Mary's Fairgrounds, Leonardtown. Antique car show, crafts, and lots and lots of crabs prepared many ways.

July: **Tidewater Archaeology Weekend** (240-895-4990; www.stmaryscity.org), Historic St. Mary's City. Get your hands dirty as you join professional archaeologists hoping to find artifacts buried in the soil.

September: **St. Mary's County Fair** (301-475-2256), fairgrounds, Leonardtown. **IHRA President's Cup Nationals** (301-449-RACE; www.mirdrag.com), Maryland International Raceway (MD 234 near Budds Creek). The largest motor-sport event in the state. More than four hundred teams.

October: **Annual Blessing of the Fleet** (301-769-2222), St. Clement's Island Museum, Colton's Point. Entertainment, arts and crafts, parade and fireworks, the Blessing of the Fleet, and boat rides to the island. **Grand Militia Muster** (301-862-0990; 1-800-762-1634; www.stmarys-city .org), Historic St. Mary's City. Believed to be the largest gathering of 17th-century reenactment units in the country. **Oyster Festival** (301-863-5015; www.usoysterfest .com), fairgrounds, Leonardtown. Carnival games and rides, arts and crafts, live entertainment, and the **National Oyster Cook-Off** and **National Shucking Championship.**

November: **Lighthouse Open House** (301-872-5688), Point Lookout Lighthouse, Point Lookout State Park, Scotland. The only day of the year visitors can tour the lighthouse. Exhibits about the site, legends, and history. **Amish Quilt Auction** (301-884-4062), MD 236, Charlotte Hall. A chance to bid on a handmade quilt.

ALONG THE POTOMAC SHORE
LA PLATA, PORT TOBACCO, AND WALDORF

A s in all of southern Maryland, water has played a major role in defining this area and its way of life. Along its eastern border is the state's longest stream, the Patuxent River, while the wide expanse of the Potomac River outlines the western edge.

Through the centuries, the Port Tobacco River has silted in and become much shallower than it once was. During the early days of colonial settlement, it was the area's most important waterway. Wide and deep enough to be navigated by oceangoing vessels, it enabled Port Tobacco to be Maryland's second largest port throughout most of the 17th and 18th centuries, and to remain an important shipment center well into the 19th century. The coming of the railroads brought about the town's decline, but a visit to historic Port Tobacco can bring those days back.

If Port Tobacco was the loser, La Plata was the winner when the railroad arrived in 1872. Coming from Baltimore and reaching all the way to the Potomac, the tracks brought prosperity to the town, which really started out as not much more than a post office and general store. Within a few years, the county seat was moved from Port Tobacco to La Plata. The coming of US 301 changed the town again, as its downtown area—now a small place worth a short stroll through (obtain the Historic La Plata Landmarks brochure from the Charles County Tourism Office)—was bypassed. Most of the commerce, primarily strip malls, chain restaurants, and convenience stores, is located on the four-lane.

The largest city in the area, Waldorf, also owes its existence to the railroads. But it was tobacco, and not county bureaucracy, that brought money into the municipal coffers. People wishing to escape living in Washington, DC, discovered the city and surrounding countryside in the mid-1900s, and it is now primarily a bedroom community for the metro area, with large shopping malls and other modern conveniences.

COMMUNITIES You need to eschew US 301 and drive the back roads if you really want to explore the area. Leaving the major highway in Waldorf and driving east on MD 5 can bring you to such out-of-the-way places as the house where Dr. Mudd, the physician who worked on John Wilkes Booth's broken leg, lived. He is buried close to his home place in St. Mary's Church cemetery in **Bryantown.** Branch off MD 5 at **Hughesville,** and you can follow MD 231 to the Patuxent River and **Benedict.** In addition to being the landing site for British troops that marched westward to burn Washington, DC, during the War of 1812, the now sleepy community bustled for more than 250 years. Established as a port in 1683, it continued to attract freight and passengers traveling on steamboats into the mid-1900s.

Along the Potomac Shore

GUIDANCE **Charles County Government Office of Tourism** (301-396-5819; 1-800-766-3386; www.charlescounty.org), 200 Baltimore St., La Plata, 20646.

The **Crain Memorial Welcome Center** (301-259-2500), US 301, Newburg, is a state- and county-operated facility and can provide information on all of Maryland as well as local attractions. It is located 1 mile north of the Governor Harry Nice Memorial Bridge over the Potomac River on US 301.

GETTING THERE *By car:* Four-lane **US 301** will bring you into the area from the north around Washington, DC. It is also the main highway coming in from the south, connecting southern Maryland with Virginia via the Governor Harry Nice Memorial Bridge (toll) across the Potomac River.

By air: The closest airport, **Ronald Reagan Washington National Airport** (703-417-8000; www.metwashairports.com/reagan/reagan.htm), is across the Potomac River in northern Virginia, but it is only about a 30- to 45-minute drive away. In another direction, but just a few minutes' longer drive away, is **Baltimore/Washington International Thurgood Marshall Airport** (1-800-I-FLY-BWI; www.bwiairport.com) near Annapolis.

By water: The **Charles County Government Office of Tourism** can supply you with a long list of marinas that will take care of you if you happen to arrive on your personal boat.

GETTING AROUND *By car:* Except for **US 301,** most of the roadways are lightly traveled.

By bus: The **Charles County Department of Community Services** (301-934-9305; www.charlescountymd.gov) administers about a dozen bus routes in the Waldorf and La Plata areas that are in operation Mon.–Sat.

MEDICAL EMERGENCY Civista Medical Hospital (301-609-4000; www.civista.org), 701 E. Charles St., La Plata.

✳ To See

COLLEGES **College of Southern Maryland** (301-934-2251; www.csmd.edu), 8730 Mitchell Rd., La Plata. The college's **Fine Arts Center** has so many things going on that it has become the cultural hub of the area. The **Walter Grove II** and **Tony Hungerford Memorial Galleries** feature works by students and staff, and the theater offers musicals, dramas, dances, concerts, and lectures throughout much of the year.

MUSEUMS **African American Heritage Society of Charles County** (301-609-9099; 301-843-2150), 7845 Crain Hwy., La Plata. Hours depend on the availability of volunteers, so call ahead of time. Donations accepted. Set in a quiet grove located off US 301, the modern home is primarily a meeting place for the heritage society, but you will find a few handmade items (ask to be told the story behind the pecan figurine collection), a tribute to Matthew Henson and other notable Charles County African Americans, and some items providing historical perspective. Your experience will probably depend upon who is volunteering when you stop by. One volunteer may give you a straight history lesson, another may talk about some of the implements on display, while another may describe how everything that went before affects the world of today.

HISTORIC HOMES ♿ **Dr. Samuel A. Mudd House** (301-274-9358; www.surratt .org), 3725 Dr. Samuel Mudd Rd. (about 6 miles east of Waldorf via MD 5 and Poplar Hill–Beantown Rd.), Waldorf. Sat. and Sun. noon–4 and Wed. 11–4,, Apr.–Nov. Small admission fee. Dr. Mudd became known to the world when he set the broken leg of John Wilkes Booth, Abraham Lincoln's assassin. This private home museum, which has been in the Mudd family since 1694, relates that story in a very personal way. Although some historians believe Mudd knew who Booth was, Mudd maintained his innocence throughout his three and a half years of imprisonment and to his death.

There is a real sense of history here, as many items in the house are original. It is easy to imagine the events when you look at the couch Booth laid on, the room in which he was operated on, Mudd's medical instruments, and furniture Mudd made while in prison.

HISTORIC SITES ♿ **Historic Port Tobacco** (301-934-4313), Chapel Point Rd. (off MD 6), Port Tobacco. Sat.–Sun. noon–4, Apr.–Oct. Small admission fee. Just a short time after the first settlers arrived in the Maryland colony at St. Mary's City, Capt. John Smith, founder of Jamestown, founded Port Tobacco. The town soon developed into the second largest port in the state but declined when the railroad arrived in the area in the 1870s.

Costumed docents lead guided tours of the Court House, providing background on the town and some of the sites still recognizable. Upstairs, the model of the town puts things into perspective. Ongoing archaeological digs continue to reveal more and more about the site.

⅃ **Port Tobacco One-Room School House** (301-934-9843), 7215 Chapel Point Rd., Port Tobacco. Open by appointment. Free. The school was built in 1876 to serve students in grades one through seven. The furnishings reflect its earliest days.

⅃ **Thomas Stone National Historic Site** (301-392-1776; www.nps.gov/thst), 6655 Rose Hill Rd. (between MD 6 and MD 225), Port Tobacco. Wed.–Sun. 9–5. Free. Thomas Stone was a contributor to the Articles of Confederation and one of Maryland's four signers of the Declaration of Independence. Guided tours take you through the five-part mansion, constructed in the 1770s. The house was nearly destroyed by fire in 1977 but has been fully restored. The original kitchen survived, and some of the original furnishings are spread throughout the house. A number of pleasant hiking trails wander through the property.

HISTORIC CHURCHES

Bryantown
St. Mary's Catholic Church (301-870-2220; http://stmarysbryantown.com). The final resting place of Dr. Samuel Mudd (see *Historic Homes*).

Hughesville
Oldfields Chapel (301-374-3796; ww.trinityepiscopalparish1744.org/oldfields.html), 15837 Prince Frederick Rd. The chapel and surrounding area were used as a campground by the British during the War of 1812. Two soldiers who died there are buried in the cemetery.

La Plata
Christ Church (301-932-1051; http://christchurchlaplata.org), 110 E. Charles St. Replacing earlier church structures, this one was originally built in Port Tobacco in 1884. In 1904, it was dismantled and its numbered stones carried by oxcart to La Plata, where it was reassembled next to the courthouse.

Port Tobacco
St. Ignatius Church (301-934-8245; www.chapelpoint.org), 8855 Chapel Point Rd. Along with St. Ignatius Church in St. Mary's County, this is the oldest Catholic parish in the country. Located on a small knoll overlooking the Port Tobacco River, it houses a Relic of the True Cross, brought by settlers across the Atlantic Ocean on the *Ark* and *Dove*. Be sure to seek out the kneelers that were needlepointed by local residents and depict scenes of interest to the area.

✷ To Do

BICYCLING Less than 25 miles from the nation's capital, this region lures many bicyclists to its quiet country roads. The **Charles County Government Office of Tourism** can provide information on three of the most popular circuit rides.

One of the rides, the longest of the three at about 27 miles, is my favorite. It follows roadways close to the **Potomac River** and passes by several opportunities to get off the bike and take to the woods on hiking trails. Another, at 16.5 miles, encounters **Historic Port Tobacco** and the sites in downtown **La Plata.** The third one is about an hour's ride and skirts the eastern edge of **Zekiah Swamp.**

Although it passes through a lot of public land (with houses only at each end), the **Indian Head Rail Trail** (301-932-3470; www.charlescountyprks.com) is quite deluxe for being as isolated as it is. Beginning in Indian Head and ending in White Plains, there is drinking water available at each terminus of the 13-mile route, benches about every 0.5 mile, and portable toilets at road crossings. Don't let that description fool you; this is a great ride or walk through some of southern Maryland's least developed natural areas. It's prime habitat for red-headed woodpeckers, bald eagles, herons, egrets, kingfishers, osprey, beavers, and muskrats. During the summer, be looking for the impressive masses of lizard's tail flowers in the wetlands area. Interpretive signs provide notes on natural and human history.

Bike Doctor (301-932-9980), 5051 Festival Wy., Waldorf. They can help you with repairs if you run into problems you can't fix yourself.

Also see *Kayaking and Canoeing*.

BIRDING Sometime around Valentine's Day every year for more than five decades, close to 2,500 great blue herons return to the **Nanjemoy Creek Great Blue Heron Sanctuary** (301-897-8570) to pair up, rehabilitate their nest, and raise their young. By July, they will have all dispersed and flown to other places. The county is also host to the state's second largest bald eagle population, while barred owls are numerous in the woodlands that border Mattawoman Creek.

Also see **Indian Head Rail Trail** under *Bicycling*.

BOAT RENTALS See **Gilbert Run Park** under *Green Space*.

BOWLING ♂ **AMC Lanes** (301-843-1494; http://amf.com/waldorflanes), 11920 Acton Ln., Waldorf. Automatic scoring and bumper bowling for the kids.

FISHING The **Potomac River** has earned a reputation as a world-class fishery, especially for largemouth bass and striped bass (known in Maryland and Virginia as rockfish). Although fishing is a year-round event in the area, spring and fall are the best times to cast for striped bass. **Mattawoman Creek** becomes a 7-mile estuary as it enters the Potomac River and is one of the bay's most productive spawning and nursery grounds.

Also see **Myrtle Grove Wildlife Management Area** under *Hiking* and **Friendship Farm Park** under *Green Space*.

GOLF

Issue

Swan Point Country and Yacht Club (301-259-0047; www.swanpointgolf.com), 11550 Swan Point Blvd. A semiprivate waterfront community with an 18-hole course designed by Bob Cupp. Great views of the Potomac River as the course goes through marshes and woodlands.

White Plains

GOLF **White Plains Golf Course** (301-645-1300; 301-843-2947; www.whiteplainsgc.com), at the intersection of DeMarr Rd. and St. Charles Pkwy. (inside White Plains Regional Park). This county-operated, tree-lined, 18-hole course is open daily.

HIKING **Myrtle Grove Wildlife Management Area** (301-743-5161; www.dnr.state.md .us/wildlife/publiclands/southern/myrtlegrove.asp), about 5 miles west of US 301 on MD 225, La Plata. In an area of the state where large tracts of public land available for outdoor recreation are somewhat sparse, this 900-acre tract provides the opportunity to enjoy natural beauty away from the traffic, strip malls, liquor stores, and other modern-day distractions along US 301. The majority of the 5 miles or so of hiking opportunities follow the routes of service roadways, but there are also a few narrow pathways.

Once home to the Piscataway Indians, the terrain is that of a typical southern Maryland landscape, with gently rolling hills of fields and forest, and natural and created wetlands. Watch for signs of beaver, woodcock, quail, and turkey. Consider bringing along tackle, as small Myrtle Grove Lake contains bluegill, pickerel, catfish, and largemouth bass.

Doncaster Forest (301-934-2282; http://dnr.maryland.gov/publiclands/southern/doncaster df.asp), 13 miles west of La Plata on MD 6. Hiking in this 1,400-acre forest is done on well-established, but sometimes unmaintained or unmarked, pathways most often used by hunters. Do not let that deter you, however. If you have a sense of adventure, you can take these routes, which add up to well over 10 miles, into forestlands and along some very pretty small streams.

Also see **Thomas Stone National Historic Site** under *To See,* **Indian Head Rail Trail** under *Bicycling,* and *Green Space.*

KAYAKING AND CANOEING The *Water Trail Adventures in Charles County Maryland* (available—also downloadable—from the Charles County Government Office of Tourism [301-396-5819; 1-800-766-3386; www.charlescounty.org]) details four trips in the area—two on the Potomac River, one along Nanjemoy Creek, and the fourth on the Port Tobacco River. All but one on the Potomac River provide access to campsites to make these trips overnighters if you wish.

Up the Creek Rentals (310-743-3733; www.upthecreekrentals.net), 108A Mattingly Ave., Indian Head. Located on the bank of Mattawoman Creek, this place is kind of a one-stop shop for getting out on the water with rentals of kayaks, canoes, paddle boats, and fishing gear. They also offer a number of guided kayak tours. In addition, they rent and service bicycles and, maybe best of all, they provide a shuttle service (whether you rent from them or not) so that you can do one-way trips on the creek or on the Indian Head Rail Trail.

Nanjemoy Creek is a tidal waterway with high banks in some places that harbor nesting sites for bald eagles. In other spots, it passes through miles of scenic marshlands with great blue herons trolling for a meal. One put-in place is at the bridge over the creek on MD 6 near **Grayton;** another is the boat ramp at **Friendship Farm Park** (301-932-3470; www.charlescountyparks.com) off MD 425 between Ironsides and Grayton. The paddling is easy, the scenery great, and obstructions few.

SKATING ⚓ **Skatepark** (301-645-1300; www.charlescountyparks.com), at the intersection of DeMarr Rd. and St. Charles Pkwy. (inside White Plains Regional Park), White Plains. Small fee. Designed by local skateboarders, in-line skaters, and bikers, the park has various-depth bowls and lots of street elements, such as rails, ledges, and banks.

✳ Green Space

BEACHES See **Purse State Park** under *Parks.*

PARKS

La Plata

Gilbert Run Park (301-932-1083; www.charlescountyparks.com), 1001 Radio Station Rd. (about 6 miles east of La Plata on MD 6). The 180-acre county-operated park offers fishing and boating (rentals in-season) on a 60-acre lake, picnic areas, a nature center, and about 4 miles of trails. Pick up a booklet at the office to learn about what you are seeing along the 1.5-mile self-guided nature route.

Marbury

Smallwood State Park (301-743-7613; www.dnr.state.md.us/publiclands/southern /smallwood.asp), 2750 Sweden Point Rd. Open daily; small admission on weekends and holidays, May–Sept. Trails of about 4 miles in total length connect at several points to form a continuous loop and pass through hardwood forests and a number of spots of historical interest. The **Smallwood Retreat House** (open Sun., May–Sept.) is the restored 18th-century home of Gen. William Smallwood, Revolutionary War figure and governor of Maryland. Nearby is a 19th-century tobacco barn. Also in the park are boat rentals (in-season), a marina on Mattawoman Creek, and a picnic area. A small campground is usually open Apr.–Oct. and has hook-ups, a central shower house, and a few small cabins for rent.

Purse State Park (contact is Smallwood State Park; see above), MD 224. Because it is so overused, I refrain from using the phrase *hidden gem*. Until now, that is. There are no improvements here (although the state is talking about some)—just a 0.25-mile trail through the forest that delivers you onto an isolated Potomac River beach. Swim (no lifeguards), stroll, search for fossils and centuries-old sharks' teeth, or do whatever comes naturally. If you go during the week, it is a good possibility you may be the only person in the entire 90-acre park.

SMALLWOOD RETREAT HOUSE IN SMALLWOOD STATE PARK

Nanjemoy

Friendship Farm Park (301-932-3470; www.charlescountyparks.com), Friendship Landing Rd. The park borders Nanjemoy Creek, providing miles of marshes, scenic water, and access to the Potomac River. A trail system wanders through 235 acres and has two birding observation platforms. The Maryland Department of Natural Resources has designated the park a free fishing area—meaning you don't have to purchase a state fishing license to enjoy the thrill of casting a line into the water.

ALONG THE BEACH IN PURSE STATE PARK

✳ Lodging
MOTELS AND HOTELS
Indian Head, 20640
🐾 **Super 8** (301-753-8100; 1-800-800-8000; www.super8.com), Indian Head Hwy. Basic rooms and few amenities in the motel, but a low rate. Free continental breakfast. Pets permitted, but you must call the local number for permission. $78–108.

La Plata, 20646
🐾 **Best Western Plus** (301-934-4900; http://bestwesternmaryland.com), 6900 Crain Hwy. Small pool and exercise room. Free continental breakfast. Small pets permitted with a deposit. $109–139.

Waldorf, 20603
♿ **Comfort Suites** (301-932-4400; www.comfortsuites.com), 11765 Business Park Dr. All rooms are suites with irons and in-room coffee. Indoor pool. $129–199.

🐾 **Days Inn** (301-932-9200; www.daysinn.com), 11370 Days Court. In-room coffee and irons. Complimentary continental breakfast. Pets permitted. $70–125.

Hampton Inn (632-9600; http://hampton inn3.hilton.com), 3750 Crain Hwy. Guests at the 100-room inn have access to the swimming pool, fitness center, and business center. $119–129.

Holiday Inn (301-645-8200; www.clarion hotel.com), 45 St. Patrick's Dr. (adjacent to the mall). Exercise room, outdoor pool, coin laundry; irons and hair dryers in the rooms. $109–189.

Super 8 (301-932-8957; www.super8.com), 3550 Crain Hwy. Low-cost motel with basic rooms and some suites. Free continental breakfast, fitness room. $74–98.

BED & BREAKFASTS
La Plata, 20646
Part of Plenty Bed & Breakfast (301-934-0707; 1-800-520-0708; www.partof plentybedandbreakfast.com), 8664 Port Tobacco Rd. Located in historic Port Tobacco, the two-story house was built around 1850 (renovated 1996), is located on 4 acres, and has five guest rooms (all

with private bath) with period antiques and reproductions. Outdoor pool. $99–139.

Port Tobacco, 29677
🐾 **Rosewood Manor** (301-534-2344; 240-640-3556; www.rosewoodmanorweddings.com), 7825 Locust Pl. This place is a truly a (modern-built) manor—in the most literal sense of the word. First of all it's huge, has a number of verandas that overlook the manicured garden, has a double staircase that Scarlett O'Hara would have been proud of, and easily fits my image of what the French kings lived in while relaxing in the countryside. In fact, it's so big that there are columns inside! Fitting such a place, quality antiques are found in every room, the guest rooms are luxurious and have modern amenities, and a continental breakfast is served in the Queen Anne dining room. This is not a run-of-the-mill B&B; you need to visit here to see for yourself. Rates start at $249. Rosewood is the site of many weddings, and the host is an expert at helping you plan yours.

COTTAGE
Charlotte Hall, 20622
Brictoria Cottage at Charlotte Hall (301-884-8699; www.brictoriacottage.com), 7535 Poplar St. Bob and Sharon Fastnaught originally built this one-bedroom

ONE OF THE MANY GRAND INTERIORS OF ROSEWOOD MANOR

cottage as an in-law residence. It is located next to the brick home they built for themselves, but as the two structures sit on 8 private acres, you will be able to sit on the outside swing and enjoy the soft sounds of the woods, isolated from the rest of the world. Bob and Sharon are also a wealth of knowledge of what to do in southern Maryland, especially if you are looking for some walking and hiking spots. The cottage's library also has a number of books relating to this area. $110.

CAMPING

Welcome, 20693

🐾 **Goose Bay Marina and Campground** (301-934-3812; www.goosebaymarina.com), 9365 Goose Bay Ln. The full-service marina, which sits on Goose Creek, an inlet of Port Tobacco River, also contains waterfront campsites, hook-ups, a swimming pool, and a camp store. Pets permitted.

Also see **Smallwood State Park** under *Green Space.*

✳ Where to Eat

DINING OUT

Port Tobacco

Blue Dog Saloon and Restaurant (310-392-1740; www.thebluedogsaloon.com), 7940 Port Tobacco Rd. Because it is a favorite watering hole with live entertainment (although with an upscale atmosphere), Blue Dog should probably be in the *Eating Out* category, but the chef's touch with the offerings pretty much elevates the place to *Dining Out* class. The menu includes nightly specials and my companion and I split an appetizer of snakehead fish bites that were quite delicious. (It's an invasive species and it happens to taste good, so we kind of felt like we were doing our part for the environment.) The cream of crab soup was full of lump crab, as was the stuffed rockfish. This is currently my favorite Charles County dining experience. Oh yeah, be sure to find out about the legend of the blue dog. $14.95–23.95.

EATING OUT

Benedict

River's Edge (301-274-2828), 7320 Benedict Ave. A local favorite that is situated almost on top of the Patuxent River. The knotty-pine walls give it a mid-1900s feel, and the menu features what could only be called Maryland/American fare. Crabcakes (market price), pork chops, and chicken Chesapeake are always on the menu. There are also daily specials like the tasty snapper sandwich I had for lunch. Most entrées $15–30.

La Plata

Casey Jones (301-932-5116; http://casey-jones.com), 417 E. Charles St. Casey Jones presents an upscale tavern atmosphere with live entertainment on a regular basis. The menu fits the atmosphere with what I would call upscale bar food. There's ahi tuna, sandwiches, salads, some tasty and innovative pizzas, and desserts made in-house. The wine list is good and there's a rotating selection of craft beers on tap. $21.95–28.95.

Newburg

🐟 **Captain Billy's Crab** (301-932-4323; www.captbillys.com), 11495 Popes Creek Rd. Open daily for lunch and dinner. Now owned by Capt. Billy Robertson's stepdaughter, this place was busy even in the middle of the afternoon on a weekday the last time I visited. It sits on the edge of the Potomac River, providing nice views as you dine on hard- or soft-shell crabs or crabcakes. Other seafood is featured on the menu, along with some sandwiches and steaks. Frozen slushies, along with some alcoholic coffee drinks, are other reasons to visit. Entrées $18.99–29.99.

Gilligan's Pier and Beach Club (301-259-4514; www.gilliganspier.com), 11535 Popes Creek Rd. With its own sandy beach on the Potomac River, some tables in the sand, outside deck, and live entertainment on the weekends, Gilligan's has the quintessential Maryland crab house party atmosphere. Boaters can even anchor just offshore and they'll send a dinghy out to get you. Seafood is prepared fresh as you order

CAPTAIN BILLY'S CRAB

it and fried items are cooked in no trans fat oil. One of the few places that still offers all-you-can-eat specials (market price). Steaks and sandwiches also available. Entrées $15.95–28.95.

CRABS ✍ **Captain John's Crab House** (301-259-2315; www.cjcrab.com), 16215 Cobb Island Rd., Cobb Island. Open daily for breakfast, lunch, and dinner. Located on the waterfront on Cobb Island, Captain John's is the typical Maryland crab house with inside and outside dining, but unlike many others, it is open year-round. The seafood platter has enough food to feed two, with a crabcake, fried scallops, fried fish, fried shrimp, fried clams, and either fried oyster or fried soft-shell crab (in-season). Fried dishes are cooked in no trans fat oil. Other sandwiches and dinners $6.95–market price.

TAKE-OUT **Randy's Ribs and BBQ** (301-274-3525; www.randysribs.com /category), MD 5 and Gallant Green Rd., Hughesville. Open daily from 10 AM. It is just a roadside stand, but anytime you drive by, there is a line of people waiting to place their order. Beef, pork, chicken, ribs, hot dogs, and a variety of platters are offered. The thing to get, however, is the BBQ sandwich. It may be the tastiest BBQ I've had in Maryland. By the way, do not make the mistake of ordering two—even if you are hungry. The size of one is almost large enough to feed two people. $5.50–19.95.

SNACKS AND GOODIES **Charles Street Bakery** (301-392-6344; www .charlesstreetbakery.com), 507 E. Charles St., La Plata. After owning a bakery in California, Deborah Taylor's baking abilities gained such renown that she became the pastry caterer for many upscale clients in the Washington, DC, area when she moved eastward. It is now the residents of and visitors to southern Maryland who get to enjoy her breads, cookies, and pies. Don't pass up the chance to do so if you pass this way.

✳ **Entertainment**

FILM **AMC St. Charles Town Center** (301-870-6058; www.amctheatres.com),

11115 Mall Circle, Waldorf. Shows first-run movies.

THEATERS

Indian Head

Black Box Theatre (301-743-3040; www .indianheadblackbox.org), Indian Center for the Arts. It's a varied schedule of productions at this hundred-seat black box theater. Those who attend are treated to comedies, musicals, dance, lectures, readings, and all manner of artistic endeavors.

La Plata

Port Tobacco Players (301-932-6819; www.ptplayers.com), 508 Charles St. Housed in an old 1940s movie theater. The Port Tobacco Players formed in 1947 as a way to raise funds for the restoration of Port Tobacco buildings. The troupe stages half a dozen or so productions each year. Most presentations are American musicals and plays, and past ones have included *A Streetcar Named Desire, You Can't Take It with You,* and Rodgers and Hammerstein's *Cinderella.* Most shows take place Fri. and Sat. evening and Sun. afternoon.

Also see *To See—Colleges.*

SPORTS **Southern Maryland Blue Crabs** (301-638-9788; www.somdblue crabs.com), Regency Furniture Stadium, Waldorf. Owned by Baseball Hall of Fame member Brooks Robinson, the Blue Crabs are an independent team, not affiliated with any team in Major League Baseball.

✳ Selective Shopping

ANTIQUES

Hughesville

Hughesville Bargain Barn (301-274-3101; 240-329-3474; http://bargainbarnofhughes ville.com), 8275 Old Leonardtown Rd. More than 140 shops crowd into two large barns selling antiques, collectibles, coins, and new and used furniture. Much of the stuff is what you would find in a flea market.

La Plata

The Royal Tea Room (301-392-1111; www.royaltearoommd.com), 110 E. Charles St. Closed Mon. It's small restaurant serving specialty sandwiches, flatbread pizzas, and soups for lunch ($9.99–13.99). No, wait, it's an antiques shop with furniture and fixtures and some Charles County–made jams and other gourmet goodies. Oh, yes, it also does a deluxe afternoon tea service that harkens back to the days of gentility.

ART GALLERIES **Mattawoman Creek Art Center** (301-743-5159; www .mattawomanart.org), inside Smallwood State Park, Marbury. Fri.–Sun. 11–4. Set off by itself with woodlands close by, and overlooking where Mattawoman Creek meets the Potomac River; I can't imagine a prettier setting for a gallery. The inside space is illuminated by natural light to accent the high quality of works by local, regional, national, and international artists. A real treasure in an out-of-the-way place.

Also see *To See—Colleges.*

FARMER'S MARKETS **Waldorf Farmer's Market** (301-934-8571), Festival Way. Produce arrives every Wed. and Sat., July–Oct.

La Plata Farmer's Market (301-934-8421; www.townoflaplata.org), corner of Charles St. and Washington Ave. Produce and other items are displayed on stands in the courthouse parking lot on Wed. 10–7 and Sat. 8–3:30.

PICK-YOUR-OWN PRODUCE FARMS **Shlagel Farms** (301-645-4554; ww.shlagelfarms.com),12850 Shalgel Rd., Waldorf. Show up in May and pick all the strawberries you can right off the vine; come in the fall for pumpkins.

✳ Special Events

March: **Children's Spring Party and Easter Egg Hunt** (301-743-5574), Indian Head village green. Live entertainment, children's activities, and photos with the Easter Bunny.

April: **Annual Potomac River Clean Up** (301-932-3599). Volunteers beautify the Potomac and other area streams.

May: **House and Garden Pilgrimage** (301-934-8819; www.mhgp.org), various sites. Every third year, the local garden club sponsors a tour of the area's best homes and gardens.

May–September: **La Plata Summer Concert Series** (301-934-8421), La Plata Town Hall, La Plata. A series of outdoor musical concerts presented each Fri. evening 7–9.

June: **Annual Juried Art Show** (301-743-5159; www.mattawomanart.org), Mattawoman Creek Art Center. Artists from Maryland, Virginia, and Washington, DC, display juried works in a wide variety of media. **Cobb Island Day** (301-259-0160), Cobb Island Field. Crab races, corn-shucking contests, many kids' activities, crafts sales, and fire-engine and carriage rides. **Artfest** (301-932-5900; www.charles countyarts.org), Indian Head. *Note:* Dates have been known to change. A day of music, visual arts, theater, and literature. Lots of entertainment.

August: **Durham Parish Festival** (301-743-7099), Christ Church, Nanjemoy. This event has taken place each year since 1847! Traditional southern Maryland ham and chicken dinner, children's games, lots of home-baked goodies, and crafts. **L'il Margeret's Bluegrass and Old-Time Music Festival** (301-475-8191; http://lilmargarets bluegrass.wordpress.com), Leonardtown. A family-friendly festival with camping available.

September: **Charles County Fair** (301-932-1234), fairgrounds, La Plata.

November: **Annual Holiday Art Show** (301-743-5159), Mattawoman Creek Art Center. Works by local member artists.

December: **Annual Holiday Festival and Craft Fair** (301-743-5574), Indian Head. Live entertainment, door prizes, crafts and children's crafts-making activities, a ginger-bread-house contest, and an antique model-train display.

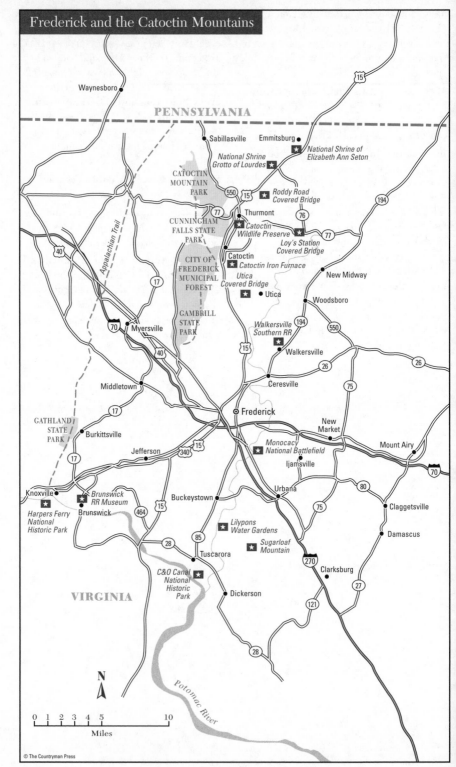

Frederick and the Catoctin Mountains

Waynesboro

PENNSYLVANIA

Sabillasville Emmitsburg

National Shrine National Shrine of
Grotto of Lourdes Elizabeth Ann Seton

CATOCTIN
MOUNTAIN
PARK

Roddy Road
Covered Bridge

Thurmont

CUNNINGHAM
FALLS STATE
PARK

Catoctin
Wildlife Preserve

Loy's Station
Covered Bridge

CITY OF
FREDERICK
MUNICIPAL
FOREST

Catoctin

Catoctin Iron Furnace

Utica
Covered Bridge

New Midway

Utica

Woodsboro

GAMBRILL
STATE
PARK

Appalachian Trail

Myersville

Walkersville
Southern RR

Walkersville

Ceresville

Middletown

Frederick

New
Market

Mount Airy

GATHLAND
STATE
PARK

Burkittsville

Monocacy
National Battlefield

Jefferson

Ijamsville

Knoxville

Brunswick
RR Museum

Urbana

Claggettsville

Harpers Ferry
National
Historic Park

Brunswick

Buckeystown

Damascus

Lilypons
Water Gardens

Sugarloaf
Mountain

Tuscarora

Clarksburg

C&O Canal
National
Historic Park

VIRGINIA

Dickerson

N

Potomac River

0 1 2 3 4 5   10

Miles

© The Countryman Press

Frederick and the Catoctin Mountains Area

FREDERICK AND THE CATOCTIN MOUNTAINS AREA

The words of Whittier's 1862 poem are just about as true today as they were then. There may be fewer meadows of corn, but the clustered spires still point skyward, framed by lush, green hillsides.

It seems that cities are always discussing ways to attract people by saving their downtown areas and historic structures; Frederick has accomplished it. Other than Annapolis, which has done an admirable job of preserving its harbor area, Frederick is the most viable, vibrant, and historic-architecture-rich city in the state.

Early-1800s Federal-style mansions may still be found in the downtown area; the Barbara Fritchie House—where the events Whittier wrote about occurred—is reconstructed with its original materials; and many of the Victorian town houses are still lived in by families and have not been turned into offices. Yet businesses thrive within the inner city without destroying it: With a minimum of changes, a complex of small shops in Everedy Square and Shab Row occupy what were once 18th- and 19th-century dwellings. Market Street and Patrick Street, the crossroads of the downtown area, are lined by renovated buildings with restaurants, antiques shops, and galleries that entice people to linger after normal business hours have expired. Also enticing people is the wonderful job the city has done with Carroll Creek Park, a mile-plus-long strip of brick walkways, water fountains, shops, restaurants, and residential buildings next to the stream it was named after. The abundance of public art and the footbridges crossing the stream that have been built in a wide variety of architectural styles add to the eye-pleasing experience of taking walks here.

The city's spirited arts and culture community has also fallen in line with protecting the old. The Delaplaine Visual Arts Education Center makes use of the renovated Mountain Mill, while the Weinberg Center for the Arts, where presentations of all forms are staged throughout the year, is in a lavish 1926 movie palace. And, of course, the steeples, spires, and towers of more than a dozen buildings provide the city with one of its most photographed scenes, its skyline.

In recent years, Frederick has become a very dog-friendly town, with many businesses putting out bowls of water for canine friends. A number of restaurants now permit you to dine with your dog if you take advantage of their outside seating.

Just northwest of Frederick are the Catoctin Mountains. The eastern rampart of the Blue Ridge Mountains, they stretch almost 40 miles from southern Pennsylvania, across Maryland, and into the northern portion of Virginia. Geologists believe the mountains once attained heights comparable to those of the Andes in South America, but wind and water over the course of millions of years have eroded Catoctin into a much lower ridgeline. Today the high point is only about 1,900 feet above sea level, while the lowest spot is a mere 500 feet. The mountain's numerous rock outcroppings are a bit more resistant to erosion, being composed of Catoctin greenstone that developed from lava flows 600 million years ago.

The mountain range's name is a derivation of Kittocton, from an Algonquian tribe that once lived near the Potomac River. Linguists believe the word translates to "land of the big mountain" or "land of the white-tailed deer." Native Americans and colonial hunters traipsed through the folded landscape in search of abundant wildlife.

Several parks in the Catoctin Mountains, and on South Mountain a bit farther to the west, along with the Chesapeake & Ohio (C&O) Canal along the southern region, have made this area a mecca for hikers, bikers, kayakers, canoeists, anglers, and others looking to experience and play in the natural world.

COMMUNITIES **Emmitsburg** has been attracting religious pilgrims ever since Father John Dubois founded Mount St. Mary's College, a Catholic four-year college and seminary, in the early 1800s. One of those attracted was Elizabeth Ann Seton, who began the country's first parochial school in Baltimore before moving to Emmitsburg and establishing the Sisters of Charity. About 150 years after her death, she was canonized as a saint, the first native-born American woman to be so recognized. A nearby spot on the side of the Catoctin Mountains, now the National Shrine Grotto of Lourdes, was one of her favorite places of meditation.

True to the translation of its name, **Thurmont** is "the Gateway to the Mountains." Nestled on the edge of the Monocacy Valley at the base of the Catoctin Mountains, it began attracting hunters, anglers, and other outdoor types when the railroad arrived in the 1870s. The establishment of Catoctin Mountain Park and Cunningham Falls State Park in the mid-1900s further enhanced its sylvan appeal. The television age has brought the little town worldwide fame, as it is used as a base camp by news agencies and journalists to keep track of events taking place in nearby Camp David. It is quite common to turn on the evening news and to see Cozy Country Inn or Mountain Gate Restaurant used as a reporter's backdrop.

During one of his many trips to the area, George Washington declared **Middletown** to be "one of the prettiest valleys I've ever seen." The town and surrounding areas are experiencing a building explosion as more and more housing developments take over former farmlands.

Despite interstates and malls growing up a few miles away, **Buckeystown** has managed to retain the look and feel of a Victorian village. Its main street, Buckeystown Pike (MD 85), remains a two-lane roadway passing by many homes and structures from the late 1800s. The town's few commercial enterprises include the upscale Alexander's.

New Market, established in 1793, flourished as a stopover point for 19th-century travelers along the National Road. Many of its early structures still exist; today the small town has a number of antiques shops occupying a number of historic buildings.

GUIDANCE The **Tourism Council of Frederick County, Frederick Visitors Center** (301-600-4047; 1-800-999-3613; www.fredericktourism.org), 151 S. East St., Frederick, 21701. Easily accessed from I-70, the visitors center is located in a refurbished historic cannery warehouse. With 2,200-square feet of interpretive exhibits highlighting the lumbering, transportation, and other aspects of the area; a theater showing an award-winning orientation movie (among others); and a staff willing to answer questions, this is the place to begin your explorations.

Maryland state welcome centers, which can provide local and statewide information, are located at mile marker 39 on I-70 near Myersville. The phone number for the center for eastbound traffic is 301-293-2526; the westbound traffic center can be reached at 301-293-4161.

The **Mason Dixon Welcome Center** (301-447-2553) is located 1 mile south of the Pennsylvania border on US 15 near Emmitsburg.

GETTING THERE *By car:* All roads may lead to Rome, but almost as many seem to converge on Frederick and this area of Maryland. **I-70** comes from Baltimore in the east and Hagerstown in the west. **I-270** is the way most people drive here from the Washington, DC, area. **US 15** arrives from Pennsylvania to the north, while **US 340** crosses the Potomac River from Virginia and West Virginia.

By air: **Washington Dulles International Airport** (703-572-2700; www.metwashairports .com/dulles/dulles.htm) in northern Virginia is the closest air facility to the area, especially if you are driving a rental car and can cross the Potomac River at either Point of Rocks on US 15, Brunswick on VA 287, or Harpers Ferry on US 340. Flying into **Ronald Reagan Washington National Airport** (703-417-8000; www.metwashairports.com/reagan/reagan.htm) enables you to take the MARC commuter train (see *By rail*) into the area. Located a little more than an hour away, between Baltimore and Washington, DC, is the **Baltimore/ Washington International Thurgood Marshall Airport** (1-800-I-FLY-BWI; www .bwiairport.com).

By bus: **Greyhound** (1-800-231-2222; www.greyhound.com) has a terminal (310-663-3311) on S. East St. Unlike many bus terminals, it is not located in some out-of-the-way, decaying part of town but is just a block or two from many of downtown's best attractions and restaurants.

By rail: **MARC** (1-800-325-RAIL; www.mta.maryland.gov) has a weekday commuter train that can bring you to a late-1800s Victorian station in Point of Rocks, to downtown Frederick, or to MD 355 close to many of the city's motels.

GETTING AROUND *By car:* The main roadways mentioned in *Getting There* will get you around quickly—except in rush hours—but use the smaller roads, such as **MD 77** and **MD 194** in the north or **MD 85** and **MD 17,** to take you on the more scenic routes.

By bus: The local bus system, **TransIT** (301-694-2065; http://frederickcountymd.gov), operates throughout Frederick and its immediate vicinity. Routes also go to Thurmont, Emmitsburg, Brunswick, and Jefferson.

By taxi: In Frederick, you can call **Bowie Taxi** (301-695-0333) or **Yellow Cab** (301-662-2250).

PARKING In Frederick, parking meters are on Mon.–Sat. 9–5. I find the municipal parking decks, especially the one at 44 E. Patrick St., to be convenient for downtown explorations without running back to feed the two-hour-limit meters. Stop by the Frederick Visitors Center to have your parking ticket validated for three free hours in any of the parking decks.

PUBLIC RESTROOMS Convenient restrooms are located in the Frederick Visitors Center and the parking decks. An information station and public restrooms can be found at 41 W. Main St. in New Market.

MEDICAL EMERGENCY **Frederick Memorial Hospital** (240-566-3300; www.fmh .org), 200 W. Seventh St., Frederick.

✳ To See

COVERED BRIDGES All three of the area's remaining covered bridges are located north of Frederick:

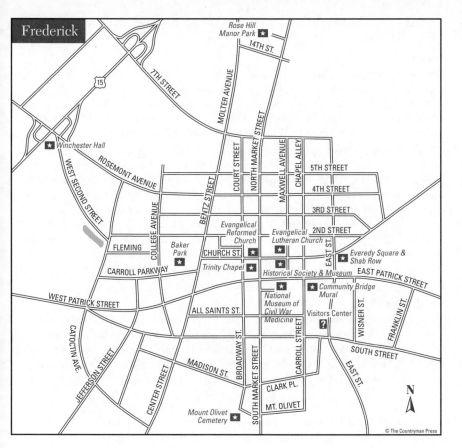

Situated off Old Frederick Rd. near Utica, the 110-foot, Burr Arch–design **Utica Covered Bridge** was originally constructed in 1850 over the Monocacy River. It was washed away in 1889, and local citizens salvaged its remains to reconstruct it over Fishing Creek in 1889.

Just south of the intersection of Old Frederick Rd. and MD 77 east of Thurmont is the **Loy's Station Covered Bridge,** built in the mid-1800s. Spanning Owen's Creek, the 90-foot bridge retains its original timbers. A small park with picnic tables and a playground enables you to enjoy the setting while giving the kids something to do.

Less than 2 miles north of Thurmont on Roddy Rd. (off US 15), 40-foot **Roddy Road Covered Bridge** was built in 1856. A small park is adjacent to the single-span Kingpost-design bridge.

You can obtain the itinerary for a self-guided driving tour/route of the covered bridges from the **Tourism Council of Frederick County, Frederick Visitors Center** (www.frederick tourism.com).

MUSEUMS

Brunswick

✂ **Brunswick Railroad Museum** (301-834-7100; www.brrm.net), 40 W. Potomac St. Fri.–Sun. Small admission fee. Railroad equipment, photographs, furnishings, toys, and other items tell of the town's early history. Of special interest to rail fans (and children) is the HO model layout of the B&O line from Washington, DC, to Brunswick. In the same building is the C&O Canal Information Center.

Frederick

Historical Society of Frederick County (301-663-1188; www.hsfcinfo.org), 24 E. Church St. Tues.–Sun. Small admission fee. Guided tours take you through an 1820s Federal-style mansion furnished with the society's collection of historic memorabilia, such as Barbara Fritchie items, furnishings of the early 1800s, and a superior collection of tall-case clocks. The society offers downtown walking tours on the weekends from Apr.–Nov.

↑ & **National Museum of Civil War Medicine** (301-695-1864; www.civilwarmed.org), 48 E. Patrick St. Open daily. Small admission fee; children 9 and younger are free. Some of the most realistic life-sized dioramas I've seen tell of the care and healing efforts during the Civil War. More than this, though, the reason to visit is the unfamiliar facts brought to light. Did you know: More than 2,000 women, disguised as men, served as soldiers? About 3,000 horses and mules perished during the Battle of Antietam? Most operations were done under anesthesia and not by "biting the bullet," as portrayed by Hollywood? Nearly ⅔ of the 62,000 soldiers who died did so from disease and not battle injuries? Interesting items include the only surviving field stretcher (and a photo of it in use during the war) and a set of war letters from Union private P. Bradford.

Walkersville

↑ **Red Cross Museum** (301-662-5131; www.redcrossmuseum.com), 2 E. Frederick St. Open Mon.–Thurs. Donations accepted. A lot is packed into this one-room museum. Uniforms, medals, badges, newspapers, photographs, and more tell the story of this volunteer organization that seems to be prepared whenever a disaster, on a large scale or to a family, happens to strike. Most outstanding to me is that they have a signed letter from Clara Barton.

HISTORIC HOMES **Barbara Fritchie House and Museum** (301-698-0630), 154 W. Patrick St., Frederick. Sadly, this historic site is open only on special occasssions; call for times.

The story goes that 95-year-old Barbara Fritchie defiantly waved the Union flag from her window as Confederate general Stonewall Jackson's troops marched through town. John Greenleaf Whittier made her famous in his poem "The Ballad of Barbara Fritchie": "Shoot if you must, this old gray head, / But spare your country's flag, she said."

Did the event really happen? Who knows; does it really matter? It is a great piece of Americana, and the museum (reconstructed out of materials from the original house) is furnished with items from the Fritchie family.

Schifferstadt (301-663-3885), 1110 Rosemont Ave., Frederick. Sat.–Sun., Apr.–mid-Dec. Small admission fee (donation). Built in 1756, the German Colonial home retains much of its original hardware and exposed oak beams. A period garden complements the scene.

HISTORIC SITES

Frederick

& **Monocacy National Battlefield** (301-662-3515; www.nps.gov/mono), 4801 Urbana Pike. Open daily. Free. An extensive visitors center provides perspective on the site of the last Southern push into Union territory. Although Confederate general Jubal Early's troops won the battle on July 9, 1864, they were delayed long enough that Federal reinforcements arrived to block the way to Washington, DC. An interactive map in the visitors center is one of the best I've ever seen in helping you understand what happened during the battle. Also, take the walk to the upstairs deck for an expansive view of the countryside.

Ranger-conducted programs and tours are presented during the summer months, while a pamphlet keyed to numbered sites along a driving-tour route lets you experience the battlefield any time of year. The **Worthington Farm Hiking Trail** consists of two connecting loops. One takes you onto **Brooks Hill** for a lesson in forest succession; the other is through bottomland to the site of the **Washington–McKinney Ford** on the Monocacy River. Each loop is about 2 miles in length. A map available from the visitors center profiles additional walking opportunities.

Thurmont

Catoctin Iron Furnace, on MD 806 (off US 15). Administered by Cunningham Falls State Park. Open daily 8 AM–sunset. Free. The iron furnace was in use 1776–1903, making it one of the state's longest-running such enterprises. It has only been about a century since it ceased operating, so its ruins are in fairly good shape; even portions of the ironmaster's home are identifiable.

The furnace is also accessible via a footpath from the state park.

HISTORIC CHURCHES The spires and steeples of Frederick have given the town much of its identity and have been immortalized and praised by luminaries such as Dr. Oliver Wendell Holmes and John Greenleaf Whittier. Among the many are:

Trinity Chapel, 10 W. Church St. Its Colonial steeple was designed by Stephen Steiner and constructed in 1807, making it Frederick's oldest spire. The 10-bell chimes in the tower's clock are still in use.

Evangelical Lutheran Church (301-663-6361; www.twinspires.org), 35 E. Church St. The present German Gothic structure was built in 1854, and its twin spires were among those Whittier referred to when he wrote the 1862 Barbara Fritchie poem that opens this chapter. The west tower contains a bell that was cast in England in 1771.

Evangelical Reformed Church (301-694-0188), 15 W. Church St. The church's two open towers, built in 1848, add to the city's skyline.

Saint John the Evangelist Catholic Church (301-662-4676; www.stjohn-frederick.org), 116 E. Second St. Built in the early 1800s, its spire has a gold-leafed dome and cross, the highest point in the city. *The Crucifixion* by Pietro Gugliardi and *The Ascension* by Baraldi are masterpieces that necessitate a visit inside.

Also see **National Shrine Grotto of Lourdes** and **National Shrine of Saint Elizabeth Ann Seton** under *Other Sites.*

MEMORIALS ♿ **National Fallen Firefighters Memorial Park** (301-447-1365; www.firehero.org), 1682 S. Seton Ave., Emmitsburg. Photo ID required for entry. Donations accepted. Located on the Federal Training Center grounds, the monument has certainly taken on more meaning and significance since the events of September 11, 2001.

OTHER SITES

Buckeystown

Lilypons Water Gardens (301-874-5133; 1-800-999-5459; www.lilypons.com), 6800 Lilypons Rd. Open daily Mar.–Oct.; Mon.–

CATOCTIN IRON FURNACE IN THURMONT

Fri., Nov.–Feb. Looking at it one way, this is just a commercial aquatic plant nursery that has been in operation since 1917. It can also be a nice outdoor experience, however. You are permitted to follow pathways beside acres of water gardens to enjoy the flowers, cattails, resident and visiting frogs, dragonflies, and dozens of species of birds, including red-winged blackbirds, geese, wild turkeys, sandpipers, and herons. (Ask at the office for the bird checklist—it identifies more than 240 species that have been seen here!) Be aware there is no shade, and walking during hot weather can be uncomfortable.

By the way, I lost my car key on one of my outings here. Please let me know if you find it. Thanks.

Emmitsburg

& **National Shrine Grotto of Lourdes** (301-447-5318; www.msmary.edu/grotto), 16300 Old Emmitsburg Rd. Open daily. Free. A short, paved, rhododendron-lined pathway leads to the Western Hemisphere's oldest replica of the Grottoes of Lourdes. The meditative, scenic beauty of the place makes a visit worthwhile, even if you happen to have no interest in the shrine. The artistic quality of the copper-relief Stations of the Cross, or mosaic scenes of the Mysteries of the Rosary along the pathway, is superb.

& **National Shrine of Saint Elizabeth Ann Seton** (301-447-6606; www.setonshrine.org), 333 S. Seton Ave. Closed Mon. Free admission. In 1975, Elizabeth Ann Seton was the first native-born American woman to be canonized a saint. Her relics lie in the basilica built in her honor in the 1990s. The adjoining museum traces her early life, the founding of the Sisters of Charity of St. Joseph's, and the establishment of the country's first parochial school. The architecture and interior of the basilica alone are worth a stop.

Frederick

The **Community Bridge Mural**, on S. Carroll St. between E. Patrick and E. All Saints Sts. If there is a more impressive work of public art in Maryland, I have yet to see it. Muralist William M. Cochran spent five years transforming what had been a plain concrete bridge. From a distance, it now appears as an old, ivy-covered stone bridge. Even when you're standing right next to it, your eyes are convinced that the stones and other items are truly three-dimensional. Cochran is also the painter of the equally impressive, and somehow calm-

AT THE NATIONAL SHRINE GROTTO OF LOURDES

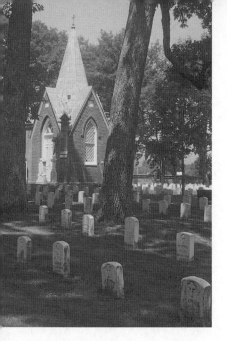

THE MORTUARY CHAPEL AT THE NATIONAL SHRINE OF SAINT ELIZABETH ANN SETON IN EMMITSBURG

ing, *Angels in Architecture* murals you find in the downtown district. More information about him, his work, and the bridge can be obtained from www.williamcochran.com.

Mount Olivet Cemetery (301-662-1164; www.mountolivetcemeteryinc.com), 515 S. Market St. The final resting place for Francis Scott Key, Barbara Fritchie, Thomas Johnson, and more than eight hundred Union and Confederate soldiers.

ZOO ✄ ⚐ **Catoctin Wildlife Preserve and Zoo** (301-271-3180; www.cwpzoo .com), 13019 Catoctin Furnace Rd. (off US 15), Thurmont. Open daily Apr.–Oct., weekends in Mar. and Nov. Adults $16.95; children 3–12 are $11.50. The 30-acre zoo began as a small snake farm in 1933. Family owned since 1966, it now includes more than three hundred animals from Australia and North and South America. Displays and enclosures are arranged to allow to you get as close as possible and still be safe.

✳ To Do

BICYCLING **C&O Canal National Historical Park** (see the sidebar on page 309 for background history and information on the canal). Approximately 20 miles of the Chesapeake & Ohio Canal pass through this area, and some of the highlights are the impressive **Monocacy River Aqueduct,** the **Victorian Railroad Station** at Point of Rocks, and access to the **Railroad Museum** in the town of Brunswick.

Three designated campsites, with vault toilets and water (in-season), are available on a first-come, first-served basis. There are also three public ramps from which you can launch a boat into the Potomac River. The **C&O Canal Visitors Center** in Brunswick (301-582-0813), 40 W. Potomac St., is located within the Brunswick Railroad Museum.

Also see **The Catoctin Trail** under *Hiking* and **Gambrill State Park** under *Green Space.*

BIRDING See the sidebar on birding, page 413.

Also see **Lilypons Water Gardens** under *To See.*

BREWERY TOUR **Flying Dog Brewery** (301-694-7899; http://flyingdogales .com), 4607 Wedgewood Blvd., Frederick. Having made its reputation in Colorado, Flying Dog moved its operations to a

THE COMMUNITY BRIDGE MURAL IN FREDERICK

business park on the southern end of Frederick and continues to attract new devotees. Tours are Thurs.–Sat. (at varying times). Small fee, but includes a tasting of five beers and a commemorative glass. The tours are quite extensive (about 45 minutes) and cover the entire aspect of the brewing process. Reservations required.

FAMILY ACTIVITIES

Frederick

🎵 **The Children's Museum of Rose Hill Manor Park** (301-600-1650; www.rosehill museum.com), 1611 N. Market St. Open daily, Apr.–Oct.; weekends only in Nov. Small admission fee for the tour. Costumed docents lead tours through the 1790s Georgian Colonial mansion of Thomas Johnson, Maryland's first governor. Hands-on exhibits invite children to help make a quilt or prepare beaten biscuits. Historic displays—and outbuildings such as the blacksmith shop, icehouse, and log cabin—help young ones gain an understanding of colonial life.

New Market

🎵 **Adventure Park USA** (301-865-6800; www.adventureparkusa.com), 11113 W. Baldwin Rd. A lot is packed into 12 acres—two go-cart tracks and two miniature golf courses; a paintball park; a 1,200-foot roller coaster; a two-story, 5,000-square-foot laser tag room; and bumper boats equipped with water cannons to ensure that you will get wet. Inside is a huge video arcade, climbing wall, and, quite unexpectedly, a high ropes course that puts you 13 feet above the ground. No admission. Tickets may be purchased for a certain number of rides or unlimited rides based on various time frames.

Thurmont

🎵 **Lawyer's Winterbrook Farm Corn Maze and Pumpkin Cannon** (240-315-8133; www.lawyersmoonlightmaze.com), 13003 Creagerstown Rd. I bet the words *pumpkin cannon* caught your eye, didn't they? Winterbrook is a hay and turkey farm, but during Sept. and Oct., they invite you to test your orientation skills on the 8 miles of trails through a corn maze. The pumpkin cannon? You get to test your aim by using compressed air to fire pumpkins (at 75 miles an hour!) at targets hundreds of feet away. Actually, who cares if you hit the

ADVENTURE PARK USA

target? It's a thrill just to pull that trigger and watch those orange orbs go flying through the air (and explode when they hit the ground).

Also see *Zoo* under *To See,* and **Candlelight Ghost Tours** under *Walking Tours.*

FISHING See **Gambrill State Park** and **Cunningham Falls State Park** under *Green Space.*

GOLF

Frederick
Clustered Spires (301-624-1295; www.clusteredspiresgolf.com), 8415 Gas House Pike. Open all year. The municipally owned course was designed by Ault-Clark and built in 1991. Look for water hazards on about half of the holes and heavily mounded fairways.

Ijamsville
Whiskey Creek (301-694-2900; www.whiskeycreekgolf.com), 4804 Whiskey Court. A dramatic course with 100-foot drops on some holes. Fees hover around $100 for weekend play.

Myersville
& **Musket Ridge** (301-293-9930; www.musketridge.com), 3555 Brethren Church Rd. The 150-acre course occupies the highest northern elevation in the Middletown Valley.

Thurmont
Maple Run (301-271-7870; www.maplerungolf.com), 13610 Moser Rd. The front nine of this family-owned course are in the open, with views of the Catoctin Mountains. The back nine are tree lined, requiring shot-making accuracy.

Urbana
& **Worthington Manor** (301-874-5400; www.worthingtonmanor.com), 8329 Fingerboard Rd. The 7,000-yard, daily-fee course has been the site of U.S. Open and U.S. Amateur Qualifiers. An Ault-Clark Signature Course, it sits in the shadow of Sugarloaf Mountain.

Walkersville
Glade Valley (301-898-5555; www.gladevalleygc.com), 10502 Glade Rd. Gently rolling terrain, with views of the Catoctin Mountains, harbors the holes, which have numerous tricky sand traps.

HIKING **The Catoctin Trail.** Public lands occupy much of the Catoctin Mountains northwest of Frederick, and in the late 1900s volunteers from the **Potomac Appalachian Trail Club** (703-242-0965; www.potomacappalachian.org), 118 Park St. SE, Vienna, VA 22180, built several miles of pathways to create the 26-mile Catoctin Trail. There are a few road crossings, but for the most part it provides a great sense of isolation. A series of extraordinary views and the opportunity to walk by Cunningham Falls are other reasons to walk the trail. Backcountry camping is not permitted, but you can stay in either of Cunningham Falls State Park's campgrounds.

The trail begins in **Gambrill State Park,** where it soon rises to the ridgeline. Weaving around streams in the **City of Frederick Municipal Forest** (whose trails are also popular with mountain bikers), it enters Cunningham Falls State Park before coming to an end in **Catoctin Mountain Park.** *50 Hikes in Maryland* (Countryman Press) gives a detailed description of the entire route.

Sugarloaf Mountain (301-874-2024; www.sugarloafmd.com), 7901 Comus Rd. (off MD 109), Dickerson. Open sunrise–sunset. No fee. Sugarloaf Mountain is such a significant feature on the rolling lands of Maryland's piedmont that it is easily visible for miles around. A monadnock—a residual hill or mountain that stands alone above a surrounding peneplain—

Sugarloaf rises more than 800 feet above the farmland below. Its upper layer is composed primarily of quartzite, an extremely erosion-resistant material that was formed by compression about 500 million years ago. In contrast, the piedmont around it is believed to be mostly metamorphic rock, much more susceptible to the erosive effects of wind and water.

A nonprofit organization, Stronghold Inc., has established a network of more than 13 miles on the mountain, with a roadway leading almost to the top. The 0.25-mile **A. M. Thomas Trail** will take you to the summit for spectacular views of the lands to the south and west. The **Northern Peak Trail** leads to other vistas, while other trails wander around the mountainside and onto valley floors. Do not miss coming here.

&. **The Trail House** (301-694-8448; www.trailhouse.com), 17 S. Market St., Frederick. Open daily. An outfitter for hiking, backpacking, cross-country skiing, and rock climbing. Also has an extensive offering of books on these activities and where to do them in the local area.

Also see *Green Space* and the sidebar on **Catoctin Mountain Park** on page 390. In addition, you'll find more hiking information under *To Do* and in the Appalachian Trail sidebar on page 414.

KAYAKING AND CANOEING The **Monocacy Scenic River** flows close to 60 miles in central Maryland before meeting up with the Potomac River a few miles south of Buckeystown, and the Monocacy River Trail lets you paddle a little more than 41 of those miles. For the most part it is an easy-flowing stream whose only natural rapid never reaches more than a Class I difficulty. Starting at the river's crossing of MD 77 a few miles east of Thurmont, you can have a nice paddle beside open fields, through deep forests, next to high bluffs, and even through downtown Frederick. There are some historical aspects to the trip, too. The LeGore Bridge was built around 1900, parts of the 1739 Michael's Mill still exist on a bank high above the river, and the river passes through the Monocacy National Battlefield. A handout map available from the Frederick Visitors Center provides a brief overview of the route and how to avoid hazards, such as when it may be necessary to portage for short distances. If water conditions are normal, the river may usually be run from spring to mid-July and again in late fall into winter.

River and Trail Outfitters (301-695-5177; 1-888-I-GO-PLAY; www.rivertrail.com), 640 Valley Rd. (off US 340), Knoxville. One of the most complete outfitters in the state, River and Trail can rent or sell you all the equipment you need to go kayaking, canoeing, rafting, tubing, biking, hiking and backpacking, and cross-country skiing. Better yet, take one of their guided trips and not only learn how to do the activity safely, but also become informed about the natural and human history of the areas you pass through.

Also see *Bicycling*.

TRAIN EXCURSIONS **Walkersville Southern Railroad** (301-898-0899; 1-877-363-9777; www.wsrr.org), 34 W. Pennsylvania Ave., Walkersville. Various excursions offered weekends from May–Oct. The one-hour-and-15-minute trip (adults $12, seniors $11, children $8) passes through the woodlands and farms north of Frederick, following a route laid out just a few years after the Civil War. A highlight is the crossing of the reconstructed bridge over the Monocacy River. It's a nice trip for a rail fan; the dinner train ($65; children 12 and under are $50) is more of a social event with couples and families conversing more with each other than looking out at the scenery. Still fun, though.

WALKING TOURS

Frederick

Guided Walking Tours of Historic Frederick (301-845-7001; www.hsfcinfo.org). Tours begin at 11 on Sat. and 1:30 on Sun., May–Oct. Small tour fee. Certified guides lead the walks to learn of the city's architecture, history, and stories. If your guide neglects to tell

THE DINING CAR OF THE WALKERSVILLE SOUTHERN RAILROAD

you, ask what happened to the state representatives who came to Frederick to discuss secession.

✂ **Candlelight Ghost Tours** (301-668-8922; www.marylandghosttours.com) depart from Brewer's Alley Restaurant at 124 N. Market St. Call for days and times. Small fee. Period-costumed tour guides take you through dark streets and alleyways to relate paranormal happenings and stories based on historic fact. A fun way to spend 90 minutes of your evening.

✳ Green Space

PARKS

Frederick

Baker Park (301-600-1493; www.cityoffrederick.com), Carroll Pkwy. and Second St. The attractive 44-acre park, with Carroll Creek flowing along its southern edge, has a public swimming pool, tennis courts, and playgrounds to provide a respite from downtown noise and traffic. Also the site of many special events and outdoor concerts.

Gambrill State Park (301-271-7574; www.dnr.state.md.us/publiclands/western/gambrill .asp), 8602 Gambrill Park Rd. The park is a gift that a group of conservationists gave to themselves and other citizens of Maryland. After using private funds to purchase land around High Knob, the group donated the tract to the city of Frederick as a municipal park. In 1934, the city turned the 1,137 acres over to the state to develop as part of the state park system.

Developed areas include picnic facilities, a campground with modern restrooms and hot showers, a nature center, a ridgeline roadway with designated overlooks, and a small pond with largemouth bass, bluegill, and channel catfish. Nature walks and campfire programs are held throughout the summer season.

Encircling the top of the mountain is a trail system of about 10 miles that takes you through a predominantly oak and hickory forest, and out to a couple of Olympian views of the Monocacy Valley. Most of the pathways are also open to mountain biking.

Thurmont

Cunningham Falls State Park (301-271-7574; www.dnr.state.md.us/publiclands/western /cunningham.asp), 14039 Catoctin Hollow Rd. There always seems to be confusion and misinformation when it comes to the height of a waterfall. A state brochure describes Cunningham Falls as a "78-foot cascading waterfall" and the highest in the state. Yet other official

CUNNINGHAM FALLS STATE PARK

sources proclaim the "sparkling water tumbling from a 51-foot ledge" of Muddy Creek Falls in western Maryland to be "Maryland's highest waterfall."

For the most part, these incongruities don't matter to those who enjoy waterfalls, and you can find the narrow grotto that Cunningham Falls flows through in the northwestern corner of the park's 5,000 acres. The **Lower Trail** is the shortest and easiest pathway to it. Other trails wander onto the ridgelines and connect with those in Catoctin Mountain Park. **Hunting Creek Lake** has swimming and boating (paddleboat and rowboat rentals during the summer), and fishing in **Big Hunting** and **Little Hunting Creeks** is permitted with artificial flies and a catch-and-return trout policy. Anglers can also fish for bass, sunfish, catfish, crappie, and bluegill in the lake.

Also see *Hiking* in "The Great Valley and Blue Ridge Region."

Catoctin Mountain Park (301-663-9388; www.nps.gov/cato), 6602 Foxville Rd., Thurmont. The federal government purchased land for Catoctin Mountain Park to demonstrate how worn-out lands could be rehabilitated. Earlier owners had clear-cut the forest or employed unsound farming practices. In 1954, 5,000 acres were deeded to Cunningham Falls State Park, while Catoctin Mountain Park retained 5,770 acres.

These lands have grown back to an eastern climax forest, much as they were in the 1700s. Barred owls, pileated woodpeckers, red-tailed hawks, and scores of other animals live in, or pass through, the park's woodlands. Close to one hundred species of wildflowers, such as bloodroot, spring beauty, Dutchman's breeches, and nodding trillium, rise from the soil.

Catoctin Mountain Park has a visitors center, picnic areas, a campground, rental cabins, and a scenic drive with viewpoints. Well hidden from view, the U.S. presidential retreat, Camp David, is within the park. **Big Hunting Creek,** along MD 77, is known to anglers for the quality of its trout fishing, and the park has some of the most diverse interpretive offerings I have come across. Programs include cross-country skiing seminars, wildflower walks, and evening programs.

Approximately 15 miles of trail, including the northern portion of the **Catoctin Trail,** reach into every corner. My favorite outings are the 2.2-mile **Chimney Rock Trail,** from which there is an impressive view of the Monocacy Valley, and the short walk to the **Blue Ridge Summit Overlook** with views northward into Pennsylvania.

✳ Lodging
MOTELS AND HOTELS

Frederick, 21703

& **Courtyard by Marriott** (301-631-9030; 1-800-321-2211; www.courtyard.com /wasfd), 5225 Westview Dr. (may be reached from I-270 Exit 31B or I-70 Exit 54). Listed for its ease of access and location close to many attractions in and around Frederick. Amenities include work desk and chair, telephones with ports, in-room iron and coffee. Indoor pool and exercise room. $149–199.

& **Fairfield Inn and Suites** (310-631-2000; www.marriott.com/fairfield-inn /travel), 5220 Westview Dr. All of the suites have refrigerator and microwave with a large working area for business travelers. Fitness room, outdoor pool, and common BBQ and picnic area. Complimentary breakfast. $149–199.

& **Hampton Inn** (301-698-2500; http:// hamptoninn3.hilton.com), 5311 Buck-eystown Pike. Conveniently located close to I-270. Swimming pool and restaurant. Rates start at $159.

Hampton Inn and Suites (301-696-1565; 1-800-426-7866; http://hamptoninn3 .hilton.com), 1565 Opossumtown Pike. Pool, fitness center, complimentary hot breakfast, guest laundry, and business center. Choice of a room or suite. About five minutes from downtown. $179–199.

Thurmont, 21788

& **Cozy Country Inn** (301-271-4301; www.cozyvillage.com), 103 Frederick Rd. (MD 806). The inn is best known as the place the national and international press, as well as many dignitaries, stay while events take place at nearby Camp David in Catoctin Mountain Park. There are the traditional motel rooms and cottages, but the standouts are the upscale rooms decorated to commemorate the styles of various past presidents.

The Carter Room reflects his penchant for hunting and fishing, the Eisenhower Room is decorated in Mamie's favorite colors, the Roosevelt Room has a bed similar to the one he was born in, and the Kennedy Room has the famous rocker. Other "presidential" rooms are similarly furnished; all are equipped with nice amenities. A bountiful continental breakfast is included. $80–180. (Also see Cozy Restaurant under *Eating Out.*)

🐾 & **Super 8** (301-271-7888; 1-877-678-9330; www.super8.com), 300 Tippin Dr. The motel's amenities are few, but its proximity to Catoctin Mountain Park and Cunningham Falls State Park is the reason to stay. $79–109.

BED & BREAKFASTS

Frederick, 21701

Hill House (301-682-4111; www.hillhouse frederick.com), 12 W. Third St. Within Frederick's historic downtown area, Taylor and Damian Branson offer four guest rooms, each with private bath. The 1870 three-story Victorian town house is filled with original artwork and many heirloom documents, pieces of furniture, and other items. I enjoy staying in the Steeple Suite on the third floor, where small windows overlook the city's spires and spur thoughts of Whittier's Barbara Fritchie poem. Damian's years of catering and gourmet cooking are evident in the breakfast she will serve to you. $145–195.

Hollerstown Hill Bed & Breakfast (301-228-3630; www.hollerstownhill.com), 4 Clarke Pl. Located just a short walk from the main downtown area, this late-Victorian home was built around the turn of the 20th century and reflects that time with carved mantels and fireplaces, period antiques, and a wraparound veranda on which to relax. Guest rooms, which are quite large, contain TV and private bath. Hosts Betty and Phillip LeBlanc prepare a full breakfast of home-baked breads, fresh fruit, tasty casseroles, and more. $135–145.

Middletown, 21769

♂ **Inn at Stone Manor** (301-371-0099; www.stonemanorcountryclub.com), 5820 Carrol Boyer Rd. Time to indulge in a bit of luxury in this rambling 1700s stone manor with a grand staircase, period antiques, gleaming wood floors, and six large guest suites, most with a fireplace and Jacuzzi. My choice would be the Hibiscus Suite because of its private porch providing a sweeping view of the grounds and pond. Guests are free to wander the scenic, manicured 114 acres where honey, hay, and grapes are grown. It's easy to see why many couples choose this as the site of their wedding. $200–225.

HOSTEL

Knoxville, 21758

American Youth Hostel (301-834-7652; www.harpersferryhostel.org), 19123 Sandy Hook Rd. The hostel is located along the C&O Canal and the Appalachian Trail, which means it is a place to meet some interesting travelers. You do not have to be a member of AYH or international hostelling organizations to stay. There are a couple of private rooms, but, for economy and companionship, most people stay in the bunk room, where you supply your own

THE TOWN HOUSES OF FREDERICK

sleeping bag or linens. As with many such hostels, it is closed to patrons during most of the daylight hours. $20–23.

VACATION RENTALS

Mount Airy, 21771

❀ **Above All Else @ Windsong** (301-831-5083; www.windsongarabians.com), 1313A Old Annapolis Rd. The vacation home, with four bedrooms and three baths—and a corral so that you can bring your own horses—sits in a private corner of a large operating horse farm. $250 per couple; $75 each additional person. If you have a group and are staying for a week, the $1,250 charge for up to eight people is a real deal.

CAMPING

Brunswick, 21706

❀ **Brunswick Family Campground** (301-834-8050; www.brunswickmd.gov), adjacent to the C&O Canal. Open early Apr.–early Nov. A municipal facility, it has trailer and tent sites, a playground area, and a bathhouse. The rates are some of the lowest you will find in the state. I like that you can walk out of your tent and onto the canal in just a few steps.

Frederick, 21701

❀ **Gambrill State Park** (see *Green Space*). The campground is located at the base of High Knob and provides access to the park's trail system. There are no hookups, and sites are quite primitive, but this makes a good, low-cost base from which to explore Frederick and the Catoctin Mountains area.

Thurmont, 21788

Catoctin Mountain Park (see the sidebar on page 390). **Owens Creek Campground** sits high on the mountain and is usually open from mid-Apr. through mid-Nov. There are flush toilets but no showers. One of the prettiest settings of all the area's campgrounds.

❀ **Crow's Nest Campground** (301-271-7632; 1-800-866-1959), 335 W. Main St. Open year-round. Swimming pool, children's playground, and trails that connect with those in Catoctin Mountain Park.

Cunningham Falls State Park (see *Green Space*). There are two campgrounds within the park. Just off US 15 are the 148 sites of the **Houck Area.** A little more isolated, and certainly quieter, are the 31 sites in the **Manor Area,** close to the falls and the lake. Be forewarned: The showers only have cold water.

Ole Mink Farm Recreation Resort (301-271-7012; www.oleminkfarm.com), 12806 Mink Farm Rd. Open year-round. Many of the 90 sites are leased on a yearly basis to RV owners, but you can still enjoy the place in your tent or in one of the deluxe camping cabins. Swimming pool.

Also see **C&O Canal National Historical Park** under *Bicycling*.

✳ Where to Eat
DINING OUT
Buckeystown
Alexander's at Buckeystown (301-874-1831; www.alexandersatbuckeystown.com), 3619 Buckeystown Pike. Open for lunch and dinner Wed.–Sun; also a brunch on Sun. Within the distinguished rooms of a late-1700s manor house, Alexander's serves a menu based on low country cooking—most often associated with Charleston, South Carolina, and the nearby coastline. All baked goods, salad dressings, and desserts are made from scratch. The last time I dined here, all meals started with sweet potato biscuits accompanied by molasses butter. I don't often get excited by a glass of lemonade, but when mixed with watermelon, it was a very tasty treat. The southern fried chicken is a customer favorite, but maybe you should consider ordering the low country shrimp in sherry cream sauce with bacon and roasted peppers over creamy stone ground grits or the beer-brined center cut pork chop. If you have never had hopping John, this is the place to try this low-country staple. $16–26.

Frederick
&. **Acacia Fusion Bistro** (301-694-3015; www.acacia129.com), 129 N. Market St. Open daily (except Mon.) for lunch and dinner, with a Sun. brunch. Although it does not have the personal-touch feeling of a chef-owned establishment, Acacia's quality and upscale atmosphere have made it a popular downtown dining destination. The menu, which changes occasionally and features locally grown organic produce and meats, consists of American fare influenced by flavors found in Eastern dishes. The Cabernet Sauvignon reduction over my bacon-wrapped filet mignon made for a wonderful mix of flavors, as did the fresh mozzarella and ripe tomatoes of my appetizer. Duck, veal, lamb, crab, and other seafood offerings round out the menu. Homemade desserts, such as a delectable key lime tart or spicy apple crisp, are reason enough to dine here. Entrées $20–38.

Dutch's Daughter (301-688-9500; www .dutchsdaughter.com), 581 Himes Ave. Considered by many to be the special-occasion place in Frederick. Seafood figures prominently on the menu, and my crab-imperial-stuffed jumbo shrimp was mouthwatering. The people at the table next to me seemed to be salivating over their filet Oscars. While eating your meal, keep in mind that desserts are made in-house. For a more casual experience, dine in the tavern downstairs (menu is the same). Entrées $18–50.

Firestone's Restaurant (301-663-0330; www.firestonesrestaurant.com), 105 N. Market St. The 1921 building that houses Firestone's was originally a department store and retains the original floors and ceiling. The establishment's fare has received a number of honors, including *Wine Spectator* awards, Best of Show in the Frederick Chocolate Fair, and best desserts from readers of *Frederick* magazine. I can attest to the desserts, as I have sampled the homemade ice cream and sorbets—and the raspberry sorbet is, without a doubt, the best that has ever melted on my tongue. Lunch is primarily salads and sandwiches, but there are always a few full entrées, and they are the same as what you would get at dinner, but at about two-thirds the price. Dinner entrées have included Kobe strip loin, pan-roasted spring lamb, and Alaskan halibut. If you like chicken and dumplings, don't pass up Firestone's. Also ask for an upstairs window table overlooking the sidewalk below so that you can do some people-watching. $26–37.

Isabella's Tavern & Tapas Bar (301-698-8922; www.isabellas-tavern.com), 44 N. Frederick St. Lunch and dinner; closed Mon. Bringing a bit of Spain to Frederick, Isabella's became a local favorite within a short time of opening soon after the turn of the 21st century by providing elegant dining at quite reasonable prices. Tapas (Spanish appetizers) include inventive items such as crispy panko-crusted asparagus "fries" with smoked tomato *aliolo,* and fried house-breaded goat cheese with almond fritters and shallot vinaigrette. Dinners are equally inventive, with a variety of paellas and meat and fish dishes costing $16.95–28.95.

The Tasting Room (240-379-7772; www.thetastingroomrestaurant.com), 101 N. Market St. Lunch and dinner; closed Sun. Owner-chef Michael Tauraso earns accolades from food critics and customers daily. An employee of the Tourism Council of Frederick County says the Sicilian rice ball appetizer—pignoli nuts and Fontinella stuffing—is one of the best things she has ever eaten and that the lobster whipped potatoes are a must-have. She calls the oak-planked rockfish with sherry roasted tomatoes and garlic cream "fantastic" and comments that the cod Mitonnée—oil-seared cod, winter greens, tomato, white beans, wine, and Gruyère croutons—on the lunch menu is "light, but really, really good with lots of flavor." Dinner entrées are $28–45.

The Wine Kitchen (301-663-6968; www.thewinekitchen.com/frederick), 50 Carroll Creek Wy. #160. After several successful years in Leesburg, Virginia, the Wine Kitchen opened its sister restaurant along the Canal Walk in Frederick. With large windows looking onto the scenery, the wine bar–restaurant features a seasonally changing menu—my watermelon soup was refreshing on an extremely hot summer day, as was the apricot salad with local arugula, charred corn, and goat cheese. Of course, do not come here without imbibing in the wine flights—a sampling of three wines (served with some entertaining and

often humorous notes). The emphasis is on fresh, locally produced items and all desserts are made in-house. Expect to spend $30 or more for dinner; the prix fixe lunch is a great deal with two courses for $18 or three for $23.

Volt (310-696-VOLT; www.voltrestaurant.com), 228 N. Market St. Open for dinner, closed Mon. Brunch Sat.–Sun. Reservations (if you can get them) are pretty much required; be prepared to have to choose a different time and day. Volt has become one of the most popular restaurants in the region ever since Chef Brian Voltaggio was a finalist on the Bravo Network's *Top Chef.* It's certainly an experience dining here, from the Houck Mansion in which the restaurant is located to the vast number of ever-changing people who will wait on you to the array of tastes you'll go through during the course of your meal. The dinner menu is a choice of five courses ($80) or seven courses ($95), with an optional wine pairing ($70 the last time I dined here). There's so much available that it would take pages to describe. Suffice it to say the goat cheese ravioli melted in my mouth; the arctic char with artichoke, pine, and sorrel was delicious; and the chocolate marshmallow with peanut and caramel a sweet way to end the most expensive meal and wine pairing I think I have ever consumed.

New Market

♣ ♂ ♿ **Mealey's Restaurant and Pub** (301-884-7454; www.mealeysrestaurantpub.com), 8 Main St. Open lunch and dinner Sat.–Sun., dinner only Wed.–Fri. Antiques fill the 1793 brick building, which has served as a general store and a hotel. The kitchen staff does an admirable job of preparing the typical American/Maryland fare. Prime rib is the specialty, but there are also many seafood choices. The atmosphere and quality of food and service are a special value, as many entrées are less than $30.

EATING OUT

Emmitsburg

♂ ♿ **Carriage House Inn** (301-447-2366; www.carriagehouseinn.info), 200 S. Seton

Ave. Open daily for lunch and dinner. With a colonial atmosphere inside and out, the inn serves what I call "upscale American" fare. Seafood, steaks, pork, chicken, and pasta all decently prepared and presented. Lots of tasty desserts, such as the chocolate mold with black raspberry ice cream inside. Entrées $22.95–32.95.

Frederick

& **Barbara Fritchie Restaurant** (301-662-2500; www.barbarafritchierestaurant .com), 1513 W. Patrick St. Open for breakfast, lunch, and dinner. I have only had breakfast here—and certainly did enjoy it—so I can't advise you on the lunch and dinner entrées, but the menu features country-cooking items at fairly low prices. $8.97–17.95.

✦ & **Brewer's Alley** (301-631-0089; www .brewers-alley.com), 124 N. Market St. Open daily for lunch and dinner. Contemporary American pub fare and wood-fired pizzas complement the fresh-brewed beer. The Southwestern grilled chicken fajita went well with the ale I chose. Other sandwiches and entrées $9.95–24.95.

Canal Bar and Grill (301-620-9898; www.canalbargrill.com), 49 S. Market St. Open for lunch and dinner and Sat. and Sun. brunch. It looks like a typical bar—narrow, with a counter, wooden floor, and several tables—yet this place must be doing something right as it has been in business since 1948, making it the oldest continuously operated family-owned restaurant in Frederick. Now with its third generation owner/operator, Chuck Kidd, the establishment is a favorite local watering hole. Chuck has modernized the menu of soups, salads, and sandwiches, making many things from scratch and serving only fresh, never frozen, items. My chicken Chesapeake was spiced with Old Bay and topped with chunks of crabmeat. $6–12.

✦ **La Paz Mexican Restaurant** (301-694-8980; www.lapazmex.com), 51 S. Market St. Open daily for lunch and dinner. The local Mexican restaurant serving the traditional dishes found in most American/Mexican establishments. Fajitas, burritos, quesadillas, tacos, and other entrées $9.95–16.95.

Quynn's Attic (301-695-9656; www.quynns attic.com), 10 E. Patrick St. Located in the historic part of the city, Quynn's is in a building whose records show it was used as a hardware store for more than two hundred years, starting as early as 1796. Lunch brings in downtown workers for soups (the old-fashioned bean stew is popular) and sandwiches (the grilled chicken, avocado, bacon, lettuce, tomato, and chipotle aioli sandwich is a nice twist on the traditional BLT). A nice use of poultry on the dinner menu is the chicken quesadilla Napoleon—marinated chicken with sautéed onions and peppers, cheddar and Swiss, guacamole, rice, salsa, and lemon crème fraîche. Other offerings that have been found on the menu include Chardonnay braised mahimahi, tuna niçoise, and a pork tenderloin with honey and maple glaze, Italian sausage stuffing, and brandy glazed apples and raisins. Entrées $15–27.

Middletown

✦ **The Main Cup** (301-371-4433; www .themaincup.com), 14 W. Main St. Open daily for breakfast, lunch, and dinner. Within a former ice cream factory and butcher shop with exposed brick walls, The Main Cup is much larger than it looks from the outside and a nice surprise to find in the out-of-the-way small village of Middletown. Also, don't be mislead by the name; this is a full-service restaurant and bar, serving a nice mix of soups, salads, sandwiches, and entrées. The fish and chips is made with rockfish, the steaks come from a farm only 10 miles away, and there's always a vegetarian dish or two available. Be sure to try the fresh squeezed lemonade—quite refreshing on a hot summer day. Regularly scheduled live entertainment and local artwork (some for sale) on the walls. Entrées $12.99–24.99.

Thurmont

✦ & **Cozy Restaurant** (301-271-7373; www.cozyvillage.com), 103 Frederick Rd. (MD 806). Open daily for breakfast, lunch, and dinner. Established in 1929 by William

Freeze and still owned by the Freeze family, the restaurant's fame parallels that of the adjacent Cozy Country Inn. Winston Churchill stopped by to play the jukebox, and Mamie Eisenhower was a frequent visitor to the pub. Display cases contain pictures, autographs, and other memorabilia from these and other famous diners.

Traditional country fare and Maryland seafood specialties are on the reasonably priced menu. The aroma of fresh-baked breads and desserts fills the air. During the growing season, the vegetables at the daily buffet were organically grown in Cozy's own garden. $10.99–18.99.

✍ ♿ **Mountain Gate** (301-271-4373; http://mountaingatefamilyrestaurant.com), 133 Frederick Rd. (MD 806). Open daily for breakfast, lunch, and dinner. Large buffets make this the place for hungry families looking for large quantities of country-cooked fare at low prices. Items from the menu include roast beef, fried ham, and a seafood platter. $9.95–20.95.

COFFEE BARS Dublin Roasters (240-674-1740; www.dublinroasterscoffee.com), 1780 N. Market St., Frederick. Open daily. Serina Roy started roasting coffee as a hobby and opened as a business on Dublin St. in 2000. Now located in a former motorcycle warehouse on the northern end of Fredericksburg, this is not a typical coffeehouse owned by someone else who employs teenagers. Serina is so serious about her coffee that she has visited many farms worldwide in search of the best organic fair trade beans. (She also sells the arts and crafts that those same farm workers create.) Of course, she roasts the beans in-house and is always happy to take customers into the back (time permitting) to explain the process. I learned more about coffee in 10 minutes than I would ever have imagined. Also, after just a few questions about my preferences, she made for me about the best cappuccino I've had. Free wi-fi, soft chairs, and live music on occasion are reasons to linger.

Frederick Coffee Company & Café (301-698-0039; www.fredcoffeeco.com), 100 N. East St., Frederick. Live music on weekend evenings.

SNACKS AND GOODIES

Frederick

The Candy Kitchen (301-698-0442), 52 N. Market St. Producing handmade chocolates, truffles, fudges, and more since 1902.

McCutcheon's Apple Products & Factory Store (301-662-3261; www.mccutcheons.com), 13 S. Wisner St. The quality of McCutcheon's cider, preserves, apple butter, juices, relishes, and other jars of tasty victuals is such that Marylanders often give them as gifts.

Sweet Memories (301-620-4202; www.sweetmemoriescandystore.com), 45 E. Patrick St. Dozens of kinds of penny candies that you can scoop out of the barrels.

Zoe's Chocolate Company (301-694-5882; www.zoeschocolate.com), 121A N. Market St. A third generation chocolatier, Zoe Tsoukatos makes the goodies fresh every day to ensure optimum taste and quality. If you're still wondering about it, you should know that Zoe's Chocolates were a part of the gift baskets given to actors at the 2011 Emmy Awards.

Middletown

✍ **South Mountain Creamery** (301-371-8565; www.southmountaincreamery.com), 8305 Bolivar Rd. Call for business hours. The milk, yogurt, cheese, ice cream, and other products sold at the retail store, located on the farm, are not only the freshest you will find but are also produced completely organically. The last time I was here, the creamery was working on a plan to enable guests to do a self-guided walking tour of the dairy and farm, but even if that has not been put into place when you visit, you and the kids are still invited to watch the cows being milked (daily 1:30–4:30) and join in on feeding the baby calves (at 4 daily). Don't leave without getting at least one scoop of the super-rich ice cream!

✳ Entertainment

FILM MDL **Holiday Cinemas** (301-662-9392; www.mdlholidaycinemas.com), 100 Baughman's Ln., Frederick. Shows films after they have been out for just a short time, at nicely reduced prices.

Regal Westview Stadium 16 (301-620-1700; www.regmovies.com), 5243 Buckeystown Pike, Frederick. First-run movies.

Also see **Weinberg Center for the Arts** under *Theaters* for classic films.

THEATERS **Maryland Ensemble Theatre** (301-694-4744; www.maryland ensemble.org), 31 W. Patrick St., Frederick. The multifaceted organization stages a number of performances during its season; most productions are new works by local talent. An added bonus is the comedy sessions presented after the Saturday-night performances. Works by regional artists are located in the lobby.

& **Way Off Broadway Dinner Theater** (301-662-6600; www.wayoffbroadway.com), 5 Willowdale Dr., Frederick. A dinner buffet accompanies the presentations of musicals, comedies, and mysteries.

✍ & **Weinberg Center for the Arts** (301-228-2828; www.weinbergcenter.org), 20 W. Patrick St., Frederick. The renovated 1926 movie palace has developed into the arts and cultural center of the region. Traveling troupes and nationally and internationally known performers present plays, musicals, concerts, and dance throughout the year. The Weinberg also has a yearly series for families and a classic-movies series.

SPORTS **Frederick Keys Baseball** (301-662-0013; www.frederickkeys.com), 6201 New Design Rd., Frederick. The Keys, Class A affiliates of the Baltimore Orioles, provide hometown action on the field of the Harry Grove Stadium Apr.–Sept. The stadium is also the site of professional wrestling, concerts, and other events.

✳ Selective Shopping

ANTIQUES

Frederick

Antique Imports (301-662-6200; 1-800-662-2014), 125 East St. Open daily. A large selection of British furniture and accessories.

Emporium Antiques (301-662-7099; www.emporiumantiques.com), 112 E. Patrick St. Open daily. More than one hundred dealers under one roof.

Old Glory Antique Marketplace (301-662-9173; www.oldgloryantiques.com), 5862 Urbana Pike. Open daily. Close to 110 dealers.

New Market

You could spend a lot of time browsing in the more than a dozen shops devoted to antiques in the small town of New Market, a few miles east of Frederick. Sometimes, places with such a large number of dealers can be overwhelming, but many of the businesses are housed within historic homes and storefronts, giving you a chance to walk around, enjoy the scenery, and recharge before entering another establishment. Recent years have seen an influx of other businesses, such as interior decorating and other specialty stores. All shops are open on the weekend; on other days, a flag flying on a storefront indicates it is open. Information about the shops can be obtained from the **Tourism Council of Frederick County, Frederick Visitors Center,** or by logging onto www.newmarketmd.com.

ART GALLERIES

Frederick

& **Delaplaine Visual Arts Education Center** (301-698-0656; www.delaplaine .org), 20 S. Carroll St. Open daily. A nonprofit organization, the center overlooks Carroll Creek and the *Community Bridge Mural.* The exhibit areas showcase local and regional talent, while the studio spaces are used for instruction and special events.

Museum Shop, LTD (301-695-0424; 1-888-678-0675; www.museumshopltd.com),

20 N. Market St. Japanese woodcuts, hand-crafted items, and original Whistler and Kornemann art.

USED BOOKS

Dickerson

Quill and Brush (301-874-3200; www
.qbbooks.com), 1137 Sugarloaf Mountain
Rd. A purveyor of signed, limited, and first
editions of collectible books. All fields and
genres are stocked, but they concentrate on
literature and mysteries.

Frederick

Wonder Book and Video (301-694-5955;
www.wonderbk.com), 1306 W. Patrick St. A
retail outlet for the chain-store company
that claims to have more than a million
new, rare, and used books available through
its Web site.

CRAFTS

Frederick

✦ ☂ **I Made This!** (301-624-4030; www
.imadethispottery.com), 10-B East St. Open
daily. Paint your own pottery. A good rainy-
day activity.

Jefferson

Catoctin Pottery (301-371-4274; www
.catoctinpottery.com), 3205 Poffenberger
Rd. Closed Sun. Susan Hanson's studio is
located in a former gristmill where she creates her vivid pieces of ceramics, tableware,
and lamps.

SPECIAL SHOPS

Frederick

✦ **Dancing Bear** (301-631-9300; www
.dbeartoys.com), 12 N. Market St. Toys,
gifts, and music for the kids. I certainly no
longer qualify as a kid, but I had a smile on
my face as I looked through children's
books written and illustrated by Maryland
residents. Its motto is "the best battery-free
toy store in the world."

Hunting Creek Outfitters (301-668-4333;
www.huntingcreekoutfitters.com), 29 N.
Market St. An authorized Orvis dealer with
fly-fishing rods and reels, accessories, and
clothing.

Terressentials (301-378-0069; www
.terressentials.com), 100 E. Patrick St. I
don't usually include chain stores in this
book, and Terressentials is essentially an
organic bath and body products company,
but this particular store has some other
interesting and distinctive products that
stand out from similar merchandise offered
in other stores. I found the acacia wood
bowls, tatum grass and sisal hemp hand-
bags, coconut shell picture frames, and
other wares to be well-crafted and eco-
friendly. It's also nice that each piece is
labeled with the materials used and country
of origin. Another shop is located in Middletown at 2650 Old National Pike (301-
373-7333).

**The Shops at Everedy Square and
Shab Row,** corner of East and Church Sts.
The 18th- and 19th-century dwellings that
once housed wheelwrights, tinkers, and
craftspeople are now a complex of small
shops filled with everything from antiques
to books to artworks and crafts supplies. As
interesting for its history and architecture as
it is for the shops. Among the standout
shops are **The Little Pottery Shop** (301-
620-7501; www.tmpottery.net), **The Perfect Truffle** (301-620-2448; www.the
perfecttruffle.com), **Sweet Angela's Cup-
cakery** (301-622-2253; www.sweetangelas
cupcakery.com), **Antique Imports** (310-
662-6200), and **Angel Cakes** (301-898-
2666; www.angelcakesandcupcakes.com).

Thurmont

Cozy Village, across from Cozy Country
Inn and Restaurant, is an assemblage of
cutesy little shops filled with handcrafted
items, antiques, and gift ideas. Most of the
shops are open until 5 daily.

FARMER'S MARKETS

Emmitsburg

Emmittsburg Farmer's Market (301-
600-6303), 302 S. Seton Ave. Open on Fri.
3–6, June–Sep.

Frederick

**Everedy Square and Shab Row
Farmer's Market** (310-898-3183), Church
and East Sts. Close to the antiques and

shopping center of town, the market is open Thurs. 3:30–6:30, early June–late Oct.

Frederick County Fairgrounds Market (301-663-5895), fairgrounds. The area's largest selection of farmer's market items is open Sat. 8–2 year-round.

West Frederick Farmer's Market (301-898-3183), 110 Baughman's Ln., Potomac Physicians parking lot (off US 40). Sat. 10–1, early May–Nov.

Thurmont

The **Thurmont Main Street Farmer's Market** (301-418-8647) is in operation Sat. 9–noon, July–Sept., at the Thurmont Carnival Grounds.

PICK-YOUR-OWN PRODUCE FARMS

Buckeystown

Maynes Tree Farm (301-662-4320; www .frederick.com), 3420 Buckeystown Pike. The strawberries are ripe from mid-May through mid-June, and the pumpkins are ready to pick by mid-Sept. Return during the holiday season to pick and/or cut your Christmas tree.

New Midway

Glade-Link Farms (301-898-7131; www .gladelink.com), MD 194. The farm grows fruit, vegetables, and gourds, so you can come here from early spring to early fall and find something to take home.

Thurmont

Catoctin Mountain Orchard (301-271-2737; www.catoctinmountainorchard.com), 15036 N. Franklinville Rd. The blackberries, blueberries, and cherries all ripen about late June and can be picked into early July.

CIDERY **Distillery Lane Ciderworks**
(301-834-8920; http://distillerylanecider works.com), 5533 Gapland Rd., Jefferson. Open Sat.–Sun. from late Aug. to Dec. and the first Sat. of the month from Jan. to late Aug. During the fall season there are signs placed around the grounds (part of a Union encampment during the Civil War) so that you can take a self-guided tour to learn

more about the cider-making process. Hard cider is more and more becoming the "in" drink of the decade and the products of the family-owned and -operated Distillery Lane are helping to lead the way. One of Maryland's first cider makers, it offers approximately six to eight ciders ranging from dry and still to sweet (about 27 percent sugar in the sweetest) and sparkling.

WINERIES The four wineries of Mount Airy are so close to one another that you could almost walk from one to the other—which is what you may want to do after tasting all they have to offer.

Black Ankle Vineyards (301-829-3338; www.blackankle.com), 14463 Black Ankle Rd., Mount Airy. Open Fri.–Sun. Free tours each Sat. at 1. Black Ankle endeavors to be as environmentally and sustainably conscious as possible. It purchases wind power, the tasting room is built with straw bales and has a sod roof, they use biodiesel-powered tractors, Piedmontese cows provide fertilizer, pigs consume the organic waste products, and chickens help keep insect populations down. The 145-acre property has 43 acres of vines and all wines are produced from grapes grown on the estate, using only French oak barrels. The guided tour not only takes in the processing part but, unlike many tours, takes you out into the vineyard with a discussion on grape varieties and how the vines are managed a bit differently than most American vineyards.

Elk Run Vineyards (410-775-2513; www .elkrun.com), 15113 Liberty Rd., Mount Airy. In its more than 30 years of production, Elk Run has garnered over 500 awards—and almost all of them the top honor in the competition entered, not just a second- or third-place finish. Most of the wines are produced from the 20 acres of vinifera grapes grown on the 42-acre estate, which includes the family home dating from the mid-1700s. Best known for its ice and sparkling wines. Tours take you through the winemaking and barrel aging area and, if time and conditions permit, a walk through the vineyard.

⍾ **Linganore Winecellars/Berrywine Plantations** (301-831-5889; www.linganore wines.com), 13601 Glissans Mill Rd., Mount Airy. With over 60 acres of grape vines, Linganore bottles about 150,000 gallons of wine annually—a little more than half of all of the wine produced in Maryland. Tours, given at noon, 2, and 4, take you through the production area and end with a tasting session unlike most others. While you can find out about the grapes that make up the wines, the emphasis here is on enlightening you to wonderful pairings or cooking techniques that you may never have thought about. I was delighted when I found that a Pinot Noir and a bite of chocolate bring out flavors not experienced when either item is consumed alone, and that Linganore's Merlot is nice complement to herbed cheeses. It is also nice to know that the winery's centrifuge eliminates the need to add chemicals during the settling process. Other bonuses are the hundred-year-old refurbished post-and-beam dairy barn where the tastings take place and the many concerts and other special events held throughout the year.

Loew Vineyards (301-831-5464; www .loewvineyards.net), 14001 Liberty Rd. (MD 26), Mount Airy. Tours, tastings, and sales Sat. 10–5 and Sun. 1–5. Estate-bottled wines.

✳ Special Events

April: **Farm Museum Spring Festival** (301-600-2743; www.rosehillmuseum.com), Rose Hill Manor Park, Frederick. Hayrides, pedal-tractor pull, petting zoo, and children's crafts.

May: **Beyond the Garden Gates Garden Tour** (301-600-2489), Frederick. Just as gardens burst forth in color, you are invited into the gardens of a number of historic homes in the downtown area.

June: **Festival of the Arts** (301-694-9632; www.frederickarts.org), Frederick. Juried arts market, children's activities, and live entertainment along Carroll Creek.

June–August: **Summer Concert Series** (301-600-2844; www.celebratefrederick .com), Baker Park, Frederick. Free outdoor concerts every Sun. evening feature local and regional acts. Expect to hear everything from New Age to country to jazz to urban music.

July: **Battle of Monocacy** (301-662-3515), Monocacy National Battlefield. Living-history portrayals of aspects of the battle.

September: **The Great Frederick (County) Fair** (301-663-5895), 797 E. Patrick St., Frederick.

October: **Oktoberfest** (301-663-3885), Schifferstadt, Frederick. Annual festival with German food, biergarten, and oompah bands. Children's events and juried arts and crafts show. **Railroad Days** (301-834-7100), Brunswick Railroad Museum, Brunswick. Scenic bluegrass train excursions, and model-railroad exhibits and demonstrations.

December: **Candlelight Tour of Historic Houses of Worship** (301-600-4047; 1-800-999-3613), Frederick. More than a dozen houses of worship participate, with each one providing a different program, such as organ recital, bell-chime demonstration, Christmas pageant, harp ensemble, and choir performances.

The Mountains of Western Maryland

6

THE GREAT VALLEY AND BLUE RIDGE REGION
Hagerstown, Antietam, and Hancock

THE ALLEGHENY PLATEAU
Rocky Gap, Cumberland, and Frostburg

AROUND DEEP CREEK LAKE
Grantsville, McHenry, Thayerville, and Oakland

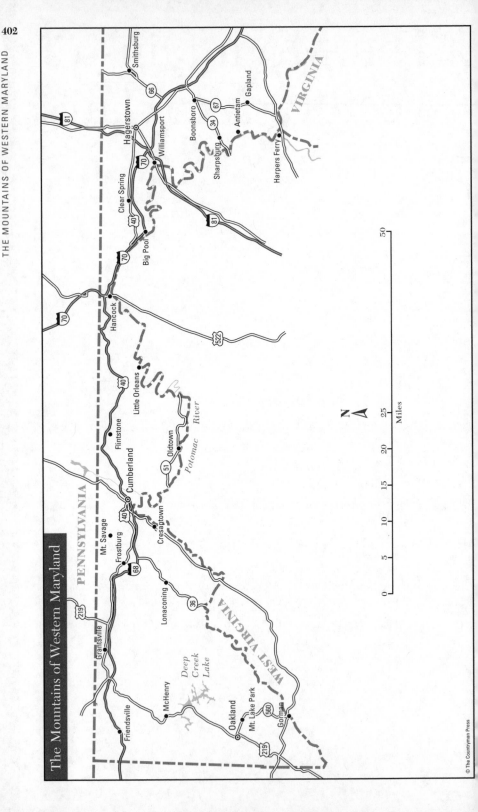

The Mountains of Western Maryland

© The Countryman Press

THE MOUNTAINS OF
WESTERN MARYLAND

The mountains of western Maryland are a world apart. Although they were the gateway through which early settlers passed on their way to America's early frontiers, they were the last area in Maryland to be settled. The construction of I-70, I-81, and I-68 has made them more accessible, yet things are still a little rough around the edges—and that is the allure.

Other than in Hagerstown and Cumberland, and their immediate vicinities, malls and supersized discount stores are few and far between, there are only a couple of large luxury resorts, home-style cooking is what you will find in many of the restaurants, and mom-and-pop enterprises are the norm. Two-lane roadways, which snake over heavily forested ridge-lines and along swiftly moving mountain streams, connect one sparsely populated community with another.

Traveling along the interstates is more scenic than you would imagine. Valley floors resemble patchwork quilts, made up of cropland, fields of cattle, and meadows all tinted by nature's own hues. West of Hancock, the Allegheny Plateau continues into West Virginia, providing mile after mile of extended mountain vistas. This is Maryland's coalfield. While driving on country roadways, you may look into your rearview mirror to see the grille of an overloaded coal truck barreling down the mountain, just inches from your rear bumper.

Due to the access provided by the interstates, much of this is changing and "economic development" is on the rise. So the time to visit western Maryland is now, before it loses its rough edges, before its roadsides are littered with the parking lots of fast-food restaurants instead of being bordered by modest homesteads. Before other folks learn of the charms of the place and come flocking to an area just waiting to be discovered. Explore now, while public lands are not well visited and can provide rambles and wanderings in relative peace and quiet with few other wayfarers.

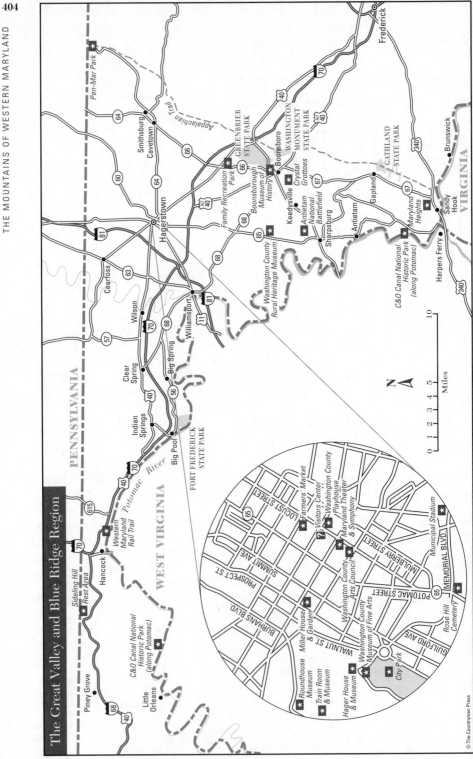

The Great Valley and Blue Ridge Region

THE GREAT VALLEY AND
BLUE RIDGE REGION
HAGERSTOWN, ANTIETAM, AND HANCOCK

As I-70 rises onto the crest of South Mountain—a part of the Blue Ridge Mountains stretching from northern Georgia to central Pennsylvania—westbound travelers gaze upon the bounteous expanse of the Great Valley.

A miles-wide and relatively flat feature in an otherwise mountainous landscape, the valley extends from mid-Pennsylvania into southern Virginia and beyond. This natural travel conduit is what Jonathan Hager and other German settlers from Pennsylvania followed into the Maryland colony, arriving in the early 1700s to establish new lives on the fertile valley floor.

During the French and Indian War in 1755, British troops (including a young George Washington) under the command of General Braddock built a wagon road through Turners Gap on South Mountain, the valley's eastern barrier. In 1806, the route was designated part of the National Road and became a major thoroughfare to the West.

Hagerstown began to grow where the two routes met, and its strategic location made it a contested site during the Civil War. Maryland was a free state, but there were many Confederate sympathizers in Hagerstown, and escaped slaves were often captured and returned to their Southern owners.

Confederate troops under the command of Robert E. Lee occupied the town prior to the Battle of Antietam in 1862, retreated after the conflict, and returned nine months later. Lee's push into Northern territory was once more thwarted, with most of the fighting this time taking place on South Mountain. Land on which these hostilities occurred has been preserved, and you can trace the events by visiting Antietam National Battlefield or walking the route of the Appalachian Trail along South Mountain.

The arrival of several railroad lines after the Civil War helped establish Hagerstown as the industrial center of the valley. The construction of I-81 (along the basic course Jonathan Hager followed) and I-70 (which parallels the route of the National Road) solidified its economic status and brought new people into the area. The downtown area, with a blend of old and new buildings, harbors a vibrant arts and cultural community, evident in the many museums, galleries, and theaters within a few blocks of one another. The Washington County Museum of Fine Arts is one of the best of its kind, and the Hager House and Museum preserve the city's former days.

On the western edge of the valley, Hancock began as an early-1700s trading post close to where Native Americans forded the Potomac River. The settlement was later named for Revolutionary War figure Edward Joseph Hancock Jr. and, like Hagerstown, started to grow when the National Road, and later the Chesapeake & Ohio (C&O) Canal, reached the town. It, too, was fought over during the Civil War, with Stonewall Jackson laying siege to it as early as December 1861. Hancock lost much of its importance in the mid-1900s when I-70 bypassed it a bit to the north. Its narrow downtown area, however, has remained an active business district with antiques shops, a C&O Canal Visitors Center, and a number of places catering to canal bikers and hikers.

COMMUNITIES Boonsboro was established in 1792 by George and William Boone. Its position along the National Road brought it growth and prosperity, as it lay about halfway between Frederick and Hagerstown. There is now another spurt of growth as the populations of the two cities migrate toward each other. A couple of museums (do not miss the Boonsborough Museum of History!), a commercial cavern, and one of the region's finest restaurants have begun to put the town on many a traveler's must-stop list.

Sleepy little **Williamsport** was once considered by George Washington as a potential site for the nation's capital, but its remoteness and inaccessibility caused him to look elsewhere. The town's fortunes grew once the C&O Canal reached it in 1834, yet declined when the waterway closed in the early 1900s. The canal and its history remain focal points, though, as people come to town to access the towpath or obtain information about it at the C&O Canal Visitors Center.

GUIDANCE The **Hagerstown/Washington County Convention and Visitors Bureau** (301-791-3246; 1-888-257-2600; www.marylandmemories.org) is located at Elizabeth Hager Center, 16 Public Square, Hagerstown, 21740, and can provide you with information if you are calling or writing when you are not in the area. The best place for guidance while in town is the bureau's **Welcome Center** at 6 N. Potomac St., Hagerstown, 21740. Information concerning the more western area of the county may be obtained from the **Hancock Museum and Visitors Center** (301-678-6236; www.hancockmd.com), 42 W. Main St., Hancock, 21750.

GETTING THERE *By air:* **Hagerstown Regional Airport** (210-313-2777; www.fly hagerstowncom).

By car: **I-81** comes into the region from Pennsylvania to the north, and West Virginia and Virginia to the south. **I-70** provides access from the east, while **I-68** (which terminates at I-70 in Hancock) is the way to arrive from the west.

By bus: **Greyhound** (1-800-231-2222; www.greyhound.com) will drop you off at its local terminal (301-739-7420), located at 354 Dual Hwy. in Hagerstown.

By rail: A **MARC** (1-800-325-RAIL; www.mta.maryland.gov) commuter train out of Washington, DC, makes stops in Harpers Ferry, which is just across the Potomac River in West Virginia.

GETTING AROUND *By car:* Many streets in Hagerstown are one way; pay attention to the signs.

By bus: The local bus service, **County Commuter** (240-313-2750; www.washco-md.net), has routes to all points in Hagerstown and to a few of the nearby communities, such as Funkstown, Maugansville, Smithsburg, Long Meadow, and Williamsport.

By taxi: **Turner Van Service** (301-733-7788) is based in Hagerstown. In and around Hancock, you can call **Valley Cab** (301-678-7767).

MEDICAL EMERGENCY Meritus Medical Center (301-790-8000; www.meritus health.com), 11116 Medical Campus Rd., Hagerstown.

MUSEUMS

Boonsboro

Boonsborough Museum of History (301-432-6969), 113 N. Main St. Sun. 1–5, May–Sept. Small admission fee. Doug Bast's late father was a fanatical collector, and Doug has followed in his footsteps. Their assortment of thousands of items is crammed into a two-story structure. It is almost impossible to describe what is here, but it is, by far, one of the most amazing personal museums I have ever seen. There are bullet carvings from the Civil War, a preserved rose from Lincoln's coffin, a pike given to a slave by John Brown, an original letter from Clara Barton, a cane carved by Geronimo, religious items dating from A.D. 800, and a clay lamp made in 1500 B.C. Do not miss this place!

Boonsboro Trolley Museum (301-432-7030; www.town.boonsboro.md.us), 214 N. Main St. Open fourth Sun. of the month, May–Oct. Donations accepted. Located within the last standing trolley station in Washington County, this small museum has a few displays that commemorate the spur line of the Hagerstown and Frederick Railroad that operated from 1902–1938. The museum was just getting started when I visited; future plans include connecting it to the Heritage Museum.

Washington County Rural Heritage Museum (240-313-2839; www.ruralheritage museum.org), 7313 Sharpsburg Pike (MD 65). Open Sat. and Sun. 1–4. Small admission fee. I thought I would be visiting a typical farm museum with a few pieces of agricultural equipment. I found this museum, which depicts the struggles and achievements of farmers of the past, to be much more. There are grain reapers, potato graders, and such, but there are also sleighs, buggies, an original Conestoga wagon, a replica of a country store, the complete interior of the old Keedysville post office—and a grain harvester that is believed to have been built in Eastern Europe nearly 1,000 years ago. A rural village, parts of which are still being constructed, showcases the area's agricultural heritage.

Hagerstown

✄ ᴅ ᵀ **Discovery Station at Hagerstown** (301-790-0076; 1-877-790-0076; www.discovery station.org), 101 W. Washington St. Closed Mon. Small admission fee. Allow a minimum of two hours (better would be four hours) to see and do as many things as possible in this multistory museum. The docent told me it is an intergenerational museum, but there is no doubt most of the exhibits and interactive displays are geared toward children. Yet, there are all kinds of things you and the kids can do together. Discover the properties of magnets, find out how dinosaurs lived, take a look inside a Mack truck engine, learn how your eyes work, and become better informed on many aspects of history, science, astronomy, agriculture, technology, and flight. Where else can you actually test your skill on a flight simulator? I'm not talking about a computer game, but the actual piece of equipment that pilots use to train.

ᴅ **Washington County Museum of Fine Arts** (301-739-5727; www.wcmfa.org), 91 Key St. (in Hagerstown City Park). Closed Mon. Donations accepted. Certainly one of the most impressive free-admission, small-city galleries you will find anywhere. The permanent collection contains more than 7,000 pieces of noted American art, old masters, European works, decorative and folk arts, and items by regional and Maryland artists. In addition, the museum brings in some of the world's finest artwork for limited exhibitions. There is also at least one music concert a month. Steel baron William H. Singer donated the building that houses the museum, and its beauty alone makes a stop here worthwhile.

✄ **Hagerstown Roundhouse Museum** (301-739-4665; www.roundhouse.org), 300 S. Burhans Blvd. Open Fri.–Sun. 1–5. Small admission fee. At one time, five railroad companies operated in the Hagerstown area, and more than 20 passenger trains a day came into the city. Inside are displays, items, and photographs from those days. The HO and O gauge model-train layouts are impressive, and children are permitted to operate the largest one, which depicts the roundhouse and nearby tracks.

Hancock

Hancock Museum and Visitors Center (301-678-6236; www.hancockmd.com), 42 W. Main St. It's just a small storefront, but does an admirable job of providing tourists with the usual needed information and acquainting them with the history of the area. Exhibits cover the local apple industry and the building of the C&O Canal, along with a few pieces that once were a great display at the Sideling Hill rest area on I-68 (see sidebar on page 411) that provided wonderful information about the geology of the mountain there.

Hancock Town Museum (301-678-6308; www.hancockmd.com), corner of High St. and Pennsylvania Ave. Open 2–4 on the second and fourth Sun., Apr.–Oct. Donations accepted. Within a small basement area of a former school, the museum chronicles the town's history with photographs (seek out the original *Harper's* magazine prints), transportation exhibits, and an early tool collection. There is even an original letter from Henry Clay postmarked 1827. All in all, it is a great collection of items, especially for a place that charges no admission fee.

HISTORIC HOMES **Miller House and Garden** (301-797-8782; www.washington countyhistoricalsociety.org), 135 W. Washington St., Hagerstown. Open Wed.–Fri. 1–4, Apr.–Dec. (Dec. hours and days may vary). Small admission fee. Guided tours of about an hour take you through the town house, which was built in various stages and is furnished as it would have been in 1825. The spiral staircase and furnishings reflect William Price's desire to let others know he was successful. The gardens are planted in period plants. One of the most interesting items is the original ledger of ransom for Hagerstown from Civil War Confederate general McCausland.

Jonathan Hager House (301-739-8393; www.hagerhouse.org), 110 Key St. (within Hagerstown City Park), Hagerstown. Thur.–Sat. 10–4 and Sun. 2–5. Small admission fee. Jonathan Hager arrived in frontier Maryland in 1739, built his house of uncut fieldstones (with 22-inch walls), married neighbor Elizabeth Kreshner, and set up a trading post in his home. The building is filled with period pieces, many of them Hager family originals. (Ask the docent to explain the origin of "pop goes the weasel.") Period plants grow all around the house. The **Hager Museum** next door contains 18th- and 19th-century items found when the Hager House was restored in 1953. I find it amazing that so many of Hager's belongings still exist—such as his *Book of Sermons* (in German) and his waistcoat.

Plumb Grove Mansion (301-842-2342; www.marylandmemories.org/museum/#), 12654 Broadfording Rd., Clear Spring. Open third Sun. June–Oct. (best to call ahead). Donations accepted. Members of the Clear Spring District Historical Association have labored long and hard to restore this 1831 mansion to its former glory. Guided tours, which can contain as much humorous and interesting folklore as historical information, take visitors through the house (all furnishing are local- or Maryland-

MILLER HOUSE

THE ENTRANCE TO PLUMB GROVE MANSION

made) and onto the grounds for glimpses of the slave quarters, four-seater outhouse, and the heirloom plant garden. Kudos to the volunteers for their fruitful labors.

HISTORIC SITES

Big Pool

Fort Frederick State Park (301-842-2155; www.dnr.state.md.us/publiclands/western/fort frederick.asp), 11100 Fort Frederick Rd. The park and the fort are open daily; other attractions have varying open dates and times. Free admission to the park; a small fee to enter the fort. The colony of Maryland constructed the fort in 1756 to protect its western frontier during the French and Indian War. It also saw action during the Revolutionary and Civil wars. With the fort restored to its earliest appearance, its stone walls enclose barracks, catwalks, and parade grounds. Costumed interpreters provide information on displays inside the barracks, and living-history demonstrations are presented on a scheduled basis. (A large reenactment with British, French, and Indian reenactors takes place each Memorial Day weekend.) A self-guided walking-tour brochure is available.

Also within the state park is a visitors center (with an excellent orientation film), a **Civilian Conservation Corps Museum,** seasonal boat rentals, a short nature trail, and a small campground scenically located on bottomland between the C&O Canal and the Potomac River.

FORT FREDERICK

Hagerstown

Rose Hill Cemetery (301-739-3630; www .rosehillcemeteryofhagerstown.org), 600 S. Potomac St. The cemetery, which still has plots available, is the final resting place for more than 2,500 Confederate soldiers killed during the Antietam and South Mountain battles. Less than 350 were able to be identified.

Beaver Creek Country School (301-797-8782), 9702 Beaver Creek Church Rd. Open by appointment. A small admission fee may (or may not) be charged. The 1904 brick building, filled with desks, books, slates, and engaging wall charts, is the third school to stand on this site. The museum room contains artifacts of early rural life. Interestingly, across the street, the refined steeple and stained glass of the 1902 **Beaver Creek Christian Church,** laid out by the same architect who designed the school, stand in stark contrast to the simple lines and windows of the 1845 **St. Matthew's Lutheran Church** next door.

THE FORMER LIVING QUARTERS AT FORT FREDERICK

Sharpsburg

Antietam National Battlefield (301-432-5124; www.nps.gov/anti). The visitors center is off MD 65 a few miles north of Sharpsburg. Open daily. Small admission fee. When Confederate general Robert E. Lee made his first push into Northern territories in September 1862, his troops clashed with Union soldiers on a battlefield that covered 30 square miles. More men were killed or wounded than on any other single day during the Civil War.

I was impressed with the way the park service had organized visitors' experiences when I first came here many years ago. It was the first Civil War battlefield I had ever visited, and I have never failed to learn something new on subsequent visits. A driving tour takes you by significant battle sites, rangers lead guided walks, and a system of trails take the more inquisitive into hidden areas of the battlefield's 3,000 acres.

Antietam National Cemetery is off MD 34 in Sharpsburg. Grand old maple, oak, and Norway spruce trees provide shade for the graves, set out in a circular fashion. It is mind-

BEAVER CREEK COUNTRY SCHOOL

THE BURNSIDE BRIDGE AT ANTIETAM NATIONAL BATTLEFIELD

boggling to walk through here and realize that only a portion of those killed during the battle are buried here.

OTHER SITES Between 1819 and 1863, more than 30 **stone bridges** were constructed along Antietam and Conococheague Creeks and their tributaries. Many of these impressive and eye-pleasing structures still exist. A brochure detailing where they are located may be obtained from the **Hagerstown/Washington County Convention and Visitors Bureau.**

CAVERN TOUR ✤ **Crystal Grottoes Caverns** (301-432-6336; www.crystalgrottoes caverns.com), MD 34 about 1.5 miles west of Boonsboro. Adults $15, children 11 years old and younger $10. A 30-minute guided tour takes you through the 250-million-year-old caverns, believed to contain more formations per square foot than any other commercial cavern in the world. Triangular pyramids of calcite have formed eight-sided crystals rarely found anywhere else.

✳ To Do

BICYCLING Western Maryland Rail Trail (301-842-2155; www.westernmaryland railtrail.org/wmrt). The paved, and nearly flat, trail follows the route of the former Western

SIDELING HILL

On I-68 west of Hancock, the Washington County–Allegany County line, the interstate makes a long climb over 1,600-foot Sideling Hill. To reduce the length and grade of the ascent, workers spent more than two years making a cut 360 feet deep into the mountain's ridgeline (the deepest road cut in Maryland).

The passageway is a great place to learn about the geology of the mountains, so you should take a few minutes' break from driving to stop at the Sideling Hill rest area, accessed directly from the interstate. Take the short trail that begins at the restrooms and find the road cut revealing fossilized plants and seashells from 350 million years ago, when the site was at the bottom of an ancient ocean. The cut also shows how the layers of sedimentary rock were folded as Africa collided with North America about 230 million years ago.

Maryland Railroad. Begins about 0.5-mile west of Fort Frederick State Park and continues westward for 23 miles into Hancock and a bit beyond. Supporters are hoping to get additional miles added to the route, bringing it even farther west. The trail parallels the C&O Canal, which makes it possible to do round-trip rides without following the exact same course.

C&O Canal National Historical Park (301-739-4200; www.nps.gov/choh). The **C&O Canal Visitors Centers** in Williamsport (301-582-0813) and Hancock (301-678-5463) can provide you with much detailed information. (Also see the sidebar on page 309 for background history and information on the canal.) Well over 50 miles of the canal pass through this area of Maryland, providing a grand opportunity for hours of easy riding and sightseeing. Some of the highlights include access to the **Appalachian Trail** and **Maryland Heights,** the Big Pool area and **Fort Frederick State Park,** and the rewatered parts of the canal at Williamsport and Hancock. Spaced along the route are a dozen designated campsites, with vault toilets and water (in-season), that are available on a first-come, first-served basis. There are also numerous ramps from which you can launch a boat into the Potomac River.

WESTERN MARYLAND RAIL TRAIL

Insider's tip: There is a free parking lot located off S. Pennsylvania Ave. in Hancock for those using the C&O Canal Towpath or the Western Maryland Rail Trail.

The small *Bicycle Tours of Washington County* brochure (available from the Hagerstown–Washington County Convention and Visitors Bureau) provides point-by-point details on eight rides in the county and one within the city limits of Hagerstown. All are circuit routes and range in length from 10 to 34 miles. A couple might be considered strenuous as they take you from the Great Valley onto the heights of South Mountain, yet others make use of the paved and flat terrain of the Western Maryland Rail Trail. My favorite is the Farm Orchard Tour, a 32-mile route that runs along the bottom of South Mountain, passing by one orchard, fruit stand, and restaurant after another.

C&O Bicycle (301-678-6665; www.candobicycle.com), located next to the C&O Canal, Hancock. Bicycle rentals, sales, and service. They will also do shuttles (schedule permitting) for you even if you have your own bike and don't rent one from them. Those of you looking for low-cost accommodations might want to consider the bunkhouse. About $10 a person gets you a bunk, bedroll, towel, and hot shower.

BOAT RENTALS See Fort Frederick State Park under *Historic Sites.*

FAMILY ACTIVITIES *✐* **Family Recreation Park** (301-733-2333; www.famrecpark .com), 21036 National Pike, Boonsboro. Open daily May–Aug.; weekends in Apr. and Sept.–

Oct. You may not know what Water Wars is, but your kids do—and they probably can't wait to start propelling liquid-filled balloons into the air. This local hot spot also offers miniature golf, batting cages, attractions for very small children, and three go-cart tracks. The figure eight is one of the most fun tracks I have ridden in many years.

Also see *Cavern Tour* under *To See*.

GOLF **Hagerstown Greens at Hamilton Run** (301-733-8630; www.hagerstownmd.org), 2 S. Cleveland Ave., Hagerstown. The nine-hole course was built in the 1930s by citizens who could not afford the fees of a private club. The entire grounds project a maturity and feel not found in newer courses.

Black Rock (240-313-2816; www.blackrockgolfcourse.com), 20025 Mount Aetna Rd., Hagerstown. Grand views of the mountains from the 6,878-yard, par 72 course.

Yingling's Golf Center (301-790-2494; www.yinglingsgolfcenter.com), 20220 Jefferson Blvd., Hagerstown. The area's only par 3 course, it is an excellent choice for beginners or those wanting to brush up on their game. Also on the premises are a miniature-golf course and batting cages.

MINIATURE GOLF See **Family Recreation Park** under *Family Activities*, and **Yingling's Golf Center** under *Golf*.

HIKING **Maryland Heights** (304-535-6029; www.nps.gov/hafe), located off Sandy Hook Rd. across the Potomac River from Harpers Ferry, West Virginia. A steep and strenuous circuit hike of 5 miles will take the hardy and adventurous past remnants of Civil War fortifications and out to a spectacular view of the confluence of the Shenandoah and Potomac Rivers. Thomas Jefferson proclaimed the vista (as seen from a spot in West Virginia) to be "one of the most spectacular scenes in Nature, and worth a voyage across the Atlantic." Luckily, you only have to drive here and take a hike to enjoy it.

Also see **Antietam National Battlefield** under *Historic Sites*, and *Bicycling*.

KAYAKING AND CANOEING **Outdoor Excursions** (1-800-77-KAYAK; www.outdoorexcursions.com), P.O. Box 24, Osage Dr., Boonsboro, 21713. A one-stop shop for

BIRDING—THE AUTUMN HAWK MIGRATION

Maryland's portion of the Appalachian Trail (see the sidebar on page 414) has overlooks along South Mountain, which are great areas from which to watch the annual autumn hawk migration. Heated air from rays of the sun striking cliffs and rock outcroppings couples with warm air rising from the lowlands to create forceful drafts, or thermals, that the hawks use to soar upward. In addition, by gliding near the crest of the ridges, they take advantage of the northwesterly winds striking the Appalachians, providing more uplift.

Sometimes as early as mid-August, ospreys, American kestrels, and a few bald eagles begin the procession southward. The migration commences in earnest in the middle of September as broad-winged hawks take to the skies. Peak daily sightings of several thousand are not uncommon. In early October, peregrine falcons join the movement, while later in the month one of the smallest hawks, the sharp-shinned, becomes the dominant migrant. Joining the procession are the larger in size but fewer in number Cooper's hawks. Red-tailed hawks, northern harriers, and red-shouldered hawks zip by leafless trees in November. Soaring over an Appalachian Trail that could be covered by December snows, northern goshawks and golden eagles bring the migratory season to a close.

water-sports trips. They can teach you what you need to know and then will take you on guided kayaking, rafting, and tubing trips along the Potomac River. You can choose from day or weekend outings and a number of lesson packages. All instructors are certified by the American Canoe Association.

Antietam Creek Canoe (240-447-0444; www.antietamcreek.com), 19005 Lappans Rd., Boonsboro. Provides the same basic services, but along a 22-mile section of Antietam Creek.

Also see **C&O Canal National Historical Park.**

SKATING *✐* **Hagerstown Ice and Sports Complex** (301-766-9122; www.hagerstown ice.org), 580 Security Rd., Hagerstown. Ice-skating lessons, rentals, and public sessions are available within the 35,000-square-foot structure.

✐ **Family Skating Center** (301-582-2020; www.rinktime.com), 1733 Virginia Ave.; and **Starland Roller Rink** (301-739-9844; www.starlandrollerrink.com), 800 Park Rd., both in Hagerstown, are both open to the public for roller-skating fun.

SKIING, CROSS-COUNTRY, AND SNOWSHOEING See the **Appalachian Trail** sidebar below.

SWIMMING **Claude M. Potterfield Municipal Pool** (301-733-2599; www.hagerstown md.org), 730 Frederick St., Hagerstown. Memorial Day–Labor Day.

TRAIN EXCURSIONS See **Hagerstown Roundhouse Museum** under *To See.*

WHITE-WATER RAFTING See *Kayaking and Canoeing.*

THE APPALACHIAN TRAIL

There may be no better introduction to backpacking and primitive camping than the Appalachian Trail through Maryland. Shelters and campsites are conveniently spaced so that you don't have to do marathon miles to find a place to spend the night, wildlife is abundant, and the trail crosses numerous roads where help may be available in case of an emergency. Even though the route has a good feeling of isolation, there are four places where it is possible to make use of modern restroom facilities—and one spot that offers free warm showers!

The gentle terrain and great scenery are what make this the perfect place to bring the kids for overnight hikes or to break friends into the pleasures of backpacking without introducing them to the rigors of a more rugged topography. Other than a couple of climbs of less than 500 feet, the trail stays along the gently undulating crest of South Mountain for nearly the entire distance, neither losing nor gaining much in the way of elevation. On the rare occasions when winter cooperates by bringing in a blanket of snow deep enough to completely cover all of the rocks and boulders, the trail can be a great cross-country skiing or snowshoeing route.

In addition to its natural beauty, South Mountain has been the scene of numerous activities in American history. George Washington crossed the mountain a couple of decades before the colonies broke from England, the first National Road coursed its way over it, and skirmishes of the Civil War were waged on its heights.

The guidebook *50 Hikes in Maryland* (Countryman Press) gives a detailed description of the trail's 40-mile route through the state.

HAGERSTOWN CITY PARK

✳ Green Space
PARKS

Hagerstown
🐾 **City Park** (301-739-8577; www.hagerstownmd.org), located along Virginia Ave. in the city's South End. One of the state's prettiest municipal parks. Three man-made lakes are surrounded by 50 acres of open and forested areas, playgrounds, tennis courts and ball fields, and short walking trails. Within the park are the **Washington County Museum of Fine Arts, Jonathan Hager House,** and the restored **1912 Engine 202 Steam Locomotive and Caboose.**

South Mountain at the Frederick–Washington County line
Five parks encompass most of the land along South Mountain's ridgeline and protect Maryland's 40 miles of the Appalachian Trail (see the sidebar on page 414). From south to north they are:

South Mountain State Park (301-791-4767; www.dnr.state.md.us/publiclands/western/southmountain.asp). It is hard to actually tell where this park is, as it was established to safeguard those lands along the mountain that were not already protected by the other parks. Be thankful the state appropriated the funds to purchase these additional acreages.

Gathland State Park (301-791-4767; www.dnr.state.md.us/publiclands/western/gathland.asp), Gapland Rd. (off MD 67). Open daily 8 AM–sunset. The park is the site of the only monument in the world to

WAR CORRESPONDENTS MEMORIAL, GATHLAND STATE PARK

war correspondents. Planned and built by George Alfred "Gath" Townsend, a journalist and columnist 1866–1910, it memorializes more than 150 reporters and artists who covered the Civil War from both sides of the conflict. The off-balance monument contains a large Moorish arch below three smaller ones of Roman design. Taking the time to look at and read the dozens of inscriptions and view the mythological figures could take up much of an afternoon. Picnic areas; also a small museum open on an irregular basis.

Washington Monument State Park (301-791-4767; www.dnr.state.md.us/publiclands /western/washington.asp), accessed from US Alternate 40 east of Boonsboro. Open daily. Home of the original Washington Monument. Built by the citizens of nearby Boonsboro in 1827, the jug-shaped tower was the first structure to be completed in honor of America's first president. Be sure to ascend the inside staircase for a grand view of the rolling Maryland countryside to the west. There are also attractive picnic sites close to the monument.

Greenbrier State Park (301-791-4767; www.dnr.state.md.us/publiclands/western /greenbrier.asp), on US 40 about 9 miles east of Hagerstown. The focal point of the park is a 42-acre lake that provides swimming, fishing, and boating. Short hiking trails, a campground, and some great nature interpretive programs are other reasons to stop by.

Pen-Mar Park (240-313-2700; www.washco-md.net), in the town of Pen-Mar. Appearing to be not much more than a community picnic grounds today, this spot was an amazingly popular resort between 1890 and 1920. Seven hotels and close to one hundred guest cottages were located nearby to cater to daily crowds of 5,000 or more drawn to an amusement park. Gas rationing during World War II forced the park to close in 1943. There is a splendid view of Hagerstown (Great) Valley to the west, and restrooms and water are available in-season.

✳ Lodging

MOTEL

Hagerstown, 21740

 ♿ **Homewood Suites** (301-665-3816; http://homewoodsuites3.hilton.com), 1650 Pullman Ln. Choice of studio, one-, two-, or three-bedroom suites with fully equipped kitchens. Complimentary hot breakfast (and dinner! Mon.–Thurs.). Business center, swimming pool, basketball court, and fitness center. More like staying in a condominium than a motel. $129–229.

♿ **Springhill Suites** (301-582-0011; www .marriott.com), 17280 Valley Mall Rd. All rooms are suites with a microwave, fridge, and sink, with a large deck and work area appreciated by business travelers. Pool, exercise room, complimentary hot breakfast. $159–189.

INN Inn Boonsboro (301-432-1188; www.innboonsboro.com), 1 North Main St. Pure luxury created by author Nora Roberts and husband/photographer Bruce Wilder. They basically gutted the 1790s building (constructed as a hotel) after a fire,

so just about everything is new on the inside, while retaining the historic exterior. It's hard to describe all of the amenities here. The eight guest rooms (named for characters in novels that have happy endings) are all lush in décor and furnishings, each with a private bath—some as large as a small apartment, and containing amenities such as a copper tub and multijet shower. A library, sitting room, back terrace, and . . . I

A ROOM AT INN BOONSBORO

THE LANDSCAPE AT STONEY CREEK FARM B&B

could go on and on. Even the breakfast you are served is something special—it's created by a chef who has an associate's degree from the Baltimore International Culinary College. $255–305.

BED & BREAKFASTS

Boonsboro, 21713

♂ **Stoney Creek Farm B&B** (301-432-6272; www.stoneycreekfarm.com), 19223 Manor Church Rd., Boonsboro. It takes a special place to be accepted onto the Select Registry and, in my opinion, Stoney Creek more than qualifies. The early-1800s brick farm home was restored and remodeled after the turn of the 21st century and offers modern amenities within the historic setting, rich furnishings, and an abundance of windows in the common areas (thoughtfully designed additions to the house) providing bright natural lighting and views of the 65-acre farm. Wood-burning fireplaces add warmth and an inviting atmosphere in winter.

Guests can hike the 5 miles of trails that wind around a wooded knoll, arrange to have a guided horseback ride of the same trails, or wander around the grounds finding benches placed in scenic, skillfully landscaped spots that invite quiet contemplation. Of the four guest rooms, I liked the

Empire Room best. Its winding staircase provided a hidden feel, yet the room opened onto the balcony (once the home's outside porch) that overlooks the common areas. Then again, I wished I had the time to luxuriate in the Equestrian Room's slipper tub. $225–250.

Hancock, 21750

1828 Trail Inn (301-678-7227; www.1828-trail-inn.com), 10 W. Main St. The restored early-1900s Craftsman home sits directly across the street from the Western Maryland Rail Trail and the C&O Canal Towpath. As such, many of its guests are bicyclists riding one or both of the routes, and the hosts have responded by developing amenities such as a guest laundry facility, large public rooms where guests can gather to tell tales of how their day went, and an alcove that is always full of complimentary beverages, fruits, and other afternoon refreshments. There's also an outside secure storage area for bicycles. One of the guest rooms has a Jacuzzi, separate shower, and a private porch. Another looks out to the canal and has a large bathroom, while the suite lets you come and go by a private entrance. $129–159.

Keedysville, 21756

Antietam Overlook Farm (301-432-4200; 1-800-878-4241; www.antietamoverlook

.com), 4812 Peterstown Rd. This place is more than a typical B&B. The manor home (and I truly mean *manor*) sits on 95 acres and has a 40-mile view that takes in not only Antietam Battlefield, but four states—Maryland, Virginia, West Virginia, and Pennsylvania. (Screened porches let you look at all of this without having to be bothered by bugs or inclement weather.) Inside the home, hand-hewn timber framing, fine furniture, crystal accessories, and a grand fireplace complement the fireplaces, inviting beds, and bubble baths in the guest suites. Not enough to entice you to stay? How about adding a full three-course country breakfast that former guests rave about in the inn's log book. Complimentary beverages, including brandy, wine, and beer, are also available 24 hours a day. $225–295.

🐌 **Inn at Red Hill** (301-730-2620; www.innatredhill.com), 4936 Red Hill Rd. Talk about planning! While still employed as a Washington County teacher, Cindy Neugebuer designed and built her home with the idea of someday running a B&B. Now that she is retired, her guests are the fortunate recipients of her planning as the modern home has only two guest rooms (making for relaxing stays and easy conversations with Cindy in the large common area) that are nicely furnished and have private baths. I would have liked to linger longer to enjoy the hammock on the back deck that looks upon a deep green forest in summer and has expansive views of Antietam when leaves are off the trees. The inn is popular with bicyclists even though it is a distance from the C&O Canal—maybe that's because Cindy will shuttle bikers if arrangements are made in advance. $110–150.

Sharpsburg, 21782

Inn at Antietam (301-432-6601; 1-877-835-6011; www.innatantietam.com), 220 E. Main St. This Eastlake Victorian home, circa 1908, has been receiving accolades since its B&B inception in the 1980s. Charles Van Metre and Bob Leblanc (memorabilia in the solarium chronicle their many years in the theater business) continue to run the inn with a touch of class. Each of the five guest suites has a private bath. I enjoyed the Rose Suite, with its antique four-poster bed and bright walk-in bay overlooking Sharpsburg's Main Street. The Smokehouse Suite is where hams and other meats were cured. Today the stone fireplace remains the focal point of the sitting room, while guests bed down in an upstairs loft. Although somewhat out of character from the rest of the house, the Penthouse Suite's resemblance to a studio apartment and grandstand view of the surrounding mountains are a great use of the remodeled third-floor attic.

If a walk around the inn's 7 acres or an evening spent rocking on the wraparound porch are too relaxing, you can always exercise your mind by playing chess with the hand-carved Civil War set. $120–185.

⚓ **Jacob Rohrbach Inn** (301-432-5079; 1-877-839-4242; www.jacob-rohrbach-inn.com), 138 W. Main St. The 1800 Federal-period inn is named for the man who lost his life defending the property from horse thieves during the Civil War. The Clara Barton guest room is decorated with furniture made by host Paul Breitenbach's grandfather. I thought that the three small steps into the elevated bathroom in the Thomas Jackson Room added a bit of historical authenticity to my stay. The restored summer kitchen house was a great place to unwind, and the eggs Benedict, a mainstay

INN AT ANTIETAM, SHARPSBURG

with many B&Bs, were some of the best I've had during my travels. Take advantage of the hammock and gardens under spreading maple trees as a place to relax. Well-behaved children permitted. $135–212.

VACATION RENTALS Rustic Retreats (202-686-5339; 1-877-787-8425; www.rusticretreats.net). They have a number of cabins (in West Virginia and in this area of Maryland) that are available for rent for the night, weekend, week, or month. Each is fully equipped and can accommodate four to six people.

CAMPING
Big Pool, 21711
♿ **Fort Frederick State Park** (301-842-2155; www.dnr.state.md.us/publiclands /western/fortfrederick.asp), 11100 Fort Frederick Rd. Apr.–Oct. Located adjacent to the Potomac River and the Big Pool area of the C&O Canal. Vault toilets and two handicapped-accessible sites.

🐾 **Indian Springs Campground** (301-842-3336), 10809 Big Pool Rd. One of the lowest-cost commercial campgrounds in the state. Limited facilities in winter.

Boonsboro, 21713
Greenbrier State Park (301-791-4767; www.dnr.state.md.us/publiclands/western /greenbrier.asp), on US 40 about 9 miles east of Hagerstown. Usually open early Apr.–late Oct. The large campground has a dump station and flush toilets. Within the state park is a lake for swimming, fishing, and boating (with paddleboat and canoe rentals).

Gapland, 21779
🐾 **Maple Tree Campground** (301-432-5585; www.thetreehousecamp.com), 20716 Townsend Rd. Open year-round. A nicely laid-back campground in which RVs and trailers are not permitted; there are only tent sites. Two camping tree houses accommodate up to six people—a fun and different way to enjoy the woods. Rates are some of the most reasonable you will find anywhere, and the campground backs up to the Appalachian Trail. Pets permitted on a leash.

Hancock, 21750
🐾 **Happy Hills** (301-678-7760; www .happyhillscampground-md.net), 12617 Seavolt Rd. Open all year. The campground's 350 acres are within easy walking distance of the C&O Canal, which means you have access to many more miles of trails in addition to those in the campground. RV and tent sites, pool, miniature golf, and activities building. Camping cabins for rent. Pets on a leash permitted.

Williamsport, 21795
🐾 🚣 **Hagerstown Antietam Battlefield KOA** (301-223-7571; 1-800-562-7607; www .hagerstownkoa.com), 11579 Snug Harbor Ln. Open year-round. The campground's 24 acres are along scenic Conococheague Creek, and some of the sites are next to the water. Canoe rentals, miniature golf, and many, many planned family activities.

McMahon's Mill (301-223-8778; www .mcmahonsmill.com), Avis Mill Rd. (at Mile 88.1 on the C&O Canal). The closest campground to Antietam National Battlefield, it has tent and RV sites next to the Potomac River. Flush toilets and hot showers. Also on the premises are a restaurant and the small **Civil War Military and American Heritage Museum** (open by appointment; small admission fee).

🐾 **Yogi Bear's Jellystone Park Camp and Resort** (301-223-7117; www .jellystonemaryland.com), 16519 Lappans Rd. Open all year. Lots of things to do on the campground's 90 acres: pool, water park, playground, basketball and volleyball courts, and miniature golf. Some sites have full hook-ups. Small camping cabins for rent.

✳ Where to Eat
DINING OUT

Boonsboro
Old South Mountain Inn (301-432-6155; www.oldsouthmountaininn.com), 6132 Old National Pike. Open for lunch Sat. and Sun., dinner Tues.–Sun. Reservations strongly recommended for dinner. The inn was established in 1732, so be sure to ask about its eventful past. The menu features Maryland dishes influenced by cuisines

from around the world. Scallops Provençale ($24), chicken Saltimbuca ($23), shrimp Mediterranean ($25), and a couple of vegetarian entrées are just a few of the savory surprises to be found in this restaurant sitting next to the Appalachian Trail. The waitstaff are friendly and knowledgeable about the many wines available. Desserts are delectable—and huge.

Hagerstown

Aqua 103 (301-393-5757; www.aqua103 .net), 12916 Conomar Dr. Open for lunch and dinner Mon.–Fri.; dinner only Sat. One of Aqua 103's owners has been in the upscale food service business for more than a quarter of a century and his experience shows. Despite being a distance from the downtown dining district, the restaurant stays busy with customers enjoying the "progressive American cuisine" based on fresh ingredients. My ahi tuna over roasted mango and peach risotto with raspberry sauce was definitely fresh and tasty. Some of the other offerings at the time I dined were surf and turf consisting of filet and crab, and maple leaf duck breast with herbs and hazelnuts marinated over asiago and bacon risotto with raspberry coulis. $18–40.

The Rhubarb House (301-733-4399; www.rhubarbhouse.com), 12 Public Square. Open 8–3 for breakfast and lunch Mon.–Fri.; 5–10 for dinner Fri. and Sat. The lunch menu has a wide choice of salads, inventive sandwiches ($4.25–7.95), and soups (the $5.95 cream of seafood is flavorful). Homemade potato chips sprinkled with grated cheese are a house specialty. Ask for the lower dining room if you want the quieter spot during lunch. Entrées are $16.95 and up.

EATING OUT

Boonsboro

Dan's Restaurant and Tap Room (301-432-5224; http://drnth.com), 3 S. Main St. In an upscale atmosphere, Dan's has a menu fitting its furnishings of exposed brick walls and wood floors. Yes, there's burgers and sandwiches, but there are also entrées like sesame salmon and cherry chicken. Beef lovers can't go wrong with the 14-ounce grilled Delmonico steak. With more than one hundred beers available, the place is a favorite tavern that often gets very busy. $14–22.

☦ **LJ's & The Kat Lounge** (301-739-7990; www.ljsandthekatlounge.com), 1130 Conrad Crt., Hagerstown. Open for dinner Tues.–Sat. Textures. That's what I remember from my dining experiences here, wonderful textures and tastes. LJ's is surrounded by parking lots, but you'll forget that as soon as you take your first bite in this upscale establishment, which has pleasant décor and an open kitchen where you can watch the chefs perform their magic. In order to take advantage of the freshest ingredients, the menu changes seasonally, while the "Market Menu" changes weekly. This ensures never-ending choices.

Don't pass up the Japanese hush puppies for an appetizer if they are on the menu. Cornmeal tempura crunchily encloses the tender sesame tuna hidden inside, the wasabi drizzle is tempered by the addition of honey, and the roe topping adds a slight hint of saltiness. Lobster meat loaf; a mushroom cannelloni full of morels, bluefoots, Madiera béchamel, and duck sausage; and tandoori-grilled wild scallops with cucumber mint hummus and cauliflower couscous are just a few of the resourceful items that have found their way to the menu. For a real texture and taste treat, order a side of the truffle scalloped potatoes. Desserts are homemade; my notes from last time here read, "passionfruit sorbet—outrageous burst of flavor!"

Without a doubt, LJ's is one my favorite western Maryland dining choices. Order anything—you won't be disappointed. Entrées $15–34.

Hagerstown

Always Ron's (301-797-7887; www.always rons.com), 29 N. Burhans Blvd. Open for lunch and dinner Mon.–Sat. Good American deli food, with many sandwiches and a few seafood and meat entrées. Worth a stop for straightforward food and atmosphere. $7.95–19.95.

Bulls and Bears (301-791-0370; www .bullsandbears.biz), 38 S. Potomac St. Open daily for lunch and dinner. A favorite with downtown employees for lunch and as an after-work watering hole. With an interior of wood and bricks, Bulls and Bears serves an upscale pub fare with all-lump crabcakes, ribs, steaks, and seafood (I like the mango-pistachio-glazed grilled Atlantic salmon). Also well-known for their fish taco appetizers and stuffed burgers. Be aware service has been known to be a little slow when the place is busy. $12.95–23.95.

The Gourmet Goat (301-790-2343; www .thegourmetgoat-ggs.com), 41 N. Potomac St. Open for breakfast, lunch, and dinner Wed.–Sat; breakfast and lunch only on Mon.–Tues. A good downtown place for a quick and reasonably priced breakfast or lunch. The gazpacho is nicely spiced and the shrimp salad has full, large-sized shrimp (not those little itty-bitty things you are often served). The place transforms in the evening into a busy bar and restaurant with some tasty entrées, such as chicken Allyson and artichoke Florentine. Lunch $5.50–7. Dinner $17–23.

The Plum (301-791-1717; on facebook), 6 Rochester Pl. Open for breakfast and lunch Mon.–Fri. 7–2:30. A gourmet deli serving hot and cold sandwiches. Hartwick's Heap has enough meat to satisfy any carnivore, while Jen's Veggie Pita is for the artery-conscious. $6.95–12.95.

Schmankerl Stube Bavarian Restaurant (301-797-3354; www.schmankerlstube .com), 58 S. Potomac St. Open for lunch and dinner; closed Mon. From the dark sculpted wooden fixtures and beams to the portrait of King Ludwig II, music on the sound system, and original Bavarian waitstaff outfits, everything in the restaurant says *Let's go to Bavaria!* Owner Charlie Sekula makes sure that the restaurant reflects his homeland, and the Kassler ripperl, Wiener schnitzel, and zwiebelrostbraten do a good job. Daily specials and an extensive selection of German brews. Entrées $17–26.

Hancock

✍ **Weaver's Restaurant and Bakery** (301-678-6346; www.weaversrestaurant andbakery.com), 77 W. Main St. Open for lunch and dinner Mon.–Fri., and breakfast, lunch, and dinner Sat.–Sun. A Hancock institution for more than 50 years, this is the kind of place that, if you were to come here often enough, you would eventually meet the town's entire population. The home-cooking menu features hot and cold sandwiches, country-cured ham, pork chops, and seafood. The peanut butter or red raspberry pies are hard to resist, as are the doughnuts, cakes, and other goodies you can take home. The most expensive entrées are around $18.95.

Keedysville

Bonnie's at the Red Byrd (301-432-5822; www.bonniesattheredbyrd.com), 19409 Shepherdstown Pike. Open daily for breakfast, lunch, and dinner. Vinyl tablecloths, chairs, and booths make this look like a plethora of other eating establishments. Yet, the country cooking menu of the Red Byrd has had a loyal following since it opened in 1960. The business became even more popular once Bonnie bought the restaurant a few years back and, with 25 years of food service experience, introduced her own recipes for her well-regarded fried chicken, pork BBQ, and crabcakes. The BBQ sandwich I had was tasty and full of chunks of tender pork. Pies and cakes are homemade, with the red velvet cake being the thing that draws many people to Bonnie's. Prices are nice, too, with the menu topping out at about $15.

Williamsport

Desert Rose Café (301-223-6400; http:// desertrosecafeandcatering.com), 42 N.

Conococheague St. Open Mon.–Sat. 8–5, Sun. 10–3. Genial Desert Rose Harris (yes, that is really her given name) does some of the cooking (much of it based on her and her mother's—a co-owner and employee— recipes), but also spends a great deal of time greeting and conversing with her customers, many of whom have now become old friends. She started the restaurant because she felt Williamsport needed a healthier alternative to the fare served in other area eateries. Sandwiches, salads, and soups are $2.99–5.99.

SNACKS AND GOODIES

Boonsboro
Icing Bakery and Café (301-432-5068; www.icingbakerycafe.com), 7 N. Main St. Closed Mon. Come here for the tarts, muffins, macaroons, scones, pies, cakes, pastries, quiches, soups, and sandwiches.

Hagerstown
Uncle Louie G's Homemade Gourmet Italian Ices and Ice Cream (301-671-3084; www.unclelouiegee.com), 34 E. Washington St.

Krumpe's Do-Nuts (301-733-6103; www .krumpesdonuts.com), 912 Maryland Ave. The same family has been making Krumpe's Do-Nuts and other baked goods since 1934.

Olympia Candy Kitchen (301-739-0221; www.olympiacandy.net), 13154 Pennsylvania Ave. The outlet for handmade chocolates produced in nearby Pennsylvania.

Sharpsburg
Nutter's Ice Cream (301-432-5809; on facebook), 100 E. Main St. A pleasant place to stop after a hot afternoon's worth of exploring nearby Antietam National Battlefield.

Also see **Weaver's Restaurant and Bakery** under *Eating Out.*

✳ Entertainment
FILM The two first-run movie theaters in the area are located in Hagerstown: **Regal**

Cinema Valley Mall (301-582-1000; www .regmovies.com), 17301 Valley Mall Rd.; and **Leitersburg Cinemas** (240-329-2093; www.leitersburgcinemas.com), Leitersburg Pike.

MUSIC Maryland Symphony Orchestra (301-797-4000; www.marylandsymphony .org), 30 W. Washington St., Hagerstown. There are at least 10 full concerts in the orchestra's year-round schedule, and many smaller venues and outreach programs.

THEATERS Maryland Theatre (301-790-3500; www.mdtheatre.org), 21 S. Potomac St., Hagerstown. The theater has been a place for the performing arts since 1915. Home to the **Maryland Symphony Orchestra,** it also brings in national and international plays and musicals, events, and performers.

Potomac Playmakers (301-797-8182; www.potomacplaymakers.com), 31 S. Prospect St., Hagerstown. The local community theater usually stages at least four productions each year and has been doing so for decades.

Washington County Playhouse (301-739-7469; www.washingtoncountyplayhouse .com), 44 N. Potomac St., Hagerstown. Open Fri. and Sat. evening, and Sun. afternoon. Year-round dinner theater with a huge buffet.

SPORTS ⚾ **Hagerstown Suns** (301-791-6266; www.hagerstownsuns.com), Municipal Stadium, 274 E. Memorial Blvd., Hagerstown. The Suns, Class A affiliates of the Washington Nationals, have some of the most loyal and colorful fans I have seen for a minor-league baseball team. Almost more entertaining than the action on the field are the comments and antics of the spectators in the stands. A low-cost (ticket prices are a bargain) and enjoyable way to spend an evening watching America's favorite pastime. Who knows? You might even see a future star, like the fans who attended Willie Mays's first professional ball game here in 1950.

✳ Selective Shopping
ANTIQUES

Hagerstown

Antique Crossroads (301-739-0858; www
.antiquexroads.com), 20150 National Pike.
Closed Wed. More than two hundred dealers display wares in separate booths and
showcases.

Hancock

Hancock Antique Mall (301-678-5959;
www.hancockantiquemall.com), 266 N.
Pennsylvania Ave. With more than 48,000
square feet of climate-controlled space in a
former London Fog factory and close to
four hundred dealers, just about anything
imaginable might be found here. There are
antiques of every shape and kind, handcrafted items, memorabilia, and lots of
other stuff/junk/pieces.

ART GALLERIES Contemporary
School of the Arts and Gallery (301-791-
6191; www.csagi.org), 4 W. Franklin St.,
Hagerstown. Open daily. Consider coming
here if you are thinking of obtaining a work
of art. Not only will you find some nice
pieces in a variety of media from local,
regional, and (sometimes) national artists,
but your purchase will help fund the primary goal of this organization—providing
after-school art programs for the children of
Washington County. The programs are free
and open to all students, and hundreds of
children have participated. There are
classes for adults, too.

Washington County Arts Council (301-
791-3132; www.washcountyartscouncil.org),
14 W. Washington St., Hagerstown. Open
daily. A renovated downtown storefront has
been turned into a bright and airy place to
showcase the best of local and regional people working in all manner of arts and crafts.
Definitely worth a stop to look around.

Just Lookin' Gallery (310-714-2278;
www.justlookin.com), 40 Summit Ave.,
Hagerstown. A commercial gallery that
specializes in the works of more than 50
living African American, African, and West
Indian artists.

Also see **Washington County Museum of
Fine Arts** under *To See.*

BOOKSTORES

Boonsboro

Turn the Page Bookstore Café (301-
432-4588; www.ttpbooks.com), 18 N. Main
St. Women's fiction author Nora Roberts
has written more than two hundred novels
and sold more than 400 million books.
Since this is her store, you should be able
to find just about everything she has ever
written—in addition to other best-sellers
and local-interest titles.

USED BOOKS Wonder Book and
Video (301-733-1888; www.wonderbk
.com), 607 Dual Hwy., Hagerstown. Open
daily. They claim to have more than a million used, new, and rare books.

SPECIAL SHOPS

Boonsboro

Gifts Inn Boonsboro (301-432-0090;
www.giftsinnboonsboro.com), 16 N. Main
St. There's a wide array of items from more
than 70 juried artists who come from within
about 60 miles of Boonsboro. Interestingly,
one of the regional authors is Antonio
Mendez, the CIA agent portrayed by Ben
Affleck in the 2012 movie *Argo.*

Clear Spring

Wilson's General Store (301-582-4718;
http://wilsongeneralstore.com), 14921
Rufus Wilson Rd. A throwback to another
era, the store sells everything from livestock
feed to denim jeans. It is like a museum,
preserving the decades from when Rufus
Wilson first opened it in 1847. Curved
wood and glass display cases are filled with
lye soap, ointments, elixirs, and spools of
sewing thread. The ornately carved wood-
and-glass refrigerator still works, keeping
meats and cheeses cold. After buying a stick
of hard candy, you could sit by the old pot-
bellied stove and play a game of checkers
with the rough, hand-carved pieces. **Wilson's School,** Washington County's only
remaining one-room schoolhouse, is

adjacent to the store and will be opened by appointment.

Hagerstown

🚂 **The Train Room** (301-745-6681; www .the-train-room.com), 360 S. Burhans Blvd. Besides being a model-train store, the shop contains a **Lionel museum** (small admission fee; children under 12 free) that is the remarkable collection of owner Charles Mozingo. More than 5,000 items include old transformers, a four-track layout, Lionel chemistry sets and microscopes, and many items made by Lionel for the World War II war effort.

OUTLETS ✴ **Premium Outlets** (301-790-0300; www.premiumoutlets.com), I-70 Exit 29, Hagerstown. The local complex of this national developer of outlet malls contains places to purchase Adidas, Bose, Izod, Jockey, Maidenform, Corning Revere, and at least 80 other companies' merchandise at so-called reduced prices.

FARMER'S MARKETS City Farmer's Market (301-739-8577; www .hagerstownmarket.org), 25 W. Church St., Hagerstown. Open Sat. year-round, 5–noon. This has been the area's gathering and gossiping spot since 1791. There are vegetables and fruits for sale, but the real draw is the opportunity to watch local residents meet, greet, and eat. There is no way you can leave here hungry, as there are baked goods, homemade chocolates, hot pretzels, fresh coffee, and a great breakfast stand to tempt you. Arts and crafts are available and become more dominant in the colder months.

PICK-YOUR-OWN PRODUCE FARMS Lewis Orchards (301-824-2962; www.lewisorchards.com), 22550 Jefferson Blvd., Cavetown. Head to the fields in mid-May to gather strawberries and return in mid-June to pick cherries.

WINERY Knob Hall Winery (301-842-2777; www.knobhallwinery.com), 14108 St. Paul Rd., Clear Spring. Tastings Thurs.–Mon. On land that has been in the same family for two centuries, Knob Hall is dif-

KNOB HALL WINERY

ferent than most wineries in Maryland. Most of the others have just a few acres of vines. Knob Hall has more than 40 acres of vines producing so many grapes that, even though it produces more than four thousand cases of wine annually, it sells some of the fruit to other vineyards. The tasting room is in a two-hundred-year old bank barn and tours will take you out to the vineyard and other parts of the farm, where you may meet one of the resident farm fowls.

✳ Special Events

March: **Flower and Garden Show** (301-790-2800), Hagerstown Community College. An annual event with more than one hundred vendors and the chance to learn about plant care from personnel of the U.S. Botanical Garden and National Arboretum.

April: **18th-Century Market Fair** (301-842-2155), Fort Frederick State Park, Big Pool. Living-history demonstrations and a chance to purchase items made by artists and craftspeople using techniques of the 1700s.

May: **Annual Sharpsburg Memorial Day Commemoration** (301-432-8410), Sharpsburg. The oldest continuous Memorial Day parade and celebration in the United States. It started after the Civil War to honor returning veterans. **National Pike Festival and Wagon Train** (301-791-

3246; www.nationalpikefestival.org), from Clear Spring to Boonsboro. Mule- and horse-drawn wagons reenact travel as it would have taken place in the early days of America's first long-distance national road.

Late May or early June: **Western Maryland Blues Fest** (301-791-3246; www .blues-fest.org), Hagerstown. Annual three-day celebration of music, a street festival, and workshops with national and international blues luminaries.

June: **Cumberland Valley Artists' Exhibit** (301-739-5727), Hagerstown. Annual juried competition in all media.

July: **Maryland Symphony Orchestra's Annual Salute to Independence** (301-532-5124), Antietam National Battlefield. Celebrate the nation's birthday with patriotic and light classical music accompanied by cannon fire and fireworks. **Washington County Agricultural Expo** (301-791-3246; 1-888-257-2600), Sharpsburg.

August: **Augustoberfest** (301-791-3246), Hagerstown. An annual celebration of the city's German heritage.

September: **Sharpsburg Heritage Festival** (301-991-0265), Sharpsburg. Guided walking tours, living-history demonstrations, period-music concerts, arts and crafts, and historical-topics workshops. **Annual Steam and Craft Show** (301-791-3246), Smithsburg. A lineup of old steam engines, gas-powered tractors, and arts and crafts vendors.

November: **Alsatia Mummers Parade** (301-739-2044), Hagerstown. An annual event with decades of history and tradition.

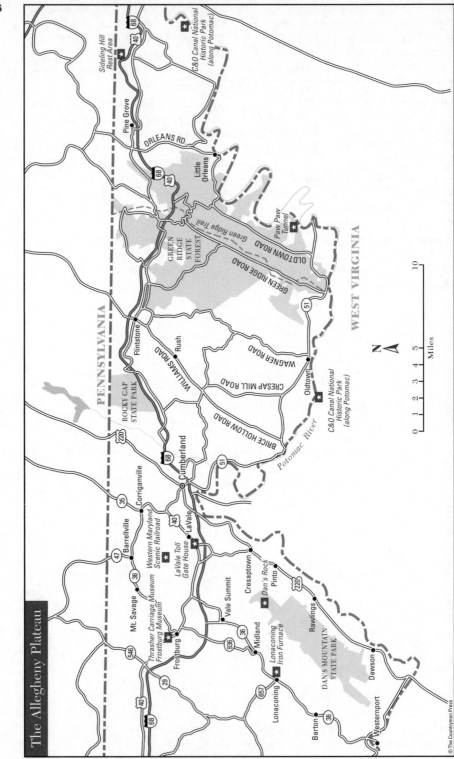

The Allegheny Plateau

© The Countryman Press

THE ALLEGHENY PLATEAU
ROCKY GAP, CUMBERLAND, AND FROSTBURG

West of Hancock, I-68 works its way over Sideling Hill to rise onto the Allegheny Plateau. Once the floor of an ancient ocean, the land was raised to new heights when Africa collided with North America 250 million years ago. Through time, water and wind have cut valleys and eroded softer rock to leave behind higher ridgelines, yet the plateau has remained essentially a mountain tableland with only minor variations in elevation. The mountain streams and ridgelines beckon those in pursuit of outdoor adventure, while the slightly rolling landscape lends itself to agricultural purposes. Some of Maryland's most extensive farms line both sides of the interstate.

Like the more famous Cumberland Gap along the Virginia-Kentucky-Tennessee border, Rocky Gap has been used for centuries by humans as an access route through the mountains. Following the tracks made by game animals, Native Americans were the first to pass through. As settlers from the Old World began pushing into western Maryland, the course was enlarged into the Old Hancock Road, a wagon route connecting Hancock in the east with Fort Cumberland to the west.

The only thing many travelers know about Cumberland is that it is the small city in which winding I-68 takes you past one church steeple after another—all of which are at eye level because of the interstate's elevated route. To get off the four-lane and do a little exploring is to find a place rich in the history of America's westward expansion, yet with a forward-looking population ready to celebrate the life it enjoys today.

The settlement began in 1787, when Gen. Edward Braddock (and a young George Washington) established Fort Cumberland (the Emmanuel Episcopal Church is built on its foundations) during the French and Indian War. Cumberland developed into a transportation center as all of the early-1800s modes of transportation converged upon it. People poured through town on the National Road on their way to the western frontier, the B&O railroad arrived in 1842, and the town became the western terminus of the Chesapeake & Ohio (C&O) Canal in 1850.

Industrialization and coal mining brought unprecedented prosperity after the Civil War, and a walk along the opulent houses of Washington Street, now a National Historic District, lets you see just how successful business leaders were. Railroading became a major employer around the turn of the 20th century, enabling more industries to establish themselves and bringing new wealth and refinement into the area. The Cumberland Academy of Music was so prestigious that it attracted luminaries such as George Gershwin. Many of the downtown's buildings date from this era, and a walking-tour brochure from the Allegany County Convention and Visitors Bureau describes some of them.

When manufacturing jobs began to disappear and city shops began to lose business to malls and outlying areas, Cumberland was one of the first places in America to establish a pedestrian mall in 1980. It has taken a while, but downtown is once again filled with restaurants, businesses, antiques stores, and eclectic shops. The mall has become the spot for the annual Summer in the City events, a farmer's market, and a pleasant place to stroll and people-watch. It is just a few blocks from the C&O Canal Visitors Center and the Western Maryland Scenic Railroad Depot.

THE WESTERN MARYLAND SCENIC RAILROAD AT THE GREAT ALLEGHENY PASSAGE TRAILHEAD

Like Cumberland, Frostburg owes much of its existence to the National Road. When stagecoach service began in 1818, an assemblage of taverns, houses, and businesses grew up around the stagecoach stop. The arrival of the railroad in the 1840s allowed the coal industry to develop, soon followed by the manufacture of bricks from the high-grade clays found in the area. The biggest employer today is Frostburg State University, established as a normal school in 1898. Frostburg may not be the railroading center it once was, but rail enthusiasts still arrive by the thousands each year on their round-trip journey from Cumberland along the Western Maryland Scenic Railroad. Baseball pitching great Lefty Grove, voted the American League's Most Valuable Player in 1931, is buried in the Frostburg cemetery.

COMMUNITIES **LaVale** was a sleepy village along US 40 until the expansion of malls and fast-food restaurants overtook many small towns in America. Two interstate exits can deliver you to the Country Club Mall and just about any national restaurant chain you can think of.

CANAL PLACE IN CUMBERLAND

Mount Savage, like many of the small towns in the western part of this area, first developed as a coal-mining community. Around the turn of the 20th century, Andrew Ramsey came upon a way to produce a special colored, glazed brick. It soon received worldwide acclaim and was bought for its smooth, bright, and easily cleaned surface. Unfortunately, Ramsey never told anyone exactly what his process was, so his factory closed when he died.

The bituminous coal underlying the mountain lands along MD 36 gave rise to so many coal-mining communities that it is almost hard to tell where one community ends and another begins. These settlements, the largest of which is **Lonaconing,** were once so isolated from the outside world that the local speech still contains slight traces of an English accent.

GUIDANCE The **Allegany County Convention and Visitors Bureau** (301-777-5132; 1-800-425-2067; www.mdmountainside.com), 13 Canal St., Suite 406, Cumberland, 21502, can be found on the ground floor of Canal Place.

GETTING THERE *By car:* **I-68** is the major highway that will bring you into the area from the east or the west. **US 220** connects with the **Pennsylvania Turnpike** as it comes into the area from the north.

By rail: Cumberland is lucky enough to be one of the dwindling number of small cities in America that can still be reached by passenger-rail service. The **AMTRAK** (1-800-872-7245; www.amtrak.com) station on Harrison St. receives passengers arriving from the west in the morning and those coming from the east in the evening.

GETTING AROUND *By car:* **I-68** is, of course, the fastest way to get around, but consider using **US 40,** which parallels it and will take you through rural areas and some of the smaller towns. It also is along the historic route of the **National Road. US 220** and **MD 26** are two-lane roadways that will take you into the more isolated southern regions of this area.

By bus: **Allegany County Transit Division** (301-772-6360; www.gov.allconet.org/act) operates numerous routes that can transport you to most of the cities and towns in the area.

By rail: See the **Western Maryland Scenic Railroad** sidebar on page 436.

By taxi: **Queen City Taxi** (301-722-2800) and **Yellow Cab** (301-722-4050) are both based in Cumberland.

MEDICAL EMERGENCY **Western Maryland Health System** (240-964-7000; www .wmhs.com), 12500 Willbrook Rd., Cumberland.

✳ To See
MUSEUMS

Cumberland
☂ **Allegany County Museum** (301-777-7200; www.alleganymuseum.org), 3 Pershing St. Open Tues.–Sun., May–Dec. Donations accepted. Within a 1932 art deco multistory building, this museum chronicles the history of the county, with an emphasis on local industries— such as breweries, glassware, and tire manufacturing—that make up the bulk of the displays. In addition, there are small collections of prehistoric artifacts, folk art, and the architecture of the county (plans were to expand these when I last visited).

☂ **Brooke Whiting House of Art** (301-777-7782; www.thewhitinghouse.org), 632 Washington St. Open second and fourth Sat. of the month May.–Oct. Small admission fee. F. Brooke Whiting II was the Curator of Rare Books for the University of California–Los Angeles for 32 years and spent much of his time traveling the world collecting objets d'art, artifacts, and curios. His sister did much the same, and their collections are displayed throughout his 1911 bungalow home. People on the tour I took were constantly commenting on the breadth and depth of the collections. There are arrowheads dating from before the birth of Christ, Greek icons, Asian works of art, early American furniture, Tiffany glass, a 1680 painting of the first Duchess of Devonshire, and miniatures that are impressive in the detail they possess.

Frostburg

& **Thrasher Carriage Museum** (301-689-3380; www.thethrashercarriagemuseum.com), 19 Depot St. (adjacent to the Western Maryland Scenic Railroad Depot). Open Thurs.–Sun. May–Oct.; Sat.–Sun. Nov.–mid-Dec. Small admission fee. Contains horse-drawn vehicles from almost every part of American life, including Theodore Roosevelt's inaugural parade carriage. Seek out the buckboard—the work the carpenter did with the wood is remarkable. Guides and interpretive signs provide detailed background.

Frostburg Museum (301-689-1195; www.frostmuseum.allconet.org), 69 Hill St. Open Tues.–Sat. Donations accepted. The volunteer-maintained museum is housed in the 1899 Hill Street School, and its exhibits preserve and portray the industrial and social past of the area.

HISTORIC HOMES **Gordon-Roberts House** (301-777-8678; www.gordon-roberts house.com), 218 Washington St., Cumberland. Open Wed.–Sat. Guided tours given on the hour; small admission fee. The Second Empire home was built in 1867 for Judge Josiah Hance Gordon, president of the C&O Canal (and a Southern sympathizer arrested during the Civil War). It was later purchased by the West Milner Roberts Sr. family, who lived there until the 1950s. It is furnished with pieces reflecting their time of occupation. A few rooms contain items of local historical interest.

After visiting the house, take a walk along the six blocks of Washington St. listed on the National Register of Historic Places, and you will glean a bit of information about Cumberland's earlier days. The Gordon-Roberts House reflects the obvious wealth of the Gordon and Roberts families, but their former home is quite simple and plain compared with the other, more extravagant houses along the street.

HISTORIC SITES

Cumberland

& **George Washington's Headquarters** (301-777-5132), Riverside Park on Greene St. Most easily accessed by a two-minute walk from Canal Place: Simply cross the railroad tracks and use the Esplanade over Wills Creek. Most places that are open by appointment only have been excluded from this guidebook, but you can get a feel for history just by walking around this small cabin and reading the interpretive signs. Local lore (which some historians question) states that Washington used the structure when he was aide-de-camp to General Braddock in the mid-1700s, and when he returned as president in 1794. The Cresap Chapter of the Daughters of the American Revolution has furnished the cabin with period replicas.

GEORGE WASHINGTON'S HEADQUARTERS IN CUMBERLAND

Oldtown

Just a few buildings and a small cemetery remain in **Oldtown** beside the C&O Canal to mark the site where the first settlement in Allegany County once stood. Thomas Cresap established a trading post in the 1740s next to the Potomac River and along the route of the Native American Warrior's Path. His son, Michael, was born in 1741, and his home—now a museum open on an irregular basis—is the only building from the early days that is still standing. (Michael was later engaged in battles with Native Americans along the Ohio River. Although Cresap was considered a hero by some, Chief Logan claimed he was the man who sparked the war by murdering, unprovoked, the chief's wife and all of his children.) Also on the site, and open on an irregular basis, is the **Lock House 70,** constructed when the C&O Canal was built in the mid-1800s.

LAVALE TOLL GATE HOUSE

Upper LaVale

LaVale Toll Gate House (301-777-5132), Old US 40. Open Sat.–Sun. 1:30–4:30, May–Oct. Times are very changeable; call ahead. The tollgate house was built in the early 1800s and is now the only surviving such structure in the state. Its seven-sided construction has windows facing all directions so that the gatekeeper could clearly see any approaching traffic. The antique furnishings reflect its earliest days; ask for the story behind the courting candle.

HISTORIC CHURCHES **Emmanuel Episcopal Church** (301-777-3364; www .emmanuelparishofmd.org), 16 Washington St., Cumberland. Constructed in the mid-1800s with a commanding view of the town, the church is one of the earliest uses of the Greek Revival style in America. Louis Tiffany extensively remodeled its interior in the early 1900s. Among other things, he carved the High Altar, and three of the stained-glass windows are his. His original design sketches are on display in the church community room.

All of these things, however, are not the only reasons to visit. The church was built upon the foundations of the mid-1700s **Fort Cumberland.** Some of the earthworks, ammunition magazines, and fort tunnels still exist and are open for public visitation. To walk these narrow passageways is to perceive the ghosts of the soldiers who helped prepare the way for western Maryland's early settlers. Call the Allegany County Convention and Visitors Bureau (301-777-5132; 1-800-425-2067), and they can make the arrangements for you to explore this historic place.

OTHER SITES

Cumberland

& **C&O Canal National Historical Park Cumberland Visitors Center** (301-722-8226; www.nps.gov/choh), 13 Canal St. (in the Western Maryland Railroad Station). Open daily 9–5. Free. Much more than just a visitors center, it has many exhibits pertaining to the history of the canal and the local area. Interactive displays with audiotapes let you become familiar with canal workers, such as lockkeeper Harvey Brant, who received $22.50 a week and was on call 24 hours a day. I found the exhibit in which Mr. Sandblount describes

LONACONING IRON FURNACE

growing up and working on a canal boat to be both enlightening and entertaining. This is a great place, especially since it is free. Don't forget to take the short walk to the *Cumberland,* a full-scale canal-boat replica. (Also see C&O National Historical Park under *To Do* for information on the canal in this area.)

The visitors center is located in **Canal Place,** which is being developed as a performing arts/historic site incorporating several buildings and locations around the canal's western terminus.

Lonaconing

Lonaconing Iron Furnace. Built in 1837, it was America's first successful coal- and coke-fired furnace to produce pig iron. Most furnaces from these days are crumbling shells, but this one is nearly intact and worth a visit.

Vale Summit

Dan's Rock, located on Dan's Rock Rd., off MD 36 near Vale Summit. It is a twisting mountain road you must negotiate to reach Dan's Rock, but the view is definitely worth it. Just a few steps from the parking area is an Olympian view of Savage Mountain rising out of the depths of George's Creek Valley. The Allegheny Mountains of West Virginia recede far to the south, while farmlands stretch eastward along the Potomac River.

GUIDED TOURS See *Walking Tours* under *To Do.*

ZOO Tristate Zoological Park (301-724-2400; www.tristatezoologicalpark.com),

GREETING A RESIDENT AT THE TRISTATE ZOOLOGICAL PARK

10105 Cottage Inn Ln. NE. Open daily Apr.–Dec. Small admission fee. Do not come here expecting a zoo with manicured grounds and specific animal habitats. As owner Bob Candy told me, "Be sure to let your readers know this is not a pretty zoo." In actuality, it is pretty much an animal rescue facility, with more than 90 percent of the animals having been given to the zoo. It operates primarily on donations, and staff members are volunteers. It's just a few acres of fenced-in areas and dirt paths. The lack of many of the usual zoo amenities works out in your favor, though, as you are able to get fairly close to most of the animals which at the time of my visit included (among others) lemurs, alligators, farm animals, Siberian tiger, Himalayan black bear, and African lion. I was able to get so close that I could hear the mountain lion purring!

✳ To Do
BICYCLING
Cumberland
C&O Canal National Historical Park (301-739-4200; www.nps.gov/choh). More than 40 miles of the canal pass through this area of Maryland. The section is more isolated than any other portion, which enables you to ride and explore without the crowds often found elsewhere. Some of the highlights include access to **Oldtown,** the **Green Ridge Hiking Trail,** and the **Paw Paw Tunnel.** About a dozen designated campsites (some free, some with a fee) are spaced along the route. Each has vault toilets and water (in-season), and is available on a first-come, first-served basis. There are also numerous ramps from which you could launch a boat into the Potomac River and paddle for several days while making use of the riverside campsites. The **C&O Canal Visitors Center** in Cumberland can provide detailed information.

Flintstone
Green Ridge State Forest (301-478-3124; www.dnr.state.md.us/publiclands/western/green ridgeforest.asp), 28700 Headquarters Dr. NE. Multiple miles of trails and dirt roads are open to mountain biking. An exceptional ride, which has a variety of terrain (and may not be suited to beginners), is the 12-mile self-guided loop trail. The state forest headquarters can provide you with a map of all the routes.

Cycles and Things (301-722-5496; http://cyclesandthings.net), 165 N. Centre St., Cumberland. Cycles and Things sells bikes, but they can also repair yours if you have a problem while in the area.

Cumberland Trail Connection (310-777-8724; www.ctcbikes.com), Canal Pl., Cumberland. These folks, located within a few yards of the C&O Canal Towpath, can rent you a bike if you don't want to have to load yours onto your automobile's bike rack and lug it all the way from home.

Also see **Inn at Decatur** under *Lodging.*

BIRDING ✐ ✦ **Dan's Mountain State Park** (301-895-5453; www.dnr.state.md .us/publiclands/western/dansmountain.asp), Water Station Run Rd. (off MD 36), Lonaconing. The park's heavily wooded acres are habitat for those species that nest only in forests. Expect to find scarlet tanagers, ovenbirds, and yellow-throated vireos.

MANY MILES OF NEARLY FLAT RIDING
The Great Allegheny Passage is a 141-mile bicycle route that begins near Pittsburgh, Pennsylvania, and connects with the C&O Canal Towpath at Cumberland. This enables you to ride more than 300 miles on pathways devoid of road traffic or other similar hazards all the way to Washington, DC.

Information on the route is available from **Allegheny Trail Alliance** (1-888-282-BIKE; www.atatrail.org), P.O. Box 501, Latrobe, PA 15650.

BOAT RENTALS See *Outdoor Adventure,* and **Rocky Gap State Park** under *Green Space.*

CARRIAGE RIDES See *Walking Tours.*

FISHING See **Rocky Gap State Park** under *Green Space.*

GOLF Rocky Gap State Park (301-784-8400; 1-800-724-0828; www.rockygapresort.com), 16701 Lakeview Rd. (accessed from I-68 Exit 50), Flintstone. The only Jack Nicklaus Signature Golf Course in Maryland. The front nine, carved out of the mountainous terrain and lined by trees, have quite dramatic elevation changes. The back nine course their way over an open, rolling meadow.

Also see **Manhattan Centre Golf and Gallery** under *Selective Shopping.*

HIKING 🐾 **Green Ridge Hiking Trail,** Green Ridge State Forest (301-478-3124; www .dnr.state.md.us/publiclands/western/greenridgeforest.asp), 28700 Headquarters Dr. NE, Flintstone. This 18-mile trail is one of the best backpacking outings in Maryland at any time of year, but to get the most fun out of it, wait for a hot summer weekend. The majority of the hike is along one creek or another, each with miles of small ripples and cascades—and a profusion of swimming holes. Even if you don't want to take a plunge, you still need to ford them well over 60 times; wait until warm weather has raised the water temperature a few degrees.

Backcountry camping is permitted; obtain a permit (and pay the fee) at the forest headquarters just off I-68 Exit 64. A pamphlet for the **Pine Lick Hollow Segment** has information describing the natural and human history of the area. (The state forest is the habitat of the rarely seen large blazing star and Kate's mountain clover.) Pets must be on a leash, and hunting is permitted during the season, so take proper precautions. Headquarters personnel can also provide information on the more than 20 miles of other pathways in the forest.

Paw Paw Tunnel, off MD 51 (at the Potomac River Bridge and the C&O Canal). Like so many other things associated with the canal, construction of the 3,118-foot tunnel faced difficulties and miscalculations from the outset. Intense friction among camps of Irish, English, and German laborers—in conjunction with a cholera epidemic—compounded the problems. Originally estimated to be built within 2 years at a cost of $33,500, it took 14 years and more than $600,000 to complete. Once finished, though, the tunnel—lined with close to 6 million bricks in layers of 7 to 11 deep—was used from 1850 to the canal's demise in 1924.

Break out the flashlights when you enter the tunnel, which is a little more than 0.5-mile long. Even after its completion, the tunnel proved to be a source of contention. Although upstream boats were supposed to have the right-of-way in the narrow channel, some boat captains would refuse to yield. Local lore tells of an occasion where two barges stayed in place for several days because neither captain would give way. Canal workers finally built a fire to smoke them out.

The pathway is usually wet and slippery, so use the provided handrail. Some of the boards are the original lumber, and your hand can feel the grooves worn into it from years of towropes sliding across. Once through, you can take a break at a small picnic area. You have the choice of going back the way you came or taking the **Tunnel Hill Trail** over the ridgeline the tunnel goes through. The round-trip journey is about 3 miles.

RIDING THE LAKE HABEEB PONTOON BOAT
WITH WESTERN MARYLAND ADVENTURES

OUTDOOR ADVENTURE

Cumberland
Allegany Expeditions Inc. (301-722-5170;
301-777-9313;
www.alleganyexpeditions.com), 10310
Columbus Ave. NE. AEI can take care of
you for just about any activity in the natural
world that you can engage in during a visit
to western Maryland. They can provide
instructions or set up guided trips for climbing, caving and rappelling, paddling excursions, skiing, fishing, and backpacking. All of
the required equipment can be rented or
purchased.

Flintstone
Western Maryland Adventures (301-876-
PLAY; www.wmdadventures.com), P.O. Box 3284, LaVale, 21504. Open year-round. Like the
other businesses in this section, WMA can take you on just about any outdoor activity you
can think of, and they have an advantage—many of their activities take place in scenic Rocky
Gap State Park (see *Parks*) or within a very short drive. They can take you for a guided
kayaking or canoeing tour on the park's lake, or give you instructions on how to become a
better white-water paddler. Rappelling (a sport that really requires little skill or physical
strength), rock climbing, fishing for bass in the lake, cross-country skiing, snowshoeing,
horseback riding, and even stagecoach and sleigh rides are just a few of the other adventures
they can take you on. Hunting for geocached stations within the park has become one of the
company's most popular family activities. Bikes are available for rent for rides around the
lake or on some of the back roads near the state park. Kayak and canoe rentals for excursions
on the lake are also available, as are shuttles for those who supply their own equipment. If all
of this sounds just a little too active for you, take the relaxing 45-minute pontoon boat tour of
Lake Habeeb.

SCUBA DIVING See **Adventure Sports** under *Outdoor Adventure.*

SWIMMING See **Rocky Gap State Park** under *Green Space.*

✳ Green Space
PARKS

Flintstone
✲ ৬ **Rocky Gap State Park** (301-784-8400; 1-800-724-0828; www.rockygapresort.com;
301-722-1480; www.dnr.state.md.us/publiclands/western/rockygap.asp), 16701 Lakeview Rd.
(accessed from I-68 Exit 50). As you descend westward on Martin Mountain on I-68, the
first thing to catch your eye will be the dramatic setting of the park's massive 220-room
resort lodge, built along the southern shore of Lake Habeeb. Below Evitt's Mountain's lush
hillside, the manicured greens of a golf course stretch between the lodge and the four-lane
highway.

WESTERN MARYLAND SCENIC RAILROAD

TRAIN EXCURSION

Western Maryland Scenic Railroad (301-759-4400; 1-800-TRAIN-50; www.wmsr.com), 13 Canal St. Railway Station, Cumberland-Frostburg. May–Sept., the diesel engine leaves Cumberland Mon.–Thurs. at 11:30 AM; the steam engine departs Fri.–Sun. at 11:30 AM. In Oct., the diesel operates Mon.–Wed., the steam Thurs.–Sun. In Nov. and Dec., there is only one departure (the steam engine) at 11:30 AM. *Please note:* The schedule has been known to change, so be wise and call first. Standard fare: adults $35, seniors $33, children $18. First class (includes lunch in the dining car): adults $55, seniors $53, children $35.

The three-hour round-trip excursions (with a 90-minute layover in Frostburg) travel through some of western Maryland's prettiest scenery by negotiating the **Narrows,** climbing over 1,900-foot Piney Mountain, and passing through 914-foot **Brush Tunnel. Helmstedder's Curve** is such a long, tight horseshoe bend that even those sitting in the very rear passenger car can look across the way and see the engine. There is some taped narration along the way, but it would be nicer if it would describe more of what you are experiencing.

THE NARROWS WEST OF CUMBERLAND

ROCKY GAP STATE PARK

(There is no doubt that this type of development adds another aspect and attraction to the state park, but there was much debate and protest in the local community, and throughout Maryland, about changing the natural character of the state park. Many people also questioned the propriety of the state's turning such a large amount of public land over to a private, profit-making corporation.)

Within the park are a campground, a camp store, laundry facilities, beaches with modern bathhouses, an outdoor pool, tennis courts, a snack bar, and boat rentals. The 243-acre Lake Habeeb attracts anglers with largemouth bass, panfish, and trout. A trail network brings hikers by the lake, up Evitt's Mountain to an old homesite, and down into scenic Rocky Gap Gorge. Thousands of visitors attend the park's annual music festivals in August. **Western Maryland Adventures** (see *Outdoor Adventure*), located in the park, can arrange for you to participate in many outdoor activities.

Lonaconing

✄ ♿ **Dan's Mountain State Park** (301-895-5453; www.dnr.state.md.us/publiclands/western /dansmountain.asp),Water Station Run Rd. (off MD 36). Open daily during daylight hours. The 485 acres have the feel of a community park, as the local population comes here in significant numbers to enjoy the Olympic-sized swimming pool with waterslide, and beautiful mountain scenery. There is a designated overlook, but the view from the children's playground is equally awe inspiring.

✳ Lodging

RESORTS

Flintstone, 21530

👣 ♿ **Rocky Gap State Park** (301-784-8400; 1-800-724-0828; www.rockygapresort .com), 16701 Lakeview Rd. (accessed from I-68 Exit 50). The accommodations within the park's lodge are pretty much standard upscale hotel/motel-type rooms—but, oh, those views. I prefer a deluxe room (with a balcony and kitchenette) overlooking the lake and Evitt's Mountain, although there is certainly nothing wrong with the view of the emerald fairways of the golf course. Staying in any room gives you access to all of the park's facilities. Pets are permitted in some rooms, but there is quite a substantial cleaning fee tacked onto your bill. The swimming pool is open year-round, as is the spa, which offers a complete range of services from manicures and pedicures to deep tissue and warm stone massages. The public areas of the lodge are quite eye-pleasing, with lots of earth tones and stone employed throughout the building, as well as the works of local artists displayed on many of the walls. $199–219. Many package deals—golf, outdoor adventure, and honeymoon—are available. Also see *Camping*.

MOTELS AND HOTELS

Cumberland, 21502

☀ ♿ **Holiday Inn** (301-724-8800; 1-800-HOLIDAY; www.hicumberland.com), 100 S. George St. The hotel overlooks the noise and activity of a busy CSX rail-freight yard—which, admittedly, is not the most scenic of places. At one time, the manager had mounted a video cam on the roof, pointed it toward the rail yard, and made the 24-hour action available on the hotel's Web site. It had been receiving more than a million hits a year. Sadly, that is no longer available. Railroading fans still make reservations for one of the rooms with a rail-yard view, though. The hotel also has an outdoor pool, a fitness room, and an on-site restaurant. $139 and up.

Frostburg, 21532

Failingers Hotel Gunter (301-689-6511; www.failingershotelgunter.com), 11 W. Main St. Like many older, grand hotels, Failingers now rents some rooms as residential apartments. However, the 17 remaining hotel rooms have been thoroughly renovated and reflect the property's glory days. Each is furnished differently with antiques and reproductions. The rooms are enjoyable enough, but wander around to appreciate the massive oak stairway in the lobby, the swing on the balcony where you can watch the rest of the world go by, and the stained-glass windows found on each stairway landing. The basement is a small museum with items found during the renovation, plus the town's original jail and a replica of a coal mine. $90–110.

♿ **Hampton Inn** (301-689-1998; http://hamptoninn3.hilton.com), 11200 New George's Creek Rd. A whirlpool, heated pool, and exercise room are available to work off the calories you consume during the free continental breakfast. All rooms have an iron and small refrigerator. $115–139.

Trail Inn (301-689-6466; www.trailinnatfrostburg.com), 20 Depot St. The best thing about the Trail Inn is that it is located a few scant steps from the Western Maryland Scenic Railroad depot and a trailhead for the Great Allegheny Passage—perfect for those who are doing overnight journeys on the rail trail. The main portion of the complex is a mid-1800s hotel built for workers constructing the railroad, while the rooms and the café (301-687-8036; breakfast and light fare) are additions. The rooms ($79; breakfast included) are small, but if you're on the trail, you're going to appreciate a soft bed and hot shower. Several larger rooms ($129–185; breakfast included) than can accommodate three to eight people are located on the second floor. There's also a hostel-style room ($30 per person) with twin beds, and camping is available in a former vineyard on the hillside behind the hotel.

LaVale, 21502

♿ **Best Western** (301-729-3300; 1-800-296-6006; www.bestwesternbraddock.com), 1268 National Hwy. One of the most meticulously maintained mainstream motels in the state. Rooms are continually being renovated and updated, tanning beds and a sauna are in the exercise room, and the large inside pool adjoins an outside sundeck. Although the motel sits next to a crossroads area, the landscaping and natural brook add an unexpected gentle quality. $69–109.

BED & BREAKFASTS

Cumberland, 21502

❀ **The Bruce House** (301-777-8860; www.brucehouseinn.com), 201 Fayette St. Possibly the classiest B&B in Cumberland, the 1840 Federal Italianate building sits on a corner and has elevated ceilings, a curving staircase, and gleaming wood floors. More than that, though, it is impeccably decorated and amenities abound. The host, who used to work for Disney Studios, told me "Everything is about creating an experience"—and she has pretty much guaranteed yours here will be a pleasant one. Wine and tea are available in the sitting area, a gourmet breakfast is served, and each guest room has its own very pleasant bathroom. A value at $129–175.

Cumberland Inn and Spa (240-362-7111; www.cumberlandinnandspa.com), 120 Greene St. The B&B is actually two adjacent town houses (circa 1820 and 1890) that have been joined together to provide 11 guest rooms and suites. Some share a bath, others have a private bath, and each conveys a bright, clean, and modern look inside this historic structure. The inn's location in the heart of Cumberland made my explorations much easier. Do not fail to schedule a massage during your stay. $109–139.

Inn at Decatur (301-722-4887; www.theinnondecatur.net), 108 Decatur St. With a down-home atmosphere (and down-home hosts), the 1970 Federal style B&B is popular with riders along the C&O Canal and Great Allegheny Passage. (In fact, the host is a major contributor to the *Trail Book,* which provides details on both routes.) Furnishings are basic, but guest rooms are large, as are the bathrooms, with claw-foot tubs custom made for soaking away trail aches. Guests are permitted to use the kitchen, but a full breakfast is provided. Complimentary laundry service and bicycle cleaning area. This place is also good for rail enthusiasts as the second floor porch overlooks Cumberland's extensive rail activity. $135.

In addition, the hosts operate **Mountainside Bike Tours** (301-722-4887; www.mountainsidebiketours.net) whose motto is "You pedal, we pamper." Along with providing a luggage shuttle and vehicle transports,

TERRA ANGELICA

THE CASTLE B&B IN MOUNT SAVAGE

these folks will help you design a custom trip of your own or you may join one of their organized outings. A great service from very knowledgeable people.

Terra Angelica (301-724-9110; 1-866-724-9110; www.terra-angelica.com), 14701 Smouse's Mill Rd. NE. Terra Angelica was built in 1845 with bricks made from clay on the 1790 land grant property. Located in the countryside a short drive from downtown Cumberland, the stately home has four guest rooms, two in the 1845 part of the home (and with working fireplaces) and two in the 1945 addition. As nice as the rooms are, you should spend your time wandering the 200 acres of field and forest and taking the short hike up to the view that overlooks two states. If walking is too taxing, take a rod and fish in the stocked (bass and catfish) spring-fed pond. Still too strenuous? Okay, then just sit on the porch and appreciate the scenery after enjoying an ample breakfast made with all organic ingredients. (Also, say hi to the nearly 300-year-old oak trees for me.) $95–105.

Mount Savage, 21545
The Castle B&B (301-264-4645; www.castlebandb.com), 15925 Mt. Savage Rd. The Castle started life in 1840 as a modest stone house, but near the beginning of the 20th century, nouveau riche owner Andrew

Ramsey turned it into a replica of Scotland's Craig Castle. You get to enjoy large verandas and terraces of glazed tile, formal gardens, and a 16-foot stone wall (built by Italian masons) surrounding the property. Six guest rooms (some with a private bath) range $149–195.

CABINS 🍴 **7Cs Lodging** (301-478-3535; www.7cs-cabins.com), 21530 National Pike NE., Flintstone. As their brochure says, "Do not let the word cabin fool you." Yes, they are nice, large log cabins—but, again as the brochure says, you'll be staying in "beautiful hotel room nestled in a cabin." Each cabin is fully furnished with a kitchen, dining area, and satellite television. The best part to me was the front porch where, despite hearing nearby interstate traffic, I could watch the western Maryland day come to an end. The business had just opened when I spent an evening and if the rate of $119 is still in effect, the cabins are a bargain.

COTTAGE

Oldtown, 21555

Alpacas at Rivers Edge (301-478-5424; www.barbsalpacas.com), 20020 Potomac Overlook. Barbara Buehl has opened an upstairs apartment on her working alpaca farm for visitors to stay the evening, enjoy the countryside, and have the opportunity

ALPACAS AT RIVERS EDGE

to interact and get to know these gentle creatures, whose ancestral home is the South American Andes Mountains. If you wish, Barbara will take you around the farm, educating you with what I called the Alpaca 101 course. The apartment, which is located on the top level of the barn, overlooks the alpaca corral and is completely equipped with everything you need, including a kitchen and washer and dryer. Guests are permitted to wander the property's 34 acres, and those who are adventurous should consider the somewhat steep walk down to the Potomac River. $100.

CAMPING

Flintstone, 21530

Green Ridge State Forest (301-478-3124; www.dnr.state.md.us/publiclands/western/greenridgeforest.asp), 28700 Headquarters Dr. NE. Primitive campsites are designated along many of the roads that snake their way through the 43,000-acre forest. A permit (and payment of a fee) can be obtained in the state forest headquarters.

🏕 **Hidden Springs Campground** (814-767-9676; www.hiddenspringscampground.com), Pleasant Valley Rd. May–Oct. The campground's 58 acres are close to Rocky Gap State Park and contain a swimming pool, playgrounds, miniature golf, and a stocked fishing pond.

🏕 **Rocky Gap State Park** (301-722-1480; www.dnr.state.md.us/publiclands/western/rockygap.asp), 16701 Lakeview Rd. (accessed from I-68 Exit 50). Nearly three hundred sites are situated among the trees along the northern shore of Lake Habeeb. Hook-ups, bathhouses with hot showers, and access to all of the park's facilities. Pets (on leashes) are permitted in two of the campground's loops.

Little Orleans, 21766

Little Orleans Campground (301-478-2325; www.littleorleanscampground.com), 31661 Green Forest Dr. SE. Located less than a five-minute walk from the C&O Canal and bordered on two sides by Green Ridge State Forest. I would classify this almost as a resort, as it contains RV and tent sites, a playground, a fishing pond, swimming pools, a game room, volleyball, basketball, and horseshoes—in addition to usual campground facilities.

Also see **Trail Inn** under *Lodging.*

✴ Where to Eat
DINING OUT
Cumberland
Ristorante Ottaviani (301-722-0052; www .ristoranteottaviani.com), 25 N. Centre St. In the heart of downtown Cumberland, family-owned and -operated Ristorante Ottaviani serves the usual Italian dishes found in America, but also features some specials from central Italy. One of the nights I dined here the special was braised rabbit, which had a nice blend of spices. I asked Tony Ottaviani how the decision is reached to place an item on the menu and he said, "It's what I like—or what my mother dictates." Desserts are made in-house. Prices are very reasonable for the portions and quality of atmosphere. $13.25–23.95.

EATING OUT
Cumberland
City Lights (301-722-9800; www.citylights americangrill.com), 59 Baltimore St. Open daily 11 AM to closing. Having relocated from the shopping mall in LaVale, City Lights has become a favorite on the Down-town Pedestrian Mall. After a meal of stuffed mushrooms, Greek spinach salad, and walnut apple pork, customers of the two-story restaurant have a tendency to linger, socialize, and imbibe in selections from the bar. Friday and Saturday nights hop. The highest-priced entrée is $34.95.

🍴 **The Crabby Pig** (301-724-7472; www .thecrabbypig.com), 13 Canal St., at Canal Place. Open daily for breakfast, lunch, and dinner. The name pretty much describes it—seafood and BBQ. The picture windows overlook a scenic portion of the C&O Canal and the Western Maryland Scenic Railroad tracks, so you can sit in air-conditioned comfort and watch the train roll in. The

BBQ sandwich I ordered had a generous portion of pork. Full dinners are also available. Sandwiches $6.95–10.95; entrées $17.95–35.95.

Curtis's Famous Wieners (301-759-9707), 35 N. Liberty St. Open 7 AM–10 PM daily. A Cumberland tradition, it has been serving hot dogs, burgers, and hand-dipped milk shakes since 1918. A favorite of downtown office workers for lunch. Most meals will cost you less than $6.

Puccini (301-777-7822; www.puccini restaurant.com), I-68 Exit 46. Open daily for lunch and dinner. Under contract to build tollhouses along the National Pike, Jacob Hoblitzell built his own home in 1819. Used for many things, including a Civil War field hospital, the house eventually fell into disrepair. Now on the National Register of Historic Places after being restored—from its Georgia pine floors to the horse-hair plaster walls—Puccini serves a widely varied menu. The wood-cooked Pizza Bianca, with spinach, artichoke hearts, mushrooms, and red peppers, proves a meal doesn't need meat to be tasty. The sauce used with the battered zucchini appetizer is rich and flavorful. Other Italian dishes include sausage and peppers diablo and pasta primavera. A choice of the restaurant's own microbrews, including ales, lagers, and dark beers, keeps the locals coming back. The upstairs is the quietest spot; the downstairs bar where the pizzas are made gets a little noisy, and many customers opt for the outside patio overlooking a trout stream. Entrées $17.95–27.95.

Frostburg
♿ **Giuseppe's Italian Restaurant** (301-689-2220; www.giuseppes.net), 11 Bowery St. Open daily for dinner. Good, traditional Italian fare, such as pizza, chicken cacciatore, shrimp scampi, lasagna, and baked ziti. Reasonable prices—the most expensive entrée is about $29; many are less than $18.

🍴 **Princess Restaurant** (301-689-1968; www.princessrestaurant.com), 12 W. Main St. Open Mon.–Sat. 6 AM–8 PM. I always take pleasure in finding places such as this—which are becoming increasingly harder to find. It is clean and well kept, but the atmosphere is nothing fancy; in fact, the place is somewhat reminiscent of a diner. Prices are so low that they have not been seen in other restaurants for years. The well-prepared food ranges from more than 40 different sandwiches to full dinners of meat loaf, broiled haddock, grilled pork chops, and T-bone steaks. The children's menu even includes an ice cream dessert in the cost of the meal.

Like his grandfather, who started the business in this location in 1939 (a portion of the original tin ceiling is still in place), George W. Pappas ensures quality by doing things the old way, such as hand-forming hamburger patties, making gravies from scratch, and fresh-cutting potatoes for the home fries. Entrées $11.95–17.50.

LaVale

& **Gehauf's** (301-729-1746; www.best westernbraddock.com), 1268 National Hwy. (inside the Best Western hotel). Closed Mon. With lush plants adding a feeling of being outdoors, Gehauf's makes all of its soups, sauces, dressings, and baked goods from scratch. Seafood entrées are prominent, joined by traditional western Maryland dishes of turkey, ham, pork chops, and steak. A few vegetarian items are a pleasant surprise. Entrées $9.95–19.95.

COFFEE BAR Café Mark and Jennifer's Desserts (301-759-0276; www.cafe markcumberland.com; 301-724-2253; www .jennifersdesserts.com), 37 Baltimore St. Open daily. Two businesses have combined to create a sum greater than their parts. The bakery makes some very special pastries, cakes, and pies, and the café serves a light fare of soups, sandwiches, and vegetarian selections, along with a full menu of coffee drinks.

SNACKS AND GOODIES

Cumberland

European Desserts & More (301-777-0404; on facebook), 17 Howard St., at Canal Place. Sasha and Jasmina Vasic have brought the best of their native Bosnia to western Maryland. Using family recipes, everything is made from scratch and hand-crafted, including the baklava, banini, sacher torte, cocoa balls, and the ever-so-yummy beinenstich cake—a German pastry with whipped cream and topped with honey and chopped nuts. The sandwiches include chicken and tuna salad, but while they are good, you really should try the Bosnian spinach pita-pie.

✆ **The Fruit Bowl** (301-777-2790), 10325 National Hwy. US 40 in the Narrows at the western end of town. Yeah, they sell fresh fruits and vegetables, but what you really want to stop for are the eight hundred bins filled with just about every kind of snack-bar-sized candy you can think of. Snickers, Milky Way, Reeses, 3 Musketeers, and dozens of others are available in bulk.

& **Queen City Creamery and Deli** (240-979-4125; www.queencitycreamery.com), 108 Harrison St. Open daily for breakfast, lunch, and dinner. They have breakfast items, deli sandwiches, and gourmet coffee, but the premium homemade frozen custard is what entices me to stop in nearly every time I pass by. The old-time soda fountain and booths create an atmosphere of yesteryear.

Flintstone

Alpine Pantry (301-478-3696), 21511 Flintstone Dr. NE, I-68 Exit 56. Open Mon.–Fri. 7:30–5:30, Sat. 7–4. A fun place in which to browse for fresh-baked pies, breads, cakes, and pastries in addition to meats, cheeses, and a vast assortment of bagged candies. The small sign on the door, THANK YOU FOR SHOPPING HERE MODESTLY DRESSED AND WELL COVERED, lets you know this is a Mennonite establishment.

Frostburg

McFarland Candies (301-689-6670; www.mcfarlandcandies.com), 22 Broadway. What a treat. The McFarland family has been making assorted chocolate candies in Frostburg since 1944. Enjoy a taste of the premium nut clusters, chewies, barks, cremes, jellies, and fudges. Ask, and they will take you on a tour of the kitchen to witness the art of homemade candy production.

Mountain City Coffeehouse and Creamery (301-687-0808; www.mtncity coffeehouse.com), 60 E. Main St. Closed Mon. It's not often you get to sip organic gourmet coffee or eat Lakeside Creamery Ice Cream (see *Snacks and Goodies* in the "Around Deep Creek Lake" chapter) in a Gothic-style building originally constructed in 1882 that was once used as a place to sell tombstones. The inside walls showcase the works of local artists, while the patio is often the scene for community events and live music.

✴ Entertainment

FILM

Frostburg

Frostburg Cinema (301-689-1100; www .rctheatres.com), Frostburg Plaza. Presents movies when they are first released.

LaVale

Country Club Cinema (301-729-4215), 1262 Vocke Rd. Shows first-run films.

See **New Embassy Theatre** under *Theaters* for information on classic films.

THEATERS ⅙ **Cumberland Theatre** (301-759-4990; www.cumberlandtheatre .com), 101–103 Johnson St., Cumberland. Western Maryland's only professional theater presents at least six musical, drama, or other theatrical productions during its season, which usually runs Apr.–Dec. The small auditorium provides an intimate setting.

⅙ **New Embassy Theatre** (301-722-4692; 1-877-722-4692; www.newembassy.org), 49 Baltimore St., Cumberland. Citizens' efforts saved this 1931 art deco movie house. Classic films, live music, dance, and theatrical productions are presented in the lovingly, and accurately, restored edifice.

✴ Selective Shopping

ANTIQUES You could spend a lot of time browsing for antiques in downtown Cumberland as there are about a dozen shops that are pretty much all within walking distance of each other.

ART GALLERIES Allegany Arts Council (301-777-ARTS; www.alleganyarts council.org), 9 N. Centre St., Cumberland. The gallery features works by local and regional artisans, and traveling exhibits. The council sponsors performing arts events throughout the year.

C. William Gilchrist Museum of the Arts (301-724-5800; http://gilchristgallery .com), 104 Washington St., Cumberland. An early-19th-century Federal-style mansion houses an art library and galleries that exhibit various media and theme-oriented presentations. Local and state history and culture are also featured, as well as art lectures and classes.

Mountain City Traditional Arts (301-367-8040; on facebook), 25 E. Main St., Frostburg. Mountain City Traditional Arts is a collaboration of the Allegany Arts Council, Folklore and Folklife Programming at Frostburg State University, and the FrostburgFirst Main Street Program. It also carries some of the most authentic, and well-executed, Appalachian arts and crafts to be found in the region. Look for quilts, pottery, musical instruments, soaps, textiles, and photography that range from simple to complex to masterpieces. All of the 50–60 artists come from within a two-hour drive of Frostburg. There are also classes available and live performances on occasion.

BOOKSTORES

Cumberland

Book Center (301-722-2284; 1-800-497-0633; www.thebookcenteronline.com), 15–17 N. Centre St., Cumberland. One of the few nonchain bookshops for many miles around, it stocks a large selection of local history, railroad, and travel titles, along with children's books and games, newspapers, and magazines.

Frostburg

Main St. Books (301-689-5605; on facebook), 2 E. Main St. The shop has been in the business of selling books, greeting cards, games, and music in this small town for close to two decades.

CRAFTS **The Country Angel** (301-722-5151), 424 Mechanic St., Cumberland. Open Tues.–Fri. 10–6, Sat. 10–3. In addition to her own handmade crafts, Betty Harvey offers a number of items from local and regional craftspeople. The surprising sculptures created from cardboard deserve special attention.

SPECIAL SHOPS & **Fort Cumberland Emporium** (301-722-4500; www.fortcumberlandemporium.com), 55 Baltimore St., Cumberland. Open daily. A multivendor shop with handmade arts and crafts, antiques, jewelry, furniture, and more.

& **Manhattan Centre Golf and Gallery** (301-777-0021; www.golfandgallery.com), 61 Baltimore St., Cumberland. Do you think someone has combined their two passions into one business? The golf part offers complete sales, service, and lessons. The gallery has limited-edition prints and some nice original artwork.

FARMER'S MARKETS **Cumberland Downtown Farmer's Market** (301-777-2800). The Downtown Pedestrian Mall becomes a beehive of activity 9:45–2 on Thurs. and Sat., June–Oct.

LaVale Country Club Mall Farmer's Market (301-876-0728). Part of the mall's parking lot becomes a farmer's market 9:30–2 on Tues., June–Oct.

Frostburg Farmer's Market (301-738-1093). Main Street is transformed into an open-air emporium 9:45–1 on Fri., June–Oct.

✳ Special Events

May: **DelFest** (301-777-5134; www.delfest.com), Allegany County Fairgrounds. Bluegrass music festival with on-site camping.

Late May–early September: **Summer in the City** (301-722-5500; www.downtowncumberland.com), Cumberland. A series of concerts featuring local and regional musicians.

June: **Heritage Days** (301-722-0037; www.heritagedaysfestival.com), Cumberland. The area's biggest street festival features entertainment, children's activities, a carnival, scenic railroad excursions, arts and crafts, and food demonstrations. **Schoolhouse Quilters Guild Quilt Show** (301-724-7889; www.schoolhousequilters.org), Frostburg State University. Western Maryland's largest quilt show. Vendors, demonstrations, and raffles.

July: **Oldtown Summer Fest** (301-777-0293; www.oldtownmdsummerfest.com), Oldtown. Eastern Woolland Indians, children's programs, arts and crafts, and reenactments along the C&O Canal. **Allegany County Fair** (301-729-1200; www.allegany cofair.org), fairgrounds, Cumberland. **Frostburg Derby Days** (301-689-6900; www.frostburgfirst.org), Frostburg. Celebrate an American tradition that seems to be disappearing—soapbox derby races on Main St.

August: **Maryland BBQ Competition and Festival** (www.district16vfd.com), Allegany County Fairgrounds. Sponsored by District 16 Volunteer Fire Department, this is the state championship BBQ competition—also with music, crafts, and food. **Cruisin' Main Street** (301-689-6900; www.frostburgfirst.org), Frostburg. A celebration of the cruisin' automobiles and days of the '50s and '60s (and more).

September: **Street Rod Roundup** (301-777-7774; www.westernmarylandstreetrod.com), fairgrounds, Cumberland. More than one thousand pre-1949 street cars show up for exhibitions and street jousting. **Appalachian Festival** (301-687-3737; www.frostburg.edu/events/festival), Frostburg State University, Frostburg. Celebrates everything Appalachian from music to food to agriculture to environmental issues.

October: **Iron Rail Days** (301-707-1114; www.mountsavagehistoricalsociety.org), Mount Savage. Attended and participated in by much of the residential population. Look for a reenacted bank robbery and jailbreak, along with guided tours of local sites.

AROUND DEEP CREEK LAKE

GRANTSVILLE, MCHENRY, THAYERVILLE, AND OAKLAND

Outdoor types have been coming here for centuries. Three Native American trails converged at a spot near Grantsville, enabling members of several tribes to use the area for hunting. In the early 1700s, Meshach Browning was one of the area's earliest settlers and known far and wide for his hunting skills. In his book *Forty-Four Years of the Life of a Hunter,* he not only describes life on America's frontier but also estimates he killed "1,800 to 2,000 deer, 300 to 400 bears, about 50 panthers and catamounts, with scores of wolves and wildcats." Self-styled vagabonds Henry Ford, Harvey Firestone, Thomas Edison, and John Burroughs came to the area for some backcountry camping in 1918 and again in 1921.

Situated upon the elevated terrain of the Allegheny Plateau, Deep Creek Lake, Maryland's largest inland body of water, was formed in the 1920s when Deep Creek was dammed as part of a hydroelectric project to provide power to the residents of Pennsylvania. It covers 3,900 acres with approximately 65 miles of shoreline and has become a destination for those who enjoy motorboating, waterskiing, sailing, and fishing, as well as those who just appreciate its scenic beauty. Six other lakes attract boaters of all kinds, while sport anglers come in search of abundant game fish. The streams that feed these lakes—the Youghiogheny, Savage, Casselman, and North Branch Potomac Rivers; Deep, Muddy, and Herrington Creeks; Buffalo, Laurel, and Hoyes Runs; and others—are considered to be some of the country's best fly-fishing destinations, brimming with brook, rainbow, and brown trout. All of the state's record trout were caught in this area. These same waterways, especially the Youghiogheny, Savage, and North Branch Potomac Rivers, are legendary to kayakers and white-water rafters.

Nearly 100,000 acres of state parks, state forests, wildlife management areas, and Wild and Scenic River lands are laced with scores of trails, ranging from easy to difficult. Most of the pathways are open to hiking, mountain biking, and cross-country skiing, with multiple miles also available to snowmobiles. There are hundreds of campsites, some in commercially developed campgrounds, others rustically situated in the state parks. Backcountry camping is permitted on thousands of acres of state forest lands.

Maryland's only downhill skiing resort is located here, but it also takes advantage of every season by having a golf course, mountain biking and mountain boarding routes, and other outdoor activities available throughout the year.

COMMUNITIES Only two to three blocks wide and surrounded by farmland, **Grantsville** began as a small settlement clustered around Stanton's Mill, built in 1797. The

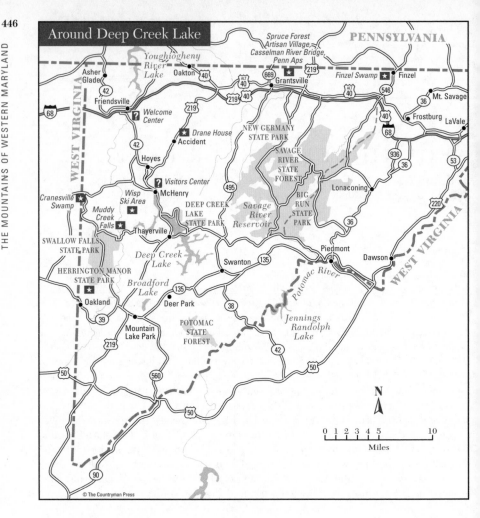

Around Deep Creek Lake

© The Countryman Press

1818 Penn Alps and 1824 Casselman Inn were constructed to service travelers along the National Road, and are both still in use. The town developed into a destination center soon after Dr. Alta Shrock established a nonprofit organization in 1957 to study and promote the way of life in the Allegheny Highlands. The Penn Alps Restaurant and Spruce Forest Artisan Village are visible symbols of her efforts.

McHenry grew up after the establishment of Deep Creek Lake and is the commercial strip that greets people as they come into the lake area from the north. **Thayerville** has many of the businesses at the center of the lake.

Oakland, with several (now defunct) grand hotels, was the area's vacation spot before the development of Deep Creek Lake. It is a modern town of two thousand people, but its brick sidewalks, 1884 Queen Anne–style train station, Victorian homes, and farmer's market in a parklike setting festooned with native plants hark to a time past. The spring next to where George Washington camped is now along a 2.5-mile hiking/biking trail, and a paved route leads to a grandstand view of the town's many architecturally outstanding buildings.

Like Oakland, the stately hotels of **Deer Park** made it a Victorian vacation destination. Before it closed in 1929, the Deer Park Hotel's guests included Presidents Cleveland, Grant, and Harrison. The town is still somewhat famous for its commercially bottled Deer Park Spring Water.

Mountain Lake Park was established in 1881 as a Chautauqua-style summer resort with religious, educational, and recreational activities. A pamphlet available from the Garrett County Chamber of Commerce will take you on a self-guided tour of its historic district.

Local legend says that **Accident** received its name in 1774 when two speculators, wanting to take advantage of Lord Baltimore's offer of land to settlers, surveyed the same acreage "by accident." To this day, it remains a small settlement of just a few hundred spread out on agricultural land.

Friendsville was the first settlement to be established in Garrett County. Although many travelers along I-68 see it as just an interstate exit, the small town sits next to the Youghiogheny River and is well known to white-water rafters and kayakers.

GUIDANCE The **Garrett County Chamber of Commerce** (301-387-4386; 1-888-387-5237; www.visitdeepcreek.com), 15 Visitors Center Dr., McHenry, 21541, is located off US 219 just as you come into the commercial strip at the north end of Deep Creek Lake. In addition to the usual information, ask them for the pamphlets and brochures that have discount coupons in them. The *Lake Front* (www.lakefrontmagazine.com) is a free monthly magazine with news, events, and features on places around the lake. You can pick up one in many business establishments.

With a grand view of Youghiogheny Lake, a **Maryland welcome center** (301-746-5979) is at mile marker 6 on I-68, east of Friendsville.

GETTING THERE *By car:* **I-68** will bring you into the area from the east or west, while **US 219** is the way to arrive from the north and south.

By air: There are scheduled flights to the airport in Morgantown, West Virginia, about 40 miles away. Of course, you will save quite a few dollars by taking the numerous national and international airline companies that fly into **Pittsburgh, Pennsylvania, International Airport** (412-472-3525; www.flypittsburgh.com), just about a two-hour drive from Deep Creek Lake.

GETTING AROUND *By car:* If coming from the east, take **US 219** to Deep Creek Lake. If from the west, take **MD 42,** which will soon intersect with US 219.

MEDICAL EMERGENCY **Garrett County Hospital** (301-533-4000; www.gcmh.com), 251 N. Fourth St. (on the corner of Fourth St. and Memorial Dr.), Oakland.

✷ To See
MUSEUMS
Accident
Drane House (301-746-6346), Cemetery Rd. (off US 219). Open by appointment and on special days. Built around 1800 and believed to be the oldest structure in Garrett County, the log-and-frame home still has some of its original mud chinking. Items inside chronicle the town's history.

Grantsville
Grantsville Community Museum (301-895-5454; www.garrettcountymuseums.com), 153 Main St. Open Thurs.–Sat. May–Oct. Donations accepted. Within the town's small former bank and former library, the museum has many of the usual type of items found in such a facility—farm implements, military uniforms, and items from the bank. Most impressive,

however, is the large exhibit of Leo J. Beachy photographs, just a small part of the three thousand plate glass negatives he left behind that provide a very detailed (and quite stirring) chronicle of the area in the early 20th century. This exhibit definitely is worth making a stop for.

Oakland

B&O Museum (http://oaklandtrainstation.org), 117 Liberty St. The 1884 B&O Railroad Station that will house the museum was still undergoing renovation as this book went to press, but it has partnered with Baltimore's B&O Railroad Museum (which is affiliated with the Smithsonian), so the rotating artifacts and exhibits should be well-displayed and informative.

Garrett County Historical Society (301-334-3226; www.garrettcountymuseums.com), 107 S. Second St. Among the many items pertaining to the human history of the area are a period newspaper containing articles on Lincoln's assassination, glassware from the Glades and Oakland hotels, and, what interested me the most, Meshach Browning's bear trap.

⬆ **Garrett County Museum of Transportation** (301-334-3226; www.garrettcounty museums.com), 107 S. Second St. Donations accepted. An amazingly high-quality museum to be found in a small town like Oakland. Occupying two floors, the museum features carriages, automobiles, and other means of conveyance (bicycles, boats, etc.) from the late 1800s to the mid-1900s. I was not only impressed with the layout of the building, but also how everything that is displayed is in great condition, despite much of it having been used more than one hundred years ago. Just a few of the many transportation apparatuses on display are the 1873 Deer Park Hotel Omnibus, Indian and Harley-Davidson motorcycles, a 1910 International Harvester Auto-Buggy, a 1920 wooden Old Town canoe, a 1941 Old Town sailing canoe, and one of the first Flying Scot sailboats (still produced in nearby Deer Park). Easy to overlook, but worth seeking out is the complete Maryland state license plate collection from 1910 to the present and the Buddy L toy cars.

REAR FACADE OF THE GARRETT COUNTY HISTORICAL SOCIETY

SPRUCE FOREST ARTISAN VILLAGE IN GRANTSVILLE

OTHER SITES **Spruce Forest Artisan Village** (301-895-3332; www.spruceforest.org), 177 Casselman Rd. (US Alternate 40), Grantsville. Demonstrations of colonial and contemporary arts and crafts. Some of the best bird carvings, pottery, stained glass, and weaving you will find anywhere. Well worth a visit, especially since it is free.

LAKES **Deep Creek Lake** is the big draw to the area, but several other lakes have their own scenic and recreational attractions.

Youghiogheny River Lake (814-395-3166; www.lrp.usace.army.mil/rec/lakes/youghiog.htm) spans the Mason-Dixon Line on the Maryland-Pennsylvania border. Powerboating and waterskiing are popular on the 16-mile body of water, and anglers come here for the variety of game and panfish, especially walleye and smallmouth bass. Picnic areas and three campgrounds (one in Maryland; see Mill Run Recreation Area under *Lodging*) are spaced around the lake. The access in Maryland is Mill Run Rd., off MD 53 north of Friendsville.

Savage River Reservoir (301-895-5759), accessed on Savage River Rd. from MD 135 at Bloomington, or from Big Run Road off New Germany Rd. One of the most spectacular settings of any of the area's lakes. Big Savage Mountain, Mount Nebo, and other ridgelines rise dramatically and quickly from the water. Trout, bass, crappie, walleye, perch, and catfish are in abundance, while a fly-fishing catch-and-release site at the dam's tailwater often yields 6- and 7-pound trout. The tailwaters are a popular kayaking spot and have even been used by those training for the Olympics.

Broadford Lake (301-334-9222), in the town of Mountain Lake Park. Non-gasoline-powered watercraft are welcome, which means the 140-acre body of water is a great place to canoe, kayak, sailboard, and fish for the stocked trout, crappie, bass, and catfish. Boat rentals during the season.

Jennings Randolph Lake (304-355-2346; www.nab.usace.army.mil/missions/damsrecreation /jenningsrandolphlake.aspx) on the North Branch of the Potomac River, which separates Maryland from West Virginia. Scenically sandwiched in by high ridges, the lake is one of the area's least used for powerboating, waterskiing, and fishing. The fly-fishing tailwater area regularly yields brown, rainbow, cutthroat, and brook trout. Mount Zion Rd., off MD 135, provides the only Maryland access to the lake. There is an inspiring view of the lake on Chestnut Grove Rd., which is also off MD 135.

Also see **New Germany State Park** and **Herrington Manor State Park** under *Green Space*.

STONE BRIDGES Casselman River Bridge, on US Alternate 40 east of Penn Alps Restaurant, Grantsville. An impressive example of the stonemason's art, the 80-foot Casselman River Bridge was the largest stone-arch bridge in the world when it was built in 1813. While standing on it, be sure to look across the road to its two modern successors, the US 40 and I-68 bridges.

✳ To Do

BICYCLING See **Swallow Falls/Herrington Manor Trail** and the text note under *Hiking,* and **New Germany State Park** and **Deep Creek Lake State Park** under *Green Space*. During the warmer months when downhill skiing is impossible, **Wisp Resort** (see *Lodging*) opens some of its ski runs and hiking trails to mountain bikers. Rentals are available.

BIRDING See *Green Space—Nature Preserves.*

BOAT RENTALS

Thayerville/Deep Creek Lake

Aquatic Personal Watercraft Center (301-387-8233; www.aquatic-center.com), 634 Deep Creek Dr. Open daily 9–8. I get annoyed when personal watercraft show up at quiet lakes, inlets, or rivers. At Deep Creek Lake, however, it seems that almost all the boaters, whether in a small or huge boat, are trying to see how fast their craft can go, so you might as well join in. I'll admit I did, and I enjoyed it. Rentals by the hour or day.

Bill's Marine Service (301-387-5536; www.billsmarineservice.com), 20721 Garrett Hwy. (US 219). Little boats with less than 10 horsepower to monsters with 190 horsepower.

CASSELMAN RIVER BRIDGE IN GRANTSVILLE

DEEP CREEK LAKE

Silver Tree Marine (301-387-5855; www .silvertreemarine.com), 455 Glendale Rd. (on the way to Deep Creek Lake State Park). Rentals of inboard/outboard power-boats, pontoon boats, and personal water-craft by the hour, half day, day, and week.

McHenry/Deep Creek Lake

Deep Creek Marina (301-387-6977; www.deepcreekmarina.com), 1899 Deep Creek Dr. (off US 219). Hourly, daily, and weekly rentals of canoes as well as fishing, pontoon, and ski boats. Stop by in winter for cross-country ski equipment rentals.

Also see *Outdoor Outfitters*.

BOAT TOURS Wisp Resort (301-387-4911; 1-800-462-9477; www.wispresort.com), 296 Marsh Hill Rd., McHenry. The resort's lake Courtesy Patrol invites guests onto their pontoon boat for tours of Deep Creek Lake. You may get to feed some ducks and catch glimpses of other birds and wildlife as you go lazily up and down the lake. About $30 for adults and $15 for children.

DOGSLEDDING Husky Power Dogsledding (301-746-7200; www.huskypowerdog sledding.com), 2008 Bumble Bee Rd., Accident. Mike and Linda Herdering have extensive experience and education in dogsledding in North America and share their experience with customers by taking them on a variety of sledding tours of one hour or more. Since they have wheeled carts, they can take you on an outing even if there is no snow. It's not just about the ride; the Herderings put as much emphasis on introducing you to and educating you about the dogs.

I have to admit that I have never gone on a trip with Mike and Linda, but having done some dogsledding in the Pacific Northwest, I can say what a grand sensation it is to feel the power and joy of the dogs as they pull you over undulating mountainous terrain. Expect to spend $195–245 (or slightly more) per person (with two people) for a trip.

FAMILY ACTIVITIES

Accident

✿ **Cove-Run Farms Corn Maze** (301-746-6111; 301-616-6111; www.coverunfarmscorn maze.com) 596 Griffith Rd. Usually open Fri.–Sun. Aug.–Oct. Small admission fee. The 10-acre maze has a different theme every year, meaning it will be something new and different on your subsequent visits.

McHenry/Deep Creek Lake

✿ **Smiley's FunZone** (301-387-0059; www.smileysfunzone.com), on US 219 across from the fairgrounds. There is enough here to keep the kids busy all day. There are batting cages (with slow-pitch softball or fast-pitch baseball), an old-time photo studio, arcade games, indoor laser tag, ice cream, pizza and other foods, and two go-cart tracks (one with a graded incline and the other with carts designed for kids as young as four years old). The bumper boats are a great way to get rid of some aggression, while the Smiley-designed miniature-golf course is different from any other you may have played on.

✿ **Funland** (301-387-6168; www.deepcreekfunland.com), US 219 across from McHenry Plaza. Go-carts, a video arcade, miniature golf, bumper cars, and a "carousel for all ages."

There is a free volleyball court and picnic tables to use while eating the burgers, pizza, or ice cream the kids insist on getting.

✔ **Wisp Mountain Coaster** (301-387-4911; 1-800-462-9477; www.wispresort.com), 296 Marsh Hill Rd. Take an alpine slide and mix it with a roller coaster, and you have a little bit of an idea of what the mountain coaster is. Riding on stainless-steel tubular tracks, your two-person cart makes a slow 1,300-foot ascent up the mountain, and then . . . it's off you go! Picking up speed, your cart winds through trees and above the ski slopes, quickly negotiating all manner of twists, turns, corkscrews, and horseshoe bends. Brake levers let you control how fast you go, but if you want to be brave and not use the manual breaks so that you reach the top speed of close to 30 miles per hour, a centrifugal braking system will ensure that you do so safely. *Yee haw!*

Swanton

✔ **Discovery Center at Deep Creek Lake State Park** (301-387-7067; www.dnr.state.md.us/publiclands/western/deepcreek.asp), 898 State Park Rd. Interactive displays about the geology, ecology, and human history of the area. There's much to see and do here, so make sure you

HEADING UP THE MOUNTAIN ON THE WISP MOUNTAIN COASTER

look up, down, and sideways, or you'll miss the live snakes, the swimming fish, and the "hidden footprints." Also, don't forget to visit the birds in the aviary—and take the walk on the constructed Forest Canopy Walkway.

FISHING **Streams and Dreams** (301-387-6881; www.streams-and-dreams.net), 8214 Oakland–Sang Run Rd., Oakland. Don Hershfeld, an aquatic ecologist, is also owner of a B&B on which a trout stream runs through the property. The Youghiogheny is a just a two-minute walk away, and Don educated me quickly during that short stroll.

Fishing Deep Creek Lake (301-859-8161; www.fishingdeepcreeklake.com), P.O. Box 2125, Mountain Lake Park, 21550. Half-day and full-day lake and fly-fishing trips.

Wisp Resort's Outdoors (301-387-4911; 1-800-462-9477; www.wispresort.com), 296 Marsh Hill Rd., McHenry. The resort's fly-fishing program is Orvis-endorsed and includes all the gear you need. Half-day and full-day guided trips with instruction.

Also see *To See*, and **New Germany State Park** and **Herrington Manor State Park** under *Green Space*.

ICE FISHING Ice fishing on **Deep Creek Lake** and **Savage River Reservoir** has become increasingly popular. Most anglers come in Jan. and Feb. in hopes of hooking yellow perch, walleye, northern pike, and a few other species.

McHenry/Deep Creek Lake

Golf Club at Wisp (301-387-4911; www.wispresort.com), 296 Marsh Hill Rd. The course has both open holes and tree-lined fairways, and shares some of the same land used by skiers in winter.

Lodestone Golf Club (301-387-4653; www.lodestonegolf.com), 2112 Marsh Hill Rd. Sitting on the ridge above Deep Creek Lake, the par-72 course has some nice views and some amazing elevation differences—110 feet from tee to green on the 13th hole alone.

Oakland

Oakland Golf Club (301-334-3883; www.golfatoakland.com), 433 N. Bradley Ln. Apr.–Oct. Established in 1937, the par-72 course has a maturity that is lacking in newer courses.

MINIATURE GOLF See **Smiley's FunZone** and **Funland** under *Family Activities.*

HIKING The **Big Savage Hiking Trail** must be one of the best-kept outdoor secrets in Maryland. It offers a fine sense of isolation, relatively minor changes in elevation, several viewpoints (the one from **High Rock** is one of western Maryland's best), and an abundance of deer and other wildlife. The route traverses the crest of Big Savage Mountain for 17 miles. In addition, visitors may set up a backcountry camp wherever they wish—yet the trail shows very few signs of use. There are no worn-out areas from too many people camping in the same spot, fire rings are almost nonexistent, and the trail's treadway is narrow and shallow.

The required backcountry camping permit (and payment of a fee) can be obtained at the forest headquarters, accessible from I-68 Exit 22 or from the New Germany State Park office (see *Green Space*).

Try the **Swallow Falls/Herrington Manor Trail** for an easier trek. The 5.5-mile pathway follows the bed of a former logging railroad on its way from one state park to the other. It is also popular with mountain bikers and cross-country skiers.

Without a doubt, 4.5-mile **Lostland Run Trail,** west of Mountain Lake Park, is the showpiece of the **Potomac/Garrett State Forest** (301-334-2038; dnr.maryland.gov/publiclands /western/potomacforest.asp). Volunteers, members of the Maryland Conservation Corps, and personnel of the forest service have lavished much attention on the route, keeping it well maintained and building a number of bridges—both simple and complex.

The attention is well deserved, as the Lostland Run area is one of the most attractive in western Maryland. The hike begins in a hemlock grove, and it soon comes into contact with three lively and gurgling mountain streams before it drops to the calmer waters of the Potomac River. Along the way are an abundance of wildflowers, numerous cascades, ripples, and waterfalls, and the possibility of seeing bobcats, opossums, deer, groundhogs, weasels, minks, and black bears. An additional draw is backcountry camping in this beautiful setting. Because of the proximity of the forest service road, you also have the option of shuttling a car to make it a one-way hike.

Note: The **Garrett County Chamber of Commerce** can provide you with information on the many other trails in this area that open up scores of miles for hiking, mountain biking, cross-country skiing, and snowmobiling.

Also see Green Space.

HORSEBACK RIDING Both **Western Trails** (310-387-6155; www.westerntrails.com), 4009 Mayhew Inn Rd., Oakland, and **Circle R Ranch** (301-387-6890; www.deepcreek lakestable.com), 4151 Sand Flat Rd., Oakland, offer hour-long trail rides.

KAYAKING AND CANOEING See **Savage River Reservoir** and **Broadford Lake** under *To See*, as well as *Outdoor Adventure, Outdoor Outfitters,* and *White-Water Rafting.*

OUTDOOR ADVENTURE

Friendsville

All Earth Eco Tours (301-746-4083; 1-800-446-7554; www.allearthecotours.com), P.O. Box 35, Friendsville, 21531. Take a trip into the woods or onto the water with All Earth, and you will be the beneficiary of the experience and knowledge that the owner of this company has gained since he first started leading tours in 1975. Some of the guided hikes include treks in the local state parks and state forests, walks to waterfalls and along the Youghiogheny River, and multiday trips atop the Savage Mountain ridgetop. All Earth was also the first company to take paddlers on guided trips of the Savage River Reservoir. All of the company's trips not only provide the instruction you will need, but the leaders will also pass on a great deal of information concerning the geology, history, and ecology of the places in which you will be recreating. In addition, you may be able to glean some tips from the owner about how to improve your picture-taking ability, as he is also a professional photographer.

McHenry/Deep Creek Lake

Wisp Resort (301-387-4911; 1-800-462-9477; www.wispresort.com), 296 Marsh Hill Rd. Wisp's outdoor-adventure program includes activities that you may either do on your own or have someone go along with you to provide instructions on how to improve your skills. The 25-foot climbing wall has three routes, providing a challenge for beginner to intermediate climbers. Guided kayak tours on Deep Creek Lake take paddlers across the flat water and into hidden coves. Rentals are available if you wish to explore the lake on your own.

OUTDOOR OUTFITTERS **High Mountain Sports** (301-387-4199; www.high mountainsports.com), 21327 Garrett Hwy. (US 219 at Trader's Landing), Thayerville. A full-service store; if it has to do with the outdoors, they can rent or sell you the equipment and teach you how to use it. This includes mountain biking, hiking, kayaking, snow skiing, water-skiing, and guided mountain bike and kayaking tours.

SAILING **Deep Creek Sailing School** (301-387-4497; www.deepcreeksailingschool .com), located in Deep Creek Yacht Club at Turkey Neck, Swanton. Low-cost group sailing lessons on small sailboats taught by U.S. Sailing–certified instructors.

SKATING **Wisp Resort** (301-387-4911; www.wispresort.com), 296 Marsh Hill Rd. Has the area's only skate park, where you can practice your skills on quarter pipes, rails, fun boxes, and more. Skates and boards are available for rent.

SKIING, CROSS-COUNTRY This area receives as much as 220 inches of snow, which can fall from November into April. **New Germany** and **Herrington Manor State Parks** (see *Green Space*) offer miles of wide, well-marked, and groomed trails. Ski rentals and warming lodges are available in both parks.

Many other miles of trails are located in the state forests; information is available from the **Garrett County Chamber of Commerce.**

Also see *Skiing, Downhill* and *Hiking.*

SKIING, DOWNHILL ✔ **Wisp Resort** (301-387-4911; www.wispresort.com), 296 Marsh Hill Rd. Maryland's only downhill skiing area has 32 runs and trails totaling 10.5 miles and 132 acres of skiable terrain. With an elevation over 3,000 feet and a 700-foot vertical drop, the resort also has facilities for ski boarding, cross-country skiing, and tubing. Night skiing is available. Like most such places, you can take lessons and buy or rent equipment; children's lessons and programs also available.

Wisp's snowmaking system is considered to be one of the most efficient in the world, so even if Mother Nature does not supply the white powder, Wisp is capable of making plenty of its own.

SNOWMOBILING There are miles and miles of marked snowmobile trails throughout the state parks and forests. One of the most popular is the route along the crest of Meadow Mountain that runs from **Deep Creek Lake State Park** to **New Germany State Park** and beyond. Another good choice is the 9.5-mile **Garrett State Forest Snowmobile System.**

Permits are required to ride some of the trails; information available from the **Garrett County Chamber of Commerce.**

SWIMMING Lifeguard-patrolled beaches are located at **Deep Creek Lake, Herrington Manor,** and **New Germany State Parks.** Many people swim in the Youghiogheny River at **Swallow Falls State Park;** be aware there are no lifeguards, and the river can have a strong current.

WHITE-WATER RAFTING

Friendsville
Precision Rafting (301-746-5290; 1-800-477-3723; www.precisionrafting.com), Maple and Morris Sts. The premier company based in Maryland that runs the Upper Youghiogheny River's Class IV and V rapids. Kayaking lessons, family float trips, and runs in West Virginia and Kentucky, too.

Wilderness Voyageurs (1-800-272-4141; http://wilderness-voyageurs.com), 276 Maple St. Established in 1964, Wilderness Voyageurs provides many of the same services as Precision Rafting.

McHenry
Adventure Sports Center International (301-387-3250; 1-877-300-2724; www.adventure sportscenter.com), 250 Adventure Sports Way. ASCI will provide you with a unique white-water experience. You will not be paddling down a river. Rather, the $24 million project, which is built atop Marsh Mountain, has a 1,700-foot constructed course with a 250,000-gallon-per-minute flow. Yes, there are other constructed white-water courses, but (as of this writing) ASCI is the only one in the country that can change the intensity of its rapids with the touch of a button. Beginners may take guided raft or kayak trips on Class II water, while more experienced water rats can challenge themselves with Class IV rapids. In addition, huge boulders (dug up during construction) line the course, giving a more natural look and not one that appears to be like a big concrete trough. Although it provides all the thrills of river whitewater, the route is designed so that if you do fall out of your craft, you will only have to swim a few feet before you can stand up. Maybe the best part: A conveyor belt takes you from the finish point back to the starting pond without you having to get out of the raft or kayak. Tickets are purchased for two-hour time slots, so you will probably run the course a number of times each session. All gear and instructions are provided; you can run the course on your own with your own equipment if you can demonstrate a level of proficiency.

ASCI also has a 550-acre property with trails for hiking and biking, and cliffs where staff offer classes in rock climbing and rappelling.

✳ Green Space

NATURE PRESERVES Two tracts of land owned by the Nature Conservancy are situated in what are known as "frost pockets." The lower-lying swamplands are surrounded by high ridges, which trap cold air and create an environment more like Canada than Maryland. They are the location of some of America's southernmost occurrences of tamarack, wild calla, Canadian burnet, and insectivorous round-leaved sundew. Each has developed trails and is open daily during daylight hours. More background information can be obtained by contacting the Maryland Chapter of the **Nature Conservancy** (301-897-8570; www.nature.org). The **Garrett County Chamber of Commerce** can supply you with directions (which are quite lengthy) to both places.

State-rare breeding birds that have been seen in the 326-acre **Finzel Swamp** are the Virginia rail, sedge wren, alder flycatcher, and saw-whet owl. Other species spotted in the swamp have included the rose-breasted grosbeak, cedar waxwing, and whip-poor-will.

Partially in West Virginia and partially in Maryland, 1,600-acre **Cranesville Swamp** has a boardwalk that will take you by bogs, cranberries, and sphagnum moss. State-rare breeding birds found here include the golden-crowned kinglet, alder flycatcher, and Nashville warbler.

PARKS

Grantsville

New Germany State Park (301-895-5453; www.dnr.state.md.us/publiclands/western/new germany.asp), 349 Headquarters Ln. The park is located off New Germany Rd. In contrast to 3,900-acre Deep Creek Lake, New Germany's lake is all of 13 acres in size. It was formed in the early 1800s when John Swauger dammed Poplar Lick Run to obtain waterpower for a sawmill and gristmill. The lake is stocked with sportfish, and rowboat and canoe rentals are available during the summer season. Other attractions include rental cabins (open year-round) with modern amenities, a campground, and a sandy beach for swimming.

The park's trail system was designed with cross-country skiers (who come to the park in large numbers) in mind, so the routes are generally wide and for the most part rise and fall at a moderate grade. A hike or a mountain bike ride will not deliver you to any spectacular waterfalls or open up any grand vistas but does provide the opportunity to meander through a quiet woodland, surveying the different small parts of the forest that come together to make up the whole.

Oakland

Herrington Manor State Park (301-334-9180; www.dnr.state.md.us/publiclands/western /herrington.asp), 222 Herrington Ln., follow signs from US 219 in Thayerville on a convoluted route to the park. Like New Germany State Park, Herrington Manor's moderately easy trails are popular cross-country ski routes, and they are groomed and tracked by park personnel. Ski rentals are available.

The park's blend of recreational opportunities makes use of many of the still-standing 1930s Civilian Conservation Corps constructions, such as rental cabins 1–10. (An exhibit in the park office profiles the corps.) **Herrington Lake,** at 53 acres, is stocked with trout, bass, crappie, bluegill, and catfish. Non-gasoline-powered watercraft only; canoes and paddleboats are rented during summer.

Swallow Falls State Park (301-334-9180; www.dnr.state.md.us/publiclands/western/swallow falls.asp), follow signs from US 219 at Thayerville. A walk of less than 1.5 miles provides you with not just one, but four distinctly different waterfalls. **Muddy Creek Falls** is considered the highest in the state (although some claim Cunningham Falls near Frederick is). The area between **Lower Falls** and **Swallow Falls** on the Youghiogheny River is a popular swimming spot, while the sandy beach at **Toliver Falls** is another inviting place. An added attraction of the hike is a shaded 37-acre, three-hundred-year-old hemlock and white pine forest. The park also has a campground and picnic facilities.

Swanton/Deep Creek Lake

Deep Creek Lake State Park (301-387-5563; www.dnr.state.md.us/publiclands/western/deepcreek.asp), 898 State Park Rd. Although you are permitted to walk the shoreline around Deep Creek Lake, much of the land beyond has been turned into housing developments, private-home lots, or commercially operated enterprises. The Maryland General Assembly recognized the need for at least a bit of public land here, and after purchasing a mile of shoreline opened the park in 1959. Its 1,800 acres provide protected terrain for resident black bears, bobcats, wild turkeys, white-tailed deer, skunks, chipmunks, squirrels, raccoons, and numerous small mammals.

In addition to a swimming beach, amenities in the park include a campground, rowboat rentals, and a boat-launch facility. Stocked trout, walleye, bass, and yellow perch keep anglers busy. Ranger-naturalists lead interpretive programs—sometimes throughout the year, but most often during summer months. The **Discovery Center** is part visitors center, part museum.

Approximately 10 miles of trails along the slopes and crest of Meadow Mountain provide an opportunity to get away from the crowds of the lake and campground, visit an old mining site, enjoy a couple of vistas, and study a mountaintop wetland. Be aware that hunting is permitted in the park's backcountry area during regular hunting seasons, and that some of the trails are popular snowmobile routes in the winter and open to mountain bikes year-round.

✸ Lodging

RESORT

McHenry, 21541

🐾 **Wisp Mountain Resort/Hotel** (301-387-4911; 1-800-462-9477; www.wispresort.com), 296 Marsh Hill Rd. The 168-room/suite hotel for the **Wisp Resort** offers an Olympic-sized heated pool, tennis courts, an exercise room, and special golf, skiing, and other package deals. A renovation has given most of the rooms sitting areas, and the king suites have leather furniture, large-screen TVs, and marble and Italian tile accents. Rooms have a choice of ski-slope, lake, or golf course views. Pets permitted with a substantial deposit. The resort's Sewickley Spa, the only dedicated spa in the Deep Creek area, offers massage and body therapies, skin care treatments, and waxing and nail services, along with a surprising amount of services geared toward men. In addition to the skiing and winter sports (see *Skiing, Downhill*), the resort has year-round activities, such as Orvis-endorsed fly-fishing lessons (see *Fishing*), the fast-paced Wisp Mountain Coaster (see *Family Activities*), paintball, disc golf, pontoon boat excursions (see *Boat Tours*), street and skate parks, mountain boarding, mountain biking, and guided kayak tours. $239–329.

MOTELS AND HOTELS

Grantsville, 21536

♪ **The Casselman Inn** (301-895-5055; www.thecasselman.com), Main St. (US Alternate 40). The Casselman was built in 1824 as a stop to serve the stagecoaches, covered wagons, and other travelers along the National Road. The décor and fixtures (Room 5 has an old-fashioned water closet) in the four inn rooms reflect the early days

ONE WISP MOUNTAIN RESORT EVENT THAT WILL NOT BE FORGOTTEN IS THE DOCK DOGS CHAMPIONSHIP

🐾 ✒ **Savage River Lodge** (301-689-3200; www.savageriverlodge.com), P.O. Box 655, 1600 Mt. Aetna Rd. (within Savage River State Forest), Frostburg, 21532. Call for directions.

The lodge, and its 45 acres surrounded by thousands of Savage River State Forest acreage, is the pet project of Jan Russell and Mike Dreisbach. I like that the facility's construction disturbed the environment as little as possible. The sites for the 18 guest cabins (which can accommodate up to four people) were carved out of the forest but left most of the trees standing. Even at the main lodge, which overlooks the land, Jan and Mike did not cut down trees just to enhance the view. The septic system employs an environmentally friendly method, rainwater is used to water plants, the roadway is designed with water conservation in mind, and wind and solar power supply close to 90 percent of the main lodge's energy needs. The restaurant (see *Dining Out*) serves as many locally produced items as possible. Although the natural world would be best served by no further development, if we must disturb the land, architects and planners would do well to emulate Savage River Lodge's example.

In addition to self-guided explorations of the 13 miles of trail (which connect with additional pathways in the state forest), the lodge can arrange all manner of guided outdoor activities: hiking, bicycling, canoeing, kayaking, geocaching (ask about the wine cache course!), fly-fishing, and more—as well as renting bicycles, sleds, and skis if you want to engage in the activities on your own. They can even arrange to shuttle you for a couple of days of bike riding or hiking on the Great Allegheny Passage. This is, by far, one of my favorite outdoor-oriented Maryland places. If you can't unwind and enjoy the outdoors here, I have my doubts if you can do so anywhere. The property is also very pet-friendly (additional $30 fee). $190 and up. Many packages available.

and rent for $70–85. Newer motel rooms have been built next door and have some of the lowest rates in the state, $65–85. The adjacent restaurant (see *Eating Out*) serves Amish/country fare.

McHenry/Deep Creek Lake, 21541

& **LakeStar Lodge** (301-387-5596; www .lakestarlodge.com), 2001 Deep Creek Dr. Years ago I inspected this property and decided that it was so unkempt that it was not worthy of being included in this guide. Then new owners had done a complete renovation, and I included it in the book. Later I had to remove it again. However, on my last visit things looked good once more. So my suggestion is to ask the right questions when making a phone reservation. The establishment does have the advantage of overlooking the lake (which is just a few yards away) and looking out across the water to the ski slopes of Wisp Resort. $159–179.

Oakland/Deep Creek Lake, 21550

♨ **Garrett Inn** (301-387-6696), 17848 Garrett Hwy. The sizes of the rooms are small by today's standards, but the owners of this well-maintained mid-1900s motel have created a nice homey ambiance with each room having décor that matches the quilts on the two queen beds. With a refrigerator and microwave in each room and a family-friendly atmosphere, the rates are pretty much a bargain at $80 during the height of the summer season.

🐾 **Inn at Deep Creek** (301-387-5534; www.innatdeepcreek.com), 19638 Garrett Hwy. At the southern end of Deep Creek, the inn offers large suites with fireplaces and full kitchens. *Insider's Tip:* Only a few of the suites have a (limited) view of the lake, so ask for one of those when making reservations. There's a private beach and floating dock to fish or launch a canoe or kayak from, a heated outdoor pool, gas grills for making an outdoor meal, and some grassy areas to walk the dog. Pets are permitted with an additional $25–50 fee. $149–199.

INNS

Deep Creek Lake/Oakland, 21550

Carmel Cove (301-387-0067; www.carmel coveinn.com), P.O. Box 644, Glendale Rd. (off US 219 near Thayerville). The inn, built in 1945 as a monastery for Carmelite Fathers, provides many complimentary items and amenities: billiards, fishing poles for use on the dock, swimming in the lake, canoes and paddleboats, mountain bikes, tennis courts and equipment, beverages and snacks (always available), cross-country skis, and snowshoes.

Some rooms have a private deck, fireplace, and whirlpool bath; all have a private bath. Wood furniture and ceilings, along with a stacked stone fireplace, add an overall warmth to the inn. $175–195.

North Glade Inn (301-387-3373; 1-877-433-6911; www.northgladeinn.com), 184 N. Glade Rd. All of the rooms, which resemble standard motel rooms, have a fireplace and a two-person jetted tub. The primary reason to stay here is that guests can take advantage of all the amenities of the country club property next to the inn. Fish in the stocked pond, play tennis on one of two courts, or enjoy a round of golf on the par 3 course. $185.

Deer Park, 21550

Deer Park Inn (301-334-2308; www.deer parkinn.com), 65 Hotel Rd. The inn was constructed as a 17-room family cottage in 1889 by Baltimore architect Josiah Pennington. Many of the family's furnishings are still here, such as a tiger maple dresser and table, a ruby-colored chandelier, and one of the first Sears & Roebuck mail-order sleigh beds. The plumbing is original (the sinks were made in nearby Mount Savage), the tile work in the bathrooms and fireplaces is quite interesting, and I always get a kick out of pulling the chain on the toilet's suspended water box. Mattresses have that

distinctive French sag in the middle. French country meals are served by candlelight in the downstairs dining rooms (see *Dining Out*). $145–165.

BED & BREAKFASTS

McHenry/Deep Creek Lake, 21541

Lake Pointe Inn (301-387-0111; 1-800-523-5253; www.deepcreekinns.com), 174 Lake Pointe Dr. The inn is the oldest house on Deep Creek Lake, actually predating the lake by several decades. It now sits just 13 feet from the water's edge, and the wraparound porch, with rocking chairs, is perfect for lazy hours of lake-watching. The 9-foot stone fireplace, rich woodwork, and handcrafted furniture, fixtures, and pottery give the feel of a rustic lodge, but one with modern amenities. All 10 guest rooms have a private bath, air-conditioning, TV with video player (an extensive collection of videos is available), and telephone. There are also bikes, canoes, kayaks, and a hot tub for guest use. It is one of my favorite Deep Creek Lake places because of the location, laid-back atmosphere, and attentive staff.

Orange juice, muffins, and snacks are available throughout the day; hors d'oeuvres are served in the early evening. Breakfast may include scrambled eggs on a puff pastry

LAKE POINTE INN

and/or a fresh strawberry-mango tart. $235–300.

McHenry/Oakland, 21550

Good Timber B&B (301-387-0097; www .goodtimber.net), 2159 Mayhew Inn Rd. I knew I was going to enjoy this place as soon as I pulled in the driveway. The log house sat just a few scant feet from Deep Creek Lake, and wet kayaks, paddles, swimming trunks, and towels were drying on the side porch. Everything about the B&B appeals to me. The hosts made an effort to employ as many local artisans as possible in the house's construction, and the stairway's handrails and even the beds are made by woodworkers. Many of the fixtures were constructed by an ironwright, and much of the furniture was locally made. Paintings that adorn the walls are from local and regional artists, and the hosts have worked hard to create a nice landscaping scheme on the small lot around the house. All of this comes together as a very eye-pleasing place to spend a day or two. Then again, you may want to leave for a few hours so that you can paddle around the lake on the supplied kayaks or canoes. The three guest rooms have private bath, and one has a two-person whirlpool tub. $175–230.

Streams and Dreams (301-387-6881; www.streams-and-dreams.net), 8214 Oak-land–Sang Run Rd. Hosted by Don Hersh-feld, an aquatic ecologist, and Karen Hersh-feld, a fisheries-science graduate and physician assistant, this little retreat sits upon 15 acres bisected by Hoyes Run, a wild trout stream. An extensive deck over-looks the parklike grounds. Guests of the three private rooms have access to refresh-ments in the parlor, a cedar sunroom, and a gazebo planted upon a small island in the stream. Don offers fly-fishing lessons for individuals and small groups by making use of any one of the four major trout rivers within a few minutes' drive (see *To Do*). Be sure to have him tell you the story of the fireflies as the two of you take an evening stroll along the Youghiogheny River. $110–170. Two cottages, capable of holding groups or five or more, are also available.

Swanton, 21561

♿ **Waters Run Guest House and B&B Suite** (301-245-4218; 1-888-536-3801; http://watersrun.tripod.com), 3146 Dry Run Rd. You have a choice here: You can stay in a suite, with a private entrance, in the hosts' home or spend the evening in a cottage of your own. Either way, you'll get to enjoy the peace and tranquility of the property's 90-acre working farm, which has been in the same family for several genera-tions. If you tire of wandering the grounds,

GOOD TIMBER B&B

HALEY FARM B&B

make use of the free pass to Deep Creek Lake State Park, where you can hike, bike, or kayak, The full breakfast always includes homemade bread and fresh fruits. $95–125.

Thayerville/Oakland, 21550

Haley Farm B&B (301-387-9050; 1-888-231-3276; www.haleyfarm.com), 16766 Garrett Hwy. (between Thayerville and Oakland on US 219). The wraparound porch looks upon the farm's 65 acres and the surrounding mountains. All of the suites and rooms have a private bath, and everybody has access to a Jacuzzi either in the room or on the deck. Wander the property, sit by the fireplace, fish or row the pond, or borrow a bike for an exploratory ride. $170–235.

The Oak & Apple Bed & Breakfast (301-334-9265; www.oakandappleinn.com), 208 N. Second St. The 1915 Colonial Revival Victorian home sits in Oakland's quiet historic preservation district and offers four guest rooms. The hosts have tastefully furnished the large rooms. From my second-floor room, I was entertained by squirrels scampering from one large oak tree branch to another just outside my windows. The rest of my time was spent on the columned front porch watching small-town life roll by. A full breakfast complete with

fresh juices, fruits, and your choice of hot beverage is served on the enclosed sunporch. $100-130.

SUITES

Oakland, 21550

Will O' the Wisp Prestige Condominiums (301-387-5503; 1-888-590-7283; www.willothewisp.com), 20160 Garrett Hwy. (US 219 near Thayerville). The one- to three-bedroom condominiums overlook the lake. Indoor pool, sauna, exercise room, and its own sand beach. $139–374.

CABINS Herrington Manor, New Germany, and Deep Creek Lake state parks have cabins that can be rented by the week Memorial Day–Labor Day, and for two-night minimum stays at other times of the year. Reservations can be made by calling 1-888-432-2267.

VACATION RENTALS There are so many rental homes and condos in the area—well over six hundred—that descriptions of them fill several large advertisement books. Everything from small, rustic cabins to nine-bedroom luxury homes are available. Many are on the Deep Creek Lake shoreline, but others are nestled in quiet, out-of-the-way places. In a sign of the times, some include free computer and Internet access. Most of the individually rented places are listed in the *Vacation Guide* available from the **Garrett County Chamber of Commerce.** However, three companies manage the bulk of the rentals:

Coldwell Banker Deep Creek Realty Rentals (301-387-6187; 1-800-769-5300; www.deepcreekrealty.com), 24439 Garrett Hwy. (US 219), McHenry/Deep Creek Lake, 21541.

Long and Foster Resort Rentals (301-387-5832; 1-800-336-7303; www.deepcreek resort.com), 23789 Garrett Hwy. (US 219), McHenry/Deep Creek Lake, 21541.

Railey Mountain Lake Vacations (301-387-2124; 1-855-264-0764; www.deepcreek .com), 5 Vacation Way, McHenry/Deep Creek Lake, 21541.

CAMPING

Friendsville, 21531

🐾 **Mill Run Recreation Area** (814-395-3242), Mill Run Rd. (off MD 53, 4 miles north of Friendsville). (Mailing address is RD 1, Box 17, Confluence, PA 15424.) Usually open May–Sept. The only Youghiogheny Lake campground in Maryland, it has a swimming beach, boat ramp, and flush toilets, but no showers. Pets permitted.

Grantsville, 21536

🐾 **Big Run State Park** (see New Germany State Park, below, for contact information). Near Savage River Reservoir, 16 miles south of I-68 Exit 24 on Savage River Rd. Basic sites with few amenities, but open year-round.

🐾 **Little Meadows** (301-895-5675; www .littlemeadowslake.com), Chestnut Ridge Rd. Offers improved and unimproved sites, along with rowboat rentals, a playground, and a dump station.

🐾 🐟 **New Germany State Park** (301-895-5453; www.dnr.state.md.us/publiclands /western/newgermany.asp), 349 Headquarters Ln. The park is located off New Germany Rd. Close to the park's small lake are 39 sites with a playground for the kids.

McHenry/Deep Creek Lake, 21541

🐾 🐟 **Double G RV Park** (301-387-5481; www.doublegrvpark.com), 76 Double G Dr. RVs only; no tents. Bathhouse, laundry facility, camp store, playground, and dump stations.

Oakland, 21550

🐾 **Swallow Falls State Park** (301-334-9180; www.dnr.state.md.us/publiclands /western/swallowfalls.asp), 9 miles northwest of Oakland on Herrington Manor–Swallow Falls Rd. Showers, modern bathhouse, sanitary facilities.

Swanton, 21561

🐾 **Deep Creek Lake State Park** (301-387-5563; www.dnr.state.md.us/publiclands /western/deepcreek.asp), 898 State Park Rd. The more than one hundred campsites, with hot showers and modern sanitary facilities, are just a short walk from the lake. Rental cabins also available.

Note: Thousands of acres of state forest lands are open to backcountry camping (after payment of a fee). Contact the **Potomac/Garrett State Forest** (301-334-2038; dnr.maryland.gov/publiclands /western/potomacforest.asp), 1431 Potomac Camp Rd., Oakland, 21550, and **Savage River State Forest** (301-895-5759; www .dnr.maryland.gov/publiclands/western /savageriverforest.asp), 349 Headquarters Ln., Grantsville, 21536, for details.

✳ Where to Eat
DINING OUT

Deer Park

Deer Park Inn (301-334-2308; www.deer parkinn.com), 65 Hotel Rd. Open for dinner, but closed some Sun. Reservations required. Pascal Fontaine moved his family to Deer Park so that he could concentrate on preparing meals influenced by methods he learned growing up in France. The menu changes often, as he makes use of seasonally available items grown locally. I dined on the succulent confit of duck, while my companion praised the beef fillet with Cabernet Sauvignon sauce. One of Pascal's signature appetizers, corn chowder with applewood-smoked bacon and crabmeat, is an example of how Maryland cuisine is blended into the offerings. $19.95–29.95.

Frostburg

🍃 **Savage River Lodge** (301-689-3200; www.savageriverlodge.com), P.O. Box 655, 1600 Mount Aetna Rd. (within Savage River State Forest), Frostburg, 21532. Call for directions. Open for lunch and dinner. Going along with Savage River Lodge's (see sidebar on page 458) environmentally friendly philosophy, its restaurant serves as many locally grown products as possible, including maple syrup that is harvested and produced on the property. The chefs employ these ingredients to make some wonderfully fresh and tasty dishes. I thought I was ordering a normal spinach salad to start my meal, but it arrived with a refreshing house-made poppy seed dressing, fresh strawberries, and toasted pine nuts. The duck breast is topped with a mango and avocado sauce and an orange-chipotle sauce. Standards, such as fillet Oscar and pork tenderloin, are also available, along with a number of vegetarian offerings. The food is reason enough to take a ride to the country, but you also get to enjoy dining on the porch, where soft breezes pass through giant fir trees and owl hoots provide the soundtrack for the evening. Entrées $19–35.

McHenry

Pine Lodge Steakhouse and Saloon (301-387-6500; www.pinelodgesteakhouse.com), 1520 Deep Creek Dr. Open for lunch and dinner. Steaks are always cut fresh and are never frozen in this steakhouse, located in an imposing and impressive multistory pine log building. The extremely tender filet mignon I had for dinner was cooked perfectly to my liking, and my dining companion was well satisfied with the house specialty, prime rib au jus. Pasta, seafood, and poultry dishes are also on the menu. Forgo all of the other dressings in favor of the one made in-house for your salad, and save room for one of the pastry chef's desserts. $13–43.

Thayerville/Deep Creek Lake

🍴 **Dutch's at Silver Tree** (301-387-0525; www.dutchsatsilvertree.com), 567 Glendale Rd. Open daily for lunch and dinner. A sister restaurant of Dutch's Daughter in Frederick, Dutch's at Silver Tree is housed in what is believed to be the first place built to cater to tourists after completion of Deep Creek Lake in the early 1900s. The large stone fireplace and log walls may recall a bygone era, but the menu is decidedly typical modern American. Appetizers have included coconut shrimp and chicken bites. The blackened/honey-glazed broiled salmon and 8-ounce filet mignon with béarnaise sauce are popular dinner items, as are the wide variety of pasta dishes. For something a little different, try the marinated chicken topped with ham and asparagus and baked with cheese. Arrive very early (or very late) to be seated at one of the lake-view tables. Entrées $20–28. The outside Inner Harbor Bar and patio have a beach/waterfront party atmosphere, especially on summer weekends.

EATING OUT

Grantsville

🍴 **The Casselman Inn** (301-895-5266; www.thecasselman.com), Main St. (US Alternate 40). Open for breakfast, lunch, and dinner; closed Sun. Straightforward, low-cost Amish/country cooking that is

SAVAGE RIVER LODGE

popular with locals. Look for fried chicken, breaded fish, grilled ham, and other entrées served with two vegetables for $8.95–12. The shoofly pie is different from what you will find in Pennsylvania Dutch country.

⚓ ♿ **Penn Alps Restaurant** (301-895-5985; www.pennalps.com), US 40. Open daily for breakfast, lunch, and dinner. Part of the Penn Alps/Spruce Forest complex, the restaurant serves what I would call an upscale country/Amish/German fare. Hickory-smoked ham, pork with sauerkraut, and cabbage rolls are representative dishes on the menu. Seemingly out of place, but I thought delicious, is the chickpea burger. Three of the dining rooms were once part of a log stagecoach inn, and the front of the restaurant showcases arts and crafts items. The restaurant is part of a nonprofit organization, so some of the money you spend goes toward good works. Entrées $12.99–18.99.

McHenry/Deep Creek Lake

⚓ **Canoe on the Run** (301-387-5933), 2622 Deep Creek Dr. Open daily until 3–4 PM for breakfast and lunch. A cross between a coffeehouse where you can grab a quick breakfast of baked goodies and a café serving soups, sandwiches, and other finger foods, such as quesadillas and focaccia. $4.75–8.25.

DC's Bar and Restaurant (301-387-4911; 1-800-462-9477; www.wispresort.com), 296 Marsh Hill Rd. Wisp Resort's main restaurant, DC's is open daily for breakfast, lunch, and dinner. The evening menu offers quite a number of dishes, including pastas, beef, chicken, seafood, and vegetarian entrées. $15–32.

⚓ **Mountain State Brewing Company Pub & Restaurant** (301-387-3360; www.mountainstatebrewing.com), 6690 Sang Run Rd. Open daily for lunch and dinner. It's a short drive in the country to reach the restaurant, but it's worth it. Yes, this is a pub that features the brews made in nearby West Virginia, but I was impressed with the quality and innovativeness of the food offerings. Certainly not typical bar food. My notes from the experience read "excellent

crab soup! great spiciness! personal size margarita flatbread (cooked in wood-fired oven) really good—and more than large enough for one person." Worth the little bit of a drive, and a nice atmosphere with wooden tables, wooden ceiling, and tree trunk posts. $7.95–13.95.

⚓ **Santa Fe Grille & Cantina** (301-387-2182; www.santafedcl.com), 75 Visitors Center Dr. (located behind the visitors center on US 219). Open daily for lunch and dinner. The Santa Fe Grille and Cantina is in the same building that used to house the Deep Creek Brewing Company (and when I last visited, the management was hoping to restart the microbrewery), so it has the feel of a tavern restaurant. The menu's focus is on south of the border items like enchiladas, fajitas, and chimichangas. There's also a full selection of ribs, steaks, pastas, and mesquite-grilled specialties. I enjoyed the blackened tilapia on flatbread for lunch, along with the zesty hot wing dip served with tortilla chips. Entrées $16.95–26.95.

Oakland

Dottie's Fountain and Grill (301-533-0000), 205 E. Alder St. Open for breakfast, lunch, and "afternoon" dinner, Mon.–Fri. 8:30–3:30, Sat. 8:30–2. Come to Dottie's to experience a time warp. Dottie, the vinyl booths, U-shaped counters, and the menu have been here for more than 30 years. Everything retains the look and feel of when it served as the fountain for a long-gone pharmacy. (The front of the store is now Englander's Antique Mall; see *Selective Shopping.*)

Breakfast is served all day, and the most expensive item you can order is just over $6. Hot dogs, cheeseburgers, grilled cheese, and good ol' PB&J are some of the standard lunch items. Try the deep-fried cauliflower instead of french fries. Dinner is a choice of fried chicken, shrimp, or fish. The hand-dipped milk shakes are not to be missed. Sandwiches and entrées $1–6.95.

Mountain Lake Park

Long Branch Saloon (301-334-4533; www.lbsaloon.com), 1501 Maryland Hwy.

Open for dinner Mon.–Sat. 5–9:30. One half of this large building is a bar; the other half serves as the restaurant (and dance hall on Fri. and Sat. nights—see *Entertainment*). Beef in all shapes—filet mignon, T bone, Delmonico, and others—is the definite house specialty and is served with salad and potato. Chicken, fish, and sandwiches also available. $9.95–23.95.

COFFEE BARS

Thayerville/Deep Creek Lake
Trader's Coffee House (301-387-9246; www.traderscoffeehouse.com), 21311 Garrett Hwy. Open daily at 7 AM. Gourmet coffees, breakfast and lunch sandwiches, and fresh-baked goodies. A few sugar-free items and wi-fi too.

SNACKS AND GOODIES

Accident
Mountain Flour Baking Company (301-750-5035; www.mountainflourbakery.com), 203 N. Main St. How can you not stop here and get something? Bagels, donuts, muffins, cakes, cookies, candy, brownies, danishes, pies, cakes, and artisan breads.

Oakland
Sugar and Spice Bakery and Cheese (301-334-1559; www.thebestamishcook books.com), 2 miles south of Oakland on US 219. Closed Sun. It looks like someone's private home, but go on in for fresh-baked Amish breads, doughnuts, cookies, pies, and some scrumptious pumpkin rolls.

McHenry/Deep Creek Lake
🐾 **Deep Creek Sweets** (310-387-7979; www.deepcreeksweets.com), 1550 Deep Creek Dr. Not only can you get a chocolaty goody for yourself, but this place has also created a dog-friendly chocolate treat for the furry members of your family.

Thayerville/Deep Creek Lake
🍦 **Lakeside Creamery** (301-387-5655; www.lakesidecreamery.com), 20282 Garrett Hwy. This is homemade ice cream at its best. There is a rotating menu of about 80 flavors and no way to choose a bad one. Bill Meagher, who oversees the operation, is so particular that he buys different vanilla extracts from around the world. He has found that Tahitian vanilla complements fruit-flavored ice creams, while an extract with a slight alcoholic taste is suited for heavier flavors. Bill is such a recognized authority that people come from other continents for·his college courses about the homemade ice cream business. Enjoy your cones or sundaes on the picnic tables overlooking the lake.

✳ Entertainment

FILM Garrett Eight Cinemas (301-387-8597; www.garrett8cinema.com), 19736 Garrett Hwy. (US 219), Thayerville/Deep Creek Lake. First-run films.

NIGHTLIFE

McHenry/Deep Creek Lake
🍸 **Black Bear Tavern** (301-387-6800; www.blackbeartavern.com), US 219, at "The Fort." Closed Sun. Live regional bands every Fri. and Sat. night. No cover charge 10 PM–1:30 AM.

Mountain Lake Park
🍸 **Long Branch Saloon** (301-334-4533; www.lbsaloon.com), 1501 Maryland Hwy. The restaurant (see *Eating Out*) tables are rolled away on Fri. and Sat. nights to create the largest dance floor in the area. Energetic crowds dance the night away to music supplied by regional musicians.

Thayerville/Deep Creek Lake
🍸 **Honi Honi** (301-387-9100; http://honi -honi.com), 19475 Garrett Hwy. This place hops both night and day, as they often have live outdoor entertainment from early afternoon on.

THEATERS Our Town Theatre (301-334-5640; http://ourtowntheatre.wix.com), 121 Center St., Oakland. The volunteer community theater, housed in a building that has served as a church, armory, and museum, provides space for teen coffeehouses, recitals, meetings, dances, classes, and theatrical performances.

✳ Selective Shopping

ANTIQUES

Oakland

Englander's Antique Mall (301-533-0000), Alder and Second Sts. Four thousand square feet of antiques and collectibles.

Mt. Panax Antiques (301-334-9249), 27 Norris Welch Rd. About 3 miles south of Oakland. Closed Sun. Glassware, clocks, and some excellent furniture finds.

Oak'tiques (301-334-1087), 109 S. Third St. Open daily. It's a small store, but they usually have some nice furniture, along with the usual antique shop items.

Red House School Antiques (301-334-2800; www.redschoolantiques.com), 3039 Garrett Hwy. More than 60 vendors peddling their wares in the 12,000-square former school.

Also see **Book Market and Antique Mezzanine** under *Bookstores.*

Note: A pamphlet available from the **Garrett County Chamber of Commerce** describes a couple of antiques driving tours in the area that will take you by scores of dealers.

ART GALLERIES **Garrett County Arts Council** (301-334-6580; www.garrettarts.com), 206 E. Alder St., Oakland. Closed Sun. The only fine-arts gallery in the region. Arts and crafts by more than 80 local and regional council members.

BOOKSTORES **Book Market and Antique Mezzanine** (301-387-8778; www.thebookmkt.com), Oakland. Open daily. A full-service bookstore with best-sellers, classics, and an excellent selection of local-interest books. One of the friendliest bookstores I have visited. Antiques on the second floor.

CRAFTS

Mountain Lake Park

Simon Pearce Glassblowing (301-334-5277; www.simonpearce.com), 265 Glass Dr. (off MD 135). Open daily. A catwalk permits visitors to watch the craftspeople at work on the factory floor. It is amazing to watch as a blob of red-hot, molten silica is turned into a crystal-clear work of glass art.

Swanton

Snowbird Creations Glass Studio (301-387-4624; www.snowbirdcreations.com), 398 Snowbird Lane. Julie S. Turrentine is a talented artist who creates jewelry, vases, clocks, tableware, and interesting sculptures out of fused glass.

FARMER'S MARKETS **Oakland Mountain Fresh Farmer's Market** (301-334-6960). In the city parking lot off Second St., Sat. and Wed. 10–1, June–Oct.

WINERY **Deep Creek Cellars** (301-746-4349), 177 Frazee Rd., Friendsville. Tours, tastings, and sales Thurs.–Sat. 11–6, late Apr.–late Nov. Deep Creek Cellars is the farthest west of the state's wineries and, even with its reputation for fine wines, offers its varieties at some of the lowest prices. It's situated on a hillside, so visitors are encouraged to linger, picnic, enjoy the scenic vineyard, and maybe shop in the farm market.

✳ Special Events

February: **Oakland Winterfest** (www.oaklandmd.com), Oakland. Ice art and family entertainment.

June: **McHenry Highland Festival** (1-800-313-0811; www.highlandfest.info), fairgrounds, McHenry. Scottish dancing and solo piping contests. The annual day-long event celebrates the heritage of Scotland, Ireland, Wales, and England and includes sheepdog demonstrations, ethnic food and music, and a military encampment. **Grantsville Days** (301-895-5177; www.grantsvillemd.us), town park, Grantsville. Parade and fireworks, tractor and horse pulls, lots of food, and continuous entertainment. **Redneck Dayz** (http://redneckdayz.webs.com), Broadford Park, Oakland. Redneck music, the redneck regatta (with anything that floats as boats), mud pit belly flop contest, and corn-hole tournament.

June–September: **Garrett Lakes Arts Festival** (301-387-3082; www.artsand entertainment.org), various sites. A summerlong celebration of visual and performing arts. Classes, workshops, and concerts with classical and contemporary music. **Music at Penn Alps** (301-895-5985; www .musicatpennalps.com), Grantsville. The annual series features classic to contemporary classical music.

July: **Independence Day Exhibition of Art** (301-746-6115), Accident. Annual juried art competition in a variety of media that has categories open to adults and children of various ages. **Friendsville Fiddle and Banjo Contest** (301-746-4246), Friendsville.

August: **Annual Western Maryland Tennis Championships** (301-334-3249),

Mountain Lake Park. The clay-court competitions have been held for more than 80 years. **Garrett County Fair** (301-387-5400; www.garrettcountyfair.org), fairgrounds, McHenry. **Country Fest and Auction** (301-245-4564; www.countryfest .org), fairgrounds, McHenry. Arts and crafts, all-day gospel music, old-time milking, weaving, and apple cider demonstrations. Hay wagon and pony rides. Petting zoo and pedal-tractor pull for the kids. Auction proceeds from homemade items support the local Mennonite school and church.

October: **Autumn Glory Festival** (301-387-4386; www.visitdeepcreek.com), various sites throughout the area. An annual five-day celebration of fall foliage. Parades, live music, arts and crafts, dances, and lots of food.

INDEX